CREATIVE CANADA

CREATIVE CANADA

Compiled by Reference Division, McPherson Library, University of Victoria, BC

A biographical dictionary of twentieth-century creative and performing artists

VOLUME TWO

Published in association with McPherson Library, University of Victoria, BC

by University of Toronto Press

© University of Toronto Press 1972
Toronto and Buffalo
Printed in Canada
ISBN 0-8020-3285-0
Microfiche ISBN 0-8020-0196-3
LC 71-151387

Preface

Your knowledge is nothing unless others know that you possess it.

Persius

As the first volume of this series was, the second also is the result of a deliberate decision to include in each a cross-section of creative and performing artists who have lived and worked in Canada and whose work has been recognized as significant in the Canadian context, although not all necessarily may have achieved international reputations. One of our most eminent reviewers, taking a contrary position, noted,

But surely there is a certain prestige in being in the first volume of *Creative Canada*, and that, true or not, there is an implied put-down in being omitted.

This is precisely what we have tried to avoid. Everyone has his own list of those whom he or she considers the best in any artistic category, but we have tried to eliminate the *crème de la crème* syndrome from our thinking and indeed we are forced to do so. Since the intention of this series is to cover those creative and performing artists who have contributed to the culture of Canada in the twentieth century, we must consider those still to come and the potential significance of those who are now children or are, as yet, unborn. To have anywhere implied that an artist's place within this series reflected his or her stature would therefore have been presumptuous in the extreme if it were not in fact impossible.

The amount of critical acclaim in print has been a guide to the compilers who have sought out data not only through the artists themselves, but also checking material discovered by examining every entry in the *Canadian periodical index* from its inception to the cut-off date for *Creative Canada* entries: 31 December 1968, *Canadian annual review, Who's who in Canada* and the *Canadian who's who* besides specialized works of a similar nature, the *Index analytique*, the BC Provincial Library's newspaper index, the *New York Times index*, *The Times (London) index*, as well as an infinity of literary, visual and performing arts books, newspapers, and magazines reached through these tools and others such as *Biographical index, Bibliographical index*, etc. Besides the over half-million volumes and 6,000 periodical files in the McPherson Library, the compilers have had access through interlibrary loan and the co-operation of a gratifyingly large number of other Canadian institutions to material not owned by the University of Victoria but pertinent to our research. From the beginning of compilation it was agreed that in this era of the media and the message no artist could conceivably be of significance if he or she has not received critical acclaim in books, journal articles, newspapers, etc. Inclusion also depends on whether a given artist has contributed significantly as an individual. For example, no member of an orchestra or choir is considered unless he or she has received recognition individually as a soloist, concert artist, or composer.

The terms of reference of the first two volumes (they may be expanded as the series progresses) limit inclusion to authors of works of the imagination (*belles lettres*, if you prefer); artists and sculptors; musicians (performers, composers, conductors, and directors), and performing artists in the fields of ballet, modern dance, radio, theatre, television, and motion pictures; directors, designers, and producers in theatre, cinema, radio and television, and the dance; choreographers; and, for cinema, cartoonists and animators. Excluded for the time being are architects, commercial artists, creators of handicrafts and patrons of the arts, as well as journalists, historians, etc., unless they have an established reputation as individual artists in one of the categories listed above.

No artist is included simply because he or she happened to have been born in Canada. He or she must have lived in Canada and contributed as an artist to its cultural life. Some may be Canadian born and trained but unless they have had their work recognized by critics and the public as significant in the Canadian context, they will not be included. Others, neither Canadian born, nor naturalized, nor indeed, long-time dwellers in Canada, may properly have their place in the series. Sir Tyrone Guthrie in volume one is such an example.

The first two volumes contain about 500 entries each and in them the breakdown among the various kinds of artists is approximately: authors, 27%; artists (painters, sculptors), 28%; musicians (including instrumentalists), 19%; performing artists, 26%. (The theoretical percentage breakdown to which the compilers were working appears in this preface.)

It is therefore important for enquirers to realize that, if the person whom they seek does not appear in the first two volumes, he or she will be in one of the succeeding volumes. The first two are, as their successors will be, cross-sections of many different kinds of artists, and within each category the compilers have attempted to include a selection of those who have achieved national or international recognition and are firmly established, those who are making a distinct contribution which has been recognized locally and will undoubtedly in time receive wider acclaim, and some, now deceased, who markedly influenced their contemporaries, locally, nationally, and/or internationally.

Because this dictionary is limited to an objective presentation of the facts of a given artist's life and career, the entry for each will depend on those facts. An artist of some stature producing very little actual material will not have as lengthy

an entry as another of equal or lesser importance who has produced a great deal. A Keats would have a brief entry but a Victor Hugo a very long one. The artist's life and involvement will influence the length of his entry, for should he have many children, have attended numerous educational institutions, have been represented in many exhibitions, his entry will be longer than someone who is unmarried, educated at home, and exhibited seldom. Some categories have posed special problems, for example, film makers, whose entries should be more succinct in future volumes.

Verification for accuracy has entailed mailing by registered post to each biographee a copy of his entry with a request for correction and return. The entries for those deceased are verified as carefully as possible from printed sources and/or through consultation with relatives. It is possible that the memory is not always accurate, so if an artist quotes a date which is in conflict with information obtained from such reliable printed sources as theatre programmes, exhibition catalogues, newspaper reviews, etc. contemporaneous with the event, the printed source is preferred to the artist's recollection. Those who have personally verified their entries are asterisked in the text.

Before reading the description in the introduction of some of the technicalities regarding the style and organization of the work, the reader may wish to know under what circumstances it was conceived. In June 1966, the Information Services Section of the Canadian Library Association resolved that the Reference Division of the McPherson Library, University of Victoria, chair a committee to investigate what was being done in Canada to collect systematically biographical information on Canadian authors, artists, and musicians. In discussing the matter, the University of Victoria Reference Division decided to go beyond mere investigation and to prepare a biographical dictionary which not only would update, revise, and expand *Canadian biographies: artists and authors* (published by the Canadian Library Association, 1948-52), but would also include within its frame of reference not only those artists born in Canada, but, as explained above, those who have made a distinct contribution, locally or nationally, to the Canadian scene. The work was envisaged as an annual or biennial series. An outline of the project prepared by the Reference Division formed the basis of the University Librarian's brief which was conveyed by the President of the University to the Board of Governors. The Board accepted the brief and approval was given to the project subject to its obtaining financial support from a foundation or other grant to defray at least part of the cost. A submission was duly made to the Canada Council which, in December 1967, made an award of $10,000 to the Library to help finance the preparation and publication of the first two volumes.

During 1966/67 three hundred possible sources of biographical material in Canada (libraries, art galleries, museums, government departments, associations, foundations, etc.) were canvassed and the seventy-four which maintained biography files agreed to co-operate, while others offered to set up files with the project in mind. Many institutions went beyond the limits of the original request in providing biographical outlines specifically for the dictionary, and several thousand files were set up in the project's headquarters.

Once files of source material were organized, Professor Peter Garvie, former Dean of the Faculty of Fine Arts, University of Victoria, and chairman of the consultant advisory panel, projected the following percentages of entries to be allotted to the various categories of artists, based partly upon various general and specialized who's whos consulted: authors, 30%; artists (painters, sculptors, etc.), 25%; musicians (including instrumentalists), 20%; performing artists (excluding instrumentalists), 20%; for a total of 95%; leaving 5% to be allocated among categories as required. As may be seen from the percentages quoted for volumes 1 and 2 earlier in this preface, the actual figures differ slightly from those Professor Garvie projected, indicating the substantial number of performing artists of significance who should and will be recognized in this series, and perhaps also reflecting the importance of television as a national medium for exploitation of performing talents.

When the theoretical percentage breakdown of categories was established we were fortunate in being able to call upon a distinguished panel of consultant-advisers (listed in the acknowledgments) to assist in selection and in helping us obtain and maintain liaison with sources of biographical information beyond those we had ourselves established. In agreeing to help us our consultant-advisers assumed an exceedingly difficult and delicate task, for they placed themselves on target for all the slings and arrows of the outraged who were not included in the first volume. The compilers ask that critics and public alike direct their barbs not against this panel and its chairman but rather against the compilers and especially the director of the project, for the final decision regarding inclusion was hers. Considering the mass of data to be culled and organized, compiled and verified, it was necessary to limit the initial volumes severely. Such a limitation does not, however, obtain in the series as a whole. Like the Gale Research Company's *Contemporary authors*, all who fall within the project's terms of reference will be included within its volumes.

This compilation does not pretend to be critical or appreciative but is meant to be an objective and factual reference tool much needed in libraries and other institutions. This second volume contains, as its successors will, a cumulative index covering all volumes to date. From the third volume onwards we hope to update earlier entries as well as to present new ones. For volumes 1 and 2, only major changes that have come to our attention, i.e. death, have been added after the cut-off date of 31 December 1968. Gathering data for future volumes will be a co-ordinated function of the project's director and compilers with those institutions which have offered their help to us both now and in the future.

Helen McGregor Rodney
Director
Head, Reference Division
McPherson Library

Acknowledgments

For the want of a nail the shoe was lost,
For the want of a shoe the horse was lost,
For the want of a horse the rider was lost,
For the want of a rider the battle was lost,
For the want of a battle the kingdom was lost
And all for the want of a horseshoe-nail.

Benjamin Franklin *Poor Richard* 1758

In the context of this biographical project the horseshoe nail was a substantial grant in aid of publication on the acquisition of which depended the support of the University of Victoria's Board of Governors. The Canada Council award of $10,000 made in December 1967 meant that the kingdom was by no means lost. In acknowledging with thanks the Council grant we wish at the same time to acknowledge the support, both financial and moral, that our Board of Governors has given. We hope that the series of volumes of which this is the second will justify their confidence. We would like also to indicate our appreciation for the excellent co-operation provided by the many institutions and individuals who have assisted us in obtaining and verifying biographical data, the comprehensiveness and accuracy of which are so essential to the users of this work. Any errors or omissions are those either of the compilers or of the biographees. Professor Peter Garvie, former Dean of the Faculty of Fine Arts at the University of Victoria, has our appreciation for his guidance, and his chairmanship of our consultant-advisory panel to whose distinguished members (listed below) we are much indebted:

Art (painting and sculpture, etc.) J. RUSSELL HARPER, Associate Professor of Fine Arts, Sir George Williams University and author of *Painting in Canada, a history*
Authors (English) ROBERT WEAVER, Editor of *Tamarack review* and Radio Network Supervisor, Drama and Special Programs, Canadian Broadcasting Corporation
Authors (French) GÉRARD R. TOUGAS, Professor of French, University of British Columbia
Cinema GUY L. COTÉ, Founder and ex-President of La Cinématheque Canadienne
Dance the late RALPH HICKLIN, Drama and Ballet Critic for the Toronto *Telegram* and Canadian correspondent for *Dance magazine*
Eskimo Art GEORGE SWINTON, Professor, University of Manitoba School of Art
Music (excluding Opera) KEITH MacMILLAN, Executive Secretary of the Canadian Music Centre
Opera HERMAN GEIGER-TOREL, General Director of the Canadian Opera Company
Performing Arts (English) ESSE W. LJUNGH, former Supervisor of Drama, Canadian Broadcasting Corporation
Performing Arts (French) JEAN GASCON, Artistic Director of the Stratford Festival of Canada

Consistency of compilation is one of the major objects of any work such as *Creative Canada*, and to this end the unflagging effort of the project co-ordinator, Mrs. Joan Lawrence, has been directed. Consistency is easier to achieve if one's staff is

constant but, for Mrs. Lawrence, this has not
been the case. Through force of circumstances
many changes among compilers occurred since
the initial team of Mrs. Elizabeth Hagmeier and
Mrs. Marta Williamson, with their assistant, Mrs.
Beverley Robertson, essayed the mass of unorgan-
ized biographical data. Their enthusiasm fired
those who followed: Liselotte Berliner, Mrs.
Gladys M. Cropp, Joseph L. Gentry, Robert M.
Gray, Robert H. Ker, Frances E. Roscoe, and Mrs.
Doris Stastny, ably assisted by Mrs. Gladys K.
Ewan, Mrs. Jennifer Clark Herfst, and Mrs.
Susanne Niemann. The patience and care of the
divisional secretary, Mrs. Judy Boultbee, made
possible the final manuscript. Our recognition
goes not only to those specified by name but also
to many others of the McPherson Library staff
whose cheerful co-operation materially assisted
completion of the first two volumes.

Special thanks for particular help go to Anthony Emery, Director, Vancouver Art Gallery,
and to two members of the University of Victoria
faculty: Carl Hare, Department of Theatre, and
especially R.G. Lawrence, Department of English.

D.W. Halliwell, the University Librarian, carried
our brief successfully to the University administration and the Canada Council. Without his encouragement, advice, and support this work would
neither have been undertaken nor completed and
to him all credit is due.

HMR

Introduction

As guides for the style manual prepared for the use of the compilers of this biographical dictionary, the Gale Research Company's series, *Contemporary authors,* and the University of Chicago's *A manual of style* were used together with the *Dictionary of Canadian English*, by W.S. Avis et al., as the authority for spelling, and F.H. Collins' *Authors' and printers' dictionary,* for abbreviations. The *Canadian almanac and directory*, 1967, was the authority for the form of citing newspapers in CAREER sections, e.g. *Times*, Victoria, BC. Each entry is as comprehensive as possible but not necessarily exhaustive (i.e., all anthologies are not listed under CONTRIBUTED). Because of the large number of possible candidates in the English-speaking theatre category, the qualifications for inclusion were strictly followed to keep the number of entries within the percentage allotted to that group of artists, and professional qualifications determined inclusion.

Each entry is found under the subject's best known name with cross references from other names under which he may have appeared. When an entire section has been omitted within an entry, the information is either unavailable, not applicable, or specifically withheld by the biographee and not readily verified from existing public records.

In every author's entry is included as complete a bibliography of his monographic works as possible. No attempt has been made to list separate articles, but titles of those periodicals to which the individual has contributed are duly noted. When a biographee has received recognition in several fields the one in which he is best known has been preferred and his entry will read, for example, "Artist, sculptor"; or "Producer, actor, author." When he has devoted his entire life to his creative vocation and has not been employed in any other field the information is cited thus, "CAREER: Purely literary." Every attempt has been made to achieve consistency but complete consistency appears to be beyond human capability.

Those entries which have been verified by the biographee have been asterisked. As noted in the preface, information regarding the deceased has been exhaustively researched and in a number of cases entries have been verified by relatives or friends.

Education information is given in general terms with emphasis on professional education. In general only those memberships relating to the creative activities of the artist or author are listed. Information regarding titles of associations, awards, positions, etc., if found in French, appears in that language rather than in English translation. Usually awards are dated by the year for which the award is given, not the year in which it was presented; for example, the Governor General's award given in spring of 1969 is for work published in 1968 and would therefore be cited as Governor General's award, 1968.

HMR

Abbreviations

*	verified by biographee
AB	Bachelor of Arts
ABC	Associated British Cinemas
ABTT	Association of British Theatre Technicians
ACTRA	Association of Canadian Television and Radio Artists
ACTT	Association of Cinematograph, Television and Allied Technicians
ACUTE	Association of Canadian University Teachers of English
AEA	Actors' Equity Association
AFM	American Federation of Musicians
AFMUSC	American Federation of Musicians of the United States and Canada
AFTRA	American Federation of Television and Radio Artists
AGEUM	Association Générale des Étudiants de l'Université de Montréal
AGMA	American Guild of Musical Artists
AGVA	American Guild of Variety Artists
Ala.	Alabama
Alas.	Alaska
Alta.	Alberta
AM	Master of Arts
AMP	Associated Music Publishers
AMPAS	Academy of Motion Picture Arts and Sciences
ANTA	American National Theatre and Academy
AOCA	Associate Ontario College of Art
ARCA	Associate of the Royal College of Art
ARCT	Associate of the Royal Conservatory of Toronto
Ariz.	Arizona
Ark.	Arkansas
ATAS	Academy of Television Arts and Sciences
ATCM	Associate of the Toronto Conservatory of Music
ATV	Associated Television
BA	Bachelor of Arts
Bac Mus	Bachelor of Music
BBC	British Broadcasting Corporation
BC	British Columbia
BCL	Bachelor of Civil Law
BD	Bachelor of Divinity
BEd	Bachelor of Education

B-ès-A	Bachelier-ès-Arts
BFA	Bachelor of Fine Arts
BHL	Bachelor of Hebrew Literature
BL	Bachelor of Letters
BLitt	Bachelor of Letters or Literature
BLS	Bachelor of Library Science
BMI	Broadcast Music Incorporated
BMus	Bachelor of Music
BPaed	Bachelor of Paedagogy
BPh	Bachelor of Philosophy
BS	Bachelor of Science
BSc	Bachelor of Science
CA	Chartered Accountant
CAAE	Canadian Association for Adult Education
CAHA	Canadian Amateur Hockey Association
Calif.	California
CAMMAC	Canadian Amateur Musicians/Musiciens Amateurs Canadiens
CAPAC	Composers, Authors and Publishers Association of Canada
CAUT	Canadian Association of University Teachers
CBC	Canadian Broadcasting Corporation
CBC IS	Canadian Broadcasting Corporation International Service
CBE	Commander of the Order of the British Empire
CBS	Columbia Broadcasting System
CIDALC	Comité International pour la Diffusion des Arts et des Lettres par le Cinéma
CIIA	Canadian Institute of International Affairs
CLA	Canadian Library Association
CM	Master in/of Surgery
CMC	Canadian Music Centre
CMG	Companion of the Order of Saint Michael and Saint George
CNIB	Canadian National Institute for the Blind
CNR	Canadian National Railway
CODL	Central Ontario Drama League
Colo.	Colorado
Conn.	Connecticut
COTC	Canadian Officers Training Corps
CPR	Canadian Pacific Railway
CTV	Canadian Television
DC	District of Columbia
DCL	Doctor of Civil Law
DD	Doctor of Divinity
DDF	Dominion Drama Festival
Del.	Delaware
DEW Line	Distant Early Warning Line
D-ès-Let	Docteur-ès-Lettres
D-ès-Jur	Docteur-ès-Jurisprudence

DFC	Distinguished Flying Cross	MB	Bachelor of Medicine
DGA	Directors Guild of America	MBE	Member of the Order of the British Empire
D Hu L	Doctor of Humane Letters		
D Lett	Docteur-ès-Lettres	MC	Military Cross
D Litt	Doctor of Letters	Md.	Maryland
D Mus	Doctor of Music	MD	Doctor of Medicine
D PEc	Doctor of Political Economy	Me.	Maine
D Ped	Doctor of Pedagogy	M Ed	Master of Education
DSO	Distinguished Service Order	MFA	Master of Fine Arts
DU	Doctor of University	Mich.	Michigan
DUC	Doctor of the University of Calgary	Minn.	Minnesota
		Miss.	Mississippi
FAO	Food and Agriculture Organization	ML	Master of Letters
Fla.	Florida	MM	Military Medal
FRAIC	Fellow of the Royal Architectural Institute of Canada	M Mus	Master of Music
		Mo.	Missouri
FRSA	Fellow of the Royal Society of Arts	Mont.	Montana
FRSC	Fellow of the Royal Society of Canada	MPD	Motion Picture Distributors
		MPE	Master of Physical Education
FRSCM	Fellow of the Royal School of Church Music	MS	Master of Science
		M Sc	Master of Science
		MSW	Master of Social Work
GB	Great Britain	Mus B	Bachelor of Music
GEMA	Gesellschaft für Musikalische Aufführungen	Mus D	Doctor of Music
Geo.	Georgia	NATAS	National Academy of Television Arts and Sciences
GM	General Motors		
GPO	General Post Office	NB	New Brunswick
		NBC	National Broadcasting Company
HMS	His/Her Majesty's Ship	NC	North Carolina
		n.d.	no date
IGNM	Internationale Gesellschaft für Neue Musik	N. Dak.	North Dakota
		Nebr.	Nebraska
IGZM	Internationale Gesellschaft für Zeitgenössische Musik	Nev.	Nevada
		Nfld.	Newfoundland
Ill.	Illinois	NH	New Hampshire
Ind.	Indiana	NJ	New Jersey
IODE	Imperial Order of the Daughters of the Empire	N. Mex.	New Mexico
		n.p.	no publisher
		NS	Nova Scotia
Kans.	Kansas	NSW	New South Wales
KC	King's Counsel	NWT	Northwest Territories
Ky.	Kentucky	NY	New York
La.	Louisiana	OBE	Order of the British Empire
L-ès-Let	Licencié-ès-Lettres	Okla.	Oklahoma
LHD	Doctor of Humane Letters	Ont.	Ontario
Litt D	Doctor of Letters	Oreg.	Oregon
LLB	Bachelor of Laws		
LLD	Doctor of Laws	Pa.	Pennsylvania
LLL	Licentiate in Laws	PEI	Prince Edward Island
L Ph	Licentiate of Philosophy	PEN	Poets, Playwrights, Essayists, Editors, Novelists
LRSM	Licentiate of the Royal School of Music		
		Pharm Lic	Licentiate of Pharmacy
L Sc Soc	Licence in Social Sciences	Ph B	Bachelor of Philosophy
		Ph D	Doctor of Philosophy
MA	Master of Arts	POW	Prisoner of War
Man.	Manitoba	p.p.	privately printed
Mass.	Massachusetts	PQ	Province of Quebec

QC	Queen's Counsel
RCAF	Royal Canadian Air Force
RCMP	Royal Canadian Mounted Police
RCN	Royal Canadian Navy
RCNVR	Royal Canadian Naval Volunteer Reserve
RI	Rhode Island
RNVR	Royal Naval Volunteer Reserve
SAG	Screen Artists Guild
Sask.	Saskatchewan
SC	South Carolina
S. Dak.	South Dakota
SODRE	Servicio Oficial de Difusion Radio Electrica
SSD&C	Society of Stage Directors and Choreographers
Tenn.	Tennessee
Tex.	Texas
UK	United Kingdom
UNESCO	United Nations Educational, Scientific and Cultural Organization
UNIATEC	Union Internationale des Associations Techniques Cinématographiques
UNICEF	United Nations Children's Fund
UNRRA	United Nations Relief and Rehabilitation Administration
USA	United States of America
USITT	United States Institute for Theater Technology
USSR	Union of Soviet Socialist Republics
Va.	Virginia
VD	Auxiliary Forces (Volunteer) Officers' Decoration
Vt.	Vermont
Wash.	Washington
WGA	Writers Guild of America
Wis.	Wisconsin
WRCNS	Women's Royal Canadian Naval Service
W. Va.	West Virginia
Wyo.	Wyoming
YMCA	Young Men's Christian Association
YMHA	Young Men's Hebrew Association
YT	Yukon Territory
YWCA	Young Women's Christian Association
YWHA	Young Women's Hebrew Association

CREATIVE CANADA

Creative Canada

ACORN, Milton   1923–
Poet; b. 1923 in Charlottetown, PEI; m. Gwendolyn MacEwen.

EDUCATION
Attended primary and secondary schools in Charlottetown.

HOME
Apt. 3, 19 Spadina Rd., Toronto, Ont.

CAREER
Canadian Army, c. 1939-45; employed part-time as industrial worker 1945–; mainly literary 1957–; resided in Maritime provinces, Montreal, PQ, Vancouver, BC, and Toronto.

WRITINGS
In love and anger, the author, 1957; *The brain's the target,* Ryerson, 1960; *Against a league of liars,* Hawkshead, 1960; *Jawbreakers,* Contact, 1963; *I've tasted my blood*, Ryerson, 1969.
CONTRIBUTED: Poems to *Poetry 62*, edited by E. Mandel and J.G. Pilon, Ryerson, 1961; *Modern Canadian verse in English and French*, edited by A.J.M. Smith, Oxford, 1967; *Canadian Literature, Evidence, Queen's quarterly, University of Toronto quarterly, Dalhousie review, Tamarack review, Canadian forum, Delta, Fiddlehead, Canadian author and bookman.*

ADAMS, Ernest   1920–
Singer (baritone); b. 17 Dec. 1920 in Winnipeg, Man.; m. Patricia; children: daughter b. c. 1958, daughter b. c. 1965.

EDUCATION
Studied voice 1936-41.

HOME
41 Lincombe Drive, Thornhill, Ont.

OFFICE
Canadian Opera Company, 129 Adelaide St. W., Suite 517, Toronto 1A, Ont.

CAREER
RCAF, 1942-45; Theatre Under the Stars, Vancouver, BC, leading roles 1945-48; Royal Conservatory Company, Toronto, baritone c. 1948; Canadian Opera Company, Toronto, leading baritone 1950–, tour manager 1950–, assistant to general director 1961-68, assistant director 1968–; soloist in many symphony and choral concerts.

MEMBER
ACTRA.

AWARDS, HONOURS
CBC "Singing stars of tomorrow" winner, c. 1947, 1948; Royal Conservatory of Music, Toronto, Opera School scholarship, 1945-48; Canada Council grant, 1966/67.

THEATRE
Sang in many productions, e.g. Nimming Ned in *The beggar's opera* (Stratford, Ont. Festival, 1958), Bartolo in *The barber of Seville* (Canadian Opera Company, tour 1958/59), *Orpheus in the underworld* (Canadian Opera Company, tour 1961).

RADIO
Sang in several CBC productions, e.g. "The Ernest Adams Show" (series, 1945-48).

TELEVISION
Sang in several CBC productions.

ADASKIN, Harry   1901–
Violinist and musical educator; b. 1901 in Riga, Latvia; son of Samuel and Neisha (Perstnov) Adaskin; came to Canada 1902 and settled in Toronto, Ont.; m. Frances Marr 1926; children: Gordon (adopted) b. 1931.

EDUCATION
Attended primary and secondary schools in Toronto; started violin studies 1908; studied with Bertha Drechsler Adamson and Luigi von Kunits, Toronto (now Royal) Conservatory of Music, 1913-22; Sametini, Chicago Musical College, Ill., 1922-23; Marcel Chailley in Paris, France, and Jacques Thibaud and Georges Enesco, summers 1938-46.

OFFICE
Department of Music, University of British Columbia, Vancouver 8, BC.

CAREER
Private violin teacher 1915-22; played in restaurant and theatre orchestras, e.g. Regent and Comedy Theatres, Toronto; Toronto Symphony Orchestra, violinist 1917-22; Academy String Quartet, Toronto, second violin 1920; Milton Blackstone's quartet, Toronto, first violin 1920-22; Hart House String Quartet, Toronto, founder-member and second violin 1923-38; toured with this quartet in USA, Canada, Britain, Austria, France, Italy, Holland, Denmark, and Sweden; Upper Canada College, Toronto, violin teacher 1938-41; concert soloist accompanied by his wife as pianist 1938-46; CBC, violinist in recitals, lecturer on musical subjects 1938-46; Toronto (now Royal) Conservatory of Music, violin teacher 1941-46; University of British Columbia, Department of Music, director, 1946–.

CONCERT STAGE
First public appearance, Moulton College, Toronto, 1913; New York debut, NY, Feb. 1947; recital, New York, 1948.

RADIO

Lecture series, "Musically speaking" (CBC, three years between 1938-46); intermission commentator for Sunday program by New York Philharmonic Orchestra (CBC, 1943-46).

COMPOSITIONS

Never forever, song, 1942.

WRITINGS

CONTRIBUTED: Articles to *Canadian music journal, Saturday night.*

ADASKIN, John 1908-64

Cellist, conductor, and producer; b. 4 June 1908 in Toronto, Ont.; son of Samuel and Neisha (Perstnov) Adaskin; m. Naomi Yanova Granatstein 28 Dec. 1934; children: Tamar Neisha Ruth b. 20 Oct. 1944, Susan Frances b. 23 Feb. 1946; d. 4 Mar. 1964 in Toronto.

EDUCATION

Attended public schools in Toronto, 1913-21; Harbord Collegiate Institute and Central Technical School, Toronto, 1921-25; studied cello with George Bruce and Boris Hambourg, Hambourg Conservatory of Music, Toronto, 1924-29; studied cello and theory with Leo Smith, conducting with Luigi von Kunits, Toronto (now Royal) Conservatory of Music, 1930-33; studied television technique with Hutchison in New York, NY.

RELIGION

Hebrew.

CAREER

Toronto Symphony Orchestra, cellist 1925-36; CBC, String Orchestra, first cello 1926-35, organiser of production department, Toronto 1934, program producer 1934-36, senior producer 1936-40, production director 1940-43; played wind instruments in restaurant and theatre orchestras, *c.*1927-34; compiled first list of Canadian composers 1940; John Adaskin Productions, proprietor 1943-61; Ryerson Institute of Technology, Toronto, organiser and teacher of radio and television production courses *c.*1950; Canadian National Exhibition Grandstand Show, Toronto, musical director, conductor, and composer of songs 1952; *Latin American bulletin*, correspondent 1961-64; Canadian Music Centre, Toronto, executive secretary 1961-64; International Association of Music Information Centres, secretary 1962; *Music across Canada,* editor 1962-64.

MEMBER

Arts and Letters Club; Royal Society of Arts, London, England (elected fellow, 1961); Toronto Musicians Association; Montreal Musicians Association; ACTRA.

AWARDS, HONOURS

Hans Kindler scholarship to study cello in Paris, France (not taken up), 1929; Beaver award for

distinguished service to Canadian radio, 1945; namesake of John Adaskin Memorial Fund to assist music students and Canadian Music Centre John Adaskin Project to further new music in education, 1964.

RADIO

Produced and directed over 4000 CBC programs, including symphony broadcasts from Massey Hall and Varsity Arena, Toronto, many series, e.g. "Shakespeare series," "Magic carpet," three seasons of Victory Loan programs from Massey Hall, Toronto, and Vancouver Arena, BC, with performers, e.g. André Kostelanetz, Paul Whiteman, Sir Henry Wood, Sir Adrian Boult, Gracie Fields, Lily Pons, and Victor Borge; with John Adaskin Productions, produced many series, e.g. "Singing stars of tomorrow" (CBC, 1944-58) including performers, e.g. Lois Marshall, Maureen Forrester, Robert Goulet, "Opportunity knocks" (CBC, 1947-57), "Voice of Victor," "The Happy Gang."

CONCERT STAGE

Gave many recitals as cellist accompanied by his wife, 1929-38; conducted Promenade Symphony Orchestra, Toronto, Aug. 1951; conducted CBC Symphony Orchestra, 1952.

AGOSTINI, Lucio 1913—

Composer, conductor, and arranger; b. 30 Dec. 1913 in Fano, Italy; son of Giuseppe Agostini; came to Canada in 1916 and settled in Montreal, PQ; m.; children: Lola b. 1939, Elio b. 1943.

EDUCATION

Started musical studies with his father, 1918; studied cello and all wind instruments; studied harmony and composition with Louis Michaels and Enrique Miro, cello with Peter van der Meerschen.

HOME

210 South Service Rd., Port Credit, Ont.

OFFICE

Canadian Broadcasting Corporation, 354 Jarvis St., Toronto, Ont.

CAREER

Giuseppe Agostini's orchestra, arranger 1928-30; Montreal Philharmonic Orchestra, cellist 1929- ?; Palace and Capitol Theatres, Montreal, saxophonist and clarinettist 1929-33; Loew's Theatre, band member 1933; CBC, arranger of incidental music 1934-40, musical director of variety shows 1943—, Light Concert Orchestra, conductor 1958-61; Associated Screen News, musical director 1940-43; National Film Board of Canada, composer 1942-43.

MEMBER

CAPAC; Toronto Musicians Association.

AWARDS, HONOURS

Nice, France, Music Festival award, 1957.

RADIO

Conductor-arranger for numerous series on CBC,

e.g. "Stage" (1944-55), "Ford Theatre," "Wednesday night," "Let there be music," "Ways of mankind," "Democracy in America," "Juliette show"; composer and director of numerous CBC feature programs.

TELEVISION

Numerous appearances on CBC, as conductor-arranger for series, e.g. "Appointment with Agostini" (1958-61), "Front page challenge" (1955-67), "Russ Thompson show"; conductor, numerous feature programs, e.g. *Another side of young* ("Show of the week," Dec. 1965), *The big sky* (Mar. 1967), *Tom Jones* ("O'Keefe Centre presents," Feb. 1968).

RECORDINGS

Action with Agostini, RCA Victor; *Mucho Lucio,* Canadian Talent Library CTL 065; *Mas mucho Lucio,* Canadian Talent Library, CTL 1109.

COMPOSITIONS

Numerous scores for radio and television programs and stage productions; music for concert orchestra, e.g. *Goldleaf, Centipedantics, Taxi, A night in Spain, Pedro Pussycat,* all recorded; *Piano concerto,* piano, voices, and orchestra, 1948; *Suite for strings,* 1948; *Élégie,* orchestra; *Pickwick papers suite,* 1948; *Subway,* orchestra; *The ghost speaks,* orchestra; *Scherzo,* orchestra; *Pizzicato rhumba,* orchestra, 1951; *Full speed ahead,* orchestra, 1951; *An eye for an eye,* orchestra, 1951; *Willie the squowse,* musical comedy, 1966.

ALBANI, Marie-Louise Émma Cécile   1847—1930
(Marie-Louise Émma Cécile Lajeunesse Gye)
Singer (soprano); b. 24 Sept. 1847 in Chambly, PQ; daughter of Joseph and Mélina (Mignault) Lajeunesse; m. Ernest Gye 1878; children: Ernest F. b. 1880; d. 3 Apr. 1930 in London, England.

EDUCATION

Early musical education by her father continued at Convent of the Sacred Heart, Sault au Recollet, Montréal; studied voice with Duprez and Benoist in Paris, France, 1865; with Lamperti in Milan, Italy.

RELIGION

Roman Catholic.

CAREER

Recitals in Montreal, Chambly, L'Assomption, Sorel, Joliette, Terrebonne, PQ; instructor in singing and piano at Kelwood, Man., 3 years; organist at Saratoga Springs, NY, 1862; Albany Cathedral, NY, soloist 1864-68; toured Italy and England 1872, Russia 1873, France, Holland, Germany, and the Scandinavian countries 1884-88, Germany 1891, 1893, USA and Mexico 1890, Canada 1889, 1890, 1896, 1901, 1903, 1906, Africa, India, and Australia 1901; sang in New York, NY, 1874, 1896, Venice, Italy, 1874, Nice, France, 1876, Montreal, 1883; sang at Händel Festival, 1877, at Colonial and Indian Exhibition, 1886; repeatedly sang for Queen Victoria and at her funeral, 22 Jan. 1901; sang at reception given to King Edward VII and Queen Alexandra at Guildhall, London, England, Jan. 1901 and at coronation of King Edward VII, 9 Aug. 1902; sang at opening of Franco-British Exposition, London, 1908; last concert 1909; some teaching during her old age.

AWARDS, HONOURS

Received title of Prima Donna at Théâtre des Italiens, Paris, France; title of Hofkammersängerin (court singer) from Emperor of Germany; title of Queen of English Festivals at Birmingham; Orders of merit from Denmark, Germany, and the King of the Sandwich Islands; Order of merit for Art, Science and Music from King Edward VII; Beethoven medal from Royal Philharmonic Society, London; badge from Amateur Orchestral Society, London; Victoria badge, Jubilee medal of 1887 with clasp for Diamond Jubilee; was made Dame Commander of the British Empire by George V, 1925.

THEATRE

First public appearance at Mechanics' Hall, Montreal, 1854; first concert, 15 Sept. 1856; opera deput as Amina in *La sonnambula* (Messina, Italy, 1870); London debut (Royal Italian Opera, London, England, 1872); sang in numerous productions, e.g. Antonida in *Ivan Sussanin,* Desdemona in *Otello,* Elisabeth in *Tannhäuser,* title role in *Tristan und Isolde,* Elsa in *Lohengrin,* Eva in *Die Meistersinger von Nürnberg,* title role in *Lucia di Lammermoor,* Marguerite in *Faust,* title role in *Mignon,* Ophélie in *Hamlet,* soloist in *Messiah* (Crystal Palace, London).

RECORDINGS

Few cylindrical recordings were made in London, 1904-05.

ALFSEN, John Martin   1902—
Artist: b. 22 Dec. 1902 in Alpena, Mich.

EDUCATION

Studied with J.W. Beatty, A. Lismer (*q.v.*), and F.H. Varley, Ontario College of Art, Toronto; studied with Hayes Miller, Art Students' League, New York, NY; studied under Bourdelle, Académie de la Grande Chaumière, Paris, France; attended Beaux-Arts, Antwerp, Belgium.

HOME

182 Main St., Markham, Ont.

OFFICE

Ontario College of Art, Grange Park, Toronto, Ont.

CAREER

Ontario College of Art, teacher 1929—.

COMMISSIONS

Portrait of the honourable Frank L. Bastedo, 1965.

MEMBER
Canadian Group of Painters; Ontario Society of
Artists (elected, 1937); Royal Canadian Academy
(Associate 1943; Academician 1959).

AWARDS, HONOURS
Art Students' League Scholarship; Forster Award,
Purchase Award, Ontario Society of Artists; Can-
ada Council senior arts fellowship, 1962/63.

EXHIBITIONS
GROUP: Represented in group exhibitions held
in Canada during his lifetime including exhibi-
tions of the Canadian Group of Painters, Montreal
Museum of Fine Arts Spring Show; represented
in group exhibitions organized by the National
Gallery of Canada, Ottawa, Ont.; Exhibition of
Contemporary Canadian Painting, arranged ...
for circulation in the Southern Dominions of the
British Empire, 1936; A Century of Canadian Art,
Tate Gallery, London, England, 1938; Carnegie
Institute, Pittsburgh, Pa., National Academy of
Design Exhibition; Great Lakes Exhibition assem-
bled by the Albright Art Gallery, Buffalo, NY,
1939; Canadian Art, Yale University Art Gallery,
New Haven, Conn., 1944.

COLLECTIONS IN WHICH REPRESENTED
National Gallery Art Students' League, USA;
Hamilton, Ont.; Art Gallery of Ontario, Toronto.

ALLEYN, George Edmund 1931—
Artist; b. 9 June 1931 in Montreal, PQ.

EDUCATION
Studied under Jean Paul Lemieux, École des
Beaux-Arts, Montreal, PQ, 1956, diplôme en
peinture, 1955; attended L'Académie Julian,
Paris, France.

HOME
49 Lincourt, Paris 14e, France.

CAREER
Lived and painted in Paris since 1955.

AWARDS, HONOURS
Grand prize, Concours Artistique of the Province of Quebec, 1955; bourse du Gouvernement
français, Paris, 1955; Alexander Therien prize,
1955; Royal Society of Canada bursary, 1956;
bronze medallion, Biennial de Sâo Paulo, Brazil,
1959.

EXHIBITIONS
ONE-MAN: Galerie Agnès Lefort, Montréal, 1955-
60; Galerie du Haut-Pavé, Paris, 1957; Théâtre
Fauteuil, Basle, Switzerland, 1958; Galerie
Denyse Delrue, Montréal, 1960; Roberts Gallery,
Toronto, Ont., 1960-64; Galerie Dresdnère, Montréal, 1962; Galerie Soixante, Montréal, 1964;
University of Toronto; Galerie Ed Smith, Paris,
1966; Galerie Blumenthal-Momaton, Paris, 1967.
GROUP: Represented in group exhibitions held
in Canada since 1956; represented in group exhibitions organized by the National Gallery of Canada, Ottawa, Ont. including the second, third,

fifth, and sixth Biennial of Canadian Painting,
1957, 1959, 1963, and 1965; travelling exhibition
through the USA and Canada, Smithsonian Institute, 1956; Obelisk Gallery, London, England,
1957; Guggenheim Exhibition, New York, NY,
1957 and subsequent years; Salon des Réalités
nouvelles, Paris, 1958 and subsequent years; International Festival of Art, New York, 1958; Musée
Rath, Geneva, Switzerland, 1959; Wallraf-Richartz
Museum, Cologne, Germany, 1959; Galerie Appia
Antica, Rome, Italy, 1959; Biennale de Venise,
1960; Six peintres canadiens, Galerie Arditi,
Paris, 1962; Galerie Levi, Milan, Italy, 1962;
Donner à voir, Galerie Creuze, Paris, 1963; Gal-
erie Le Gendre, Paris, 1963; La Boîte, Galerie Le
Gendre, Paris, 1964; Rythmes et Réflexion, Gal-
erie A., Paris, 1964; La figuration narrative,
Galerie Creuze, Paris, 1965; Artistes latino-amé-
ricains, Musée d'art moderne, Paris, 1965; Galerie
J. Massol, Paris, 1965; Zero Point, La Roue,
Paris, 1966; 50 peintres de l'École de Paris,
Gmünd, Darmstadt, Germany, 1966.

COLLECTIONS IN WHICH REPRESENTED
National Gallery of Canada, Ottawa; Montreal
Museum of Fine Arts; Musée de Québec, PQ;
Vancouver Art Gallery, BC; Musée d'Art Contem-
porain, Montréal; Art Gallery of Ontario, Toronto.

ALLISTER, William* 1919—
Author and artist; b. 1919 in Benito, Man.; son
of Solomon and Luba Allister; m. Mona June
1946; children: Dorrianne b. 1951, Ada b. 1955.

EDUCATION
Attended Baron Byng High School, Montreal, PQ;
studied painting at Instituto Allende, Mexico.

HOME
2085 Noel St., St. Laurent, PQ.

CAREER
Commercial artist in Montreal; Canadian Army,
served in expedition to Hong Kong, China, 1941;
prisoner-of-war 1941-45, released in Japan, 1945;
actor in Hollywood, Calif., 1945-48; returned to
Montreal c.1950; writer for an advertising agency;
CBC, National Film Board, and Westminster Films,
Toronto, Ont., script writer; resided one year in
Mexico.

AWARDS, HONOURS
Dominion Drama Festival acting award, 1939; 1st
prize for literary merit, 1962; Canada Council
senior arts fellowship, 1962-63.

EXHIBITIONS
ONE-MAN: In Canada, 1968.
GROUP: Represented in a group exhibition held
in San Miguel de Allende, Mexico, 1963.

WRITINGS
A handful of rice (novel), Secker and Warburg,
1961; Knowing your market (film script, Westminster Films; certificate of merit, Vancouver
Film Festival, BC, 1962); The inner mind of

Milton Whitty (screenplay, Westminster Films; bronze plaque, National Committee on Films for Safety, Chicago, Ill., 1963; Chris award, Columbus Film Festival, Ohio, 1964); *The return of Milton Whitty* (screenplay, Westminster Films; bronze plaque, National Committee on Films for Safety, Chicago, Ill., 1966; Chris award, Columbus Film Festival, Ohio, 1966; certificate of merit, Fifth International Labour and Industrial Film Triennial, Brussels, Belgium, 1966; blue ribbon certificate, American Film Festival, New York, NY, 1967); *The changing of the gods* (radio play, "Summer Stage," CBC, 18 July 1965).

CONTRIBUTED: Articles to *Saturday night*.
WORK IN PROGRESS: "Time to unmask the clown" (novel).

ALMOND, Paul* 1931–
Director, producer, and author; b. 26 Apr. 1931 in Montreal, PQ; son of Eric and Irene Clarice (Gray) Almond; m. Angela Leigh (*q.v.*) 1958 (marriage dissolved); m. Geneviève Bujold 18 Mar. 1967; children (second marriage) James Matthew b. 1968.

EDUCATION
Attended Roslyn primary school in Westmount, Montreal; Bishop's College School, Lennoxville, PQ; McGill University; Balliol College, Oxford University, BA, MA in philosophy, politics, and economics, 1949-52.

RELIGION
Anglican.

HOME
212 Briar Hill Ave., Toronto 12, Ont.; 42 Cambridge St., London, S.W.1, England.

CAREER
Oxford and Cambridge Players Company, England, founder 1953; CBC, Toronto, television director and producer 1954-66; Associated British Cinemas, BBC, and Granada, London, television director and producer; freelance film director and producer 1966–.

TELEVISION
Directed and produced over 100 programs, e.g. wrote and produced *The hill* (1956; reproduced 1959; reproduced for BBC 1957; Ohio State University award, 1956); adapted and produced *Under Milkwood* (based on Dyland Thomas' play; 1957; Ohio State University award, 1957), *Point of departure* (based on Anouilh's play; 1958; Ohio State University award, 1958), *Julius Caesar* (based on Shakespeare's play; "Festival," 19 Dec. 1960); produced *The watchers* ("GM presents," 25 Dec. 1960), *Return journey* ("Q for Quest," 28 Feb. 1961), *The town that didn't care* ("Q for Quest," 21 May 1961), *Standard of dying* ("Q for Quest," 23 May 1961), *Power by proxy* ("GM presents," 25 June 1961); wrote (with Rudi Dorn) and produced *The*

broken sky ("Playdate," 8 Nov. 1962); produced *Venus observed* ("Festival," 7 Jan. 1963); directed *The dark did not conquer* (12 Apr. 1963); produced *Antigone* (Anouilh, "Festival," 9 Oct. 1963); devised and directed *Mother and daughter* (ballet, "Telescope," 14 Feb. 1964); directed and produced *Seven-up* (England; special diploma of merit at Prague International Television Festival, 1964); produced *The close prisoner* ("Festival," 11 Nov. 1964), *Neighbours* ("Show of the week," 7 Dec. 1964), *The birthday party* ("Festival," 6 Jan. 1965), *Departure and arrival* ("Festival," 1964/65), *The labyrinth* ("Festival," 1964/65), *A spring song* ("Festival," 12 May 1965), *Roméo and Jeannette* (Anouilh, "Festival," 6 Oct. 1965); directed and produced *Horror of darkness* ("Festival," 13 Oct. 1965), *The murderer* ("Festival," 23 Feb. 1966); adapted and directed *Dylan revisited* (based on Dylan Thomas' writings; "Festival," 20 Apr. 1966), *A doll's house* (based on Ibsen's play; "Festival," 4 May 1966); directed *All aboard for Candyland* ("Wojeck," 27 Sept. 1966), *The puppet caravan* ("Festival," 1 Mar. 1967).

FILMS
Wrote, directed, and produced *Isabel* (Quest Film Productions Ltd., Toronto, distributed by Paramount, 1968).

WRITINGS
Television and film scripts.
CONTRIBUTED: Poems and short stories to *Isis, Gambit, Oxford poetry, Family herald,* and various women's magazines.
WORK IN PROGRESS: Film for Quest Film Productions set in Montreal.

AMBROSE, Katherine Charlotte
see AMBROSE, Kay

AMBROSE, Kay
(Katherine Charlotte Ambrose)
Designer, author, and illustrator; b. in Surrey, England, came to Canada in 1951.

EDUCATION
Attended Reading University, England.

CAREER
Illustrated *Ballet* by Arnold Haskell, Pelican, 1938 and *A theatre for everybody* by Edward J. Dent, Boardman, 1945; Ram Gopal's Company, India, art director, lecturer, and dancer; National Ballet of Canada, Toronto, artistic designer and adviser 1951-62.

MEMBER
ACTRA (life member).

AWARDS, HONOURS
Scholarship for fine arts at Reading University; awards in drama, elocution, and dance.

THEATRE
Designed costumes for *Giselle* (1952), (with James Pape) *Coppelia,* act I, II (1952), *Casse-*

noisette, act II (1952), *L'après-midi d'un faune* (1952), *Le pommier* (1952), *Dances from the classics* (1953); decor and costumes for *Le lac des cygnes*, act II (1953), *Le jardin aux lilas* (1953), *Gala performance* (1953), *Dark of the moon* (1953), *Le lac des cygnes* (1954), *Barbara Allen* (1954; Palace, Hamilton, Ont., 26 Oct. 1960), *Offenbach in the underworld* (Palace, St. Catharines, Ont., 17 Jan. 1955), *Casse-noisette* (1955); costumes for *Lady from the sea* (1955); decor and costumes for *The fisherman and his soul* (1956), *Le carnaval* (1957), *Winter night* (1957), *Coppelia* (Capitol, Ottawa, Ont., 29 Oct. 1958), *The mermaid* (Hamilton, 5 Nov. 1959), *Princess Aurora* (Palace, Hamilton, 24 Oct. 1960).

TELEVISION
Designed costumes for *Pineapple Poll* ("Ford startime," CBC, 22 Dec. 1959).

WRITINGS
(with A. Haskell) *Balletomane's sketch-book* A & C Black, 1941; *Ballet – to Poland*, A & C Black, 1941; *The ballet-lover's pocket book*, A & C Black, 1943; *Ballet impromptu, variations on a theme*, Golden Gallery, 1946; *Ballet-lover's companion*, A & C Black, 1949; *Classical dances and costumes of India*, A & C Black, 1950; *The story of Ram Gopal*, Dilworth, 1951; (with Celia Franca) *Beginners, please!*, A & C Black, 1953 (published in USA under title *The ballet student's primer*, Knopf, 1954 [c. 1953]).

AMESS, Frederick Arthur* 1909–
Artist; b. 1909 in London, England.
EDUCATION
Studied under C.H. Scott, J.W.G. MacDonald (*q.v.*), and F.H. Varley, Vancouver School of Art; studied under Austin Cooper and Stanley Herbert, Reimann School of Art, London.
OFFICE
Vancouver School of Art, 249 Dunsmuir, Vancouver, BC.
CAREER
Vancouver School of Art, lecturer 1930–, director of Saturday morning children's classes and night school classes, principal 1954–; University of Victoria, teacher, summer sessions; freelance commercial artist; organizer of Art in Living Group; University of British Columbia Fine Arts Advisory Committee.
COMMISSIONS
Mural, Pacific Mills Paper Company.
MEMBER
BC Industrial Design Committee (charter member); British Columbia Society of Artists; Federation of Canadian Artists (honourary life member).
AWARDS, HONOURS
Canada Council senior fellowship to Europe, 1959.

EXHIBITIONS
ONE-MAN: Vancouver Art Gallery, 1951; Victoria Arts Centre; The Bau Xi Gallery, Vancouver, 1966.
GROUP: Represented in group exhibitions held in Canada including annual exhibitions of the Canadian National Exhibition, Toronto, Ont.; represented in group exhibitions organized by the National Gallery of Canada, Ottawa, Ont.
COLLECTIONS IN WHICH REPRESENTED
Vancouver Art Gallery.
WRITINGS
CONTRIBUTED: To *Canadian art*.

ANDERSON, Patrick* 1915–
Poet; b. 1915 in England; came to Canada in 1940 and became Canadian citizen in 1945.
EDUCATION
Attended Oxford University; Columbia University.
CAREER
Taught in a private school, Montreal, PQ, 1940-46; *Preview*, Montreal, co-founder 1942; *Northern review*, Montreal, co-founder 1945; McGill University, assistant professor of English 1949-50; left Canada for Singapore in 1950; Malaya University, lecturer in English 1950-52; returned to England in 1952; BBC, commentator; University of London, tutor; travelled in Europe, including Spain and Greece.
MEMBER
Oxford University Union (past president).
AWARDS, HONOURS
Commonwealth fellowship to attend Columbia University; *Poetry magazine* fellowship prize, 1943.
WRITINGS
A tent for April (poems), First Statement Press, 1945; *The white centre* (poems), Ryerson, 1946; *The colour as naked* (poems), McClelland & Stewart, 1953; *Snake wine*, Chatto & Windus, 1955; *Search me* (autobiography), Chatto & Windus, 1957; *First steps in Greece* (travel), Chatto & Windus, 1958; *Finding out about the Athenians* (non-fiction), F. Muller, 1961; *The character ball* (autobiography), Clarke, Irwin, 1963; *Dolphin days* (travel), Gollancz, 1963; *The smile of Apollo* (travel), Chatto & Windus, 1964.
EDITED: (with A.E. Sutherland) *Eros, an anthology of friendship*, Blond, 1961.
CONTRIBUTED: Poems and articles to *The book of Canadian poetry*, 3rd ed., edited by A.J.M. Smith, Gage, 1957; *Other Canadians*, edited by John Sutherland, First Statement Press, 1947; *Canadian forum, Canadian poetry, First statement, Here and now, Preview,* and *Spectator*, London.

ANDERSON, William Henry 1882-1955
Composer and organist; b. 21 Apr. 1882 in
London, England; came to Canada in 1910 and
settled in Winnipeg, Man.; d. 1955 in England.
EDUCATION
Studied voice and composition privately in
England; attended Guildhall School of Music,
London.
CAREER
Church chorister in London to 1910; music
teacher and examiner in Winnipeg; Central
Church, Winnipeg, organist and choirmaster;
St. Andrew's Church, River Heights, Man.,
organist and choirmaster; Canadian National
Railway Choir, conductor; CBC, conductor
of The Choristers choral group 1939–c. 52.
MEMBER
CAPAC; Men's Musical Club, Winnipeg; Manitoba
Choral Society.
AWARDS, HONOURS
Guildhall School of Music scholarship.
RADIO
Conducted church music on CBC.
COMPOSITIONS
(All published by Western Music unless otherwise
indicated) *The little king is sleeping,* women's
voices, 1935; *Come, I pray thee,* mixed choir,
1938; *Born of Marie,* mixed choir and piano,
1938; *Sleep, little Jesus,* women's voices, 1938;
Old shepherd's prayer, medium voice and piano,
1938; *The bird in the nest,* women's voices,
1940; *Little Jesus came to town,* medium voice
and piano, 1940; *The piper wind,* women's
voices, 1941; *The sea-blue gardens,* women's
voices, 1942, Oxford; *Soldier's song,* men's
voices and piano, 1943; *The white dove,*
women's voices and piano, 1943; *Twilight,*
women's voices, 1943; *Spring is here,* soprano,
alto, and piano, 1943; *Give ear to my words,*
mixed choir, 1944; *Two Christmas carols,*
mixed choir and solo, 1944; *Wind in the lilacs,*
women's voices, 1945; *Christmas gifts,* women's
voices, 1945; *Long, long ago,* women's voices,
1945; *As I walked in Bethlehem,* mixed choir,
1947; *O little children, lead us,* mixed choir or
women's voices, 1947; *Five introits or vespers,*
mixed choir, 1947; *As Mary sings,* women's
voices, 1947; *In the morning, O Lord,* mixed
choir and solo, 1948, C. Fischer; *Hospitality,*
medium voice and piano, 1948; *Song of Mary,*
medium voice and piano, 1948; *Come, Holy
Ghost,* mixed choir, 1953, C. Fischer; many other
choral works and arrangements of folk songs,
etc., published by H.W. Gray, G. Schirmer, C.C.
Birchard, T. Presser, Galaxy Music, W. Paxton,
Arnolds, Boosey & Hawkes, Stainer & Bell.

ANHALT, Istvan 1919–
Composer and musicologist; b. 12 Apr. 1919 in
Budapest, Hungary; son of Arnold and Katalin
Anhalt, m. Beate Frankenberg; children: Helen,
Carol; came to Canada in 1949, settled in Montreal.
EDUCATION
Studied piano and conducting, composition
with Zoltan Kodaly, Royal Hungarian Academy
of Music, Budapest, 1937-41; conducting with
Louis Fourestier, Conservatoire National de
Musique, Paris, France, laureate, 1946; compo-
sition with Nadia Boulanger in Paris, 1946.
RELIGION
Jewish.
HOME
464 Claremont Ave., Montreal, PQ.
OFFICE
Department of Music, McGill University,
Montreal, PQ.
CAREER
Opera of Budapest, assistant conductor 1945;
McGill University, associate professor of music
and chairman of the department of theory
1949–; helped to organise the first public
concert of electronic music in Canada, McGill
University 1959; carried out research in electronic
music, at National Research Council of Canada
Electronic Music Laboratory, Ottawa, Ont.
1959-61, Columbia-Princeton Electronic Music
Center, Columbia University 1961, Bell Tele-
phone Laboratories, Murray Hill, NJ.
MEMBER
Canadian League of Composers; Montreal
Jewish Music Council (hon. vice-president).
AWARDS, HONOURS
Budapest Academy of Music first prize in
composition; Lady Davis fellowship, 1949;
Canada Council grant, 1960/61; Columbia-
Princeton Electronic Music Center grant, 1961.
RADIO
Discussed Arnold Schoenberg's music ("Wed-
nesday night," CBC, 8 Aug. 1962); commented
on Canadian music ("Sunday night," CBC, Sept.
1964).
COMPOSITIONS
Six songs from Na Conxy Pan, baritone and piano,
1948; *Interludium,* strings, piano and timpani,
1949; *Psalm XIX,* baritone and piano, 1951;
Three songs of love, women's voices a cappella,
1951; *Sonata for piano,* 1951; *Arc en ciel,*
ballet suite, two pianos, 1951; *Journey of the
Magi,* baritone and piano, 1952; *Trio,* violin,
cello, and piano, 1953; *Fantasia for piano,* 1954;
Funeral music, woodwinds and strings, 1954, first
performed 1954 by McGill University Orchestra
under the composer; *Three songs of death,* mixed
choir a cappella, 1954; *Comments,* suite, contralto,
violin, cello, and piano, 1954; *Sonata for violin
and piano,* 1955, recorded by RCA Victor with
Hyman Bress, violin; *Chansons d'aurore,* soprano,
flute, and piano, 1955; *Symphony,* 1958, first

performed Nov. 1959 in Montreal under the composer as conductor, dedicated to the bicentenary of Canadian Jewry; *Electronic music composition no. 1, 1959, no. 2, 1959, no. 3, 1960, no. 4, 1961,* all first realized at National Research Council of Canada Elmus Laboratory; *Cento on Eldon Grier's "An ecstasy,"* 12 speakers and tape, 1966, first realized in the electronic music studio at McGill University; *Symphony of modules,* electronic sounds, 1967.

ANKA, Paul   1941–

Singer and composer; b. 30 July 1941 in Ottawa, Ont.; son of Andrew and Camilia (Tannis) Anka; m. Anne de Zagheb 16 Feb. 1963; children: Alexandra.

EDUCATION

Attended Fisher Park High School in Ottawa.

OFFICE

200 W. 57th St., New York, NY.

CAREER

The Bobbysoxers, founder 1955; singer in major cities of the world 1956–; TV, radio, and film entertainer 1959–; musical comedy artist 1964–; Spanka Music Corporation, proprietor 1958–; Flanka Music Corporation, proprietor 1958–; Camy Productions Inc., proprietor 1961-66; RCA Victor, singer on world tour 1963.

AWARDS, HONOURS

Fifteen Gold Record awards.

THEATRE

Title role in *What makes Sammy run?* (Broadway, New York, 1964).

FILM

Guest singer in *Let's rock* (Columbia, 1958); *Girls' town,* (MGM, 1959); *The private lives of Adam and Eve* (Universal-International, 1960); *Look in any window* (Allied Artists, 1960); *The longest day* (Twentieth Century Fox, 1962); *Lonely boy* (1962).

CONCERT STAGE

Singer, Sahara Hotel, Las Vegas, Nev.; Copacabana Restaurant, New York; Carib Hilton Hotel, San Juan, Puerto Rico; Cocoanut Grove, Hollywood, Calif.; Forum, Montreal, PQ; Maple Leaf Gardens, Toronto, Ont.; San Remo Music Festival, Italy, 1964.

TELEVISION

Guest appearances on "Ed Sullivan show," "Danny Thomas show," "Perry Como show," "Dean Martin show," "Open mind," "Hollywood palace."

RECORDINGS

Many recordings, RCA Victor, 1957–.

COMPOSITIONS

Popular songs e.g. *My heart sings,* recorded by RCA Victor; *Diana,* 1957; *Crazy love; Lonely boy; Put your head on my shoulder; Time to cry; The longest day,* film score, 1962.

ANNE-MARIE, pseud.

see DAVID, Nellie Maillard

APINÉE, Irene*

(Irene Apinée Gotshalks; Irene Apiné)
Dancer; b. in Riga, Latvia; m. Jury Gotshalks (marriage dissolved Dec. 1967).

EDUCATION

Studied ballet in Riga.

OFFICE

c/o Les Grands Ballets Canadiens, 5415 Chemin de la Reine Marie, Montréal 248, PQ.

CAREER

Founded ballet school in Halifax, NS; National Ballet of Canada, Toronto (charter member), leading dancer 1951-56; Les Ballets Chiriaeff (now Les Grands Ballets Canadiens), Montreal, soloist 1956-59, 1965-67; American Ballet Theater, New York, NY, soloist 1959, 1961; City Center Opera Company, New York, leading dancer 1962; Jacob's Pillow Dance Festival, Lee, Mass., 1962.

THEATRE

Danced Swanhilda in *Coppelia* (St. Leon, 1952), Sugar Plum Fairy in *Casse-noisette,* act II (Ivanov, 1952), French ballerina in *Gala performance* (Tudor, Capitol, Ottawa, Ont., 18 Nov. 1953), title role in *Giselle* (Coralli-Perrot, 1954), Pas de deux and Mazurka in *Les sylphides* (Fokine, 1954), Odette-Odile in *Le lac des cygnes* (Petipa-Ivanov, 1954/55); created Debutante in *Offenbach in the underworld* (Tudor, Palace, St. Catharines, Ont., 17 Jan. 1955); danced in *Theme and variations* (Balanchine, 1959, 1961), *Design for strings* (Taras, 1959, 1961), Valse in *Les sylphides* (Fokine, 1959, 1961), title role in *L'oiseau de feu* (Nault, 1965-67), Sugar Plum Fairy in *Casse-noisette* (Nault, 1965-67), Girl in *Gehenne* (Nault, 1965-67), *The three sisters* (Les Grands Ballets Canadiens Workshop, summer 1965).

TELEVISION

Danced in many CBC productions.

ARBUCKLE, Franklin*   1909–

(George Franklin Arbuckle)
Artist; b. 17 Feb. 1909 in Toronto; son of George Lyons and Isebel Jane (Gier) Arbuckle; m. Frances-Anne Johnston 15 June 1934; children: Robin b. 6 Feb. 1937; Candace b. 25 June 1949.

EDUCATION

Attended Huron Street Public School, Davenport and Harbord High Schools, Toronto; studied under J.W. Beatty, F.S. Challener, Frank H. Johnston, and J.E.H. MacDonald (*q.v.*), Ontario College of Art, Toronto, graduated 1931.

HOME
278 Lawrence Ave. E., Toronto 12, Ont.
CAREER
Painted and lived in Montreal, PQ, 1940-58;
illustrated for *Maclean's* 1944-62; illustrated
historical series for Hudson's Bay Company,
Maclean's, Labatts Brewery Co., Distillers Corporation and Dow Chemicals; illustrated T.B.
Costain's *The white and the gold*, Doubleday,
1954, serialized in *Maclean's*, 1954; illustrated
Labatt Brewery's *Old names in Quebec*,
1957-59; Ontario College of Art, Department
of Advertising and Editorial Design, director
1962–; travelled widely throughout Canada on
painting assignments; illustrated *Great
Canadians*, Canadian Centennial Publishing Co.,
1965.
COMMISSIONS
Mural, commissioned by Steel Company of
Canada for the Hamilton City Hall, Ont.,
1960; design for two tapestries, Royal Bank of
Canada, Toronto, 1965; design for two tapestries,
Château Champlain, Montreal, 1966 (supervised
weaving of the four tapestries in Aubusson,
France); mural, New Parliament Building Annex,
Province of Ontario, 1968.
MEMBER
Ontario Society of Artists (elected, 1933);
Royal Canadian Academy (Associate 1936;
Academician 1943; president, 1960-64);
Canadian Society of Book Illustrators (elected,
1967).
AWARDS, HONOURS
Two Jessie Dow prizes, Montreal Museum of
Fine Art Spring Show; four prizes, Montreal
Directors' Club; medal, International Business
Machines; Canada Council grant *c.*1968.
EXHIBITIONS
ONE-MAN: Art Gallery of Toronto, *c.*1940;
Laing Gallery, Toronto; T. Eaton Company
Gallery, Toronto, many times; Continental
Gallery, Montreal; Roberts Gallery, Toronto.
GROUP: Represented in group exhibitions held
in Canada including annual exhibitions of the
Royal Canadian Academy and the Ontario
Society of Artists; World's Fair, New York,
NY, 1939.
COLLECTIONS IN WHICH REPRESENTED
Art Gallery of Ontario, Toronto; Musée du
Québec, PQ; International Business Machines;
Canadian Pacific Railway; Imperial Oil Company,
Toronto; Seagram Distillers, Montreal; Canadian
Club of New York, NY; Canadian Pulp and
Paper Association; Canadian Starch Ltd.;
Union Carbide of Canada Ltd.; Shell Oil of
Canada, Toronto; National Gallery of Canada,
Ottawa, Ont.

ARBUCKLE, George Franklin
see ARBUCKLE, Franklin

ARCHAMBAULT, Gilles* 1933–
Author; b. 19 Sept. 1933 in Montreal; son of
Paul and Colombe (Poirier) Archambault; m.
Lise Martel 10 May 1958; children: France
b. 25 June 1959; Sylvain b. 23 Aug. 1962.
RELIGION
Agnostic.
HOME
11975 Guertin St., Montreal 9, PQ.
OFFICE
Room 618, 1410 Stanley, Montreal 2, PQ.
CAREER
CBC, Montreal, 1958–.
MEMBER
Association des réalisateurs de radio (Radio-
Canada).
WRITINGS
Une suprême discrétion (novel), Cercle du Livre
de France, 1963; *La vie à trois* (novel), Cercle du
Livre de France, 1965.
CONTRIBUTED
Articles and stories to *Le devoir*, *Maclean's*,
Revue d'histoire.

ARLES, Henri d' 1870-1930
(Henri Beaudé; Henri Beaudet)
Author; b. 1870 in Arthabaskaville, PQ; d. 1930
in Rome, Italy.
EDUCATION
Séminaire de Québec.
RELIGION
Roman Catholic.
CAREER
Entered the Dominican Order 1890; ordained
priest 1895; parish priest in New York and New
Hampshire; travelled extensively in France, the
Holy Land, USA; secretary of Cardinal Canutelli
in Rome.
WRITINGS
Propos d'art, 1903; *Pastels*, 1905; *Tête d'étude*,
Paris, 1906; *Le collège sur la colline*, Rudeval,
1908; *Essais et conférences*, 1910; *Lacordaire,
l'orateur et le moine* (biography), Manchester,
1912; *Eaux fortes et tailles douces, essais*, La-
flamme et Proulx, 1913; *Nos historiens* (cours
de critique littéraire), Bibliothèque de
l'Action française, 1921; *Arabesques*, Dorbon-
Aîné, 1923; *Louis Fréchette* (biography),
Ryerson, 1924; *Laudes*, Paul Lefèbvre, 1925;
Estampes, Bibliothèque de l'Action française,
1926; *Miscellanées*, Mercure, 1927; *Horizons*,
Librairie d'Action, 1929.
EDITED
*Acadie: reconstitution d'un chapitre perdu de
l'histoire d'Amérique: ouvrage publié d'après
le ms. original, entièrement refondu*, 3v.,
1916-18.

BALDWIN, Catherine Janet
see BALDWIN, Janet

BALDWIN, Janet* 1912–
(Catherine Janet Baldwin Volkoff)
Dancer, teacher, and choreographer; b. 5 Dec.
1912 in Toronto; daughter of William Willcocks
and Kathleen (Gordon) Baldwin; m. Boris
Volkoff June 1936 (marriage dissolved
c.1951).

EDUCATION
Attended private schools in Ontario, Florence,
Italy, and Paris, France; studied ballet with
Boris Volkoff in Toronto; Adolph Bolm in San
Francisco and Hollywood, Calif.; Gweneth
Lloyd in Winnipeg, Man.; Aubrey Hitchins in
New York, NY; Andrew Hardie and Anna North-
cote in London, England.

HOME
Apt. 206, 94 Crescent Rd., Toronto 5, Ont.

OFFICE
Janet Baldwin School of Ballet, 9 Price St.,
Toronto 5, Ont.

CAREER
Janet Baldwin School of Ballet, Toronto, founder
and director; Canadian Dance Teachers Associations, co-founder; Canadian Ballet Festival,
co-founder 1948.

MEMBER
Royal Academy of Dancing.

THEATRE
Choreographed *Ballet cycle* (Canadian Ballet
Festival, Toronto, 1954).

BALES, Gerald Albert 1919–
Composer and organist; b. 12 May 1919 in
Toronto; m. June Liddell 1941.

EDUCATION
Studied music with his mother, 1924; studied
orchestral and choral conducting, composition,
piano, and organ, with Healey Willan (*q.v.*), and
Albert Proctor, Royal Conservatory of Music,
Toronto.

HOME
Apt. 302, 110 Wellesley Cres., Toronto, Ont.

CAREER
St. Ann's Anglican Church, Toronto, organist
and choirmaster 1937-41; Rosedale United
Church, Toronto, organist and choirmaster
1941-43; RCAF 1943-45; Brant Ave. United
Church, Brantford, Ont., organist and choir-
master 1945-46; Royal Conservatory of Music,
Toronto, teacher of piano, organ, and theory
1946- ?; St. Mark's Cathedral, Minneapolis,
Minn., organist and choirmaster.

MEMBER
BMI Canada.

CONCERT STAGE
First public appearance as pianist, 1926, as
organist, 1932; formal debut, Eaton Auditorium,
Toronto, 1937; recitals across Canada 1943-45;

many concert appearances 1945–; soloist with
Ottawa Philharmonic Orchestra, Ont., and Chicago
Philharmonic Orchestra, Ill.

RADIO
Organ recitalist in CBC series, e.g. "Sunday night"
(23 Aug. 1964), "Canadian organists in recital"
(25 Feb. 1966).

COMPOSITIONS
Thou art so like a flower, vocal; *Prelude in E
minor*, organ, 1939, BMI Canada, also arranged
for strings, 1951; *Prelude in C major*, organ;
Nocturne, orchestra; *Reverie*, piano; *Fantasy
for piano and orchestra*; *Suite for piano*;
Two improvisations, organ; *Lazarus*, mixed
choir; *Suite for orchestra*; *Summer idyll*,
orchestra; *Toccata*, piano, BMI Canada; *Your
tears*, vocal; *Revelry for orchestra*; *Invention*,
piano; *Essay for strings*, 1947, score available
from Canadian Department of External Affairs,
recorded by CBC IS with Jean-Marie Beaudet;
Petite suite, organ, BMI Canada; *Te deum*,
mixed choir, organ, brass, and percussion,
1962; *Jubilate*, mixed choir, organ, 3 trumpets,
and timpani, 1967.

BARBEAU, Charles Marius
see BARBEAU, Marius

BARBEAU, Christian Marcel
see BARBEAU, Marcel

BARBEAU, François* 1935–
(François Dominique)
Actor and costume designer; b. 1935 in Montreal;
son of Paul and Gabrille (Rochon) Barbeau; m.
Carmen Tremblay 28 Oct. 1964; children:
Valery b. 28 Aug. 1965.

EDUCATION
Attended l'Académie de Trois Rivières, PQ;
Cour la Roque, Montréal; Sir George Williams
University; studied with Cotnoir and Capponi,
Montreal, for 3 years; studied acting with Tania
Fédor, Montreal, for 3 years and Paul Buisson-
neau, Montreal, for 6 years.

RELIGION
Roman Catholic.

HOME
4397 Ave. de l'Esplanade, Montréal 131, PQ.

OFFICE
355 Gilford, Montreal, PQ.

CAREER
Montreal Parks and Playground Department,
costume designer for 5 seasons; Le Théâtre de
Quat'sous, Le Théâtre Club, Le Théâtre de L'Égrégore, Théâtre du Nouveau Monde, Montréal, costume designer; Le Théâtre du Rideau Vert, Montréal, resident designer; National Theatre School,
Montreal, teacher 1962–; assistant to Robert Pré-

vost, Claudette Picard, Solange Légendre; travel-
led extensively in Europe, USSR, and Japan.
MEMBER
Union des Artistes de Montréal; Canadian
Theatre Centre; International Theatre Institute.
AWARDS, HONOURS
Canada Council arts scholarship, 1960/61;
costume prizes from Congrès du Spectacle, 1965.
THEATRE
Played in several productions, e.g. Snug in *Le
songe d'une nuit d'été* (Rideau Vert, 15 Sept.
1965); designed costumes for *Le soldat au
briquet* (Parks and Playgrounds, 1958), *Long
day's journey into night* (Nouveau Monde, 1959),
Les dialogues des Carmélites (Rideau Vert, 1959),
Une femme douce (l'Égrégore, 1959), *Clérembard*
(Nouveau Monde, 1959), *Fin de partie* (l'Égrégore,
1959), *Pierre et le loup* (Parks and Playgrounds,
1959), *Le baladin du monde occidental* (Nouveau Monde, 1959), *Les taupes* (Nouveau
Monde, 1959), *Pantagleize* (Nouveau Monde,
1960), *Horace* (Théâtre Universitaire, 1960),
Chacun sa vérité (Nouveau Monde, 1960), *Le
manteau de Galilée* (Quat'sous, 1960), *Barbe
bleue* (Parks and Playgrounds, 1960), *L'école
des femmes* (Théâtre Universitaire, 1960), *Le
pélican* (l'Égrégore, 1960), *Été et fumée*
(l'Égrégore, 1961), *L'annonce faite à Marie*
(Théâtre Universitaire, 1961), *Celles qu'on
prend dans ses bras* (Théâtre Club, 1961), *Orion
le tueur* (Parks and Playgrounds, 1961), *Georges
Dandin* (Nouveau Monde, 1962), *Le médecin
malgré lui* (Nouveau Monde, 1962), *Irma la
douce* (Nouveau Monde, 1963), *L'Alcalde de
Zalamea* (Rideau Vert, 1963), *Le pain dur*
(Nouveau Monde, 1963), *L'orpheline Russe*
(Nouveau Monde, 1963), *L'heureux stratagème*
(Rideau Vert, 1963), *L'ombre d'un franc-
tireur* (Nouveau Monde, 1963), *Le roi se meurt*
(l'Egrégore, 1963), *L'avare* (Nouveau Monde,
1963), *Les gueux au paradis* (Rideau Vert,
1964), *La guerre de Troie n'aura pas lieu*
(Rideau Vert, 1964), *Iphigénie* (Nouvelle Compagnie, 1964), *On ne badine pas avec l'amour*
(Rideau Vert, 1964), *Un otage* (Rideau Vert,
1964), *Un mois à la campagne* (Rideau Vert,
1964), *Les jouets* (Rideau Vert, 1964), *Victor
ou les enfants au pouvoir* (l'Égrégore, 1964),
Jeanne et les juges (Nouvelle Compagnie, 1965),
Oncle Vania (l'Égrégore, 1965), *Chat en poche*
(Rideau Vert, 1965), *Les fourberies de Scapin*
(Rideau Vert, 1965), *Le Cid* (Nouvelle Com-
pagnie 1965), *La double inconstance* (Nouvelle
Compagnie, 1965), *La répétition ou L'amour
puni* (Rideau Vert, 1965), *Le tableau,* (l'Égrégore, 1965), *Une maison ... un jour* (Rideau
Vert, 11 Sept. 1965), *Fleur de cactus* (Rideau
Vert, 15 Oct. 1965), *L'effet Glapion* (l'Égrégore,
21 Oct. 1965), *La locandiera* (Nouvelle Com-

pagnie, Nov. 1965), *On ne sait comment*
(Rideau Vert, 15 Nov. 1965), *On grève ... de
rire* (Rideau Vert, 15 Dec. 1965), *La vie est un
songe* (Rideau Vert, 1966), *Du vent dans les
branches de Sassafras* (Rideau Vert, 1966),
Carmina burana (Les Grands Ballets Canadiens,
Montréal, 1966; Expo 67, Place des Arts,
Montréal, June 1967), *Le soulier de satin*
(Nouveau Monde, 1966), *Don Juan* (Nouvelle
Compagnie, Mar. 1966), *Croque Monsieur*
(Rideau Vert, 15 Mar. 1966), *Les trois soeurs*
(Rideau Vert, 15 Apr. 1966), *La grande Roue*
(Quat'sous, 2 June 1966), *Encore cinq minutes*
(Rideau Vert, 1967), *Dona Rosita* (Rideau Vert,
1967), *La p... respectueuse* (Rideau Vert, 1967),
Huis clos (Rideau Vert, 1967), *Terre d'aube*
(Rideau Vert, 1967), *Le malentendu* (Rideau
Vert, 1967), *L'oiseau bleu* (Rideau Vert, 1967),
Je veux voir Mioussov (Rideau Vert, 15 Feb.
1967), *La poudre aux yeux* (Rideau Vert, 18 May,
1967), *L'amant* (Rideau Vert, 1968), *La collec-
tion* (Rideau Vert, 1968), *Drôle de couple*
(Rideau Vert, 15 Jan. 1968), *L'exécution*
(Rideau Vert, 15 Mar. 1968), *Partage de midi*
(Rideau Vert, 15 Apr. 1968), *Le cheval évanoui*
(Rideau Vert, 15 May 1968), *Les belles soeurs*
(Rideau Vert, 28 Aug. 1968), *Ce soir on
improvise* (Rideau Vert, 16 Oct. 1968).
FILM
Designed costumes for several films, e.g. *Con-
flict* (Crawley Films, 1966); designed costumes
and played in *Festin des morts* (National Film
Board of Canada).
TELEVISION
Played Polichinel in *Boîte à surprise* (CBC, 1959/
60−1960/61).

BARBEAU, Marcel* 1925−
(Christian Marcel Barbeau)
Artist; b. 18 Feb. 1925 in Montreal, PQ; son of
Philippe Barbeau; m. Elizabeth St. Antoine
(marriage dissolved); children: Manon b. 8 Mar.
1949.
EDUCATION
Studied with Paul-Émile Borduas, l'École du
Meuble, Montréal, Diplôme d'ébéniste, 1941-46.
RELIGION
None.
HOME
41 Union Square, Room 1101, New York, NY,
USA.
CAREER
Painter; participated in the International Op Art
Seminar, Fairleigh Dickinson University, Madison,
NJ, 1965.
MEMBER
Contemporary Art Society.
AWARDS, HONOURS
Samuel Zacks Award, Royal Canadian Academy

of Arts, 1963; Canada Council fellowship, 1962; Purchase Award, Royal Canadian Academy, 1963; Conseil des Arts bursary, 1966.

EXHIBITIONS

ONE-MAN: *Le comptoir de l'art et du livre*, Ottawa, Ont., 1951; Wittenborn and Shutz, New York, 1952; Galerie Agnès Lefort, Montréal, 1952 and 1955; Palais Montcalm, Québec, PQ, 1955; Galerie l'Actuelle, Montréal, 1955; Galerie Denyse Delrue, Montréal, 1961, 1962, and 1963; Galerie Iris Clert, Paris, France, 1964; Dorothy Cameron Gallery, Toronto, Ont., 1964; Galerie du Siècle, Montréal, 1964, 1965, and 1967: East Hampton Gallery, New York, 1964, 1965, 1966, and 1967; Jerrold Morris Gallery, Toronto, 1965.

GROUP: Represented in group exhibitions organized by the National Gallery of Canada, Ottawa; Luxembourg Gallery, Paris, France, 1947; Einaudi, Rome, Italy, 1962; Festival of Two Worlds, Spoleto, Italy, 1963; Op from Montreal, Robert Hall Fleming Museum, University of Vermont, 1965; Walter Chrysler Museum, Provincetown, Mass., 1965; Penthouse Show, Museum of Modern Art, New York, 1965; Op Art, Foley's Gallery, Houston, Texas; Ohio State University and other mid-west universities, 1965; 1+1=3, Retinal Painting, University of Texas Museum, Austin, 1965; The Deceived Eye, Fort Worth Texas Art Center, 1965; Op Art Seminar Show, Fairleigh Dickinson University, Madison, NJ, and Riverside Museum, New York, 1965; International Artists Seminars, Empire State Building Art Gallery, New York, 1965; Optical 66, Argus Gallery, Madison, 1966; International Exhibition, Hilton International Hotel, New York, 1966; National Arts and Antiques Show, Madison Square Garden, New York; Boston Museum, Massachusetts Institute of Technology, 1968.

COLLECTIONS IN WHICH REPRESENTED

National Gallery of Canada, Ottawa, Ont.; Stedelijk Museum, Amsterdam, Netherlands; Chrysler Museum, Provincetown, Mass.; New Brunswick Museum, Saint John, NB; Montreal Museum of Fine Arts; Hart House, University of Toronto; Canada House, Paris, France; Rose Art Museum, Brandeis University, Waltham, Mass.; University of Massachusetts Museum; Galerie du Siècle and Musée d'Art Contemporain, Montréal.

BARBEAU, Marius* 1883—1969

(Charles Marius Barbeau)
Author; b. 5 Mar. 1883 in Ste. Marie de Beauce, PQ; son of Charles and Marie Virginie (Morency) Barbeau; children: Dalila b. 1920, Hélène b. 1922; d. 27 Feb. 1969 in Ottawa, Ont.

EDUCATION

Attended Collège Ste. Anne de la Pocatière; Laval University, BA, LL L, 1907; Oxford University, B Sc, 1910; University of Montreal, PhD; attended La Sorbonne.

CAREER

National Museum of Canada, ethnologist and folklorist 1911-58.

MEMBER

Royal Society of Canada (elected fellow, 1950); L'Académie canadienne-française (co-founder); International Folk Music Council, Unesco (vice-president); La Société canadienne de musique folklorique (president).

AWARDS, HONOURS

Rhodes scholar, 1907; Oriel College, Oxford (honorary fellow); D Litt from Laval University; Lorne Pierce medal for literature, 1950; D Litt from Oxford University, 1952; Canada Council grant for preparation of material on Canadian folk-songs 1957/58, for completion of *Répertoire de la chanson* ... 1958/59, 1959/60, to prepare and continue work on a glossary and grammar of the Huron-Wyandot language 1961/62, 1962/63; Canada Council medal, 1961/62; University of Alberta gold medal for music, 1965; Companion of the Order of Canada, 1966; Centennial medal, 1967.

WRITINGS

Huron and Wyandot mythology, Geological Survey, 1915; *Indian days in the Canadian Rockies*, Macmillan, 1923; *The downfall of Temlaham* (novel), Macmillan, 1928; *Totem poles of the Gitksan*, National Museum, 1929; *Au coeur de Québec,* Zodiaque, 1934; *Cornelius Krieghoff*, Macmillan, 1934; *La merveilleuse aventure de Jacques Cartier*, Lévesque, 1934; *Grand'mère raconte,* Beauchemin, 1935; *Il était une fois*, Beauchemin, 1935; *Quebec where ancient France lingers*, Macmillan, 1936; *The kingdom of Saguenay*, Macmillan, 1936; *Assomption Sash*, National Museum, 1937; *Québec où survit l'ancienne*, Garneau, 1937; *Henri Julien*, Ryerson, 1941; *Maîtres artisans de chez nous*, Zodiaque, 1942; *Les rêves des chasseurs*, Beauchemin, 1942; *Côté the wood-carver*, Ryerson, 1943; *Les enfants disent*, Paysana, 1943; (with G. Melvin) *The Indian speaks*, Macmillan, 1943; (with R. Lasnier) *Madones canadiennes*, Beauchemin, 1944; *Modalité dans nos mélodies populaires*, Société royal du Canada, 1944; *Mountain cloud* (novel), Macmillan, 1944; *Saintes artisanes*, Fides, 1944; *Ceinture fléchée*, Paysana, 1946; *Painters of Quebec*, Ryerson, 1946; *L'arbre des rêves*, Lumen, 1947; *Alaska beckons*, Macmillan, 1947; *Le rêve de Kamalmouk* (novel), Fides, 1948; *Les contes du grand-père Sept-heures,* Chantecler, 1950-53; *Totem poles*, National Museum, 1950-51; *Haida myths*, National Museum, 1953; *The tree of dreams*, Oxford, 1955; *Haida carvers in argillite*, National Museum, 1957; *I have seen*

Quebec, Macmillan, 1957; *Indian days on the western prairies*, National Museum, 1957; *J'ai vu Québec*, Garneau, 1957; *Trésor des anciens Jésuites*, National Museum, 1957; (with M. Hornyansky) *The golden phoenix* (fairy tales), Oxford, 1958; *Medicine-men on the North Pacific coast*, National Museum, 1958; *Pathfinders in the north Pacific*, Caxton, 1958; *Huron-Wyandot traditional narratives*, National Museum, 1961; *Répertoire de la chanson folklorique française au Canada*, National Museum, 1962; *Histoire des peaux-rouges*, Beauchemin, 1964-66; *Folklore*, L'Académie canadienne-française, *c.*1965; *Comment on découvrit l'Amérique*, Beauchemin, 1966; *Le Saguenay légendaire*, Beauchemin, 1967; *Louis Jobin, statuaire* (biography), Beauchemin, 1968. EDITED: *Folksongs of French Canada*, Yale, 1925; *Folksongs of old Quebec*, National Museum, 1935; *Chansons populaires du vieux Québec*, National Museum, 1936; *Romancero du Canada*, Beauchemin, 1937; *Alouette*, Lumen, 1946; *Come a-singing!*, National Museum, 1947; *Roundelays*, National Museum, 1958; *Jongleur songs of old Quebec*, Ryerson, 1962; *Le rossignol y chante*, Queen's Printer, 1962. CONTRIBUTED: "Folk-song" in *Music in Canada*, edited by E. MacMillan, University of Toronto, 1955; articles to various publications of the National Museum of Canada, the Royal Society of Canada, Canadian and American periodicals, etc. WORK IN PROGRESS: "Indian captivities," McClelland & Stewart, *c.*1968.

BARKIN, Leo   1905–
Pianist; b. 18 May 1905 in Warsaw, Poland; son of Abraham and Sonia Barkin; came to Canada in 1926 and settled in Toronto; m. Fannie Barkin; children: Stella, Kiva, Henry.
EDUCATION
Studied piano with his father.
HOME
319 Warren Rd., Toronto, Ont.
CAREER
First appearance as accompanist in Poland 1913; Rialto Theatre, Toronto, pianist 1926; CBC, pianist 1926-34; Promenade Symphony (now Toronto Philharmonic) Orchestra, pianist and accompanist 1934-44; Toronto Symphony Orchestra, pianist 1949–.
CONCERT STAGE
Accompanied many concert artists, e.g. Ruggiero Ricci (Flint, Mich.), Mario Lanza (Toronto), Lawrence Tibbett, Jan Peerce, Robert Merrill; accompanied brother, Jack Barkin (Pittsburgh, Pa., 15 Mar. 1961); accompanied chamber groups in Toronto;

soloist in recitals, especially interpreting music by George Gershwin.
RADIO
Pianist on CBC on numerous occasions, 1926–; accompanied many internationally famous artists in CBC series "Distinguished artists," e.g. Jiri Tancibudek (1964), Albert Pratz (1964, 1965, 1967), Jennifer Vyvyan (1966), Marta Hidy (1967), "Canadian recitalist," e.g. Harvey Seigel, Abraham Galper, Peter Smith, "Sunday night," "Wednesday night"; accompanied Festival Singers of Toronto (7 Apr. 1964); soloist with CBC String Orchestra (24 June 1964); soloist, *Concerto for piano* by Lucio Agostini (26 Aug. 1965); performed on every private radio station in Toronto.
TELEVISION
Accompanied *The endless echo* ("Festival," CBC, 11 Mar. 1963).

BARRINGTON, Josephine*   1910–
(Josephine Barrington Tatlow)
Actress, director, and teacher; b. 9 Aug. 1910 in Toronto; daughter of Joseph William and Agnes (Campbell) Barrington; m. Kenneth Garnett Tatlow 18 Aug. 1964.
EDUCATION
Studied theatre at Margaret Eaton School, Toronto; Hart House Theatre, University of Toronto; Central School of Speech and Drama, London, England, 1930-32.
HOME
Apt. 1902, Park Towers W., 400 Walmer Rd., Toronto 10, Ont.
CAREER
John Holden's Summer Theatre, Bala, Muskoka, Ont., actress 1935-36; WRCNS, 1944-46; International Players, Kingston, Ont., leading lady 1948-51; Niagara Summer Theatre, Ont., actress 1951-53; taught many theatre and television personalities, e.g. Lloyd Bochner, Donald Davis, William Davis, Angela Fusco, John Kastner, Peter Kastner, Frank Perry, Sandra Scott, Alan Waxman.
MEMBER
AEA (Canada and UK); ACTRA; Canadian Theatre Centre; Toronto Heliconian Club.
THEATRE
Made debut as Olivia in *Twelfth night* (Hart House, 1928); played title role in *The swan* (Hart House, 1929), Mrs. Gibbs in *Our town* (Vancouver Little Theatre, BC, 1946), Mrs. Clandon in *You never can tell* (Toronto, 1948), *The vinegar tree* (International Players, 1948-51), *Claudia* (International Players, 1948-51) *The fatal weakness* (International Players, 1948-51), Capulet in *Ring round the moon* (Jupiter Theatre, Toronto, 1954), Beulah Moulsworth in *Romanoff and Juliet* (Piccadilly, London,

1956-57), Mrs. Higgins in *Pygmalion* (Crest Theatre, Toronto, 1959), *La bonne soupe* (Crest Theatre, Toronto, 1961).

FILM

The concert (H.M. Tennent, London, 1956), "Mark Sabre" (series, London, 1956).

RADIO

Played in numerous CBC dramas and feature programs, e.g. "Stage" (series).

TELEVISION

Played in numerous CBC productions, e.g. *Uncle Harry* (1953), Martha Pepperleigh in *Sunshine sketches* (series, 1953), *Teach me how to cry* (1953), *Guest in the house* (1953), *The man who ran away* ("GM theatre," 1954), *Laburnum grove* ("GM theatre," 1954), Mrs. Carlyle in *Carlyle and Mill* ("Scope," 1955), *Aunt Mary* ("On stage," 1957), *The little sweep* ("On stage," 1957), *Dark of the moon* ("Folio," 1958), *Three to get married* ("On camera," 1958), *Family reunion* ("Folio," 1959), *The inquest* ("GM theatre," 1960), *Mr. Arcularis* ("Encore," 21 Aug. 1960), *Call me a liar* ("Playdate," 1963), *No sand for the ostrich* ("Playdate," 1963), *A suitable case for treatment* ("Playdate," 1963), *The boy king* ("The time of your life," 1963).

BASTIEN, Hermas* 1896–

Author; b. 4 May 1896 in Montreal; son of Clovis and Amanda (Asselin) Bastien; m. Marie-A. Lamothe 1921; children: Andrée, Yolande, Mireille.

EDUCATION

University of Montreal, MA, 1925, PhD, 1927, DPed, 1951.

RELIGION

Roman Catholic.

HOME

Apt. 18, 4251 Marcil Ave., Montreal 28, PQ.

CAREER

Le devoir, Montréal, staff member 1920; Collège Mont-Saint-Louis, Montréal, professor of Latin 1927-38; Université de Montréal, professor of history of American philosophy 1928-41, professor of psychology of learning 1953-67; National Defence Headquarters, Ottawa, Ont., major 1941-45.

MEMBER

Académie des sciences morales et politiques de Montréal.

WRITINGS

Les eaux grises, poèmes, Editions du Devoir, 1919; *Les énergies rédemptrices*, l'Action française, 1923; *Essai sur la psychologie religieuse de William James*, thèse de doctorat en philosophie, 1928; *Itinéraires philosophiques*, ACF, 1929; *La défense de l'intelligence*, A. Lévesque, 1932; *Témoignages*, A. Lévesque, 1933; *Conditions*

de notre destin national, A. Lévesque, 1935; *L'enseignement de la philosophie*, A. Lévesque, 1937; *Le bilinguisme au Canada*, ACF, 1938; *Olivar Asselin*, Bernard Valiquette, 1938; *Les méthodes scientifiques dans l'éducation*, Légion canadienne, 1945; *L'Ordre hospitalier de Saint-Jean-de-Dieu au Canada*, Lumen, 1948; *Psychologie de l'apprentissage pédagogique*, Les frères des Écoles chrétiennes, 1951 (translated into Italian and Portuguese); *philosophies et américains*, Les Frères des Écoles chrétiennes, 1959; *La motivation et l'apprentissage*, Institut pédagogique Saint-Georges, 1964; *Images et paroles canadiennes*, 1968.

CONTRIBUTED: Articles to *Notre américanisation*, L'oeuvre de presse dominicaine, 1937; *Pour une société chrétienne*, École sociale populaire, 1939; *Courtes biographies canadiennes*, Éditions Éoliennes, 1951, 1953; *Cahiers*, edited by Académie canadienne-française, 1958; many periodicals.

BATES, Maxwell Bennett* 1906–

Artist; b. 14 Dec. 1906 in Calgary, Alta.; son of William Stanley and Marian Montford (Thomasson) Bates; m. Charlotte Grace Kintzle 1954.

EDUCATION

Studied under Lars Haukaness, Provincial Institute of Art and Technology, Calgary, 1926-27; Max Beckmann and Abraham Rattner, Brooklyn Museum Art School, NY, 1949-50.

RELIGION

Anglican.

HOME

827 Royal Oak Ave., Victoria, BC.

CAREER

Institute of Art and Technology, Calgary, instructor of evening classes and children's classes 1926-27; travelled to England, 1931, painted and worked at odd jobs; J. Harold Gibbons, England, architect 1934-39; British Army, Kensington Regiment 1939-45, private; Thuringia, Germany, prisoner of war 1940-45; A.W. Hodges, ecclesiastical architect and designer, partner 1951-57.

COMMISSIONS

Design, St. Mary's Cathedral, Calgary, 1954.

MEMBER

Twenties Group, England; Institute of Registered Architects, UK; Alberta Society of Artists (vice-president, 1952-53; now honorary member); Canadian Group of Painters (elected, 1957); Canadian Society of Graphic Art (elected, 1947); BC Society of Artists; Canadian Society of Painters in Water Colour (second vice-president, 1953); Canadian Section of the International Plastic Arts Society (vice-president, 1960); Royal Architectural Institute of Canada;

Fellow of the International Institute of Arts and Letters; Royal Canadian Academy (Associate 1961).

AWARDS, HONOURS

Honourable mention for watercolour, Montreal Art Association, 1957; honourable mention, Winnipeg Show, 1957; Purchase Award, Winnipeg Show, 1957; annual honour award, Canadian Society of Painters in Watercolour, 1957; award, Biennial Exhibition of Art, Minneapolis, Minn., 1958; Haspel Seguin Memorial Award, Canadian Society of Graphic Art, 1960.

EXHIBITIONS

ONE-MAN: Wertheim Galleries, Manchester, England, 1934; London, England, 1938; Vancouver Art Gallery, BC, 1947; Saskatoon Art Centre, Sask., 1947; Canadian Art Galleries, Calgary, 1947 and 1948; Queen's University, 1950; University of Manitoba Art School, 1956 and 1967; Ego Interiors, Victoria, 1963.

GROUP: Represented in Canadian group exhibitions including annual exhibitions of the Canadian Federation of Arts; represented in group exhibitions organized by the National Gallery of Canada, Ottawa, Ont. since 1931; Opportunity Gallery, New York, NY, 1930; New York Art Center, 1931; Bloomsbury Gallery, London, 1932; Chelsea Studio, London, 1935; Artists International, 1937; Royal Academy, London, 1938; Directions for 1950, Laurel Gallery, New York; First International Biennial of Prints, Tokyo, Japan, 1957; Philadelphia Print Club, Pa., 1958; Fifth International Biennial of Color Lithography, Cincinnati, Ohio, 1958; New Directions in Print Making, Chicago, Ill., 1960; Canadian Paintings and Graphics, Mexico City and Guadalajara, Mexico, 1960-61; Canadian Art, Mexico City, 1960; Coloured Graphics, Grenchen, Switzerland, 1961; Second International Biennial Exhibition of Prints, Tokyo, 1960.

COLLECTIONS IN WHICH REPRESENTED

Wertheim Gallery, Manchester; Department of External Affairs, Ottawa; National Gallery of Canada, Ottawa; Art Gallery of Ontario, Toronto; Norman Mackenzie Art Gallery, Regina, Sask.; Calgary Allied Arts Centre; National Gallery of New Zealand, Auckland; University of Victoria; Confederation Centre, Charlottetown, PEI; Winnipeg Art Gallery, Man.; Memorial University.

WRITINGS

Faraway flags (poems), the author, 1964.

CONTRIBUTED: To *Canadian art*.

BEAMENT, Harold* 1898–
(Thomas Harold Beament)
Artist; b. 23 July 1898 in Ottawa, Ont.; son of Herman Joseph and Lillian (Perkins) Beament; m. Ida Lawson McDougal 14 Oct. 1939; children: Thomas Harold b. 17 Feb. 1941.

EDUCATION

Attended Model School, Ottawa, 1905-09; Ottawa Collegiate Institute, 1910-1915; Osgoode Hall, Toronto, Ont., barrister-at-law, 1922; studied under J.W. Beatty, Ontario College of Art, Toronto, 1922.

RELIGION

Anglican.

HOME

183 St. Paul St. E., Montreal 1, PQ.

CAREER

RCNVR, 1917-18 ordinary seaman, warrant officer, officer from 1924, commander Montreal Division 1930-35, lieutenant commander 1935-43, commander 1943, senior naval war artist 1943-47, awarded VD; called to the bar, Ontario, 1923; National Gallery of Canada, Ottawa, Canadian Fine Arts Representative, British Empire Exhibition 1924; Montreal Museum of Fine Art, teacher 1936; private art teacher 1936-57; Newfoundland Government Art Competition, sole judge 1954-57; Nova Scotia College of Art, Halifax, instructor 1962, fellow of the Nova Scotia College of Art.

COMMISSIONS

Design for the ten cent Canadian Eskimo stamp, Canadian Government, 1955; mural for scenic dome scenes, CPR.

MEMBER

Royal Canadian Academy (Associate 1936; Academician 1946; honorary treasurer, 1958; secretary-treasurer, 1960 and 1961; president, 1963-67).

AWARDS, HONOURS

Jessie Dow prize for oils, Art Association of Montreal, 1935; Centennial medal.

EXHIBITIONS

ONE-MAN: Watson Gallery, Montreal, 1932-39; Laing Gallery, Toronto, 1948 and 1949.

GROUP: Represented in Canadian group exhibitions since 1922 including annual exhibitions of Royal Canadian Academy and Ontario Society of Artists; represented in group exhibitions organized by National Gallery of Canada since 1926; Canadian Section of Fine Arts, British Empire Exhibition, Wembley, England, 1924-25; *Exposition d'art canadien*, Musée du Jeu de Paume, Paris, France, 1927; Buenos Aires, Brazil, 1929; Exhibition of Contemporary Canadian Paintings, arranged for circulation in the Southern Dominions of the British Empire, 1936; A Century of Canadian Art, Tate Gallery, London, England, 1938; World's Fair, New York, NY, 1939; National Gallery, London, 1944; Olympic Games, Helsinki, Finland, 1952; An Exhibition of

Canadian Paintings held at Fortnum and Mason Ltd., London, 1955.

COLLECTIONS IN WHICH REPRESENTED
National Gallery of Canada; Musée du Québec, PQ; Montreal Museum of Fine Arts; London Public Library and Art Museum, Ont.; Dominion Archives, Ottawa; Art Gallery of Hamilton, Ont.; Queen's University; Canadian Club, New York; Canadian Industries Ltd., Montreal; Seagram Collection, Montreal.

BEAMENT, Thomas Harold
see BEAMENT, Harold

BEATTIE, Jessie Louise* 1896—
Author; b. 2 Oct. 1896 in Blair, Ont.; daughter of Francis Walker and Janet (Fleming) Beattie.

EDUCATION
Attended Tassie Hall, Galt, Ont.; studied editorial work at University of Buffalo, 1925; drama at Hart House Theatre, Toronto, 1935; attended School of Social Work, University of Toronto, 1943.

RELIGION
Protestant.

CAREER
Kitchener Public Library, Ont., library assistant 1922-24; Buffalo Public Library, NY, library assistant 1925-27; Preston Public Library, Ont., librarian 1927-29; Atlantic City Library, NJ, library assistant 1929; conducted a private school at Blair 1930-34; Community Welfare Council, Toronto, director of recreation 1935-36; Ontario Girls' Training School, Galt, social worker 1938-40; Vancouver Public Library, BC, library assistant 1941; Big Sister Association, Toronto, social worker 1942-43; Ontario Training College for Technical Teachers, Hamilton, librarian 1945-46; Easthaven School for Retarded Children, Hamilton, teacher 1957—.

MEMBER
Canadian Authors Association; Canadian Women's Press Club.

WRITINGS
Blown leaves (poems), Ryerson, 1929; *Shifting sails* (poems), Ryerson, 1931; *Hilltop* (novel), Macmillan, 1935; *Three measures* (novel), Macmillan, 1938; (with D.M. Green) *White wings around the world* (travel), Ryerson, 1953; *Along the road* (autobiography), Ryerson, 1954; *John Christie Holland* (biography), Ryerson, 1956; *Black Moses, the real Uncle Tom* (biography), Ryerson, 1957; *The split in the sky* (novel), Ryerson, 1960; *Hasten the day* (short stories), United Church of Canada, 1961; *Strength for the bridge* (novel), McClelland & Stewart, 1966; *A season past* (autobiography), McClelland & Stewart, 1968; *The call of the*

caravan (operetta); *The four-leafed clover* (play; produced in Ontario and Quebec).

CONTRIBUTED: Poetry, short stories, and articles to *Canadian magazine, Canadian poetry, Chatelaine, Farmer's magazine, Saturday night,* and other Canadian and American magazines.

BEAUCHEMIN, Nérée 1850-1931
Poet; b. 20 Feb. 1850 in Yamachiche, PQ; d. 1931 in Yamachiche.

EDUCATION
Attended Séminaire de Nicolet, PQ; Université Laval, MD, 1874.

RELIGION
Roman Catholic.

CAREER
Country doctor in Yamachiche.

AWARDS, HONOURS
Université Laval, D Lett, 1928; poet laureate of Trois Rivières, 1928; silver medal of the Académie de médecine, 1930.

WRITINGS
Les floraisons matutinales, Ayotte, 1897; *Patrie intime, harmonies*, Librairie d'Action canadienne française, 1928; *Un choix de poésies*, Éditions du Bien public, 1950.

CONTRIBUTED: Poems to *Anthologie des poètes canadiens*, edited by J. Fournier and O. Asselin, Granger, 1922; *Les fleurs de la poésie canadienne*, 4th ed. Beauchemin, 1924; *Quinze ans de poésie française à travers le monde*, edited by J. Artrey, La France universelle, 1927; *Action canadienne-française, Canada-français, Journal de l'instruction publique, L'opinion publique, Revue de Montréal.*

BEAUDÉ, Henri
see ARLES, Henri d'

BEAUDET, Henri
see ARLES, Henri d'

BEAULNE, Guy* 1921—
Director and actor; b. 23 Dec. 1921 in Ottawa, Ont.; son of Léonard and Yvonne (Daoust) Beaulne; m. Pauline Beaudry 15 Sept. 1948; children: Pascale b. 1949, Martine b. 1952, Vincent b. 1954.

EDUCATION
Attended Garneau School, Ottawa, 1927-34; University of Ottawa High School, 1934-38; Lisgar Collegiate, Ottawa, 1938-40; University of Ottawa Normal School, teacher's diploma, 1940-41; University of Ottawa, BA, BPh, 1946; Le Conservatoire National d'Art Dramatique de Paris, France; l'Institut de Phonétique de la Sorbonne, Paris, France; studied with Denis D'Inès, La Comédie Française, Paris, 1948-50.

RELIGION
Roman Catholic.

HOME
1155 Bougainville, Québec, PQ.
OFFICE
Le Grand Théâtre de Québec, 269 est, Boul. St. Cyrille, Québec, PQ.
CAREER
Le Caveau and Ottawa Little Theatre, actor and director 1938-48; Canadian Officers Training Corps, lieutenant 1940-46; University of Ottawa High School, teacher 1941-42; Ontario Department of Education, teacher 1945-48; University of Ottawa, artistic director 1945-48; Canadian Repertory Theatre, Ottawa, Montreal Repertory Theatre, Les Festivals de Montréal, La Jeune Scène, Mountain Playhouse, Le Théâtre d'Été Chantecler and Le Rideau Vert, Montreal, actor and director; *Le Droit*, Ottawa, drama editor 1945-48; Radio-Télévision française, Paris, France, Canadian correspondent 1948-50; *Points de vue*, Montreal, drama editor; *Theatre in the world*, Canadian correspondent 1949-63; International Theatre Institute, Second Conference, Zurich, Switzerland, Canadian delegate 1949; Third Conference, Paris (UNESCO), Canadian delegate 1950; Dominion Drama Festival, governor 1952, member of the executive 1956-, regional adjudicator 1960-, adjudicator 1965, 1967; CBC, French network radio drama producer 1950-56, TV drama producer 1957-63; Les Jeunesses Musicales du Canada, Summer Theatre School, Mount Orford, PQ, resident director 1958-64; Société Saint-Jean-Baptiste de Montréal, lecturer on Les conférences Duvernay, 1960-63; 5th International Congress of the International Amateur Theatre Association and 2nd Festival of Amateur Theatre, Monaco, Canadian representative 1961; Université de Montréal, teacher 1961-62; *Canadian annual review*, drama editor 1961-63; École des Beaux-Arts de Québec, teacher 1963-66; Ministère des Affaires Culturelles, director of theatre 1963, director-general of artistic training 1965, director-general of theatre 1967; Prague Quadriennale of Theatre, commissioner-general of Quebec 1967; Université Laval, teacher 1968; *Culture vivante*, member of editorial staff; travelled extensively in Europe and across Canada.
MEMBER
L'Association canadienne du théâtre d'amateurs (founder and honorary director, 1958-); Canadian Theatre Centre (past president); Théâtre Populaire du Québec (member of board of directors).
AWARDS, HONOURS
Dominion Drama Festival, best actor and adjudicator's award 1948, best director 1955; Canadian Radio Award, 1952; Canadian Drama Award, 1955; Trophée Laflèche, CBC radio, 1956;

Trophée Frigon, CBC TV, 1959; Trophée Congrès du Spectacle, CBC TV, 1961; Centennial medal, 1967.
FILM
Commentaries for National Film Board of Canada and Crawley Films.
RADIO
Created and directed *Nouveautés dramatiques* (CBC French radio workshop, 1950-56); produced *La famille Plouffe* (serial, CBC, 1952-55); *Les grands romans canadiens, Le théâtre canadien, Contes de mon pays, Le théâtre du grand prix* (CBC).
TELEVISION
Produced and directed *La famille Plouffe* (French and English serial, CBC, 1956-57); "Théâtre populaire" (CBC, 1957-58); *Shoestring theatre* (English experimental series, CBC, 1958-63).
WRITINGS
CONTRIBUTED: Numerous articles to leading theatre magazines in Canada and around the world.
WORK IN PROGRESS: "Notre théâtre, conscience d'un peuple" (essay).

BEGIN, Catherine Agnès Marie* 1939-
Actress; b. 22 Apr. 1939 in Bois-Colombes, Seine, France; daughter of Lucien and Marie-Louise (Van Havre) Begin.
EDUCATION
Attended Notre Dame de Grâce, Montréal, 1944-53; Esther-Blondin High School, Montreal, 1953-56; studied dramatic art at Mrs. J.L. Audet School, Montreal, 1955-56; with Jean Doat and Jean Valcour (*q.v.*), Conservatory of Music and Dramatic Art, Montreal, 1956-59.
OFFICE
Union des Artistes, 1434 St. Catherine St. W., Montreal, PQ.
CAREER
Toured extensively in the province of Quebec, 1964-67; Théâtre Anjou, Montréal, actress 1960-; Théâtre du Nouveau Monde, Montréal, 1963-.
MEMBER
Union des Artistes de Montréal.
AWARDS, HONOURS
First prize in tragedy and classical comedy, second prize in modern theatre from Conservatory of Music and Dramatic Arts, Montreal, 1956-59.
THEATRE
Played in many productions, e.g. Fulvie in *Cinna* (Théâtre Club, Montréal, 1959), Sonia in *Crime et châtiment* (Théâtre de la Poudrière, Montréal, 1959), Isabelle in *Soif d'aimer*(Anjou, 1960), Betty in *Virginie* (Anjou, 1960), Genevieve in *Blaise* (Anjou, 1961), Francine in *Le printemps de la Saint-Martin* (Théâtre de l'Anse, PQ, 1961), Catherine in *Guillaume le confident* (Théâtre de l'Anse, 1961), Véronique in *Patate* (Théâtre du

Rideau Vert, Montreal, 1962), Yvonne in *Les glorieuses* (Théâtre du Rideau Vert, Montreal, 1962), Suzon in *Huit femmes* (Nouveau Monde, 1963), Junie in *Britannicus* (Théâtre Populaire du Québec, Montréal, 1963), Cyrenne in *La crécelle* (Théâtre de la Poudrière, 1964), Olga in *Le complexe de Philémon* (Théâtre de l'Estérel, PQ, 1964), Catherine Ginari in *Lorenzaccio* (Nouveau Monde, 21 Nov. 1965), Camille in *Horace* (Théâtre Populaire, 1965), Missia in *Une folie* (Théâtre de l'Égrégore, Montréal, 1966), Franny in *Au revoir Charlie* (Le Piggery, 1966), Dorimène in *Le bourgeois gentilhomme* (Nouveau Monde, 15 May 1967), Bianca in *Anatole* (Nouveau Monde, 7 Dec. 1967); created Claudia in *Un matin comme les autres* (La Comédie Canadienne, Montréal, 1968); played Chimène in *Le Cid Maghane* (Festival de Ste-Agathe, PQ, 1968).

FILM
Played in several productions, e.g. *Délivrez-nous du mal* (Cooperatio, 1964).

RADIO
Played in many productions, e.g. "Sur toutes les scènes du monde" (series, CBC), *La côte de sable* (CKAC, Montreal, 1964/65), *Le survenant* (CKVL, Verdun, PQ, 1964/65), *Vous baissez, Monsieur Fareinght* (CBC, 1966), *Marie Tellier, avocate* (CBC, 1966–).

TELEVISION
Appeared in many CBC productions, e.g. *En haut de la pente douce* (1959-60), *The town above* (1959-60), *La côte de sable* (1960/61-1961/62), *Comme tu me veux* (1961), *La mort dans l'âme* (1963), *Le feu sacré* (1963), *Monsieur Lecoq* (Jan.-June 1964), Gwendoline in *Il est important d'être aimé* (1964), Judith Anderson in *Le disciple du diable* (1964), *Septième nord* (1965/66-1966/67), *Table tournante* (1968), *Partie remise* (1968).

WORK IN PROGRESS: New role in *Le paradis terrestre* (serial, CBC TV); episodic appearances in *Langue vivante* (serial, CBC TV); participation in a research and experimentation workshop for theatre.

BELL, Alistair Macready* 1913–
Artist; b. 21 Oct. 1913 in Darlington, England; son of Archibald and Gladys Mary (Vassie) Bell; came to Canada in Nov. 1922 and settled in Toronto, Ont.; m. Lorna Beatrice Streatfield 5 July 1941; children: Alan Streatfield b. 30 Aug. 1944.

EDUCATION
Attended two private schools in England, 1918-22; two public schools in Toronto, 1922-24; public school in Galt, Ont., 1925-26; Galt Collegiate Institute and Vocational School, 1927-28; Vancouver School of Art, evening life drawing classes, 1936-37, 1939-40; Central School of Arts and Crafts, London, England, etching and lithography classes, autumn term 1959; mainly self-taught as artist.

HOME
2566 Marine Drive, W. Vancouver, BC.

CAREER
Worked at a variety of jobs 1928-36; freelance commercial artist 1936-42; Hamilton Bridge Western Ltd. (now Western Bridge Division, Canada Iron Foundries, Ltd.), Vancouver, employed in the drawing office 1942-58, squad leader in the drawing office 1958-67; travelled and worked in England, Scotland, Holland, France, and Italy 1959/60; since April 1968 devotes time entirely to artistic work, principally print making.

MEMBER
Canadian Society of Graphic Art (elected, 1947; vice-president, Western, 1951-52; resigned, 1959); Canadian Society of Painter-Etchers and Engravers (associate, 1952; full member, 1954); British Columbia Society of Artists (elected, 1949; executive member about ten years; president, 1953-54); Royal Canadian Academy of Arts (Associate 1965); Canadian Group of Painters (elected, 1949; president, 1961; resigned, 1963).

AWARDS, HONOURS
Honourable mention, Northwest Print Makers International Exhibition, Seattle, 1946; C.W. Jefferys award, Canadian Society of Graphic Art, 1956; Lemoine Fitzgerald Memorial Award (shared), Winnipeg Show, Man., 1957; purchase prize, Winnipeg Show, 1958; Canada Council senior arts fellowship, 1959; honourable mention, Winnipeg Show, 1960; honourable mention, Calgary Graphics Exhibition, Alta., 1963; purchase prize, Calgary Graphics Exhibition, 1964; Canada Council arts award for a year to work at print-making, 1967.

EXHIBITIONS
ONE-MAN: Vancouver Art Gallery, 1951, 1957, and 1961; Hart House, University of Toronto, 1954; Art Gallery of Greater Victoria, BC, 1959; University of New Brunswick, 1962; Mount Allison University, 1963; Provincial Library, Victoria, 1964; Pandora's Box Gallery, Victoria, 1966; Unitarian Church, Vancouver, 1967.
GROUP: Represented in group exhibitions organized by the National Gallery of Canada, Ottawa, Ont., including the second and fourth Biennial of Canadian Painting, 1957 and 1961; Northwest Print Makers International Exhibition, Seattle, Wash., 1950, 1953, 1956, and 1959; First International Graphic Biennial, Tokyo and Osaka, Japan, 1957; Second and Third International Graphic Biennial, Ljubljana, Yugoslavia, 1957 and 1959; Sixth International Graphic Biennial, Lugano, Switzerland, 1960; First

American Biennial of Graphics, Santiago, Chile, 1963; Second American Biennial of Graphics, Santiago, Chile and Lima, Peru, 1965; Canadian Drawings and Prints Exhibition, Commonwealth Arts Festival, Cardiff, Wales, 1965; Canada 1967, Graphics Exhibition, Museum of Modern Art, New York, NY, 1967.

COLLECTIONS IN WHICH REPRESENTED
National Gallery of Canada; Victoria and Albert Museum, London, England; Winnipeg Art Gallery; Royal Ontario Museum, Toronto; Vancouver Art Gallery; Art Gallery of Greater Victoria; Art Gallery of Hamilton, Ont.; London Public Library and Art Museum, Ont.; Kitchener-Waterloo Art Gallery, Ont.; Alberta College of Art Gallery, Calgary; University of Victoria; Brandon University, Man.; Colby College, Waterville, Me.; Owens Art Gallery, Mount Allison University; Museum of Modern Art, New York.

BELL, Donald* 1934–

Singer (bass-baritone); b. 19 June 1934 in South Burnaby, BC; son of Charles Clare and Jessie Jane (Munro) Bell; m. Erika Brugger 26 Aug. 1960 (d. in car accident); m. Ingrid von Krannhals 2 Apr. 1968; children: (first marriage) Donald Sebastian b. 17 July 1961.

EDUCATION
Attended Inmen Ave. School and Burnaby South Secondary; studied voice with Nancy P. Benn, Vancouver, BC; Royal College of Music, London, England, 1952-54; H. Weissenborn, Städtische Oper, Berlin, Germany, 1955-57; Edith Boros-check, Buederich, Germany.

RELIGION
Church of England.

HOME
13504-112th Ave., North Surrey, BC; Olympia Str. 12, 404 Neuss, Germany.

OFFICE
c/o Walter Homburger, 12 Sheppard St., Toronto 1, Ont.

CAREER
Vancouver Symphony Orchestra, 1948; Glynde-bourne Opera Company, England, 1955; Staats Oper Berlin, 1955; Deutsche Oper am Rhein, Düsseldorf, Germany, 1964-67; music festivals in Bath and London, England, Basel and Lausanne, Switzerland, Bergen, Norway, Berlin, 1958, Bayreuth, Germany, 1958, 1960, Lucerne, Swit-zerland, 1959, Glyndebourne, 1964, Tanglewood, Mass., 1964; toured Canada 1958, 1964, 1968, Israel 1959 and 1964, USSR and Europe 1963, Spain 1967, England 1968.

MEMBER
ACTRA; AGMA.

AWARDS, HONOURS
Junior festival prizes; AOTS scholarship, 1947; BC Teacher's Federation scholarship, 1947; Vancouver Women's Musical Club scholarship,

1947; BC Music Festival, highest marks for singers, 1948; Royal College of Music, London, 3-year scholarship, 1952, Arnold Bax memorial medal for most outstanding student of the Commonwealth, 1954; Städtische Oper, Berlin, 2-year scholarship, 1955.

THEATRE
Lieder debut (Wigmore Hall, London, England, 22 Apr. 1958), opera debut in *Die Meistersinger von Nürnberg* (Bayreuth Festival, 1958-61); sang in many productions, e.g. Count di Luna in *Il trovatore* (Dortmund, Germany), Robinson in *The secret marriage* (Mannheim, Germany), *Abstrakte Oper* (Berlin, 1957), *Parsifal* (Bayreuth Festival, 1958-61), *St. Matthew passion* (Berlin Philharmonic Orchestra, 1958; New York Phil-harmonic Orchestra under Leonard Bernstein, NY, 28 Apr. 1962), *Requiem* by Brahms (London Philharmonic Orchestra, c.1959), New York debut in *Christmas oratorio* (1959; Israeli Philharmonic Orchestra, 1964), opening concert of Lincoln Center (New York, 23 Sept. 1962), *Intermezzo* (New York, 1963), Wolfram in *Tannhäuser* (Basel, 1967), *Messiah* (Toronto Mendelssohn Choir and Toronto Symphony Orchestra under Elmer Iseler, Massey Hall, Toronto, 22 Dec. 1968).

RADIO
Sang in many CBC productions, e.g. "Winnipeg pops concert" (29 June 1957), "Winnipeg Sunday concert" (30 June 1957), "Distinguished artists" (2 July 1957), soloist in *Cantata no. 86* by Bach (1 Nov. 1959), *Symphony no. 9* by Beethoven (20 Dec. 1959), lieder recital ("Dis-tinguished artists," 22 Dec. 1959), *Neue Liebe, neues Leben* ("Wednesday night," 8 June 1960), "Wednesday night" ("Celebrity concerts," 1960/61), *St. Matthew passion* (28 Apr. 1962), *Strauss in retrospect* ("Sunday night," 7 June 1964), recital (12 Mar. 1967), "CBC Thursday music" ("Celebrity centennial concerts," 23 Mar. 1967), "Tuesday night" (28 Mar. 1967), "En-core," part I (2 Apr. 1967), *War requiem* ("Tuesday night," 11 Apr. 1967), all Beethoven program ("Distinguished Canadian artists," 27 Aug. 1967), "Friday concert" (20 Oct. 1967), *Messiah* (22 Dec. 1968); recitals (BBC, London, 1958), recital (WDR, Cologne, Germany, July 1967).

TELEVISION
Sang in many CBC productions, e.g. "Music in miniature," "Emphasis on youth" (13 May 1962), "Youth concert" (c.Feb. 1962), Master Ford in *Falstaff* by Verdi ("Festival," 15 May 1961).

RECORDINGS
Liebeslieder waltzes by Brahms, Capitol G7189, 1959; Seraphim 60033, 1967; His Master's Voice ALP 1789. *Belshazzar's feast,* Philharmonia Chorus and Philharmonia Orchestra, London,

Angel Records, ANG 35681, 1960; Columbia SAX 2319. *Symphony no. 9* by Beethoven, Cleveland Orchestra under George Szell, Epic SC 6041 (LC 3799-3800) 1961; London Symphony Orchestra, 8-EV 6065, 3065; EV 6110, 3110. *Serenade: Donald Bell sings Schubert and Loewe*, Columbia ML 5743, 1962; Columbia MS 6343, 1962. *The crucifixion,* His Master's Voice ALP 1885, 1962; Leeds Philharmonic Choir, Angel 35984. *Opening concert at Lincoln Center,* New York, under Leonard Bernstein, Columbia L2L 1007. *St. Matthew passion,* New York Philharmonic Orchestra under Leonard Bernstein, Columbia M3S 692 (MS 6501-6503) 1963; Columbia M3L 292 (ML 5901-5903) 1963. *Three favorite Beethoven symphonies,* Epic SC 6063 (LC 3960-3962) 1967.

BELL, Leslie Richard 1906-62

Choir conductor; b. 1906 in Toronto, Ont.; son of George Bell; m. Leona; children: Leslie Richard, Janet; d. 19 Jan. 1962 in Toronto.

EDUCATION
Attended school in Toronto, 1917-25; studied clarinet, saxophone, and piano, Toronto (now Royal) Conservatory of Music; University of Toronto, BA, MA in English, 1932, PhD in music, 1940; University of Montreal; Ontario College of Education, 1933-34.

CAREER
Dance band leader in Toronto 1925-34; Parkdale Collegiate School, Toronto, teacher 1934-39; Ontario College of Education, chairman of music 1939-46; Leslie Bell Singers, founder and conductor 1939-62; University of Toronto, supervisor and director of choral technique 1946- ?; *Star,* Toronto, music columnist to 1962; Canadian Music Educators' Association, executive secretary to 1962; *Canadian music journal,* assistant editor 1956-62; Toronto Parks Board, music director 1959-62.

MEMBER
Canadian Bureau for the Advancement of Music; Canadian Music Council.

CONCERT STAGE
Conducted the Leslie Bell Singers in numerous stage performances, 1939-62; toured US with this group annually, *c.*1948-55; conducted them in Canadian National Exhibition Grandstand Show, Toronto, *Star* concerts, Toronto, and at Madison Square Garden, New York, NY.

FILM
Conducted Leslie Bell Singers in three films (National Film Board of Canada, 1940s).

RADIO
Conducted Leslie Bell Singers in numerous broadcasts on CBC and commercial networks, in series and feature programs; originated and appeared in music appreciation series on CBC,

e.g. "Music won't hurt you," "Speaking of music"; wrote script of *History of music* (CBC, Oct. 1948); commentator on music with CFRB, Toronto.

RECORDINGS
Made over 20 recordings with the Leslie Bell Singers, for CBC IS and RCA Victor.

COMPOSITIONS
In winter cold, mixed choir and piano, 1950, Canadian Music Sales; *Marilyn,* voice and piano, 1954, Canadian Music Sales; *Glorious is the land,* band or chorus and band, 1954, Canadian Music Sales; *Two's too many,* voice, piano, and guitar, 1955, Canadian Music Sales; *Awakening,* unison song, 1957, Canadian Music Sales; also many arrangements of Canadian, French-Canadian, English, Scots, Irish, and American-negro songs, for various vocal groups accompanied or unaccompanied, 1940-62, some published by Canadian Music Sales; collections of arrangements: (with J.M. Gibbon) *Canada in song,* G.V. Thompson, 1941; *Festival song book,* books 1-4, Canadian Music Sales, 1954-57.

WRITINGS
The chorister, Gage, 1947-50.
CONTRIBUTED: "Popular music" in *Music in Canada,* edited by E. MacMillan, University of Toronto, 1955; articles to *Saturday night, Maclean's, Canadian music journal,* and *Star,* Toronto.

BELL-SMITH, Frederick Martlett 1846-1923

Artist; b. 26 Sept. 1846 in London, England; son of John and Georgina Maria (Boddy) Bell-Smith; m. Anna Myra Dyde; children: two sons; d. 23 June 1923 in Toronto, Ont.

EDUCATION
Attended South Kensington Art School, London; studied with his father; attended Colarossi Académie, Paris, France, 1896; studied with Courtois, Blanc, and Dupain, Paris, 1891.

RELIGION
Methodist.

CAREER
Victoria Rifles No. 5 Company, member till 1867; illustrated for newspapers, 1872-84; public schools of London, Ont., drawing instructor 1882-89; illustrated for *Picturesque Canada,* 1882; photographer in Montreal, PQ, *c.*1891; Alma College, St. Thomas, Ont., art director 1881-90, 1897-1910.

COMMISSIONS
Portrait of H.M. Queen Victoria, at Windsor, England, 1895.

MEMBER
Society of Canadian Artists (founder member, 1867); Ontario Society of Artists (elected, 1872; president, 1904-08); Pallete Club; Dickens' Fellowship, Toronto; Arts and Letters Club; Royal Canadian Academy (Associate 1880; Academican

1886); Royal British Colonial Society of Painters, (elected, 1908).

AWARDS, HONOURS
Jessie Dow prize for water colour, Montreal Art Association, 1892 and 1909; gold medal, Halifax, NS, 1881.

EXHIBITIONS
GROUP: Represented in Canadian group exhibitions since 1911 including annual exhibitions of Ontario Society of Artists, Royal Canadian Academy, and Canadian National Exhibition; represented in group exhibitions organized by National Gallery of Canada, Ottawa, Ont.; Canadian Section of Fine Arts, British Empire Exhibition, London, 1924; A Century of Canadian Art, Tate Gallery, London, 1938; An Exhibition of Canadian Paintings held at Fortnum and Mason Ltd., London, 1955.

COLLECTIONS IN WHICH REPRESENTED
Art Gallery of Ontario, Toronto; National Gallery of Canada.

BENOIT, Réal*   1916–

Author and film producer; b. 14 May 1916 in Ste. Thérèse de Blainville, PQ; son of Rosaire and Gabrielle (Cinq-Mars) Benoit; children: Christian.

EDUCATION
Classical studies.

RELIGION
None.

HOME
516 Bloomfield, Outremont, Montréal, PQ.

OFFICE
Canadian Broadcasting Corporation, Box 6000, Montreal, PQ.

CAREER
Travelled extensively abroad, in Brazil 1946-47; L'Assiette à Musique (record club), founder 1942; Réal Benoit Film Productions, 1947-60; CBC, film reporter two years, film director 1960–; *Revue architecture,* editor; *Le Jour,* music reporter; *Le Devoir,* Montreal, film reporter; International Film Festival, Montreal, 1966, board of directors; Le Centre International d'Étude des Problèmes Humains (cinéma et civilisation), Monaco, Canadian correspondent at annual meetings.

AWARDS, HONOURS
Brazilian government scholarship to study artistic life in Brazil, 1946-47; Quebec government literature award 1963; Montreal $3000 grand prize in literature for *Quelqu'un pour m'écouter* (novel), 1966.

FILMS
Produced *Marius Barbeau; l'art totémique* (National Film Board, 1959); *Marius Barbeau; le folklore canadien-français* (National Film Board, 1959); *Cyrius Ouellette.*

RADIO
Reported on films for CBC program *La revue des arts et des lettres*; master of ceremonies at CBFT, Montreal, for Ciné-club.

WRITINGS
Nézon, contes, Parizeau, 1945; *La Bolduc* (biography), Éditions de l'homme, 1959; *Quelqu'un pour m'écouter* (novel), Cercle du livre de France, 1964; *Le marin d'Athènes* (TV play), Cercle du livre de France, 1966 (produced summer 1965, awarded trophy for best TV drama of the year); *La saison des artichauts* (novel), Cercle du livre de France, 1968.

CONTRIBUTED: Articles to *Les Écrits du Canada français.*

BENSON, Nathaniel Anketell Michael   1903-66
(Pegasus, pseud.)

Poet; b. 11 Oct. 1903 in Toronto, Ont.; son of Thomas and Catherine (Sheehan) Benson; m. Emma Wright 4 Oct. 1930; children: Julian David Thomas, Charles William Michael; d. 1966 in Detroit, Mich.

EDUCATION
University College, University of Toronto, BA with honours in modern languages, 1927, MA, 1928; Ontario College of Education, University of Toronto, 1932.

RELIGION
Anglican.

CAREER
Mail and empire, Toronto, contributor 1928; *Evening telegram,* Toronto, contributor 1929; *Manitoba free press,* Winnipeg, junior editor 1929; freelance journalist 1930-31; Weston Vocational School, Ont., teacher 1932-33; Danforth Technical School, Ont., teacher of English 1933-37; *Canadian poetry magazine,* managing editor 1937-43; worked for various advertising companies, New York, 1940-48; *Saturday night,* Toronto, drama critic in New York 1946-49; R.H. King Collegiate Institute, Scarborough, Ont., English Department, teacher 1955.

MEMBER
Canadian Literary Club (past president, 1936-38); Canadian Authors Association (national vice-president, president Toronto branch, 1941-43; founder New York branch, 1943-44); Poetry Society of America 1944; Lincoln Fellowship, New York; Sigma Delta Chi.

AWARDS, HONOURS
Jardine prize poem for *Twenty and after,* 1926.

WRITINGS
Poems, Robertson, 1927; *Twenty and after,* Ryerson, 1927; *The wanderer,* Ryerson, 1930; *Three plays for patriots,* Graphic, 1930; *Dollard, a tale in verse,* Nelson, 1933; *Ode on the death of George V,* Ryerson, 1936; *The glowing years,* Nelson, 1937; (with F.A. Hall) *Improve your skiing,* McLeod, 1936; *The maple's praise,* 1945; *In memoriam principis,* Toronto, 1951;

None of it came easy (biography), Burns &
MacEachern, 1955; Words for (K.W. Bissell)
Ballad of the Rawalpindi, Thompson, 1959;
One man's pilgrimage, Nelson, 1963.
EDITED: *Modern Canadian poetry*, Graphic, 1930;
Canadian stories of action and humour, Nelson,
1955-57.
CONTRIBUTED: Poems and articles to *Canadian
magazine, Canadian music journal, Dalhousie
review, Forbes magazine, Saturday night*, and
other periodicals.

BENY, Roloff* 1924—
(Wilfred Roy Beny)
Artist, photographer, and writer; b. 7 Jan. 1924
in Medicine Hat, Alta; son of Charles John
Francis Beny and Rosalie M. (Roloff) Beny.
EDUCATION
Attended elementary and high school in
Medicine Hat; School of Fine Arts, Banff, Alta.,
1939; Trinity College, University of Toronto, BA,
BFA, 1941-45; studied under Mauricio Lasansky,
State University of Iowa, MA, MFA in graphic
arts, 1946-47; attended Columbia University and
Institute of Fine Art, New York University, con-
tinued work toward PhD, 1947-48; studied in
Greece, Italy, and France, May 1948-Nov. 1949;
studied in Spain, England, Italy, and Germany,
May 1951-Dec. 1952.
RELIGION
Anglican.
HOME
Lungotevere Ripa 3-B, Rome, Italy; 432-13th St.
S., Lethbridge, Alta.
CAREER
Travelled in Europe 1948-49 and 1951-52; pro-
duced "An Aegean Note Book," twenty litho-
graphs, 1950; worked seriously with photography
since 1956; illustrated Dame Rose Macaulay's
Pleasure of ruins, Thames and Hudson, 1964;
travelled and worked on a commission in India
1967-68.
COMMISSIONS
Photographic illustrations, *Queen*, Cromwell,
1958; book dealing with India, commissioned
by Thames and Hudson, McGraw-Hill, and
government of India, 1968—; 38 murals,
Federal Pavillion of Expo 67, Montreal, PQ,
1967.
MEMBER
Knight of Mark Twain (elected, 1967).
AWARDS, HONOURS
Banff School of Fine Arts scholarship, 1939;
2-year fellowship, State University of Iowa,
1946-47; scholarship to Columbia University
and New York University, 1947-48; John Simon
Guggenheim fellowship for print making and
painting, 1953; Centennial medal, 1967; international prize for design for *The thrones of*
earth and heaven, Leipzig Book Fair, 1958; one
of the fifty great books of 1965, *A time of gods*,
Comité des Arts Graphiques, 1962; world's finest
book award, for *Japan in colour*, International
Book Fair, Leipzig, Germany, 1968.
PHOTOGRAPHIC EXHIBITS
"A time of gods," shown in Rome, Royal Ontario Museum, Toronto, Ont., University of
Lethbridge (1962); "Metaphysical monuments,"
shown in Rome and Toronto; "Pleasure of photography," shown in National Gallery of Canada,
Ottawa, Ont., Art Gallery of Ontario, Toronto,
Vancouver Art Gallery, BC, Confederation Art
Gallery and Museum, Charlottetown, PEI, Mont-
real Museum of Fine Arts (1966); "Sculpture of
the renaissance," (1967); "Renaissance," shown
in University of Toronto (1968); "A visual
odyssey," Gallery of Modern Art, New York, NY,
1968.
EXHIBITIONS
ONE-MAN: More than 25 one-man exhibitions
since 1941 including Hart House, University of
Toronto, 1941, 1944, and 1951; Weyhe Gallery,
New York, 1947; Art Gallery of Palazzo
Strozzi, Florence, Italy, 1949; Fine Art Gallery,
Eaton's College Street, Toronto, 1950 and 1951;
Knoedler Gallery, New York, 1950, 1951, and
1954; Gallery del Corso, Merano, Italy, 1951;
Paul Morihien Gallery, Palais Royal, Paris, France,
1952; Galleria del Milione, Milan, Italy, 1952; Art
Gallery of Toronto, 1954; Robertson Gallery,
Ottawa, 1954; Waldorf Galleries, Montreal, 1954;
Tour, Western Canada Art Circuit, 1955; The Con-
temporaries Gallery, New York, 1956; Institute of
Contemporary Art, London, England, 1955; Sagit-
tarius, Rome, 1956; Paolo Barazzi Galleries, Venice,
Italy, 1967.
GROUP: Represented in Canadian group exhibi-
tions since 1939 including annual exhibitions of
Manitoba Society of Artists, Saskatoon Society of
Artists, Canadian Society of Painters in Water
Colour, Ontario Society of Artists; represented
in group exhibitions organized by National Gal-
lery of Canada; National Print Show, Wichita,
Kan., 1946; Philadelphia Print Club, Pa., 1946;
International Exhibition, New Delhi, India, 1956;
Palace of the Legion of Honor, San Francisco,
Calif.; San Francisco Museum; Pennsylvania Acad-
emy of Fine Arts, Philadelphia; Art Institute of
Chicago, Ill.; National Academy, New York; Lib-
rary of Congress, Washington, DC; Brooklyn Mu-
seum, NY; Carnegie Institute, Museum of Art,
Pittsburgh, Pa.; Walker Art Center, Minneapolis,
Minn.; Cincinnati Art Museum, Ohio; Dallas
Museum of Fine Art, Texas; Expo 67, Montreal.
COLLECTIONS IN WHICH REPRESENTED
National Gallery of Canada; Art Gallery of Ont-
ario, Toronto; Fogg Museum, Boston, Mass.;
Yale University Museum; Knoedler Gallery, New

York; Brooklyn Museum, NY; New York Public Library; Museum of Modern Art, New York; Wesleyan University, Middletown, Conn.; Milione Gallery, Milan; Redfern Gallery, London; Bezalel Museum, Jerusalem, Israel; University of Lethbridge.
WRITINGS
(with Freya Stark and others) *The thrones of earth and heaven*, Thames and Hudson, 1958; *A time of gods*, Thames and Hudson, 1962; *To every thing there is a season*, Thames and Hudson, 1967 (number one on Canada's Best Seller list); (with Anthony Thwaite) *Japan in colour*, Thames and Hudson, 1967.
CONTRIBUTED: To *Chatelaine, Canadian art, Harper's bazaar, Maclean's, Mayfair, Sunday times, Vogue, La revue des voyages*.

BENY, Wilfred Roy
see BENY, Roloff

BERENDS, Hans Engel* 1908–
Designer; b. 30 Sept. 1908 in Nymegen, The Netherlands; son of Frank Engel and Henrietta Johana (Dekok) Berends; came to Canada in 1925 and settled in Montreal, PQ.
HOME
124 Tyndall Ave., Apt. 108, Toronto, Ont.
CAREER
National Ballet of Canada, Toronto; Montreal Opera Guild, designer 1938-53; Repertory Theatre, Montreal, designer 1939-52; Canadian National Exhibition, Grandstand Show designer 1950-67; Canadian Opera Company, Toronto, scenic designer 1951-61.
AWARDS, HONOURS
Canadian drama award, 1952.
THEATRE
Designed sets for many productions, e.g. *The consul, School for fathers, Madama Butterfly, The abduction from the seraglio, Tosca.*
EXHIBITIONS
Art Association of Montreal, 1930, 1932, 1934, 1936, 1943.

BERESFORD-HOWE, Constance Elizabeth* 1922–
(Constance Elizabeth Pressnell)
Novelist; b. 10 Nov. 1922 in Montreal; daughter of Russell and Marjory Mary (Moore) Beresford-Howe; m. Christopher W. Pressnell, 1960; children: Jeremy Howe b. 18 Mar. 1967.
EDUCATION
West Hill High School, Montreal; McGill University, BA, 1945, MA, 1946; Brown University, PhD, 1950.
RELIGION
Anglican.
HOME
42 Burton Ave., Westmount, Montreal, PQ.

OFFICE
Department of English, McGill University, Montreal, PQ.
CAREER
McGill University, assistant professor of English 1949-64, associate professor 1965–.
MEMBER
Humanities Association of Canada; PEN Club (past president, Montreal centre); Phi Beta Kappa.
AWARDS, HONOURS
McGill University Shakespeare Gold medal, Dorothy Peterson prize, 1945; Province of Quebec scholarship; Dodd, Mead Inter-collegiate literary fellowship for *The unreasoning heart*, 1945.
WRITINGS
The unreasoning heart, Dodd, Mead, 1946; *Of this day's journey*, Dodd, Mead, 1947; *The invisible gate*, Dodd, Mead, 1949; *My Lady Greensleeves*, Dodd, Mead, 1955.
CONTRIBUTED: Short stories and articles to *Canadian home journal, Maclean's, The Montrealer, Saturday night, The writer.*

BERGMAN, Henry Eric 1893-1958
Artist; b. 10 Nov. 1893 in Dresden, Germany; came to Canada in 1913 and settled in Toronto, Ont.; d. 8 Feb. 1958 in Winnipeg, Man.
EDUCATION
Attended trade school in Germany for three years; studied under Fred Brigden and W.J. Phillips, 1922.
CAREER
Started work in a commercial art·studio in Germany c.1907; Brigden's of Winnipeg, wood engraver, retoucher, and photo engraver 1914-58; illustrated James A. Roy's *The heart of the Highland*, Toronto, 1942.
MEMBER
Manitoba Society of Artists (president, 1939-40); Canadian Society of Painters in Water Colour; Society of Canadian Painter-Etchers, and Engravers (elected 1935); Canadian Handicrafts Guild (honourary life member).
AWARDS, HONOURS
Diploma for wood engraving, International Exhibition of Woodcuts, Warsaw, Poland, 1937.
EXHIBITIONS
ONE-MAN: Winnipeg Art Gallery, 1924 and 1940; De Young Museum, San Francisco, Calif., 1933; Robert Simpson Art Gallery, Toronto, 1935; Royal Canadian Academy, Toronto Art Gallery, 1941; Memorial Exhibition, Winnipeg Art Gallery, 1960; Memorial Exhibition touring Canada, 1960-61.
GROUP: Represented in group exhibitions held in Canada since c.1924 including annual exhibitions of Manitoba Society of Artists, Canadian Society of Painters in Watercolour, Society of

Canadian Painter-Etchers and Engravers, Canadian National Exhibition, Montreal Museum of Fine Arts, Canadian Society of Graphic Art; represented in group exhibitions organized by the National Gallery of Canada, Ottawa, Ont.; International Printmakers Show, Los Angeles, Calif., 1933; International Exhibition of Woodcuts, Warsaw, 1933; Exhibition of Contemporary Canadian Paintings Arranged ... for Circulation in the Southern Dominions of the British Empire, 1936; International Exhibition of Printmakers, Poland, 1936; International Exhibition of Prints, Art Institute of Chicago, Ill., 1937 and 1939; Royal Scottish Water Colour Society, Edinburgh, Scotland, 1938; Royal Canadian Academy Exhibition, Philadelphia, Pa., 1943; Rio de Janeiro, Brazil, 1945.

COLLECTIONS IN WHICH REPRESENTED
National Gallery of Canada.

BERNARD, Harry* 1898–

Author; b. 9 May 1898 in London, England; son of J. Horace and Alexandra (Bourdeau) Bernard; m. Louella Tobin 1923; m. Alice Sicotte 1957; children: (first marriage) Louella b. 1924, Marcelle b. 1933.

EDUCATION
Attended Collège Rollin, Paris, France; University of Montreal, D-ès-Let.

RELIGION
Roman Catholic.

HOME
2950, rue Lafontaine, St. Hyacinthe, PQ.

OFFICE
Le Courrier, 655 rue Saint-Anne, St. Hyacinthe, PQ.

CAREER
Le Droit, Ottawa, correspondent, assistant to the editor, 1919-23; Le Courrier, editor 1923–; Quebec French press representative at the International Convention of the Catholic Press, Rome, Italy, 1950, Vienna, Australia, 1957.

MEMBER
Royal Society of Canada; Association des Hebdomadaires français du Canada (director).

AWARDS, HONOURS
Prix David de Roman, 1924, 1925; Grand Prix David de Littérature for Juana, mon aimée, 1931; Prix d'Action Intellectuelle for La Terre vivante, 1926; Rockefeller Foundation travel grant, 1943; Prix des Lecteurs, Le Cercle du livre de France, 1951; Pierre Chauveau medal, 1959.

WRITINGS
L'Homme tombe (novel), L'Action française, 1924; La Terre vivante (novel), L'Action française, 1925; La Maison vide (novel), L'Action française, 1926; La Dame blanche (novel), L'Action française, 1927; Essais critiques,

L'Action canadienne-française, 1929; La Ferme des pins (novel), L'Action canadienne-française, 1930; Juana, mon aimée (novel), L'Action canadienne-française, 1931; Dolores (novel), L'Action canadienne-française, 1932; ABC du petit naturaliste canadien (non-fiction); "Le Roman régionaliste aux États-Unis" (thesis), 1949; Les Jours sont longs, Le Cercle du livre de France, 1951; Portages et routes d'eau en Haute-Mauricie, Éditions du Bien public, 1953.
CONTRIBUTED: Articles to Action nationale, Canada français, Liberté, Revue de l'université Laval, Transactions of the Royal Society of Canada.

BESRÉ, Jean* 1938–

Actor; b. 22 June 1938 in Sherbrooke, PQ; son of Adolphe Joseph and Aline (Tremblay) Besré; m. Lise Lasalle 1963.

EDUCATION
Studied theatre with François Rozet and Henri Norbert in Montreal, 1955-57; with Pierre Bertin, André Voisin, and Raymond Girard in Paris, France, 1957-60; Conservatoire de Paris, France, auditor.

HOME
4546 Old Orchard Ave., Montreal 28, PQ.

CAREER
Travelled extensively in Europe and the Middle East.

MEMBER
Union des Artistes de Montréal.

AWARDS, HONOURS
Prix Festival Provincial, Trois Rivières, PQ, meilleur acteur, 1957; Prix Festival National, Edmonton, Alta., meilleur acteur de soutien, 1957.

THEATRE
Played title role in Milot (Théâtre Récamier, Paris, 1957-60), 5 roles in Les Cenci (Théâtre de l'Alliance Française, Paris, 1957-60), père Dima Licasi in La jarre (Théâtre Universitaire, Paris, 1957-60), Marinoni in Fantasio (Théâtre Universitaire, Paris, 1957-60), Georges in Lorsque l'enfant paraît (Théâtre du Rideau Vert, Montréal, 1961), Pas d'âge pour l'amour (Théâtre du Rideau Vert, 1961), Béranger in Tueur sans gages (Centre Theatre, Montreal, 1962), fils de Deburau in Deburau (Théâtre du Rideau Vert, 1962), Arlequin in La double inconstance (Théâtre du Nouveau Monde, Montreal, 1963), Le diable in L'amour des 4 colonels (Théâtre de Marjolaine, Montréal, 1963), Lancelot in Le marchand de Venise (Théâtre Club, Montréal, 1964), lead in Le vol rose de Flamand (La Comédie Canadienne, Montréal, 1964), Le bijoutier in Il est une saison (La Comédie Canadienne, 1965), Jonathan in Le placard (Théâtre de l'Égrégore, Montréal, 1965/66), Lui in Ciel de lit (Théâtre de Quat'sous, Montréal, 1966), Mufti in Le bourgeois gentilhomme

(Théâtre du Nouveau Monde, 1967), Olivier in *Elle tournera la terre* (La Comédie Canadienne, 17 Nov. 1967), Freddy in *Pygmalion* (Théâtre du Nouveau Monde, Dec. 1967), Bérenger in *Rhinocéros* (Théâtre du Nouveau Monde, Apr. 1968), *Le Tartuffe* (Théâtre du Nouveau Monde, 8 Nov. 1968).

FILM

Played in various films, eg. lead in *L'homme à l'oreille cassée* (Niagara Film, 1963), lead in *13, impasse Lucrèce* (Niagara Film, 1964), Maricourt in *D'Iberville* (1966-67).

RADIO

Played in numerous programs, e.g. title role in *Tintin* (serial, 1962-64).

TELEVISION

Appeared on numerous programs, e.g. Étudiant en médecine in *Filles d'Ève* (1960-64), Étudiant en médecine in *Le Bonheur des autres* (1965-67), Medical student in *Shoestring Theatre* (1964-65), Animateur in *Tour de terre* (1964), Journaliste in *La dernière heure*, Étudiant in *Tuez le veau gras* (CBC, 1963/64), Diable in *L'amour des 4 colonels*.

BETTS, Lorne 1918–

Composer; b. 1918 in Winnipeg, Man.

EDUCATION

Studied piano with Filmer Hubble, organ with W.H. Anderson, voice and theory with Hunter Johnson in Winnipeg; studied composition with John Weinzweig, Royal Conservatory of Music, Toronto, Ont.; Ernst Krenek in Austria, Alan Rawsthorne in England, and Roy Harris in USA.

HOME

Apt. 18, 123 Bold St., Hamilton, Ont.

CAREER

Hamilton Philharmonic Orchestra, director; Hamilton Conservatory of Music, principal; St. Paul's Presbyterian Church, Hamilton, director of music to 1964; Melrose United Church, Hamilton, organist and choirmaster 1964–; *Spectator*, Hamilton, music critic 1965–.

MEMBER

CAPAC; Canadian League of Composers.

COMPOSITIONS

Suite for strings, 1948, first performed 1950 in Vancouver, BC, by CBC Orchestra under John Avison; *Sonata for violin and piano*, 1948, first performed 1948 at the Royal Conservatory of Music; *Sonata for orchestra*, 1948-49, first performed 1950 by the student orchestra, Royal Conservatory of Music; many songs for high and medium voice and piano, 1949–; *David*, mixed choir, 1949; *Elegy*, horn and strings, 1949, first performed 1950 in Vancouver by CBC Orchestra under Albert Steinberg; *Prelude, pastoral and dance*, woodwinds, 1949; *Joe Harris 1913-42*, men's voices and orchestra, 1950, first performed

1952 in Vancouver by CBC Orchestra under John Avison; *Two dances for orchestra*, 1950, first performed by Juilliard School of Music Orchestra, New York, NY, under Jean Morel; *Music for theatre*, small orchestra, 1950, first performed at Royal Conservatory of Music; *String quartet no. 1*, 1950; *String quartet no. 2*, 1951; *Prelude for spring*, mezzo-soprano and baritone with flute, harp, and string quartet, 1951; *Suite da chiesa*, winds and percussion, 1952, first performed 1954 in Montreal, PQ, at concert of Canadian League of Composers; *Suite for small orchestra*, 1954, first performed 1955 in Vancouver by CBC Orchestra under John Avison; *Symphony no. 1*, 1954; *Riders to the sea*, chamber opera, 1955; *The souls of the righteous*, mixed choir and organ, 1960, Waterloo Music; *The woodcarver's wife*, chamber opera, 1960; *Two abstracts for orchestra*, 1961, first performed 1961 by St. Catharine's Civic Orchestra, Ont., under Leonard Pearlman; *Symphony no. 2*, 1961; *Kanadario: music for a festive occasion*, orchestra, 1966, first performed Jan. 1967 by London Symphony Orchestra, Ont., commissioned by Ontario Federation of Symphony Orchestras for Canada's centennial; *Vespers*, mixed choir, 1967, first performed 17 Mar. 1968 by McMaster University Choir under Frank Thorolfson, commissioned by McMaster University for Canada's centennial.

BIÉLER, André* 1896–

Artist; b. 8 Oct. 1896 in Lausanne, Switzerland; son of Charles and Blanche (Merle d'Aubigné) Biéler; came to Canada with his parents in 1908; m. Jeanette Munier 27 Apr. 1931; children: Nathalie b. 23 Jan. 1934, Sylvie b. 18 Feb. 1937, André (Ted) b. 23 July 1938, Peter b. 2 Nov. 1943.

EDUCATION

Attended Lycée Carnot, Paris, France, 1905-08; Stanstead College, PQ, 1909-13; studied under Eugene Speicher, Charles Rosen, and George Bellows, Art Students' League, Woodstock, NY, 1921; attended École du Louvre, Paris, 1920s; studied with Paul Sérusier and Maurice Denis, Académie Ranson, Paris, 1923; studied with Ernest Biéler, Switzerland, 1920s.

HOME

Twelve Pines, RR 1, Glenburnie, Ont.

CAREER

Canadian Army, Princess Patricia's Canadian Light Infantry, 1915-18, Canadian Corps Headquarters, topographical section, 1918, became sergeant, awarded Meritorious Service Award, 1918; assisted Ernest Biéler with frescoes, Town Hall of Le Locle, Jura Mountains, 1922; The Atelier, Montreal, PQ, teacher 1931-34; Queen's University, head of art department and resident artist 1936-63, emeritus professor 1963–, Agnes

Etherington Art Centre director 1957-63; travelled and lectured under the auspices of the National Gallery of Canada, 1940-41; organized and chaired "Conference of Canadian Artists" held at Kingston, Ont., 1941; Banff School of Fine Arts, Alta., teacher summers 1940, 1947, 1949 and 1952; illustrated part of the booklet, *10 pulp and paper paintings*, 1948.

COMMISSIONS
Mural, St. Sauveur, PQ, 1931; mural, Aluminum Co. of Canada, Kingston, 1947; mural, Aluminum Co. of Canada, Shipshaw, PQ, 1948; mosaic, Chalmers Church Hall, Kingston; mosaic, Frontenac Tile Company, Kingston.

MEMBER
Canadian Group of Painters (charter member, 1933; vice-president, 1943); Canadian Society of Painters in Water Colour; Ontario Society of Artists (elected, 1937); Federation of Canadian Artists (organizer, 1941; president, 1942-44); Royal Canadian Academy (Associate 1942; Academician 1955).

AWARDS, HONOURS
Won mural competition, Aluminum Co. of Canada, Shipshaw, 1946; won mural competition, Veteran's Building, Ottawa, Ont., 1954; J.W.L. Forster award, Ontario Society of Artists, 1957.

EXHIBITIONS
ONE-MAN: Cour St. Pierre, Geneva, Switzerland, 1924; Montreal Museum of Fine Art, 1924 and 1952; Ritz-Carlton Hotel, Montreal, 1926; Kingston Art Association, 1937, 1955, and 1960; tour of Montreal and Quebec, PQ, Ottawa, Edmonton, Alta., Calgary, Alta., Banff, and Winnipeg, Man., 1940; Le Caveau, Ottawa, 1940; École des Beaux-Arts, Québec, 1941; Winnipeg Art Gallery, 1942; Dominion Gallery, Montreal, 1946; Hart House, University of Toronto, Ont., 1946; Eaton's College Street, Toronto, 1946; Garfield Gallery, Toronto, 1950; Robertson Art Gallery, Ottawa, 1954; Agnes Etherington Art Centre, Queen's University, 1955, 1960, and 1965; Galebia San Miguel Allende, Mexico, 1964; Glenburnie, 1964.
GROUP: Represented in group exhibitions held in Canada since 1924 including annual exhibitions of Montreal Museum of Fine Arts Spring Show, Canadian Society of Graphic Arts, Royal Canadian Academy, Ontario Society of Artists, Canadian National Exhibition, Group of Seven, Canadian Group of Painters, and Canadian Society of Painters in Water Colour; represented in group exhibitions organized by National Gallery of Canada, Ottawa; *Exposition Internationale,* Paris, 1937; Coronation, England, 1937; A Century of Canadian Art, Tate Gallery, London, England, 1938; International Water Colour Exhibition, Brooklyn Museum, NY, 1941; Aspects of Contemporary Painting in

Canada, Addison Gallery, Andover, Mass., 1942-43; Canadian Art 1760-1943, Yale University Art Gallery, 1944; *Pintura Canadense Contemporanea*, Rio de Janeiro, Brazil, 1946; Exhibition of International Modern Art, Musée d'Art Moderne, Paris, originated by UNESCO, 1946; Boston Museum of Fine Arts, Mass., 1946; Contemporary Canadian Painting, Canadian Club, New York, 1949; Painters of Canada ... 1668-1948, Virginia Museum of Fine Arts, Richmond, 1949; Brazil, 1950; San Francisco, Calif., 1956; An Exhibition of Canadian Paintings held at Fortnum and Mason Ltd., London, 1955.

COLLECTIONS IN WHICH REPRESENTED
Art Gallery of Ontario, Toronto; Musée du Québec, PQ; Queen's University; Montreal Museum of Fine Art; National Gallery of Canada, Ottawa; Winnipeg Art Gallery; Hart House, University of Toronto; Edmonton Art Gallery; Windsor Art Association, Ont.; Art Collector Society of Kingston.

WRITINGS
(with Elizabeth Harrison) *The Kingston conference*, Carnegie Corporation, 1941.
CONTRIBUTED: To *Maritime art, Canadian art,* and other publications.

BIRD, William Richard*   1891—
Novelist; b. 11 May 1891 in East Mapleton, NS; son of Stephen and Augusta Caroline Bird; m. Ethel May Sutton 18 June 1919; children: Betty Caroline, Stephen Stanley (killed in action 8 July 1944).

EDUCATION
Attended Cumberland County Academy, Amherst, NS.

RELIGION
United Church.

HOME
963 Marlborough Ave., Halifax, NS.

CAREER
Homesteaded in Alberta; Canadian Army, 42nd Royal Highlanders, 1916-20, awarded MM; freelanced; visited World War I battlefields for *Maclean's magazine*, 1931; lecture tour of eastern and central provinces, 1931-33; Nova Scotia Bureau of Information, clerk 1933, assistant director 1934-50; Nova Scotia Historic Sites Advisory Council, appointed chairman 1950.

MEMBER
Canadian Club; Nova Scotia Historical Society; Haliburton Society of King's College (elected fellow, 1956); Canadian Authors Association (national president, 1949-50, Nova Scotia branch, honorary president); St. George's Society, Halifax (president, 1958).

AWARDS, HONOURS
Ryerson fiction award, co-winner for *Here stays good Yorkshire*, 1945; for *Judgment glen,* 1947;

DLitt from Mount Allison University, 1949; Queen's Coronation medal; Canada Council fellowship, 1961/62; national award in letters from University of Alberta, 1965; short stories listed in *O. Henry memorial award prize stories* and in *O'Brien's best short stories.*

WRITINGS
A century at Chignecto (non-fiction), Ryerson, 1928; *And we go on* (biography), the author, 1930; *Private Timothy Fergus Clancy,* Graphic, 1930; *Thirteen years after* (non-fiction), Maclean, 1932; *Story of Vimy-ridge* (non-fiction), the author, 1932; *The communication trench* (non-fiction), the author, 1935; *Maid of the marshes,* the author, 1936; *Here stays good Yorkshire,* Ryerson, 1945; *Sunrise for Peter,* Ryerson, 1946; *Judgment glen,* Ryerson, 1947; *The passionate pilgrim,* Ryerson, 1949; *This is Nova Scotia* (non-fiction), Ryerson, 1950; *So much to record,* Ryerson, 1951; *To love and to cherish,* Ryerson, 1953; *No retreating footsteps,* Kentville, 1953; *The two Jacks* (biography), Ryerson, 1954; *Done at Grand Pré,* Ryerson, 1955; *The shy Yorkshireman,* Ryerson, 1955; *Off-trail in Nova Scotia* (non-fiction), Ryerson, 1956; *Tristram's salvation,* Ryerson, 1957; *These are the Maritimes* (non-fiction), Ryerson, 1959; *Despite the distance,* Ryerson, 1961; *The north shore regiment* (non-fiction), Brunswick Press, 1963; *Ghosts have warm hands* (autobiography), Clarke, Irwin, 1967.
EDITED: *Atlantic anthology,* McClelland & Stewart, 1959.
CONTRIBUTED: Articles and short stories to veteran's publications in the British Commonwealth and USA, *Maclean's, Collier's, Family herald,* and other magazines.

BISSON, Napoleon 1923—
Singer (baritone); b. 1923.
HOME
733 Champagneur, Montréal, PQ.
CAREER
THEATRE: Sang in many productions, e.g. *The diary of a madman* (Berlin Festival, 30 Oct. 1958), *Le magicien* (Les Jeunesses Musicales du Canada, trans Canada tour, 1960/61), Amonasro in *Aida* (Canadian Opera Company, Toronto, 22 Sept. 1964), Bonze in *Madama Butterfly* (Vancouver Opera Association, BC, 28 Oct. 1965), Father in *Hansel and Gretel* (Vancouver Opera Association, 29 June 1966), *Benvenuto Cellini* (Royal Opera House, Covent Garden, London, England, 1966), *Das Rheingold* (Royal Opera House, Covent Garden, Oct. 1966), Agamemnon in *La belle Hélène* (Théâtre Lyrique de Montréal, 19 Apr. 1967), *Barber of Seville* (Vancouver Opera Association, 14 Nov. 1968).

RADIO
Sang in several CBC productions, e.g. *Le magicien* ("Wednesday night," 6 June 1962), *Music of the sun king* ("Wednesday night," 28 June 1961).
TELEVISION
Sang in several CBC productions, e.g. Dr. Bartolo in *The barber of Seville* ("L'heure du concert," Mar. 1965; "Festival," 3 Nov. 1965).

BLACKBURN, Maurice 1914—
Composer and pianist; b. 22 May 1914 in Quebec City, PQ; m. Marthe Morisset.
EDUCATION
Studied organ with Henri Gagnon, piano and composition with Jean Beaudet, harmony with George-Emile Tanguay, École de Musique, Laval University, to 1939; studied counterpoint with Quincy Porter, New England Conservatory of Music, Boston, Mass., 1939; studied orchestration and conducting with Francis Findlay; studied with Nadia Boulanger in Paris, France, 1954.
HOME
549, rue Chester, Montréal, PQ.
CAREER
National Film Board of Canada, staff composer 1942—.
MEMBER
CAPAC.
AWARDS, HONOURS
Jean Lallemand national competition, second prize for *Les petites rues de vieux Québec,* 1938; Quebec government scholarship for studies abroad, 1939; New England Conservatory of Music George Allan prize for *Sonatine for piano,* 1940; Canada Council fellowship, 1954; Canada Council award, 1967/68.
COMPOSITIONS
Les petites rues de vieux Québec, orchestra, 1938; *Digitales,* piano, 1940, F. Harris; *Sonatine,* piano, 1940; *Fantaisie en mocassins,* orchestra, 1941, performed 1941 by Quebec Symphony Orchestra under the composer; *Maple sugar,* film score, 1942; many other film scores for National Film Board of Canada documentary films, 1942—, e.g. *A phantasy* (synthetic music), *Blinkety blank* (chance music), *Lignes verticales* (electronic improvisations), *Jour après jour* (concrete music), *Je* (organized sound-effects); *Concertino in C major for piano, woodwind and brass,* 1948, Canadian Music Centre, first performed 1949 in Montreal by CBC Orchestra under Jean Beaudet with Yvon Barette, piano, recorded by CBC IS; *Soir d'hiver,* low voice and piano, 1949; *Une mesure de silence* or *Silent measures,* comic opera, 1954, first performed 1955 on CBC television; *Suite for strings,* 1960, first performed 1960 in Toronto, Ont., by Hart House Orchestra

under Boyd Neel, commissioned by Hart House Orchestra; *Pirouette*, chamber opera, 1960, first performed by Jeunesses Musicales du Canada, commissioned by the same group; scores for productions of Le Théâtre du Nouveau Monde, Montréal.

BLANTON, Jeremy* 1939–
Dancer; b. 31 Dec. 1939 in Memphis; son of Clarence James and Octavia (Dell) Blanton; came to Canada in 1962.

EDUCATION
Attended Memphis State University, 1957; studied ballet with Charles Kirby and Manolo Agullo, Memphis, 1952-59; Robert Joffrey, New York, NY, 1959-60; Antony Tudor, New York.

HOME
c/o 735 Breedlove St., Memphis, Tenn., 38107, USA.

OFFICE
National Ballet of Canada, 157 King St. E., Toronto 1, Ont.

CAREER
Robert Joffrey Ballet, New York, soloist 1959/60; Metropolitan Opera Ballet, New York, feature dancer 1960/61; Academy of Ballet Arts, Memphis, teacher 1961/62; National Ballet of Canada, Toronto, soloist 1962-67, principal 1967–.

MEMBER
ACTRA; AEA; AGMA.

AWARDS, HONOURS
School of American Ballet scholarship, New York.

THEATRE
First danced Lead male in *Serenade* (Balanchine, 1962/63), title role in *L'après-midi d'un faune* (Franca, 1962/63), Lead boy in *One in five* (Powell, 1962/63), Lover in *Winter night* (Gore, 1962/63), Count Paris in *Romeo and Juliet* (Cranko, 1963/64), Orestes in *The house of Atreus* (Strate, 1963/64), Poet in *Les sylphides* (Fokine, 1963/64), Painter in *Offenbach in the underworld* (Tudor, 1963/64), Lead male in *Les rendez-vous* (Ashton, 1963/64), *Concerto barocco* (Balanchine, 1963/64), Prince in *Casse-noisette* (Franca after Ivanov, 1964/65), *Triptych* (Strate, 1964/65), Lead peasant boy in *La sylphide* (Bruhn, 1964/65), Her Lover in *Le jardin aux lilas* (Tudor, 1965/66), title role in *The rake's progress* (de Valois, 1965/66), Lead male in *Solitaire* (MacMillan, 1965/66), *Adagio cantabile* (Poll, 1965/66), *Pulcinella* (Strate, 1965/66), Prince Siegfried in *Le lac des cygnes* (Bruhn, 1966/67), Danseur in *La prima ballerina* (Heiden, 1966/67); created Prince in *Cinderella* (Franca, O'Keefe Centre, Toronto, 15 Apr. 1968).

TELEVISION
Danced in *One in five* (Powell, "Festival," CBC, 6 May 1964), Count Paris and Carnival King in *Romeo and Juliet* (Cranko, "Festival," CBC, 15 Sept. 1965), Pas de deux in *And then we wrote* ("Music Canada," CBC, 8 Feb. 1967), Neapolitan dance in *Le lac des cygnes* (Bruhn, "Festival," CBC, 27 Dec. 1967), Prince in *Cinderella* (Franca, CBC, 22 Dec. 1968).

WORK IN PROGRESS: Lead male in new Strate ballet.

BLISS, Sally Brayley
see BRAYLEY, Sally

BLOORE, Ronald L. 1925–
(Win Hedore)
Artist; b. 29 May 1925 in Brampton, Ont.

EDUCATION
University of Toronto, BA, 1945-49; attended New York University, 1949-51; Washington University, St. Louis, Mo., MA, 1953; Belgium Art Seminar, 1955; Courtauld Institute, London, England, 1955-57.

OFFICE
Room 206, Vanier College, York University, Toronto 12, Ont.

CAREER
Served in the Canadian Army and the RCAF during the second world war; Washington University, St. Louis, instructor 1953-55; University of Toronto, instructor 1957-58; University of Saskatchewan, Regina College, instructor 1958; Norman Mackenzie Art Gallery, Regina, Sask., director 1958-66 (except May 1962 to Aug. 1963); studied and painted in Egypt and Greece 1962-63; *The Vikings* (musical drama), government-sponsored project for Denmark, Norway, and Sweden, visual designer and adviser 1965; *Canadian art*, editorial advisory committee member 1966; York University, director of art 1966–.

COMMISSIONS
Mural, Confederation Centre, Charlottetown, PEI.

MEMBER
Federation of Canadian Artists (student committee of Ontario Region, 1948-49); Canadian Museum Directors Association (vice-president, 1964-65); Regina Group of Painters.

AWARDS, HONOURS
Canada Council grant, 1962 and 1965.

EXHIBITIONS
ONE-MAN: Here and Now Gallery, Toronto, 1962; Dorothy Cameron Gallery, Toronto, 1965. GROUP: Represented in group exhibitions held in Canada including annual exhibitions of Montreal Museum of Fine Art Spring Show, Canadian Society of Painters in Water Colour; represented in group exhibitions organized by National Gallery of Canada, Ottawa, Ont.,

including the fourth and fifth Biennial of Canadian Painting; Sâo Paulo Biennial, Brazil, 1961; Albright-Knox Gallery, Buffalo, NY, 1962 and 1963; Art of Spain and The Americas, Madrid, Spain, 1963; Tate Gallery, London, England, 1964.

COLLECTIONS IN WHICH REPRESENTED National Gallery of Canada; Art Gallery of Ontario, Toronto; Agnes Etherington Art Centre, Queen's University.

WRITINGS
CONTRIBUTED: To *Canadian art*.

BLOUIN, Paul*   1928–
Director; b. 11 July 1928 in Dauphin, Man.; son of Amedée and Odile (Belliveau) Blouin.

EDUCATION
Attended North Battleford Separate School, Sask.; Roecliffe School, Denholm, Sask.; École Émard, Valleyfield, PQ; St. Joseph Academy, Hawkesbury, Ont.; studied diction and dramatic art with Eleanor Stuart (*q.v.*); voice and singing with Albert Cornellier.

HOME
Apt. 24, 2150 Sherbrooke St., West, Montreal, PQ.

OFFICE
1625 Maisonneuve Boul., Montréal, PQ.

CAREER
CBC, Montreal, radio actor 1948-54, TV producer and director 1955–; Negro Theatre Guild, stage director 1953-54; Théâtre du Rideau Vert, Montréal, director 1965–; National Theatre School, Montreal, instructor 1968.

MEMBER
Canadian Theatre Centre; Association des Réalisateurs.

AWARDS, HONOURS
Imperial Relations Trust bursary, 1964; Canada Council senior arts fellowship for studies in England and continental Europe, 1964.

THEATRE
Directed *Vent d'est* (Théâtre Populaire, Montréal 1960), *View from the bridge* (Centre d'Art, Percé, PQ, 1961), *Le cid* (La Nouvelle Compagnie Théâtrale, Montréal, 1965), *On ne sait comment* (Rideau Vert, 15 Nov. 1965), *La vie est un songe* (Rideau Vert, 1967), *La collection* (Rideau Vert, 15 Jan. 1968), *L'amant* (Rideau Vert, 15 Jan. 1968).

RADIO
Played in many CBC programs, e.g. "Wednesday night", "Way of the spirit."

TELEVISION
Produced many CBC programs, e.g. *Au coeur de la rose, Il neigera dans l'île, Un cas de paresthénie, Martine, Otage, La cellule, Mesure de guerre, Vent d'est, Yerma, The little moon of Alban, La dame aux camélias, Colombe, Le temps des lilas,* *Bousille et les justes, The three sisters, La pensée, Blues pour un homme averti, Quelqu'un parmi vous, The importance of being earnest, The Aspern papers, Un caprice, L'amant, The heiress, Cap-aux-sorciers* (series; Frigon Award, 1957), *L'échéance de vendredi* (Congrès du Spectacle award, 1960), *Bilan* (Congrès du Spectacle award, 1961), *Death of a salesman* (Congrès du Spectacle award, 1963), *La maison de Bernarda* (14 Mar. 1963); produced and directed *Doux sauvage* (colour feature film).

BLUME, Helmut   1914–
Pianist and musicologist; b. 12 Apr. 1914 in Berlin, Germany; son of Gustav and Romana (Sachs) Blume; came to Canada in 1942 and settled in Toronto, Ont.; m. Mignon Hickson-Elkins 23 May 1955.

EDUCATION
Attended University of Berlin, 1932-33; studied under Paul Hindemith, Berlin College of Music, 1933-38; studied under Louis Kentner in London, England; Toronto (now Royal) Conservatory of Music, 1942-43.

RELIGION
Lutheran.

HOME
20 Windsor Ave., Westmount, PQ.

OFFICE
Dept. of Music, McGill University, Montreal, PQ.

CAREER
Canadian Wartime Information Board, editor of German broadcasts 1942-44; Hambourg Conservatory of Music, Toronto, head of piano department 1942-46; toured Canada and USA as concert pianist; CBC IS, head of German-language section 1944-60, music consultant 1960–; McGill University, instructor in piano 1946-55, associate professor and chairman of department of keyboard and vocal music 1955-64, dean of faculty of music 1964–.

AWARDS, HONOURS
22nd American Exhibition of Educational Radio-Television Programs, Ohio State University, first prize for "Music to see," 1958.

RADIO
Made numerous appearances on CBC radio as writer, commentator, and critic of musical programs; wrote and lectured series: "The musical mind" (1961), "Opera stars and story." "The story of music"; produced four programs in "Footloose" series; many appearances in "Wednesday night" series.

TELEVISION
Appeared in many CBC programs as commentator and compère; wrote and appeared in three educational series "Music to see" (1958-61).

RECORDINGS
Form in music, 1960.

COMPOSITIONS

Piano accompaniments, *Canada's story in song*, by E. Fowke and A. Mills, W.J. Gage, 1960, 2nd ed. 1965.

WRITINGS

The piano, no 10 in series *Let's explore music*, G.V. Thompson, 1961.

CONTRIBUTED: Articles and reviews to national and local periodicals, e.g. *Saturday night*.

BOBAK, Molly* 1922–

(Molly Lamb Bobak)
Artist; b. 25 Feb. 1922 in Vancouver, BC; daughter of Harold Mortimer Lamb and Alice Mary Price; m. Bruno Bobak 1945; children: Alexander b. 12 Oct. 1946, Anny Mary b. 25 Mar. 1957.

EDUCATION

Studied under Jack L. Shadbolt (*q.v.*), Vancouver School of Art, 1938-41.

RELIGION

None.

HOME

97 Grey St., Fredericton, NB.

CAREER

CWAC, became lieutenant 1942-46; appointed official war artist with the Canadian Army in Europe 1945-46; Vancouver School of Art, instructor in painting 1947-50; Vancouver Art Gallery, art teacher for the Women's Auxillary 1954-58; participated in a CBC TV series on teaching drawing and art appreciation *c.*1956; University of British Columbia Extension and Summer School, instructor 1958-59; University of New Brunswick Art Centre, instructor 1960-61, 1962-67; CHSJ TV in Saint John, NB, instructor in a televised art course 1964-65.

MEMBER

Canadian Group of Painters; Canadian Society of Graphic Art.

AWARDS, HONOURS

Prize, Canadian Army Art Competition, 1944; first prize, Graphic Art Society, 1966; French Government scholarship for study in France, 1950-51; Canada Council fellowship for study in Europe, 1960-61.

EXHIBITIONS

ONE-MAN: Vancouver Art Gallery, *c.*1940; Vancouver Art Gallery and New Design Gallery, Vancouver and Waddington Gallery, Montreal, PQ, sometime during the period 1950-60; Wells Gallery, Ottawa, Ont., 1965; National Gallery Travelling Show, 1965; Dalhousie University, 1966; Douglas Gallery, Vancouver, 1967; Roberts Gallery, Toronto, 1967.
GROUP: Represented in group exhibitions held in Canada; second, third, and fourth Biennial Exhibitions of Canadian Painting, National Gallery of Canada, Ottawa, 1957, 1959, and 1961; Exhibition of Canadian Painting, Rio de Janeiro and São Paulo, Brazil, 1944; Canadian Women Artists, Riverside Museum, New York, NY, 1947; Canadian Section, São Paulo Biennial exhibition, Museo de Arte Moderna, 1951; Festival of Britain, London, England, 1951; German Industries Fair, Berlin, 1953; exhibition of Canadian paintings shown Pakistan, India, and Ceylon, 1954-55; International Print Exhibition, Lugano, Switzerland.

COLLECTIONS IN WHICH REPRESENTED

Art Gallery of Greater Victoria, BC; Art Gallery of Ontario, Toronto; Art Museum, Jerusalem, Israel; Confederation Art Gallery, Charlottetown, PEI; Montreal Museum of Fine Arts; National Gallery of Canada; New Design Gallery, Vancouver; Sir George Williams University; University of British Columbia; University of New Brunswick; University of Victoria; Vancouver Art Gallery; Owens Museum, Mount Allison University.

WRITINGS

CONTRIBUTED: To *Canadian art*.

BODSWORTH, Charles Frederick

see BODSWORTH, Fred

BODSWORTH, Fred* 1918–

(Charles Frederick Bodsworth)
Author; b. 11 Oct. 1918 in Port Burwell, Ont.; son of Arthur John and Viola (Williams) Bodsworth; m. Margaret Neville Banner 8 July 1944; children: Barbara b. 6 May 1945, Nancy b. 22 Aug. 1946, Neville b. 8 Feb. 1950.

EDUCATION

Port Burwell Public and Continuation Schools.

HOME

294 Beech Ave., Toronto, Ont.

CAREER

Times journal, St. Thomas, Ont., reporter 1940-43; *Daily star* and *Star weekly*, Toronto, reporter and editor 1943-46; *Maclean's magazine*, assistant editor 1952-55; freelance writer 1959–.

MEMBER

Federation of Ontario Naturalists (past president); Ornithological Club, Toronto; Brodie Club; Toronto Field Naturalists (past president).

AWARDS, HONOURS

Doubleday Canadian prize novel award for *The sparrow's fall*, 1967.

WRITINGS

Last of the curlews (novel), Dodd, Mead, 1954 (Reader's digest condensed book club selection); *The strange one* (novel), Dodd, Mead, 1959 (Literary Guild of America selection, published in the USA under title *The mating call*, Pocket Books, 1961); *The atonement of Ashley Morden* (novel), Dodd, Mead, 1964; *The sparrow's fall* (novel), Doubleday, 1967 (Literary Guild of America selection).

CONTRIBUTED: Articles to *Forest and outdoors, Canadian nature, Maclean's, Saturday night,* and other Canadian and American periodicals.

BOISJOLI, Charlotte
Actress.
HOME
4182 Beaconsfield Ave., Montreal 261, PQ.
CAREER
La Compagnie du Masque, Montréal, co-founder and actress 1948; Théâtre du Nouveau Monde, Montréal, actress 1952–.
MEMBER
Union des Artistes de Montréal.
THEATRE
Played in numerous productions, e.g. *Maison de poupée* (Théâtre de l'Ermitage, Montréal, 194?), *L'échange* (Théâtre de l'Ermitage, 1942), Hélène in *Le songe d'une nuit d'été* (L'Équipe, Montréal, 1945), *Le pain dur* (Théâtre du Gesù, Montréal, 1947?), title role in *Antigone* (Cocteau, Masque, 1950), *L'honneur de Dieu* (Les Compagnons de Saint-Laurent, Montréal, 1952), *Les noces de sang* (Les Compagnons de Saint-Laurent, 1952), *La nuit du 16 janvier* (Nouveau Monde, 1952/53), Elmire in *Le Tartuffe* (Nouveau Monde, 1952/53), Elvire in *Don Juan* (Molière, Nouveau Monde, 1953/54), Olivia in *La nuit des rois* (Le Théâtre Club, Montréal, 15 Feb. 1956), Masha in *La mouette* (Nouveau Monde, 1955/56), *Les taupes* (Nouveau Monde, 1959), Armande in *Les femmes savantes* (Nouveau Monde, 1960), *Oreste* (Nouveau Monde, 1960), *Naïves hirondelles* (Théâtre de l'Égrégore, Montréal, 1963), *Le roi se meurt* (Nouveau Monde, 1963), Hortense in *La locandiera* (La Nouvelle Compagnie Théâtrale, Montréal, Nov. 1965), *La mouette* (La Nouvelle Compagnie Théâtrale, Montréal, 8 Mar. 1968).

BOKY, Colette 1937–
(Colette Mary Elizabeth Giroux)
Singer (coloratura soprano); b. *c.*1937 in Montreal, PQ; daughter of Mr. and Mrs. Giroux; m.; children: 1 daughter b. *c.*1956.
EDUCATION
Studied drama; attended École Supérieure de Musique de Vincent d'Indy, Montréal, 1953-55; studied with Ernesto Barbini and Herman Geiger-Torel, Royal Conservatory of Music, Toronto, Ont.; with Raoul Jobin and Dr. Wilfrid Pelletier, Conservatory of Music and Dramatic Art, Montreal, 1958-61.
HOME
10819 Waverly St., Montreal, PQ; c/o Vienna Volksoper, Vienna, Austria.
CAREER
Vienna Volksoper, Austria; Munich State Opera, Germany; Bremen Stadttheater, Germany,

Metropolitan Opera Company, New York, NY, 1967-68.
AWARDS, HONOURS
Winner of singing contest, 1953; scholarship for studies at Conservatory of Music and Dramatic Art, Montreal, from Montreal radio station, 1958; prix de solfège and first prize from Conservatory of Music and Dramatic Art, Montreal, 1961; Prix d'Europe from Quebec Government, 1962; medal from international contests in Geneva, Switzerland, and Munich, Germany, *c.*1963; Canada Council arts scholarship 1963/64.
THEATRE
French debut in operetta at Grand Théâtre de Bordeaux; sang in numerous productions, e.g. soloist in outdoor concert (Montreal Symphony Orchestra, 17 June 1962; 1968), *Romeo and Juliet* (Montreal, 1962), *L'apothicaire* (Théâtre de France, Paris, France, 1964), *La belle Hélène* (Théâtre Lyrique de Montréal, 19 Apr. 1967), Rosina in *The barber of Seville* (Canadian Opera Company, Toronto, 18 Sept. 1967), Giulietta and Antonia in *The tales of Hoffmann* (Canadian Opera Company, Toronto, 20 Sept. 1967).
RADIO
Sang in several productions, e.g. *Die Gärtnerin aus Liebe* (5 Dec. 1965), *Les trois valses* (fall 1967).
TELEVISION
Sang in many productions, e.g. Violetta in *La traviata* (CBC, 7 Dec. 1966), Gilda in *Rigoletto* (BBC, Easter week 1968).

BONNIERE, René* 1928–
Film maker; b. 10 Mar. 1928 in Lyon, France; son of Jean Louis and Madeleine (Danel) Bonniere; came to Canada 20 Oct. 1955 and settled in Ottawa, Ont.; m. Claude Caubet 26 May 1952; children: Christophe b. 11 Dec. 1956, Pascal b. 22 Feb. 1962.
EDUCATION
Attended Pensionnat St. Louis, Lyon, until 1939; École du Molard, Rive de Gier, France, 1939, 1944; University of Lyon, 1944, 1947.
RELIGION
Roman Catholic.
HOME
23 Roxboro W., Toronto, Ont.
CAREER
French Army, chasseurs alpins 1948-49; apprentice to Henri Colpi, editor, France 1949-50; Force et Voix de France, freelance assistant editor, editor, and director; Société parisienne de l'industrie cinématographique, freelance director-photographer 1950; Cinétest, freelance director-editor 1954; Radiodiffusion Télévision Française, assistant director of drama 1954-55; Belgian American Banking Corporation, New York, NY, 1955; Crawley Films, Ottawa 1955-65; freelance in Toronto 1965–.

MEMBER
Association Professionelle des Cinéastes;
Directors Guild of Canada.

FILMS
Directed and edited *Éclaireurs skieurs in
Austria* (1950), *Les joueurs d'ondes* (1952),
Routes de France (1954); edited *Legend of the
raven* (Crawley Films sponsored by Imperial
Oil Ltd., 1957; award of merit, art and experi-
mental films category, Canadian Film Awards,
Toronto, 1958; certificate of participation,
International Film Festival, Stratford, Ont.,
1958; certificate of participation, International
Documentary Film Festival, Yorkton, Sask.,
1958; certificate of participation, International
Film Festival, Vancouver, BC, 1958; certificate
of participation, Brussels World Fair, Belgium,
1958; blue ribbon award [first prize], films for
children category, American Film Assembly,
New York, 1959), *Beaver dam* (Crawley Films,
1957; award, International Film Festival,
Venice, Italy, 1958; blue ribbon award [first
prize], films for children category, American
Film Assembly, New York, 1962; award,
International Children's Film Festival,
Necochea, Argentina, 1965); directed *Craftsmen
of Canada* (Crawley Films sponsored by BA Oil
Co., 1958; award, best Canadian films of the
last fifteen years, Canadian Library Association,
1960); directed and edited *Winter crossing at
l'Ile-aux-Coudres* (Crawley Films for CBC, 1958;
award, TV films category, Canadian Film Awards,
Toronto, 1959); photographed and directed
Manitoba trails (Crawley Films sponsored by
Manitoba Trail and Publicity Branch, 1959);
directed and edited *St. Lawrence north*
(Crawley Films for CBC [12 episodes], 1960),
Au pays de Neuve-France (Crawley Films,
1958-60), *Land of Jacques Cartier* (Crawley
Films), *Attiuk* (Crawley Films), *Kakekiku*
(Crawley Films), *Jean Richard* (Crawley
Films), *Turlutte* (Crawley Films), *Soirée at St.
Hilarion* (Crawley Films), *Whalehead* (Crawley
Films), *Winter sealing at La Tabatière* (Crawley
Films), *Three seasons* (Crawley Films), *Canadian
diamonds* (Crawley Films), *On the sea* (Crawley
Films), *Anse aux Basques* (Crawley Films),
Abitibi (Crawley Films, 1961-62; award,
Canadian Film Awards, Toronto), *False faces*
(Crawley Films, 1962), *Les Annanacks* (Crawley
Films for "Camera Canada," CBC, 17 June 1963;
award, Canadian Film Awards, Toronto);
originated, directed, and edited *Amanita pestilens*
(Crawley Films, 1964); directed and edited *A
matter of attitudes* (Crawley Films, 1966);
directed "Telescope" (fourteen episodes of
series, CBC, 1966), *You have been very kind*
("Wojeck," CBC, 1967); directed and edited
Molecules for burning and a million other
things (Crawley Films sponsored by Imperial Oil
Co., 1968).
WORK IN PROGRESS: A portrait of Newfoundland, Matthew ("Telescope," CBC); a story of a
copper development in British Columbia
(Crawley Films).

BORNSTEIN, Eli* 1922–
Artist, sculptor; b. 28 Dec. 1922 in Milwaukee,
Wis.; came to Canada in 1950 and settled in
Saskatoon.

EDUCATION
Attended Art Institute of Chicago, Ill., and the
University of Chicago briefly in 1943; University
of Wisconsin, BS, 1945, MS in art, 1954; studied
with Fernand Léger, Académie Montmartre,
Paris, France, summer, 1951; attended Académie
Julian, Paris, summer, 1952.

OFFICE
Department of Art, University of Saskatchewan,
Saskatoon, Sask.

CAREER
Milwaukee Art Institute, Wis., teacher 1943-47;
University of Wisconsin, teacher 1949; University of Saskatchewan, teacher 1950-63, professor
and head of department 1963–; painted in France
1951 and 1952; travelled and painted in Europe
1957 while on sabbatical leave; *The structure*,
co-editor and co-publisher with Baljeu 1958 (one
issue); *The structurist* (annual), founder, 1960–.

COMMISSIONS
Metal sculpture, Saskatchewan Teachers Feder-
ation Building, Saskatoon, 1956; structurist relief,
Arts and Science Building, University of
Saskatchewan, 1958; structurist relief, Internatio-
nal Air Terminal, Winnipeg, Man., 1963.

MEMBER
Wisconsin Painters and Sculptors (1945).

AWARDS, HONOURS
Second award and Pepsi Cola purchase prize for
marble head, 4th annual Six State Regional
Sculpture Show, Walker Art Center, Minneapolis,
Minn., 1947; third award, 5th Annual Six State
Regional Sculpture Show, Walker Art Center,
Minneapolis; Allied Arts Medal, Royal Architec-
tural Institute of Canada, 1968.

EXHIBITIONS
ONE-MAN: Mendel Art Gallery, Saskatoon,
1965; K. Kazimer Gallery, Chicago, 1965 and
1967.
GROUP: Represented in group exhibitions
held in Canada since 1943; Annual International
Exhibition of Water-colors, Prints, and Drawings,
Pennsylvania Academy of the Fine Arts, Philadelphia; Annual Exhibition of Artists of Chicago
and Vicinity, Art Institute of Chicago; Fourth
Biennial of Painting and Prints from the Midwest,
Walker Art Center, Minneapolis; Wisconsin Salon
of Art, Wisconsin Union, University of Wisconsin;

University of Wisconsin Exhibition of Semigraphs, travelling on Canada's Western Art Circuit.
COLLECTIONS IN WHICH REPRESENTED
Walker Art Center, Minneapolis; National Gallery of Canada, Ottawa, Ont.
WRITINGS
CONTRIBUTED: To *Art international, Statements - 18 Canadian artists, 1967*, Norman Mackenzie Art Gallery, 1967; *Chicago midwest review, Arbos; Data:directions in art, theory, and aesthetics,* edited by Anthony Hill, Faber & Faber, 1968.

BOSCO, Monique* 1927–
Novelist; b. 8 June 1927 in Vienna, Austria; daughter of Robert and Stella (Mènassé) Bosco.
EDUCATION
Attended school in France; came to Canada in 1948; University of Montreal, MA, PhD, 1953.
HOME
4105 Côte des Neiges, Montréal, PQ.
OFFICE
Department of French, University of Montreal, Montreal, PQ.
CAREER
CBC, Montreal, 1952-59; travelled extensively in Europe; contributed to National Film Board of Canada, CBC; University of Montreal, assistant professor of French.
WRITINGS
Un Amour maladroit, Gallimard, 1961; *Les Infusoires*, Éditions HMH, 1965.
CONTRIBUTED: Articles and stories to *Châtelaine, Le Devoir* (Montreal), *Les Écrits du Canada français, Maclean's.*

BOUCHARD, Victor 1926–
Pianist and composer; b. 11 Apr. 1926 in Ste. Claire, PQ; m. Renée Morisset.
EDUCATION
Studied theory with Alphonse Tardif, Quebec Conservatory of Music; Laval University, BA; Académie de Musique de Québec, laureate in piano, 1950; studied with Alfred Cortot and Antoine Reboulet in Paris, France, 1950-?
CAREER
International Congress of Folk Music, Venice, Italy, Canadian delegate 1949; Archives de Folklore de Québec, member of editorial committee; Laval University, assistant professor; duo-pianist with Renée Morisset 1957–; toured England, France, Portugal, Holland, Belgium, Switzerland, and Italy.
MEMBER
International Council for Folk Music.
AWARDS, HONOURS
Rotary prize for piano, 1949; Quebec Provincial Conservatory first prize for piano, 1950.
CONCERT STAGE
Guest pianist with principal Canadian orchestras;

pianist, Montreal Festival, 1956; Port Royal Theatre, Montreal, Oct. 1967; Toronto Festival concert, City Hall, July 1968.
RADIO
Appearances on CBC in series e.g. "Young Canadian artists" (11 Nov. 1965), "Canadian chamber music" (11 July 1967), "Tuesday night" (Oct. 1967); recitals (25 Dec. 1965, 13 June 1967); concerts e.g. *Canada Day concert* (1 July 1967).
RECORDINGS
Sonata pour deux pianos by Pierre Hétu, RCA Victor CC 1021; *Duetto für 2 Claviere* by Müthel, RCA Victor CC 1021; recordings of two-piano music for National Record Club, Paris.
COMPOSITIONS
Danse Canadienne, violin and piano, 1945, also for two pianos, recorded by RCA Victor CC 1021; *Toccata*, two pianos, recorded by RCA Victor CC 1021.

BOUCHER, André-Pierre 1936–
Poet; b. 12 Apr. 1936 in Montreal, PQ.
CAREER
Mainly literary; travelled throughout USA and Canada; assisted in productions and directed at the Théâtre de la Poudrière, Montréal, PQ.
WRITINGS
Fuites intérieures, Orphée, 1956; *Matin sur l'Amérique*, Orphée, 1958; *L'Astrologie et vous* (non-fiction), Jour, 1965; *Ces mains qui vous racontent* (non-fiction), Jour, 1965; *Chant poétique pour un pays idéal*, Jour, 1966; *Votre destin par les cartes* (non-fiction), Jour, 1966.
CONTRIBUTED: Short stories and articles to *Châtelaine, Écrits du Canada français.*

BOURINOT, Arthur Stanley* 1893–
Poet and artist; b. 3 Oct. 1893 in Ottawa; son of Sir John and Isabelle (Cameron) Bourinot; m. Nora Sherwood 1920; children: Suzette b. 1922, Esmé b. 1926.
EDUCATION
University of Toronto, BA, 1915; Osgoode Hall Law School, Toronto, Ont., 1920.
RELIGION
Anglican.
HOME
290 Acacia Ave., Rockcliffe, Ottawa 2, Ont.
CAREER
Canadian Army, 1915-18; practised law 1920–; Metropolitan Life Insurance Co., assistant general counsel; Village of Rockcliffe Park, councillor 1928-33; *Canadian poetry magazine*, editor 1948-54, 1965-68; *Canadian author and bookman*, editor 1953-54; *Canadian bar review,* assistant editor; Council of Education and Canadian Institute of International Affairs, Ottawa branches, secretary; Governor General's literary awards, occasional judge.

MEMBER
Canadian Authors Association (honorary
counsel, 1942-43; honorary life member,
1965); Canadian Club, Ottawa; Royal Society of
Literature (elected fellow, 1950); Canadian
Writers' Foundation (president, 1964-65);
Nova Scotia Poetry Society (honorary life
member, 1967); PEN Club.

AWARDS, HONOURS
Governor General's prize in national poetry
competition for poem *Canada's fallen*, 1919;
Winnipeg Free Press Diamond Jubilee competi-
tion 2nd prize for poem *The Canadian federation*,
1927; Governor General's literary award in
poetry for *Under the sun*, 1939; DCL from
King's College, Halifax, NS, 1955; Canada
Council award for research and writing, 1960;
Centennial medal, 1967.

EXHIBITIONS
ONE-MAN: Last one in 1963.
GROUP: Represented in group exhibitions held
in Canada, and in many private collections.

WRITINGS
Laurentian lyrics, Copp Clark, 1915; *Poems*,
Best, 1921; *Lyrics from the hills*, Hope, 1923;
Ottawa lyrics and verses for children, Graphic,
1924; *Pattering feet* (juvenile poetry), Graphic,
1925; *Sonnets in memory of my mother*, Hope,
1931; *Selected poems*, Macmillan, 1935; *Rhymes
of the French regime*, Nelson, 1937; *Eleven
poems*, the author, 1937; *Under the sun*,
Macmillan, 1939; *Discovery*, Ryerson, 1940;
What far kingdom, Ryerson, 1941, *Canada at
Dieppe*, Ryerson, 1942; *Five poems*, Ryerson,
1944; *True harvest*, Ryerson, 1945; *Lines from
Deepwood*, Heaton Print., 1946; *Collected
poems*, Ryerson, 1947; *Riding to Brittany*,
Dalhousie Review, 1948; *More lines from
Deepwood*, Shepard Print., 1949; *The treasures
of the snow*, Ryerson, 1950; *This green earth*,
the author, 1953; *Tom Thomson and other
poems*, Ryerson, 1954; *Five Canadian poets*
(essays), the author, 1954; *Everything on
earth must die*, the author, 1955; *Ten narrative
poems*, the author, 1955; *The quick and the
dead* (essays), the author, 1955; *Edward William
Thomson, a bibliography with notes*, the author,
1955; *A gathering of poems*, the author, 1959;
*Paul Bunyan, three Lincoln poems and other
verse*, the author, 1961; *Harvest from Deepwood*,
the author, 1962; *To and fro in the earth*, the
author, 1963; *Some personal recollections of
Kingsmere*, the author, 1963; *John Donne was
right*, the author, 1964; *He who has looked on
beauty*, the author, 1965; *Watcher of men*,
the author, 1966.
EDITED: Sir John Bourinot's *How Canada is
governed*, 12th ed., Copp Clark, 1928; Archibald
Lampman's *Letters to Edward William Thompson*

(1890-1898), the editor, 1956; Edward William
Thomson's *Letters to Archibald Lampman*, the
editor, 1957; *At the Mermaid Inn*, selections from
the *Globe*, Toronto, 1892-93, the editor, 1958;
*Some letters of Duncan Campbell Scott, Archi-
bald Lampman and others*, the editor, 1959;
More letters of Duncan Campbell Scott, the
editor, 1960; *Two letters of Sir John A.
Macdonald to Sir John Bourinot*, the editor, 1961.
TRANSLATED: (with Marius Barbeau and Arthur
Lismer) *Come a-singing*, National Museum, 1947.
CONTRIBUTED: Poems to *Twentieth century
Canadian poetry*, edited by E. Birney, Ryerson,
1953; *Oxford book of Canadian verse*, edited by
A.J.M. Smith, Oxford, 1960; *A century of
Canadian literature*, edited by H.G. Green, Ryer-
son, 1967; *Atlantic advocate, Canadian poetry,
Dalhousie review, Fiddlehead, Queen's quarterly*,
and numerous other anthologies and Canadian
periodicals; many legal annotations.
WORKS IN PROGRESS: "Letters of Sir John
Bourinot to his wife" with biographical material,
to be published c.1968.

BOYLE, Harry Joseph* 1915—
Author, director, and producer; b. 7 Oct. 1915 in
Huron County, Ont.; son of William A. and
Madeline (Leddy) Boyle; m. Marian Lucille;
children: Patricia Ann b. 6 Oct. 1939, Michael b.
13 Mar. 1946.
EDUCATION
Attended Wingham High School and St. Jerome's
College, Kitchener, Ont.
RELIGION
Roman Catholic.
HOME
174 Melrose Ave., Toronto 12, Ont.
OFFICE
354 Jarvis St., Toronto, Ont.
CAREER
CKNX, Wingham, Ont., 1936-41; *Beacon-Herald*,
Stratford, Ont., 1941-42; CBC, Toronto, commen-
tator, director, executive producer 1942-68;
Telegram, Toronto, columnist 1958-67; Banff
School of Fine Arts, Alta., sessional lecturer
1966—; *Star*, Montreal, PQ, editorial contributor
1967—; Board of Broadcast Governors (now
Canadian Radio and Television Commission) pro-
gram committee 1967-68, vice-chairman 1968—.
AWARDS, HONOURS
Leacock medal for humour for *Homebrew and
patches*, 1963.
RADIO
Directed and produced numerous CBC series,
e.g. "Wednesday night," "Project," "Venture,"
"Assignment."
TELEVISION
Produced several CBC programs, e.g. "Across
Canada."

WRITINGS
Peter's other mother, Manitoba Dept. of
Agriculture, 1948; *The Macdonalds of Oak
Valley* (radio play; produced on "Stage," CBC,
in 1948 and performed under title *The inheritance* by Museum Theatre, Toronto, 1950);
Mostly in clover (autobiography), Clarke, Irwin,
1961; *Homebrew and patches* (autobiography),
Clarke, Irwin, 1963 (adapted for radio by George
Salverson, and produced on "Stage," CBC, 23 Oct.
1966); *A summer burning* (novel), Doubleday
1964; *With a pinch of sin* (novel), Doubleday,
1966; numerous other plays for radio and stage.
CONTRIBUTED: Articles to *Canadian author
and bookman*, *Saturday night*, and other
magazines.
WORK IN PROGRESS: "Dreams stronger than
night" to be published *c*.1969.

BRADEN, Bernard 1916–
Actor, director, and author; b. 16 May 1916
in Vancouver, BC; son of Edwin Donald and
Mary Evelyn (Chasten) Braden; m. Barbara
Kelly 13 Apr. 1942; children: Christopher,
Kelly, Karma.
    EDUCATION
Attended Magee High School, Kerrisdale,
Vancouver.
    OFFICE
British Broadcasting Corporation, Broadcasting
House, Portland Place, London, W.1, England.
    CAREER
CJOR, Vancouver, singer and announcer 1935;
CBC, Vancouver and Toronto, Ont., actor 1936-
49; BBC, London, actor 1949–.
    AWARDS, HONOURS
2 La Fleche awards for distinguished dramatic
radio performances; British TV award for
factual personality of the year, 1963.
    THEATRE
Played Harold Mitchell in *A streetcar named
Desire* (Aldwych, London, 12 Oct. 1949), Bert
Hutchins in *The biggest thief in town* (Fortune,
London, Dec. 1951), Howard Wilton in *The man*
(Her Majesty's, London, 30 Dec. 1952; St.
Martin's, London, 16 Feb. 1953), Mr. Roberts in
Now news from father (Lyceum, Edinburgh,
Scotland, Aug. 1954; Cambridge, London, Sept.
1954), Bud Walters in *Anniversary waltz* (Opera
House, Manchester, England, Sept. 1955; Lyric,
London, Nov. 1955), Alva Newton in *The
gimmick* (Grand, Leeds, England, Mar. 1959),
The Spoon River anthology (London); directed
Angels in love (Savoy, London, 11 Feb. 1954),
The ghost writers (Arts, Cambridge, England,
Jan. 1955; Arts, London, Feb. 1955), *The
money-makers* (London).
    FILM
Played in *Love in pawn* (England, 195?), *Hold*

my husband (England, 1951), *Jet stream*
(Pendennis Productions, 1959).
    RADIO
Played in numerous programs, e.g. Sam Honey in
The Carsons ("BC Farm Broadcast," CBC), Old
man in *Stag party* (series, CBC, 1941-42),
"Buckingham Theatre" (series, CBC, 1943–),
"Stage" (series, CBC, 1943-49), Gabby in *Wayne
and Shuster Show* (series, CBC), *Bernie Braden
tells a story* (series, CBC, 1949), *Breakfast with
Braden, Bedtime with Braden, Barbara with
Braden* (series, BBC, 1949–).
    TELEVISION
Early to Braden, On the Braden beat (series, BBC).
    WRITINGS
These English (radio scripts), McClelland &
Stewart, 1948; numerous radio scripts, e.g. *John
and Judy* (serial, CBC, 1945–), "Stage" (series,
CBC, 1944-48).

BRAITHWAITE, John Victor Maxwell
see BRAITHWAITE, Max

BRAITHWAITE, Max* 1911–
(John Victor Maxwell Braithwaite; Victor
Maxwell, pseud.)
Author; b. 7 Dec. 1911 in Nokomis, Sask.; son of
George Albert Warner and Mary (Copeland)
Braithwaite; m. Ida Marguerite Aileen Treleaven
12 Oct. 1934; children: Beryl Marie b. 1936,
Sharon Maxine b. 1942, Christopher Maxwell b.
1944, Sylvia Aileen b. 1950, Colin Scott b. 1953.
    EDUCATION
Attended public schools in Prince Albert and
Saskatoon, Sask.; Nutana Collegiate Institute,
Saskatoon, 1926-30; Saskatoon Normal School;
University of Saskatchewan.
    RELIGION
Protestant.
    HOME
51 Sunset Drive, Orangeville, Ont.
    CAREER
Taught school in Saskatchewan, 1932-40;
RCNVR, 1941-45, became instructor lieutenant;
freelance writer, 1945–.
    MEMBER
ACTRA.
    AWARDS, HONOURS
Twelve Ohio State University awards; Cairo
Television Festival award for one script, 1966.
    WRITINGS
(with R.S. Lambert) *We live in Ontario* (textbook),
Book Society of Canada, 1957; (with R.S.
Lambert) *There's no place like home* (textbook),
Book Society of Canada, 1959; *Land, water and
people* (textbook), Van Nostrand, 1961; *Voices
of the wild* (juvenile non-fiction), McClelland &
Stewart, 1962; *The cure searchers*, Ryerson,
1962; *The mystery of the muffled man* (juvenile

fiction), Little, Brown, 1962; *The valley of the vanishing birds* (juvenile fiction), Little, Brown, 1963; *The young reporter* (juvenile fiction), Ryerson, 1963; *Why shoot the teacher?* (autobiography), McClelland & Stewart, 1965; *Canada, wonderland of surprises* (juvenile), Dodd, Mead, 1967; *Servant or master? A case book of mass media,* Book Society of Canada, 1968; numerous radio and TV plays as well as scripts for school broadcasts and CBC children's programs.

CONTRIBUTED: Articles to *Canadian geographical journal, Maclean's, Saturday night*, and other Canadian magazines.

BRAITSTEIN, Marcel* 1935–

Sculptor; b. 11 July 1935 in Charleroi, Belgium; son of Arthur and Paula (Eckstein) Braitstein; came to Canada in 1951 and settled in Montreal, PQ; m. Deidra Ryshpan 15 Feb. 1957 (marriage dissolved 1959); m. Dianne Carol Farrar 2 Oct. 1965.

EDUCATION
Attended primary school in Charleroi, 1941-44 and in Brussels, Belgium, 1944-51; Strathcona Academy, Montreal, graduated 1953; École des Beaux-Arts, Montréal, school diploma and teaching certificate, 1953-59; studied under Lothar J. Kestenbaum, Institute Allende, San Miguel, Mexico, 1959-60.

HOME AND STUDIO
1061 Richelieu North, St. Hilaire sur Richelieu, PQ.

CAREER
Young Men's Hebrew Association, Montreal, art instructor 1955-58; Camp Oleanna, Mt. Laurier, PQ instructor summers 1959 and 1960; travelled and worked in Mexico 1960-61; travelled and worked in Europe 1961-62; Montreal Museum of Fine Arts, instructor 1963-65; "Young Contemporaries," London Public Library and Museum, Ont., jury member 1964; École des Beaux-Arts, Montréal, instructor 1965–; "Sculpture 1968," Jeunesses Musicales Camp, Mt. Orford, PQ, jury member 1968; mainly involved with the production of sculpture, drawings, and prints.

COMMISSIONS
Designed diving board, school in Mont-de-la-Salle, Laval Des Rapides, PQ, 1964; collaborated in architectural conception with architect Louis LaPierre of "Montreal Fireman's Bank," 1965; monument to Rt. Hon. Arthur Meighen, commissioned by Canadian Government, National Gallery of Canada, Ottawa, Ont., 1966-67.

MEMBER
Quebec Sculptors Association (elected, 1962; vice-president and president, 1963-64); Canadian Sculptors Society (elected, 1963).

AWARDS, HONOURS
Prize for sculpture, Quebec Provincial Competition, 1959; prize for sculpture, Salon de la Jeune Sculpture et Peinture, Montréal, 1961; prize for sculpture, Montreal Museum of Fine Arts Spring Exhibition, 1961; Popular Artist prize, Winnipeg Show, Man., 1961; Canada Council grant, 1961/62 and 1962/63.

EXHIBITIONS
ONE-MAN: Gallery Ptah, Brussels, 1960; Galerie Agnès Lefort, Montréal, 1961, 1963, and 1965; Gallery Glantz, Mexico, 1961; Gallery XII (two-man), Montreal, 1963.
GROUP: Represented in group exhibitions held in Canada since 1956 including annual exhibitions of Montreal Museum of Fine Arts Spring Exhibition, Contemporary Canadian Painting, Sculpture, Graphics, Art Gallery of Toronto, Ont., Winnipeg Show, Man., Quebec Sculptors Association, and Royal Canadian Academy; *Exposicion Internacional*, San Angel, Mexico, 1961; Adams Morgan Gallery, Washington, DC, 1963; Sculpture Center, New York, NY, 1966, 1967, and 1968.

COLLECTIONS IN WHICH REPRESENTED
Montreal Museum of Fine Arts; Art Gallery of Ontario, Toronto; Winnipeg Art Gallery; National Gallery of Canada, Ottawa; Confederation Centre, Charlottetown, PEI; Galerie Dresdnère, Montreal; Sculpture Center, New York.

WRITINGS
Marcel Braitstein: 12 Sculptures, Graph, 1966.

BRANDTNER, Fritz* 1896–

Artist; b. 28 July 1896 in Free City of Danzig, Prussia; son of Richard and Martha (Regel) Brandtner; came to Canada in 1928 and settled in Winnipeg, Man.; m. Mieze Preuss 30 Nov. 1929.

EDUCATION
Attended High School of Technology in Danzig; studied under Fritz August Pfuhle in Danzig, 1925-27.

RELIGION
Protestant.

HOME
Apt. 12, 4840 Plamondon Ave., Montreal 26, PQ.

CAREER
German Army, 1914-20; prisoner of war in France 1916-20; commercial artist in Danzig 1920-25; High School of Technology, Danzig, assistant to professor of art and instructor in the life classes in the Architectural Department 1925-27; commercial artist in Winnipeg 1928-34; designed and executed the decoration of the Ice Carnival for Winnipeg Winter Club 1933; art teacher in community centres, YMCA branches and adult education groups in Montreal 1937-50; held children's art classes in Inverley Settlement, Negro Community Centre, Griffintown Club, and Neighbourhood House in Montreal 1937-50;

Miss Edgar's and Miss Cramp's School, Montreal, art master 1944-66; School of Social Work, McGill University, lecturer 1947-56; Observatory Art Centre, University of New Brunswick Summer School, director 1949-53.

COMMISSIONS

Mural, Province of Saskatchewan exhibit, World's Grain Exhibition, Regina, Sask., 1933; decorations in stone, Bishop's College, Lennoxville, PQ, 1936; decorations, Bell Telephone Co., Ottawa, Ont., 1937; decorations, Berkeley Hotel, Montreal, 1938-39; decorations, Hotel Vancouver, BC, 1939; stone reliefs, Central Station, Montreal, 1943; mural, Roxbury Boy's Club, Boston, Mass., 1945; decorations, Trans Canada Airlines Office, Montreal, 1947; mural, St. John's Hotel, Nfld., 1952; carved linoleum panels, Queen Elizabeth Hotel, Montreal, 1957; decorations, Jasper Park Lodge, Alta., 1959; decorations, John Inglis Co., London, England, 1960; mural, Place Ville Marie, Montréal, 1962-63.

MEMBER

Canadian Group of Painters (elected, 1942; vice-president, 1944-48, 1953); Canadian Society of Graphic Art (elected, 1937; vice-president, 1938-40; resigned, 1952); Canadian Society of Painters in Water Colour (elected, 1935; vice-president, 1941-43; resigned, 1955); International Institute of Art and Letters (elected life fellow, 1960).

AWARDS, HONOURS

Jessie Dow prize for water colour, Montreal Museum of Fine Arts, 1946; elected for first place, Canadian Olympic Contest, 1948; first honourable mention, Painting and Graphic Art Section of the XIV Olympiad, London, 1948; second prize, competition for the design for the five-cent piece issued in commemoration of the 200th anniversary of the isolation of nickel.

EXHIBITIONS

ONE-MAN: Winnipeg School of Art, 1928 and 1936; Winnipeg Art Gallery, 1934; Morgan's Galleries, Montreal, 1936; Picture Loan Society, Toronto, 1938; Gallery Robert Oliver, Montreal, 1946; McGill University School of Social Work, 1953.

GROUP: Represented in group exhibitions held in Canada including annual exhibitions of Canadian Group of Painters, Canadian Society of Graphic Art, Canadian Society of Painters in Water Colour, and Spring Exhibitions of Montreal Museum of Fine Arts; represented in group exhibitions organized by National Gallery of Canada, Ottawa, including its first and third Biennial Exhibition of Canadian Painting, 1955 and 1959; Exhibition of Contemporary Canadian Painting Arranged ... for Circulation in the Southern Dominions of the British Empire,

1936; World's Fair, New York, NY, 1939; Exhibition of Water Colours by Canadian Artists, Gloucester, England, 1939; Aspects of Contemporary Painting in Canada, Addison Gallery, Andover, Mass., 1942-43; Canadian Art 1760-1943, Yale University Art Gallery, 1944; Canadian Group of Painters exhibition, Moscow, USSR, 1945; Canadian Water Colors, Arnot Art Gallery, Elmira, NY, 1946; Exhibition of Canadian Graphic Arts, São Paulo and Rio de Janeiro, Brazil, 1946; Philadelphia Water Colour Club, 1946, Pa.; Six Canadian Painters, Norton Gallery, Palm Beach, Fla., 1948; Forty Years of Canadian Painting, Museum of Fine Arts, Boston, Mass., 1949; Canadian Painting, National Gallery of Art, Washington, DC, 1950; An Exhibition of Canadian Paintings held at Fortnum and Mason Limited, London, England, 1955.

COLLECTIONS IN WHICH REPRESENTED

Art Gallery of Ontario, Toronto; Hart House Permanent Collection, University of Toronto; National Gallery of Canada, Ottawa; Vancouver Art Gallery.

BRAYLEY, Sally* 1937–

(Sally Brayley Tobias; Sally Brayley Bliss) Dancer; b. 18 Sept. 1937 in London, England; daughter of Jack and Zeversa Lorraine (Gibbon) Brayley; m. Norman Tobias 1959 (marriage dissolved 1965); m. Anthony A. Bliss 1967.

EDUCATION

Studied ballet with Mary Beetles, Montreal, PQ; Gwen Osborne (q.v.) and Nesta Toumine, Ottawa, Ont.; Irene Apinée (q.v.), Jury Gotshalks, and Hilda Strombergs, Halifax, NS, 1949-54; National Ballet School of Canada, Toronto, 1952-62; Antony Tudor and Margaret Craske at Metropolitan Opera Ballet School and Robert Joffrey, Perry Brunsen, and Hector Zaraspe at American Ballet Center, New York.

RELIGION

Church of England.

HOME

c/o "Coach House," Prince's Lodge, Halifax County, NS; One W. 72nd St., New York, NY, USA.

CAREER

Halifax Theatre Ballet, leading 1950-52; Canadian Ballet Festival in Montreal 1950, Toronto 1951 and 1953, Ottawa 1952; NS Festival of the Arts, Tatamagouche, guest artist 1954, 1964; Canadian National Exhibition, Toronto, soloist 1953; Les Ballets Concertantes, 1955; National Ballet of Canada, Toronto, corps de ballet 1956-61, soloist 1961-62; Metropolitan Opera Ballet, New York, soloist 1962-67; Jacob's Pillow Dance Festival, Lee, Mass., 1967; American Ballet Theater, New York, guest artist 1967; City Center Joffrey

Ballet, New York, guest artist 1968.
MEMBER
AEA.
THEATRE
Danced in *Bonanza* (1950), *Countess Maritza*
(1950), *Song of Norway* (1951), *Brigadoon*
(1952), *The merry widow* (1955), *Faust*
(1962-67), *La périchole* (1962-67), *La giaconda*
(1962-67), Prelude in *Les sylphides* (Fokine,
1962-67), Girl in *One in five* (Powell, 1962-67);
created role in *Concerning oracles* (Tudor, 1966),
Echoing of trumpets (Tudor, American premiere,
1966), female role in *Profile of silence* (Clouser,
Jacob's Pillow, 1967); danced Taglioni in *Pas
des déesses* (Joffrey, 1968), Venus in *Cakewalk*
(Boris, 1968), Wife in *Elegy* (Arpino, 1968),
Pas de deux in *Viva Vivaldi* (Arpino, 1968),
Sylph in *Scotch symphony* (Balanchine, 1968),
one of the Three graces in *Jinx* (Christensen,
1968).
TELEVISION
Danced in several CBC productions, e.g. *Anne of
Green Gables, Casse-noisette, The lady and the
logger* ("Folio," 12 Feb. 1956), *Le lac des cygnes*
(Petipa-Ivanov, "Folio," 19 Dec. 1956),
Coppelia (St. Leon, "Folio," 2 Jan. 1958),
Bathilde in *Giselle* ("Festival," 17 Dec. 1962).

BRESS, Hyman 1931–
Violinist; b. 30 June 1931 in Cape Town, South
Africa; son of Mendel and Dora (Nachman) Bress;
came to Canada in 1951 and settled in Montreal,
PQ; m. Patricia Bagrit 7 July 1960; children:
Reda.
EDUCATION
Studied music in Cape Town with his father,
1934-37, and other teachers, 1937-46; Curtis
School of Music, Philadelphia, Pa., 1946-51.
CAREER
First public appearance in South Africa 1938;
formed quartet in Montreal 1951; Montreal
Symphony Orchestra, concert master c.1956-
60; Montreal String Quartet, leader c.1958-60;
tours of North America and Europe as violinist
1958–; gave audio-visual recitals with score
visible on a screen; gave recitals accompanied
by an upright piano fitted with a lutheal.
AWARDS, HONOURS
Seven gold medals before 1946; Concert
Artists Guild award, 1956; Jascha Heifetz
award, 1957; Canada Council travel grant, 1958.
CONCERT STAGE
Gave many recitals and played as soloist in
concerts in South Africa, 1938-46, in North
America and Europe 1946–; recitalist,
Philharmonia Hall, New York, NY (30 Nov.
1965, 26 Oct. 1967), Expo 67, Montreal (14 and
15 Oct. 1967), Charlottetown Confederation
Theatre Centre, PEI (1968).

RADIO
Many broadcasts on CBC, including programs of
taped recitals and recorded music; violinist with
Montreal String Quartet ("Wednesday night");
violinist featured in "Artists of today" (25 June
1966), other series, e.g. "Tuesday night";
violinist in world premiere of *Violin concerto*,
Opus 41 by Udo Kasemets (*q.v.*; 13 Apr. 1967).
RECORDINGS
Over 30 records with orchestras, e.g. Royal
Philharmonic Orchestra, London, England,
Vienna Symphony Orchestra, Austria, English
Chamber Orchestra, Montreal String Quartet,
Symphonia Orchestra; sonatas by Brahms and
Istvan Anhalt, with suite by Kelsey Jones, RCA
Victor CC 1014; *Sonata no. 1* by Bela Bartok, RCA
Victor RB 6650.
COMPOSITIONS
Violin pieces; *Fantasy*, violin, piano, and electronic
sound, 1961, recorded in *The violin* v.5, Folkways
FM 3355.

BRITANNICUS, pseud,
see KIRBY, William

BRITTAIN, Donald Code* 1928–
Film writer, director, and producer; b. 10 June
1928 in Ottawa, Ont.; son of Abram Code and
Elise Adrienne (Duclos) Brittain; m. Barbara
Ellen Tuer 8 Apr. 1950 (deceased); m. Brigitte
Irmgard Halbig 6 July 1963; children: (second
marriage) Christopher b. 27 Jan. 1965, Jennifer
b. 14 July 1967.
EDUCATION
Attended primary schools and Glebe Collegiate
in Ottawa; Queen's University, 1947-51.
HOME
5048 Notre Dame de Grâce, Montréal, PQ.
OFFICE
c/o National Film Board of Canada, Box 6100,
Montreal 3, PQ.
CAREER
Journal, Ottawa, reporter and feature writer
1947-54; *Queen's journal*, Kingston, Ont., editor-
in-chief 1950-51; part-time employee of CBC,
Harvard University, Francis Thompson Associates,
and Multiscreen Incorporated; National Film
Board of Canada, Montreal, writer, director, and
producer 1954–; Canadian Conference of the Arts,
executive member 1968.
MEMBER
American Newspaper Guild; Canadian Society of
Film Makers (president, 1964); Ottawa Press
Club (secretary, 1953); Syndicat Général du
Cinéma et de la Télévision (director, 1965).
AWARDS, HONOURS
Centennial medal, 1967.
FILMS
Wrote and directed *A day in the night of*

Jonathan Mole (National Film Board, 1959); wrote and co-produced "Canada at war" series (National Film Board for CBC, 1962); wrote, directed, and produced *Fields of sacrifice* (National Film Board for the Department of Veteran Affairs, 1963; certificate of merit, general information category, Canadian Film Awards, Toronto, Ont., 1964-65; Chris certificate award, information-education category, Twelfth Annual Columbus Film Festival, Ohio, 1964-65; second prize, Victoria International Film Festival, BC, 1964-65; Mulholland awards for writing and directing; chosen for exhibition at Montreal, Edinburgh, Scotland and Sydney, Australia International Film Festivals); co-directed, co-produced, and joint author of *Bethune* (National Film Board, 1964 for "Festival," CBC, 13 Jan. 1965; first prize, Fourth International Documentary and Short Film Festival, Leipzig, Germany, 1965-66; gold medal, International Red Cross and Health Film Festival, Sofia, Bulgaria, 1967-68; diploma of merit, Short Film Competition, Melbourne Film Festival, Australia, 1966-67; diploma, Nineteenth International Film Festival, Edinburgh, 1965-66); wrote, directed, and produced *The campaigners* ("This hour has seven days," CBC, 1964); *Buster Keaton rides again* (National Film Board, 1965; best general information film, Canadian Film Awards, Montreal, 1966-67; special prize - CIDALC, Seventeenth International Exhibition of the Documentary and Short Film, Venice, Italy, 1966-67; silver trophy, documentary category, Tenth San Francisco International Film Festival, Calif., 1966-67; first prize [ex-aequo], medium length films, Festival of Canadian Films, Montreal International Film Festival, 1966-67; nominated for British Academy Award; special prize for best biographical documentary, Melbourne International Film Festival, Australia, 1967-68; first prize, music, literature, and films category, American Film Festival, New York, NY, 1967-68); wrote and directed *Ladies and gentlemen: Mr. Leonard Cohen* (National Film Board, 1965; blue ribbon award, literature category, American Film Festival, New York, 1966-67; award, television information category, Canadian Film Awards, Montreal, 1966-67; award for exceptional merit, International Festival of Short Films, Philadelphia, Pa.); co-directed and joint author of *Memorandum* (National Film Board, 1966 for CBC, 16 Mar. 1966; lion of St. Marc [first prize], Seventeenth International Exhibition of the Documentary Film, Venice, Italy, 1966-67; Golden Gate award [first prize], essay category, Tenth San Francisco International Film Festival, 1966-67; certificate of merit, TV films category, Ninth Vancouver International Film Festival, 1966-67; special mention, medium length films, Festival of Canadian Films, Montreal International Film Festival, 1966-67; outstanding film, London Film Festival, England), *Never a backward step* (National Film Board, 1967; first prize, biography, American Film Awards, New York; Redwood award for special merit, San Francisco Film Festival, 1967-68; best documentary over thirty minutes, Canadian Film Awards, Toronto, 1968; notable film award, Calvin Workshop Awards, New York).

WRITINGS

Stravinsky (screenplay; National Film Board, 1965; special mention, short films category, Festival of Canadian Films, Montreal International Film Festival, 1965-66; nominated for Robert J. Flaherty award, British Film Academy Awards, London, 1965-66; award, television information category, Canadian Film Awards, Montreal, 1966-67); (joint author) *Helicopter Canada* (screenplay; National Film Board, 1966; nominated for best feature documentary, Academy of Motion Picture Arts and Sciences, Hollywood, Calif., 1967-68; Canuck award [first prize], Canadian Travel Film Awards, Toronto, 1967-68; best general information film [ex-aequo] and special prize, Canadian Film Awards, Toronto, 1967-68,; *What on earth* (screenplay; National Film Board, 1967; nominated for award, Academy of Motion Picture Arts and Sciences, Hollywood; silver seal of the City of Trieste, International Festival of Science-Fiction Films, Trieste, Italy, 1967-68); *Labyrinthe* (screenplay; National Film Board for Expo 67, Montreal, 1967; award for technical development and innovation, Canadian Film Awards, Toronto, 1968); *To be young* (screenplay; Canadian Pacific Railway-Cominco for Expo 67, Montreal, 1967).

BRITTAIN, Miller Gore 1912-68

Artist; b. 12 Nov. 1912 in West Saint John, NB; son of J. Firth and Margaret Bartlett (Lord) Brittain; m. Constance Starr 1951; children: Jennifer. b. 1952; d. Jan. 1968 in Saint John.

EDUCATION

Began to study art under Miss E.R. Holt in Saint John in 1922; graduated from Saint John High School 1930; studied under Harry Herman Wickey, Art Students' League in New York, NY, 1930-32.

RELIGION

Anglican.

CAREER

Various odd jobs including part-time art teaching and portrait commissions in Saint John, 1932-42; RCAF, 1942-46, became flight lieutenant, awarded DFC; appointed official war artist, 1945; painted in Saint John, 1946-68.

COMMISSIONS
Mural, Lady Beaverbrook Gymnasium, University of New Brunswick; murals (not completed), Saint John Tuberculosis Hospital; mural, Convent of the Good Shepherd, Saint John; mural, Veterans Hospital, Saint John, c.1949.

MEMBER
Canadian Society of Graphic Art (elected, 1937); Contemporary Art Society.

AWARDS, HONOURS
Jury prize, Canadian Society of Graphic Art, 1941; Rous & Mann Award, Canadian Society of Graphic Art 1947; Canada Council senior grant, 1967.

EXHIBITIONS
ONE-MAN: Dayton Art Institute, Ohio, 1949; New Brunswick Museum, Saint John, 1949 and 1966; George Binet Gallery, New York, 1950; Ferguson's Antique Shop, Saint Andrew's, NB, 1952; L'Atelier, Ottawa, Ont., 1953; Hartert Galleries, New York, 1953 and 1955; Macdonald College, 1954; Greenwich Gallery, Toronto, 1957; Burgos Gallery, New York, 1965; Dalhousie University, 1965; Cenci Palace, Rome, Italy, 1966; Palm Beach Gallery, Fla., 1966; La Margutta Gallery, Rome, 1968.
GROUP: Represented in group exhibitions held in Canada during his lifetime including annual exhibitions of Maritime Art Association and Canadian Society of Graphic Art; fifth Biennial Exhibition of Canadian Painting, National Gallery of Canada, Ottawa, 1963; World's Fair, New York, 1939; Clearwater Museum of Art, Fla., 1950; International Art Exhibition, Florida Southern College, 1950; Canadian Section, Sâo Paulo Biennial exhibition, Brazil, 1953.

COLLECTIONS IN WHICH REPRESENTED
Beaverbrook Art Gallery, Fredericton, NB; Confederation Art Gallery and Museum, Charlottetown, PEI; Hartert Galleries, New York; Owens Museum, Mount Allison University; National Gallery of Canada, War Art Collection, Ottawa; New Brunswick Museum, Saint John; Winnipeg Art Gallery, Man.

BROCHU, André 1942–
Poet; b. 3 Mar. 1942.
EDUCATION
University of Montreal, MA.
HOME
41, rue Labrie, St. Eustache, PQ.
CAREER
Cours du Gesù, Montréal, taught French-Canadian Literature; AGEUM publishing house, founder; Cahiers de l'AGEUM, co-editor.
WRITINGS
(with J.-André Contant and Yves Dubé) Étranges domaines, Cascade, 1957; Privilèges de l'ombre: poèmes, L'Hexagone, 1961; Délit contre délit, AGEUM, 1965.
CONTRIBUTED: Articles, stories, and poems to Action nationale, Liberté.

BROTT, Alexander 1915–
Conductor, violinist, and composer; b. 14 Mar. 1915 in Montreal; son of Samuel and Anna (Fuchsman) Brott; m. Lotte Goetzel (q.v.) 11 Mar. 1943; children: Boris b. 14 Mar. 1944, Denis b. 1951.
EDUCATION
Studied violin, piano, composition, and music history in Montreal; McGill Conservatorium of Music, licentiate 1932; Académie de Musique de Québec, laureate 1933; Juilliard School of Music, New York, NY, 1934-38, diploma in composition and orchestration, 1937, in violin, 1938.
HOME
5459 Earnscliffe Ave., Montreal 29, PQ.
OFFICE
3426 McTavish St., Montreal, PQ.
CAREER
Montreal Orchestra, violinist 1930- ?, guest conductor summer concerts; McGill Conservatorium, instructor in violin, orchestration, and conducting 1939, associate professor and chairman of department of orchestral instruments 1949-67, professor 1967–; McGill String Quartet (now McGill Chamber Orchestra), co-founder, conductor, and musical director 1939–; Montreal Symphony Orchestra, concertmaster and assistant conductor 1945–; Prague Music Festival, Czecho-slovakia, Canadian composer representative 1946; Les Petites Symphonies de Radio-Canada, assistant conductor 1948–; Montreal Festivals, guest conductor 1959; Stratford, Ont. Festival, guest conductor 1959; Kingston Symphony Orchestra, Ont., conductor 1965–.
MEMBER
CAPAC; Canadian League of Composers; Canadian Music Council; Lapitsky Foundation; Musicians Guild of Montreal.
AWARDS, HONOURS
Five scholarships from McGill Conservatorium before 1928; Juilliard School of Music, five-year scholarship, 1934-39; Royal College of Music, London, England, Lord Strathcona scholarship, 1939 (not taken up); Chicago Conservatory College Ill., honorary doctorate for contribution to Canadian music, 1950; Pan American Conductors Competition first prize, 1957; Canadian Friends of the Hebrew University travel grant, 1959; Canada Council travel grant, 1959; Montreal Symphony Orchestra annual prize for a new composition for Spheres in orbit, 1960; Sir Arnold Bax gold medal as composer of the Commonwealth, 1961; Royal Society of Arts, London, fellow; two Olympic medals for

composition; Elizabeth Sprague Coolidge award for chamber music compositions, two consecutive years; Loeb memorial award for chamber music performance, two consecutive years; three CAPAC awards.

CONCERT STAGE

Conducted orchestras on tours in many countries since 1948, including England, Holland, Switzerland, Sweden, Norway, France, Belgium, Israel (1959, 1962), Mexico, and USSR (1959, 1962, 1966); conducted London Philharmonic Orchestra (Royal Albert Hall, London, 1953); National Symphony Orchestra of Mexico (Mexico City, two concerts, 1957); opening concert of Montreal Festivals (1957); Kol Israel Orchestra (Jerusalem, 1959); Orchestra of America (Carnegie Hall, New York); McGill Chamber Orchestra on tour of Russia (1966); Montreal Orchestra (Man and His World, 1968).

RADIO

Conducted McGill Chamber Orchestra and other orchestras on numerous occasions on CBC series, e.g. "Wednesday night," "Centenary concerts" (1967), "Concerts from two worlds."

TELEVISION

Several appearances on CBC.

RECORDINGS

Numerous recordings as conductor of orchestral music, especially Canadian compositions.

COMPOSITIONS

Oracle, orchestra, 1938; *Innovation and dance,* violin and piano, 1939-41, recorded by CBC IS with George Lapenson and Edmund Assaly; *Lullaby and procession of the toys,* string orchestra, 1939-43, first performed in Montreal by CBC Orchestra under Jean Beaudet, *Lullaby* recorded by CBC IS; *Lament,* string orchestra, 1939, first performed in Montreal by McGill Chamber Orchestra under the composer; *Ritual,* string quartet and string orchestra, 1939-42, first performed in Montreal by McGill Chamber Orchestra under the composer; *String quartet,* 1940; *Quintet,* recorders and string quartet, 1940; *Piano suite,* 1941; *War and peace,* orchestra, 1944, first performed by Montreal Symphony Orchestra under Désiré Defauw; *Laurentian idyll,* symphonic band or string orchestra, 1945; *Songs of contemplation,* soprano and string orchestra, 1945, first performed 1945 in Montreal by McGill Chamber Orchestra with Lois Marshall, recorded by CBC IS no. 116; *From sea to sea,* orchestra, 1946, first performed in 1947 in Montreal by CBC Orchestra under the composer, commissioned by CBC; *Concordia,* orchestra, 1947, first performed at Prague International Festival, Czecho-slovakia, recorded by CBC IS with CBC Orchestra under Jean Beaudet; *Concerto,* violin and orchestra,

1950, first performed 1950 in Montreal by Little Symphony Orchestra under Georges Schick with Noël Brunet, recorded by CBC IS no. 71 with Toronto Symphony Orchestra and John Dembeck under Geoffrey Waddington, commissioned by the Little Symphony Orchestra; *Critic's corner*, string orchestra or string quartet and percussion, 1950, first performed 1950 in Montreal with McGill String Quartet and Michel Perrault; *Delightful delusions*, overture, 1950, first performed 1950 by Montreal Symphony Orchestra under Désiré Defauw, commissioned by Désiré Defauw; *Prelude to oblivion,* orchestra, 1951, first performed in Toronto by CBC Orchestra under John Adaskin, recorded on air-check tape with the same performers, commissioned by John Adaskin for CBC; *Vignettes,* piano, 1952; *Royal tribute*, orchestra, 1953, first performed 1953 in Toronto by Toronto Symphony Orchestra under the composer, commissioned by CBC for the coronation of Queen Elizabeth II; *Fancy and folly,* orchestra, 1953; *Sept for seven*, strings, winds, and narrator, 1954, first performed in Montreal 1954 by a McGill University ensemble under the composer, recorded by CBC IS no. 131, commemorating the fiftieth anniversary of McGill Conservatorium of Music; *Canadiana*, mixed choir a cappella, 1955; *Analogy in anagram*, 1955, first performed 1956 in Toronto by CBC Symphony Orchestra under the composer; *Israel*, choir and strings, 1956; *Arabesque*, cello and piano or orchestra, 1956, first performed 1956 in Montreal on CBC with Lotte Brott, cello and Charles Reiner, piano, recorded by CBC IS no. 187 with Zara Nelsova and McGill Chamber Orchestra under the composer; *Rhapsody*, cello and piano, 1958; *Three astral visions*, string orchestra, 1960, Canadian Music Centre, first performed 1960 in Montreal with McGill Chamber Orchestra under the composer, recorded by CBC on air-check tape with the same performers, commissioned by Lapitsky Foundation for the McGill Chamber Orchestra; *Vision of dry bones*, baritone, strings, and piano, 1960, first performed in Montreal by McGill Chamber Orchestra with Cantor S. Gisser, baritone; *The prophet*, cantata, tenor, soprano, and piano, 1960; *Spheres in orbit*, orchestra, 1960, first performed 1961 by Montreal Symphony Orchestra under the composer, recorded by CBC on air-check tape with CBC Symphony Orchestra under the composer, also by Baroque BU 1831 with Greater Symphony Orchestra of Soviet Radio and Television under the composer, commissioned by Montreal Symphony Orchestra; *Three acts for four sinners,* saxophone quartet, 1961, first performed 1961 in Montreal in the McGill Faculty Series, recorded on air-check tape by Romano Saxophone

Quartet of Montreal; *Martlet's muse*, overture, 1962; *Three on a spree*, trio for various combinations of instruments, 1962; *Mutual salvation orgy*, brass quintet, 1962, first performed 1962 at Montreal Festival by Montreal Brass Quintet, commissioned by Montreal Brass Quintet through a Canada Council grant; *World sophisticate*, brass quintet, 1962, first performed 1962 on CBC radio with Montreal Brass Quintet; *Circle, triangle, four squares*, string orchestra, 1963, recorded by RCA Victor CC 1010 with McGill Chamber Orchestra under the composer, written for McGill Chamber Orchestra; *Profundum praedictum*, string orchestra with string soloist, 1964, first performed 1965 with Gary Karr, double-bass, recorded; *Centennial colloquy*, 15 wind instruments and percussion, 1967, first performed 13 Feb. 1967 on CBC radio with CBC Woodwind Orchestra under Boris Brott, commissioned by CBC for Canada's centennial; *Centennial celebration*, small orchestra, 1967, commissioned by McGill Chamber Orchestra for Canada's centennial; *Pristine prisms in polychrome*, violin, 1967, written for Ida Handel for Canada's centennial; *La Corriveau*, ballet suite, 1967, first performed 1967 at Expo 67 by Les Grands Ballets Canadiens, commissioned for Canada's centennial; *Paraphrase in polyphony*, orchestra, 1967, first performed 3 Nov. 1967.

BROTT, Charlotte
see BROTT, Lotte

BROTT, Lotte
(Charlotte Goetzel; Charlotte Brott)
Cellist; b. in Germany; daughter of Walter Goetzel; came to Canada in 1941 and settled in Montreal; m. Alexander Brott (*q.v.*) 11 Mar. 1943; children: Boris b. 14 Mar. 1944, Denis b. 1951.
EDUCATION
Commenced musical studies in Germany; Zurich Conservatory of Music, Switzerland, diploma; studied cello with Emanuel Feuermann in Switzerland.
HOME
5459 Earnscliffe Ave., Montreal 29, PQ.
CAREER
McGill String Quartet, cellist 1941–; Montreal Symphony Orchestra, cellist 1941–; Les Petits Symphoniques, cellist.

BROWN, Audrey Alexandra*   1904–
Poet; b. 29 Oct. 1904 in Nanaimo; daughter of Joseph Miller and Rosa Elizabeth (Rumming) Brown.
EDUCATION
Attended St. Ann's Convent School and Nanaimo Public School.

RELIGION
Catholic Apostolic.
HOME
Nanaimo, BC.
CAREER
Mainly literary.
MEMBER
Queen Alexandra Solarium, Mill Bay, BC. (honorary staff member, 1934-35); Canadian Club, Nanaimo branch (honorary member, 1932); University Women's Club, Victoria, BC. (honorary member, 1932); Canadian Club, Victoria Branch (honorary member, 1949); Canadian Authors Association (honorary member, 1949); Nanaimo Native Daughters, Post no. 2 (honorary member, 1966).
AWARDS, HONOURS
Canadian Women's Press Club memorial award, 1936; Lorne Pierce medal, 1944; Medal of service of the Order of Canada, 1967.
WRITINGS
A dryad in Nanaimo, Macmillan, 1931; *A dryad in Nanaimo, with eleven new poems*, Macmillan, 1934; *The tree of resurrection*, Macmillan, 1937; *The log of the lame duck* (autobiography), Macmillan, 1938; *Poetry and life* (an address), Macmillan, 1941; *Challenge to time and death*, Macmillan, 1943; *V-E Day*, Ryerson, 1947; *All Fool's day*, Ryerson, 1948.
CONTRIBUTED: Poems and articles to *Canadian poetry, Saturday night.*

BROWNELL, Peleg Franklin   1856-1946
Artist; b. 27 July 1856 in New Bedford, Mass.; son of Leander and Annice Willard (Snow) Brownell; came to Canada 1886 and settled in Ottawa, Ont.; m. Louise Nickerson Jan. 1889; children: Lois Sybil; d. 13 Mar. 1946 in Ottawa.
EDUCATION
Studied under Thomas W. Dewing, Boston Museum of Fine Arts, Mass.; studied under Tony Robert-Fleury and W.A. Bouguereau, Académie Julian, Paris, France; later studied under Léon Bonnat.
RELIGION
Protestant.
CAREER
Ottawa Art School, principal 1886-98; head of the Women's Art Association, which became the Art Association of Ottawa, until 1937; teacher, landscape and portrait painter in Ottawa 1886-1946.
MEMBER
Royal Canadian Academy (Associate 1894; Academician 1895; councillor, 1906; retired, 1916); Canadian Art Club (co-founder).
AWARDS, HONOURS
Bronze medal, Paris Exposition, 1900.
EXHIBITIONS
ONE-MAN: National Gallery of Canada, Ottawa, 1927; a number of exhibitions at the James

Wilson and Company Gallery, Ottawa.

GROUP: Represented in group exhibitions held in Canada including annual exhibitions of Royal Canadian Academy, Canadian Art Club, and Ontario Society of Artists; represented in group exhibitions organized by National Gallery of Canada, including its Annual Exhibitions; World's Columbian Exposition, Chicago, Ill., 1893; Paris Exposition, 1900; Paintings by Canadian Artists, City Art Museum, St. Louis, Mo., 1918; Canadian Section of Fine Arts, British Empire Exhibition, Wembley, England, 1924 and 1925; exhibition of Canadian art at the International Exposition, Ghent, Belgium, 1925; *Exposition d'art canadien*, Musée du Jeu de Paume, Paris, 1927; exhibition of Canadian art at the British Empire Trade Exhibition, Buenos Aires, Argentina, 1931; A Century of Canadian Art, Tate Gallery, London, England, 1938; Canadian Art 1760-1943, Yale University Art Gallery, 1944.

COLLECTIONS IN WHICH REPRESENTED
National Gallery of Canada.

BRYMNER, William 1855-1925

Artist; b. 14 Dec. 1855 in Greenock, Scotland; son of Douglas and Jean (Thompson) Brymner; came to Canada with his parents in 1857 and settled in Melbourne, PQ; m. Mary Caroline Massey 12 Sept. 1917; d. 18 June 1925 in Wallasey, Chester, England.

EDUCATION
Attended St. Francis College, Richmond, PQ, and Collège Ste. Thérèse de Blainville, PQ; studied architecture in the chief government architect's office in Ottawa, Ont.; studied under Tony Robert-Fleury and W.A. Bouguereau, Académie Julian, Paris, France, for five years and also under Carolus Duran in Paris, 1878-85.

RELIGION
Anglican.

CAREER
Art Association of Montreal, PQ, director of classes 1886-1921; painter and teacher in Montreal 1886-1921; travelled in Europe 1921-25.

COMMISSIONS
Series of paintings of the Rocky Mountains, CPR, 1892.

MEMBER
Ontario Society of Artists (elected, 1886); Royal Canadian Academy (Associate 1883; Academician 1886; vice-president, 1907; president, 1909-18).

AWARDS, HONOURS
Gold medal, Pan-American Exposition, Buffalo, NY, 1901; silver medal, Louisiana Purchase Exposition, St. Louis, Mo., 1904; CMG, 1916.

EXHIBITIONS
ONE-MAN: Art Association of Montreal, 1926.

GROUP: Represented in group exhibitions held in Canada from 1884 on including annual exhibitions of Royal Canadian Academy, Canadian Art Club, and Ontario Society of Artists, Spring Exhibitions of Art Association of Montreal and Canadian National Exhibitions; represented in the Paris *Salon* and exhibitions of the Royal Academy, London, England, on several occasions; World's Columbian Exposition, Chicago, Ill., 1893; Pan-American Exposition, Buffalo, 1901; Detroit, 1904; Louisiana Purchase Exposition, St. Louis, 1904; Paintings by Canadian Artists, City Art Museum, St. Louis, 1918; Canadian Section of Fine Arts, British Empire Exhibition, Wembley, England, 1924; *Exposition d'art canadien*, Musée du Jeu de Paume, Paris, 1927; A Century of Canadian Art, Tate Gallery, London, 1938; Canadian Painting, National Gallery of Art, Washington, DC, 1950.

COLLECTIONS IN WHICH REPRESENTED
Art Gallery of Hamilton, Ont.; Art Gallery of Ontario, Toronto; Montreal Museum of Fine Arts; Musée du Québec, PQ; National Gallery of Canada, Ottawa.

WRITINGS
CONTRIBUTED To *University magazine.*

BUCKLER, Ernest* 1908–

Author; b. 19 July 1908 in Dalhousie West, NS; son of Appleton and Mary Elizabeth (Swift) Buckler.

EDUCATION
Dalhousie University, BA, 1929; University of Toronto, MA, 1930.

RELIGION
Anglican.

HOME
RR3, Bridgetown, NS.

CAREER
Insurance company in Toronto, Ont., actuary 1931-36; returned to Nova Scotia 1936; farmer 1936–; mainly literary, 1952–; CBC, radio commentator 1954-59.

AWARDS, HONOURS
Prize for article in *Coronet*, 1938; *Maclean's* fiction contest first prize, 1948; University of Western Ontario President's medal for best Canadian short story, 1957 and 1958; Canada Council arts scholarship, 1960, senior arts fellowships, 1963/64 and 1965/66; Centennial medal, 1968.

WRITINGS
The mountain and the valley (novel), Holt, 1952; *The cruellest month* (novel), McClelland & Stewart, 1963; *Ox bells and fireflies; a memoir*, McClelland & Stewart, 1968; *By sun and candlelight* (radio play; produced "Midweek theatre," CBC, 14 Feb. 1968).

CONTRIBUTED: Short stories and articles to

Maclean's, Saturday night, Chatelaine, Country gentleman, Atlantic monthly, Atlantic advocate, Week-end; book reviews to the *New York times* and *Los Angeles times.*

BUGNET, Georges* 1879–

(Henri Doutremont, pseud.)
Author; b. 23 Feb. 1879 in Chalon sur Saône, France; son of Claude and Josephine (Sibut) Bugnet; came to Canada in 1905; m. Julia Ley 29 Apr. 1904; children: Charles, Joseph, Marie, Marthe, Jean, Thérèse, Madeleine, Maurice, Louise.

EDUCATION
Attended secondary school in Dijon, France; Université de Dijon, 1900-01; La Sorbonne, 1902-03; Université de Lyon, France, 1904; BA. Taught himself English, studied German in Karlsruhe, Germany.

RELIGION
Roman Catholic.

HOME
CP 136, Legal, Alta.

CAREER
French army volunteer, 1899, became corporal; farmer, horticulturist in northern Alberta 1905-54; school trustee 1916-49; *L'Union* (Alberta) editor 1924-29.

MEMBER
Western Canadian Society for Horticulture (honorary member).

AWARDS, HONOURS
Prix Carnégie for *La Défaite,* c.1930.

WRITINGS
Le lys de sang (novel), Garand, 1923; *Nipsya* (novel), Garand, 1924 (translated into English); *Siraf* (novel), Gar nd, 1934; *La forêt* (novel), Totem, 1935; *Les voix de la solitude* (poems), Totem, 1938; *La défaite* (play, produced CKVA c.1930).
CONTRIBUTED: Articles, stories, and poems to *Annales politiques et littéraires, Canada français, Revue des poètes.*

BUISSONNEAU, Paul* 1926–

Director and actor; b. 24 Dec. 1926 in Paris, France; son of Lucien and Andréa (Martin) Buissonneau; m. Françoise Charbonneau 1949; came to Canada in 1950 and became Canadian citizen; children: François-Martin b.1956.

EDUCATION
Attended École Beaudricourt, Paris, 1933-40; studied dramatic art with Henry Cordreau, Hubert Gignoux, Yves Joly, Leon Chancerel in Paris, 1955; with Maximilian Decroux, Paris, 1961-62; with Raymond Rouleau, Paris, 1962; l'Université du Théâtre des Nations, Paris, 1962.

HOME
1911 Dorchester Boul. W., Apt. 3, Montreal 25, PQ.

CAREER
Le Théâtre de la Ville et des Champs, France, director on tours, 1946; Les Compagnons de la Chanson, international tour, 1946-50; Service des Parcs de Montréal, director of La Roulette children's theatre 1952-67; Théâtre de Quat'sous, Montréal, founder 1953, director 1953–; toured Europe, USA, Egypt, Syria, Lebanon.

MEMBER
Union des Artistes de Montréal; Canadian Theatre Centre.

AWARDS, HONOURS
Calvert Trophy, Edmonton Festival, 1956; Calvert Trophy, Montreal Festival, 1956; best actor, best director awards, Dominion Drama Festival, Edmonton, 1958; Canada Council senior arts fellowship, 1961; Canada Council travel grant 1967/68.

THEATRE
Directed *Orion le tueur* (Quat'sous, 1953; 2 trophies, regional Drama Festival, 1953), *La tour Eiffel qui tue* (Quat'sous, 1956), *Voulez-vous jouer avec moâ?* (Quat-sous, 1957), *Le tableau des merveilles* (Quat'sous, 1957), *Les oiseaux de lune* (Quat'sous, 1958), *Le manteau de Galilée* (Théâtre Orpheum, Montréal, 1959-60), *La bande à Bonnot* (Quat'sous, 1959-60), *Marlborough s'en va t'en guerre* (Théâtre de la Poudrière, Montréal, 1959-60), *Les Éphémères* (Place des Arts, Montréal, 24 Sept. 1963), *Le cirque aux illusions* (Centre d'Art, Repentigny, PQ, 1964), *La jument du roi* (Centre d'Art, Repentigny, PQ, summer 1964), *La Florentine* (Quat'sous, 5 Dec. 1965), *La grande roue* (Quat'sous, 2 June 1966), *Love* (Quat'sous, 1966-67, tour of Quebec, 1967), *Le knack* (Quat'sous, 1967), *La promenade du dimanche* (Quat'sous, 1967), *Les Louis d'or* (Quat'sous, 6 Nov. 1968).

FILM
Played in *Neuf garçons, un coeur* (commercial, 1947), *Roule ta boule* (1956), *Yul* (National Film Board of Canada, 1965), *Dimension* (National Film Board of Canada, 1965-66; winner of Palme d'Or, Toronto, 1967; prize in Poland, 1965; Silver Sombrero for best experimental film and Silver Medal for best photography in experimental films, 2nd International Festival of Short Films, Guadalajara, Mexico, 1966; first prize in Spain, 1966); wrote and played *Picolo* (1960).

RADIO
Played in many programs 1952-60.

TELEVISION
Directed many CBC productions, e.g. *Mariage de Gogol* (one act, 1957), *Barbier de Séville* (CBC, 1964; Emmy award, New York, 1964), *Aran* (opera, TV Festival de Montréal, 1965), excerpts from *Paillasse, Traviata, Faust, Boris Godunov* (CBC, 1966).

WRITINGS
Les Éphémères (play; produced Place des Arts, Montréal, 24 Sept. 1963).

WORK IN PROGRESS: Directing *Le chemin du roy* for le Théâtre de l'Égrégore, 1968.

BUNJE, pseud.
see MOWAT, Farley McGill

BURNFORD, Sheila Every 1918—
Author; b. 11 May 1918 in Scotland; daughter of Wilfrid G.C. and Ida Philip (Macmillan) Every; m. David Burnford Feb. 1941; children: Peronelle Philip b. 1943, Elizabeth Jonquil b. 1944, Juliet Sheila b. 1947; came to Canada c.1951 and settled in Ontario.
EDUCATION
Attended St. George's School, Edinburgh, Scotland; Harrogate College, England; studied in Germany.
RELIGION
Anglican.
HOME
Loon Lake, by Pass Lake PO, Ont.
CAREER
Served in Royal Naval Hospitals, England, Voluntary Aid Detachment 1939-41; ambulance driver 1941-42.
MEMBER
Canadian Authors Association; Authors Guild, USA; Society of Authors, England.
AWARDS, HONOURS
Book-of-the-year for children medal from the Canadian Library Association, 1963; Aurianne award from the American Library Association, 1963; Dorothy Canfield Fisher Memorial Children's Book award, 1963; William Allen White Children's Book award, 1964; International Andersen award, 1964; Young Readers' Choice award from the Pacific Northwest Library Association for *The incredible journey*, 1964.
WRITINGS
The incredible journey (novel), Little, Brown, 1961 (translated into eight languages; filmed by Walt Disney, 1962); *The fields of noon* (essays), Little, Brown, 1964.
CONTRIBUTED: Articles, poems, stories to *Punch, Blackwood's, Canadian poetry, Atlantic monthly, Ladies home journal*, and other magazines.

BUTLER, Suzanne Louise 1919—
(Suzanne Louise Butler Perréard)
Author; b. 30 May 1919 in London, England; daughter of Hubert Oswald and Louise Ingeborg Anna (Jones) Butler; m. Victor Perréard.
EDUCATION
Attended private schools in France, England, and St. Clement's School in Toronto, Ont.; Provincial Normal School, Victoria, BC.
RELIGION
Anglican.

HOME
Geneva, Switzerland.
CAREER
Taught school for one year in Victoria; The Study, private school for girls, Montreal, PQ, 1942-49; Association of Canadian Clubs National Office, Ottawa, Ont., secretary 1949-53; resided in England, France, and Switzerland.
MEMBER
Canadian Authors Association; Canadian Women's Club, London, England.
WRITINGS
My pride, my folly (novel), Little, Brown, 1953; *Vale of tyranny* (novel), Little, Brown, 1954; *Portrait of Peter West* (novel), Little, Brown, 1958 (published in England under title *Portrait of the painter*, Hodder, Stoughton, 1959); *Starlight in Tourrone* (juvenile fiction), Little, Brown, 1965; *The chalet at Saint-Marc*, Little, Brown, 1968.

CAHÉN, Oscar 1916-56
Artist; b. 8 Feb. 1916 in Copenhagen, Denmark; came to Canada in 1940; m.; children: one son b. 1945; d. 26 Nov. 1956 in Oakville, Ont.
EDUCATION
Studied in Denmark, Sweden, Czecho-slovakia, and Italy; attended Kunstakademie, Dresden, Germany.
CAREER
Rotter School, Prague, Czecho-slovakia, professor; *Standard*, Montreal, PQ, and National Film Board of Canada, freelance commercial artist; illustrated for *Creative living, Maclean's, Canadian home journal, Chatelaine, and Mayfair.*
COMMISSIONS
Mural, Imperial Oil Building, Toronto, Ont.
MEMBER
Ontario Society of Artists; Canadian Society of Painters in Water Colour (elected, 1953); Canadian Society of Graphic Art; Canadian Group of Painters; Art Directors Club, Toronto; Painters Eleven.
AWARDS, HONOURS
Medals, Toronto Art Directors Club, 1950, 1951, 1953, and 1955; medal, Montreal Art Directors Club, 1952; nine merit awards, Montreal Art Directors Club, 1950-55; Taber Dulmage Fehelez purchase award, 1953; purchase award, Canadian National Exhibition, 1955; purchase award, Canadian Society of Graphic Art, 1955; award, Winnipeg Show, Man., 1955.
EXHIBITIONS
ONE-MAN: Art Gallery of Hamilton, Ont.; Art Gallery of Windsor, Ont.; London Public Library & Art Museum, Ont.; Montreal Museum of Fine Art.

GROUP: Represented in Canadian group exhibitions including annual exhibitions of Canadian National Exhibition, Ontario Society of Artists, Royal Canadian Academy, Canadian Society of Graphic Art, Canadian Group of Painters; represented in exhibitions organized by National Gallery of Canada, Ottawa, Ont., including the first Biennial, 1955; Copenhagen, 1934; Prague, 1937; Canadian Section, São Paulo Biennial Exhibition, Museo de Arté Moderna, Brazil, 1953; California Water Color Society, 1955; American Abstract Artists, Painters Eleven, Riverside Museum, New York, NY, 1956.

COLLECTIONS IN WHICH REPRESENTED
National Gallery of Canada; Art Gallery of Ontario, Toronto; London Public Library and Art Museum.

CAILLOUX, André* 1920—
Actor and author; b. 30 May 1920 in France; became Canadian citizen in 1959.
HOME
4252 Old Orchard Ave., Montreal 28, PQ.
CAREER
Au jardin de Grand-Père, children's drama course, founder and director 1961—; La Compagnie du Théâtre du Rideau Vert, Montréal, actor 1956—.
MEMBER
Canadian Theatre Centre; Union des Artistes de Montréal.
THEATRE
Played in *Le complexe de Philémon* (1956), Grand-père in *Une maison ... un jour* (11 Sept. 1965), Lecoing in *Le songe d'une nuit d'été* (15 Sept. 1965), Cochet in *Fleur de cactus* (15 Oct. 1965), Trufaldi in *L'étourdi* (15 Jan. 1966), Pacarel in *Chat en poche* (15 Feb. 1966), Feraponte in *Les trois soeurs* (15 Apr. 1966), *Les assassins associés* (14 Oct. 1966), *Le cheval évanoui* (15 May 1968), *Drôle de couple* (15 Jan. 1968), *Partage de midi* (15 May 1968).
TELEVISION
Played in *Ulysse et Oscar* (series, CBC, French network, June to Sept. 1964-68).
WRITINGS
Fredons et couplets (poems), Beauchemin, 1958; *Caroline, la petite souris blanche,* Centre de psychologie et de pédagogie, 1965; *Raphaël et son voilier,* Centre de psychologie et de pédagogie, 1965; *Lapin-Agile, le petit Indien,* Centre de psychologie et de pédagogie, 1965; *Stella, la petite étoile,* Centre de psychologie et de pédagogie, 1965.
RECORDINGS
Grand-père Cailloux raconte (RCA Victor);

Grand-père Cailloux, contes du samedi (Select M 298, 122, 1967); *Le grand Manitou* (SMM 733-014, 1968).

CALLAGHAN, Morley Edward* 1903—
Novelist; b. 22 Feb. 1903 in Toronto; son of Thomas and Mary (Dewan) Callaghan; m. Lorette Florence Dee 16 Apr. 1929; children: Michael b. 20 Nov. 1932, Barry b. 5 July 1937.
EDUCATION
St. Michael's College, University of Toronto, BA, 1925; Osgoode Hall Law School, Toronto.
RELIGION
Roman Catholic.
HOME
20 Dale Ave., Toronto, Ont.
CAREER
Star, Toronto, reporter 1923-28; admitted to the Ontario Bar 1928; resided in Paris, France 1929; resided in New York, NY, 1930; purely literary 1929—.
AWARDS, HONOURS
Governor General's award for *The loved and the lost*, 1951; *Maclean's* fiction award for *The man with the coat*, 1955; Lorne Pierce medal, 1960; Canada Council medal, 1966/67.
RADIO
Participated in many CBC series, e.g. chairman on "Things to come," "Citizen's forum" (1943-47), "Beat the champs" (1947), "Now I ask you" (1950).
TELEVISION
Played in several CBC programs, e.g. panelist on "Fighting words" (series, 1952—), narrator on *A tale of three cities: Montreal,* ("Camera Canada," 19 Feb. 1962), guest on "Quest" (31 Mar. 1963; 12 May 1963).
WRITINGS
Strange fugitive, Scribner, 1928; *Native argosy* (short stories), Scribner, 1929; *It's never over*, Scribner, 1930; *No man's meat* (novella), the author, 1931; *Broken journey*, Scribner, 1932; *Such is my beloved*, Scribner, 1934; *They shall inherit the earth*, Macmillan, 1935; *More joy in heaven*, Random House, 1937, (translated into Italian); *Now that April's here* (short stories), Random House, 1936; *The varsity story*, Macmillan, 1948; *Luke Baldwin's vow* (juvenile fiction), Winston, 1948; *The loved and the lost*, Macmillan, 1951; *Stories*, Macmillan, 1959; *The many coloured coat*, Macmillan, 1960 (published and serialized by *Maclean's* under the title *The man with the coat*, 1955); *A passion in Rome*, Macmillan, 1961; *That summer in Paris* (non-fiction), Macmillan, 1963; *Just ask for George* (play), 1939 (produced under title *To tell the truth*, New Play Society, Museum Theatre Stage, Toronto, 1949); *Turn again home* (play), 1939

(produced under title *Going home*, New Play Society, Museum Theatre Stage, Toronto, 1950).
CONTRIBUTED: Short stories and articles to *Ten for Wednesday night*, edited by R. Weaver, McClelland & Stewart, 1961; *Atlantic monthly, Cosmopolitan, Esquire, Harper's bazaar, Maclean's, New world magazine* (subsequently *National home monthly*), *Scribner's, Yale review*.
WORK IN PROGRESS: "Thumbs down on Julien Jones" (novel).

CAMPBELL, Wilfred   1858-1918

(William Wilfred Campbell)
Author; b. 1 June 1858 in Berlin, Upper Canada (now Kitchener, Ont.); son of Thomas and Matilda (Wright) Campbell; m. Mary Louisa DeBelle in 1885; children: one son, three daughters; d. 1 Jan. 1918 near Ottawa, Ont.
EDUCATION
Attended Owen Sound High School, Ont., 1877-79; Wycliffe College, University of Toronto; Episcopal theological school, Cambridge, Mass.
RELIGION
Anglican.
CAREER
Taught school, 1879-80; ordained in the Church of England, 1886; served three parishes as a clergyman in New Hampshire, New Brunswick, and Ontario, 1885-91; retired from the ministry, 1891; Dominion Archives, Ottawa, civil servant 1891-1918.
MEMBER
Royal Society of Canada (elected fellow, 1893).
AWARDS, HONOURS
LLD from University of Aberdeen, 1906.
WRITINGS
Snowflakes and sunbeams (poems), St. Croix Courier Press, 1888; *Lake lyrics and other poems*, J. & A. McMillan, 1889; *The dread voyage* (poems), Briggs, 1893; *Mordred and Hildebrand* (drama), Durie, 1895; *Departure* (poems), Ottawa, 1899; *Beyond the hills of dream* (poems), Houghton, 1899; *Night, The house of dreams; two poems*, issued privately, 1903; *The collected poems of Wilfred Campbell*, Revell, 1905; *The poems of Wilfred Campbell*, Briggs, 1905; *A sheaf of winter lyrics*, the author, 1906; *Ian of the Orcades* (novel), Oliphant, 1906; (with T.M. Martin) *Canada* (travel), Black 1907; *Poetical tragedies*, Briggs, 1908; *A beautiful rebel* (novel), Westminster, 1909; *Report of manuscript lists in the Archives relating to the United Empire Loyalists, with reference to other sources*, Archives Branch, 1909; *The beauty, history, romance and mystery of the Canadian lake region*, Musson, 1910; *Requiem: Edward the peacemaker*, the

author, 1910; *The Scotsman in Canada*, v.1, *Eastern Canada* (non-fiction), Sampson Low, 1911; *December lyrics*, Ottawa, 1913; *Sagas of vaster Britain*, Musson, 1914; *War lyrics*, the author, 1915; *Lyrics of iron and mist*, the author, 1916; *Lyrics of the dread redoubt*, the author, 1917; *Langemarck and other war poems*, St. Andrew's Church, Ottawa, 1917.
EDITED: *Poems of loyalty by British and Canadian authors*, Nelson, 1912; *Oxford book of Canadian verse*, Oxford, 1914.
CONTRIBUTED: Poems and articles to *Atlantic monthly, Century, Christian guardian, Cosmopolitan, Evening journal* (Ottawa), *Independent, Harper's, Globe* (Toronto), *Varsity*.

CAMPBELL, William Wilfred

see CAMPBELL, Wilfred

CAPLAN, Rupert*   1896—

Producer and director; b. 3 Oct. 1896 in Montreal; son of Isaac and Esther (Margolick) Caplan; m. Liebe Caplan 23 Dec. 1926.
EDUCATION
Attended Aberdeen primary school and Commercial and Technical High School, Montreal.
RELIGION
Jewish.
HOME
Apt. 49, 3421 Drummond St., Montreal, PQ.
OFFICE
Canadian Broadcasting Corporation, Box 6000, Montreal, PQ.
CAREER
Community Players, Montreal; Provincetown Players, NY, actor; Montreal Theatre Guild, co-founder and producer-director; CBC, Montreal, 1936—, senior drama producer; taught at Bishop's University 1966 and National Theatre School, Montreal 1967.
MEMBER
ACTRA (life member); Municipal Arts Council of Greater Montreal (charter member).
AWARDS, HONOURS
Ohio State University awards, 1947, 1949, 1953, 1954, 1956, 1960, 1961; ACTRA lifetime gold membership (first recipient), 1955.
THEATRE
Produced and directed many plays for Montreal Theatre Guild, Théâtre du Nouveau Monde and Comédie Canadienne, Montréal, e.g. *The trial, Come back little Sheba, Long day's journey into night* (Canadian première, Nouveau Monde, 1956), *The lark* (Comédie Canadienne, c.1959).
RADIO
Produced numerous CBC programs, e.g. donated services for "Victory Loan Shows" (1939-45); produced *Laura Limited* (serial), *The house of Horton* (serial), "Drama in sound" (series), "In

His service" (series), "Happy time" (series), *The Odyssey* (13-week serial), *The Iliad* (13-week serial), *An appreciation of Eugene O'Neill* (Wednesday night," 10 Mar. 1954), *Long day's journey into night* ("Wednesday night," 23 Sept. 1959), *The school friend* ("Wednesday night," 8 Feb. 1961), *A touch of the poet* ("Wednesday night," 5 Dec. 1962), "Famous Canadian trials" (13 week series, 20 Jan. 1963-), *The lark* ("Wednesday night," 27 Feb. 1963), *Look homeward angel* ("Sunday night," 2 Feb. 1964), *Peace as long as it lasts* ("Sunday night," 10 May 1964), *The gimmick* ("Summer stage," 11 Sept. 1964), *Emile and the devil* ("Sunday night," 20 Sept. 1964), *The fate of a poet* ("Sunday night," 31 Jan. 1965), *The black spider* ("Sunday night," 2 May 1965), *Two-faced angel* ("Mid-week theatre," 12 May 1965), *Pastures of plenty* ("Mid-week theatre," 9 June 1965), *A study in black and white and other colours* ("Mid-week theatre," 23 Feb. 1966), *Of mice and men* ("Mid-week theatre," 13 July 1966).

CARBOTTE, Gabrielle Roy
see ROY, Gabrielle

CARLYLE, Florence   1864-1923
Artist; b. 1864 in Galt, Ont.; daughter of William and Ella (Youmans) Carlyle; d. 7 May 1923 in Crowborough, Sussex, England.

EDUCATION
Attended Woodstock, Ont., public schools; studied art in her own home under tutors; studied under A.-J. Delecleuse, W.A. Bouguereau, and L.-A. Lhermitte, Paris, France, 1890; Jules Lefebvre and Tony Robert-Fleury, Académie Julian, Paris, 1890.

CAREER
Moved to Woodstock as a child; travelled to France 1890; spent two summers at Barbizan; studied in Italy; returned to Canada 1896; Havergal College, Toronto, Ont., teacher, 1896; set up studios in London, Ont. and Toronto; opened a studio in New York, NY, 1899; last twenty years of her life spent mainly in Europe with visits to Canada; settled in Crowborough, 1913; engaged in hospital work in France, 1914; later turned her Sussex home into a nurses' rest home; took up literary work in 1918 and stopped painting.

COMMISSIONS
Portrait of Lady Drummond, War Memorials Committee, Canadian Government, for the Parliament Buildings, Ottawa, Ont.

MEMBER
Ontario Society of Artists (elected, 1896); Royal Canadian Academy (Associate 1897; re-elected, 1912).

AWARDS, HONOURS
Silver medal, World's Fair, Chicago, Ill., 1893;

$500 prize, annual artists competition, 1904; silver medal, St. Louis World's Fair, Mo., 1904.

EXHIBITIONS
ONE-MAN: Jenkins Art Gallery, Toronto.
GROUP: Represented in group exhibitions held in Canada during her lifetime including annual exhibitions of Royal Canadian Academy and Ontario Society of Artists; *Salon*, Paris, 1893; World's Fair, Chicago, 1893; *Salon des Champs-Élysées,* Paris; Royal Academy, London, England; St. Louis World's Fair, 1904.

COLLECTIONS IN WHICH REPRESENTED
National Gallery of Canada, Ottawa; Art Gallery of Ontario, Toronto.

CARMICHAEL, Franklin   1890-1945
Artist; b. 1890 in Orillia, Ont.; d. 1945 in Toronto, Ont.

EDUCATION
Studied under G.A. Reid (*q.v.*) and William Cruikshank, Ontario College of Art, Toronto, *c.* 1911; studied under Gustav Hahn, Central Technical School, Toronto; studied under Isador Opsomer and G. van der Veber, Académie Royale des Beaux-Arts, Antwerp, Belgium, 1914-15.

CAREER
Grip Ltd. Toronto, commercial artist 1911-12; Rous and Mann Ltd., Toronto, commercial artist 1912-13; Ontario College of Art, instructor 1932-45.

MEMBER
Group of Seven (original member, 1919); Canadian Group of Painters (elected, 1933); Canadian Society of Painters in Water Colour (founder, 1925; president, 1932-34); Royal Canadian Academy (Associate 1935; Academician 1938); Ontario Society of Artists (elected, 1917); Arts and Letters Club.

AWARDS, HONOURS
Silver medal, Sesqui-Centennial Exposition, Philadelphia, Pa., 1926.

EXHIBITIONS
ONE-MAN: Art Gallery of Toronto, 1947; Mount Slaven School, Orillia.
GROUP: Represented in Canadian group exhibitions including annual exhibitions of Group of Seven, Canadian National Exhibition, Ontario Society of Artists, and National Gallery of Canada, Ottawa, Ont.; Canadian Section of Fine Arts, British Empire Exhibition, London, England, 1925; *Exposition d'art canadien,* Musée du Jeu de Paume, Paris, France, 1927; A Century of Canadian Art, Tate Gallery, London, 1938; Canadian Painting, National Gallery of Art, Washington, DC, 1950; International, New Delhi, India, 1954; An Exhibition of Canadian Paintings held at Fortnum and Mason Ltd., London, 1955.

COLLECTIONS IN WHICH REPRESENTED
Art Gallery of Ontario, Toronto; McMichael Con-

servation Collection of Art, Kleinburg, Ont.; Hart House, University of Toronto; National Gallery of Canada; National Gallery of South Africa, Cape Town.

CARRIER, Louis-Georges* 1927–

Producer, director, and author; b. 25 June 1927 in Detroit, Mich.; son of Fortunat and Cora (Gélinas) Carrier; came to Canada in 1932.

EDUCATION
Attended Collège Ste. Marie, Montréal; Université de Montréal, MA; La Sorbonne, Paris, France, 1952-53.

RELIGION
Roman Catholic.

HOME
1300 Ave. des Pins, Apt. 6, Montréal, PQ.

OFFICE
Canadian Broadcasting Corporation, 1625 Boul. de Maisonneuve, chambre 302, Montréal, PQ.

CAREER
Comédiens Routiers, director; CBC, Montreal, radio and TV producer and scriptwriter 1953–; National Film Board of Canada, film director 1958- ?; Théâtre de Marjolaine, Eastman, PQ, stage director 1960–.

AWARDS
Canadian Amateur Hockey Association scholarship for studies abroad, 1953; Canada Foundation grant, 1954; Canada Council fellowship for studies in Italy, France, England, 1959-60; several radio and TV awards.

THEATRE
Directed *Témoin à charge* (Théâtre Club, Montréal, 1956), *Le roi ivre* (Théâtre de Dix Heures, Montréal [?], 1957), *Zone* (Marjolaine, 1960), *Florence* (La Comédie Canadienne, Montréal, 1960), *Balmaseda* (Théâtre de Percé, PQ, 1961); wrote and directed *Soif d'aimer* (Théâtre de l'Anjou, Montréal, 1961), directed *Requiem pour une nonne* (La Comédie Canadienne, 1961), *Pour cinq sous d'amour* (Marjolaine, 1961), *L'amour des quatre colonels* (Marjolaine, 1962), *Meurtre en fa dièse* (Marjolaine, 1962), *Monsieur Chasse* (Marjolaine, 1963), *Les monstres sacrés* (Marjolaine, 1963); wrote libretto and directed *Doux temps des amours* (Marjolaine, 1964), *Il est une saison* (Marjolaine, 1965), *Ne ratez pas l'espion* (Marjolaine, 1966); directed *Les beaux dimanches* (La Comédie Canadienne, 1966), *Encore cinq minutes* (Théâtre Stella, Montréal, 1967); wrote libretto and directed *On n'aime qu'une fois* (Marjolaine, 1967), *Elle tournera la terre* (La Comédie Canadienne, 17 Nov. 1967); directed *Un matin comme les autres* (La Comédie Canadienne, 1968), *L'arche de Noé* (Marjolaine, 29 June 1968).

FILM
Directed *Au bout de ma rue* (National Film Board of Canada, 1958; prix international du Festival Locarno, Switzerland, 1958), *Les nomades* (National Film Board of Canada, 1959), *Papineau* (National Film Board of Canada, 1960), *Le monde parallèle* (1966), *Le Misanthrope* (Office du film de la province de Québec, 1966).

RADIO
Produced many CBC productions, e.g. wrote and directed *Bigot* ("Histoire du Canada," 1953), *Jean Talon* ("Histoire du Canada," 1953), *Esquisse pour un Prométhée* ("Nouveautés dramatiques," 1953), *La France n'aura pas lieu* ("Nouveautés dramatiques," 1953), *La machine* ("Nouveautés dramatiques," 1953), *L'enfant prodigue* ("Nouveautés dramatiques," 1953), *L'ascenseur* ("Nouveautés dramatiques," 1953), *Le cheval de Troie* ("Nouveautés dramatiques," 1953), *Le fil des parques* ("Nouveautés dramatiques," 1953), *Le château d'eau* ("Nouveautés dramatiques," 1953), *Les mondes illusoires* ("Nouveautés dramatiques," 1953), *Du soleil plein la tête* (1957), *Quelque part dans la ville* (1958); directed series "Histoire," "Litterature," "Initiation à la musique" (1953), "Théâtre radiophonique de Radio Canada," "Nouveautés dramatiques" (1953).

TELEVISION
Produced many CBC programs, e.g. directed *Fantasio* (1954/55), *La fée* (1954/55), *Chambre à louer* (1954/55), *Les vivants* (1954/55), *Sincèrement* (1955/56), *Un cas intéressant* (1955/56), *La nuit se lève* (1955/56), *Une maison de singe* (1955/56), *Le surveillant* (1955/56), *Passé antérieur* (1955/56), *Le procès* (1955/56); wrote and directed *Pour cinq sous d'amour* (1956/57), directed *Hamlet* (1956/57), *Cendres* (1956/57), *L'orme de mes yeux* (1956/57), *Les grands départs* (1957/58), *L'étoile de mer* (1957/58), *Le malentendu* (1957/58), *Médée* (1957/58), *Une maison dans la ville* (1957/58), *Empereur Jones* (1957/58), *Roméo et Juliette* (16 Oct. 1958), *Le feu sur la terre* (1958), *La côte de sable* (1960/61), *Antigone* (Anouilh, 1962/63), *Inquisition* (1962/63), *Dernière heure* (1962/63); wrote and directed *L'indiscret* (1963/64); directed *Une marche de soleil* (1963/64), *Miss Mabel* (1963/64), *Tuez le veau gras* (1963/64), *Un cri qui vient de loin* (1965), *Pleins feux sur Pauline Julien* (1965), *Table tournante* (1968).

WRITINGS
Many radio and TV scripts, e.g. *Le jeu de boules, Mémoire d'une image, L'intrus, Mouvement perpétuel, On demande un souvenir, Madama est servie, De Rome à domicile; Les griffes de l'ennemi* (novel) c.1960; *Les posters* (libretto, produced at Rideau Vert, Montréal, 27 Nov. 1968).

CARRIER, Roch* 1938—
Author; b. 13 May 1938 in Quebec, PQ; son of
Georges and Marie (Tanguay) Carrier; m. Diane
Gosselin; children: Capucine, Fréderique.
EDUCATION
Attended Collège Saint-Louis in Edmundston,
NB, University of Montreal, University of Paris,
France.
HOME
84 Lareau, Longueuil, PQ.
OFFICE
Collège Militaire Royal, Saint-Jean, PQ.
CAREER
University of Montreal, professor; Collège
Militaire Royal de Saint-Jean, lecturer in
English.
AWARDS, HONOURS
Quebec government literary prize for *Jolis
deuils*, 1965.
WRITINGS
Les Jeux incompris (poems), Nocturnes,
1956; *Cherche tes mots, cherche tes pas*
(poems), Nocturnes, 1958; *Jolis deuils*
(stories), Éditions du Jour, 1964; *La Guerre,
yes sir!* (novel), Éditions du Jour, 1968.

CARTER, Alexander Scott 1881—
Artist; b. 7 Apr. 1881 in Harrow, Middlesex,
England; son of Alexander and Sarah Elizabeth
(Walton) Carter; came to Canada in 1912 and
settled in Toronto.
EDUCATION
Attended Royal Academy School of Archi-
tecture and Heatherley's in London, England
and Bournemouth School of Architecture in
England.
RELIGION
Anglican.
HOME
2 Washington Ave., Toronto, Ont.
CAREER
Practised architecture in London until 1912;
illustrated for *Royal architectural institute of
Canada journal* 1927, 1928, 1929 and for
Canadian homes and gardens 1928; illustrated
war memorial book for Bank of Nova Scotia
and memorial book in honour of Sir John
Eaton; decorated presentation volume to
Dr. Frederick P. Keppel of the Carnegie
Foundation; book plate of the library, Art
Gallery of Ontario.
COMMISSIONS
Heraldic decoration, Great Hall, Trinity
College, University of Toronto; designed
silver chalice and paten, St. Michael and All
Angels church, Toronto; panel, University
Club, Montreal, PQ; designed memorial
casket and commemorative booklet presented
to Mrs. Eaton; designed memorial gold

plaque presented to the late Sir John Eaton and
Lady Eaton.
MEMBER
Royal Canadian Academy (Associate 1922;
Academician 1927); Royal Society of Arts,
London (fellow); Essex Archeological Society;
Royal Architectural Institute of Canada; Society
of Genealogists, London; Faculty Club, University
of Toronto (honorary member); Arts and Letters
Club.
AWARDS, HONOURS
Two silver medals and various prizes, Royal
Academy School of Architecture; silver medal,
Bournemouth School of Architecture; Allied
Arts medal, Royal Architectural Institute of
Canada, 1959.
EXHIBITIONS
GROUP: Represented in group exhibitions held
in Canada from 1921 on including annual
exhibitions of Royal Canadian Academy, Canadian
Society of Graphic Art, and Canadian National
Exhibition; represented in exhibitions organized
by National Gallery of Canada, Ottawa, Ont.;
Royal Academy, London, prior to 1912; Los
Angeles Museum, Calif.
COLLECTIONS IN WHICH REPRESENTED
Wycliffe College, University of Toronto; Trinity
College, University of Toronto; York University;
University Club, Montreal; Hart House, University
of Toronto; McMaster University; St. Thomas
Church, Toronto; Royal Ontario Museum,
Toronto; National Gallery of Canada; Royal
Canadian Yacht Club; Art Gallery of Ontario;
Grace Church, Toronto; St. Michael and
All Angels church, Toronto; T. Eaton Company,
Toronto; Imperial Oil Company, New York, NY;
Bank of Nova Scotia, Toronto; Bank of Montreal,
Montreal, PQ; Canadian Imperial Bank of
Commerce, Toronto; National Club, Toronto;
Alpine Club, Banff, Alta.; Standard Oil Company,
New York; Timothy Eaton Memorial Centre,
Toronto.

CARTIER, Michel* 1932—
Choreographer; b. 10 Dec. 1932 in Montreal; son
of Yvan and Rose-anna (Laurin) Cartier; m. Marie-
Berthe Bourdages 7 June 1958; children:
Dominique b. 1957, Yves b. 1959, Francois b.
1960, Pierre b. 1965.
EDUCATION
Attended Collège de Longueuil and École Le
Plateau in Montréal; École des Arts Graphiques
and École des Beaux-Arts, Montréal, Diplôme de
Grande Distinction des Arts Graphiques.
RELIGION
Roman Catholic.
HOME
10-265 Hamelin, Montreal, PQ.

CAREER
Parks and Recreation Department, Montreal; Les Feux-Follets, Montréal, founder and director amateur company 1952-64, professional company 1964-68; *Ques 'Kai?*, founder 1954; travelled extensively in Europe 1957–; Atelier Folklorique de la Cité de Montréal, founder 1958; Festival International des Danses Folkloriques, Vienna, Austria, vice-president of jury 1959; Olympic Games, Mexico, choreographer 1968.

FILM
Choreographed *Les Feux-Follets* (National Film Board of Canada 0166013).

THEATRE
Created *Mosaïque canadienne* (1964), *Légendes du Canada* (1968); choreographed *La plaine, Les néo-Canadiens, La côte du Pacifique, Le nord, L'ouest* (with Brian Macdonald), *L'Acadie* (with Brian Macdonald), *Kebec* (with Brian Macdonald), *La crosse* (1968/69), *Milling frolic* (1968/69), *Mardi Gras* (1968/69), *Shanties* (1968/69).

TELEVISION
Choreographed several CBC productions, e.g. "Où chante l'alouette" and "Filles et garçons" (1956-57).

CASSON, Alfred Joseph* 1898–
Artist; b. 17 May 1898 in Toronto; son of John Edwin and Henrietta Casson; m. Margaret Alexandria Petry 1924; children: Margaret Isobel b. 1931.

EDUCATION
Studied under J.S. Gordon, Hamilton Technical School, Ont., c.1912; Alfred Howell, Central Technical School, Toronto, 1916-18; Harry Britton, 1918; Franklin Carmichael (*q.v.*), 1919; J.W. Beatty, Ontario College of Art, Toronto, c.1920.

RELIGION
Protestant.

HOME
43 Rochester Ave., Toronto 12, Ont.

CAREER
Laidlaw Lithography Co., Hamilton, apprentice 1912; Rous and Mann, Toronto, assistant designer 1920-26; Sampson Matthews Ltd., Toronto, member of art staff 1927–; vice-president and art director, 1946-57; illustrated *The visits of royalty to Canada* by G.W. Jeffereys, North American Life Assurance Co., 1939; War Records Committee, 1940-45; National Academy of Design, New York, NY, non-resident member; Art Gallery of Ontario, Toronto, council member; Ontario College of Art, Toronto, council member, vice-president, 1955-59; O'Keefe Centre, Toronto, chairman of the art committee, 1960–; Ontario Provincial Police, art adviser, 1962–.

COMMISSIONS
Honour rolls, Department of National Defence, 1943; paintings, Canadian Pulp and Paper Association, 1947 and 1951; booklet, *Six trees;* posters, Salada Tea Company, c.1950; mural, CPR's scenic dome; design of mining stamp and pulp and paper stamp, Canadian Government.

MEMBER
Group of Seven (elected, 1926); Graphic Arts Club; Arts and Letters Club, Toronto; Canadian Society of Painter-Etchers and Engravers; Ontario Society of Artists (elected, 1923; president, 1941-45); Royal Canadian Academy (Associate 1926; Academician 1939; vice-president, 1943-48; president, 1948-52); Canadian Society of Painters in Water Colour (founder member, 1926).

AWARDS, HONOURS
Bronze medal, International Business Machines Corporation, 1940; gold medal, Canadian Association of Advertisers, 1953; gold medal, University of Alberta; prize, Dominion Government, 1941; Rolph-Clark-Stone award, seventy-fifth Annual Ontario Society of Artists Exhibition, 1947; Province of Ontario Award, Ontario Society of Artists, 1948; Centennial medal, 1967.

EXHIBITIONS
ONE-MAN: Victoria College, University of Toronto, 1951; Roberts Gallery, Toronto, 1959, 1962, and 1965.
GROUP: Represented in Canadian group exhibitions since 1921 including annual exhibitions of Royal Canadian Academy, Ontario Society of Artists, Group of Seven, Canadian Group of Painters, Canadian National Exhibition; represented in exhibitions organized by National Gallery of Canada, Ottawa, Ont. since 1931; Canadian Section of Fine Art, British Empire Exhibition, London, England, 1924; Exhibition of Canadian Art, International Exposition, Ghent, Belgium, 1925; Pittsburgh, Pa., 1925; Boston Art Club, Mass., 1926; Baltimore, Md., 1931; Gloucester, England, 1934; Toledo, Spain, 1936; Exhibition of Contemporary Canadian Painting, arranged for circulation in the Southern Dominions of the British Empire, 1936; Coronation, England, 1937; A Century of Canadian Art, Tate Gallery, London, 1938; Royal Scottish Society of Painters in Water Colour, Edinburgh, Scotland, 1938; Gloucester, 1939; New York's World Fair; NY, 1939; Golden Gate Exhibition, San Francisco, Calif., 1939; University of Washington, 1942; Canadian Art, 1760-1943, Yale University Art Gallery, 1944; Wembley, England, 1945; Rio de Janeiro, Brazil, 1944; UNESCO ... *Exposition internationale d'art moderne, peinture, graphique et décoratif, architecture,* Musée d'Art Moderne, Paris, France, 1946; Painters of Canada,

1668-1948, Virginia Museum of Fine Arts, Richmond, 1944; Canadian Painting, National Gallery of Art, Washington, DC, 1950; Exhibition of Canadian Paintings shown in India and Pakistan, 1954-55; Exhibition of Canadian Paintings held at Fortnum and Mason Ltd., London, 1955.

COLLECTIONS IN WHICH REPRESENTED
Sarnia, Ont.; London, Ont.; Montreal Museum of Fine Arts, PQ; Beaverbrook Art Gallery, Fredericton, NB; Art Gallery of Ontario, Toronto; Art Gallery of Hamilton; Tom Thomson Gallery, Owen Sound, Ont.; Hart House, University of Toronto; National Gallery of Canada; McMichael Conservation Collection of Art, Kleinburg, Ont.; Agnes Etherington Art Centre, Queen's University.

WRITINGS
Contributed to *Canadian art.*

CAVAZZI, Juliette Augustina Sysak
see JULIETTE

CHAMBERLAND, Paul 1939—
Poet.
does not wish to be included.

CHAMBERS, Jack
see CHAMBERS, John

CHAMBERS, John* 1931—
(Jack Chambers)
Artist; b. 25 Mar. 1931 in London; son of Frank Richard and Beatrice (McIntyre) Chambers; m. Olga Maria Sanchez; children: John b. 19 May 1964, Diego b. 7 Oct. 1965.

EDUCATION
Attended H.B. Beal Technical School, London, 1945-48; studied under Don Julio Moises, Don Juaquin Valveilde, and Don Gregorio Toledo, Real Academia de Bellas Artes de San Fernando, Madrid, Spain, doctorate of fine arts, 1954-59.

RELIGION
Roman Catholic.

HOME
1055 Lombardo, London, Ont.

CAREER

COMMISSIONS
Portrait of Dr. Frank Stiling, University of Western Ontario.

AWARDS, HONOURS
Western Ontario younger artists award, 1949; state prize for painting, Royal Academy, Madrid, 1958; honourable mention, Winnipeg Show, Man., 1962; Canada Council painting fellowship, 1965, 1966, and 1968.

EXHIBITIONS
ONE-MAN: Forum Gallery, New York, NY, 1965; Isaacs Gallery, Toronto, Ont., 1963 and 1965, 1965, and 1967.

GROUP: Represented in group exhibitions organized by National Gallery of Canada, Ottawa, Ont.; Forum Gallery, New York, 1961 and 1962; London Public Library and Art Museum, 1963.

COLLECTIONS IN WHICH REPRESENTED
Vancouver Art Gallery, BC; National Gallery of Canada; Montreal Museum of Fine Arts, PQ; London Public Library and Art Museum; Art Gallery of Ontario, Toronto.

CHAMPAGNE, Claude 1891-1965
(Claude-Adonai Champagne)
Composer and teacher; b. 27 May 1891 in Montreal, PQ; son of Arthur Desparrois *dit* Champagne and Melina (Normandin) Champagne; m. Jeanne Marchal 1922; children: two daughters; d. 21 Dec. 1965 in Montreal.

EDUCATION
Commenced piano studies, 1910; studied organ with R.O. Pelletier, violin with Albert Chamberland in Montreal; Dominion College of Music, Montreal, diploma 1906; Conservatoire National de Musique, Montréal, graduated 1909; studied violin with Jules Conus, counterpoint and fugue with André Gedalge, composition and orchestration with Raoul Laparra in Paris, France 1921-28; Conservatoire National de Musique, Paris, diploma.

CAREER
Worked in Paris for the Canadian Archives 1921-28; Collège de Varennes and Collège de Longueuil, Paris, part-time teacher 1921-28; École Supérieure de Musique d'Outremont, Montréal, teacher 1930-?; École Normale de Westmount, Montréal, music curriculum adviser; McGill Conservatory of Music, teacher, 1934-?; CKAC Montreal, choir director 1935; Conservatoire de Musique de la Province de Québec, co-founder and teacher of composition, assistant director 1942-?, vice-director; L'École Vincent d'Indy, Montréal, curriculum adviser and teacher; Commission of Catholic Schools of Montreal, director of music teaching; Conservatory of Rio de Janeiro, Brazil, lecturer 1945; International Conference of Folk Music, Basle, Switzerland, Canadian representative 1948; BMI Canada Inc., Montreal, editor-in-chief; School of Young Composers, founder 1949.

MEMBER
BMI Canada; Canadian League of Composers; Canadian Association of Adult Education; Canadian Arts Council (honorary president, 1951); Académie de Musique de Québec (honorary member).

AWARDS, HONOURS
Quebec government scholarship, 1921; International Folklore Award, for *Suite canadienne,* 1928; Beatty International Award, for *Suite canadienne;* honorary DMus from University of

Montreal; namesake of Salle Claude Champagne, Montréal; Canada Council medal and award of $2000, 1962.

CONCERT STAGE

Conducted Brazil Symphony Orchestra, Rio de Janeiro, 1945.

RADIO

Guest conductor, CKAC Orchestra (CKAC, 1935); lecturer in music series "Radio collège" (CBF, Montreal, 1940-44).

COMPOSITIONS

Hercule et Omphale, symphonic poem, 1918, BMI Canada, first performed 1926 in Paris by Orchestre Symphonique du Conservatoire, recorded by CBC IS; *Habanera,* violin and piano, 1924, first performed 1940 in Montreal by Annette Lasalle-Leduc, recorded by CBC; *Suite canadienne*, choir and orchestra, 1928, Durand, Paris, first performed 1928 in Paris by Concerts Pasdeloup, recorded by RCA Victor; *Danse villageoise*, violin and piano, 1930, BMI Canada, first performed 1930 in Montreal by Annette Lasalle-Leduc, recorded by Acadia 3000 CB with Arthur LeBlanc and Charles Reiner, also two versions for orchestra, recorded on air-check tape and by CBC IS; *Berceuse*, small orchestra, 1933, BMI Canada, first performed in Montreal by CBC Orchestra, recorded on air-check tape; *Images du Canada français*, choir and orchestra, 1943; *Symphonie gaspésienne*, 1945, BMI Canada, first performed 1949 in Montreal by Les Concerts Symphoniques, recorded by CBC IS; *Concerto in D*, piano and orchestra, 1948, BMI Canada, first performed 1950 in Montreal by Neil Chotem and CBC Orchestra under Roland Leduc, recorded by CBC IS; *Quatuor à cordes*, 1951, first performed in Montreal at Salle de l'Ermitage by Jeunesses Musicales Quartet; *Paysanna*, small orchestra, 1953, first performed 1953 in Montreal by CBC Orchestra under Roland Leduc, commissioned by CBC for broadcasts of Queen Elizabeth II's coronation; *Suite miniature*, or *Trio*, flute or violin, cello, harpsichord, or piano, 1958, also under title *Concerto grosso*, string quintet; *Altitude*, mixed choir, orchestra, and ondes martenot, 1959, BMI Canada, first performed 1960 in Toronto by CBC Symphony Orchestra and Chorus under Charles Houdret, recorded by CBC IS on Dominion Day record, 1961; *A la mémoire d'Henri Gagnon*, organ, Université Laval; *Quadrilha brasileira*, piano, BMI; *Prélude et filigrane*, piano, BMI Canada; *Petit scherzo*, piano, G.V. Thompson; *Messe brève*, three voices, BMI Canada; *Ave Maria*, three voices, BMI Canada; *Le rosier, Isabeau s'y promène, V'la l'bon vent, C'est la belle Françoise*, all for four voices, Waterloo Music; *A Paris, P'tit Jean, Marianne s'en va*, all for solo voice, F. Harris; *Voici le temps, Le nez*

de Martin, both for solo voice, Waterloo Music; *Scoutisme, Laurentienne*, unison songs, Archambault; *Ils sont un peuple sans histoire*, orchestra; *Évocation*, orchestra; *La ballade des lutins*, band; *Huron noël*, mixed choir and orchestra; also many arrangements of folk songs, for solo voice and piano, choir with various accompaniments, or orchestra.

WRITINGS

Initiation au solfège, Archambault; *Solfège pratique*, Archambault; *Solfège pédagoque*, Archambault; *Solfège scolaire*, Archambault; *Solfège manuscrits à changements de clefs*, Archambault, 1961.

CHAPMAN, William   1850-1917

Poet; b. 1850 in St. François de la Beauce, PQ; d. 1917 in Ottawa, Ont.

CAREER

Worked in the Civil Service, Ottawa.

AWARDS, HONOURS

French Academy award for *Les Aspirations*, 1904; *Les Rayons du nord*, 1910.

WRITINGS

Les Québecquoises, Darveau, 1876; *Les Feuilles d'érable*, Gebhardt-Berthiaume, 1890; *A propos de la guerre hispano-américaine* (poems and prose), Léger Brousseau, 1898; *Les Aspirations*, Motteroz-Martinet, 1904; *Les Rayons du nord*, Revue des Poètes, 1912; *Les Fleurs de givre*, Revue des poètes, 1912.

CONTRIBUTED: Poems and articles to *La Poésie française au Canada*, compiled by Louis-H. Taché, Courrier de St.-Hyacinthe, 1881; *Anthologie des poètes canadiens*, edited by J. Fournier and O. Asselin, Granger, 1920, 3rd ed., Granger, 1933; *Le Glaneur, Journal de l'instruction publique, Minerve, Opinion publique, La Patrie, Revue canadienne, Revue de Montréal, Revue france-américaine, Revue nationale*.

CHARBONNEAU, Hélène   1894–

(Marthe des Serres, pseud.)

Author; b. 1894.

HOME

6728 de Lorimier, Montréal, PQ.

WRITINGS

Châteaux de cartes (novel), Ducharme; *Opales* (prose poems), Ducharme, 1924; *L'Albani, sa carrière artistique et triomphale*, Cartier, 1938.

CHARBONNEAU, Robert   1911-67

Author; b. 3 Feb. 1911 in Montreal, PQ; son of Joseph-Arthur and Alma (Robert) Charbonneau; m. Madeleine Brisset 10 June 1944; children: André, Marie, Thérèse, Jeanne; d. 26 June 1967 in St. Jovite, PQ.

EDUCATION
Collège Sainte Marie, Montréal, BA, 1933; University of Montreal, Dip. Journ., 1934.

RELIGION
Roman Catholic.

CAREER
La Relève, co-founder and director 1934-41; La Nouvelle Relève, Director 1941-48; Le Droit, editor 1937; Le Canada, associate director 1938; Éditions de l'Arbre, co-founder 1940, literary director 1940-48, president; CBC, Montreal, director of Press and Information Department 1950-55, script supervisor 1955–.

MEMBER
Académie canadienne-française (vice-president, 1944-60); Société des Éditeurs canadiens (president, 1945-48); Société des Écrivains canadiens (treasurer, 1946-48); PEN Club.

AWARDS, HONOURS
David award, 1942; Duvernay award for Fontile, 1946; Chauveau medal of the Royal Society of Canada, 1965.

WRITINGS
Ils posséderont la terre (novel), L'Arbre, 1941; Petits poèmes retrouvés, 1944; Connaissance du personnage (non-fiction), L'Arbre, 1945; Fontile (novel), L'Arbre, 1947; La France et nous (non-fiction), L'Arbre, 1947; Les Désirs et les jours (novel), L'Arbre, 1948; Vers d'été, L'Arbre, 1948; Aucune créature (novel), Beauchemin, 1961; Chronique de l'âge amer (novel), Sablier, 1967.
CONTRIBUTED: Short stories and essays to Action nationale, Cahiers de l'Académie canadienne-française, Culture, Here and now, Relations industrielles, Transactions of the Royal Society of Canada.

CHARPENTIER, Gabriel 1925–
Composer, poet, and television adviser; b. 1925 in Montreal.

EDUCATION
Studied in Paris with Nadia Boulanger, 1947-53.

OFFICE
c/o Radio-Canada TV, CP 6000, Montréal, PQ.

CAREER
CBC Montreal, TV program organizer, producer, and consultant 1962–; Le Théâtre du Nouveau Monde, Montréal, music director.

MEMBER
Canadian Theatre Centre.

AWARDS, HONOURS
Paris Prix de Poésie Moderne for Aire, 1948; Canada Council grant, 1968/69.

THEATRE
Artistic adviser for Orphée by Gluck (Vancouver International Festival, BC, 1960).

RADIO
Director of choir of speakers in première of Psaume pour abri by Pierre Mercure (CBC, 15 May 1963).

TELEVISION
Assistant producer of "Heure du concert" (CBC Montreal); artistic consultant for The dialogues of the Carmelites (CBC, 16 Apr. 1960).

COMPOSITIONS
Missa brevis, three equal high voices, 1952; Sept chansons enfantines, high voices a cappella; Trois poèmes de St. Jean-de-la-Croix, contralto, violin, and cello; film scores, e.g. The fall of the house of Usher; incidental music for plays especially for Stratford, Ont. Festival, e.g. Tartuffe, 1968, The alchemist, 1968-69; music for Stratford, Ont. Festival chamber music workshop, 1968; Orphée, short opera, 1968, commissioned for the opening of the National Arts Centre, Ottawa, Ont. in 1969.
WORK IN PROGRESS: "Le cantique spirituel" commissioned by Pierrette Alarie and Léopold Simoneau (q.v.).

WRITINGS
Les amitiés errantes, Seghers, 1951; Le dit de l'enfant mort, Seghers, 1954; Cantata pour une joie (libretto), music by Pierre Mercure (q.v.), recorded by G. Ricordi, 1960.

CHATEAUCLAIR, Wilfred, pseud.
see LIGHTHALL, William Douw

CHILD, Philip Albert* 1898–
(John Wentworth, pseud.)
Author; b. 19 Jan. 1898 in Hamilton, Ont.; son of William Addison and Elizabeth Helen (Harvey) Child; m. Gertrude Hélène Potts 1925; children: John b. 10 Apr. 1928, Elizabeth b. 13 Oct. 1930.

EDUCATION
Attended elementary schools in Germany, Switzerland, Canada; Trinity College, University of Toronto, BA, 1921; Cambridge University, 1921-22; Harvard University, AM, 1924, Ph D, 1928.

RELIGION
Anglican.

HOME
40 Heathdale Rd., Toronto, Ont.

OFFICE
Trinity College, Hoskin Ave., Toronto 5, Ont.

CAREER
Canadian Army, 1917-18, became lieutenant; Trinity College, Toronto, lecturer 1923-26, special lecturer 1941-42, chancellor's professor of English 1942-67, special lecturer 1967–; University of British Columbia, assistant professor of English 1928-29; Harvard University, tutor, instructor 1929-36; University of Toronto quarterly, co-editor 1940-49; University of Toronto, member of Senate 1947-51.

MEMBER
Canadian Authors Association (vice-president, 1945-47); International Institute of Arts and Letters (elected life fellow, 1962); Arts and Letters Club; Modern Language Association.

AWARDS, HONOURS
Ryerson fiction award for *Day of wrath*, 1945, *Mr. Ames against time*, 1949; Governor General's award for *Mr. Ames against time*, 1949; Canada Council senior arts fellowship, 1960/61.

WRITINGS
The village of souls (novel), Butterworth, 1933; *God's sparrows* (novel), Butterworth, 1937; (with J.W. Holmes) *Dynamic democracy*, CAAE and CIIA, 1941; *Blow wind – come wrack* (novel), Jarrolds, 1945; *Day of wrath* (novel), Ryerson, 1945; *Mr. Ames against time* (novel), Ryerson, 1949; *The Victorian house and other poems*, Ryerson, 1951; *The wood of the nightingale* (poems), Ryerson, 1965.
CONTRIBUTED: Articles to *University of Toronto quarterly*, *Dalhousie review*, *Queen's quarterly*.

CHIOCCHIO, Fernande
Singer (mezzo soprano); b. in Montreal.
HOME
4268 St. Hubert St., Montreal 34, PQ.
AWARDS, HONOURS
Canada Council arts scholarship, 1966/67; Canada Council award, 1967/68.
THEATRE
Sang in many productions, e.g. Mara in *Opera d'Aran* (Montreal Festival, 1965), Sousouki in *Madama Butterfly* (Vancouver Opera Association, 28 Oct. 1965), Charlotte in *Werther* (1965), *Centennial celebration* (McGill Chamber Orchestra and l'Ensemble Vocal de l'École Normale, 1967), Marthe in *Faust* (Gounod, Montreal Symphony Orchestra, Expo 67, 8 July 1967).
RADIO
Sang in several CBC productions, e.g. *Music of the sun king* ("Wednesday night," 18 June 1961), *Le Martyre de St. Sébastien* ("Wednesday night," 22 Aug. 1962), *St. John the baptist* ("Sunday night," 28 June 1964), *Hippolyte et Aricie* ("Sunday night," 18 Oct. 1964), "Summer concert" (series, 10 Aug. 1966), *Medium* (9 July 1967), "Encore," part I (series, 17 Nov. 1968).
TELEVISION
Sang in several CBC productions, e.g. Mother Jeanne in *The dialogues of the Carmelites* (16 Apr. 1960), *The barber of Seville* ("Festival," 3 Nov. 1965).

CHOPIN, René 1885-1953
Poet; b. 1885 in Sault-au-Récollet, Montréal, PQ; d. 1953.

EDUCATION
Attended Collège Sainte Marie, Montréal; studied voice in Paris, France.
CAREER
Worked as notary public.
WRITINGS
Le Coeur en exil, Crès, 1913; *Dominantes*, Lévesque, 1933.

CHOQUETTE, Ernest 1862-1941
Novelist; b. 18 Nov. 1862 in Beloeil, PQ; son of Joseph and Maria T. (Audet) Choquette; m. Eva Perrault 1889; d. 29 Mar. 1941 in Montreal, PQ.
EDUCATION
Attended Séminaire de St. Hyacinthe, PQ; Université Laval, MB, MD.
CAREER
St. Hilaire, PQ, physician and mayor; Legislative Council of Quebec, elected 1910.
MEMBER
Royal Society of Canada (elected fellow, 1914).
WRITINGS
Les Ribauds, Sénécal, 1898; *Carabinades*, Déom, 1900; *Claude Paysan*, Casterman, 1916; *La Terre*, Beauchemin, 1916.

CLARKE, George Frederick* 1883–
Author; b. 29 Dec. 1883 in Woodstock; son of Abram Edwin and Maria Lucy (Harris) Clarke; m. Mary Schubert 12 Oct. 1912; children: Jane Schubert, Mary Elizabeth Pedrick, Frederick.
EDUCATION
Attended grammar school in Woodstock; Medico-Chirurgical College, Philadelphia, Pa., Doctor of Dental Surgery, 1913.
RELIGION
Protestant.
HOME
Box 155, Woodstock, NB.
CAREER
Practised dentistry until 1953 in Woodstock.
AWARDS, HONOURS
LLD from University of New Brunswick, 1969.
WRITINGS
The magic road (novel), Mills & Boon, 1925; *Chris in Canada* (novel), Blackie, 1925; *The best one thing* (novel), Mills & Boon, 1926; *Thetis Saxon* (novel), Longmans, 1927; *The Saint John River and other poems*, Ryerson, 1933 (Ryerson poetry chap-book); *David Cameron's adventures* (novel), Blackie, 1950; *Return to Acadia* (novel), Brunswick Press, 1952; *Adventures of Jimmy Why* (juvenile fiction), Brunswick Press, 1954; *Expulsion of the Acadians* (non-fiction), Brunswick Press, 1955; *Too small a world; the story of Acadia*, Brunswick Press, 1958; *Noel and Jimmy Why* (juvenile fiction), Brunswick Press, 1959; *Six salmon rivers and another*, Brunswick Press,

1960 (also published in England under title *Six salmon rivers and another in Canada*); *The song of the reel,* Brunswick Press, 1963; *Someone before us,* Brunswick Press, 1968.
CONTRIBUTED: Poems, short stories, and articles to several anthologies, e.g. *Canadian poetry in English,* edited by Bliss Carman and others, rev. and enl. ed., Ryerson, 1954; *Atlantic advocate, Maclean's, Canadian home journal, Canadian courier, Canada monthly, St. Nicholas, The novel, Blackie's boy's annual, Trail, Bulletin of Natural History Society of New Brunswick.*

CLOUTIER, Albert   1902-65
(Albert Edward Cloutier)
Artist; b. 12 June 1902 in Leominster, Mass.; son of Louis Arthur and Diana (Turcotte) Cloutier; came to Canada in 1903; m. Guila Possnet 7 July 1930 (deceased); d. 9 June 1965.

EDUCATION
Attended Olier and Plateau schools, Montreal, PQ; studied under Edmond Dyonnet (*q.v.*) and Joseph St. Charles (*q.v.*), Monument National, Montréal; studied with A.Y. Jackson (*q.v.*) and Edwin H. Holgate.

RELIGION
Roman Catholic.

CAREER
Opened a school in Montreal 1930; Canadian Government, Wartime Information Board, art director; RCAF, 1943-46, official war artist; sketched throughout Quebec; tour of Europe, 1951; freelance design consultant 1955-65; École des Beaux-Arts, Montréal, teacher 1955-57; Inter-national Design Conference, Aspen, Colo., member; since 1960 worked full time at painting, metal work, and wood work.

COMMISSIONS
Mural, (with Edwin Holgate) Canadian Pavilion, World's Fair, New York, NY, 1939; designed mural, Salle Bonaventure, Queen Elizabeth Hotel, Montreal; mural, Astra Dome observation car, CPR; graphic designs for books, posters and decorations for fairs and exhibitions.

MEMBER
Royal Canadian Academy (Associate 1951; Academician 1956); Canadian Society of Painters in Water Colour (vice-president, 1956); Canadian Society of Graphic Art; National Society of Art Directors (second vice-president; president, 1953); Art Directors Club of Montreal (president, 1953); Federation of Canadian Artists.

AWARDS, HONOURS
Jessie Dow prize, Montreal Museum of Fine Art,

1949 and 1951; Canada Council senior fellowship, 1962/63.

EXHIBITIONS
ONE-MAN: Arts Club, Montreal, 1935, 1952, 1957, 1958, and 1959; Little Gallery, Ottawa, Ont., 1948; S.S. Acadia, stopped at Ireland, England, France, and Germany, 1959; Montreal Museum of Fine Arts (organized by Gallery XII), 1961; Gemst Gallery, Montreal, 1962.
GROUP: Represented in group exhibitions held in Canada including annual exhibitions of Montreal Museum of Fine Arts, Royal Canadian Academy, and Canadian Group of Painters; represented in group exhibitions organized by National Gallery of Canada, Ottawa; Exhibition of Contemporary Canadian Painting Arranged ... for circulation in the Southern Dominions of the British Empire, 1936; World's Fair, New York, 1939.

COLLECTIONS IN WHICH REPRESENTED
National Gallery of Canada; Canadian Pulp and Paper Association, Montreal; Seagram Collection, Montreal; Imperial Oil Ltd., Toronto; External Affairs Department, Ottawa.

WRITINGS
CONTRIBUTED: To *Canadian art.*

COBURN, Frederick Simpson   1871-1960
Artist; b. 18 Mar. 1871 in Upper Melbourne, PQ; son of Newlands and Laurie Anna (Thomas) Coburn; m. Malvina Scheepers; d. 26 May 1960 in Upper Melbourne.

EDUCATION
Attended St. Francis College, Richmond, PQ; studied with C.S. Stevenson, Arts and Crafts School, Montreal, PQ; graduated from Carl Hecker School, New York, NY; studied with Erhentraut and Skarbina, Royal Academy, Berlin, Germany, graduated; studied under Gérome, École des Beaux-Arts, Paris, France; Henry Tonks, Slade School, London, England; Abrecht de Vrient, Institut des Beaux-Arts, Antwerp, Belgium.

CAREER
Illustrated works of several authors, e.g. William Henry Drummond's *The habitant and other French-Canadian poems, Phil-o-rum's canoe and Madeleine Vercheres, Johnnie Courteau and other poems, The voyageur and other poems, The great fight, poems and sketches,* Putnam, 1897-1908, Charles Dickens' *Cricket on the hearth* and *A Christmas carol,* Washington Irving's *Rip Van Winkle,* Robert Browning's *Our last ride together,* and Louis Fréchette's *Noël au Canada;* illustrated

for *London sporting and dramatic news, London News,* and *Quebec daily telegraph.*

MEMBER

Pen and Pencil Club (honorary member); Royal Canadian Academy (Associate 1920; Academician 1927).

AWARDS, HONORS

.DCL from Bishop's University, 1936; École des Beaux-Arts scholarship, Paris; government subsidy to Institut des Beaux-Arts, Antwerp.

EXHIBITIONS

GROUP: Represented in Canadian group exhibitions since 1922 including annual exhibitions of Royal Canadian Academy and Canadian National Exhibition; A Century of Canadian Art, Tate Gallery, London, 1938; An Exhibition of Canadian Paintings held at Fortnum and Mason Ltd., London, 1955.

COLLECTIONS IN WHICH REPRESENTED

National Gallery of Canada, Ottawa, Ont.; National Archives, Ottawa; Montreal Museum of Fine Art; Musée du Québec, PQ; Vancouver Art Gallery, BC; National Art Gallery, Brisbane, Australia; Art Gallery of Ontario, Toronto.

COBURN, Kathleen Hazel* 1905—

Author; b. 7 Sept. 1905 in Stayner, Ont.; daughter of John and Susannah Wesley (Emerson) Coburn.

EDUCATION

Attended Harbord Collegiate Institute, Toronto; University of Toronto, BA, 1928, MA, 1930; St. Hugh's College, University of Oxford, B Litt, 1932.

HOME

39 Elgin Ave., Toronto, Ont.

OFFICE

English Department, Victoria College, University of Toronto, Toronto 5, Ont.

CAREER

Victoria College, University of Toronto, assistant to Dean of Women 1932-35; instructor in English, assistant professor 1932-53, professor 1953—; *The collected Coleridge,* general editor 1968—.

MEMBER

Charles Lamb Society, London, England; Royal Society of Literature (fellow, 1952); Royal Society of Canada (elected fellow, 1958).

AWARDS, HONOURS

Regents' gold medal in philosophy and English, 1928; IODE war memorial scholarship for Ontario, 1930; International Federation of University Women senior fellowship, 1947; Leverhulme award, 1948; Guggenheim fellowship, 1953/54, 1957/58; Rosemary Crawshay prize of the British Academy, 1958; Commonwealth visiting fellowship, University of London, 1962-63; LLD from Queen's University, 1964.

WRITINGS

The grandmothers((novel) Oxford, 1949.

EDITED: *The philosophical lectures of S.T. Coleridge,* Philosophical Library, 1949; *Inquiring spirit, a new presentation of Coleridge,* Routledge & Paul, 1951; *The Sara Hutchinson letters,* University of Toronto, 1954; *The notebooks of Samuel Taylor Coleridge,* Routledge & Paul, 1957-61; *Coleridge: a collection of critical essays,* Prentice-Hall, 1967.

CONTRIBUTED: Articles to *Review of English studies, Canadian forum, Gazette des beaux-arts, University of Toronto quarterly, Times* (London).

CODERRE, Émile* 1893-1970

(Jean Narrache, pseud.)

Poet; b. 10 June 1893 in Montreal; son of Émile and Jeanne (Marchand) Coderre; m. Rose-Marie Delys Tassé Sept. 1922; d. 6 Apr. 1970.

EDUCATION

Attended Séminaire de Nicolet, PQ; University of Montreal, Pharm. Lic.

RELIGION

Roman Catholic.

CAREER

University of Quebec, assistant professor of pharmacy, 1954-64.

MEMBER

Quebec College of Pharmacists (registrar, 1945-61; honorary member, 1961—).

AWARDS, HONOURS

Silver medal and certificate of the Société des Poètes canadiens-français, 1933.

WRITINGS

Les Signes sur le sable, L'Auteur, 1922; *Quand j'parl' tout seul,* Lévesque, 1932; *La Corvée* (play) 1933; *La grande demande* (play), 1934; *La Guignolée* (play), 1935; *Histoires du Canada,* Valiquette, 1937; *J'parle pour parler,* Valiquette, 1939; *Bonjour les gars,* Pilon, 1948; *J'parle tout seul quand Jean Narrache* (poems), Homme, 1961; *Jean Narrache chez le diable* (non-fiction), Homme, 1963.

CONTRIBUTED: Radio scripts to several CKAC and CBF programs, Montreal, e.g. *Le Village de par chez nous, Les trois mousquetaires, Le Vagabond qui chante, Amour d'automne, Jean Narrache, pharmacien; Bonjour les gars;* poetry and articles to *Canadian pharmaceutical journal, Drug topics, La Patrie du dimanche* (Montreal), *Le Pharmacien* (Quebec).

CODY, Hiram Alfred 1872-1948

Novelist; b. 3 July 1872 in Cody's, NB; son of George Redmond and Loretta Augusta Cody; m. Jessie Margaret Flewelling 19 Sept. 1905; children: Douglas Flewelling, Kenneth White, Norman Redmond, George Albert, Frances Margaret Lillian; d. 9 Feb. 1948 in Saint John, NB.

EDUCATION
Attended Saint John grammar school; University of King's College, Windsor, NS, BA, 1897, MA, 1908.

RELIGION
Anglican.

CAREER
Ordained as deacon 1896; travelling missionary in the Yukon Territory and rector of Christ Church, Whitehorse, YT, 1905-10; St. James Church, Saint John, rector 1910-27, archdeacon 1927-43.

MEMBER
Canadian Authors Association (honorary member); Canadian Club.

WRITINGS
An apostle of the north (biography), Musson, 1908; *The frontiersman,* Briggs, 1910; *The fourth watch*, Briggs, 1911; *On trail and rapid by dogsled and canoe* (biography), Musson, 1911; *The long patrol*, Briggs, 1912; *The chief of the ranges*, Briggs, 1913; *If any man sin*, Briggs, 1915; *Rod of the lone patrol*, McClelland, 1916; *Under sealed orders*, McClelland, 1917; *The unknown wrestler*, McClelland, 1918; *The touch of Abner*, McClelland, 1919; *Glen of the high north*, McClelland, 1920; *Jess of the rebel trail*, McClelland, 1921; *The king's arrow*, McClelland, 1922; *The trail of the Golden Horn*, McClelland, 1923; *The master revenge*, McClelland, 1924; *Songs of a Bluenose* (poems), McClelland, 1925; *The fighting slogan*, McClelland, 1926; *Fighting stars*, McClelland, 1927; *The stumbling shepherd*, McClelland, 1929; *The river fury*, McClelland, 1930; *The red ranger*, McClelland, 1931; *The girl at Bullet Lake*, McClelland, 1933; *The crimson sign*, McClelland, 1935; *Storm king banner*, McClelland, 1937.

CONTRIBUTED: Poems and articles to *Canadian magazine, Canadian courier, Literary digest, The Westminster.*

COGHILL, Joy* 1926—

(Joy Coghill Thorne)
Actress and director; b. 13 May 1926 in Findlater, Sask.; daughter of J.G. and Dorothy (Pollard) Coghill; m. John Thorne 6 May 1955; children: Debra Dorothy b. 18 Aug. 1956, Gordon Alexander b. 8 July 1958, David Michael John b. 1 Mar. 1967.

EDUCATION
Attended King's Park School and Queen's Park High School in Glasgow, Scotland; Kitsilano High School in Vancouver; University of British Columbia, BA, 1949; Goodman Theatre, Art Institute, Chicago, Ill., MFA, 1951.

HOME
4672 W. 6th Ave., Vancouver 8, BC.

OFFICE
Playhouse Theatre Company, 560 Cambie St., Vancouver 3, BC.

CAREER
Taught privately in Vancouver 1943-46; Canadian Players, Kingston, Ont., director and actress 1950; University of British Columbia, teacher of drama 1951-52, 1954-66, Players' Club director 1951-52, Extension Department acting drama director 1954-55, Frederick Wood Theatre, artistic director 1954-55; Tenthouse Theatre, Rhinelander, Wis., director and actress 1951-52; Everyman Theatre, Vancouver, director and actress 1951-53; Goodman Theatre, Art Institute, Chicago, teacher 1953-54; De Paul University, Chicago, teacher 1953-54; Holiday Theatre, Vancouver, founder and artistic director 1954-66; Vancouver Festival, director 1960; National Theatre School, Montreal, PQ, guest director and teacher 1966; Holiday Playhouse, Vancouver, artistic director 1966-67; Centennial Commission, Ottawa, Ont., director 1967; Playhouse Theatre Company, Vancouver, artistic director 1967-69, artistic consultant 1969—.

MEMBER
AEA; ACTRA; Canadian Conference of the Arts; Canadian Theatre Centre (board member); Dominion Drama Festival (board member); National Theatre School (BC representative); Vancouver Community Arts Council; Vancouver Festival (board member); Vancouver Opera Association (board member).

AWARDS, HONOURS
Dominion Drama Festival acting award, 1947; Koerner Foundation grant to travel to Stratford, Ont., 1962; Canadian drama award, 1963; Canada Council grant to travel to Europe to observe children's theatres, 1963; Canadian Confederation Centennial Committee of British Columbia certificate of merit, 1967; Centennial medal, 1967.

THEATRE
Played in many productions, e.g. title role in *I remember Mama* (Frederick Wood, 1946), Mrs. Phelps in *The silver cord* (Dominion Drama Festival, Vancouver, 1947), title role in *Candida* (Goodman, 1950), Mrs. Alving in *Ghosts* (Everyman, 1951), Mother in *This happy breed* (Goodman, 1950), Puck in *A midsummer night's dream* (Britten, Vancouver Festival, 1961; San Francisco Opera Company, 1961), Clare in *The visit* (Frederick Wood, 1965), Winnie in *Happy days* (Frederick Wood, 1966), Mrs. Castleton in *Big soft Nellie* (Playhouse Theatre Company, Vancouver Festival, 1 July 1966); directed numerous productions, e.g. *School for scandal* (Players' Club, 1948), *King Midas* (Goodman, 1950), *Antigone* (Goodman, 1951), *The flies* (Everyman, 1952), *Much ado about nothing* (Players' Club, 1952),

The seagull (Frederick Wood, 1954), *East Lynne* (Goodman, 1954), *The swan* (De Paul University, 1954), *Beauty and the beast* (Vancouver Festival, 1960), *Christmas in the market place* (Playhouse, 1964), *Androcles and the lion* (Holiday Theatre, 11 Sept. 1965; Playhouse, 1967), *A month in the country* (Playhouse, 14 Oct. 1965), *Awake and sing* (National Theatre School, 1966), *The country wife* (Frederick Wood, 1966), *Beware the quickly who* and *The riddle machine* (Holiday Theatre national tour, 1967), *The beaux' stratagem* (Playhouse, 1968), *A streetcar named Desire* (Playhouse, 1968).

RADIO
Played in many CBC productions, e.g. Gertrude in *Hamlet*, Madame Arkadin in *The seagull*, Margaret in *Richard III*, Marjorie in *The knight of the burning pestle, The summer people* ("Wednesday night," 24 May 1961; "Saturday evening," 22 Feb. 1964), Alice in *The evening colonnade* ("Vancouver theatre," 14 Nov. 1961), Mary Jacobi in *The third day* ("Wednesday night," 25 Apr. 1962), *Philemon and Baucis* ("Theatre of the air," 20 Mar. 1963), Jocasta in *Oedipus Rex* ("Saturday evening," 14 Dec. 1963; 29 May 1965), Alice in *The dance of death* ("Saturday evening," 25 Jan. 1964), Cleopatra in *Antony and Cleopatra* ("Sunday night," 26 Apr. 1964), Volumnia in *Coriolanus* ("Saturday evening," 26 Sept. 1964), Agatha in *The family reunion* ("Saturday evening," 26 June 1965), *Count Flippo* ("Wednesday night," 18 Oct. 1967).

TELEVISION
Played in several CBC productions, e.g. title role in *Anyone for Alice* ("Studio Pacific," 14 Oct. 1959), Emily Carr in *The heart of the thing* ("Discovery," 11 Feb. 1962; "Camera west," 22 Aug. 1965), Mary Jacobi in *The third day* (22 Apr. 1962).

COGSWELL, Frederick William*   1917—
Poet; b. 8 Nov. 1917 in East Centreville, NB; son of Walter Scott and Florence (White) Cogswell; m. Margaret Hynes 1944; children: Carmen Patricia b. 1945, Kathleen Mary b. 1948.

EDUCATION
University of New Brunswick, BA, 1949, MA, 1950; University of Edinburgh, PhD, 1952.

RELIGION
Protestant.

OFFICE
English Department, University of New Brunswick, Fredericton, NB.

CAREER
Canadian Army, 1940-45; University of New Brunswick, assistant professor of English 1952-57, associate professor 1957-62, professor 1962—; *Fiddlehead,* editor 1952-66; *Humanities Associa-*

tion bulletin, editor 1967—; *Fiddlehead poetry books,* publisher.

MEMBER
ACUTE; Humanities Association of Canada; Institute of International Affairs; Canadian Legion.

AWARDS, HONOURS
IODE scholar for New Brunswick, 1950-52; Nuffield fellow, 1959/60; Canada Council senior fellowship 1967/68.

WRITINGS
The stunted strong, University of New Brunswick, 1954; *The haloed tree,* Ryerson, 1956; *Descent from Eden,* Ryerson, 1959; *Lost dimensions,* Outpost Publications, 1960; *Star-people,* Fiddlehead, 1968.
EDITED: *A Canadian anthology,* Fiddlehead, 1961; (with R.A. Tweedie and W.S. McNutt) *The arts in New Brunswick,* Brunswick Press, 1967; (with T.R. Lower) *The enchanted land,* Gage, 1967.
TRANSLATED: Robert Henryson's *The testament of Cresseid,* Ryerson, 1957.
CONTRIBUTED: Poems and articles to *Five New Brunswick poets,* Fiddlehead, 1962; *Literary history of Canada,* edited by C.F. Klinck, University of Toronto, 1965; *Encyclopedia Canadiana; Atlantic advocate, Canadian author and bookman, Canadian literature, Canadian poetry, Fiddlehead,* and many British and American periodicals.

COLLIER, Ron*   1930—
(Ronald William Collier)
Trombonist, composer, and conductor; b. 3 July 1930 in Coleman, Alta.; son of Vincent and Dorothy (Burns) Collier; m. Kathryn Jean MacKinnon 24 Oct. 1959; children: Matthew b. 9 Dec. 1963, Jason b. 13 Apr. 1968.

EDUCATION
Attended Coleman Public School; Alexander Public School, Vancouver, BC; British Columbia Institute of Technology, Burnaby, BC; studied composition with Gordon Delamont (*q.v.*), Toronto, 1951-55, and George Russel, New York, NY, 1961/62; harmony and orchestration with Hall Overton, New York, 1961/62.

HOME
7 Windmill Road, Toronto 17, Ont.

CAREER
Kitsilano Boys' Band, Vancouver, 1943-50; National Ballet of Canada, Toronto, *c.*1951-55; Mart Kenny Band, Toronto, *c.*1951-55; Norman Symonds (*q.v.*) Jazz Octet, Toronto, *c.*1953; Canadian Opera Company, Toronto, 1966; Ron Collier Quartet, Toronto, founder and director 1955; Ron Collier Tentet, Toronto, founder and director 1960; CBC, Toronto, executive director for "Ten centuries concerts" series 1966-69, musical director for "O'Keefe Centre presents"

TV series 1967/68, audio consultant; Canadian National Exhibition Grandstand Show, Toronto, conductor and musical director 1969.

MEMBER
Toronto Musicians Association (executive member); Jazz Arts (executive member).

AWARDS, HONOURS
Canada Council study grant, 1961/62, short-term grant, 1968/69.

CONCERT STAGE
Played with several orchestras, e.g. CBC Symphony, Tri-City-Symphony, Shenectedy, NY, 1957, Winnipeg Symphony, Man. 1962, Toronto Symphony, 1966.

RADIO
Played in several CBC series, e.g. "Summer concerts" (1958-60), "Wednesday night" (c. Sept. 1959).

TELEVISION
Played in several CBC programs, e.g. *All-Canadian jazz show* (4 Nov. 1960), *The Canadian jazz show* (10 May 1961).

COMPOSITIONS
Stratford adventure, 1956 and *Opus for trombone and saxophone*, 1956, performed at Stratford, Ont., Festival, 1956. *Sextet*, 1957 and *Adagio*, 1957, performed at Stratford, Ont., Festival, 1957. *Cambodian suite*, performed on CBC radio series "Wednesday night," 16 Sept. 1959. *Quintet*, 1959, performed on CBC TV *Canadian Timex jazz show*, 1959. *The city*, for orchestra, narrator, and singer, 1960, performed on CBC radio, selected entry for Italia prize competition, 1960, commissioned by CBC. *The myth of Marsyas*, 1960, performed on CBC TV, 1960. *Four moods*, 1960, performed on CBC radio, 1960. *Two shades of blue*, performed on CBC TV series "Music in the mirror," 15 Apr. 1962. *Autumn haze*, 1962 and *Requiem for JFK*, 1963, Kendor Publishing Co., performed on CBC TV series "A la carte," 1964. *Impressions*, 1963, performed on CBC radio, 1963. *Ad libitum*, 1963 (?), first performed on CBC radio series "Ten centuries concerts," c.1966. *Hear me talkin' to ya*, 1964, performed at Crest Theatre, Toronto, 1964, commissioned by CBC TV for *Jazz at the Crest*, "Eye opener" series, 1964. *Blue boy* and *Blues of one theme*, recorded by CBC IS, 1965. *Just about now, Lee's lament, Walking out*, and *Relaxin'*, recorded by Canadian Talent Library, 1965. Several drama scores, e.g. *The mechanic*, 1965, CBC radio series "Ten centuries concerts," c.1966, commissioned by CBC; *Silent night, lonely night*, 1965, CBC TV series "Festival," Dec. 1965, 1966, CBC radio series "Ten centuries concerts," c.Mar. 1967, recorded on *In Canada* with Duke Ellington on Decca 75069, 1968, commissioned by CBC; *Demirgian*, CBC radio series "Tuesday night," 8 July 1968. Several film scores, e.g. *Seven*

criteria, Westminster Films, Dec. 1967; *Bell Telephone film*, Westminster Films, Feb. 1968; *Rye on the rocks*, Westminster Films, Nov. 1968; *Life lines*, Westminster Films, Aug. 1969. *Short piece for workshop performance*, performed at Stratford, Ont., Festival, Aug. 1967, commissioned by R. Pannell. *Aurora borealis*, jazz ballet, 1967, performed on CBC TV centennial show series "One hundred years young," 1 Jan. 1967, recorded on *In Canada* with Duke Ellington on Decca 75069, 1968, commissioned by CBC. *The carnival*, for orchestra, narrator, and trumpet soloist, first performed at Detroit-Windsor International Freedom Festival, Ford Auditorium, Detroit, Mich., 2 July 1969, CBC radio series "Tuesday night," 8 July 1969, commissioned by CBC.

WORK IN PROGRESS: "Lyric for trumpet," suite for trumpet soloist and concert band.

COLMAN, George, the younger, pseud.
see GLASSCO, John

COLOMBO, John Robert* 1936–
(Ruta Ginsbert, pseud.)
Poet; b. 24 Mar. 1936 in Kitchener, Ont.; m.; children: two.

EDUCATION
University College, University of Toronto, graduate.

HOME
60 Ellis Park Rd., Toronto 3, Ont.

CAREER
Ryerson Press, editorial consultant 1960-64; *Tamarack review*, editorial board member 1960-68, managing editor 1966–; McClelland and Stewart, Toronto, editor-at-large and senior editor 1965–; Atkinson College, York University, tutor 1966-67.

AWARDS, HONOURS
Commonwealth Arts Festival in Wales, delegate, 1965.

MEMBER
Arts and Letters Club; Celebrity Club.

WRITINGS
Fragments, p.p., 1957; *This citadel in time*, Hawkshead, 1958; *This studied self*, Hawkshead, 1958; *Two poems*, Hawkshead, 1958; *Variations*, Hawkshead, 1958; *Fire escapes*, Hawkshead, 1959; *The impression of beauty*, Hawkshead, 1959; *In the streets*, Hawkshead, 1959? ; *Poems and other poems*, Hawkshead, 1959; *Poems to be sold for bread*, Hawkshead, 1959; *This is the work entitled Canada* (poems), Purple Partridge, 1959; *Three poems in two colours*, Hawkshead, 1959; *Towards a definition of love*, Hawkshead, 1959; *Lines for the last day*, Hawkshead, 1960; *Millenium*, Hawkshead, 1960; *The Great Wall of China: an entertainment* (poems and prose), Delta,

1966; *Miraculous montages*, H. Heine, 1966; *The Mackenzie poems*, Swan, 1966 (also published under title *William Lyon Mackenzie rides again!*, Guild of Hand-printers, 1967); *Abracadabra*, McClelland & Stewart, 1967.

EDITED: *Chiaroscuro*, Purple Partridge, 1957; *Rubato*, Purple Partridge, 1958; *The Varsity chapbook*, Ryerson, 1959; (with J. Godbout) *Poésie/Poetry 64*, Ryerson, 1964; (with R. Souster) *Shapes and sounds: poems of W.W.E. Ross*, Longmans, 1968.

CONTRIBUTED: Poems and articles to *Alphabet, Atlantic monthly, Canadian art, Canadian author and bookman, Canadian forum, Canadian literature, Canadian poetry, Continuous learning, Dalhousie review, Delta, Fiddlehead, Graphics, Liberté, Queen's quarterly, Saturday night, Tamarack review, Waterloo review.*

COLSON-HAIG, S., pseud.
see GLASSCO, John

COMFORT, Charles Fraser*   1900–
Artist; b. 22 July 1900 in Edinburgh, Scotland; son of Charles and Jean (Annan) Comfort; came to Canada in 1912; m. Louise Chase 1924; children: Ruth b. 1927, Anne b. 1931.

EDUCATION
Studied under Alexander Musgrove (*q.v.*), Winnipeg School of Art, Man. 1916-22; Robert Henri and Euphrasius Allen Tucker, Art Students League, New York, NY, 1921-22; William S. Heckscher, Kunsthistorich Instituut te Utrecht, The Netherlands, 1955-56.

RELIGION
Presbyterian.

HOME
28 Boul Alexandre Taché, Hull, PQ.

CAREER
Commercial designer, Toronto, Ont., 1925-38; Ontario College of Art, Toronto, department of mural painting, director 1935-38; University of Toronto, department of fine art, lecturer 1938-40, assistant professor 1940-46, department of art and archaeology, associate professor 1946-60; Senior combat war artist, historical section GS (discharged with rank of major) 1943-46; National Gallery of Canada, Ottawa, Ont., director 1960-65; resumed professional career as artist on retirement from National Gallery of Canada, 1965.

COMMISSIONS
Mural, North American Life Building, Toronto, 1932; mural, Toronto Stock Exchange, 1937; mural, Canada Life Building, Exposition Internationale, Paris, France, 1937; mural, Hotel Vancouver, BC, 1938; stone frieze, exterior Toronto Stock Exchange, 1937; stone rondels, Dorchester Street Station, Montreal, PQ, 1941; stone interior, Dorchester Street Station, Montreal, 1942; mural, Toronto-Dominion Bank, Vancouver, 1951; mural, Veterans Affairs Building, Ottawa, 1955; mural, Neurological Division, Toronto General Hospital, 1957; mural, National Library & Archives Building, Ottawa, 1967; mural, Academy of Medicine, Toronto, 1968; numerous portrait commissions.

MEMBER
Arts and Letters Club, Toronto (1920); Canadian Art Directors Museum Organization (honorary member); Art Directors of Canada (honorary member); Canadian Society of Education through Art (honorary member); Canadian Society of Graphic Art (secretary, 1925); Ontario Society of Artists (elected, 1928); Canadian Society of Painters in Water Colour (charter member; vice-president, 1930-31); Canadian Group of Painters (founder member, 1933; secretary, 1937-39; president, 1950); Royal Canadian Academy (Associate 1936; Academician 1942; president, 1957-60); Federation of Canadian Artists (elected, 1942); Fellow of the Royal Society of Arts, London, England (elected, 1957); Arts Club, Montreal (honorary member); Hart House, University of Toronto (honorary member); Manitoba Society of Artists (honorary member).

AWARDS, HONOURS
First prize, exhibition of drawings, YMCA, Winnipeg, Man. 1914; art award, T. Eaton Co. 1919 and 1921; honourable mention, Willingdon Art Competition, 1927; first award, Great Lakes Exhibition, Buffalo, NY, 1938; first award, Ontario Society of Artists, 1951; Royal Society fellowship, 1955-56; LLD from Mount Allison University, 1958; Medaglio al Merito Culturale, Italian Government, 1963; gold medal for painting and allied arts, University of Alberta, 1963.

EXHIBITIONS
ONE-MAN: Winnipeg Art Gallery, 1920; Richardson Gallery, Winnipeg, 1923; Art Gallery of Ontario, Toronto, 1933; Hart House, University of Toronto, 1936; Arts and Letters Club, 1946; Victoria College, University of Toronto, 1949; Robertson Galleries, Ottawa, 1967.

GROUP: Represented in group exhibitions held in Canada since 1924 including annual exhibitions of Canadian Society of Graphic Art, Canadian National Exhibition, Ontario Society of Artists, Canadian Society of Painters in Water Colour, Royal Canadian Academy, Group of Seven, Canadian Group of Painters; represented in exhibitions organized by National Gallery of Canada since 1927; American Federation of Arts, 1930-31; Contemporary Painting, circulated in Southern Dominions of British Empire, 1936; Great Lakes Exhibition, Albright Art Gallery, Buffalo, NY, 1938-39; World's Fair, New York, 1939; Century of Canadian Art, Tate Gallery,

London, 1938; Water Colours by Canadian Artists, Gloucester, England, 1939; Aspects of Contemporary Painting in Canada, Addison Gallery, Andover, Mass., 1942-43; Canadian Art 1760-1943, Yale University Art Gallery 1944; National Gallery, Edinburgh, Scotland, 1946; Stedelijk Museum, Amsterdam, The Netherlands, 1946; UNESCO, 1946; *Exposition internationale d'art moderne, peinture graphique et décoratif, architecture,* Musée d'Art Moderne, Paris, France, 1946; Forty Years of Canadian Painting, Museum of Fine Art, Boston, Mass., 1949; Canadian Painting, National Gallery of Art, Washington, DC, 1950; Coronation, 1953, National Gallery of Canada.

COLLECTIONS IN WHICH REPRESENTED
National Gallery of Canada; Art Gallery of Ontario, Toronto; Art Gallery of Hamilton, Ont.; London Public Library and Art Museum, Ont.; Winnipeg Art Gallery; Hart House, University of Toronto; Owens Gallery, Mount Allison University; Agnes Etherington Art Centre, Queen's University.

WRITINGS
Canadian painting, Massey Report, 1951; *Artist at war,* Ryerson, 1956; contributed to *Canadian art, University of Toronto quarterly, Journal of the Royal Architectural Institute of Canada, American artist.*

CONSTANTINEAU, Gilles 1933—
Poet; b. 1933.

HOME
880 Rockland Ave., Montreal 8, PQ.

CAREER
Magazine Maclean, member of editorial board.

AWARDS, HONOURS
Prix du concours from Union Canadienne des Journalistes de Langue Française, 1963/64.

WRITINGS
La pêche très verte, 1954; *Simples poèmes et ballades,* Hexagone, 1960.
CONTRIBUTED: Poems and articles to *Liberté, Magazine Maclean, Le Devoir.*

CONSTANTIN-WEYER, Maurice 1881-1964
Author; b. 1881 in France; came to North America 1902; d. 1964.

CAREER
Cowboy, trapper, lumberman in USA and Canada; farmer in Manitoba; served in World War I.

AWARDS, HONOURS
Prix Goncourt for *Un Homme se penche sur son passé,* 1928.

WRITINGS
Vers l'ouest (novel), Renaissance du Livre, 1921 (translated into English); *La Bourrasque* (novel), Rieder, 1925 (translated into English); *Cavelier de La Salle* (novel), Rieder, 1927; *Cinq éclats de silex* (stories), Rieder, 1927; *Un Homme se penche sur son passé* (novel), Rieder, 1928 (translated into English); *Manitoba* (essays), Rieder, 1928; *Morvan* (non-fiction), Rieder, 1929; *Clairière, récits du Canada,* Stock, 1929; *P.C. de compagnie* (non-fiction), Rieder, 1930; *Napoléon* (fiction), Rieder, 1931; *Une Corde sur l'abîme* (novel), Rieder, 1933; *Un Sourire dans la tempête* (novel), Rieder, 1934; *La Demoiselle de la mort* (novel), Champs Elysées, 1936; *Telle qu'elle était en son vivant* (novel), Champs-Elysées, 1936; *Les tragiques amours de Bianca* (non-fiction), Fayard, 1958.

CONTANT, Alexis 1858-1918
Composer and teacher; b. 12 Nov. 1858 in Montreal, PQ; son of Pierre and Malvina (David) Contant; m. Marie Étudienne Durand 1881; children: seven; d. 28 Nov. 1918 in Montreal.

EDUCATION
Studied with Joseph A. Fowler and Guillaume Couture in Montreal; Calixa Lavallée in Boston, Mass., 1882-91.

CAREER
St. Jean Baptiste church, Montreal, organist for thirty-one years; Collège de l'Assomption, Montréal, professor of music 1880; Mont-Saint-Louis College, teacher; Convent of the Soeurs Jésus-Marie, Hochelaga, PQ, teacher; among his pupils were Wilfrid Pelletier (*q.v.*), J.J. Gagnier (*q.v.*), Rodolphe Mathieu (*q.v.*), and Claude Champagne (*q.v.*).

COMPOSITIONS
La lyre enchantée, piano, Archambault; *Mass no. 1,* soloists, choir, and orchestra, first performed 1897 in Montreal; *Vive Laurier!,* march, piano, 1897, first performed by J.G. Yon; *Angelus,* choir and orchestra, 1898, first performed 1903; *Mass no. 2,* soloists, choir, and orchestra, first performed 1903; *Patrie,* patriotic song, first performed 1903; *Marche du Sacre de Pie X,* orchestra, 1903, first performed 1903; *Missa brevis,* choir and organ, 1903, first performed 1903 at Monument National by a choir under Edmond Hardy; *Tarantelle,* cello and piano, 1903, first performed 1903; *Quatre cantiques de Noël,* vocal, 1904, Beauchemin; *Caïn,* oratorio, 1905, first performed 1905 in Montreal under Joseph-Jean Goulet; *Le Canada,* patriotic song, choir and orchestra, first performed 1906; *Vision de Jeanne d'Arc,* vocal first performed 1906; *Trio,* violin, cello, and piano, 1906, first performed 1907; *Salut au Canada,* vocal, 1907, first performed 1907; *Musique,* vocal, 1908, J. Hamelle, Paris; *Les deux âmes,* symphonic poem, narrator, choir, and orchestra, 1909, first performed 1913 in Montreal; *Seul sur la route,* baritone and choir, 1911; *Méditation,* cello or violin and piano, 1913, Belgo-Canadienne; *L'Aurore,* orchestra, first per-

formed 1913; *Marche héroïque*, orchestra, 1914, Archambault; *Domine Jesu Christe*, male quartet, first performed 1918; *Fête du Christe-Roi à Ville Marie*, choir and organ, Passe-Temps; *Variations on "God save the king,"* piano; *Variations on "Un Canadien errant,"* piano; *Ballade*, piano; *Yvonne*, piano, Archambault; *Alice*, piano, Archambault; *Romance sans paroles*, cello and piano, Belgo-Canadienne; *La charmeuse*, violin or cello and piano, Archambault; *Vision*, vocal; *Désespérance*, vocal, first performed 1922; *Six mélodies*, vocal, Archambault; *Cinq cantiques religieux,* vocal, Archambault; *Veronica*, overture to unfinished opera, 1918.

CONTE, Michel* 1932–
Choreographer, dancer, and composer; b. 17 July 1932 in Villeneuve-sur-Lot, France; came to Canada in 1955.
EDUCATION
Paris Conservatory, BA; studied ballet with Alexandre Volinine, Paris, France, 1950.
HOME
Apt. 1, 947 rue Cherrier, Montréal 132, PQ.
OFFICE
c/o #223, 5871 Ave. Victoria, Montréal 26, PQ.
CAREER
Strasbourg Opera Ballet, France, corps de ballet 1951; Vichy Opera Ballet, France, corps de ballet 1951; Les Ballets Parisiens, France, corps de ballet 1952; CBC, Montreal, choreographer and director.
MEMBER
Union des Artistes de Montréal.
AWARDS, HONOURS
Paris Conservatory first prize in harmony and composition and second prize in piano; Canada Council senior arts fellowship, 1964/65.
THEATRE
Choreographed and composed *Un et un font deux* (Montréal Théâtre Ballet, Mar. 1957); choreographed *Variations on a lonely theme* (Royal Winnipeg Ballet, Playhouse, Winnipeg, Man., 18 Mar. 1960).
TELEVISION
Choreographed many CBC productions, e.g. *Manon* (Massenet, "Heure du concert," 11 Feb. 1960), *Variations on a lonely theme* (Royal Winnipeg Ballet, 14 Aug. 1961), *Un et un font deux* (Royal Winnipeg Ballet, 26 Aug. 1962), *The season of love* ("Festival," 26 May 1965).
COMPOSITIONS
Monica La Mitraille (musical, Place des Arts, Montréal, 2 July 1968).
WORK IN PROGRESS: "Le survenant" (musical).

CORMACK, Barbara Villy* 1903–
Author; b. 25 Jan. 1903 in Manchester, England; daughter of Ernest and Edith Anna (Lloyd) Villy; came to Canada in 1914 and settled in Calgary, Alta.; m. Eric Wyld Cormack 20 Aug. 1925; children: Douglas Villy b. 1926, David b. 1928, Ernest Eric b. 1943.
EDUCATION
Attended Manchester High School for Girls; Hillhurst, Connaught schools and Crescent Heights High School, Calgary; University of Alberta, BA, 1924.
HOME
RR1, Ardrossan, Alta.
CAREER
Taught in rural schools, Alta. 1920-24; schools for retarded children, Edmonton, Alta. 1953-67.
MEMBER
Canadian Authors Association, Edmonton branch (past president); Canadian Women's Press Club, Edmonton branch.
AWARDS, HONOURS
IODE special awards for *Local rag*, 1951 and for unpublished juvenile novel *When I grow up*, 1953.
WRITINGS
Seed time and harvest (poems), Ryerson, 1942; *Ruth, a tale of new beginnings* (poems), the author, 1948; *Local rag* (novel), Ryerson, 1951; *The house* (novel), Ryerson, 1955; *Red Cross lady* (biography), Institute of Applied Art, 1960; *Happy music to you*, Institute of Applied Art, 1963; *Westward ho! 1903* (juvenile novel), Burns & McEachern, 1967; *Landmarks, a history of the Girl Guides of Alberta*, 1968; TVscripts for the Alberta Department of Education.
CONTRIBUTED: Poems and articles to *Country guide, Canadian banker, Canadian author and bookman.*
WORK IN PROGRESS: "Perennials and politics," biography of Hon. Irene Parlby, LLD.

COSGROVE, Stanley 1911–
(Stanley Morel Cosgrove)
Artist; b. 23 Dec. 1911 in Montreal.
EDUCATION
Studied under Charles Maillard, Henri Charpentier, Maurice Felix and Joseph St. Charles (*q.v.*), École des Beaux-Arts, Montréal, 1930-37; Edwin Holgate, Art Association of Montreal, 1938; Roderigue Lozano, École des Beaux-Arts, Mexico, 1939-44; studied with José Clemente Orozco, Mexico for eight months, 1942/43.
OFFICE
École des Beaux-Arts, 125 Sherbrooke St. W., Montréal, PQ.
CAREER
Painted around the Gaspé Coast 1938-39; assisted Edwin Holgate with mural decorations for Canadian pavilion at the World's Fair, New York, NY, 1939; École des Beaux-Arts, Montréal, teacher 1943-53, 1954–; travelled to France 1953; painted in Mexico 1954.

MEMBER
Royal Canadian Academy (Associate 1951); Canadian Group of Painters.

AWARDS, HONOURS
Quebec provincial scholarship to study in France (used for extended study in Mexico), 1939-44; Canadian government fellowship to study in France, 1953; medal, École des Beaux-Arts de Montréal.

EXHIBITIONS
ONE-MAN: Mexico, 1943; Art Association of Montreal, 1944; Dominion Gallery, Montreal, 1949; Montreal Museum of Fine Arts, 1961.
GROUP: Represented in group exhibitions held in Canada including exhibitions of Montreal Museum of Fine Arts Spring Show; represented in group exhibitions organized by National Gallery of Canada, Ottawa, Ont., including the first and second Biennial of Canadian Painting, 1955 and 1957; Canadian Art 1760-1943, Yale University Art Gallery, 1944; Rio de Janeiro, Brazil, 1946; Exhibition of International Modern Art, Musée d'Art Moderne, Paris, France, originated by UNESCO, 1946; Canadian Club, New York, 1948; Forty Years of Canadian Painting, Museum of Fine Arts, Boston, Mass., 1949; Painters of Canada ... 1668-1948, Virginia Museum of Fine Arts, Richmond, 1949; Canadian Painting, National Gallery of Art, Washington, DC, (later shown in San Francisco, Calif.), 1950; São Paulo Bienal, Brazil, 1951; An Exhibition of Canadian Paintings held at Fortnum and Mason Ltd., London, England, 1955; International Festival of Art, New York, 1958; Mexico, 1960.

COLLECTIONS IN WHICH REPRESENTED
National Gallery of Canada; Vancouver Art Gallery, BC; Museum of Modern Art, New York; Winnipeg Art Gallery, Man.

COSTAIN, Thomas Bertram 1885-1965
Novelist; b. 8 May 1885 in Brantford, Ont.; son of John Herbert and Mary (Schultz) Costain; m. Ida Randolph Spragge 1910; children: Molly, Dora; d. 8 Oct. 1965 in New York, NY.

EDUCATION
Attended public schools in Brantford.

RELIGION
Episcopal.

CAREER
Courier, Brantford, reporter 1902; Mercury, Guelph, Ont., reporter 1908-10; Maclean Publishing Company, editor of trade journals 1910-15; Maclean's, editor 1915-20; Saturday evening post, assistant editor, senior associate editor 1920-34; 20th Century Fox Film Corporation, story editor 1934-36; American cavalcade, editor 1937; Doubleday and Company, advisory editor 1939-46; purely literary 1946-65.

AWARDS, HONOURS
D Litt from University of Western Ontario, 1952; Canadian Club of New York gold medallion, 1965.

WRITINGS
(with H.S. Eayrs) Amateur diplomat, Hodder & Stoughton, 1917; For my great folly, Putnam, 1942 (Book League of America selection); Ride with me, Doubleday, 1944 (Sear's People's Book Club selection); The black rose, Doubleday, 1945 (Literary Guild selection); The moneyman, Doubleday, 1947 (Book of the Month alternate selection); (with R. MacVeagh) Joshua (biography), Doubleday, 1948; The pageant of England (non-fiction): v.1 The conquerors, v.2 The magnificent century, v.3 The three Edwards, v.4 The last Plantagenets, Doubleday, 1949-62; High towers, Doubleday, 1949 (Dollar Book Club selection); Son of a hundred kings, Doubleday, 1950 (Literary Guild and People's Book Club selection); The silver chalice, Doubleday, 1952 (Literary Guild, People's, Dollar, and Family Book Clubs selection); The white and the gold, Doubleday 1954 (Canadian history series, v.1); The Mississippi bubble (non-fiction), Random House, 1955; The tontin, Doubleday, 1955; Below the salt, Doubleday, 1957; The darkness and the dawn, Doubleday, 1959; William the Conqueror (juvenile), Random House, 1959 (published in England under title All about William the Conqueror, Allen, 1961); The chord of steel, the story of the invention of the telephone, Doubleday, 1960; The last love (non-fiction), Doubleday, 1963. Works have been extensively translated.

EDITED: Canadian history series, Doubleday, 1954-61; (with J. Beecroft) Stories to remember, Doubleday, 1956; (with J. Beecroft) More stories to remember, Doubleday, 1958; Twelve short novels, Doubleday, 1961; (with J. Beecroft) 30 stories to remember, Doubleday, 1962; Read with me, Doubleday, 1965.

CONTRIBUTED: Articles and short stories to many magazines, e.g. American magazine, Ellery Queen's mystery magazine, McCall's, Saturday evening post, Maclean's.

COX, Elford Bradley* 1914–
Sculptor; b. 16 July 1914 in Botha, Alta.; son of John and Eva (Tabb) Cox; m. Elizabeth Campbell 18 Nov. 1949; children: Alice Margaret b. 25 June 1950, Kathleen Mary b. 27 July 1951.

EDUCATION
Attended Bowmanville public and Bowmanville high school, Ont.; University of Toronto, BA, 1938; mainly self-taught.

HOME
520 Finch Ave. E., Willowdale, Ont.

CAREER
Ontario Summer School for Arts and Crafts,

teacher 1946-52; with Canadian Intelligence Corps overseas for three years; full-time sculptor since 1952.

COMMISSIONS
(partial list) sculpture, University of Toronto, 1955; sculpture, McMaster University, 1957; sculpture, York University, 1960; School for Deaf in Milton, Ont.

MEMBER
Sculptors' Society of Canada (elected, 1950; vice-president, 1950-52; Ontario representative, 1952-56); Ontario Society of Artists (elected, 1950); Royal Canadian Academy (Associate 1955).

EXHIBITIONS
ONE-MAN: Montreal, PQ, Toronto, Ont., Kitchener, Ont., Windsor, Ont., Quebec, PQ, Stratford, Ont.
GROUP: Represented in group exhibitions held in Canada since 1946 including annual exhibitions of Art Association of Montreal, Sculptors' Society of Canada, Ontario Society of Artists, Royal Canadian Academy.

COLLECTIONS IN WHICH REPRESENTED
Art Gallery of Ontario, Toronto; Vancouver Art Gallery, BC; London Public Library and Art Museum, Ont.

CRAWLEY, Judith* 1914–
(Judith Rosemary Sparks)
Film editor and writer; b. 21 Apr. 1914 in Ottawa, Ont.; daughter of Roderick Percy and Rheba (Fraser) Sparks; m. Frank Radford Crawley 1 Oct. 1938 (marriage dissolved); children: Michael b. 3 July 1940, Patrick b. 1 Aug. 1943, Roderick b. 10 June 1946, Alexander b. 7 Dec. 1947, Jennifer b. 11 July 1951.

EDUCATION
Attended primary schools in Ottawa; Ottawa Ladies' College; McGill University, 1933-36.

RELIGION
Presbyterian.

HOME AND OFFICE
Meach Lake Road, Old Chelsea, PQ.

CAREER
Crawley Films, Ottawa, co-founder 1938, sound recordist and camera woman 1938-43, writer, editor, director, and producer 1938-67; National Film Board of Canada, Montreal, PQ, camera woman and freelance 1941-43; freelance writer 1968–.

AWARDS, HONOURS
Frank Radford Crawley-Judith Crawley special award, Canadian Film Awards, Toronto, Ont., 1957.

FILMS
Wrote and edited L'Ile d'Orléans (Crawley Films, 1938; Hiram Percy Maxim award, best amateur film in the world, 1939); photographed and edited Study of spring wild flowers (Crawley Films, c.1938); wrote and edited Ottawa on the river (National Film Board, c.1939), History of Canadian power (Crawley Films sponsored by the Canadian Geographical Society, c.1940); wrote and directed Who sheds his blood? (Crawley Films sponsored by the Canadian Red Cross, c.1941); wrote, edited and co-photographed Birds of Canada [no. 1] (Crawley Films, c.1943); edited Canadian landscape (National Film Board, c.1945); photographed and edited West wind (National Film Board, c.1946); wrote, directed, and edited Know your baby (Crawley Films, 1947), Why won't Tommy eat? (Crawley Films sponsored by the Department of Health and Welfare, 1948; second prize for nutrition films, US State Health Department, 1950); directed and edited He acts his age (Crawley Films sponsored by the Department of National Health and Welfare, 1948; first prize, sociological class, International Documentary Film Festival, Yorkton, Sask., 1950; award of merit, Scholastic Teachers' Annual Film and Filmstrip Awards, New York, NY, 1951); wrote, directed, and edited Creative hands series (International Film Bureau, Chicago, Ill., 1948); wrote and edited The loon's necklace (Crawley Films sponsored by Imperial Oil Ltd., 1948; Canadian film of the year, Canadian Film Awards, Toronto, 1949; certificate of participation, International Film Festival, Edinburgh, Scotland, 1949; silver medal [first prize], International Film Festival, Venice, Italy, 1949; Ente del Gera cup [first prize], colour films category, International Cinema Festival, Gardone, Italy, 1949; first prize for art and music films, Cleveland Film Festival, Ohio, 1949; award for best short film exhibited in Canada, New Liberty Magazine Awards, 1950; award for best experimental film, International Congress of Art Films, Brussels, Belgium, 1950; award of merit as one of the ten best educational films of the year, Scholastic Teachers' Annual National Film and Filmstrip Awards, New York, 1950; award for best North American film, First International Art Films Festival, Woodstock, NY, 1951; certificate of participation, International Film Festival, Salzburg, Austria, 1951; award for standards of excellence best demonstrating intelligent audio-visual communication, Illinois Institute of Technology, USA, 1952; certificate of participation, International Exhibition of Short Films sponsored by Ministry of Education, Buenos Aires, Argentina, 1958; diploma of honour, Eleventh International Film Festival, Locarno, Switzerland, 1958; award as one of the best Canadian films in the last fifteen years, Canadian Library Association, 1950; first award for entertainment films, International Film Festival, Victoria, BC, 1962); directed Terrible twos and trusting threes (Crawley Films sponsored by the Department of National Health and Welfare,

1950; award, Scholastic Teachers' Annual National Film and Filmstrip Awards, New York, 1951); wrote and directed *Child development* series (McGraw-Hill Text Films, New York, 1950; honourable mention, Canadian Film Awards, Toronto, 1951; award of merit for one of the ten best educational films of the year, Scholastic Teachers' Annual National Film and Filmstrip Awards, New York, 1951); directed *Frustrating fours and fascinating fives* (Crawley Films sponsored by the Department of National Health and Welfare, 1953; award of merit for one of the ten best educational films of the year, Scholastic Teachers' Annual National Film and Filmstrip Awards, New York, 1953; honourable mention, International Festival of Children's Films, Buenos Aires, 1962; award of merit, Boston Film Festival, Mass., 1953; Golden Reel award, [first prize], home and family category, American Film Assembly, Chicago, 1954; award of merit, Stamford, Conn. Film Festival, USA, 1954); wrote and directed *Food for Freddy* (Crawley Films sponsored by the Department of National Health and Welfare, 1953; special award, Canadian Film Awards, Toronto, 1954; award of merit, sociological class, International Documentary Film Festival, Yorkton, 1954); directed and edited *From sociable six to noisy nine* (Crawley Films sponsored by the Department of National Health and Welfare, 1954; award for one of the ten best educational films of the year, Scholastic Teachers' Annual National Film and Filmstrip Awards, New York, 1955); wrote and edited *Destination UK* (Crawley Films sponsored by Trans Canada Air Lines, 1955); produced *From ten to twelve* (Crawley Films, 1957; silver reel award [second prize], American Film Assembly, New York; award of merit, Canadian Film Awards, Toronto, 1958; award for one of the best Canadian films of the last fifteen years, Canadian Library Association, 1960); wrote and produced *Legend of the raven* (Crawley Films sponsored by Imperial Oil, 1957; award of merit, art and experimental films category, Canadian Film Awards, Toronto, 1958; certificate of participation, International Film Festival, Stratford, Ont., 1958; certificate of participation, International Documentary Film Festival, Yorkton, 1958; certificate of participation, International Film Festival, Vancouver, BC, 1958; certificate of participation, Brussels World Fair, Belgium, 1958; blue ribbon award [first prize], films for children category, American Film Assembly, New York, 1959), *Beaver dam* (National Film Board, 1957; award, International Film Festival, Venice, Italy, 1958; blue ribbon award [first prize], films for children category, American Film Assembly, New York, 1962; award, Fourth International Children's Film Festival, Necochea, Argentina, 1965); *St. Law-*

rence north series (CBC, 1960); wrote and directed *Top of a continent* (Crawley Films sponsored by Shell Oil Co., 1961; Ministry of Works cup, International Documentary Review, Milan, Italy, 1966); wrote and produced *Quality of a nation* (Crawley Films sponsored by the E.B. Eddy Company for Canadian Centennial Council, 1962); *The wonder of photography* (Crawley Films for the Kodak Pavilion feature at Expo 67, Montreal, 1966).

WORK IN PROGRESS: Film on the National Library for the National Film Board.

WRITINGS

Safeguarding the mental health of children (screenplay; Crawley Films *c.* 1942); *Adolescent development* series (screenplays; Crawley Films sponsored by McGraw-Hill Text Films, New York, 1953; award of merit for one of the ten best educational films of the year, Scholastic Teachers' Annual National Film and Filmstrip Awards, New York, 1954; award of merit, Stamford, Film Festival, 1954; award of merit, Boston Film Festival, 1954; award of merit, International Documentary Film Festival, Yorkton, 1954); *Dangerous journey* (screenplay; Crawley Films sponsored by the All Island Banana Growers Association, Jamaica, 1956); *Sibling relations and personality* (screenplay; McGraw-Hill Text Films, New York, 1956; honourable mention, Canadian Film Awards, Toronto, 1956; award of merit, International Documentary Film Festival, Yorkton, 1956; award of merit, Bluenose Film Festival, 1957); *Skywatch on 55* (screenplay; Crawley Films sponsored by the Bell Telephone of Canada, 1957; award, Vancouver Film Festival, 1958); *Winter crossing at l'Ile aux Coudres* (TV play; CBC, 1958; award, TV films category, Canadian Film Awards, Toronto, 1959); *Craftsmen of Canada* (screenplay; Crawley Films sponsored by the BA Oil Co. Ltd., 1958; award for one of the best Canadian films of the last fifteen years, Canadian Library Association, 1960); *Safe bicycling* (screenplay; Crawley Films sponsored by the Raleigh Bicycle Co., 1959; award for one of the ten best films of the year, Scholastic Teachers' Annual National Film and Filmstrip Awards, New York, 1960); *The new baby* (screenplay; Crawley Films sponsored by the Department of National Health and Welfare, 1961; Chris award certificate, Columbus Film Festival, Ohio, 1963); *Saguenay* (screenplay; Crawley Films sponsored by the Aluminum Company of Canada, 1962; diploma, International Film Festival, Vancouver, 1962; diploma, International Film Festival, Edinburgh, 1962; diploma, Venice Film Festival, 1962; diploma, Cannes Film Festival, France, 1962; diploma, Canadian Film Awards, Toronto, 1963; diploma, Film Festival, Sydney, Australia, 1963; diploma, Melbourne Film Festival, Australia, 1963;

diploma, Commonwealth Festival of the Arts, London, England and Cardiff, Wales, 1965); *Brampton builds a car* (screenplay; Crawley Films sponsored by American Motors Ltd., 1963; public relations award and award for best colour cinematography, Canadian Film Awards, Toronto, 1964; diploma, International Film Festival, San Francisco, Calif., 1964); *Growing up safely* (screenplay; Crawley Films sponsored by the Department of National Health and Welfare, 1965; award, Third International Festival of Scientific Documentary Films dealing with Medicine and Public Health, 1966; top honours, home safety films category, National Committee on Films for Safety, National Safety Council, Chicago, 1967); *The perpetual harvest* (screenplay; Crawley Films sponsored by the MacMillan Bloedel Company Ltd., 1966; gold medal, International Film Festival, New York, 1966; first award, sales and promotion films category, Canadian Film Awards, Toronto, 1967); *Global village* (screenplay; Crawley Films sponsored by the Volkswagon Canada Ltd., c.1966; public relations award, Canadian Film Awards, Toronto, 1967); *Go find a country* (screenplay; Crawley Films sponsored by the BA Oil Co. Ltd., 1966); *Menu* (screenplay; Crawley Films sponsored by the Department of National Health and Welfare, 1966); *Motion* (screenplay; Crawley Films for CN Pavilion feature at Expo 67, Montreal, c.1966; silver medal, public relations films category, International Film and TV Festival, New York, 1967); *New dimensions* (screenplay; Crawley Films sponsored by Acres Ltd., 1968).

CREIGHTON, Luella Sanders Bruce*   1901–
Novelist; b. 25 Aug. 1901 in Stouffville, Ont.; daughter of James Walter and Luella (Sanders) Bruce; m. Donald Grant Creighton 23 June 1926; children: Philip b. 18 May 1929, Cynthia b. 17 Sept. 1940.
EDUCATION
University of Toronto, BA, 1926; La Sorbonne.
HOME
15 Princess St., Brooklin, Ont.
CAREER
Taught in an Ontario rural school 1920-21; real estate saleswoman in Toronto, Ont. 1933-37.
AWARDS, HONOURS
Canadian forum fiction prize; O'Brien Honour Roll citation for outstanding short stories.
WRITINGS
High bright buggy wheels, McClelland & Stewart, 1951 (adapted and produced "Stage," CBC radio, 17 Feb. 1952); *Turn east, turn west,* McClelland & Stewart, 1954; *Canada: the struggle for Empire* (non-fiction), Dent, 1960; *Canada: trial and triumph* (non-fiction), Dent, 1963; *Tecumseh, the story of the Shawnee chief* (juvenile biography),

Macmillan, 1965; *Miss Multipenny and Miss Crumb* (juvenile), Peal, 1966; *The elegant Canadians* (non-fiction), McClelland & Stewart, 1967.

CSELENYI, Jozsef*   1928–
Designer; b. 10 Mar. 1928 in Budapest, Hungary; son of Jozsef and Friderika (Dresszmann) Cselenyi; m. Judith Mezo 15 July 1948; children: Joseph b. 13 July 1957; came to Canada in 1967.
EDUCATION
Attended Corvin Matyas Gimnazium, Matyasfold, Hungary, 1938-46; Budapest Academy of Applied Arts, diploma 1955.
RELIGION
Protestant.
HOME
267 St. George St., Apt. 502, Toronto 5, Ont.
CAREER
Kaltona J. Theatre, Kecskemet, Hungary, designer and technical director 1956-58; National Theatre, Szeged, Hungary, designer 1958-60; Gaiety Theatre, Budapest, resident designer 1960-67; Deryne Theatre, Budapest, resident designer 1960-67; Teatr Ziemi Mazowiectiej, Warsaw, Poland, guest designer 1961, 1965; Bratislava National Theatre, guest designer 1964; Interscena Conference, Prague, Czecho-Slovakia, member 1966; National Theatre, Belgrade, Yugoslavia, guest designer 1966; Wagner Festival, Bayreuth, Germany, master class 1967.
MEMBER
Canadian Theatre Centre; International Theatre Institute; ANTA.
AWARDS, HONOURS
British Council grant for studies in London, England, 1963; Jaszay State Prize for designs for *Romeo and Juliet*, 1964.
THEATRE
Designed sets for many productions, e.g. *The chemmy circle* (Shaw Festival, Niagara-on-the-Lake, Ont., 8 Aug. 1968).

CULLEN, Maurice Galbraith   1866-1934
Artist; b. 6 June 1866 in St. John's, Nfld.; son of James and Sarah (Ward) Cullen; m. Barbara (Merchant) Pilot 1910; stepchildren: Robert W. Pilot b. 9 Oct. 1898, John Pilot, and three other children; d. 28 Mar. 1934 in Chambly, PQ.
EDUCATION
Attended public schools in Montreal, PQ; studied sculpture under Louis Philippe Hébert, Monument National, Montréal, 1880s; studied sculpture, then painting in Paris, France, 1888; studied painting under Elie Delaunay and Alfred Roll, École des Beaux-Arts, Paris, 1889-92.
CAREER
Galt Brothers, Montreal, apprentice, 1881; aided Louis Philippe Hébert with the façade of St. James Cathedral, Montreal; travelled to Paris,

1889, remained in Europe till 1895; Art Association of Montreal, instructor, 1895–; travelled in Europe and North Africa, 1900-1902; returned to Canada; served overseas as an official war artist in the First World War.

MEMBER
Société National des Beaux-Arts (associate, 1895); Royal Canadian Academy (Associate 1899; Acadamician 1907).

AWARDS, HONOURS
Medal, International Exposition, St. Louis, Mo., 1904; bronze medal, Pan American Exposition, 1901.

EXHIBITIONS
ONE-MAN: Arts Club, Montreal, 1922; École des Beaux-Arts, Montreal, 1931; Hamilton Art Gallery, Ont., 1956; National Gallery of Canada, Ottawa, Ont., 1956; Montreal Museum of Fine Arts, 1956; Art Gallery of Toronto, Ont., 1956. GROUP: Represented in group exhibitions held in Canada since 1894 including annual exhibitions of Royal Canadian Academy, Montreal Museum of Fine Arts Spring Show, Canadian Art Club, Ontario Society of Artists, Canadian National Exhibition; represented in group exhibitions organized by National Gallery of Canada; Paris Salon, 1894, 1895, and 1904; Pan American Exposition, 1901; International Exposition, St. Louis, 1904; Paintings by Canadian Artists, City Art Museum, St. Louis, 1918; A Century of Canadian Art, Tate Gallery, London, England, 1938; Canadian Painting, National Gallery of Art, Washington, DC, 1950; An Exhibition of Canadian Paintings held at Fortnum and Mason Ltd., London, 1955.

COLLECTIONS IN WHICH REPRESENTED
Musée des Beaux-Arts de Pithivers, France; National Gallery of Canada; Watson Art Galleries, Montreal; Hamilton Art Gallery; Continental Galleries of Fine Art, Montreal; Art Gallery of Ontario, Toronto; Montreal Museum of Fine Arts; Musée du Québec, PQ; Agnes Etherington Art Centre, Queen's University.

CUNDARI, Emilia   1933–
(Emilia Cundari Pezzetti)
Singer (soprano); b. 1933 in Detroit, Mich.; daughter of Frank Cundari; m. Sergio Pezzetti 28 Aug. 1965.

EDUCATION
Attended St. Mary's Academy, Windsor; Marygrove College, Detroit, BMus and BA, 1953; studied with Edith Piper, Juilliard School of Music, New York, NY.

HOME
Piazza Vesuvio 23, 1-20144 Milano, Italy; c/o 753 Bruce Ave., Windsor, Ont.

CAREER
New York City Opera, 1953-55; Metropolitan Opera House, New York, 1955-61, Texas tour, 1956, Toronto and Canada tour, 1957; toured extensively in Europe.

AWARDS, HONOURS
Detroit Grinnel award, 1953; runner up in "Singing stars of tomorrow," 1954; Women's Canadian Club, New York, scholarship, 1956.

THEATRE
New York debut (Metropolitan Opera House, 6 Feb. 1956); sang in numerous productions, e.g. Xenia in *Boris Godunov* (understudy, 1956), First genie in *The magic flute* (Metropolitan Opera, 1956), Barbarina in *The marriage of Figaro* (Metropolitan Opera, 1956), Milliner in *Der Rosenkavalier* (Metropolitan Opera, 1956), Micaela in *Carmen* (Metropolitan Opera, 1957), Mimi in *La bohème* (Zürich Opera House, Switzerland, 1964), Norina in *Don Pasquale* (Zürich Opera House, 1964), Recital (Cleary Auditorium, Windsor, 1964; Toronto, 1964), Recital (Florence May Musical Festival, Italy, 1964), Lieder concert (Lyceum de Milano, 1964), Franz Schubert Lieder (Teatro Alla Scala, Milano, 1964), Lieder concert (Mozart Festival, Cologne, Germany, 1964.)

RADIO
Sang in several productions, e.g. *L'inganno felice* (Naples, Italy, 1964), Mozart Festival (Rhine Hall, Düsseldorf, Germany, 1964).

RECORDINGS
Ascanio in Alba, Dischi Angelicum. *Betulia liberata,* Dischi Angelicum. *Symphony no. 2* by G. Mahler, Columbia M2L-256 (ML 5303-5304) 1958; Columbia M2S-501 (MS 6008-6009) 1960. *The nine symphonies* by Beethoven, Columbia D7L 265 (ML 5398, 5320, 5365, 5284, 5404, M2L 264: ML 5421-5422) 1959; Columbia D7S 610 (MS 6078, 6036, 6055, 6012, 6082, M2S-608: MS 6098-6099) 1959. *Nisi Dominus* by Vivaldi, Music Guild M-11, 1961.

CUNNINGHAM, Louis Arthur   1900-54
Novelist; b. 28 Sept. 1900 in Saint John, NB; son of William John and Sarah (McGrath) Cunningham; m. Hortense Marie Mooney 10 July 1929; d. 13 June 1954 in Hammond River, NB.

EDUCATION
Attended St. Malachi's Hall and Saint John High School; University of St. Joseph, Memramcook, NB, BA, 1922, MA, 1923; Catholic University of America, Washington, DC; University of Notre Dame, Ind.

RELIGION
Roman Catholic.

CAREER
University of Notre Dame, teacher of French; mainly literary.

AWARDS, HONOURS
Fellow of Catholic University of America; Fellow of University of Notre Dame.

WRITINGS
Yvon Tremblay, Graphic, 1927; *This thing called love*, Carrier, 1929; *The king's fool,* Graphic, 1931; *Tides of the Tantramar*, Copp Clark, 1935; *Fog over Fundy*, Copp Clark, 1936; *Moon over Acadie*, McLeod, 1937; *Discords of the deep*, Quality, 1938; *Vallery of the stars*, McLeod, 1938; *Of these three loves*, McLeod, 1939; *The sign of the burning ship*, McLeod, 1940; *Marionette*, McLeod, 1941; *The forest gate*, Locker, 1947; *The wandering heart*, Gramercy, 1947; *Evergreen cottage*, Arcadia House, 1949; *Sultry love,* Archer, 1950; *Wherever you are*, Hurst & Blackett, 1950; *Beside the laughing water,* Jenkins, 1953; *In quest of Eden*, Arcadia House, 1953; *Airmail to Eden,* Jenkins, 1954; *Key to romance*, Arcadia House, 1954; *Should thy love die*, Jenkins, 1954; *The lily pool,* Arcadia House, 1955; *Sweet constancy*, Jenkins, 1955; *Meg Shannon*, Arcadia House, 1956; *Stars over Seven Oaks*, Arcadia House, 1957; *You are the dream*, Arcadia House, 1957; *Whisper to the stars*, Arcadia House, 1958; *A sunlit grove*, Arcadia House, 1959.
TRANSLATED: Albert Flament's *Private life of Lady Hamilton*, Carrier, 1929.
CONTRIBUTED: Short stories and articles to *Canadian home journal, National home monthly, Maclean's*, and other British, American and Australian magazines.

DALLAIRE, Jean-Philippe   1916-65
Artist; b. 9 June 1916 in Hull, PQ; m.; d. 27 Nov. 1965 in Vence, France.
EDUCATION
Studied art under Clapin, Hull Technical School; studied painting under Charles Goldhamer and Peter Hawarth (*q.v.*) and sculpture under Elizabeth Wyn Wood, Central Technical School, Toronto, Ont.; studied at the school of Museum of Fine Arts, Boston, Mass., *c.*1938; studied at the École des Beaux-Arts, Montreal, PQ, 1938 and *c.*1945; studied under Maurice Denis, Atelier d'Art Sacré, Paris, France, 1938; under André Lhote, Académie André Lhote, Paris, 1938-40; studied tapestry design with Jean Lurçat, Aubusson, France, 1949.
CAREER
Muralist and student in Dominican Monasteries in Ottawa, Ont., and Fall River, Mass., 1936-38; painted in France on a Quebec Government Fellowship, 1938-40; interned by the Germans in Stalag 220 at St. Denis, France, 1940-44; École des Beaux-Arts, Québec, PQ, teacher 1946-52; National Film Board of Canada, Ottawa and Montreal, illustrator on film of French-Canadian songs and Canadian history for use in schools 1952-57;

painted in Montreal 1957-59; painted in France 1959-65.
COMMISSIONS
Murals, Madame Burger's restaurant, Hull; mural, Chapel of the Dominican Monastery, Ottawa, 1936-38; mural, Dominican Monastery, Fall River, 1936-38; mural for an insurance building, *c.*1950; design for an Aubusson tapestry, *c.*1955.
AWARDS, HONOURS
Province of Quebec Scholarship, 1938-40; third prize for painting, Concours artistiques de la Province de Québec, 1951; Canada Council fellowship, 1959.
EXHIBITIONS
ONE-MAN: Galerie des Beaux-Arts, Paris, 1945; Cercle universitaire, Montréal, 1947; L'Atelier, Québec, 1949; Dominion Gallery, Montreal, 1954 and 1966; Robertson Gallery, Ottawa, 1955; Galerie Dresdnere, Montreal, 1960; Musée du Québec, 1966; Vancouver, BC, 1967.
GROUP: Represented in group exhibitions held in Canada including Spring Exhibitions of Montreal Museum of Fine Arts; represented in group exhibitions organized by National Gallery of Canada, Ottawa; Canadian Painting, National Gallery of Art, Washington, DC, and elsewhere in USA, 1950; Biennial of Sâo Paulo, Brazil, 1953.
COLLECTIONS IN WHICH REPRESENTED
Art Gallery of Ontario, Toronto; Musée d'Art Contemporain, Montréal; Bethzebel Museum, Jerusalem, Israel; Musée du Québec; National Gallery of Canada; Agnes Etherington Art Centre, Queen's University; Ottawa City Museum.

DALMAIN, Jean
Actor and director; m. Monique Leyrac (*q.v.*).
HOME
3570 Ridgewood Ave., Apt. 303, Montreal 247, PQ.
CAREER
Théâtre du Nouveau Monde, Montréal, actor 1951–.
MEMBER
Union des Artistes de Montréal.
THEATRE
Played in numerous productions, e.g. Compagnon in *Philippe et Jonas* (1953/54), Sganarelle in *Don Juan* (Molière, 1953/54), Don Alvaro Dabo in *Le maître de Santiago* (1954/55), *Boulingrin* (Théâtre de la Poudrière, Montréal, 1959), *Le dindon* (Montreal Festival, 1959), *La peur des coups* (Théâtre Anjou, Montréal, 1964), Philippe Strozzi in *Lorenzaccio* (21 Nov. 1965), *Sacrès fantômes* (Les Comédiens de l'Escale, Montréal, 30 Nov. 1967); directed *Maître après Dieu* (1951), *Une nuit d'amour* (1953/54); co-directed *Le mariage forcé, Sganarelle, La jalousie du barbouillé* (Montreal Festival, 1954; Paris, France, Festival, 1955; Stratford, Ont. Festival, 1956); directed *Dialogues des*

Carmélites (Théâtre du Rideau Vert, Montréal, 1959), *Monsieur Masure* (Théâtre de Dix Heures, Montréal, *c.*1959); directed and played Mascarille in *L'Étourdi* (Théâtre du Rideau Vert, 15 Jan. 1966), Monsieur Bécot in *Croque Monsieur* (Théâtre du Rideau Vert, 15 Mar. 1966), *Oscar* (Théâtre Anjou); directed *Georges Dandin* (Nouveau Monde), *Le Médecin malgré lui* (La Nouvelle Compagnie Théâtrale, Montréal, 8 Jan. 1968).

DALMAIN, Monique Tremblay
see LEYRAC, Monique

D'AMOUR, Rolland* 1913—
Actor, singer, and composer; b. 26 July 1913 in Mont-Tremblant, PQ; son of Jean Baptiste and Delvina (Maher) D'Amour; m. Madeleine Brais 1942; children: Pierre b. 1943, Andrée b. 1944, Jean Guy b. 1946, Josée b. 1953, Céline b. 1958.
EDUCATION
Attended Saint-Isidore, Laprairie, PQ; Collège Bourget, Rigaud, PQ; studied phonetics and drama with Mme. Jean Louis Audet; Conservatoire National, Montréal.
RELIGION
Roman Catholic.
HOME
7611 Ave. Louis Hébert, Montréal 329, PQ.
CAREER
Freelance.
MEMBER
CAPAC; L'Union des Artistes Lyriques et Dramatiques; Union des Artistes de Montréal.
AWARDS, HONOURS
Prizes for his songs, e.g. *Nuage dans le bleu, Vent d'automne, La croix de Mont Royal.*
THEATRE
Played in many productions, e.g. l'Ogre in *Le grand poucet* (l'Équipe, Montréal, 1946), *Le héros et le soldat* (l'Équipe, 1946), *Altitude 3200* (l'Équipe), *La cuisine des anges* (Théâtre du Nouveau Monde, Montréal), *Une nuit d'amour* (Théâtre du Nouveau Monde), *Philippe et Jonas* (Théâtre du Nouveau Monde), *Le baladin du monde occidental* (Théâtre du Nouveau Monde), *Bienheureuse Anais* (Théâtres des Marguerites, Trois Rivières, PQ), *Mary, Mary* (Théâtre des Marguerites).
FILM
Played in many productions of National Film Board of Canada, Crawley Films, Robert Lawrence Studios, e.g. *Le père Chopin, La forteresse, Aurore, Le curé de village, La corde au cou, Jobidon, Les brûlés* (1957/58).
RADIO
Played in many productions on CBC and CKAC, Montreal, and CKVL, Verdun, PQ, e.g. *Madeleine et Pierre, Grande soeur, L'ardent voyage, Un*

homme et son péché, Le ciel par-dessus les toits, "Les Plouffes," "Théâtre Ford."
TELEVISION
Played in many CBC and CFTM, Montreal, productions, e.g. "Je vous ai tant aimé," "Cap-aux-sorciers," *Le Pèlerin de Kranine,* "Les Plouffes," "Rue de l'Anse," "Les belles histoires," "Rue de pignons," *The Ernie game* ("Festival," co-production of CBC and NFB, world première, 8 Nov. 1967); played and wrote score for *Lie de vin, Philippe et Jonas.*
COMPOSITIONS
Wrote music for his songs *Nuage dans le bleu, Vent d'automne, La croix de Mont Royal,* and for *Cyclone* (TV play), *Céline* (musical comedy, 31 Dec. 1959); wrote music and lyrics for *Gatineau* (musical comedy, 14 Oct. 1961).
WORK IN PROGRESS: "Chasse-gallerie" (musical comedy).

DANBY, Kenneth Edison* 1940—
Artist; b. 6 Mar. 1940 in Sault Ste. Marie, Ont.; son of Milton Gordon Edison and Gertrude Lillian (Buckley) Danby; m. Judith Ellen Harcourt 20 Mar. 1965; children: Sean Edison b. 15 Dec. 1965.
EDUCATION
Attended Cody public school, Sault Ste. Marie, 1945-52; Sault Ste. Marie Technical and Commercial High School and Sault Ste. Marie Collegiate Institute, 1952-58; studied with J.W.G. Macdonald (*q.v.*), Fred Hagan, and John Alfsen (*q.v.*), Ontario College of Art, Toronto, 1958-60.
HOME
RR4, Guelph, Ont.
OFFICE
c/o Gallery Moos, 138 Yorkville Ave., Toronto, Ont.
CAREER
CJIC TV, Sault Ste. Marie, set designer summer 1960; CFTO TV, Toronto, set painter fall and winter 1960; Bradshaws Packaging Co., Toronto, package designer spring 1961; *Telegram*, Toronto, Promotion Department, graphic designer May 1961-Nov. 1962; freelance designer for TV, etc., e.g. art director for the Mariposa Folk Festival, Nov. 1962-Dec. 1963; illustrated Bank of Montreal's *Canada's first bank, Bank of Montreal history,* v.2, McClelland & Stewart, 1962.
COMMISSIONS
Portrait of Prime Minister Trudeau, *Time* magazine cover, 1968.
AWARDS, HONOURS
Purchase award, Four Seasons Exhibition, Toronto, 1962; Jessie Dow award, Montreal Museum of Fine Arts Spring Show, 1964; award, Hadassah Exhibition, 1965.
EXHIBITIONS
ONE-MAN: Pollock Gallery, Toronto, 1961;

Gallery Moos, 1964, 1965, 1966, and 1967;
Galerie Agnès Lefort, Montreal, PQ, 1966.
GROUP: Represented in group exhibitions held
in Canada including Western Ontario Exhibitions; represented in group exhibitions organized
by National Gallery of Canada, Ottawa, Ont.;
Cardiff Festival, Wales, 1965.

COLLECTIONS IN WHICH REPRESENTED
Vancouver Art Gallery, BC; Canadian Industries
Limited, Montreal; Saskatoon Art Centre, Sask.;
National Gallery of Canada; Montreal Museum of
Fine Arts; Gallery Moos.

DANSEREAU, Fernand*   1928–
Film director; b. 5 Apr. 1928 in Montreal; son of
Adolphe and Eva (Larivée) Dansereau; m. Jeanne
Desrochers 23 June 1951; children: Anne b. 6
Aug. 1952, Hélène b. 23 Oct. 1954, Jean-Pierre
b. 31 Mar. 1956, André b. 23 Feb. 1958,
Bernard b. 7 Nov. 1960, Philippe b. 25 Nov. 1965.
EDUCATION
Attended Collège de Lévis, PQ; Collège Ste. Marie,
Montréal.
RELIGION
None.
HOME
260 Logan St., Lambert, PQ.
OFFICE
National Film Board of Canada, PO Box 6100,
Montreal 3, PQ.
CAREER
Le devoir, Montréal, labour reporter 1950-55;
National Film Board of Canada, Montreal, film
director 1955–; Cooperatio Film Company Inc.,
Montreal, vice-president 1966/67.
MEMBER
Association Professionnelle des Cinéastes (secret-
ary, 1966/67).
AWARDS, HONOURS
Canadian Arts Council scholarship to study film
in Paris, 1960.
FILMS
Directed *La communauté juive de Montréal*
(National Film Board, 1957), *La canne à pêche*
(National Film Board, 1957; award, Monte Carlo,
Monaco, 1960), *Le maître de Pérou* (1958), *Pays
neuf* (National Film Board, 1958), *John Lyman*
(National Film Board, 1959), *Pierre Beaulieu*
(National Film Board, 1959), *Les administrateurs*
(1960); produced *Temps présent* series (National
Film Board, c. 1960; statuette, best documentary
series, Gala des Splendeurs, Montréal, 1960/61);
directed *Congrès* (National Film Board, 1962);
produced *Pour la suite du monde* (National Film
Board, c. 1963; feature prize, Evian, 1964);
directed *Le festin des morts* (1966; feature film
award, Canadian Film Awards, Toronto, Ont.,
1966), *Ca n'est pas le temps des romans* (1967;

award, International Bureau du Court Métrage,
Tours, France, 1967), *St. Jérôme* (1967).
WRITINGS
La communauté chinoise de Montréal (screenplay;
1956); *Alfred J.* (screenplay; National Film
Board, 1956; second prize, Second International
Labour Film Festival, Vienna, Austria, 1957);
Les mains nettes (screenplay; National Film
Board, 1958; Frigon Trophy, Gala des Splendeurs,
Montréal, 1960-61).

DAVEY, Frank*   1940–
(Frankland Wilmot Davey)
Poet; b. 19 Apr. 1940 in Vancouver, BC; son of
Wilmot Elmer and Doris (Brown) Davey; m. Helen
Edith Simmons 27 Dec. 1962.
EDUCATION
Attended Abbotsford Elementary School, BC,
1946-52, Abbotsford Junior High School, 1952-
55, Abbotsford Senior High School, 1955-57;
University of British Columbia, BA, 1961, MA,
1963; University of Southern California, Ph D,
1968.
HOME
Toronto, Ont.
OFFICE
Department of English, York University, Toronto,
Ont.
CAREER
Tish, co-founder 1961, editor 1961-63; University
of British Columbia, teaching assistant in English
1961-63; Royal Roads Military College, lecturer
in English 1963-66, assistant professor 1967–;
The open letter, founder and editor 1965–.
MEMBER
ACUTE; Philological Association of the Pacific
Coast.
AWARDS, HONOURS
British Columbia Electric Company special
scholarship, 1957, 1958, 1959, and 1960; Mac-
millan prize for poetry from University of British
Columbia, 1962; Canada Council pre-doctoral
fellowship, 1965/66.
WRITINGS
D-day and after, Rattlesnake Press for Tishbooks,
1962; *City of the gulls and sea*, the author, 1964;
Bridge force, Contact, 1965; *The scarred hull*,
Imago, 1966; *Four myths from Sam Perry*, Talon
Books, 1968.
CONTRIBUTED: Articles and poems to *Poésie/
poetry 64*, edited by J. Godbout, Ryerson,
1964; *The making of modern poetry in Canada*,
edited by L. Dudek, Ryerson, 1967; *British
Columbia library quarterly, Canadian commen-
tator, Canadian forum, Canadian literature, El
corno emplumado, Delta, Evidence, Fiddlehead,
Imago, Island, Magdalene syndrome gazette,
The open letter, Prism, Sum, Tamarack review,
Tish.*

DAVID, Nellie Maillard 1917—
(Anne-Marie, pseud.)
Novelist; b. 1917 in Lyon, France; came to Canada in 1919; m. Paul David; children: six.
EDUCATION
Attended McGill University.
RELIGION
Roman Catholic.
HOME
3 McCulloch, Montreal, PQ.
CAREER
Mainly literary; lectures on marriage preparation for Foyers Notre-Dame.
MEMBER
Jeunesses littéraires du Canada français (executive committee).
WRITINGS
L'aube de la joie, Cercle du Livre de France, 1959; *La nuit si longue*, Cercle du Livre de France, 1960; *Maintenant et toujours*, Cercle du Livre de France, 1967.
CONTRIBUTED: Articles to *Relations*.

DAVIDSON, Hugh 1930—
Composer; b. 1930 in Montreal.
EDUCATION
Studied composition and harmony with Godfrey Ridout (*q.v.*), piano with George Crum, Toronto (now Royal) Conservatory of Music, 1945-48; studied with Ernest White, School of Church Music, London, Ont., 1948; studied harmony and counterpoint with Bernard Stevens, piano with Frank Merrick, Royal College of Music, London, England, 1951; studied with Neil Chotem in Montreal, 1955.
OFFICE
c/o Radio-Canada, 1425 Dorchester St. W., PO Box 6000, Montreal, PQ.
CAREER
CBC, Montreal, music producer 1956, supervisor of music programming for French network.
AWARDS, HONOURS
CAPAC award for *Three preludes for piano*, 1946.
COMPOSITIONS
Three preludes, piano, 1946; *Five epitaphs*, voice and piano, 1950; *Introduction and scherzo*, symphony orchestra, 1951; *Two motets*, choir of eight parts, 1952; *Sonata*, piano, 1953; *His Eminence of England*, incidental music for drama, 1953, composed for Canterbury Coronation Festival, England; *Divertissement*, three wind instruments, 1954; *Cymbeline*, incidental music, 1954, composed for Bristol Old Vic, England; *Psalm C*, soloists, choir, organ, brass, and percussion, 1955; *Grand pas de deux*, orchestra, 1956; *Ballet-hoo*, eight instruments, 1956; *Afternoons with Baedeker*, mixed choir, 1956; *Adagio*, string quartet, 1959, composed for Eric McLean's 40th birthday; *Variations en G*, sym-

phony orchestra, 1961; *Dances from Hydra*, small orchestra, 1961.

DAVIGNON, Grace, pseud.
see GLASSCO, John

DAVIS, Donald George 1928—
Actor and director; b. 26 Feb. 1928 in Newmarket, Ont.; son of Elihu James and Dorothy (Chilcott) Davis, Jr.
EDUCATION
Newmarket Public School, 1941; St. Andrew's College, Aurora, Ont., 1946; University of Toronto, BA, 1950; studied drama with Josephine Barrington (*q.v.*), Toronto, Ont.
HOME
41 King St., New York, NY 10014, USA.
OFFICE
c/o Peter Witt Associates, 37 W. 57th St., New York, NY 10019, USA.
CAREER
Straw Hat Players, Port Carling, Muskoka, Ont., co-founder and co-producer 1948-55; Glasgow Citizens' Theatre, Scotland, Bristol Old Vic Theatre, and Wilson Barrett Company, England, actor 1950-53; Crest Theatre, Toronto, co-founder and co-producer 1953-59; Stratford, Ont. Festival, actor 1954-56; American Shakespeare Festival, Stratford, Conn., actor 1960-61.
MEMBER
AEA (Canadian advisory committee, 1956-59); AFTRA; SAG.
THEATRE
Amateur debut as Sir Toby Belch in *Twelfth night* (Josephine Barrington's Juveniles, Hart House, Toronto, 1 Dec. 1937); professional debut as Henry Bevan in *The Barretts of Wimpole Street* (Woodstock Playhouse, NY, summer 1947); played title role in *Papa is all* (Straw Hat Players), Crocker-Harris in *The Browning version* (Straw Hat Players), Mr. Winslow in *The Winslow boy* (Straw Hat Players), Sir Henry Harcourt Reilly in *The cocktail party* (Straw Hat Players), *The wind and the rain* (Southern Ontario tour, 1950), title role in *Noah* (Canadian Repertory Theatre, Ottawa, Ont., 1951), Claudius in *Hamlet* (Canadian Repertory Theatre, Ottawa, 1951), Baptista in *The taming of the shrew* (UK), *The river line* (UK), Bassanio in *The merchant of Venice* (UK), Joseph Surface in *School for scandal* (UK), Thomas à Becket in *Murder in the Cathedral* (Crest), Malvolio in *Twelfth night* (Crest), Creon in *Antigone* (Crest), Vershinin in *The three sisters* (Crest), *Haste to the wedding* (Crest), Jack the skinner in *A jig for the gypsy* (Crest, Sept. 1954), Mr. Stuart in *Hunting Stuart* (Crest), Angelo in *Measure for measure* (succeeded James Mason, Stratford, Ont. Festival, 1954), Tiresias in *Oedipus Rex* (Strat-

ford, Ont. Festival, 1954-55), Mark Antony in *Julius Caesar* (Stratford, Ont. Festival, 1955), Agydas in *Tamburlaine the great* (Winter Garden, New York, 19 Jan. 1956), Westmoreland in *Henry V* (Stratford, Ont. Festival, 1956), Pistol in *The merry wives of Windsor* (Stratford, Ont. Festival, 1956), Angus McBane in *The glass cage* (Piccadilly, London, England, 26 Apr. 1957), narrator in *Oedipus Rex* (Stravinsky, City Center, New York, 24 Sept. 1959), title role in *Krapp's last tape* (US première, Provincetown Playhouse, Mass., 14 Jan. 1960; Arena Theatre, Washington, DC, Apr. 1961), Orsino in *Twelfth night* (American Shakespeare Festival, 8 June 1960), Domitius Enobarbus in *Antony and Cleopatra* (American Shakespeare Festival, 31 July 1960), *Roar like a dove* (Royal Poinciana Playhouse, Palm Beach, Fla., Feb. 1961), Jaques in *As you like it* (American Shakespeare Festival, 15 June 1961), Duncan in *Macbeth* (American Shakespeare Festival, 16 June 1961), Achilles in *Troilus and Cressida* (American Shakespeare Festival, 23 July 1961), Gustav in *The creditors* (Mermaid, New York, 25 Jan. 1962), title role in *Becket* (Goodman, Chicago, Ill., Oct. 1962), Sam in middle age in *Photo finish* (Brooks Atkinson, New York, 12 Feb. 1963), George in *Who's afraid of Virginia Woolf?* (Billy Rose, New York, matinee company 10 July 1963, evening company 13 Jan. 1964; Manitoba Theatre Centre, Winnipeg, 1965/66), *An evening's Frost* (Theatre de Lys, New York, 11 Oct. 1965), Lord Essex in *Elizabeth the Queen* (City Center, New York, 3 Nov. 1966), *The Oresteia* (Ypsilanti Greek Theatre, Mich., 1966), *The birds* (Ypsilanti Greek Theatre, 1966); directed *Laura* (Straw Hat Players), *French without tears* (Straw Hat Players); co-produced *The drunkard* (trans-Canada tour, 1948), *There goes yesterday* (trans-Canada tour, 1949); directed *Bright sun at midnight* (Crest), *The Crest revue* (Crest), *Toy for the clowns* (Richard Barr's Theatre '62 Playwright series, Cherry Lane, New York, 11 Dec. 1961), *Deathwatch* (Richard Barr's Festival of the Absurd, Cherry Lane, 25 Feb. 1962).

FILM
Played Tiresias in *King Oedipus* (Oedipus Rex Productions, Toronto, 1957).

RADIO
Played in many CBC productions, e.g. "Stage," "Wednesday night," "Buckingham theatre," "Ford theatre," "National school broadcasts," 1946-59.

TELEVISION
Played in many productions, e.g. Sir Henry Watton in *The picture of Dorian Gray* (CBC), Young Marlow in *Gay deceivers* (CBC), Alcibiades in *Socrates* (CBC), Raleigh in *Elizabeth the Queen* (CBC), FBI agent in *I made news* (BBC, 1951),

Hector in *Tiger at the gates* ("Play of the week," WNTA, Feb. 1960), title role in *Henry IV*, part I ("Play of the week," WNTA, Sept. 1960), *Sound of murder* ("Play of the week," WNTA, Feb. 1961), title role in *The trial and death of Socrates* ("Robert Herridge theatre," CBC, 1961), *The indelible silence* ("The defenders," CBS, 1962), *Night sounds* ("The nurses," CBS, 1962), *Death watch* ("The defenders," CBS, 1963), Abraham Lincoln in *A season of war* ("Chronicle," CBS, 1963).

DELAMONT, Gordon Arthur*   1918–
Composer and teacher; b. 27 Oct. 1918 in Moose Jaw, Sask.; son of Arthur William and Lily (France) Delamont; m. Vina Smith 5 June 1952; children: Susan b. 22 July 1953, Debna b. 26 Apr. 1955, Gordon b. 14 May 1963.

EDUCATION
Attended General Gordon School and Kitsilano High School, Vancouver, BC; studied music in Vancouver and with Dr. Maury Deutsch, New York, NY, graduate diploma, 1949.

HOME AND OFFICE
2 Kempsell Crescent, Willowdale, Ont.

CAREER
Kitsilano Boys' Band, Vancouver, solo trumpet; professional trumpet player with leading dance and studio orchestras of Canada 1939-59; own band *c.* 1945-49; Gordon Delamont Studios, Willowdale, Ont., teacher of harmony, counterpoint, composition, and arranging *c.* 1949– ; CBC, Toronto, "Ten centuries concerts" series founding member and vice-president 1962, executive member 1966-69.

MEMBER
Jazz Arts (president, *c.* 1966).

COMPOSITIONS
Memoirs of Huron county, suite for jazz octet. *Five miniatures. A portrait of Charles Mingus,* first performed on CBC. *Allegro and blues,* first performed on CBC. *Three entertainments,* saxophone quartet, recorded by New York Saxophone Quartet. *Saxophone quartet. Walden,* jazz quartet, performed on "Ten centuries concerts." *Compositions on the theme of Bach's musical offering,* performed on "Ten centuries concerts." *Ontario suite,* Kendor Music Inc., 1967, performed daily at Ontario pavilion, Expo 67, Montreal 1967, recorded by Hallmark Studio, 1965, commissioned by Ontario government, May 1965. *Collage no. 3* and *Song and dance,* Kendor Music Inc., recorded on *In Canada* with Duke Ellington on Decca 75069, 1968. *Centum,* first performed on "Ten centuries concerts," Feb. 1967, recorded by Ron Collier (*q.v.*) on CAPAC-CAB, commissioned by CBC for Canadian centennial.

WRITINGS
Modern harmonic technique, vols. I and II, Ken-

dor Music Inc., 1965; *Modern arranging technique*, Kendor Music Inc., 1965; *Modern contrapuntal technique*, Kendor Music Inc., 1969.
CONTRIBUTED: Articles to *Canadian music journal, Music across Canada, Crescendo, Jazz monthly, Saturday night.*

DE LA ROCHE, Mazo 1879-1961
Novelist; b. 15 Jan. 1879 in Newmarket, Ont.; daughter of William Richmond and Alberta (Lundy) De la Roche; children: (adopted) René, Esmé; d. 12 July 1961 in Toronto, Ont.
EDUCATION
Attended schools in Galt, Ont. and Toronto; Parkdale Collegiate Institute, Toronto; University of Toronto.
CAREER
Purely literary; resided in England 1929-39.
AWARDS, HONOURS
Daughters of the British Empire competition, 2 prizes, 1925; *Atlantic monthly* $10,000 prize for *Jalna*, 1927; Lorne Pierce medal, 1938; National award medal for signal contribution to letters, painting, music by University of Alberta, 1951; LL D from University of Toronto, 1954.
WRITINGS
Explorers of the dawn (short stories), Macmillan, 1922; *Possession*, Macmillan, 1923; *Delight*, Macmillan, 1926; *Jalna*, Little, Brown, 1927 (filmed as *Jalna*, RKO Radio Pictures, 1935); *Whiteoaks of Jalna*, Little, Brown, 1929; *Portrait of a dog*, Little, Brown, 1930; *Finch's fortune*, Macmillan, 1931; *The thunder of new wings*, Little, Brown, 1932; *Beside a Norman tower;* Macmillan, 1932; *Lark ascending*, Macmillan, 1932; *The master of Jalna*, Macmillan, 1933; *Young Renny*, Macmillan, 1935; *Whiteoak harvest*, Macmillan, 1936; *The very house,* Macmillan, 1937; *Growth of a man*, Macmillan, 1938; *The sacred bullock and other stories of animals*, Macmillan, 1939; *Whiteoak heritage*, Little, Brown, 1940; *Wakefield's course*, Little, Brown, 1941; *The two saplings,* Macmillan, 1942; *The building of Jalna*, Little, Brown, 1944; *Quebec, historic seaport* (non-fiction) Doubleday, 1944; *Return to Jalna*, Little, Brown, 1946; *Mary Wakefield*, Little, Brown, 1949 (Literary Guild selection); *Renny's daughter*, Little, Brown, 1951; *A boy in the house*, Little, Brown, 1952; *Whiteoak brothers, Jalna-1923*, Macmillan, 1953; *Variable winds at Jalna*, Macmillan, 1954; *The song of Lambert* (juvenile), Macmillan, 1955; *Ringing the changes* (autobiography), Macmillan, 1957; *Bill and Coo* (juvenile), Macmillan, 1958; *Centenary at Jalna*, Macmillan, 1958; *Morning at Jalna*, Macmillan, 1960; *Low life* (play), Macmillan, 1925 (produced Trinity Memorial Hall, Montreal, PQ, 14 May 1925); *Come true* (play), Macmillan, 1927 (produced Hart House Theatre,

Toronto, 16 May 1927); *The return of the emigrant* (play), Little, Brown, 1929 (produced Hart House Theatre, 12 Mar. 1928); *Low life and other plays,* Macmillan, 1929; *Whiteoaks* (play), Macmillan, 1936 (produced Little Theatre, John Street, The Adelphi, London, England, 13 Apr. 1936; H.M. Theatre, Montreal, 23 Feb. 1938; Hudson Theatre, New York, NY, 24 Mar. 1938); *The mistress of Jalna* (play; produced New Theatre, Bromley, Kent, England, 12 Nov. 1951). Works translated into many languages, including French, German, Norwegian, and Braille.
CONTRIBUTED: Short stories, poems, articles to many magazines, e.g. *Atlantic monthly, Canadian author and bookman, Canadian forum, Good Housekeeping, Harper's bazaar, London mercury, Maclean's, Munsey's, Tatler, Woman's home companion.*

DELFOSSE, Georges 1869-1939
Artist; b. 8 Dec. 1869 in St. Henri de Mascouche, PQ; son of Mélaine and Joséphine (Mount) Delfosse m. Aline Constant 14 May 1908; d. 24 Dec. 1939 in Montreal, PQ.
EDUCATION
Attended school in St. Henri de Mascouche; École Saint-Jacques in Montreal, 1883; École Saint-Laurent in Montreal; studied art under Abbé Chabert, Institut National des Beaux-Arts, c.1885; William Brymner (*q.v.*), and Edmond Dyonnet (*q.v.*); Alexis Harmaloff and Léon Bonnat in Paris, France, 1908.
CAREER
Decorated church in St. Henri de Mascouche, 1890; engaged in designing streets in Montreal 1893, 1894, and 1899; illustrated *Contes vrai*, by Léon Pamphile Lemay, Beauchemin, 1899, *Femmes rêvées*, by Albert Ferland, the author, 1899 and *Florence*, by Rodolphe Girard, 1900; studied, painted, and worked on seven paintings for St. James Cathedral, Montreal, in Paris 1908; sold twelve paintings of old Montreal to the municipality of Maisonneuve, PQ; painted in Paris 1914; painted, decorated churches on commission in Quebec, Ontario, New York, NY, Chicago, Ill., and elsewhere in the USA; painted portraits and taught in Montreal c.1890-1939.
EXHIBITIONS
GROUP: Represented in group exhibitions held in Canada from 1888 on including annual exhibitions of Royal Canadian Academy and Art Association of Montreal; represented in exhibitions of Royal Academy, London, England.
COLLECTIONS IN WHICH REPRESENTED
National Gallery of Canada, Ottawa, Ont.

DENTAY, Elizabeth Benson Guy
see GUY, Elizabeth Benson

DÉSAULNIERS, Gonzalve 1863-1934
(Gonzalve Lesieur-Désaulniers)
Poet; b. 1863 in Saint-Guillaume d'Upton, PQ;
son of Antoine and Hélène (Letellier) Lesieur-
Désaulniers; d. 5 Apr. 1934 in Montreal, PQ.
EDUCATION
Attended Collège Sainte-Marie, Montréal; Univer-
sity of Montreal, LLL, 1895.
RELIGION
Roman Catholic.
CAREER
L'étendard, Montréal, journalist; Le national,
owner and editor 1889-96; King's counsel 1902;
Superior Court of Quebec, judge 1923.
MEMBER
Royal Society of Canada (elected fellow, 1932);
Alliance française de Montréal (president).
WRITINGS
Pour la France, Beauchemin, 1918; Les bois qui
chantent, Beauchemin, 1930.

DESILETS, Alphonse 1888-1956
(Jacquelin, pseud.)
Poet; b. 1888; d. 1956.
EDUCATION
Attended college.
CAREER
Mainly literary.
WRITINGS
Heures poétiques, Écho des bois, 1910; Mon pays,
mes amours, l'auteur, 1913; Dans la brise du
terroir, l'auteur, 1922; Pour la terre et le foyer
(non-fiction), 1926.
CONTRIBUTED: Articles and poetry to Canada-
français, Culture, Revue de l'Université Laval.

DESROCHES, Francis* 1895—
(Frandero, pseud.)
Poet.
HOME
1074 Louis-Jobin, Québec 10, PQ.
CAREER
Canadian Army, 1915, became sergeant; Quebec government, publicist for department of
agriculture 1917-37, for department of provincial secretary 1938-48; L'événement, Québec,
translator, reporter, and editor, 1920-48; La
revue des éleveurs, founder; La vie rurale,
founder; Tout-sport, founder; À travers tout,
founder; Contact, founder; Le bulletin de la Mu-
tuelle-Vie des Fonctionnaires du Québec, founder;
Le message des poètes, founder.
MEMBER
La Société des Poètes Canadiens-Français (co-
founder, 1923; secretary, director, vice-president,
president, executive secretary, and treasurer,
1954-65).
WRITINGS
En furetant, 1919; Brumes du soir, Action sociale, 1920; Chiquenaudes, 1924; Pascal Berthi-

aume (novel), Élite, 1932; Propos d'un rôdeur,
1942; Cendres chaudes, Garneau, 1963.
CONTRIBUTED: Poetry to Poésie (Paris), Poésie
(Québec), Revue de l'Université Laval.

DESROSIERS, Léo-Paul 1896-1967
Author; b. 11 Apr. 1896 in Berthierville, PQ; son
of Louis and Marie (Oliver) Desrosiers; m. Marie
Antoinette Tardif June 1922; children: Louis,
Claude, Michelle; d. 20 Apr. 1967.
EDUCATION
Attended Séminaire de Joliette, PQ; University of
Montreal, LLL, 1919.
RELIGION
Roman Catholic.
CAREER
Le devoir, Montréal, PQ, journalist 1920-28; Pro-
ceedings and orders, House of Commons, Ottawa,
Ont., French editor 1929-41; Montreal Civic
Library, chief librarian 1941-52; retired to Saint-
Sauveur-des-Monts, PQ, in 1953.
MEMBER
Société des "Dix" (elected, 1941); Royal Society
of Canada (elected fellow, 1942); Académie
canadienne-française (co-founder, 1944); Société
historique de Montréal.
AWARDS, HONOURS
Prix d'Action intellectuelle for Ames et paysages,
1922; Vermeille medal of the Académie fran-
çaise, 1931; Quebec province prize for Les engagés
du Grand Portage, 1938; Prix Duvernay, 1951;
Lorne Pierce medal, 1963.
WRITINGS
Ames et paysages (stories), Devoir, 1922; Nord-
Sud (novel), Devoir, 1931; Le livre des mystères
(short stories), Devoir, 1936; L'accalmie (non-
fiction), Devoir, 1937; Les engagés du Grand
Portage (novel), Gallimard, 1938; Commence-
ments (non-fiction), Action canadienne-française,
1939; Les opiniâtres (novel), Devoir, 1941;
Sources (novel), Devoir, 1942; Iroquoisie 1534-
1646 (non-fiction), Études de l'Institut d'Histoire
de l'Amérique française, 1947; L'ampoule d'or
(novel), Gallimard, 1951; Les dialogues de Marthe et de Marie (biography), Fides, 1957; Vous
qui passez (novel), Fides, 1958; Les angoisses et
les tourments (novel) Fides, 1959; Rafales sur les
cimes (novel), Fides, 1960; Dans le nid d'aiglons,
la colombe: vie de Jeanne Le Ber, la recluse,
Fides, 1963; Paul de Chomedey, Sieur de Maisonneuve (biography), Fides, 1967.
CONTRIBUTED: Articles and stories to La croix
du chemin, edited by Société Saint-Jean-Baptiste
de Montréal, 1916; Ville ô ma ville, edited by
the Société des Écrivains canadiens, 1941; Histoire véritable et naturelle des moeurs et productions du pays de la Nouvelle-France, edited by
the Société historique de Boucherville, 1964;
L'action française, L'action nationale, L'action
universitaire, Annales de la Bonne Sainte Anne,

Aujourd'hui Québec, Cahiers de l'Académie canadienne-française, Cahiers de Nouvelle-France, Cahiers des Dix, Canada français, Culture, Lectures, Liaison, Liberté 60, Monde nouveau, Québec 64, Revue de l'Université d'Ottawa, Revue dominicaine, Revue d'histoire de l'Amérique française.

DES SERRES, Marthe, pseud.
see CHARBONNEAU, Hélène

DE TONNANCOUR, Jacques
see TONNANCOUR, Jacques Godefroy de

DEVAUX, Richard
Dancer; b. in Guatemala; son of Jean G. and Madame Bonge de Devaux.
EDUCATION
Studied ballet with his mother in Guatemala.
CAREER
Guatemala Ballet, corps de ballet; International Exhibition, Berlin, Germany, 1964; Les Grands Ballets Canadiens, Montreal, soloist 1965–?
MEMBER
AEA.
THEATRE
Danced Soldat mécanique and Trepak Ivan in *Casse-noisette* (Nault, 1965), *Suite canadienne* (Chiriaeff, 1965).

DEVENSON, Rosemary
see DEVESON, Rosemary

DEVESON, Rosemary *c.*1922–
(Rosemary Devenson; Natasha Sobinova, pseud.; Rosemary Deveson Westerfield; Rosemary Deveson Hamilton)
Dancer and teacher; b. *c.*1922 in Winnipeg, Man.; daughter of Bertram L. Deveson; m. James Westerfield; m. Gerald Hamilton.
EDUCATION
Studied ballet with June Roper, Vancouver, 1935-38; movement with Eileen O'Connor in New York, NY.
HOME
1584 W. 29th St., Vancouver, BC.
CAREER
Commodore Cabaret, Vancouver, dancer; de Basil's Ballet Russe de Monte Carlo, corps de ballet, soloist 1938–? ; Rosemary Deveson Dance Studio, Vancouver, founder 1941–?
THEATRE
Danced in *Le lac des cygnes* (Petipa-Ivanov), *Le coq d'or* (Fokine), *Perpetual motion* (Lichine), *Natasha* (Orpheum, Vancouver, 17 Nov. 1939); choreographed series of operettas (Danbury, Conn., 1949).

DEWDNEY, Selwyn Hanington* 1909–
Author and artist; b. 22 Oct. 1909 in Prince

Albert, Sask.; son of Alfred Daniel Alexander and Alice A. (Hanington) Dewdney; m. Irene Maude Donner 3 Oct. 1936; children: Donner b. 3 Dec. 1939, Alexander Keewatin b. 6 Aug. 1941, Peter North b. 14 Dec. 1943, Christopher b. 9 May 1951.
EDUCATION
Attended King George School, Prince Albert, 1913-21; Kenora High School, Ont., 1922-27; Wycliffe College, University of Toronto, 1928-29; University College, University of Toronto, BA, 1931; studied with Annette Marsh, Ontario College of Education, art specialist, 1931-32; J. W. Beatty, Ontario College of Art, AOCA (honours), 1932-36; Emmanuel Hahn 1935-36.
RELIGION
Humanist.
HOME
27 Erie Avenue, London, Ont.
CAREER
Travelled extensively in Canadian hinterland by canoe, packhorse, and aircraft, especially in the Canadian Shield region; Anglican mission to Ojibway, Lac Seul, Ont., student-in-charge 1929-30; Collegiage-Vocational Institute, Owen Sound, Ont., teacher of art, geography, and English 1932-34; Sir Adam Beck Secondary School, London, Ont., teacher of art, geography, and English 1936-45; book illustrator and muralist 1945-55; Westminster (DVA) Hospital, London, psychiatric art therapist 1947–; illustrated *Kristli's trees* by M. Dunham, McClelland & Stewart, 1948; Artist's Workshop of London, director 1960-62; Quetico Foundation, Royal Ontario Museum, Glenbow-Alberta Institute, and National Museum of Canada, field work and research on aboriginal rock paintings, petroglyphs, and birchbark pictography 1957–; Royal Ontario Museum, Toronto, research associate 1966; Indian-Eskimo Association of Canada, Ontario Division, board of directors 1967–; travelled to Russia to lecture on Canadian pictography and to consult Soviet specialists on Siberian art and pictography 1968; Artist's Workshop, London, executive director.
COMMISSIONS
Murals, Sir Adam Beck Secondary School, 1945-48; reproductions of Canadian Indian rock paintings in the Ontario Pavilion, Expo 67, Montreal, PQ; mural, Odeon Theatre, London; mural, Bell Telephone Building, Brantford, Ont.; mural, Waterloo Trust Building, Kitchener, Ont.
MEMBER
Ontario College of Art (associate); Western Art League (president).
AWARDS, HONOURS
Canada Council joint grant with Frank Arbuckle (*q.v.*), 1964; Royal Ontario Museum, research associate, 1966.

EXHIBITIONS
GROUP: Represented in group exhibitions held in Canada.

WRITINGS
(with G.A. Cornish) *Social studies for Canadians* (non-fiction), Copp Clark, 1938; *Wind without rain* (novel), Copp Clark, 1946; *The map that grew* (non-fiction), Oxford, 1960; (with K.E. Kidd) *Indian rock paintings of the Great Lakes* (non-fiction), University of Toronto, 1962; *Stone age paintings* (non-fiction), Manitoba Dept. of Mines and Natural Resources, Parks Branch, 1965; *Magic on the rocks* (film script; "The world around us," CFPL-TV, London, Nov. 1967).
EDITED: N. Morriseau's *Legends of my people, the great Ojibway*, Ryerson, 1965.
CONTRIBUTED: Articles to *The school, Beaver, Canadian art, Journal of the Canadian Psychiatric Association, Bulletin of art therapy, Canadian forum, Maclean's.*
WORK IN PROGRESS: "Christopher Breton" (novel); working on book length study of Canada's native cultures.

DICKENSON, Jean 1914—
Singer (soprano); b. 10 Dec. 1914 in Montreal; daughter of Ernest and May Louise (Freud) Dickenson.
EDUCATION
University of Denver, Colo., BMus, 1935; studied with Florence Hinman, Lamont School of Music, University of Denver.
RELIGION
Roman Catholic.
HOME
5640-7 Ave., Montreal, PQ.
CAREER
Denver Opera Company; San Carlos Opera Company, Calif.; Milwaukee Symphony Orchestra, Wis.; Denver Symphony Orchestra; Little Symphony, Montreal; toured USA and Canada.
THEATRE
Debut as Philine in *Mignon* (Metropolitan Opera, New York, NY, 26 Jan. 1940).
RADIO
Sang in several productions, e.g. "American album of familiar music" (NBC, 1937-50); "Hollywood hour."

DI GIOVANNI, Edoardo, pseud.
see JOHNSON, Edward

DINSDALE, Patricia Joudry
see JOUDRY, Patricia

DISSMANN, Patricia Rideout
see RIDEOUT, Patricia

DOLIN, Samuel Joseph 1917—
Composer and teacher; b. 22 Aug. 1917 in Montreal, PQ; son of Joseph and Frieda Dolin; m. Leslie Pidgeon; children: Elizabeth Leslie, John.
EDUCATION
Royal Conservatory of Music, Toronto, 1935-42; University of Toronto, BMus, 1942, DMus, 1957; studied with E.R. Schmitz in Denver, Colo., 1945, 1947, in San Francisco, Calif., 1948, 1949; with John Weinzweig (*q.v.*) in Toronto, 1949; with Ernst Krenek, 1952.
HOME
12 Reigate Rd., Islington, Ont.
OFFICE
Royal Conservatory of Music, 273 Bloor St. W., Toronto, Ont.
CAREER
Pianist in Montreal 1933-35; taught music privately; Ontario counties of Durham and Northumberland, music supervisor 1942-45; Royal Conservatory of Music, teacher of piano and theory.
MEMBER
BMI Canada; Canadian League of Composers (co-founder).
COMPOSITIONS
Three piano preludes, 1949; *Four miniatures for piano*, 1949; *Sonata for piano*, 1949-50; *Sinfonietta*, orchestra, 1950, scherzo first performed 1951 at Yale University by University Symposium Orchestra, scherzo recorded by CBC IS no. 71 with Toronto Symphony Orchestra under Geoffrey Waddington; *Serenade for strings*, 1951, first performed 1952 in Helsinki, Finland on Finnish National Radio, recorded by CBC IS no. 86 with CBC Symphony Orchestra under Geoffrey Waddington; *Sonatina*, violin and piano, 1951; *Three songs*, 1951; *Little sombrero*, violin and piano, BMI Canada; *Symphony no. 1*, or *Elk Falls symphony*, orchestra, 1956, first performed 1957 by CBC Symphony Orchestra under Albert Pratz; *Symphony no. 2*, 1957, first performed 1958 in Toronto by CBC Symphony Orchestra under Walter Susskind, recorded on air-check tape with the same performers; *Sonata for violin and piano*, 1960, first performed 1960 on CBC by Albert Pratz, recorded 1966 on air-check tape with David Zafer; *Portrait*, string quartet, 1961; *Chloris*, medium voice and piano, 1961, BMI Canada; *Sonata for string orchestra*, 1962; *The hills of Hebron*, mixed voices and piano.

DOMINIQUE, François
see BARBEAU, François

DOMVILLE, James de Beaujeu* 1933—
Director, producer, teacher; b. 23 June 1933 in Cannes, France; son of Henry de Gaspé and Elsie Welsh (Saltus) Domville; m. Patricia Joan Irvine 1961; children: Marc-Henri de Beaujeu b. 1963, Philippa de Beaujeu b. 1965.

EDUCATION

Attended Selwyn House School, Montreal, 1942-48; Trinity College, Port Hope, Ont., 1948-50; Université de Fribourg, Switzerland, diplôme de français, 1950; McGill University, BA, 1954, BCL, 1957; University of Montreal.

HOME

50 Holton Ave., Montreal 6, PQ.

CAREER

Quince Ballet productions, co-founder and president 1959; National Theatre School of Canada, Montreal, co-founder 1960, administrative director 1960-62, teacher 1960-68, executive director, director general 1963–, board of governors, consultant, and member of executive committee 1968; Dominion Drama Festival, governor and member of executive 1961; Canadian Centenary Council, chairman of festivals and cultural activities subcommittee 1963; International Theatre Institute, member of committee for professional training 1966, co-chairman of Theatre of tomorrow panel, New York, NY, 1967, Canadian representative of executive committee, Paris, France, 1967, program co-ordinator for International Colloquium on theatre design, Montreal, 1967; theatre consultant for Canadian Centre for the Performing Arts, Ottawa, for Wascana Centre Auditorium, Regina, Sask., for Saskatoon, Sask., Auditorium, for twin theatre at Mackay Pier, Montreal; Canadian Federal Pavilion Expo 67, Montreal, adviser and consultant for the Entertainment Branch; University of Ottawa, adviser for the Fine Arts Department, 1967; Théâtre du Nouveau Monde, Montreal, adviser and member of executive committee 1967–, executive director 1968–; Canada Council, member of advisory arts panel 1968–; Centre Culturel International, panellist in international colloquium on Canada, Cérisy La Salle, France, 1968; guest lecturer at various university theatre departments; travelled extensively in Europe, USSR, North America, Caribbean, and within Canada.

MEMBER

Canadian Theatre Centre (treasurer and director, 1962; secretary, 1964; representative at international symposions in Rumania, Germany, Austria, Sweden, and Czecho-Slovakia, 1964-67); United States Institute of Theatre Technology (director, 1966); American Educational Theatre Association; Quebec Society for Education through Art (director, 1968).

AWARDS, HONOURS

Centennial medal, 1967; Canada Council travel grant, 1967/68.

THEATRE

Produced and wrote most of the music for *My fur lady* (McGill Red & White Revue, 1957; Canada tour, 1957-58); co-produced *Summer of the seventeenth doll* (Crest Theatre, La Comédie Canadienne, Montreal, 1959); produced *Jubilee!* (Vancouver Festival; Royal Alexandra, Toronto, 1959); co-produced *Spring thaw '60* (Ontario tour; Odeon-Fairlawn Theatre, Toronto, 1960).

FILM

Appeared in documentary films.

RADIO

Produced *Maple sauce* (revue, CBC, 1960); devised and hosted "Curtain time" (series, CBC, 1960-61).

TELEVISION

Appeared on panel shows.

DOUTREMONT, Henri, pseud.
see BUGNET, Georges

DOWNES, Gwladys Violet* 1915–
Poet; b. 22 Apr. 1915 in Victoria; daughter of Gordon and Gwendolyn (Bywater-Jones) Downes.

EDUCATION

Attended Willows and Monterey primary schools, Victoria, 1921-27; Oak Bay High School, Victoria, 1927-30; Victoria College (now University of Victoria), 1930-31; University of British Columbia, BA, 1934, MA, 1940; École de Préparation des professeurs de français à l'étranger, Paris, France, 1935; University of Toronto, 1941-42, 1945-46; Université de Paris, docteur, 1953.

RELIGION

Anglican.

HOME

2621 Lincoln Rd., Victoria, BC.

OFFICE

Department of French Language and Literature, University of Victoria, Victoria, BC.

CAREER

University of British Columbia, lecturer in French and English 1940-41, 1946-49; University of Victoria, instructor in French 1951-c.53, assistant professor c.1953-57, associate professor 1957-67, professor 1967–; BC Department of Education Summer School, lecturer in creative writing 1955-56.

MEMBER

Art Gallery of Greater Victoria, director.

AWARDS, HONOURS

IODE bursary for undergraduate education, 1930-34; University Women's senior fellowship for doctoral studies, 1950-51; Canada Council senior fellowship, 1968/69.

WRITINGS

Lost diver, University of New Brunswick, 1955 (Fiddlehead poetry books, no. 2).

TRANSLATED: French-Canadian poems which have appeared in *Edge* and *Tamarack review*.

CONTRIBUTED: Poems and articles to *British Columbia: a centennial anthology*, edited by

R.E. Watters, McClelland & Stewart, 1958; *Alphabet, Canadian forum, Canadian poetry, Canadian literature, Edge, Fiddlehead, Prism, Tamarack review, Times* (Victoria).
WORK IN PROGRESS: Translations of French-Canadian poetry to be published by Oxford University Press.

DRAINIE, John   1916-66

Actor; b. 1 Apr. 1916 in Vancouver, BC; m. Claire Murray Apr. 1942; children: Bronwyn, Kathryn, Michael, Jocelyn, Philip, David; d. 30 Oct. 1966 in Toronto, Ont.
  EDUCATION
Attended North Vancouver High School.
  CAREER
CJOR and CKWX, Vancouver, announcer and actor 1937-41; CBC, announcer and actor in Vancouver 1941-43, in Toronto 1943-66; Academy of Radio Arts, Toronto, teacher of acting and sound effects.
  MEMBER
AEA; ACTRA.
  AWARDS, HONOURS
Ohio State University award; La Flèche award for best actor; John Drainie scholarship established by Ontario Arts Council, 1966.
  THEATRE
Played in productions by Vancouver Little Theatre (later Community Playhouse), New Play Society, Jupiter Theatre, and Earle Grey Players, Toronto; *Red and white* (London, England, 1963), *Laugh with Leacock* (Charlottetown Festival, PEI, 1965).
  FILM
Played in *Family circle* (National Film Board of Canada, 1949), *The performer* part II (National Film Board 0159050), Professor Hunter in *The incredible journey* (Buena Vista, 1963); dialogue director in *Bush Pilot* (Dominion Productions Ltd., 1947).
  RADIO
Played in numerous CBC productions, e.g. Sam Honey in *The Carsons* ("BC farm broadcast," *c.* 1942), *Maybe in a thousand years, Scoop, The precipice,* Julius Monk in *For the time is at hand, Hoghead's last run* ("Men at work"), 6 parts in *Portrait of a year* ("Wednesday night"), valet in *The way of the world, Stories with John Drainie* (series), title role in *The black bonspiel of Wullie MacCrimmon* ("Stage"), Mr. Winkle in *Pickwick papers* ("Stage," 1948/49), Mort Clay in *Allan and me* (serial, *c.*1950), title role in *The investigator,* title role in *Coming to terms with Tolstoy* ("Wednesday night," 19 Aug. 1959), narrator in *The fall of Quebec* ("Wednesday night," 11, 18 Nov. 1959), Obadiah in *Under the sun* ("Wednesday night," 23 Dec. 1959), *Spark in Judea* ("Wednesday night," 13 Apr. 1960), Sailor in *Christopher Columbus* ("Wednesday

night," 4 May 1960), *The Melos affair* ("Four's company," 18 June 1960), *Theme and variations* ("Four's company," 6 May 1961), *The rise and fall of witchcraft*("Four's company," 1 July 1961), title role in *A 14th century life of Christ* ("Four's company," 22 July 1961), *A life of the poor* ("Four's company," 19 Aug. 1961), *God so loved the world* ("Sunday night," 30 May 1965), Brampton Shipley in *The stone angel* ("Sunday night," 15 Aug. 1965), Clarence Darrow in *Hot days in Dayton* ("Sunday night," 19 Sept. 1965), Dr. Amos Harping in *A new dialogue on two world systems* ("Tuesday night," 30 Aug. 1966), *The voices of John Drainie* ("Stage," 11 Dec. 1966), *Just for love* ("Tuesday night," 27 Dec. 1966), *Yeats in Dublin* ("Tuesday night," 14 Mar. 1967), title role in *Turvey* ("Theatre 10:30," 14-22 Oct. 1968).
  TELEVISION
Played in numerous CBC productions, e.g. title role in *Mr. Arcularis* ("Encore," 21 Aug. 1960), *The day of the dodo* ("Festival," 8 Jan. 1962), title role in *The black bonspiel of Wullie MacCrimmon* ("Playdate," 7 Mar. 1962), Hector in *Grand exits* ("Festival," 16 Apr. 1962), Peter in *The devil's instrument* ("Festival," 5 Nov. 1962), Cook in *Mother Courage* ("Festival," 20 Jan. 1965), Father in *A spring song* ("Festival," 12 May 1965), narrator in *At the moment of impact* ("Document," 7 Nov. 1965), Baptista in *The taming of the shrew* ("Festival," 11 Jan. 1967), *A sense of truth* ("Telescope," 23 Feb. 1967).
  RECORDINGS
Played title role in *The investigator*, Discuriosities 6834, 1954.
  WRITINGS
Several radio scripts, e.g. (with Claire Drainie) *Flow gently sweet Limbo* ("Stage," 1947/48). EDITED: *Stories with John Drainie*, Ryerson, 1963.

DRENTERS, Yosef Gertrudis*   1929-

Sculptor; b. 25 Nov. 1929 in Poppel, Flanders, Belgium; son of Yozeph Antonius and Hendrika Maria (Swinkels) Drenters; came to Canada 11 Oct. 1951 and settled in Oyama, BC.
  EDUCATION
Attended nun's school for children in Poppel, Belgium, 1936-37; attended Jongens (Boys) School in Poppel, 1937-41; attended boys school in Nijnsel, Sint Oedenrode, Noord-Brabant, The Netherlands 1941-43; classical studies for the priesthood at Twello, Gelderland, The Netherlands, 1943-44, at Bergen op Zoom, Brabant, The Netherlands 1944-47, at Turnhout and Antwerp, Belgium, 1947-48 and at Kortryk, West Flanders, Belgium, 1948-50; self-taught as sculptor.
  RELIGION
Roman Catholic.

HOME
Old Academy, Rockwood, Ont.
CAREER
Employed as a cowboy in Oyama, 1951-53; engaged in factory work in Vancouver, BC, 1953; employed as a miner in the Yukon 1953-54; worked on his father's farm in Eramosa, near Rockwood, Ont., 1954-62; sculptor and painter in Rockwood, 1962–;
COMMISSIONS
Two chapels and other works, University of Windsor, 1964, 1965, 1966, 1967, and 1968; sculpture commemorating Canadian wheat growing, Tokyo International Trade Fair, Japan; sculpture, Ontario pavilion, Expo 67, Montreal, PQ; sculpture, La Ronde, Expo 67, Montreal.
MEMBER
Ontario Society of Artists; Sculptors' Society of Canada.
AWARDS, HONOURS
Award, Five Counties Artists Association; first prize for sculpture, Winnipeg Show, Winnipeg Art Gallery, Man., 1961; Canada Council arts scholarship, 1961/62.
EXHIBITIONS
ONE-MAN: Here and Now Gallery, Toronto, Ont., 1960; Norman Mackenzie Art Gallery, Regina, Sask., 1961; Dorothy Cameron Gallery, Toronto, 1962; Galerie Dresdnere, Montreal, 1963.
GROUP: Represented in group exhibitions held in Canada since 1954 including annual exhibitions of Ontario Society of Artists.
COLLECTIONS IN WHICH REPRESENTED
Assumption University; Edmonton Art Gallery, Alta.; Queen's University; Princeton University; Willistead Art Gallery, Windsor, Ont.; Ontario Government, Toronto; Canadian Government, Ottawa.

DUDEK, Louis* 1918–
Poet; b. 6 Feb. 1918 in Montreal; son of Vincent and Rozynski (Stasia) Dudek; m. Stephanie Zuperko 1943.
EDUCATION
Montreal High School, senior matriculation, 1936; McGill University, BA, 1939; Columbia University, MA in history, 1947, Ph D in English and comparative literature, 1955.
HOME
3476 Vendôme Ave., Montreal, PQ.
CAREER
Employed as advertising writer 1939-c.1945; *First statement*, copy writer and editorial board 1941-43; New York City College, NY, instructor in English 1946-51; McGill University, lecturer in English 1951-52, assistant professor 1953-61, associate professor 1962–; *CIV/n*, co-founder and editor 1955-56; *McGill poetry series*, founder and editor 1956–; *Delta*, founder and editor 1957-66;

Contact Press, Montreal, co-founder and publisher *c.*1951–.
AWARDS, HONOURS
Northern review poetry award, 1951; Canada council senior arts fellowship, 1959/60.
WRITINGS
East of the city, Ryerson, 1946; (with I. Layton and R. Souster) *Cerberus*, Contact, 1952; *The searching image*, Ryerson, 1952; *Twenty-four poems*, Contact, 1952; *Europe*, Contact, 1955; *The transparent sea*, Contact, 1956; *En Mexico*, Contact, 1958; *Laughing stalks*, Contact, 1958; *Literature and the press* (non-fiction), Ryerson, 1960; (with M. Régnier) *Montréal, Paris d' Amérique – Paris of America* (Non-fiction), Éditions du Jour, 1961; *Atlantis*, Contact, 1967; *The first person in literature* (radio script), CBC, 1967 (produced "Ideas," 8 Nov. 1966).
EDITED: (with I. Layton) *Canadian poems, 1850-1952*, Contact, 1952; *Poetry of our time*, Macmillan, 1965; (with M. Gnarowski) *The making of modern poetry in Canada*, Ryerson, 1967.
CONTRIBUTED: Poems and articles to *Unit of five*, edited by R. Hambleton, Ryerson, 1944; *Other Canadians*, edited by J. Sutherland, First Statement, 1947; *Canadian forum, Canadian poetry, Contemporary verse, Culture, Dalhousie review, Delta, Here and now, Queen's quarterly, Saturday night, Tamarack review*.

DUGAS, Jean-Paul
Actor.
HOME
3335 Ridgewood Ave., Apt. 7, Montreal 247, PQ.
CAREER
MEMBER
Union des Artistes de Montréal.
THEATRE
Played in many productions, e.g. Valère in *Le Tartuffe* (Théâtre du Nouveau Monde, Montréal, 1952/53), *Le corsaire* (Théâtre du Nouveau Monde, 1953), *Le monsieur de cinq heures* (Monument National, Montréal, 1953), Fortunio in *Le chandelier* (Le Théâtre Club, Montréal, Apr. 1955), *La petite hutte* (Théâtre du Rideau Vert, Montréal, 1956).

DUMBRILLE, Dorothy* 1897–
(Dorothy Dumbrille Smith)
Author; b. 25 Sept. 1897 in Crysler, Ont.; daughter of Rupert John and Minnie (Fulton) Dumbrille; m. James Travers Smith 27 Dec. 1924.
EDUCATION
Attended Kemptville High School, Ont.; business college in Philadelphia, Pa.
RELIGION
Anglican.
HOME
Alexandria, Ont.

CAREER
Department of Militia and Defence, Ottawa, Ont. 1916-21; Provident Mutual Life Insurance Co., Philadelphia, secretary to the vice-president 1921-24.

MEMBER
Canadian Authors Association (past executive); Ontario-St. Lawrence Development Commission (now The St. Lawrence Parks Commission); Glengarry Historical Association, Ont. (life member); Glengarry National Institute for the Blind (honorary member).

WRITINGS
We come! we come! (poems), Crucible, 1941; *Deep doorways* (novel), Allen, 1947 (first published in *The standard*, Montreal, PQ, 1941); *Last leave* (poems), Ryerson, 1942; *Watch the sun rise* (poems), Massey, 1943; *All this difference* (novel), Progress Books, 1945; *Stairway to the stars* (poems), Allen, 1946; *Up and down the glen* (non-fiction), Ryerson, 1954; *Braggart in my step* (non-fiction), Ryerson, 1956; *All the difference* (novel), Harlequin, 1963; (with H. Nelson) *La lo and lullaby* (poems), G.V. Thompson, 1964; *The battle of Crysler's Farm*, p.p., 1967; *A boy at Crysler's Farm*, p.p., 1968; radio plays.
CONTRIBUTED: Poems, stories, articles to *Flying colours*, edited by C.G.D. Roberts, Ryerson, 1942; *Canadian tribute to Mary*, compiled by Notre Dame College, Toronto, Ont., under the auspices of Canadian Federation of Convent Alumnae and the Marian Literary Research Committee, 1947; *So long ago, so well remembered*, Kemptville Centennial Committee, 1957; *Poems for boys and girls*, book 3, compiled by G. Morgan, Copp Clark, 1958; *Lyric and longer poems*, book 1, edited by A.H. Humble, Macmillan, 1959; *Rubaboo*, compiled by K. and L. Rix, Gage, 1964; many Canadian magazines, e.g. *Canadian author and bookman, Canadian poetry, National home monthly.*

DUNCAN, Norman 1871-1916
Novelist; b. 2 July 1871 in Brantford, Ont.; son of Robert Augustus and Susan (Hawley) Duncan; d. 18 Oct. 1916 in Buffalo, NY.

EDUCATION
Attended University of Toronto, 1891-95.

CAREER
Bulletin, Auburn, NY, journalist 1895-97; *New York evening post*, NY, journalist 1897-1900; *McClure's magazine*, correspondent for Newfoundland and Labrador coasts 1900-04; Washington and Jefferson College, Washington, Pa., professor of rhetoric 1901-06; *Harper's magazine*, Middle East correspondent 1907, Palestine, Egypt, Arabia, Australia, New Guinea, and Malaya correspondent 1912-13; University of Kansas, professor of English 1909-11.

WRITINGS
The soul of the street (short stories), McClure Phillips, 1900; *The way of the sea* (short stories), McClure Phillips, 1903; *Doctor Luke of the Labrador*, Revell, 1904; *Dr. Grenfell's parish: the deep sea fishermen* (biography), Revell, 1905; *The mother*, Revell, 1905; *The adventures of Billy Topsail* (juvenile fiction), Revell, 1906; *The cruise of the Shining Light*, Harper, 1907; *Every man for himself*, Harper, 1908; *Going down from Jerusalem* (non-fiction), Harper, 1909; *Higgins, a man's Christian* (biography), Harper, 1909; *The suitable child*, Revell, 1909; *Billy Topsail and company* (juvenile fiction), Revell, 1910; *Christmas Eve at Topmast Tickle*, Revell, 1910; *The measure of a man*, Revell, 1911; *The best of a bad job*, Frowde, 1912; *Finding his soul*, Harper, 1913; *The bird store man*, Revell, 1914; *Australian byways* (non-fiction), Harper, 1915; *Christmas Eve at Swamp's End*, Revell, 1915; *Billy Topsail, M.D.*, Revell, 1916; *Battles royal down north* (juvenile), Revell, 1918; *Harbour tales down north*, Revell, 1918.
CONTRIBUTED: Stories to *Atlantic monthly, Century, Delineator, Harper's monthly, Ladies' home journal.*

DUNHAM, Bertha Mabel
see DUNHAM, Mabel

DUNHAM, Mabel 1881-1957
(Bertha Mabel Dunham)
Novelist; b. 29 May 1881 in Harriston, Ont.; daughter of Martin and Magdalena (Eby) Dunham; d. 21 June 1957 in Kitchener, Ont.

EDUCATION
Attended public schools in Berlin, Ont. (now Kitchener); Toronto Normal School, Ont.; Victoria College, University of Toronto, BA, 1908; McGill University Library School.

RELIGION
United Church of Canada.

CAREER
Taught school 1898-1904; Berlin Public Library, chief librarian 1908-44; Waterloo College (now University of Waterloo), lecturer in library science 1932-45; travelled extensively in Canada, USA, and Europe.

MEMBER
Waterloo Historical Society, Ont. (president, 1947-50); Ontario Library Association (past president); Kitchener University Women's Club (1st president); Kitchener Business and Professional Women's Club (1st president); KW Quota Club (honorary president).

AWARDS, HONOURS
D Litt from University of Western Ontario, 1947; Book of the year for children medal from Canadian Library Association for *Kristli's trees*, 1948.

WRITINGS
Trail of the Conestoga, Macmillan, 1924; *Toward*

Sodom, Macmillan, 1927; *The trail of the king's men*, Ryerson, 1931; *So great a heritage* (nonfiction), Cober Printing Service, 1941; *Grand River* (non-fiction), McClelland & Stewart, 1945; *Kristli's trees* (juvenile), McClelland & Stewart, 1948.
CONTRIBUTED: Articles to *Ontario library review*.

DUVAL, Pierre
Singer (tenor).
EDUCATION
Studied with Dina Narici, Conservatory of Music and Dramatic Art, Montreal; St. Cecilia's Academy, Rome, Italy; studied with Maestro Alberto Volonnino for 3 years.
HOME
1992 Nice St., Ville de Laval, PQ.
CAREER
New York City Opera, NY; Philadelphia Opera, Pa.
AWARDS, HONOURS
Quebec Government scholarship, *c.*1962; Canada Council arts scholarship, 1963/64.
THEATRE
Debut in *The nightingale* (Rome Opera House, 1962); sang in many productions, e.g. Alfredo in *La traviata* (Théâtre Lyrique de Nouvelle France, Québec, PQ, 23 Oct. 1965), *Carmina burana* (concert version, Los Angeles, Calif., Apr. 1966; Les Grands Ballets Canadiens, Place des Arts, Montréal, 12 Nov. 1966; World Festival, Salle Wilfrid Pelletier, Montréal, 23 June 1967), lead in *La sonnambula* (Hartford, Conn. *c.*1966), Gérald in *Lakmé* (Les Jeunesses Musicales du Canada, Feb. 1967), *La belle Hélène* (Théâtre Lyrique de Montréal, 19 Apr. 1967) *Rigoletto* (Vancouver Opera Association, BC, 21 Oct. 1967), *Requiem* by Verdi (50th anniversary of Cleveland Symphony Orchestra, Ohio, 1968), Rodolfo in *La bohème* (Canadian Opera Company, Toronto, Ont., 23 Sept. 1968), *Tosca* (Théâtre Lyrique du Québec, Québec, 23 Nov. 1968).
TELEVISION
Sang in several CBC productions, e.g. *The barber of Seville* ("Heure du concert," Mar. 1965; "Festival," 3 Nov. 1965).

DYONNET, Edmond   1859-1954
Artist; b. 25 June 1859 in Crest, France; son of Ulysse-Alexandre and Albine (Goullioud) Dyonnet; came to Canada 1875 and settled in Montreal, PQ; d. 9 July 1954 in Montreal.
EDUCATION
Attended municipal schools in Turin, Italy, 1868-73; attended Collège de Crest in France, 1873-75; studied under Gilardi and Gastaldi at the Reale Accademia Albertina, Turin, 1880; studied under Morelli in Naples, Italy, and at Scuola Libera in Rome, Italy for four years *c.*1882.

CAREER
Council of Arts and Manufactures (Monument National), Montreal, head teacher of drawing 1891-1922; École Polytechnique, Montréal, professor 1907-23; McGill University, Department of Architecture, professor 1920-36; École des Beaux-Arts, Montréal, teacher 1922-24; school of the Art Association of Montreal, head 1925-30; conducted evening classes of Royal Canadian Academy in Montreal for many years; travelled to England with Royal Canadian Academy exhibition shown at the Festival of the Empire, London, England, 1910; teacher and portrait painter in Montreal *c.*1885-1954.
MEMBER
Royal Canadian Academy (Associate 1892; Academician 1901; secretary, 1910-48).
AWARDS, HONOURS
Silver medal, Pan-American Exposition, Buffalo, NY, 1901; silver medal, Louisiana Purchase Exposition, St. Louis, Mo., 1904; appointed Officier d'Académie by French government, 1910.
EXHIBITIONS
GROUP: Represented in group exhibitions held in Canada during his life time including annual exhibitions of Royal Canadian Academy; Pan-American Exposition, Buffalo, 1901; Louisiana Purchase Exposition, St. Louis, 1904; A Century of Canadian Art, Tate Gallery, London, England, 1938.
COLLECTIONS IN WHICH REPRESENTED
National Gallery of Canada, Ottawa, Ont.; Montreal Museum of Fine Arts; Musée du Québec, PQ; Owens Museum, Mount Allison University.

EADY, W.P.R., pseud.
see GLASSCO, John

EBERT, Peter   1918-
Stage director; b. 1918 in Frankfurt, Germany; son of Carl Ebert; children: 5 girls, 4 boys; came to Canada 1 Jan. 1967.
EDUCATION
Formal education in England.
OFFICE
Royal Conservatory of Music, Opera School, 273 Bloor St. W., Toronto, Ont.
CAREER
Director of opera productions in Britain, Denmark, Holland, Switzerland, Germany, Italy, USA and Canada; Academy of Music, Hannover, Germany, director of opera classes; Canadian Opera Company, Toronto, stage director 1967-; Royal Conservatory of Music Opera School, Toronto, director 1967-; Städtische Bühnen, Augsburg, Germany, general intendant 1968-.
THEATRE
Directed many productions, e.g. *Salome* (Music

Center, Los Angeles, Calif., 1965), *The tales of Hoffman* (Canadian Opera Company, Toronto, 20 Sept. 1967), *Oedipus rex* (Royal Conservatory of Music Opera School, 1967/68), *The magic flute* (Royal Conservatory of Music Opera School, 1967/68), *The devils* (Hart House Theatre, Toronto, 1967/68).

FILM
Directed several productions in England until 1939; directed documentary film on operas in Glyndebourne, England, Edinburgh and Glasgow, Scotland, Johannesburg, South Africa, and Los Angeles (BBC, summer 1967).

TELEVISION
Produced operas and music programs for BBC.

EDDY, Albert, pseud.
see GLASSCO, John

ELOUL, Rita Letendre
see LETENDRE, Rita

EWEN, Paterson   1925–
Artist; b. 7 Apr. 1925 in Montreal; m. Françoise Sullivan.

EDUCATION
Attended McGill University, 1948-49; studied under John Lyman (*q.v.*) for two years; at Montreal Museum of Fine Arts, 1950-51; under Goodridge Roberts (*q.v.*) and Arthur Lismer (*q.v.*) for two years.

HOME
823 Vinet, Montreal, PQ.

CAREER
Employed at one time by the Province of Quebec; painter in Montreal.

MEMBER
L'Association des Artistes non-figuratifs de Montréal.

AWARDS, HONOURS
Prix des Laurentides, 1958; second prize, Concours artistique de la Province de Québec, 1958; purchase award, Spring Exhibition, Montreal Museum of Fine Arts, 1961; Canada Council senior arts fellowship, 1964.

EXHIBITIONS
ONE-MAN: Gallery XII, Montreal Museum of Fine Arts, 1955 and 1963; Parma Gallery, New York, NY, 1956 and 1958; Galerie Denyse Delrue, Montréal, 1958, 1960, 1961 and 1962; Association des Architectes, Montréal, 1962; Galerie du Siècle, Montréal, 1963 and 1966; Dunkelman Gallery, Toronto, Ont.
GROUP: Represented in group exhibitions held in Canada; International Water-colour Exhibition, Brooklyn Museum, NY, 1959; Aspects of Canadian Painting, Canada House, New York, NY, 1959; Little international, toured USA, 1960; *Festival des Deux Mondes*, Spoleto, Italy, 1962.

COLLECTIONS IN WHICH REPRESENTED
Montreal Museum of Fine Arts; Musée du Québec, PQ; Stedelijk Museum, Amsterdam, The Netherlands; National Gallery of Canada, Ottawa, Ont.; Sir George Williams University.

FARRALLY, Betty*   1915–
(Betty Hey)
Dancer and teacher; b. 1915 in Bradford, England; daughter of Arthur and Ada (Sugden) Hey; came to Canada in 1938; m. John Hudson Farrally Nov. 1942; children: Richard Blaise b. 14 Feb. 1944.

EDUCATION
Attended Harrogate Ladies College in England; Torch School of Dance, Leeds, England.

OFFICE
Canadian School of Ballet (Okanagan Valley), RR 4, Kelowna, BC.

CAREER
Canadian School of Ballet, co-founder and director 1938–; (now Royal) Winnipeg Ballet, Man., co-founder, director, producer, and ballet mistress 1938-57; Banff School of Fine Arts, Alta., co-director of ballet division; Banff School Festival Ballet, co-director and company manager.

MEMBER
AEA.

FAUCHER, Jean*   1924–
Producer; b. 19 Oct. 1924 in Vésinet, Seine et Oise, France; son of Leonard and Aimée (Pulby) Faucher; m. Françoise Faucher 1950; children: Philippe b. 1951, Sophie b. 1958, François b. 1959, Catherine b. 1963.

EDUCATION
Attended Lycée Charlemagne, Paris, France; Université de Droit, Paris; studied drama with René Simon, Paris.

RELIGION
Roman Catholic.

HOME
4415 Circle Rd., Montreal, PQ.

OFFICE
Canadian Broadcasting Corporation, 1425 Dorchester St. W., Montreal, PQ.

CAREER
CBC, Montreal, TV producer; Théâtre du Rideau Vert, Montréal, actor 1960–.

THEATRE
Directed *Mary, Mary* (Théâtre International de Montréal), *Les gueux au paradis* (Rideau Vert), *On ne badine pas avec l'amour* (Rideau Vert), *Un couple parfait* (Théâtre de la Poudrière, Montréal), *Du vent dans les branches de sassafras* (Rideau Vert), *Piphagne* (Les Compagnons de

Saint-Laurent, Montréal, 1951), *La mamma* (Rideau Vert, 1959), *Week end* (Théâtre de Marjolaine, Eastman, PQ, 1960), *Partage de midi* (Rideau Vert, 1962; trophy for best theatre production, 1962), *Pour Lucrèce* (Rideau Vert, 1963), *Fleur de cactus* (Rideau Vert, 1965).

RADIO

Wrote numerous scripts for CBC programs, e.g. *Paris a mon coeur* (1951/52), several scripts for "Nouveautés dramatiques" (1952/53).

TELEVISION

Produced numerous CBC productions, e.g. *La chasse aux corbeaux, Humiliés et offensés, Volpone, La danse de mort, L'éternel mari, Par delà les âges, Marius, La reine morte, Madame Maura, Chacun son amour, Le disciple du diable, Béthanie, Hyménée, Les quatre coins du monde* (1953/54), *Anne-Marie* (series, 1954/55), *Quatuor* (series, 1955/57), *Le Léviathan* (1957), *La mercière assassinée* (1957), *Le dimanche j'attends* (1957), *Les noces de sang* (21 Jan. 1960), *L'échange* (1960), *Un mois à la campagne* (trophy for best TV production, Congrès du Spectacle, 1960), *Les frères Karamazov* (trophy for best TV production, Congrès du Spectacle, 1961).

FELDBRILL, Victor* 1924–

Conductor and music director; b. 4 Apr. 1924 in Toronto; son of Nathan and Helen (Ledermann) Feldbrill; m. Zelda Mann 30 Dec. 1945; children: Deborah Geraldine b. 24 Mar. 1951, Aviva Karen b. 19 May 1954.

EDUCATION

Attended Harbord Collegiate Institute in Toronto; Royal College of Music and Royal Academy of Music (studied with Sir Adrian Boult), London, England, 1943-45; Royal Conservatory of Music, Toronto, artist's diploma in violin and conducting 1949; studied with Pierre Monteux in Maine, 1949-50; studied conducting with Willem van Otterloo in Hilversum, The Netherlands, 1956; studied in Salzburg, Austria, 1956.

RELIGION

Hebrew.

HOME

170 Hillhurst Boul., Toronto, Ont.

CAREER

Conducted school performances of Gilbert and Sullivan operas 1938-41; Toronto Convocation Hall, formal debut conducting University of Toronto Symphony Orchestra, Feb. 1942; University of Toronto Symphony Orchestra, conductor 1942; RCNVR, 1942-45, leading bandsman; Toronto Symphony Orchestra, guest conductor 1943, 1948, violinist 1949-57, assistant conductor 1956-58; Royal Conservatory Symphony Orchestra and Opera Company, Toronto, concert master and assistant conductor

1945-49; Royal Conservatory Summer School Orchestra, conductor 1946-50; CBC Symphony Orchestra, violinist and guest conductor 1952–; Toronto Chamber Players, founder 1952, conductor 1952-53; Canadian Ballet Festival, conductor 1952; BBC, London, guest conductor 1957, annually 1960–; World's Fair, Brussels, Belgium, conductor 1958; Winnipeg Symphony Orchestra, Man., conductor and musical director, 1958-68; International Symposium of Contemporary Music, Stratford, Ont., conductor 1960; National Youth Orchestra of Canada, conductor and music director for four sessions 1960-63; Brussels Radio, guest conductor 1961; conducted in USSR 1963, 1966; guest conductor with orchestras in Toronto, Montreal, PQ, Vancouver, BC, Edmonton, Alta., Quebec, PQ, Ottawa, Ont., Regina, Sask., and Saskatoon, Sask.; Royal Winnipeg Ballet, guest conductor; Canadian Opera Company, conductor; University of Manitoba, lecturer in music.

MEMBER

AFMUSC, Toronto and Winnipeg centres; American Symphony Orchestra League (board member, 1960-67).

AWARDS, HONOURS

Concert Artists Guild of the USA award for encouragement of young musicians, 1964; Canadian League of Composers' Canada Music Citation for outstanding achievement in the furthering of performance of Canadian music, 1967; honorary citizen of the cities of Brandon and Dauphin, Man.; Manitoba, membership in Order of the Buffalo; Winnipeg community service award; Centennial medal, 1967; Canada Council senior arts award, 1968.

CONCERT STAGE

Conducted Canadian Opera Company in world première of *Louis Riel* by Harry Somers (q.v.) and Mavor Moore (q.v.; O'Keefe Centre, Toronto, Sept. 1967); conducted Winnipeg Symphony Orchestra in world première of *The democratic concerto* by Norman Symonds (1967).

RADIO

Conducted Winnipeg Symphony Orchestra, Toronto Symphony Orchestra, CBC Montreal Orchestra, CBC Vancouver Chamber Orchestra, CBC Symphony Orchestra, CBC Festival Orchestra in many programs and series on CBC, 1949–; commentator and speaker in many CBC series, e.g. "Music diary," "Music in education"; creator and conductor of two music appreciation series, 1952-60; conducted opening concert of "Focus" (CBC, 1955); conducted CBC Symphony Orchestra in world première of *Concerto for piano and orchestra* by Violet Archer (Toronto, 1958); conducted Toronto Symphony Orchestra in world première of *Eulogy in memory of John Fitzgerald Kennedy* by George Fiala, *The name-*

less hour by Norman Symonds, and *Piano concerto* by John Weinzweig (*q.v.*; "Concerts from two worlds," 1966); conducted Winnipeg Symphony Orchestra in world première of *Grant, warden of the plains* by Murray Adaskin (18 July 1967).

TELEVISION
Conducted in many concerts; conducted in many CBC series e.g. "Scope," "Folio," "Concert hour."

RECORDINGS
Conducted works for "Canadian music," series, RCA Victor; symphonic music on Canadian folk themes, Heritage Records; concerts, CBC IS.

FERLAND, Albert 1872-1943
Poet; b. 1872 in Montreal, PQ; d. 1943.

CAREER
Montreal, free evening schools, professor of graphic arts 1891; Ferland Studio of Poetry and Art, Montreal, 1894; Post Office Department, Montreal, artist 1910.

MEMBER
École littéraire de Montréal (past president); Royal Society of Canada.

WRITINGS
Mélodies poétiques, Bédard, 1893; *Femmes rêvées*, the author, 1899; *Le Canada chanté*, 4v. Granger, 1908-10; *Montréal, ma ville natal*, the author, 1946.
CONTRIBUTED: Poetry to *Franges d'autel*, 1900; *Les soirées du Château de Ramezay*, edited by l'École littéraire de Montréal, Dénécal, 1900; *Les soirées de l'École littéraire de Montréal*, 1925; *Anthologie des poètes canadiens*, edited by J. Fournier and O. Asselin, Granger, 1920; *Action canadienne-française, Canada-français, Le pays laurentien, Revue canadienne, Revue nationale, Transactions of the Royal Society of Canada*.

FILION, Jean-Paul* 1927—
Author, chansonnier, and artist; b. 24 Feb. 1927 near St. André Avellin, PQ; son of Napoléon and Laurenza (Desormeaux) Filion; m.; children: Josée, Claude.

EDUCATION
Attended École des Beaux-Arts, Montréal, PQ, 1945-52.

RELIGION
Agnostic.

HOME
22, rue de la Mairie, L'Ange Gardien, Montmorency, PQ.

OFFICE
560 boul. Hamel, Québec, PQ.

CAREER
Literary, artistic, and musical; spent 15 months in Paris, France; CBC, Montreal, assistant set designer.

THEATRE
Sang in theatres and "boîtes à chansons" throughout Quebec province.

MEMBER
CAPAC; Union des Artistes de Montréal; Société des Écrivains du Québec.

AWARDS, HONOURS
Grand prix de la chanson canadienne for *La folle*, 1958; Canada Council senior arts fellowship, 1959; Quebec province literature prize for *Un homme en laisse*, 1963.

COMPOSITIONS
Les îles de la Madeleine, film score, National Film Board of Canada; *Vivre en ce pays*, film score, CBC.

RECORDINGS
Chansons by Pathé, 1949; Gamma, 1967.

WRITINGS
Du centre de l'eau (poems), Hexagone, 1955; *C'est mon oeil: 12 chansons de Jean-Paul Filion*, Archambault, 1958; *Demain les herbes rouges* (poems), Hexagone, 1962; *Un homme en laisse* (novel), Jour, 1962; *La grandgigue* (TV play; produced CBC); *Une marche au soleil* (TV play; translated into English and produced "Playdate," CBC, 27 Apr. 1946); *Quand meurt l'image* (TV play); *Les amours neuves* (TV play); *La maison de Jean-Bel* (TV play).
CONTRIBUTED: Articles to *Culture vivante, Liberté*.

FINCH, Robert Duer Claydon* 1900—
Poet, artist, musician; b. 14 May 1900 in Freeport, Long Island, NY; son of Edward C.J. and Ada F. Finch; came to Canada in 1908.

EDUCATION
Attended private school in USA, public schools in Toronto; University College, University of Toronto, BA in French and German, 1925; attended La Sorbonne, Paris, France, 1926-27; studied music with Paul Wells and Alberto Guerrero in Canada; with Paul le Flem, Marcel Gautier, Croiza, and Landowska in France.

RELIGION
Anglican.

HOME
Massey College, 4 Devonshire Place, Toronto, Ont.

OFFICE
University College, Toronto, Ont.

CAREER
Ridley College, St. Catharines, Ont., teacher 1920-22; Hart House Theatre, Toronto, actor 1922-41; University College, University of Toronto, lecturer in French 1928-30, assistant professor 1931-42, associate professor 1943-51, professor 1952—; several lecture recitals in music, Heliconian Club and Alliance Française, Hart House Theatre and

Royal Ontario Museum, Toronto, 1930-33;
Leonard Foundation, Toronto, board of trustees;
Hart House Theatre, board of syndics; travelled
extensively in Canada, eastern USA, and Europe.
MEMBER
Royal Society of Canada (elected fellow, 1963).
AWARDS, HONOURS
Jardine memorial prize for poetry, 1924; Gover-
nor General's medal for languages, 1925; Québec
Bonne Entente prize, 1925; French government
scholarship for studies in French, 1926-27;
Governor General's literary award for *Poems*,
1946 and *Acis in Oxford*, 1960; Lorne Pierce
medal, 1968.
EXHIBITIONS
ONE-MAN: British Empire Gallery, Toronto,
1932; Picture Loan Society, Toronto, 1937, 1947,
1953, and 1959.
GROUP: Represented in group exhibitions held
in Canada including annual exhibitions of St.
Catharines Art Association and Society of Gra-
phic Art; Salon Nautique International, Grand
Palais, Paris, 1927; World's Fair, New York, NY,
Canadian Section, 1939.
WRITINGS
Poems, Oxford, 1946; *The strength of the hills*,
McClelland & Stewart, 1948; *Acis in Oxford*,
New Bodleian, 1959; *Dover beach revisited*,
Macmillan, 1961; *The sixth sense* (non-fiction),
University of Toronto, 1966; *Silverthorn bush
and other poems*, Macmillan, 1966; *A century
has roots, a masque ...* , University of Toronto,
1953 (produced Hart House Theatre, 1953).
EDITED: (with C.R. Parsons) F.A.R. Chateau-
briand's *René*, University of Toronto, 1957.
CONTRIBUTED: Poems to *New provinces*,
edited by F.R. Scott, Macmillan, 1936; *Oxford
book of Canadian verse in English and French*,
edited by A.J.M. Smith, Oxford, 1960; *Pen-
quin book of Canadian verse*, rev. ed., edited by
R. Gustafson, Penguin, 1967; *Canadian poetry,
Fiddlehead, Here and now, Saturday night,
Tamarack review.*
COMPOSITIONS
Incidental music for *Antigone* (Sophocles, Hart
House Theatre, 1936).

FIRMIN, Angela
see LEIGH, Angela

FISHER, Brian*   1939—
Artist; b. 10 Mar. 1939 in Uxbridge, England; son
of Joseph Henry and Lillian (Southam) Fisher;
came to Canada in 1940 and settled in Sask.; m.
Carole Itter 20 May 1964.
EDUCATION
Attended Regina, Sask., public schools until 1957;
studied under Ronald Bloore (*q.v.*), Arthur F.
McKay (*q.v.*), Kenneth Lochhead, and Roy
Kiyooka, Regina College School of Art,

University of Saskatchewan, 1957-59; studied
under Donald Jarvis, Vancouver School of Art,
BC, 1959-61; studied under Montanarni and
Macari, Accademia di Belle Arti, Rome, Italy,
1961-63.
HOME
218 W. 6th Ave., Vancouver 10, BC.
CAREER
Painter in Vancouver 1965—.
COMMISSIONS
Mural, Dorval Airport, Montreal, PQ, 1967.
AWARDS, HONOURS
Governor General's bronze medal, 1957; Reeves
scholarship, Vancouver School of Art, 1961; Ita-
lian government scholarship for study and travel,
1962; Canada Council junior fellowship for
study and travel in Italy, 1963; purchase award,
Young BC Painters exhibition, University of
Victoria, 1966; major award winner, Perspective
'67, Centennial Art Exhibition, 1967.
EXHIBITIONS
ONE-MAN: New Design Gallery, Vancouver,
1965 and 1966; Calgary Allied Arts Council, Alta.,
1966; Art Gallery of Greater Victoria, BC , 1966;
University of Manitoba School of Art, 1966;
York University, 1967; (with Claude Breeze) Nor-
man Mackenzie Art Gallery, Regina, 1967.
GROUP: Represented in exhibitions in British
Columbia and elsewhere in Canada; two-man
show, Gallerie Bilco, Rome, 1963; Pacific North-
west Annual Exhibition, Seattle, Wash., 1965.
COLLECTIONS IN WHICH REPRESENTED
Art Gallery of Greater Victoria; Art Gallery of
Ontario, Toronto; Brock Hall Collection, Univer-
sity of British Columbia; Canadian Industries
Limited Collection, Montreal; Canada Council,
Ottawa, Ont.; Department of External Affairs,
Ottawa; Memorial University Art Gallery; Mon-
treal Museum of Fine Arts; Norman Mackenzie
Art Gallery, Regina; Agnes Etherington Art
Centre, Queen's University; University of Calgary;
University of Victoria; University of Western
Ontario; Vancouver Art Gallery; Willistead Art
Gallery, Windsor, Ont.; York University.

FORBES, Kenneth Keith*   1892—
Artist; b. 4 July 1892 in Toronto, Ont.; son of
John Colin and Laura Gertrude (Holbrooke)
Forbes; m. Jean Mary Edgell 6 June 1919; chil-
dren: Laura June.
EDUCATION
Attended Westmount Academy, Montreal, PQ;
studied at St. John's Wood Art School, London,
England; Stanhope Forbes, Newlyn Art School,
Cornwall, England; Hospital Field Art School,
Arbroath, Scotland; H.H. Tonks and Wilson
Steer, Slade School of Art, London; Orchardson,
London and New Art School, 1912.
ADDRESS
153 Burbank Drive, Willowdale, Ont.

CAREER

Lived and studied in England 1908-24; champion boxer in England 1912-14; 10th Royal Fusiliers and 32nd Machine Gun Company, 1914-18, became captain, mentioned in dispatches twice; portrait, figure and landscape painter in Toronto 1924-.

MEMBER

Ontario Institute of Painters (co-founder, 1958; president, 1958); Ontario Society of Artists (elected, 1930; resigned, 1951); Royal Canadian Academy (Associate 1927; Academician 1933; resigned, 1959).

AWARDS, HONOURS

Four-year scholarship for study at Hospital Field Art School, 1910; William M. Chase scholarship, 1913; prize for portrait, National Academy of Design, New York, NY, 1932 and 1940; prize, Sanity in Art exhibition, Chicago, Ill., 1938; Medal of service of the Order of Canada, 1967.

EXHIBITIONS

ONE-MAN: Art Gallery of Ontario, Toronto, 1936; Norman Mackenzie Art Gallery, Regina, Sask., 1962.

GROUP: Represented in group exhibitions held in Canada from 1924 on including annual exhibitions of Royal Canadian Academy and Ontario Society of Artists; represented in group exhibitions organized by National Gallery of Canada, Ottawa, Ont., including its Annual Exhibitions; represented in group exhibitions held in England from 1915 on including exhibitions of Royal Academy, London; represented in exhibitions of National Academy of Design, New York; represented England in the International Exhibition, Carnegie Institute, Pittsburgh, Pa., 1924; Royal Glasgow Institute, Scotland, 1937; A Century of Canadian Art, Tate Gallery, London, 1938; World's Fair, New York, 1939.

COLLECTIONS IN WHICH REPRESENTED

Art Gallery of Ontario; Columbus Gallery of Fine Art, Ohio; National Gallery of Canada; University of Saskatchewan; Walker Art Gallery, Liverpool, England; Owens Museum, Mount Allison University.

FORRESTER, Maureen 1931–

(Maureen Kathleen Stewart Forrester Kash) Singer (contralto); b. 25 July 1931 in Montreal; daughter of Thomas and May Forrester; m. Eugene Kash (*q.v.*) July 1954; children: Paula b. *c.*1956, Gina Deborah b. *c.*1959, Daniel Joshua b. *c.*1960, Linda Valerie b. 17 Jan. 1962, daughter b. 18 Dec. 1965.

EDUCATION

Attended Sir William Dawson High School, Montreal, until 1943; studied voice with Sally Martin, 1946-49; with Frank Rowe, 1949-51; with Bernard Diamant, 1951–.

HOME

338 Roslyn St., Westmount, Montreal, PQ.

CAREER

Fairmount-Taylor Presbyterian Church, Montreal, regular soloist; York Concert Society Orchestra, Toronto, under Dr. Heinz Unger; Ottawa Philharmonic Orchestra; Halifax Symphony Orchestra; Chalet Symphony Orchestra under Milton Katims; CBC Symphony Orchestra; Sherbrooke Symphony Orchestra, PQ; St. Catharines Orchestra and Kitchener Orchestra, Ont.; New York Philharmonic Orchestra, NY; Royal Philharmonic of London, BBC Symphony, Liverpool Symphony, Bournemouth Symphony Orchestras, England; Concertgebouw Orchestra, Amsterdam, The Netherlands; Berlin Philharmonic Orchestra, Germany; Tivoli of Copenhagen Symphony Orchestra, Denmark; Oslo Philharmonic Orchestra, Norway; Lamoureux of Paris Orchestra, France; Music Festivals at Stockholm, Sweden, Berlin, Montreux, Switzerland, Bournemouth, England, Vancouver, BC, and Montreal; Montreal Symphony's Mozart Festival, *c.*1955; Edinburgh International Festival, Scotland, 1957; Paris Festival, France, 1957; Israel Festival, Jerusalem, 1960, Aug. and Sept. 1961; Festival Casals, Puerto Rico, 1960, 1961, and 1963; Stratford, Ont. Festival, 30 July 1961; Festival Maggio Musicale, Florence, Italy, 1963; Vienna Festival, Austria, May 1964; Salzburg Festival, Austria, Aug. 1965; Marlborough Festival, England, 1965; Hollywood Bowl, Calif., 1965; Les Jeunesses Musicales du Canada, Canadian tour, 1953 and European tour, 1955; toured USA, 1954, 1957, 1965; Europe annually; North Africa, 1957, Scandinavia, 1957, Australia, fall 1961, 1962, USSR, 1961/62; private coaching 1965; Royal Conservatory of Music, Summer School, Toronto, instructor of master classes, July 1965, 1966; Academy of Music, Philadelphia, Pa., chairman of voice department and artist-in-residence 1966.

AWARDS, HONOURS

Ladies Morning Music Club scholarship; Montreal Social Club scholarship; CBC "Opportunity knocks" finalist; International Nickel Company of Canada centennial scholarship, 1967; University of Alberta national award in music, 1967; Companion of the Order of Canada, 1967.

THEATRE

Formal Canadian debut (YWCA, Montreal, Mar. 1953); sang in numerous concerts and opera productions, e.g. *Xerxes, Rodelinda,* leading role in *El pesebre, Le roi David, Israel in Egypt, L'enfance du Christ, Requiem* by Mozart, *Requiem* by Verdi, *St. John's passion, Messiah* (Toronto Mendelssohn Choir under Sir Ernest MacMillan), *Elijah* (St. James United Church, Montreal, 1953), *The consul* (Cornwall, Ont., May 1953), *Symphony no. 9* by Beethoven (Montreal Symphony

Orchestra under Otto Klemperer, c.1953; under Zubin Mehta, Sept. 1963), European debut in Paris (Salle Gaveau, 1955), New York recital debut (Town Hall, New York, 12 Nov. 1956), *Resurrection symphony* (New York Philharmonic Orchestra under Bruno Walter, Carnegie Hall, New York, 17 Feb. 1957), Gala Spring Festival (Paris, 1957), London debut (Royal Philharmonic Orchestra under Sir Thomas Beecham, Royal Festival Hall, England, 1957), guest artist (Berlin Philharmonic Orchestra, May 1957), Nancy in *Albert Herring* (summer 1957), *Symphony no. 2* by Mahler (New York, 1957), *Concert* (Montreal Symphony Orchestra, 14 Oct. 1957), *La demoiselle élue* (New York Philharmonic Orchestra and choir under Leonard Bernstein, Carnegie Hall, New York, 14 Nov. 1957), Recital (Town Hall, New York, 1 Dec. 1957), Lieder recital (Town Hall, New York, 15 Dec. 1957), *Symphony no. 3* by Mahler (Concertgebouw Orchestra under E. von Beinum, Holland Music Festival, c.1957), *Das Lied von der Erde* (Berlin Philharmonic Orchestra, 1958; Toronto Symphony Orchestra, 1958; Cleveland Orchestra, Ohio, 1960; New York Philharmonic Orchestra, Apr. 1960; Montreal Symphony Orchestra, Place des Arts, Montréal, Feb. 1964), Recital (Toronto Symphony Orchestra, Massey Hall, Toronto, Mar. 1958), New York opera debut as Cornelia in *Julius Caesar* (American Opera Society, 18 Nov. 1958; New York City Opera, Lincoln Center, Oct. 1966), *Alto rhapsody* (Casals Festival, Puerto Rico, 1960), *Bar Mitzvah* (world première, Israel Music Festival, Jerusalem, 1961), *Italienisches Liederbuch* (Dumbarton Oaks, DC, 1962), Orfeo in *Orfeo ed Euridice* (O'Keefe Centre, Toronto, 28 May 1962), Brangaine in *Tristan and Isolde* (Teatro Colon, Buenos Aires, Argentina, 1963), *Missa solemnis* (Vienna Festival, 1966), 7 Concerts (Carnegie Hall, New York, 1966), *The confession stone* (world première, 21 July 1966), *Otello* (opening of concert hall, Expo 67, Montreal, 1967), Recital (Stratford, Ont. Festival, 1967), *Dido and Aeneas* (Chicago Opera, June 1967), La Cieca in *La gioconda* (San Francisco Opera, fall 1967), Recital (2 Oct. 1967), Concert (Carnegie Hall, New York, 2 Feb. 1968).

FILM

Guest soloist in *Festival in Puerto Rico* (National Film Board of Canada, 1961).

RADIO

Sang in numerous CBC productions, e.g. *Messiah* ("Concert hour," 2 Jan. 1957), *La demoiselle élue* (17 Nov. 1957), *Recital* (Mar. 1958), *Symphony no. 9* by Beethoven (20 Dec. 1959), *Recital* ("Summer Festival," 6 Aug. 1961), *Stratford, Ont. Festival* ("Wednesday night," 29 Aug. 1962; 12 June 1967), *Lieder eines fahrenden*

Gesellen (24 Nov. 1963), *Chants de Buchenwald* ("Concerts from two worlds," 7 Mar. 1964), *St. Matthew Passion* ("Sunday night," 29 Mar. 1964), *Ten centuries concert* (12 Apr. 1964), "Celebrity concerts" (26 July 1964), "Opera time" (21 Nov. 1964), *Music of the church* (31 Jan. 1965), *Cinderella* ("Opera time," 30 Oct. 1965), *The music of Mannheim* ("Tuesday night," 2 Nov. 1965), "University celebrity series" ("Tuesday night," 12 Apr. 1966; 21 Apr. 1967), *The patient Socrates* (29 May 1966), "This week's artist" (11, 12, 13, 14 July 1966), "Centennial concerts" ("Thursday music," 16 Feb. 1967), *Das Lied von der Erde* (25 May 1967), "Distinguished Canadian artists" (10, 30 July 1967), *Music from Expo* (20 Aug. 1967), *Friday concert* (27 Oct. 1967), "Centenary concerts" (7 Dec. 1967), *Celebrity recital* (15 Dec. 1967; "Thursday music," 11 July 1968), *Saturday evening* (9 Mar. 1968), *Music* (19 July 1968).

TELEVISION

Sang in *St. Matthew Passion* (NBC, New York, 1962) and in many CBC productions, e.g. *Les Jeunesses Musicales du Canada* (12 Mar. 1963), "Praise of great performers" ("Festival," 30 June 1965), *Spanish love songs* (6 July 1966), "Centennial performance" (4 Oct. 1967), "Telescope" (winter 1967; 1 Aug. 1968).

RECORDINGS

Hercules, Julius Caesar, Orfeo ed Euridice, Symphony no. 3 by Mahler, *Selections* by Purcell, *A charm of lullabies, Frauenliebe und Leben. Symphony no. 9* by Beethoven, Decca DXB 157 (DL 10,002-10,003) 1959; RCA Victor LM 6066, 1959; RCA Victor LSC 6066, 1959; RCA Victor LSC 6066, 1959; 2-Victor VIC 6003, 1965; 2-Victor VICS - 6003, 1965. *Lieder* by Brahms, RCA Victor LSC 2275, 1959; RCA Victor LM 2275, 1959. *Symphony no. 2* by Mahler, New York Philharmonic Orchestra, Columbia M2L 256 (ML 5303-5304) 1958; Columbia M2S-501 (MS 6008-6009) 1960. *Das Lied von der Erde,* Chicago Symphony Orchestra under Fritz Reiner, RCA Victor LM 6087, 1960; RCA Victor LSC 6087, 1960. *Lieder eines fahrenden Gesellen,* Boston Symphony Orchestra under Charles Munch, RCA Victor, LM 2371, 1960; RCA Victor LSC 2371, 1960. *Songs to Shakespeare's plays* by Arne, Vienna Radio Orchestra, Westminster 19075; 17075. *4 arias by Bach, 4 arias by Händel,* solisti di Zagreb, Bach 669, 70699. *Cantata no. 35 and 42* by Bach, Vienna Radio Orchestra, Westminster 19080, 17080. *Cantata 53, 54, 169* by Bach, solisti di Zagreb, Bach 670, 70670. *Cantata 170* by Bach, *Salve regina* by Scarlatti, Vienna solisti, Bach 683, 70683. *Easter oratorio* by Bach, Philadelphia Orchestra, Columbia ML 5938, MS 6539. *Rodelinda* by Händel, Vienna Radio Orchestra, 3-West-

minster 3320, 320. *Excerpts of Rodelinda,*
Westminster 19102, 17102. *Serse* by Händel,
Vienna Radio Orchestra, 3-Westminster 3321-321.
Youth's magic horn, Vienna Festival Symphony
Orchestra, Vanguard 1113, 2154. *After hours*
by Mozart, Vienna State Opera Orchestra, Van-
guard 9165, 79165. *Operatic arias and songs*,
Vienna State Opera Orchestra, Westminster
19074, 17074. *Requiem* by Verdi, Philadelphia
Orchestra, 2-Columbia M2L-307, M2S-707.

FORSTER, Francis Michael   1907–
(Michael Forster)
Artist; b. 4 May 1907 in Calcutta, India; came to
Canada in 1933.
EDUCATION
Attended school in London, England; studied
with Bernard Meninsky and William Roberts in
Paris, France.
CAREER
Worked in New York, NY and Hollywood, Calif.;
returned to Canada, 1939; RCN, 1944-46,
official war artist; painted in the Virgin Islands,
1946-47; Jesuit University, Mexico, worked on
murals and taught.
EXHIBITIONS
ONE-MAN: Picture Loan Society, Toronto, Ont.,
1941.
GROUP: Represented in group exhibitions held
in Canada; represented in group exhibitions or-
ganized by National Gallery of Canada, Ottawa,
Ont.; World's Fair, New York, 1939; Rio de
Janeiro, Brazil, 1946; *UNESCO ... Exposition internationale d'art moderne, peinture, graphique
et décoratif, architecture*, Musée d'Art Moderne,
Paris, 1946; Aspects of Contemporary Painting
in Canada, Phillips Academy, Andover, Mass.,
1942.
COLLECTIONS IN WHICH REPRESENTED
National Gallery of Canada; Art Gallery of Ontario, Toronto.
WRITINGS
CONTRIBUTED: To *Canadian art; Montreal
standard.*

FORSTER, Michael
see FORSTER, Francis Michael

FORTIN, Marc-Aurèle   1888-1970
Artist; b. 14 Mar. 1888 in Sainte Rose, PQ; son
of Thomas Fortin; d. 2 Mar. 1970 in Macamic, PQ.
EDUCATION
Attended primary school in Sainte Rose; attended École du Plateau in Montreal, PQ; studied
under Ludger Larose (*q.v.*) and Edmond Dyonnet (*q.v.*), Monument National evening classes in
Montreal; Ludger Larose at Le Plateau, Montréal,
1904-08; Tarbell, Timmons, Vanderpoel, and
Alexander, Art Institute of Chicago, Ill., and in

Alexander, Art Institute of Chicago, Ill., and in
Boston, Mass., 1909-14; Sir Alfred East in London, England and in Paris, France, 1920-22.
RELIGION
Roman Catholic.
CAREER
Employed in the Post Office Department in Mon-
treal and in a bank in Edmonton, Alta., 1908-14;
painted in Quebec 1914-20, 1922-35; studied and
painted in Europe 1920-22; painted in southern
France and northern Italy 1935; painted in the
Baie-Saint-Paul region and in the Gaspé in PQ
1935-42; painted in Sainte-Rose, in the Gaspé,
and in the Lac Saint-Jean region 1946-55; almost
ceased painting due to ill health 1955-62; resumed
painting briefly in 1962.
MEMBER
Royal Canadian Academy (Associate 1942).
AWARDS, HONOURS
Scholarship for study in London and Paris, 1920;
Jessie Dow prize for water colour, Spring Exhibi-
tion, Art Association of Montreal, 1938; bronze
medal, World's Fair, New York, NY, 1939; grand
prize, Concours Provincal de Québec, 1945.
EXHIBITIONS
ONE-MAN: Several exhibitions at T. Eaton Company gallery, Montreal, 1935 and subsequent
years; exhibitions every two years at La Galerie
L'Art Français, Montréal, PQ, 1942-57; Musée du
Québec, PQ, 1944; C.J. Van Der A.A., Almelo,
The Netherlands, 1948; Montreal Museum of Fine
Arts, 1954; Queen Elizabeth Hotel, Montreal,
1958; National Gallery of Canada, Ottawa, Ont.,
and later on tour in NB, PQ, Ont., and Sask., 1963-
64; Centre culturel de Verdun, PQ, 1968.
GROUP: Represented in group exhibitions held
in Canada including annual exhibitions of Royal
Canadian Academy and Spring Exhibitions of
Montreal Museum of Fine Arts; represented in
group exhibitions organized by National Gallery
of Canada including its annual exhibitions; represented in group exhibitions held in Chicago,
1929, Pretoria, South Africa, 1930, and National
Gallery of Japan, Osaka; A Century of Canadian
Art, Tate Gallery, London, England, 1938; Exhi-
bition of Water Colours by Canadian Artists,
Gloucester, England, 1939; World's Fair, New
York, 1939; Exhibition of Canadian Graphic
Arts, São Paulo and Rio de Janeiro, Brazil,
1946; UNESCO ... *Exposition internationale d'art
moderne, peinture, graphique et décoratif, arch-
itecture*, Musée d'Art Moderne, Paris, 1946.
COLLECTIONS IN WHICH REPRESENTED
Montreal Museum of Fine Arts; National Gallery
of Canada; Musée du Québec; Agnes Etherington
Art Centre, Queen's University; Séminaire de
Joliette, PQ; Collège Grasset, Montréal; Musée
d'Art Contemporain, Montréal.

FOX, Beryl* 1931–
Film maker; b. 10 Dec. 1931 in Winnipeg, Man.;
daughter of Meyer and Sipora (Shliefman) Fox.
EDUCATION
University of Toronto, BA, 1951.
RELIGION
Jewish.
HOME
21 Woodlawn Ave. E., Toronto, Ont.
CAREER
CBC, Toronto, editor and director 1960-66; CBS,
New York, NY 1966-67; Public Broadcast Labs,
New York 1967–.
FILMS
Co-produced *The servant of all* (CBC, 1962),
Three on a match (CBC, 1962), *One more river*
(CBC, 1963; Wilderness award, CBC, 1963),
Balance of terror (Talent Association Para-
mount, New York, 1963), *The chief* (CBC, 1964;
award, Vancouver Film Festival, BC); directed
"Living camera" (series, CBC, 16 May - 13 June
1964); produced "Compass" (series, CBC, 1965);
directed and produced *The single woman and
the double standard* (1965); directed "This hour
has seven days" (series, CBC, 1965; [*Summer in
Mississippi* episode, 1965] award, Canadian Film
Awards, Toronto; award, Ohio Film Awards;
award, Commonwealth Film Festival, Cardiff,
Wales; award, Vancouver Film Festival; award,
Film Festival Oberhausen, Germany; special
mention, Montreal Film Festival, PQ;. [*The mills
of the gods* episode, 1965] Wilderness award, CBC,
1965; George Polk memorial award, Department
of Journalism, Long Island University, 1966;
certificate of merit and film of the year award,
Canadian Film Awards, Toronto; award, Vancouver Film Festival); produced and directed
Saigon (CBS, 1967), *Last reflections on a war*
("The way it is," CBC, 10 Mar. 1968).

FRANCHÈRE, Joseph Charles 1866-1921
Artist; b. 4 Mar. 1866 in Montreal, PQ; d. 12 May
1921 in Montreal.
EDUCATION
Studied under M. Chabert, Institut national des
Beaux-Arts, Montréal; Gérôme, École des Beaux-
Arts, Paris, France; Joseph Blanc in Paris; at
Académie Colarossi, Paris.
CAREER
Painted pictures for Sacré-Coeur Chapel, Mon-
treal in the 1890's; painted in Montreal 1890-
1921.
MEMBER
Royal Canadian Academy (Associate 1902).
AWARDS, HONOURS
Three honourable mentions, École des Beaux-
Arts, Paris; two first prize medals, evening schools
in Paris.

EXHIBITIONS
GROUP: Represented in group exhibitions held
in Canada during his lifetime including annual
exhibitions of Royal Canadian Academy and
Spring Exhibitions of Art Association of Montreal;
Paintings by Canadian Artists, City Art Museum,
St. Louis, Mo., 1918; Morse Gallery, Winter Park,
Fla., 1943.
COLLECTIONS IN WHICH REPRESENTED
National Gallery of Canada, Ottawa, Ont.; Musée
du Québec, PQ.

FRANDERO, pseud.
see DESROCHES, Francis

FRASER, Carol Lucille* 1930–
(Carol Lucille Hoorn)
Artist; b. 5 Sept. 1930 in Superior, Wis.; daughter
of Arvid Ferdinand and Alice Hazel (Mereness)
Hoorn; m. John Fraser 8 Sept. 1956; came to
Canada 10 Aug. 1961 and settled in Halifax.
EDUCATION
Attended Peter Cooper School and Central High
School in Superior; Gustavus Adolphus College,
St. Peter, Minn., BS, 1951; studied theology at
Göttingen University, Germany, 1952-53; Univer-
sity of Minnesota, MFA, 1958.
HOME
1352 Queen St., Halifax, NS.
CAREER
University of Minnesota, instructor in painting,
sculpture, and art history 1955-61; illustrated
Folk tales of Liberia, by J. Luke Creel, Dennison,
1960; painter in Halifax, 1961–.
COMMISSIONS
Painting, Waegwoltic Club, Halifax, 1967.
AWARDS, HONOURS
First prize and purchase award, Walker Art Center
Biennials, Minneapolis, Minn., 1956 and 1958;
first prize for painting, Spring Biennial, Minneapolis
Institute of Art, 1959; purchase award, Sixteen
Minnesota Artists, Walker Art Center, 1960;
Canada Council arts award, 1966/67.
EXHIBITIONS
ONE-MAN: Penthouse Gallery, Montreal, PQ,
1964; Atlantic Provinces Art Circuit, 1965, 1966,
and 1967; Wells Gallery, Ottawa, Ont., 1967.
GROUP: Represented in group exhibitions held
in Canada from 1961 on including Spring Exhibi-
tions of Montreal Museum of Fine Arts; fifth and
sixth Biennial Exhibitions of Canadian Painting,
National Gallery of Canada, Ottawa, 1963 and
1965; Walker Art Center Biennials, 1956 and
1958; University of Minnesota Gallery 1956,
1957, 1958, 1959, and 1960; UNESCO Travelling
Show, 1958-59; Spring Biennial, Minneapolis
Institute of Art, 1959; Sixteen Minnesota Artists,
Walker Art Center, 1960; Minneapolis First

National Bank Exhibition, 1961; Drawing, USA, St. Paul Gallery, St. Paul, Minn., 1963.

COLLECTIONS IN WHICH REPRESENTED
Walker Art Center; University of Minnesota; Minneapolis Public Library; Sir George Williams University; National Gallery of Canada; Confederation Art Gallery and Museum, Charlottetown, PEI; Canada Council, Ottawa; Mount Allison University; Dalhousie University; University of New Brunswick.

FREEDMAN, Harry 1922—
Composer and horn player; b. 5 Apr. 1922 in Lodz, Poland; came to Canada in 1925 and settled in Medicine Hat, Alta.; m. Mary Morrison (q.v.) 15 Sept. 1951; children: Karen Liese b. 21 Oct. 1953, Cynthia Jane b. 27 Sept. 1956, Lori Ann b. 19 Mar. 1958.

EDUCATION
Studied clarinet with Arthur Hart in Winnipeg, Man., c.1938-42; studied oboe with Perry Bauman, composition with John Weinzweig (q.v.), Toronto (now Royal) Conservatory of Music, 1945-47, 1949-50; studied with Ernst Krenek, 1953.

HOME
35 St. Andrews Gdns., Toronto 5, Ont.

CAREER
RCAF during World War II; Toronto Symphony Orchestra, English horn player 1946—; CBC Symphony Orchestra, English horn player 1952—.

MEMBER
CAPAC; Toronto Musicians Association.

AWARDS, HONOURS
Toronto Conservatory of Music scholarship, 1949-50; Canada Council grant, 1960, 1965.

RADIO
Compiler and narrator, *Parodies and paraphrases* ("Wednesday night," CBC, 12 Dec. 1962); gave 6 programs *Bach, Brubeck and all that jazz* ("Wednesday night," CBC, 1963); host "Thursday music" (series, CBC, 1968—).

COMPOSITIONS
Divertimento, oboe and strings, 1947, first performed 1949 in Toronto by Royal Conservatory Orchestra under Victor Feldbrill, with composer as oboist; *Symphonic suite*, orchestra, 1948; *Trio*, 2 oboes and English horn, 1948; *Nocturne*, orchestra, 1949, first performed 1952 in Toronto at Canadian League of Composers concert, recorded by CBC IS no. 71 with Toronto Symphony Orchestra under Geoffrey Waddington; *Five pieces for string quartet*, 1949, first performed 1949 in Toronto by Conservatory String Quartet, recorded by CBC IS no. 43 with Parlow String Quartet; *Piano suite*, 1950; *Scherzo*, piano, F. Harris; *Six French-Canadian folksongs*, 1950, violin and piano; *March; pastoral*, woodwinds, 1951; *Matinee suite*, orchestra, 1951-55; *March for small types*, orchestra, 1952, first performed

1952 by CBC Symphony Orchestra under John Adaskin, recorded on air-check tape, commissioned by John Adaskin for CBC; *Tableau*, string orchestra, 1952, G. Ricordi, first performed 1952 in Toronto by Canadian Chamber Players under Victor Feldbrill, recorded 1956 by CBC Strings under Thomas Mayer, commissioned by Forest Hill Community Centre; *Two vocalises*, soprano, clarinet, and piano, 1953, first performed 1954 in Toronto on CBC by Mary Morrison, Abraham Galper, and Leo Barkin; *Fantasia and dance*, violin and orchestra, 1955, revised 1959, first performed 1956 in Toronto by Royal Conservatory Orchestra with Jack Groob; *Images*, string orchestra, 1957, first performed 1958 by McGill Chamber Music Society, Montreal, PQ, commissioned by Lapitsky Foundation, also for orchestra, 1957-58, BMI Canada, first performed 1960 by Toronto Symphony Orchestra under Walter Susskind, recorded by Columbia with same performers; *Symphony no. 1*, 1960-61, first performed 1961 in Washington, DC, at Inter-American Music Festival by CBC Symphony Orchestra under Geoffrey Waddington, recorded on air-check tape by same performers; *Fantasy and allegro*, string orchestra, 1962, commissioned by Brantford Music Society, Ont., for Hart House Orchestra; *Quintet for winds*, 1962, first performed 1962 in Toronto on CBC by Toronto Woodwind Quintet, recorded on air-check tape by same performers, specially written for this quintet; *Trois poèmes de Prévert*, soprano and strings or piano, 1962, recorded; *Totem and taboo*, choir, written for Festival Singers, Toronto; *Tokaido*, choir, 1964, first performed 1964 on CBC by Festival Singers, Toronto, commissioned by Festival Singers; *Chaconne*, strings, 1964, recorded; *Variations for flute, oboe, and harpsichord*, 1965, first performed 28 Oct. 1965 by Baroque Trio, Montreal, recorded and commissioned by Baroque Trio; *A little symphony*, 1966, first performed 26 Feb. 1967 by Saskatoon Symphony Orchestra, commissioned for Saskatoon Symphony; *Rose Latulippe*, ballet suite, 1966, music first performed 1966 at Stratford, Ont. Festival, commissioned by Royal Winnipeg Ballet for Canada's centennial; *Anerca*, setting of Eskimo poems, soprano, 1967, commissioned by Lois Marshall; *Armana*, orchestra, 1967, first performed 1967 at CBC Toronto Festival, commissioned by CBC for Canada's centennial; *Tangents for orchestra*, 1967, commissioned by National Youth Orchestra for Canada's centennial; many film scores for CBC productions, e.g. *The dark did not conquer*, *Journey to the centre*, *Let me count the ways*, *October beach*; scores for radio programmes, e.g. *Vincent Massey and his times*.

WORK IN PROGRESS: Film scores; set of 80 graded pieces for high school orchestras.

FREEDMAN, Mary Morrison
see MORRISON, Mary

FRIPP, Thomas William 1864-1931
Artist; b. 23 Mar. 1864 in London, England; son
of George Arthur Fripp; came to Canada in 1893
and settled in Hatzic, BC; d. 30 May 1931 in Van-
couver, BC.
EDUCATION
Attended London University School; studied at
St. John's Wood Art School, London; Royal
Academy Schools, London, 1887-90; studied
under his father.
CAREER
Travelled and painted in northern Italy; pioneer
farmer in Hatzic 1893-c.1900; painter, mainly
in watercolour, c.1900-31.
MEMBER
British Columbia Society of Fine Arts (co-
founder, 1908; president, 1909-16 and 1926-31);
British Columbia Art League; Island Arts and
Crafts Society, Victoria, BC.
AWARDS, HONOURS
Gold medal, Winnipeg, 1905.
EXHIBITIONS
ONE-MAN: Vancouver Art Gallery, 1952.
GROUP: Represented in group exhibitions held
in Canada during his lifetime including annual
exhibitions of Royal Canadian Academy; Annual
Exhibitions of National Gallery of Canada,
Ottawa, Ont.
COLLECTIONS IN WHICH REPRESENTED
Legislative Buildings, Toronto, Ont.; National
Gallery of Canada; Vancouver Art Gallery; Arch-
ives, Victoria; Government House, Victoria;
Vancouver Museum.

FRY, Lynette
Dancer; b. in Pretoria, South Africa.
EDUCATION
Studied ballet with Andrew Hardie, Maria Fay,
Marie Rambert, Northcote School, Zeglovsky,
Audrey de Vos, and Royal Ballet School, London,
England.
CAREER
Western Theatre Ballet, Bristol, England; Royal
Winnipeg Ballet, Man., corps de ballet, soloist.
MEMBER
AEA.
AWARDS, HONOURS
Adeline Genee silver cup, South Africa; Ruby
Jenner floating trophy for Greek dancing, London.

FUGERE, Jean-Paul* 1921—
Producer and author; b. 25 June 1921 in Montreal.
HOME
11625 Guertin, Cartierville, PQ.
OFFICE
La Société Radio Canada, CP 6000, Station "H,"
Montréal 25, PQ.

CAREER
Les Compagnons de Saint-Laurent, Montréal,
actor 1945-49; CBC, Montreal, director and pro-
ducer 1952—.
AWARDS, HONOURS
Canada Council senior arts fellowship, 1959.
THEATRE
Directed and produced many plays, e.g. *Un
simple soldat* (La Comédie Canadienne, Montréal,
1958).
WRITINGS
Les terres noires (novel) Éditions HMH 1965.

GADOUAS, Robert
Actor and director.
HOME
3465 Redpath St., Apt. 105, Montreal 109, PQ.
CAREER
Théâtre du Nouveau Monde, Montréal, director
1952-53; L'Équipe, Montréal, actor, 1955—.
MEMBER
Union des Artistes de Montréal.
THEATRE
Played in many productions, e.g. Puck in *Le
songe d'une nuit d'été* (l'Équipe, 1945), title
role in *Le grand poucet* (l'Équipe, fall 1946),
Notaire in *L'école des femmes* (l'Équipe, 1947),
Les parents terribles (l'Équipe, 1947), *Polichinelle*
(1950), La Flèche in *L'avare* (Nouveau Monde,
1951), *Un inspecteur vous demande* (Nouveau
Monde, Nov. 1951), *Maître après Dieu* (Nouveau
Monde, 1952), *Une nuit d'amour* (Nouveau Monde,
1953-54); Dauphin Charles in *L'Alouette* (La
Comédie Canadienne, Montréal, 1958), Comédien
in *Les Temples* (La Comédie Canadienne, 10 Jan.
1966); directed and played in *Poil de carotte*
(Théâtre du Gesù, Montréal, 1953); co-directed
Trésor (Théâtre l'Anjou, Montréal, 1959); direc-
ted and played title role in *Caligula* (Le Théâtre
Club, Montréal, 1960).
RADIO
Played in several productions, e.g. *D'une certaine
manière* (weekly show, CBUF, Nov. 1967).

GAGNIER, Gérald Ray D'Iese 1926-51?
Composer; b. 14 Oct. 1926 in Montreal, PQ; son
of René and Dora (Carmier) Gagnier; d. c.1951.
EDUCATION
Attended St. Vincent Ferrier primary school in
Montréal; Séminaire des Trois Rivières, PQ, 1939-
45; Conservatoire de Musique de la Province de
Québec, 1945-51; three years study with Pierre
Monteux; studied music in England.
CAREER
Studied Labelle, Montréal, music teacher 1946-

49; Orchestre de Radio-Canada, cornet and cello player 1947; leader of various orchestras; Fusiliers de Mont-Royal, bandmaster 1950-51; Mont St.-Louis College, Montreal, music teacher 1951; Opera National, assistant leader 1951.

COMPOSITIONS

Poème symphonique; Polyphème; Prélude, piano 1947, first performed 26 June 1947 at Palais Montcalm, Montréal; *Élégie,* trumpet and piano, 1947 first performed 26 June 1947 at Palais Montcalm, Montréal; collection of six songs; *Sonata,* flute; *Gavotte,* small orchestra, 1947, performed 1947 on Radio-Canada networks; band music.

GAGNIER, Joséphat Jean 1885-1949

Conductor and composer; b. 2 Dec. 1885 in Montreal, PQ; son of Joseph and Élise (Caron) Gagnier; m. Diane Delaunay-Hudson; children: one son; d. 16 Sept. 1949 in Montreal.

EDUCATION

Attended Collège de Montréal and Collège Ste.-Marie, Montréal; studied clarinet, bassoon, piano, harmony, fugue, and counterpoint with A. Contant (*q.v.*), R.O. Pelletier, O. Arnold and others; University of Montreal, DMus, 1934.

RELIGION

Roman Catholic.

CAREER

Local theatres in Montreal, clarinettist 1899; Montreal Symphony Orchestra, bassoonist 1899; Montreal Opera, bassoonist 1899; began conducting 1904; Capitol Theatre orchestra, conductor; L' Harmonie Concordia de Montréal, founder and director 1910; Canadian Grenadier Guards, bandmaster 1913-49; Canadian Expeditionary Force, bandmaster of 60th, 87th, 199th, and 245th regiments 1914-18; Parc Sohmer, Montréal, musical director 1917-20; Théâtre Saint-Denis and Théâtre Français, Montréal, opera conductor 1921; Montreal Symphony Orchestra, re-organizer and conductor 1924-?; Montreal Little Symphony, founder and conductor 1924-?; Mont St.-Louis College, Montreal, teacher; Collège de Montréal, teacher; Conservatoire Nationale, teacher; guest conductor of US orchestras in New York, NY, Chicago, Ill., Boston, Mass., Washington, DC, Cincinnati, Ohio, etc.; Académie de Musique de Québec, Prix d'Europe adjudicator; judge at festivals of military music in Canada and USA; CBC French network, musical director 1934-49.

MEMBER

American Bandmasters Association; American Conductors Association; CAPAC.

COMPOSITIONS

Orchestral works: *Journey,* recorded by CBC Winnipeg Orchestra under Eric Wild, Capitol ST 6261; 1968; *In the shade of the maples; Mélodie brève,* also arranged for piano; *Suite for harp,* S. Fox; *Three preludes; Reflets,* string orchestra, Parnasse; *Têtes d'enfants,* string orchestra, Parnasse; *The wind in the leafless maples; Goatfooted Pan; Suite in the olden style,* string quintet, orchestra, or band; *Currente calamo; Queen of hearts,* Carl Fischer; *Toronto Bay,* Carl Fischer; *Victoire,* march. Marches for band: *Skip along,* Carl Fischer; *Hands across the border,* Remick; also many unpublished military marches. Incidental music: *Dans le marais,* orchestra; *Panache sur la neige,* oboe and band; *Le bandit,* English horn, band, and timpani; *Coucher de soleil,* 3 French horns, English horn, and band; *La paix soit avec vous,* harp; *Le faux rossignol,* flute, oboe, clarinet, and band; *Le rival,* orchestra; *Cinq petits lapins,* 3 oboes, English horn. Keyboard works: *Petite suite,* oboe and piano; *Ten studies in concert form,* piano, Archambault; *Trois esquisses musicales,* piano, Parnasse; *Soliloque,* piano; *Prélude,* organ, Parnasse. Choral works: *Tritons et sirènes; Pyrame et Thisbe,* Parnasse; *Hamac dans les voiles,* Parnasse.

GAGNON, Charles* 1934—

Artist; b. 23 May 1934 in Montreal; son of Jean and Jeanne (Geoffrion) Gagnon; m. Machiko Yajima 25 June 1960; children: Monika b. Mar. 1961, Erika b. Apr. 1963, Eames Charles b. Aug. 1964.

EDUCATION

Attended Collège Stanislas, Montréal, 1942-48; attended Loyola College, Montreal, 1948-50; attended École Supérieure de Préparation Scientifique, Montréal, 1950-51; studied graphic art and interior design, Parsons School of Design, New York, NY, 1956-57; evening classes, Art Students League, New York, 1956; studied under Paul Brach, evening classes, New York University, 1957; New York School of Interior Design, graduate, 1957-59.

RELIGION

Christian.

HOME

3510 Addington, Montreal 28, PQ.

CAREER

Artist, photographer, and film maker in Montreal 1960—; designed exhibits for Man the Provider pavilion and Christian pavilion for Expo 67 in Montreal; made the film *The eighth day* for the Christian pavilion at Expo 67; Loyola College, professor of cinematography 1967—.

COMMISSIONS

Sculpture, Department of Trade and Commerce, Tokyo Trade Fair, Japan, 1965.

MEMBER

Association of Canadian Industrial Designers; Association of Quebec Industrial Designers (director).

AWARDS, HONOURS

Canada Council fellowship, 1961; honourable mention, Spring Exhibition, Montreal Museum of

Fine Arts, 1963 and 1965; award for outstanding use of photography, Christian pavilion at Expo 67, 1967.

EXHIBITIONS

ONE-MAN: Galerie Artek, Montréal, 1958; Galerie Denyse Delrue, Montréal, 1961 and 1962; Jerrold Morris Gallery, Toronto, Ont., 1962; Norton Gallery, Montreal Museum of Fine Arts, 1963; Galerie Camille Hébert, Montréal, 1964; Galerie Agnès Lefort, Montréal, 1966.

GROUP: Represented in group exhibitions in Montreal area and elsewhere in Canada since 1960 including Spring Exhibitions of Montreal Museum of Fine Arts; fourth, fifth, and sixth Biennial Exhibitions of Canadian Painting, National Gallery of Canada, Ottawa, Ont., 1961, 1963, and 1965; Art USA, New York, 1958; Paris Biennale, Musée d'Art Moderne, Paris, France, 1961; *Festival des Deux Mondes*, Spoleto, Italy, 1962; Canadian Contemporary Painting, toured Africa, 1962; Canadian Painting, Speed Museum, Louisville, Ky., 1962; Canadian Painting, Rochester Memorial Institute, NY, 1962; *El Arte Actual de America y Espana*, Madrid and Barcelona, Spain, Paris, France, Brussels, Belgium, London, England, Amsterdam, The Netherlands, Berlin, Munich, Germany, 1962; members loan acquisition exhibition, Albright-Knox Art Gallery, Buffalo, NY, 1963; International Exhibition, Washington Square Gallery, New York, 1964; Tokyo International Trade Fair, 1965; First Salon of Pan American Painting, Columbia, 1965; *Canada-Art d'aujourd' hui*, Paris, Rome, Italy, Geneva, Switzerland, 1967-68.

COLLECTIONS IN WHICH REPRESENTED

Art Institute of Ontario, Toronto; Canada Council Art Collection, Ottawa; Department of External Affairs, Ottawa; Department of Trade and Commerce, Ottawa; Montreal Museum of Fine Arts; National Gallery of Canada; Sir George Williams University.

GAGNON, Maurice* 1912—

Novelist and playwright; b. 13 Aug. 1912 in Winnipeg, Man.; son of Émile and Hedwige (Fiset) Gagnon.

EDUCATION

Attended schools in England, France, Belgium and Canada; Université Laval, BA.

HOME

App. 1014, 165 est Grande Allée, Québec, PQ.

CAREER

Freelance journalist; N.W. Ayer & Sons, Philadelphia, Pa., copy-writer and publicity man; RCNVR, c.1939-45, training officer and executive officer, became lieutenant-commander.

WRITINGS

L'échéance (novel), Cercle du Livre, 1955; *Rideau de neige* (novel), Cercle du Livre, 1957; *L'anse aux brumes* (novel), Cercle du Livre, 1958; *Les chasseurs d'ombres* (novel), Cercle du Livre, 1959; *Entre tes mains* (novel), Cercle du Livre, 1960 (published in France under title *Les chirurgiennes*, Laffont, 1960); *L'Inspecteur Tanguay, meurtre sous la pluie* (novel), Jour, 1963; *Unipax intervient* (juvenile fiction), Lidec, 1965; *Les savants réfractaires* (juvenile fiction), Lidec, 1965; *Opération Tanga* (juvenile fiction), Lidec, 1966; *Le trésor de la "Santissima Trinidad"* (juvenile fiction), Lidec, 1966; *Une aventure d'Ajax* (juvenile fiction), Lidec, 1966; *Alerte dans le Pacifique* (juvenile fiction), Lidec, 1967; *Un complot à Washington* (juvenile fiction), Lidec, 1968; *Servax à la recousse* (juvenile fiction), Lidec, 1968; *Marie Tellier, avocate* (radio serial, CBC, Montreal); and TV plays (produced CBC, Montreal).

CONTRIBUTED: Short stories and articles to *Liberté, Magazine Maclean, Saturday night.*

WORK IN PROGRESS: "Carib" and "Carib II" (novels to be published in England and France simultaneously c.1969); "Les nuits de Beaumesnil" (non-fiction) to be published in English and French.

GALLANT, Mavis de Trafford 1922—

Author; b. 1922 in Montreal, PQ; m. (marriage dissolved).

EDUCATION

Attended school in Canada and USA.

HOME

Paris, France.

CAREER

Mainly literary; *Standard*, Montreal, film critic c.1940; *New Yorker*, regular contributor from Paris; resided in France 1951—.

WRITINGS

The other Paris (short stories), Houghton Mifflin, 1956; *Green water, green sky* (novel), Houghton Mifflin, 1959; *My heart is broken* (short stories), Random House, 1964 *(Bernadette* and *The ice wagon going down the street* produced CBC radio, "Stage," 31 Oct. 1965); *An unmarried man's summer* (short stories), Heinemann, 1965.

CONTRIBUTED: Stories to *Canadian short stories*, 2nd series, edited by R. Weaver, Oxford, 1968; *Canadian winter's tales*, edited by N. Levine, Macmillan, 1968; *Esquire, Glamour, Harper's bazaar, New Yorker, Texas review.*

GARANT, Albert Antonio Serge
see GARANT, Serge

GARANT, Serge 1929—
(Albert Antonio Serge Garant)

Composer, pianist, and clarinettist; b. 22 Sept. 1929 in Quebec, PQ.

EDUCATION

Studied piano with Sylvio Lacharité and Yvonne Hubert, harmony with P. Robicloux, composition with Claude Champagne (*q.v.*), Montreal; musical analysis with Olivier Messiaen and counterpoint with Mrs. Arthur Honegger, Paris, France, *c.*1951-52; counterpoint with Jocelyn Binet, Montreal, *c.*1952.

HOME
4560 St. Catherine St. W., Apt. 34, Montreal 6, PQ.

CAREER
Sherbrooke Symphony Orchestra, PQ, clarinettist; Music of our time, co-founder 1957?; La Société de Musique Contemporaine du Québec, founder, musical director, and sometime conductor 1966–; Université de Montréal, Music Faculty, Membre du Conseil, assistant professor 1967–; Ensemble de Musique Contemporaine, founder and conductor 1968.

MEMBER
Canadian League of Composers.

AWARDS, HONOURS
Composition prize from Youth Festival of Sherbrooke, 1950.

RADIO
Music critic on "La revue des arts et des lettres" (series, CBC, *c.*1953); participated in many CBC programs, e.g. "Premières" (series, 1954), "Wednesday night" (series, 1956/57), "Summer festival" (series, 1961), *Psaume pour abri* (world première, "Wednesday night," 15 May 1963), "Music of today" (series, 12 Jan. 1965), "Chamber music" (series, July-Aug. 1968.)

TELEVISION
Conducted several CBC programs, e.g. *Loving* ("Festival," 25 May 1966).

COMPOSITIONS
Several jazz works, e.g. *Jazz suite* in 3 movements. *Un grand sommeil noir*, voice, 1949. *Music for saxophone alto and band*, 1950, transcribed for symphony orchestra. *Sonatine*, piano, 1950. *Fantaisie*, clarinet and piano, 1950. *Ta forme monte comme la blessure du sang*, string orchestra, 1950. *Concerts sur terre*, soprano and piano, 1951, recorded by CBC IS. *Et je prierai ta grâce*, soprano and piano, 1952, recorded by CBC IS, 1954. *Caprices*, soprano and piano, *c.*1953, recorded by CBC IS. *Pièce no. 1*, piano, 1953. *Musique pour la mort d'un poète*, strings and piano, 1954. *Variations for piano*, 1954, recorded by CBC IS. *Musique rituelle*, piano, 1954. *Nucléogame*, for septet and tape, 1954. *Canon VI*, for ten musicians, 1957. *Pièces pour quatuor à cordes*, chance music, 1958. *Asymétries*, piano, 1958. *Asymétries no. 2*, clarinet and piano, 1959, commissioned by Dartmouth College and first performed at Dartmouth College Festival for English, Canadian, and American Music, Hanover, NH, 1959. *Anerca*, soprano and 8 instruments, 1961, first performed at Festival of Contemporary Music, Montreal, 1962; revised 1963, and

performed by Mary Morrison (*q.v.*), CBC, 13 Sept. 1964, recorded by RCA IS no. CL 1011 and issued as a centennial project, 1967, BMI 1967. *Pièce no. 2, Cage d'oiseau*, soprano and piano, 1962, première recital series "Groupe des rencontres musicales," 1967, BMI 1968. *Ouranos*, orchestra, chance music, 1963, first performed by Quebec Symphony Orchestra. *Ennéade*, orchestra, 1964. *Phrases I*, mezzo-soprano, piano, and percussion, 1967, first performed by Société de Musique Contemporaine du Québec, 17 Nov. 1967. *Phrases II*, for 2 orchestras, 1968, commissioned by the Junior Committee of the Montreal Symphony Orchestra. *Jeu à quatre*, first performed on CBC "Chamber music" series, 25 July 1968, commissioned by Stratford, Ont. Festival. *Amuya*, orchestra, world première CBC Toronto Festival "Music of Quebec" series, Sept.-Oct. 1968, commissioned by the CBC. Several radio, TV, and film scores, e.g. *Man in the polar regions* (National Film Board of Canada, Expo 67, Montreal, 1967).

RECORDINGS
Several compositions taped by CBC IS, released on RCA "Canada-International" label.

WRITINGS
CONTRIBUTED: Articles to *Canadian art, Liberté*.

GARDNER, David Emmett* 1928–
Director, producer, and actor; b. 4 May 1928 in Toronto, Ont.; son of David and Madeleine Vera (Cunningham) Gardner; m. Dorothy Rosemary Wood Kerr 30 July 1965; children: Jennifer Kathleen b. 23 Apr. 1968.

EDUCATION
Annette Street Public School, Toronto, 1934-38; Bedford Park Public School, Toronto, 1938-41; Lawrence Park Collegiate, Toronto, 1941-46; Victoria College, University of Toronto, BA in art and archaeology 1946-50; studied speech with Jeanette Reddick, Lawrence Park Collegiate, 1945-46; Clara Salisbury Baker, Royal Conservatory of Music, Toronto, 1947-48; Eleanor Stuart (*q.v.*), Toronto, 1953; Esme Crampton, Toronto, 1955-56; studied drama with Robert Gill, Hart House Theatre, Toronto, 1946-50.

RELIGION
United Church.

OFFICE
Playhouse Theatre Company, 560 Cambie St., Vancouver 3, BC.

CAREER
Hart House Theatre, Toronto, actor 1946-53, director 1963-67; University Alumnae, Toronto, actor 1948, 1953, 1955; Straw Hat Players, Port Carling, Muskoka, Ont., actor 1948-52; New Play Society, Toronto, actor 1949-51, 1955; International Players, Kingston, Ont., actor 1951; University of Toronto, assistant to warden of Hart House, 1951-52; Jupiter Theatre, Toronto, actor

1951-53; Crest Theatre, Toronto, actor 1954-56, director 1960; Brae Manor Theatre, Quebec, PQ, actor 1954; Canadian Repertory Theatre, Ottawa, Ont., actor 1955; Globe Theatre, Chatham, Ont., actor 1955; Stratford, Ont. Festival, actor 1955-56; Canadian Players, Toronto, actor 1956-57, director 1961; CBC, Toronto, contract TV producer and director 1958–; Dominion Drama Festival, governor 1960–, regional adjudicator 1961–; National Theatre School, Montreal, PQ, member of board of governors, 1966–; Playhouse Theatre Company, Vancouver, artistic director 1969–.

MEMBER

AEA; ACTRA; Canadian Theatre Centre (former vice-president; chairman of committee to found National Theatre School and co-author of the blueprint to set up the School); Society of Filmmakers; TV Producers Association.

AWARDS, HONOURS

First prize in Ontario verse-speaking competition, 1946; Tyrone Guthrie award from Stratford, Ont. Festival, 1956; Wilderness award for direction of *The paper people*, 1968.

THEATRE

Played title role in *Othello* (Hart House, 1946-50), title role in *Macbeth* (Hart House, 1946-50), Mark Antony in *Julius Caesar* (Hart House, 1946-50), Constantin in *The seagull* (Hart House, 1946-50), *Spring thaw* (Museum Theatre, Toronto, 1951) Jesse Fewtrell in *A jig for the gypsy* (Crest, Sept. 1954), various role in *Julius Caesar* (Stratford, Ont. Festival, 1955), Chorus in *Oedipus Rex* (Stratford, Ont. Festival, 1955; Stratford, Ont. Festival Company, Edinburgh Festival, Scotland, 1956), various roles in *Tamburlaine the great* (Winter Garden, New York, NY, 19 Jan. 1956), Captain Gower in *Henry V* (Stratford, Ont. Festival, 1956; Stratford, Ont. Festival Company, Edinburgh Festival, 1956; Old Vic Theatre Company, North American tour, 1957/58); Robert in *The merry wives of Windsor* (Stratford, Ont. Festival, 1956), Horatio in *Hamlet* (Canadian Players, tour 1956/57), various roles in *Peer Gynt* (Canadian Players, tour 1956/57), Governor in *Requiem for a nun* (Royal Court, London, England 26 Nov. 1957), Sea Captain in *Twelfth night* (Old Vic Theatre Company, North American tour 1957/58), Fortinbras in *Hamlet* (Old Vic Theatre Company, North American tour 1957/58), David Rudderman in *Hunter's moon* (Winter Garden, London, 26 Feb. 1958), *Clap hands* (Hart House, 1958); directed *Gigi* (University Alumnae, Toronto, 1955), scenes from *The seagull* (Stratford, Ont. Workshop, 1955-56), *King Lear* (Crest Theatre, Toronto, 1960; Eskimo version, Canadian Players, 1961), *The lady's not for burning* (Canadian Players, 1961), *Masterpieces of comedy* (Canadian Players, 1962/63), *Look back in anger* (Hart House, 1965), *Under Milkwood* (Neptune Theatre, Halifax, NS, 1965), *The father* (Hart House, 1967).

FILM

Played juvenile boy in *Family circle* (National Film Board of Canada, 1949), *It's in the cards* (Crawley, 1954), Chorus in *King Oedipus* (Oedipus Rex Productions, Toronto, 1957).

RADIO

Played over 150 roles in CBC productions on "Wednesday night," "Ford theatre," "Stage," "Summer fallow," "Once upon a time," "National school broadcast," etc.

TELEVISION

Played in several productions, e.g. Lieut. Bob Martin in *The field* ("Navy log," USA, 1958), Producer in *Who crucified Christ* ("Heritage," CBC 11 Apr. 1965; 8 Apr. 1966); produced over 60 CBC programs, e.g. *The face of God* ("Heritage," 1960), *Some are so lucky* ("First person," 1960; award for outstanding half hour show of the year), five episodes of "Jake and the kid" (series, 1961), *Village wooing* ("GM presents," 2 July 1961), four episodes of "Wings of night" (series, 1962), *Mr. Oblomov* ("Playdate," 1962), *The greatest man in the world* ("Playdate," 1962), *The applecart* ("Festival," 1962), *Doctor's dilemma* ("Festival," 1963), *With my head tucked underneath my arm* ("Playdate," 1963), *Ivan* ("Festival," 11 Feb. 1963), *A resounding tinkle* and *I spy* ("Festival," 13 Nov. 1963), *Uncle Vanya* ("Festival," 26 Feb. 1964), *Dear liar* ("Playdate," 1964), *Train of murder* ("The serial," 24 Dec. 1964–), *The reluctant agent* ("The serial," 28 Jan. 1965–), *The kite* ("Show of the week," 26 Apr. 1965), *Mr. Member of Parliament* ("The serial," 7 Oct. 1965–), *Spirit of the deed* ("Festival," 26 Oct. 1966); produced and directed "Quentin Durgens, MP" (series, 1966–); directed *The paper people* ("Festival," 13 Dec. 1967); produced and directed *Yesterday the children were dancing* ("Festival," 6 Nov. 1968).

WRITINGS

CONTRIBUTED: "Drama in English-speaking Canada" to *Canadian annual review*, edited by J.T. Saywell, University of Toronto, 1961-63; articles to *Saturday night, Arts Canada, Canadian architect, Acta Victoriana, Theatre Canada.*

WORK IN PROGRESS: Preparation of TV version of Stratford, Ont. Festival's *The three musketeers.*

GARNEAU, Joseph René Sylvain
see GARNEAU, Sylvain

GARNEAU, Sylvain 1930-53
(Joseph René Sylvain Garneau)
Poet; b. 29 June 1930 in Saint-Germain d'Outremont, Montreal, PQ; d. 7 Oct. 1953.

EDUCATION
Attended Collège Stanislas, Montréal.

CAREER
La presse, Montréal, reporter; CKVM, Ville Marie, PQ, announcer; CBC, Montreal, announcer.

AWARDS, HONOURS
Prix David for *Objets trouvés*, 1951.

WRITINGS
Objets trouvés, Malte, 1951; *Les trouble-fête*, Malte, 1952; *Objets retrouvés; poèmes et prose*, Déom, 1965.

CONTRIBUTED: Poetry to numerous anthologies, e.g. *Twelve modern French Canadian poets*, translated by G.R. Roy, Ryerson, 1958; *Anthologie de la poésie canadienne-française*, edited by G. Sylvestre, Beauchemin, 1963; *Amérique française, Autorité, Le jour, Journal des Jeunesses musicales canadiennes, Notre temps*.

GAUCHER, Yves* 1934–
Artist; b. 3 Jan. 1934 in Montreal; son of Tancrède and Laure (Elie) Gaucher; m. Germaine Chaussé 17 Oct. 1964.

EDUCATION
Attended a classical college, BA; Montreal Museum of Fine Arts School for two months in 1954; attended École des Beaux-Arts, Montréal, taking the general course, 1954-55; self-taught as an artist.

RELIGION
Agnostic.

HOME
7094 Christophe Colomb, Montréal 10, PQ.

CAREER
Imperial Oil Limited, Montreal, clerk; employed in various occupations in Montreal 1954-60; print maker in Montreal 1960-64; jury member, Spring Exhibition, Montreal Museum of Fine Arts, 1964; jury member, Perspective '67, Toronto, Ont.; judge, BC Annual Exhibition, Vancouver Art Gallery, 1968; Sir George Williams University, assistant professor of fine arts 1965–; painter in Montreal 1964–.

AWARDS, HONOURS
Graphic art prize, *Salon de la Jeune Peinture*, Montreal, 1959; premier prix de gravure, École des Beaux-Arts, Montréal, 1960; second prize, National Print Competition, Vancouver, 1961; first prize, art graphique, Concours Artistique de Québec, 1961 and 1963; purchase award, Winnipeg Biennial, Winnipeg Art Gallery, Man., 1962; honourable mention, *La Primera Bienal Americana de Grabado de Santiago de Chile*, 1963; exhibition prize, Thomas Moore Institute, Montreal, 1963; purchase prize, Montreal Spring Exhibition, Montreal Museum of Fine Arts, 1963; second international grand prize, International Exhibition of Prints, Grenchen, Switzerland, 1964; exhibition award, Hadassah Exhibition, Montreal, 1964; exhibition award, Ladies' Committee Art Sale, Montreal Museum of Fine Arts, 1965; Canada Council fellowships, 1962, 1963, and 1967; grand prize, Survey '68, Montreal Museum of Fine Arts.

EXHIBITIONS
ONE-MAN: Galerie de l'Échange, Montréal, 1957; Galerie Agnès Lefort, 1963, 1965, 1966, and 1967; Gallery Moos, Toronto, 1963 and 1966; Martha Jackson Gallery, New York, NY, 1963 and 1966; Benjamin Galleries, Chicago, Ill., 1964; Winnipeg Art Gallery, 1967.

GROUP: Represented in group exhibitions held in Canada including Spring Exhibitions, Montreal Museum of Fine Arts; represented in exhibitions organized by National Gallery of Canada, Ottawa, Ont., including its sixth Biennial Exhibition of Canadian Painting, 1965; International Exhibition of Graphic Arts, Ljubljana, Yugoslavia, 1961, 1963, and 1965; Paris *Biennale*, Musée d'Art Moderne, France, 1961; International Exhibition of Prints, Tokyo, Japan, 1962; Canadian Contemporary Painting, toured Africa, 1962; International Exhibition of Drawings and Prints, Lugano, Switzerland, 1962; Canadian Painting, Albright-Knox Art Gallery, Buffalo, NY, 1962; Contemporary Art of Americas, Madrid, Spain, Brussels, Belgium, Paris, 1963; *Junge Kunst der Welt*, Vienna, Austria, 1963; International Print Exhibition, Osaka, Japan, 1963; *La Primera Bienal Americana de Grabado de Santigo de Chile*, 1963; Members' Loan Acquisitions, Albright-Knox Art Gallery, Buffalo, 1963; International Collection of Prints, Albertina Museum, Vienna, 1963; Selection of Prints, Victoria and Albert Museum, London, England, 1963; International Exhibition of Prints, Grenchen, Switzerland, 1964; Art Today, Albright-Knox Art Gallery, Buffalo, 1964; Contemporary Painters and Sculptors as Printmakers, Museum of Modern Art, New York, 1964; 1 plus 1 Equals Three, University of Texas, 1965; Optics and Kinetics, Ohio State University, 1965; Optics, Illusion and Art, University of Kansas, 1965; The Deceived Eye, Fort Worth Art Center, Tex., 1965; Vibrations Eleven, Martha Jackson Gallery, New York, 1965; Art with Optical Reaction, Des Moines Art Center, Iowa, 1966; International Selection of Prints, Prague, Czecho-Slovakia, 1966; Canadian Section, *Biennale*, Venice, Italy, 1966; *Biennale Internationale de Gravure*, Cracow, Poland, 1966; Young International Artists, Tokyo, 1967; Canada '67, Museum of Modern Art, New York, 1967; Pittsburgh International, Carnegie Institute, Pa., 1967; Nine Canadians, Institute of Contemporary Art, Boston, Mass., 1967; Eleven Printmakers, Dartmouth College, Hanover, NH, and Cordova Museum, Lincoln, Mass., 1967; *Art d'Aujourd'hui*, Paris, Brussels, Geneva, Switzerland and Milan, Italy, 1968.

COLLECTIONS IN WHICH REPRESENTED
Albright-Knox Art Gallery; Art Gallery of Ontario, Toronto; Art Institute of Chicago; Bundy Art

Museum, Wakefield, Vt.; Library of Congress, Washington, DC; Martha Jackson Gallery, New York; Montreal Museum of Fine Arts; Musée du Québec, PQ; Museum of Modern Art, New York; National Gallery of Canada, Ottawa; Agnes Etherington Art Centre, Queen's University; Robert Hull Fleming Museum, Burlington, Vt.; Rose Art Museum, Brandeis University; Sir George Williams University; Museum of Modern Art, Skopje, Yugoslavia; William Humphrey's Gallery, Kimberley, South Africa; Willistead Art Gallery, Windsor, Ont.; Winnipeg Art Gallery; Kansas State University; Victoria and Albert Museum; Norman Mackenzie Art Gallery, Regina, Sask.; Vancouver Art Gallery; Saskatoon Art Centre, Sask.; American Potash and Chemical Company, New York, Canadian Industries Ltd., Montreal; Kensington Industries Ltd., Montreal; Singer Corporation, Montreal; York University; University of British Columbia; Musée d'Art Contemporain, Montréal; Canada Council, Ottawa.

GAUVREAU, Claude* 1925–
Poet, playwright, and artist; b. 19 Aug. 1925 in Montreal.

HOME
2100 rue Saint-Denis, Montréal 18, PQ.

CAREER
Mainly literary; *Le haut-parleur*, theatre critic 1950; CBC, Montreal, scriptwriter; *La matière chante*, travelling art show organized 1954; poetry recitals, including *Poèmes et chansons de la Résistance*, Théâtre du Gesù, Montréal, 1968.

WRITINGS
Sur fil métamorphose (poems and plays), Erta, 1956; *Brochuges* (poems), Erta, 1957; *Bien-être*, (play, produced Montreal, 1947); *Le rose enfer des animaux* (TV play, 1958); *La jeune fille et la lune* (play, produced École des Beaux-Arts, Montréal, 1959); *Les grappes lucides* (play, produced École des Beaux-Arts, Montréal, 1959); *La charge de l'original épormyable* (play, read Centre d'essai des auteurs dramatiques, Montréal, 1967); *Six ouïes* (radio script); *Faisceau d'épingles* (radio script); *L'imagination règne* (radio script); *Le coureur de Marathon* (radio script).
CONTRIBUTED: Poetry to *La poésie canadienne*, edited by Alain Bosquet, Seghers, 1962; *Liberté*.
WORK IN PROGRESS: "Les oranges sont vertes" (play); "Jappements à la lune" (poems).

GÉLINAS, Gratien* 1909–
Actor and author; b. 1909 in St. Tite, PQ; son of Mathias and Geneva (Davidson) Gélinas; m. Simone Lalonde 1935; children: Sylvie, Michel, Yves, Pierre, Alain, Pascal.

EDUCATION
Attended College of the Brothers at St. Jérome, PQ; Collège de Montréal; School of Higher Commercial Studies, Montreal.

OFFICE
84 St. Catherine St. W., Montreal 18, PQ.

CAREER
La Sauvegarde Insurance Company, accountant 1929-37; National Film Board of Canada, member of board of governors 1950-52; La Comédie Canadienne, Montréal, founder and artistic director 1957–, president 1968–.

MEMBER
Association Canadienne du Théâtre Amateur (president, 1950-61); Greater Montreal Arts Council (vice-president, 1957-62); Canadian Theatre Institute (president, 1959-60); Canadian Theatre Centre; Royal Society of Canada (elected fellow).

AWARDS, HONOURS
Grand Prix de la Société des Auteurs Dramatiques for *Tit-coq*, 19? ; award, Dominion Drama Festival, 193– and 193–; D Litt from University of Montreal, 1949; D Litt from University of Toronto, 1951; LL D from University of Saskatchewan, 1966; Medal of Service of the Order of Canada, July 1967; St. Jean-Baptiste Society, Victor Morin prize, 1967.

THEATRE
Played Dr. Caius in *Merry wives of Windsor* (Montreal Repertory Theatre; Stratford, Ont. Festival, 1956), *Télévise-moi-ça* (St. Denis Theatre, Montreal, 1936), title role in *Fridolinons* (revues, Cabaret Mon Paris, Montréal, 1938; Orpheum Theatre, Montreal, 1956), *St. Lazares pharmacy* (Chicago, Ill., 1945); wrote, directed, and played title role in *Tit-coq* (Monument National, Montréal, 22 May 1948; translated into English, Broadhurst, New York, NY, 9 Feb. 1951); played Charles VI in *Henry V* (Stratford, Ont. Festival, 1957); directed and played Charles VII in *The lark* (Feb. 1958); directed *L'alouette* (Feb. 1958); wrote, directed, and played title role in *Bousille et les justes* (16 Aug. 1959; translated into English, Royal Alexandra, Toronto, Ont. Jan. 1962; World's Fair, Seattle, Wash., 1962; Vancouver International Festival, 1962); played and produced *Le diable à quatre* (1964); wrote and directed *Hier les enfants dansaient* (11 Apr. 1966; translated into English, Charlottetown Festival, PEI, July 1967; French, played Pierre Gravel and co-directed with Mavor Moore at Théâtre l'Escale, Montreal, 7 Sept. 1967); co-produced *The Katimavik review* (Expo 67, Montreal); directed and played in *Docile* (Comédie Canadienne, 10 May 1968).

FILM
Wrote and played title role in *Tit-coq* (1952; film of the year award, Canadian Film Awards, 1952).

RADIO
Wrote and played *Fridolin* ("Carousel de la gaieté," later "Le train de plaisir," 1937-38), *Bousille and the just* (CBC, spring, 1962; BBC, 1964).

TELEVISION
Wrote and played in *Les quatre fers en l'air* (serial,

CBC, 1954/55); wrote and played title role in *Bousille et les justes* ("Festival," CBC, 26 Feb. 1962); wrote, directed, and played Pierre Gravel in *Yesterday the children were dancing* ("Festival," CBC, 6 Nov. 1968).

WRITINGS

Tit-coq (play), Beauchemin, 1950; (translated into English by K. Johnstone and the author, Clarke, Irwin, 1967); *Bousille et les justes* (play), Institut littéraire du Québec, 1960; (translated into English by K. Johnstone, Clarke, Irwin, 1961); *Le diable à quatre* (revue, 1964); *Yesterday the children were dancing* (plays; translated into English by Mavor Moore), Clarke, Irwin, 1967.

GÉLINAS, Pierre* 1925–
Novelist. Does not wish to be included.

GENCSY, Eva von
See VON GENCSY, Eva

GEORGE, Graham* 1912–
Composer, analyst, conductor, and organist; b. 11 Apr. 1912 in Norwich, England; son of Alfred Robert and Ethel Elizabeth (Graham) George; came to Canada in 1928 and settled in Ottawa, Ont.; m. Tjot Coster 5 Sept. 1945; children: Charles Robert Brian b. 27 June 1949, Paul Philip Graham b. 12 Jan. 1953, Jan Michael b. 9 Feb. 1955, Derek Norman b. 19 Feb. 1956.

EDUCATION

Attended Woodroughs Preparatory School in Birmingham, England, 1921-24, and grammar schools in Birmingham and Dorset, England, 1924-28; McGill University, 1932-33; studied architecture for 3 years in Ottawa; Royal Conservatory of Music, Toronto, Ont., BMus, 1936, DMus 1939; studied with Alfred Whitehead, composition with Paul Hindemith, conducting with Willem van Otterloo; Canadian College of Organists, fellow; Royal College of Organists, associate.

RELIGION

Anglican.

HOME

151 Earl St., Kingston, Ont.

OFFICE

Queen's University, Kingston, Ont.

CAREER

Mount Royal Church, Montreal, PQ, organist 1932-34; Church of the Ascension, Montreal, organist 1935-37; St. Peter's, Sherbrooke, PQ, organist and choirmaster 1937-40; St. Francis Madrigal Singers, Sherbrooke, conductor 1938-40; Sherbrooke Protestant schools, musician 1938-40; St. Matthew's, Hampstead, PQ, organist and choirmaster 1940-41; Montreal Protestant schools, musician 1940-41, 1945-46; 7th Canadian Reconnaissance Regiment, 1941-45, counter-intelligence in Canada, United Kingdom, and n.w. Europe, became captain; Queen's University, professor and head of music department 1946–; Queen's Symphony Orchestra, conductor 1946-54; Queen's University Musical Theatre, conductor 1946–; St. James', Kingston, organist and choirmaster 1946-47, Sydenham St. Church, Kingston, organist and choirmaster 1949-54; Kingston Choral Society, conductor 1953-58; Civic Symphony Orcestra, Kingston, organizer 1954, conductor 1954-58; St. Paul's, Kingston, organist and choirmaster 1957-60; Grace Church, Gananoque, Ont., organist and choirmaster 1963-66; Edith Rankin Memorial Church, Collins Bay, Ont., organist and choirmaster 1968–.

MEMBER

American Musicological Society; BMI Canada; Canadian Folk Music Society (president, 1965-68); Canadian Music Council; Canadian Music Educators' Association; Canadian Philosophical Association; College Music Society.

AWARD, HONOURS

Prix Lallemand, Montreal, for *Variations on an original theme*, 1938; CAPAC prize for *Variations for strings*, 1943, and *Jabberwocky*, 1947; Canada Council arts fellowship 1965/66, travel grant 1966/67.

RADIO

Conducted CBC String Orchestra (summer series of concerts, 1957); appeared in various CBC panel programs.

COMPOSITIONS

Principal works: *String quartet 1936*; *Variations on an original theme*, orchestra, 1938, first performed by Les Concerts Symphoniques de Montréal under Wilfrid Pelletier (*q.v.*); hymn tunes, e.g., *The King's majesty* in *American Episcopal hymnal*, 1940 and *Grace Church, Gananoque* in *American Methodist hymnary*, 1967; *Dorian fugue*, string orchestra, 1942; *Variations for strings*, 1943; *Jabberwocky*, ballet suite, 1947; *String quartet 1948*; *String quartet 1951*; *Hymn for Christmas Day*, mixed choir and orchestra, 1954; *Evangeline*, opera, before 1955, first performed at Queen's University; *Experiences of a self-made theme*, orchestra, 1956; *Songs of the Salish*, orchestral suite, 1961, first performed by Quebec Symphony Orchestra under Sir Ernest MacMillan, recorded on air-check tape, commissioned by Canadian Folk Music Society; *Concerto for flute and strings*, 1963-64, first performed 23 Sept. 1964 by CBC String Orchestra with Wolfgang Kander, flute, commissioned by Wolfgang Kander; *Quintet for piano and strings*, 1966, commissioned by Kingston Music Club; *Sonatina for organ*, 1967, commissioned for Expo 67; *Kingston suite*, orchestra, first performed by Kingston Civic Symphony Orchestra; *Queen's jig*, orchestra, first performed at Queen's University; *Way out*, opera, first performed at Queen's University; *The king, the pigeon and the hawk*, ballet suite, first performed at Queen's University; *Pas-*

sacaglia: Lobe den Herren, organ, H.W. Gray;
Two preludes on theme The King's majesty, organ, H.W. Gray; *Elegy in memory of Vaughan
Williams*, organ, H.W. Gray; *Suite on 'Grace
Church, Gananoque,'* organ, Abingdon; *Three
fugues*, organ, BMI Canada; *Four short pieces*,
organ; *Prologue, chaconne and epilogue*, organ;
Introduction and fugue, organ, also arranged for
string quartet, first performed by CBC String
Quartet; church music including anthems, service
arrangements, and music for junior choirs, some
published by H.W. Gray, Abingdon, Augsburg,
and BMI Canada.

RECORDINGS
St. John Passion by Alessandro Scarlatti, continuo realisation, organist, with Yale Symphony Orchestra, Overtone, 1958.

WRITINGS
Two theories of musical structure, Faber and
Faber, 1969.
CONTRIBUTED: Articles to journals and newspapers, e.g. *Journal of International Folk Music
Council, Musical quarterly, Queen's quarterly.*
WORK IN PROGRESS: "Twelve-toned harmony
for beginners," in preparation; series of books on
the relevance of composers' lives; a study of musical structure from plainsong to the 16th century;
study of the nature of operatic libretto as preliminary to composition of a third opera; proposed edition of first-rate Canadian church music
1630-1930.

GIGUÈRE, Roland* 1929–
Artist and poet; b. 4 May 1929 in Montreal; son
of Maurice and Jeanne (Bourgoin) Giguère; m.
Denise Marsan.

EDUCATION
Attended École Supérieure Saint-Viateur, Montréal; Institut des Arts Graphiques, Montréal, diploma, 1951; Ateliers de Gravure J. Friedlander,
1954-55 and Ateliers de Lithographie Desjobert,
Paris, France, 1957.

RELIGION
None.

HOME
3417 Ste.-Famille, Montréal, PQ.

CAREER
Artistic and literary; Éditions Erta, founder 1959;
illustrated his books *Adorable femme des neiges,
Les armes blanches, Le défaut des ruines est d'avoir des habitants.*

AWARDS, HONOURS
Royal Society of Canada scholarship, 1957; Canada Council grants, 1959, 1966/67, 1967/68; Quebec government poetry award, France-Canada
prize, and Grand Prix Littéraire de la Ville de
Montréal for *L'âge de la parole*, 1966.

EXHIBITIONS
ONE-MAN: Galerie l'Actuelle, Montréal, 1955;
Galerie Denyse Delrue, Montréal, 1957 and 1959;
Galerie Libre, Montréal, 1960, 1961, 1962, and
1964; Galerie du Ranelagh, Paris, 1962; Musée
d'Art Contemporain, Montréal, 1966; Musée du
Québec, PQ, 1966.

GROUP
Represented in group exhibitions organized by
National Gallery of Canada, Ottawa, Ont., including its second, third, and fourth Biennial of Canadian Painting, 1957, 1959, and 1961; *Phases de
l'Art Contemporain*, Galerie Creuze, Paris, 1955;
International Exhibition of Graphic Art, Mexico,
1955; *Exposition de Gravures à Ljubljana*, Jugoslavia, 1957; International Exhibition, Kyoto,
Japan, 1957; *Bienniale de Lugano*, Switzerland,
1958; *Expositions du Mouvement Phases*, Buenos
Aires and Santa Fé, Argentina, and Montevideo,
Uruguay, 1958 and 1959; American Federation
of Arts, 1959 and 1960; *Arte Canadiense*, Mexico,
1960; International Surrealism Exhibition, D'Arcy
Gallery, New York, NY, 1960; *La Face Inconnue
de la Terre*, Brussels, Belgium, 1960; *Solstice de
l'Image*, Galerie du Ranelagh, Paris, 1961; *Exposition de quatre peintres*, Galerie Bellechasse, Paris,
1962; *Exposition de Peinture Canadienne*, Spoleto, Italy, 1962.

COLLECTIONS IN WHICH REPRESENTED
Musée d'Art Contemporain, Montréal.

WRITINGS
Faire naître, Erta, 1949; *Trois pas*, Erta, 1950;
Les nuits abat-jour, Erta, 1950; *Yeux fixes* (prose
poems), Erta, 1951; *Images apprivoisées*, Erta,
1953; *Les armes blanches*, Erta, 1954; *Le défaut
des ruines est d'avoir des habitants* (prose poems),
Erta, 1957; *Adorable femme des neiges*, Erta,
1959; *L'âge de la parole*, Hexagone, 1965; *Pouvoir du noir* (exhibition catalogue), Musée d'Art
Contemporain, 1966.
CONTRIBUTED: Poem to *Pouvoir du noir*, edited
by Musée d'Art Contemporain, 1966; poems and
articles to *Cité libre, Tamarack review.*

GILBERT, Herbert* 1926–
(William Herbert Gilbert)
Artist; b. 19 Dec. 1926 in Regina, Sask.; son of
Alfred and Ella (Rankin) Gilbert; m. Anna Rosemary Theo Mason 15 Aug. 1959; children. Ellawyn Saffron Theo b. 28 May 1962.

EDUCATION
Attended Thompson Public School and Connaught Public School, Regina, 1932-39; Kimberley High School, Regina, 1939-42; Luther College,
Regina, 1942-45; studied at Vancouver School of
Art, 1946-47; University of British Columbia, BA,
1947-50; Institute of Design, Chicago, Ill., 1951;
studied under Elmer Bischoff, California School
of Fine Arts, San Francisco, summer 1951; studied with John Bernhardt in Mexico, 1957-58.

HOME
3309 Point Grey Road, Vancouver, BC.

CAREER

Travelled and studied in Europe 1953-54; Vancouver School of Art, design instructor 1954-57; travelled in the USA and Mexico 1958; travelled in Europe, the Middle East, and Africa 1960-61; engaged in freelance design in South Africa 1961-64; painter in Vancouver 1964–.

MEMBER

Canadian Group of Painters (elected, 1957); BC Society of Artists (elected, 1957); Federation of Canadian Artists.

AWARDS, HONOURS

Emily Carr scholarship, 1957.

EXHIBITIONS

ONE-MAN: Hart House, University of Toronto, 1960; Montreal, PQ, 1960; Western Canada Art Circuit, 1960; Leichi Gallery, Durban, South Africa, 1962; 101 Gallery, Johannesburg, South Africa, 1963; New Design Gallery, Vancouver, 1963; Studio Gallery, Durban, 1964.

GROUP: Represented in group exhibitions held in Canada including exhibitions of Canadian Federation of Artists, Canadian Group of Painters, and BC Society of Artists; Mary P. Stone Gallery, San Rafael, Calif., 1965.

COLLECTIONS IN WHICH REPRESENTED

National Gallery of Canada, Ottawa, Ont.; Vancouver Art Gallery, Brock Hall Collection, University of British Columbia; University of Natal, South Africa.

GILBERT, Kenneth*   1931–

Harpsichordist and organist; b. 16 Dec. 1931 in Montreal; son of Albert George and Reta Mabel (Welch) Gilbert.

EDUCATION

Attended Stanstead College and Westmount High School in Montreal; Conservatoire de Musique de la Province de Québec, 1945-53; studied theory with Nadia Boulanger and organ with Gaston Litaize, Conservatoire National Supérieur de Musique, Paris, France, 1953-55; studied harpsichord with Ruggero Gerlin, Accademia Musicale Chigiana, Siena, Italy, 1955-56, 1960; International Summer Academy for Organists, Haarlem, The Netherlands, 1961.

HOME

1280 St. Mark St., Apt. 1107, Montreal 25, PQ.

OFFICE

Dept. of Music, McGill University, Montreal, PQ.

CAREER

Queen Mary Rd. United Church, Montreal, organist and director of music 1953-68; Conservatoire de Musique de la Province de Québec, harpsichord instructor 1957, professor 1967–; toured eastern Canada under auspices of Les Jeunesses Musicales, giving over fifty recitals and lecture-recitals 1959, 1960-61; played a major role in introducing the modern European concepts of organ design to Canada, 1959–; toured France under auspices of Les Jeunesses Musicales de France 1963; Jeunesses Musicales Summer Camp, Mount Orford, PQ, harpsichord instructor 1963-66; McGill University, harpsichord and organ lecturer 1964–; McGill University Organ Summer School, instructor 1966; concert tour of England, France, Germany, and Switzerland 1968.

MEMBER

Académie de Musique de Québec; Ars Organi (founder-member); Royal Canadian College of Organists.

AWARDS, HONOURS

Quebec government prix d'Europe, 1953; Canada Council grant, 1961/62, senior arts fellowship, 1968/69.

CONCERT STAGE

Harpsichord soloist with Orchestra de Camera, Montreal, 4, 6 Dec. 1959; gave inaugural recital in "Ars organi" series, Jan. 1960; organ soloist, Bach Festival, Aeolian Hall, London, Ont., 7 Apr. 1961; organ soloist, Berlin Festival, Kirche zum Heilsbronen, Germany, 23 Sept. 1961; harpsichord soloist, Pro Musica Society, Ottawa, Ont. 3 Dec. 1962; harpsichord soloist with Vancouver Chamber Orchestra, Nov. 1964; harpsichord soloist with Quebec Symphony Orchestra, 4 Mar. 1965; harpsichord recital, Carnegie Hall, New York, NY, 10 May 1965; harpsichord soloist with Chicago Symphony Orchestra, Ill., 4 June 1966, 1, 3 June 1967, and at Fair Lane Festival, Detroit, Mich., 4 June 1967; conducted complete cycle of harpsichord concertos by J.S. Bach from the keyboard, McGill University, fall 1966; harpsichord soloist with orchestra, Ten Centuries Concerts, Toronto, 16 Oct. 1966; organ soloist, American Guild of Organists, Charlotte, NC, 28 Nov. 1966; harpsichord soloist in complete cycle of violin and keyboard sonatas by J.S. Bach, McGill University, 3, 17 Feb. 1967; harpsichord soloist with McGill Chamber Orchestra, Montreal, 27 Feb. 1967; organ soloist, inaugural series of recitals, Canadian Pavilion, Expo 67, Montreal, 28 Apr.-4 May 1967; organ soloist, International Organ Festival, St. Joseph's Oratory, Montreal, 28 June 1967; harpsichord recitals, Expo 67, Montreal, 5, 6 Aug. 1967; harpsichord recitals, Queen Elizabeth Hall, London, England, 16 Jan., 3 Feb. 1968, Tonhalle, Hamburg, Germany, 19 Jan. 1968, and Zunfthaus zur Meisen, Zürich, Switzerland, 24 Jan. 1968; organ recital, Royal Canadian College of Organists, Toronto, 25 Mar. 1968; organ soloist, National Convention of American Guild of Organists, Denver, Colo., 1 July 1968; organ recitals, University of Colorado, 6, 7 July 1968.

FILM

Played background music, all by Bach or Couperin, on organ or harpsichord, for several National Film Board of Canada films, e.g. *Waiting for Caroline, La bourse et la vie* (1965).

RADIO

Recital of Canadian organ music (RTF, Paris, spring 1955); eleven recitals in "Complete organ works of Bach" (series, CBC, 1960/61); two organ recitals (RIAS, Berlin, Germany, Sept. 1961); two recitals recorded on Bach organ at Lüneburg, Germany (Norddeutscher-Rundfunk/CBC, Oct. 1961); played harpsichord with a chamber group in world première of *Psaume pour abri* by Pierre Mercure ("Wednesday night," CBC, 15 May 1963); numerous organ and harpsichord recitals in CBC series, e.g. "Tuesday night," "Distinguished artists," "Concert hall"; harpsichordist and conductor in many CBC concerts of chamber music.

TELEVISION

Played in *Concerto for three harpsichords* by J.S. Bach ("Heure du concert," CBC, 1963); harpsichord soloist with CBC Toronto Symphony Orchestra under Hermann Scherchen (CBC, Dec. 1965); frequent appearances as harpsichord solo and continuo, and in organ recitals (CBC, 1956–).

RECORDINGS

Twelve records by RCA Victor, Baroque, Janus, Philips (Germany), Oryx (England).

WRITINGS

CONTRIBUTED: Articles and reviews to *Canadian music journal, Journal des Jeunesses Musicales, Journal musical canadien.*

WORK IN PROGRESS: Preparing an edition of complete harpsichord works of François Couperin-le-Grand, to be published by Heugel (Paris) in four volumes, vol. I to appear 1968; recording the same works for commercial release.

GILBERT, William Herbert
see GILBERT, Herbert

GILMOUR, Glenn Harvey 1939–
Dancer; b. 30 May 1939 in Hamilton, Ont.; son of Steve and Ann Bertrand (Parker) Gilmour; m. Charmain Turner 11 May 1964.

EDUCATION

Attended school in Windsor, Ont.; studied ballet with René Russel, Windsor, 1954; Leon Danielian and Edward Caton at Ballet Russe de Monte Carlo School, New York, NY, 1957; National Ballet of Canada, Toronto, 1958; Maria Fay, Stanislas Idzikowski, and Kathleen Crofton, London, England, 1961, 1964/65.

RELIGION

Protestant.

HOME

32 Rosehill Ave., Toronto 7, Ont.

OFFICE

National Ballet of Canada, 157 King St. E., Toronto 1, Ont.

CAREER

National Ballet of Canada, corps de ballet 1958-61; soloist 1963-64, 1965-67; principal 1967–;

Walter Gore's London Ballet, soloist 1961-63; Ballet Rambert, London, soloist 1964/65.

MEMBER

AEA.

AWARDS, HONOURS

Ballet School, Windsor, scholarship for study in New York; Windsor Ballet Guild grant for study with the National Ballet of Canada, 1958.

THEATRE

First danced Phaser in *The remarkable rocket* (Gillies, 1960), Pas de trois in *Le lac des cygnes* (Petipa-Ivanov, 1961), Scottish variation in *Scottish suite* (1961), Thedius in *Ballad* (Strate, 1963), *One in five* (Powell, 1963), Peasant pas de deux in *Giselle* (Coralli-Perrot, 1963), Pas de trois in *Les rendez-vous* (Ashton, 1963), Jasper in *Pineapple Poll* (Cranko, 1964), Benvolio in *Romeo and Juliet* (Cranko, 1964), Tavern dancer, Torreador, and Gypsy pas de deux in *Don Quixote* (Gorsky, 1964/65), Betrothal dance in *Coppelia* (St. Leon, 1964/65), Second boy's variation in *La sylphide* (Bournonville, 1964/65), Wilfrid in *Giselle* (Corrali-Perrot, 1964/65), Mercutio in *Romeo and Juliet* (Cranko, Nov. 1965), Gurn in *La sylphide* (Bruhn, Nov. 1965), Boy's variation in *Solitaire* (Macmillan, Nov. 1965), Cavillio in *Pulcinella* (Strate, Nov. 1965), Master of ceremonies and Trepak in *Casse-noisette* (Franca after Ivanov, Dec. 1965), Officer in *Offenbach in the underworld* (Tudor, 1966), Lead bandit and Artist in *La prima ballerina* (Heiden, Oct. 1967), Spanish dance in *Le lac des cygnes* (Bruhn, Dec. 1967).

TELEVISION

Danced in *One in five* (Powell, "Festival," CBC, 6 May 1964), Spanish dance in *Le lac des cygnes* (Bruhn, "Festival," CBC, 27 Dec. 1967).

GINSBERG, Ruta, pseud.
see COLOMBO, John Robert

GIOVANNI, Edoardo di, pseud.
see JOHNSON, Edward

GIRARD, Benoît* 1932–
Actor; b. 26 Jan. 1932 in Montreal; son of Uldéric and Marguerite (Lavoie) Girard; m. Monique Joly; children: Christian.

EDUCATION

Attended Collège Mont-Saint-Louis, Montréal; Université de Montréal.

HOME

4535 Oxford Ave., Montreal 28, PQ.

CAREER

Théâtre Club, Montréal, actor 1956–; Théâtre du Rideau Vert, Montréal, actor 1958–; toured France, USSR, and Canada.

MEMBER

Canadian Theatre Centre; Union des Artistes de Montréal.

AWARDS, HONOURS
Best actor award from Congrès du Spectacle,
1965.

THEATRE
Played in *Doux temps des amours, Elle tournera
la terre, Encore cinq minutes, Les taupes*, Sir
Andrew in *Twelfth night* (Théâtre Club, 1956),
Coelio in *Les caprices de Marianne* (Rideau Vert,
1958), Gowan in *Requiem pour une nonne*
(Théâtre Club, Mar. 1962), Perdigan in *On ne
badine pas avec l'amour* (Rideau Vert, Mar.
1964), Vincent in *Une maison ... un jour* (Rideau
Vert, 11 Sept. 1965), Démétrios in *Le songe
d'une nuit d'été* (Rideau Vert, 15 Sept, 1965),
Giorgio Vanzi in *On ne sait comment* (Rideau
Vert, 15 Nov. 1965), Prozorov in *Les trois soeurs*
(Rideau Vert, 15 Apr. 1966), Richard in *L'amant*
(Rideau Vert, 15 Feb. 1968), James in *La collec-
tion* (Rideau Vert, 15 Feb. 1968), *Bilan* (Théâtre
du Nouveau Monde, Montréal, 4 Oct. 1968),
Hamlet, prince du Québec (Théâtre de l'Escale,
Montréal, 17 Jan. 1968).

TELEVISION
Played leading roles in many productions, e.g.
*Colombe, Quelqu'un parmi vous, Montserrat,
L'héritière, Mort d'un commis-voyageur, Toa, Le
feu sur la terre* (CBC, 1958), *Bilan* (CBC, 1961),
L'inquisition (CBC, 1962/63), *Tuez le veau gras*
(CBC, 1963/64), Lui in *Loving* ("Festival," CBC,
25 May 1966).

GIROUX, Antoinette
Actress.

HOME
2055 Lincoln Ave., Apt. 5, Montreal 108, PQ.

CAREER
Théâtre l'Arcade, Montréal, actress; Compagnons
de Saint-Laurent, Montréal, actress; Théâtre du
Nouveau Monde, Montréal, actress 1951–.

MEMBER
Union des Artistes de Montréal.

THEATRE
Played in many productions e.g. *Les mal aimés*
(l'Arcade), *Tessa ou la nymphe au coeur fidèle*
(L'Équipe Montréal, 1943), *La cathédrale*
(Théâtre du Monument National, Montréal,
1950), *Neiges* (Théâtre du Rideau Vert, Montréal,
1950), *Un inspecteur vous demande* (Nouveau
Monde, Nov. 1951), *Le corsaire* (Nouveau Monde,
1952/53), Dorine in *Le Tartuffe* (Nouveau Monde,
1952/53), *Les assassins associés* (Théâtre du Rideau Vert, 14 Oct. 1966), *Pygmalion* (Nouveau
Monde, 12 Jan. 1968).

GIROUX, Colette Mary Elizabeth
see BOKY, Colette

GIROUX, Germaine
Actress and singer.

HOME
2055 Lincoln Ave., Apt. 5, Montreal 108, PQ.

CAREER
Compagnons de Saint-Laurent, Montréal, actress;
Théâtre du Nouveau Monde, Montréal, actress
1955–?; CBC, Montreal, actress; Théâtre du Rideau Vert, Montréal, actress 1965–.

MEMBER
Union des Artistes de Montréal.

THEATRE
Played in many productions, e.g. *The spider, Ladies of the jury, The circus, Ladies all, Madame
sans gêne, Mademoiselle, Mon homme, Le châtiment, Maman, Paris, L'emprise, Frénésie, Les hus-
sards, Family blues* (New York, NY), *Le testament
du père Leleu* (l'Équipe, Montréal, 1946), *Philippe
et Jonas* (Nouveau Monde, 1953/54), *Gigi* (Mountain Playhouse, Montreal, 1954), *Le mariage forcé,
Sganarelle, La jalousie du barbouillé* (Nouveau
Monde, Montreal Festival, 1954; Paris Festival,
France, 1955; Stratford, Ont. Festival, 1956),
Fridolinades (1956), Alice in *Henry V* (Stratford,
Ont. Festival, June 1956), *On grève ... de rire* (Rideau Vert, 15 Dec. 1965), Amandine in *Chat en
poche* (Rideau Vert, 15 Feb. 1966), *Les assassins
associés* (Rideau Vert, 14 Oct. 1966), *En rire et
en couleur* (Rideau Vert, 15 Dec. 1966), *Je veux
voir Mioussov* (Rideau Vert, 15 Mar. 1967), *La
poudre aux yeux* (Rideau Vert, 18 May 1967),
Les belles soeurs (Rideau Vert, 28 Aug. 1968).

GLADSTONE, Gerald*   1929–
Sculptor; b. 1929 in Toronto; son of Ralph and
Dora Gladstone; m. Sheila 27 Jan. 1953; chil-
dren: five.

EDUCATION
Attended Lansdowne School, Toronto to seventh
grade; mainly self-taught as sculptor.

HOME
47 Colborne St., Toronto, Ont.

CAREER
Travelled to England in 1961; sole judge to select
three sculptures for Atlas Alloys Metal Company;
Toronto International Sculpture Symposium, organizer and guide, 1965 and 1967.

COMMISSIONS
Fountain, William Lyon MacKenzie Federal
Building, Toronto, c.1961; concrete and bronze
pylon, East York Library, Ont., c.1961; fountain,
Winnipeg Airport, Man.; fountain, Toronto Telegram Newspaper Building; bas-relief, Trinity College, University of Toronto; hydraulically-oper-
ated sea monster, St. Lawrence River, Canadian
Government Participation Pavilion; space column
with fountain, Expo 67, Montreal, PQ; sculpture,
Expo 67 amusement area; forty sculptures, Provincial Government Buildings, Toronto, 1967-68;
eight pieces of sculpture, rented by MGM for TV
series *Man from Uncle*, 1967.

AWARDS, HONOURS
Canada Council grant, 1961/62 and 1962/63.

EXHIBITIONS
ONE-MAN: Art Gallery of Toronto, 1957; Isaacs Gallery, Toronto, 1958, 1959, and 1960; Molton Gallery, London, England, 1962; Montreal Museum of Fine Arts, 1962; Dorothy Cameron Gallery, Toronto, 1963, 1964-65; Hamilton Galleries, London, 1964; Graham Gallery, New York, NY, 1964; Norman Mackenzie Gallery, University of Saskatchewan, Regina, 1965; Coomera Gallery, Los Angeles, Calif., 1965.

GROUP
Represented in group exhibitions held in Canada including annual exhibitions of Montreal Museum of Fine Arts and Winnipeg Show; represented in group shows organized by National Gallery of Canada, Ottawa, Ont.; Carnegie International, Pittsburgh, Pa., 1958; Graham Gallery, New York, 1962; Commonwealth Institute, London, 1962; Museum of Modern Art, New York, 1963; Contemporary Canadian Painting and Sculpture, Rochester Memorial Art Gallery, NY, 1963; Long Beach City College Sculpture Show, Los Angeles, Calif., 1963.

COLLECTIONS IN WHICH REPRESENTED
Art Gallery of Ontario, Toronto; Vancouver Art Gallery, BC; British Arts Council; York University; National Gallery of Canada; Montreal Museum of Fine Arts; Fry-Drew Associates, London; Victoria and Albert Museum, London; Loborough High School, England; Scarborough College, Ont.; Loyola College, Montreal; Sir George Williams University; Israel National Gallery; Billy Rose Sculpture Court, Israel.

GLASSCO, John* 1909–
(George Colman the younger, pseud.; Grace Davignon, pseud.; W.P.R. Eady, pseud.; Albert Eddy, pseud.; Silas N. Gooch, pseud.; S. Colson-Haig, pseud.; George Henderson, pseud.; Nordyk Nudleman, pseud.; Hideki Okada, pseud.; Jean de Saint-Luc, pseud.; Miles Underwood, pseud.)
Author; b. 15 Dec. 1909 in Montreal, PQ; son of Archibald P.S. and Beatrice (Rawlings) Glassco; m. Elma von Colmar 10 Sept. 1963.

EDUCATION
Attended Selwyn House School, Montreal, 1916-23; Bishop's College School, Lennoxville, PQ, 1923-24; Lower Canada College, Montreal, 1924-25; McGill University, 1925-28.

RELIGION
Church of England.

HOME
Jamaica Farm, Foster, Eastern Townships, PQ.

CAREER
Mainly literary; resided in Europe 1928-31.

AWARDS, HONOURS
Borestone Mountain poetry award, 1955, 1958;

Canada Council grant to complete a translation, 1959/60, senior arts fellowship, 1964/65; Quebec government prize for best work in English literature written between 1959 and 1961 and prize for poetry, 1964.

WRITINGS
Contes en crinoline (novel), Gaucher, 1930; *The deficit made flesh* (poems), McClelland & Stewart, 1958; (with A. Beardsley) *Under the hill* (novel), Olympia Press, 1959; *The English governess* (novel), Olympia Press, 1960 (published also under title *Under the birch* and *The authentic confession of Harriet Marwood, governess*, Orpheus Books, 1967; pirated under title *The governess*, Collectors Publications, 1967; expurgated version published under title *Harriet Marwood, governess*, Grove Press, 1967); *A point of sky* (poems) Oxford, 1964; *Squire Hardman* (poem), Pastime Press, 1967.

EDITED: *English poetry in Quebec*, McGill, 1965 (Foster Poetry Conference proceedings, PQ, 1963).

TRANSLATED
L. von S. Masock's *Venus in furs*; S.D. Garneau's *Journal*, McClelland & Stewart, 1962; words for H. Willan's *Hymne à l'occasion du centenaire de la Confédération canadienne*, BMI, 1966.

CONTRIBUTED: Poems and stories to *Alphabet*, *Avant garde* (Paris), *Canadian forum*, *Canadian literature, Delta, Fiddlehead, McGill fortnightly review, Queen's quarterly, Saturday night, Tamarack review, This quarter, Transition, Yes.*

WORK IN PROGRESS: "Memoirs of Montparnasse" (1928-30); "The art of pornography"; translation of S.D. Garneau's *Poésies complètes*; edition of "Poetry of French Canada in translation" to be published by Oxford University Press.

GLYDE, Henry George 1906–
Artist; b. 18 June 1906 in Luton, England; son of George Glyde; came to Canada in Sept. 1935 and settled in Calgary, Alta.; m. Hilda Mabel Allwood; children: two sons, one daughter.

EDUCATION
Attended Brassey Institute of Arts and Sciences, Hastings, England, 1920-26; Royal College of Art, London, England, 1926-30.

HOME
RR1, Port Washington, BC.

CAREER
Royal College of Art, student demonstrator 1929-30; Croydon School of Arts and Crafts, England, art instructor 1929-31; Polytechnic, London, instructor 1929-31; High Wycombe School of Art, England, instructor 1931-35; Institute of Technology and Art, Calgary, head of art department 1935-46; University of Alberta, head of department of fine arts 1946-66; Banff School of Fine Arts, Alta., head of painting division 1937-66; il-

lustrated *Alberta golden jubilee anthology*, Mc-Clelland & Stewart, 1955; illustrated *Three Icelandic sagas*, Princeton, 1950; travelled in Europe 1967-68; painting on Pender Island, BC 1968–.

COMMISSIONS
Mural, University of Alberta Library; mural, Medicine Hat Public Library, Alta., 1958; mural, Student Union Building, University of Alberta; design for bas-relief in stone, University of Alberta; design for bas-reliefs, Victoria Composite High School, Edmonton, Alta.; design for frieze, Edmonton City Hall; paintings for Stations of the Cross, St. Patrick's Church, Medicine Hat.

MEMBER
Alberta Society of Artists (president, 1940-46); Canadian Society of Graphic Arts; Federation of Canadian Artists (president, 1954); Canadian Arts Council (Alberta representative, honorary vice-president, 1950); Royal Canadian Academy (Associate 1942; Academician 1949).

AWARDS, HONOURS
Lewis Berger scholarship, Royal Society of Artists, 1928; scholarship, Royal College of Art, 1929; Honorary Associate of the Royal College of Art, 1929; Canada Council senior overseas fellowship, 1958; University of Alberta national award in painting, 1966.

EXHIBITIONS
ONE-MAN: Hudson's Bay Store, Calgary, 1937; Coste House, Calgary; Canadian Art Galleries, Calgary; Edmonton Art Gallery; Jacox Galleries, Edmonton.
GROUP: Represented in group exhibitions held in Canada including annual exhibitions of Royal Canadian Academy, Ontario Society of Artists, Canadian Society of Graphic Arts, Canadian Society of Painters in Water Colour, and exhibitions sponsored by National Council of Jewish Women; represented in group exhibitions organized by National Gallery of Canada, Ottawa, Ont., including second Biennial Exhibition of Canadian Painting, 1957; Student's International Exhibition, Prague, Czecho-Slovakia, 1938; Canadian International Exhibition, New York, NY; Royal Academy, London; Royal Society of British Artists.

COLLECTIONS IN WHICH REPRESENTED
Art Gallery of Ontario, Toronto; Edmonton Art Gallery; National Gallery of Canada.

GODIN, Jacques* 1930–
Actor; b. 14 Sept. 1930 in Montreal; son of Alphonse and Jeanne (Picard) Godin.

EDUCATION
Attended École St. Zotique, Montréal, 1936-45; École St. Henri, Montréal, 1945-48; Collège Mont-Saint-Louis, Montréal, 1948-50; École des Hautes Études Commerciales, Montréal, 1950-53; studied drama with Georges Groulx, Théâtre du Nouveau Monde, Montréal.

RELIGION
Roman Catholic.
HOME
281 Riverside Drive, Apt. 906, St. Lambert, PQ.
CAREER
Théâtre du Nouveau Monde, actor, 1967–.
MEMBER
Union des Artistes de Montréal.
THEATRE
Played in many productions, e.g. *Fin de partie, Monsieur Bonhomme et les incendiaires*, Mountjoy in *Henry V* (Stratford, Ont. Festival, June 1956), *Le roi se meurt, Balmaseda, L'amour des 4 colonels, Quadrille, L'alouette, Venise sauvée, Nemo, Chacun sa vérité, Chant du cygne, Nuit des rois, On n'a pas tué Joe Hill* (Nouveau Monde, 18 Feb. 1967), *Le bourgeois gentilhomme* (Nouveau Monde, 15 May 1967), *On n'aime qu'une fois* (Théâtre de Marjolaine, Montréal, 24 June, 1967), *Bois-brûlés* (Nouveau Monde, 3 Nov. 1967).

FILM
Played in several productions, e.g. *The luck of Ginger Coffey* (National Film Board of Canada), *Festin des morts* (National Film Board of Canada), *Pas de vacances pour les idoles*.

RADIO
Played in several productions on CKVL, Verdun, PQ and CKAC, Montreal.

TELEVISION
Played in many productions, e.g. *La mort du commis voyageur, Noces de sang* (CBC, 21 Jan. 1960), *Yerma, Volpone, Pari d'un milliardaire, Disciple du diable, Deux tours d'horloge, Antigone* (Anouilh, CBC, 1962/63), *Dernière heure, Au-dessus de tout, Madame Nora, L'étrangère, Blues pour un homme averti, Équation à deux inconnus, L'otage, Little loaves of Ste-Geneviève, Absalom mon père, Le veau d'or, L'exilé, Le cheval blanc, Radisson* (serial), *Courrier du roi* (serial), *Belles histoires* (serial), *7ième nord* (serial), "Entre deux eaux" (series), *Des fourmis et des hommes* (serial), *Ile au trésor* (serial), *Les martins* (serial), several productions of "Shoestring theatre" (1958/65), "Boîte à surprises" (CBC, 1958), "Agence Jobidon" (series).

GOETZEL, Charlotte
see BROTT, Lotte

GOLDBERG, Eric* 1890–
Artist; b. 28 Oct. 1890 in Berlin, Germany; son of Richard and Claire Goldberg; came to Canada in 1928, settled in Montreal, PQ and became Canadian citizen in 1935; m. Regina Seiden 3 July 1928.

EDUCATION
Attended Koenigstädtsche Gymnasium, Berlin, until 1906; studied under Tony Robert-Fleury, Jean

Paul Laurens, and Jules Lefebvre, Académie Julian, Paris, France, 1906-10; École des Beaux-Arts, Paris, 1906-10; studied under Lovis Corinth, Akademie Levin Funke, Berlin 1915-17.

HOME
331 Clarke Ave., Westmount, PQ.

CAREER
Bezalel Art School, Jerusalem, Israel, teacher 1911-15; Akademie Levin Funke, art teacher 1915-17; lived in Chicago, Ill., 1921-24; opened art school in Montreal 1949, teacher there 1949–; painter in Montreal 1928–.

COMMISSIONS
Portrait of Robert Taschereau, Supreme Court of Canada.

MEMBER
Eastern Group.

EXHIBITIONS
ONE-MAN: Berlin, 1911; Jerusalem, 1928; *Sacre du Printemps*, Paris, 1928; Montreal Museum of Fine Arts, 1929, 1948, 1951, 1958, 1963; Wise Center, Cincinnati, Ohio, 1930 and 1936; Montross Gallery, New York, NY, 1930; Noonan Kocian Galleries, St. Louis, Mo., 1936; Ehrich-Newhouse Galleries, New York, 1936; Carroll Carstaire Gallery, New York, 1938; Scott Gallery, Montreal, 1938; Eaton's Fine Art Galleries, Toronto, Ont., 1942; Dominion Gallery, Montreal, 1943, 1950, 1953, 1955, and 1963.
GROUP: Represented in group exhibitions held in Canada from 1929 on including exhibitions of Eastern Group and Spring Exhibitions of Montreal Museum of Fine Arts; Paris *Salons*; represented in group exhibitions held at Chicago Art Gallery and Whitney Museum, New York; World's Fair, New York, 1939; Aspects of Contemporary Painting in Canada, Addison Gallery, Andover, Mass., 1942-43; Canadian Art 1760-1943, Yale University Art Gallery, 1944; *Pintura Canadense Contemporanea*, Rio de Janeiro, Brazil, 1944; Contemporary Canadian Painting, Canadian Club, New York, 1948; Painters of Canada ... 1669-1948, Virginia Museum of Fine Arts, Richmond, 1949; 400th Anniversary Exhibition, São Paulo, Brazil, 1954; exhibition of Canadian painting shown in Pakistan, India, and Ceylon, 1954-55.

COLLECTIONS IN WHICH REPRESENTED
Beaverbrook Art Gallery, Fredericton, NB; Cincinnati Museum Association, Ohio; Edmonton Art Gallery, Alta.; Bezalel National Art Museum, Jerusalem; Montreal Museum of Fine Arts; National Gallery of Canada, Ottawa, Ont.; Seminary of Joliette, PQ; Vancouver Art Gallery, BC.

GOOCH, Silas N., pseud.
see GLASSCO, John

GORDON, Hortense 1887-1961
(Hortense Crompton Mattice) Artist; b. 24 Nov. 1887 in Hamilton, Ont.; daughter of James

Harvey and Sarah Louise (Crompton) Mattice; m. John G. Sloan Gordon 3 Aug. 1920; d. 6 Nov. 1961 in Hamilton.

EDUCATION
Attended Collegiate Institute in Hamilton; studied with A.M. Fleming and Marion E. Mattice in Chatham, Ont.; studied in London, England, Paris, France, and Vienna, Austria; studied under Hans Hofmann; attended School of Design, Normal School, Detroit, Mich.; mainly self-taught.

RELIGION
Presbyterian.

CAREER
Moved to Chatham, Ont. 1904; Hamilton Institute of Technology, instructor in art 1916, succeeded her husband, as head of the Art School 1932-61; Sixth International Congress of Art Education, Prague, Czecho-Slovakia, organized an exhibition of art and design 1928; travelled and painted extensively in Europe with her husband.

MEMBER
Royal Canadian Academy (Associate 1929); Painters Eleven; Women's Art Association of Hamilton (president); Canadian Society of Graphic Art; North Shore Art Association of Gloucester, Ont.; International Federation of Art of Zurich, Switzerland; Contemporary Artists of Hamilton; Art Teacher's Guild, London (elected, 1928); Ontario Secondary School Teachers' Federation.

AWARDS, HONOURS
Special honours presented by President Jan Masaryk, Sixth International Congress of Art Education, Prague 1928.

EXHIBITIONS
ONE-MAN: Park Gallery, Montreal, PQ; Glenhyrst Arts Centre, Brantford, Ont. (with John S. Gordon); Moos Gallery, Toronto; New York, NY; Detroit, Mich.; Hamilton, 1962; University of New Brunswick; Michigan State College, 1953.
GROUP: Represented in group exhibitions held in Canada since 1906 including annual exhibitions of Ontario Society of Artists, Royal Canadian Academy, Painters Eleven.

COLLECTIONS IN WHICH REPRESENTED
Art Gallery of Hamilton; Art Gallery of Ontario, Toronto.

GOTLIEB, Phyllis Fay Bloom* 1926–
Author; b. 25 May 1926 in Toronto; daughter of Leo and Mary (Kates) Bloom; m. Calvin Carl Gotlieb 12 June 1949; children: Leo Ronald b. 8 Mar. 1950, Margaret Susan b. 11 Apr. 1952, Jane Elizabeth b. 9 Apr. 1956.

EDUCATION
Attended Kew Beach Public School, 1931-34, Withrow Avenue Public School, 1934-39, Jarvis Collegiate Institute, 1939-40, and Forest Hill Secondary School, 1940-44, in Toronto; University of Toronto, Victoria College, BA, 1948, University College, MA, 1950.

RELIGION
Jewish.
HOME
29 Ridgevale Dr., Toronto 19, Ont.
CAREER
Mainly literary.
MEMBER
Science Fiction Writers of America.
WRITINGS
Who knows one? (poems), Hawkshead, 1962; *Sunburst* (novel), Fawcett, 1964; *Within the zodiac* (poems), McClelland & Stewart, 1964. CONTRIBUTED: Poems and stories to many periodicals, e.g. *Alphabet, Amazing, Canadian forum, Canadian literature, Fantastic, Fantasy, If, Queen's quarterly, Science fiction, Tamarack review.*
WORK IN PROGRESS: "Why should I have all the grief? " (novel), Macmillan, *c.*1969; "Ordinary, moving" (collection of poetry); "Time pieces" (science fiction stories).

GOTSHALKS, Irene Apinée
see APINÉE, Irene

GOULD, Glenn 1932–
(Glenn Herbert Gould)
Pianist and composer; b. 25 Sept. 1932 in Toronto; son of Russell Herbert and Florence (Greig) Gould.
EDUCATION
Taught by private tutor, 1939-40; attended Williamson Rd. primary school in Toronto, 1940–? ; studied piano with Alberto Guerrero, organ with Frederick Silvester, composition with Leo Smith, Royal Conservatory of Music, Toronto, 1943-52, associate, 1944; Malvern Collegiate Institute, Toronto, graduated 1951.
OFFICE
Canadian Broadcasting Corporation, 354 Jarvis St., Toronto 5, Ont.
CAREER
First piano recital 1946; formal debut with Toronto Symphony Orchestra 1947; toured USA 1954, annually 1956-59; American debut, Washington, DC 1955; Columbia Records, long-term contract 1955–; Stratford, Ont. Music Festival, composer, conductor, and pianist 1956, co-director.1961; European debut with Moscow Philharmonic Orchestra, USSR 1957; toured USSR and Germany 1957, Israel 1958; University of Cincinnati, Ohio, lecturer 1962; final concert tour 1962; composer, lecturer, broadcaster, and recording artist 1962–.
MEMBER
CAPAC; Toronto Musicians Association.
AWARDS, HONOURS
Harriet Cohen Music Awards, London, England, Bach medal, 1959; LLD from University of To-

ronto, 1964; Canada Council Molson prize of $15,000, 1968.
CONCERT STAGE
Pianist, New York Town Hall, NY, 1955; piano soloist with Berlin Philharmonic Orchestra under Herbert von Karajan, Berlin, Germany, 1957; pianist, Vienna International Music Festival, Austria, 1957; piano soloist with Concertgebouw Orchestra of Amsterdam under Dimitri Mitropoulos, Salzburg Festival, Austria, 1958; pianist, Vancouver International Festival, BC, 1960; piano soloist with New York Philharmonic Orchestra, symphony orchestras throughout USA, e.g. Detroit, Mich., Pittsburgh, Pa., Dallas, Tex., St. Louis, Mo., Cleveland, Ohio, San Francisco, Calif., and in Canada at Vancouver, Montreal, PQ, and Toronto.
FILM
Featured performer in *Glenn Gould off the record, Glenn Gould.on the record* (National Film Board of Canada).
RADIO
Played and commented on numerous CBC series, e.g. "Tuesday night," "Wednesday night," "Sunday supplement"; pianist with New York Philharmonic Orchestra (14 Apr. 1962); devised and performed in *Arnold Schoenberg – the man who changed music* (8 Aug. 1962); compiled and narrated *Dialogues on the prospects of recordings* ("Sunday night," 10 Jan. 1965); played in "The art of Glenn Gould" (series, 1966/67).
TELEVISION
Played and commented on numerous CBC series, e.g. "Festival"; played in "Documentary 60" (22, 29 Nov. 1959), *The subject is Beethoven* ("Festival," 6 Feb. 1961); lectured in *Glenn Gould and the music of the U.S.S.R.* (14 June 1962), *Glenn Gould on Bach* (8 Apr. 1962), *Glenn Gould features Richard Strauss* (15 Oct. 1962), *The art of fugue* ("Festival," 4 Mar. 1963); played in *Concerti for four Wednesdays* ("Festival," June 1964); presented music and discussion with Yehudi Menuhin ("Festival," 18 May 1966); videotaped series of four "musical conversations" (BBC, 1966); played *Centennial performance* (CBC, 15 Nov. 1967); hosted *A world of music* (CBC, 18 Feb. 1968).
RECORDINGS
Goldberg variations by J.S. Bach, Columbia ML 5060, 1956; *Italian concerto* and *Partitas nos. 1 and 2* by J.S. Bach, Columbia ML 5472, 1960; *The well-tempered clavier* by J.S. Bach, Columbia ML 5808, 5938, 6176, MS 7099, 1963-68; *Canadian music in the twentieth century*, CBC Masterworks 32 11 0046, 1967; *Sonata*, K.330, and *Fantasia and fugue*, K.394, by Mozart, Columbia MS 7097; *Sonatas*, Opus nos. 109, 110, 111, and *Piano concertos in D minor and F minor* by Beethoven, Columbia; *Sonata no. 1* in E flat by Haydn, Columbia; *Sonata,* Opus 1, by Alban Berg,

Columbia, also Hallmark; *Sonata no. 3* by
Krenek, Columbia; *Complete music for solo piano
and Songs for voice and piano* by Schoenberg,
Columbia M 2L 336; *Instrumental music* by
Schoenberg, Columbia M 2S 767, 1967; *Music by
Brahms*, Columbia ML 5637; *Partita no. 5* by J.S.
Bach, and *Quintet in F minor* by Brahms, CBC IS.

WRITINGS
Arnold Schoenberg; a perspective, University of
Cincinnati, 1964.
CONTRIBUTED: Articles to *Saturday night, Saturday review*; album notes for recordings.

COMPOSITIONS
String quartet no. 1, 1953-55, Barger & Barclay,
first performed 1956 in Montreal by Montreal
String Quartet, recorded by CBC IS with Montreal
String Quartet, also by Columbia ML 5578 with
Symphonia Quartet; *Twelve-tone piano pieces*;
Cadenzas to Beethoven's piano concerto no. 1,
Barger & Barclay; *So you want to write a fugue?* ,
string quartet, also mixed choir and piano, 1964,
G. Schirmer, first performed 8 Mar. 1966 on CBC
Toronto by Festival Singers; *A letter from Stalingrad*, soprano, 1964, written for Lois Marshall.

GOULDING, Dorothy* 1898–
(Dorothy Massey Goulding)
Director; b. 4 Apr. 1898 in Toronto; daughter of
Walter and Susan Maria (Denton) Massey; m.
Arthur M. Goulding 3 Oct. 1916; children:
Helen b. 1917, Ann b. 1919, Susan b. 1921,
Dorothy-Jane b. 1923.

EDUCATION
Privately educated; studied stage design in Vienna,
Austria.

HOME
305 Dawes Rd., Toronto 17, Ont.

CAREER
Children Players of Hart House Theatre, Toronto,
director 1931-35; Toronto Children Players, director 1935-42, designer-director 1942-59; Junior
Players, Toronto, director 1937-38; taught summer classes at Dentonia Park, Toronto, 1942-60;
Caravan Players, Toronto, designer-director 1947.

AWARDS, HONOURS
Central Ontario Drama Festival best play award,
1947.

THEATRE
Directed more than 330 productions for children
at Hart House, 1931-35, Margaret Eaton Hall,
Toronto, 1935-42, Dentonia Park, 1942-60,
Eaton Auditorium, Toronto, 1942-59; directed
Beauty and the beast (Hart House, Dec. 1952);
Runabout royal (Hart House, 1958).

GRAY, Simon James Holliday 1936–
(Hamish Reade, pseud.)
Author; b. 21 Oct. 1936 in Hayling Island, Hampshire, England; son of J.D. and Barbara Mary Cecelia (Holliday) Gray; came to Canada in 1953; m.
Beryl Mary Kevin 10 Aug. 1965; children: Benjamin b. 10 July 1966.

EDUCATION
Attended Westminster School, London; Dalhousie
University, BA; Université de Clermont-Ferrand,
France, 1958-59; University of Cambridge, 1959-61.

RELIGION
None.

HOME
67 Aberdare Gardens, London, N.W.6, England.

OFFICE
Queen Mary College, University of London, Mile
End Road, London, E.1, England.

CAREER
Collège Technique, Clermont-Ferrand, instructor
in English 1958-59; resided in Spain 1961-62;
University of Cambridge, instructor 1962-63,
Trinity College, supervisor in English 1964-66;
University of British Columbia, instructor in English 1963-64; Queen Mary College, University of
London, lecturer in English 1966–; *Delta* (Cambridge), editor.

AWARDS, HONOURS
Harper Wood travelling scholarship, 1961; Trinity
College senior scholar, Cambridge University,
1962-64; Writer's Guild scroll for best TV play in
1967, Apr. 1968.

WRITINGS
Colmain (novel), Faber & Faber, 1963 (adapted
and produced CBC radio, Halifax, NS, 1963);
Simple people (novel), Faber & Faber, 1965
(translated into Spanish); *Little Portia* (novel),
Faber & Faber, 1967; *A comeback for Stark*
(novel), Faber & Faber, 1968; *The candidate*
(radio play; produced CBC Halifax, 1962); *Up in
Pigeon Lake* (radio play; produced CBC, Halifax,
1962); *The caramel crisis* (TV play; "Thirty minute theatre," BBC, Jan. 1966); *Death of a teddy
bear* (TV play; "Wednesday play," BBC, Feb.
1967); *Away with the ladies* (TV play; "Wednesday play," BBC, July 1967); *Sleeping dog* (TV
play), Faber & Faber, 1968 ("Wednesday play,"
BBC, Oct. 1967); *Wise child* (play), Faber & Faber,
1968 (translated into German; produced Wyndham's, London, 14 Oct. 1967; to be filmed by
British Lion).
EDITED: (with K. Walker) *Selected English prose*,
Faber & Faber, 1967.
CONTRIBUTED: Stories and book reviews to
Voices, 2, edited by M. Ratcliffe, Joseph, 1966;
*Delta, The listener, New society, New statesman,
Spectator, Times literary supplement*.
WORK IN PROGRESS: "Autobiography of James
Haydon-Sprigg" (novel); "Dutch uncle" (play); a
biography of Dickens (TV script to be produced
on London Weekend TV); film script for Fitzroy
Film.

GREENE, Lorne*   1915–
Actor; b. 12 Feb. 1915 in Ottawa, Ont.; son of
Daniel and Dora Greene; m. Rita Hands 1940
(marriage dissolved 1960); m. Nancy Anne Deale
Dec. 1961; children: (first marriage) Belinda Susan and Charles b. 1944; (second marriage)
daughter b. Jan. 1968.

EDUCATION
Queen's University, BA, 1932-37; attended Neigh-
bourhood Playhouse School of the Theatre and
Martha Graham School of Contemporary Dance,
New York, NY, 1937-39.

RELIGION
Jewish.

HOME
2090 Mandeville Canyon Rd., Los Angeles, Calif.
90049, USA.

OFFICE
National Broadcasting Company, 3000 W. Alame-
da Ave., Burbank, Calif. 91505, USA.

CAREER
CBC, Toronto, Ont., chief newscaster and actor
1939-42, 194? -53; National Film Board of Cana-
da, Ottawa, official theatre release commentator
1940-45; Canadian Army; Academy of Radio
Arts, Toronto, founder and director 1946–? ;
Jupiter Theatre, Toronto, co-founder and actor;
New Play Society, Toronto, actor; Earle Grey
Players, Toronto, actor; NBC, Hollywood, Calif.,
actor 1959–.

MEMBER
AEA; ACTRA; AFTRA; AGVA; SAG; Canadian
Theatre Centre.

AWARDS, HONOURS
Fellowship to Neighbourhood Playhouse School
of the Theatre, 1937; H.P. Davis award of NBC
for best announcer in his field, 1942; Canada's
man of the year, 1965; DHL from Missouri Valley
College, Marshall.

THEATRE
Played in many productions by New Play Society,
Earle Grey Players, and Jupiter Theatre; Elliott
Clark in *The Prescott proposals* (Broadhurst, New
York, 16 Dec. 1953), Doc in *Come back little
Sheba* (Théâtre du Nouveau Monde, Montréal, PQ,
17 May 1954), Marcus Brutus in *Julius Caesar*
(Stratford, Ont. Festival, 1955), Prince of Morro-
co in *The merchant of Venice* (Stratford, Ont.
Festival, 1955), Charles Ashton in *Speaking of
murder* (Royale, New York, 19 Dec. 1956), Wil-
liam Winter in *Edwin Booth* (46th Street, New
York, 24 Nov. 1958).

FILM
Narrator in *Churchill's island* (Warwick Pictures,
1942); played Apostle Peter in *The silver chalice*
(Victor Saville Productions, 1955), Costain in
Tight spot (Columbia, 1955), Mr. Hanson in *Autumn leaves* (Columbia, 1956), Prosecutor in *Pey-
ton Place* (Twentieth Century Fox, 1957), *Hard

man* (Columbia, 1957), *The buccaneer* (Paramount, 1958), Grant Allan in *The gift of love*
(Twentieth Century Fox, 1958), Davis in *The
trap* (Paramount, 1958).

RADIO
Played in numerous CBC productions, e.g. "Stage,"
"Saturday night," *25th anniversary of CBC News
Service* ("As time goes by," 3 Jan. 1966).

TELEVISION
Played in many productions, e.g. title role in
Othello (CBC, Feb. 1953), Conductor in *Arietta*
("Studio one," CBS, spring 1953), O'Brien in
1984 ("Studio one," CBS, 23 Sept. 1953), *Ren-
dezvous* ("Studio one," CBS, 1953), *Driftwood*
("Elgin hour," ABC, 3 May 1955), Dr. Walter
Reed in *Yellow Jack* ("Producer's showcase,"
NBC, 1955), "Sailor of fortune" (series, UK, 1955-
56), *Mayerling* ("Producer's showcase," NBC,
1957), *The unburied dead* ("Folio," CBS, 24 Apr.
1957), guest star on "You are there," "Omnibus,"
"Danger," "Alfred Hitchcock presents," "Play-
house 90," "Wagon train," Ben Cartwright in
"Bonanza" (series, NBC, 12 Sept. 1959–), host in
Lorne Greene's American West (NBC, 3 May
1965), *A sense of truth* ("Telescope," CBC, 23
Feb. 1967).

RECORDINGS
*Destiny; Five card stud; Ringo; Welcome to the
Ponderosa,* RCA Victor LPM 2843, 1964; *Peter
and the wolf,* RCA Victor LM & LSC 2783, 1965;
Have a happy holiday, RCA Victor LPM 3410,
1965; *Lorne Green's American West,* RCA Victor
LPM & LSP 3409, 1966; *Portrait of the West,* RCA
Victor LPM & LSP 3678, 1966.

GREICIUS, Betty-Jean
see HAGEN, Betty-Jean

GRIER, Eldon Brockwill*   1917–
Poet and artist; b. 13 Apr. 1917 in London, England; son of Charles Brockwill and Kathleen Phyllis (Black) Grier; m. Elizabeth Temple Jamieson
1944 (marriage dissolved); m. Sylvia Tait 29 June
1954; children: (first marriage) Sharon Temple
Brockwill b. 9 Jan. 1948; (second marriage) Brock
Eldon b. 23 July 1956, Alexa Phyllis b. 12 Sept.
1960.

EDUCATION
Attended Selwyn House and other private schools
in Montreal, PQ; Ashbury College and St. Andrew's College in Ontario; studied with Goodridge Roberts (*q.v.*) and John Lyman (*q.v.*); with
Diego Rivera, 1945.

HOME
6221 St. George's Place, West Vancouver, BC.

CAREER
Engaged as a painter 1935–; Montreal Museum
of Fine Arts School, teacher 1946-61; travelled
extensively in Europe and Mexico.

COMMISSIONS
Mural for a drug-store restaurant in Montreal
*c.*1948.

MEMBER
Graphic Arts Society; Contemporary Arts Society (charter member, 1939).

EXHIBITIONS
Exhibited widely till 1955.

WRITINGS
A morning from scraps (poems), 1955; *Poems*, 1956; *Manzanillo and other poems*, 1957; *The ring of ice* (poems), Cambridge, 1957; *A friction of lights* (poems), Contact, 1963; *Pictures on the skin* (poems), Delta, 1967.
CONTRIBUTED: Poems to *The Penguin book of Canadian verse*, edited by R. Gustafson, Penguin, 1958; *English poetry in Quebec*, edited by J. Glassco, McGill, 1965; *Poetry of our time*, edited by L. Dudek, Macmillan, 1965; *Modern Canadian verse in English and French*, edited by A.J.M. Smith, Oxford, 1967; *Canadian forum, Delta, Fiddlehead, International, New: American and Canadian poetry, Prism, Tamarack review.*

GRIER, Sir Edmund Wyly
see GRIER, Sir Wyly

GRIER, Sir Wyly 1862−1957
(Sir Edmund Wyly Grier)
Artist; b. 26 Nov. 1862 in Melbourne, Australia; son of Charles and Marie Agnes (Monro) Grier; lived in England 1866-76 and 1878-91 and in Canada 1876-78; returned to Canada 1891 and settled in Toronto, Ont.; m. Florence Geale Dickson 4 Sept. 1895; children: Crawford G.M., Stella Evelyn, Sylvia E., E. Geoffrey, John Edmund; d. 7 Dec. 1957 in Toronto.

EDUCATION
Attended Pridham's school, Bristol, England; attended Upper Canada College, Toronto, 1876-78; studied under Legros, Slade School of Art, London, England, 1879-81; studied at the Scuola Libera, Rome, Italy, 1881-82; studied under W.A. Bouguereau and Tony Robert-Fleury, Académie Julian in Paris, France, 1882-84.

RELIGION
Christian Science.

CAREER
Taught for a year at Havergal Ladies College, Toronto; art editor of *The week*, Toronto, for fourteen months; Royal Canadian Field Artillery, 1897-1905, became major; portrait painter in Toronto, painting many eminent Canadians of his day, 1891-1947.

MEMBER
Royal Canadian Academy (Associate 1893; Academician 1894; president, 1930-39; resigned, 1939); Ontario Society of Artists (elected, 1898; president, 1905-10); Canadian Authors Association; National Academy of Design, New York, NY (corresponding member); Arts and Letters, Toronto.

AWARDS, HONOURS
Gold medal, Paris *Salon*, 1890; silver medal, Pan-American Exposition, Buffalo, NY, 1901; King's Jubilee medal, 1935; DCL from Bishop's College, Lennoxville, PQ, 1935; Knight Bachelor, 1935.

EXHIBITIONS
GROUP: Represented in group exhibitions held in Canada during his lifetime including annual exhibitions of Ontario Society of Artists, Royal Canadian Academy, and Canadian National Exhibitions; represented in several annual exhibitions of Royal Society of British Artists, Paris *Salon*, and National Academy of Design, New York; annual exhibitions of Royal Academy, 1886-95; *Exposition d'art canadien*, Musée du Jeu de Paume, Paris, 1927; Exhibition of Canadian Art at the British Empire Trade Exhibition, Buenos Aires, Argentina, 1931; A Century of Canadian Art, Tate Gallery, London, 1938; Painting in Canada, a Selective Historical Survey, Albany Institute of History and Art, NY, 1946.

COLLECTIONS IN WHICH REPRESENTED
Art Gallery of Ontario, Toronto; Bodleian Library, University of Oxford; Institute of Mining and Metallurgy, London; National Gallery of Canada, Ottawa, Ont.; Osgoode Hall, Toronto; law courts in Halifax, NS, Winnipeg, Man., Hamilton, Ont., and Victoria, BC; University of Toronto; Upper Canada College, Toronto; Bishop's College School; City Hall, Toronto; Parliament Buildings, Toronto.

WRITINGS
CONTRIBUTED: Articles to *Christian Science monitor, The week.*

GRIGNON, Claude-Henri* 1894−
(Valdombre, pseud.)
Author; b. 8 July 1894 in Sainte-Adèle; son of Wilfrid and Eugenie (Baker) Grignon; m. Thérèse Lambert 1916; children: Claire (adopted).

EDUCATION
Attended Collège de Saint-Laurent, PQ.

HOME
Sainte-Adèle, PQ.

CAREER
L'avenir du nord, Saint Jérôme, PQ, 1916−? , *Le Canada, Le matin, La minerve, Le nationaliste, L'ordre, La renaissance,* Montréal, journalist; *Les pamphlets de Valdombre*, publisher 1936-42; *En avant*, literary editor 1937-39; Sainte-Adèle, major; Terrebonne county, prefect; CKAC, Montréal, PQ, commentator.

MEMBER
Royal Society of Canada (elected fellow, 1961).

AWARDS, HONOURS
Prix David for *Un homme et son péché*, 1935.

WRITINGS
Le secret de Lindbergh (non-fiction), 1928;
Ombres et clameurs (non-fiction), 1933; *Un
homme et son péché* (novel), Totem, 1933 (produced as film, 1949, 1950; produced on radio
CKVL, 1963); *Le déserteur* (short stories), Vieux
Chêne, 1934 (produced on radio); *Le restaurant
d'en face* (produced on radio); "Rhumba des
radio-romans" (series, produced on radio); *Les
belles histoires des pays d'en haut* (TV serial).
CONTRIBUTED: Articles and short stories to
Bulletin des agriculteurs, Photo-journal.

GROULX, Gilles* 1931–
Film director; b. 30 Aug. 1931 in Montreal, PQ;
m. 21 Apr. 1953; m. 31 Jan. 1964; children:
(first marriage) Eric b. 28 Mar. 1954, Cyril b. 8
July 1958; (second marriage) Sara-Raphaêlle b.
20 Nov. 1967.
EDUCATION
Attended École des Beaux-Arts, Montréal.
HOME
Rue Principale, St. Antoine sur le Richelieu, PQ.
CAREER
CBC, French network, editor 1955; National Film
Board of Canada, Montreal, director, producer,
and editor 1958; Les Cinéastes Associés, founder
1964; freelance film maker.
FILM
Les raquetteurs (National Film Board, 1958; silver plaque of the Italian Radio, Florence, Italy,
1960); directed *Normétal* (National Film Board,
1960); edited *La France sur un caillou* (National
Film Board, 1960), *Le vieil âge* (National Film
Board, 1961); photographed *A Saint-Henri le
cinq septembre* (National Film Board, 1961);
directed *Golden gloves* (National Film Board,
1961); edited *Seul ou avec d'autres* (AGEUM,
1962; first film to represent Canada at Critics
Week, Cannes Film Festival, France, 1963);
Vivre en ce pays (CBC); *Québec sans parenthèse*
[*Québec?* – new title] (National Film Board);
edited and directed *Voir Miami* (National Film
Board, 1962; best film award, Congrès du Spectacle, Montréal, 1963), *Un jeu si simple* (National
Film Board, 1964; first prize, Film Festival,
Tours, France, 1965; first prize, Film on Sport,
Paris, France, 1965; special award, Canadian Film
Awards, Toronto, Ont., 1966; diploma, International Film Festival, Locarno, Switzerland, 1966;
first prize, Film Festival, Florence, Italy, 1966);
wrote, directed, and edited *Chat dans le sac* (National Film Board, 1964; first prize, feature films
category, Festival of Canadian Films, Montreal
International Film Festival, 1964; special prize
for best direction, Cinematographic Festival of
Thessaloniki, Greece, 1966; shown at Critics
Week, Cannes Film Festival, 1965; shown at
Young Cinema Week, Berlin, Germany, 1968).

GUITON, Helen* 1894–
Author; b. 10 May 1894 in Jersey, Channel Islands; daughter of James Philip and Eliza (LeMasurier) Guiton; came to Canada in 1903.
EDUCATION
Attended primary school in Jersey; Fairmount
School and High School for Girls, Montreal; Macdonald College, McGill University.
RELIGION
Anglican.
HOME
Apt. 602, 2300 St. Matthew St., Montreal 25, PQ.
CAREER
University Settlement of Montreal, head social
worker 1920-27; MacVicar School, Montreal,
principal 1929-45; *Provincial teachers' magazine*,
editor-in-chief 1932-35; Delormier School, Montreal, principal 1945-46; Côte des Neiges School,
Montreal, principal 1946-51; High School for
Girls Alumnae, recording secretary 1948-50; travelled extensively in Europe; *Vistas for volunteers*,
editor.
MEMBER
Women Teachers' Association, Montreal (past
president); Association of Women Principals,
Montreal (past president); PEN Club (Canadian
centre, past president); Provincial Association of
Protestant Teachers (honorary life member);
Montreal Council of Women (past vice-president);
Association of Protestant Women Teachers (president, 1932); Montreal Girls' Association (president, 1949-50); Canadian Authors Association
(Montreal branch, past president); Zonta Club,
Montreal (past president).
AWARDS, HONOURS
King George VI Coronation medal, 1937; Quebec
Department of Education Order of scholastic
merit, 1942; Centennial medal, 1967.
WRITINGS
A country lover (novel), Dent, 1948 (translated
into French).
CONTRIBUTED: Poems, articles, and stories to
*Provincial teacher's magazine, Farmer's advocate,
Family herald and weekly star.*

GUSTAFSON, Ralph Barker* 1909–
Author; b. 16 Aug. 1909 in Lime Ridge, PQ; son
of Carl and Gertrude (Barker) Gustafson; m. Elisabeth Renniger 4 Oct. 1958.
EDUCATION
Bishop's University, BA with honours in English
and history, 1929, MA, 1930; University of Oxford, BA with honours, 1933, MA, 1963.
RELIGION
Anglican.
HOME
North Hatley, PQ.
OFFICE
Department of English, Bishop's University, Lennoxville, PQ.

CAREER

Bishop's College School, music master 1929-30; St. Alban's School for Boys, Brockville, Ont., teacher of English 1933-34; resided in London, England as tutor and journalist 1935-38; British Information Services, New York, NY, 1942-46; Bishop's University, lecturer 1963-64, poet-in-residence 1965–; assistant professor 1965-66, associate professor 1967–; CBC, Montreal, music critic 1960–.

MEMBER

ACUTE; CAUT; Humanities Association of Canada; Keble Association, Oxford (life member).

AWARDS, HONOURS

Governor General's medal from Bishop's University, 1930; Prix David for *The golden chalice*, 1935; Canada Council senior fellowship, 1959/60 and grant, 1968.

WRITINGS

The golden chalice(poems), Nicholson & Watson, 1935; *Alfred the great* (play), Joseph, 1937; *Epithalamium in time of war* (poems), the author, 1941; *Lyrics unromantic*, New York, 1942; *Flight into darkness* (poems), Pantheon, 1944; *Poetry and Canada; a guide to reading*, Canadian Legion Educational Services, 1945; *Rivers among rocks* (poems), McClelland & Stewart, 1960; *Rocky Mountain poems*, Klanak, 1960; *Sift in an hourglass*, McClelland & Stewart, 1966.

EDITED

Anthology of Canadian poetry (English), Penguin, 1942; *A little anthology of Canadian poets*, New Directions, 1943; *Canadian accent*, Penguin, 1944; *The Penguin book of Canadian verse*, Penguin, 1958.

CONTRIBUTED: Stories, articles, and poems to *Best American short stories, 1948 and 1950*, edited by M. Foley, Houghton Mifflin, 1949-51; *A book of Canadian stories*, edited by D. Pacey, Ryerson, 1952; *Canadian short stories*, edited by R. Weaver, Oxford, 1960; numerous periodicals, e.g. *Argosy* (London), *American scholar, Atlantic monthly, Canadian forum, Epoch, Fantasy, Fiddlehead, New Mexico quarterly, Prism, Queen's quarterly, Story, Tamarack review, Tomorrow*. WORK IN PROGRESS: "Ixion's wheel," McClelland & Stewart, c.1969.

GUY, Elizabeth Benson* 1928–
(Elizabeth Benson Guy Dentay)
Singer (soprano); b. 7 Dec. 1928 in Halifax, NS; daughter of Thomas and Sarah Louise (Anderson) Guy; m. John Theordore Dentay 11 June 1949; children: Guy Nicholas Theodore b. 19 Feb. 1951, Suzanne Elizabeth b. 11 June 1954.

EDUCATION

Attended Netherwood School for Girls, Rothesay, NB; Dalhousie University, 1944-45; studied with Dr. Ernesto Vinci, University of Toronto; with Lotte Leonard, Juilliard School of Music, New York, NY.

HOME

60 Wimpole Dr., Willowdale, Ont.

CAREER

CBC, singer 1947–; sang at Milwaukee Festival, Wis., 1949; Stratford, Ont. Music Festival, Marlboro Festival, England, 1968; Banff School of Fine Arts, Alta., instructor and singer; Les Jeunesses Musicales du Canada, Mt. Orford, PQ, instructor and singer; taught privately.

AWARDS, HONOURS

First prize from "Singing stars of tomorrow," 1948; Canada Council arts scholarship, 1967/68.

THEATRE

Debuts at Carnegie Hall, New York, 10 May 1959, Amsterdam, The Netherlands, 27 Oct. 1967, Wigmore Hall, London, England, 31 Oct. 1967; Festival concert (Stratford, Ont. Festival, 1964, 1965).

RADIO

Sang in numerous productions, e.g. "Northern Electric hour" (13 Oct. 1947; 18 Oct. 1948), recital ("Wednesday night," 25 July 1948; 21 Apr. 1954; 26 May 1954; 23 Feb. 1955; 12 Oct. 1955; 30 May 1956; 26 Dec. 1956; 20 May 1959; 13 Apr. 1960; 31 Jan. 1962), *La traviata* (9 Feb. 1949; "Wednesday night," 27 Jan. 1954), *Don Giovanni* (20 Apr. 1949; "Wednesday night," 11 Jan. 1950; 12 Jan. 1955), "Distinguished artists" ("Wednesday night," 27 July 1949; 9 Nov. 1952; 16 Nov. 1952; 13 Apr. 1959; 25 May 1959; 20 Dec. 1960; 19 Aug. 1962; 23 Nov. 1964), *Music by O. Morawetz* ("Wednesday night," 19 Oct. 1949; 30 Nov. 1949), *Summer strings* (25 June 1950; 2 July 1950), *Music by Schubert* ("Wednesday night," 16 Aug. 1950), *Turandot* ("Wednesday night," 18 Oct. 1950), *Sunday morning recital* (13 Jan. 1952), *Stars of the CBC Opera Company* (2 July 1952), *Gianni Schicchi* ("Wednesday night," 28 Jan. 1953), *Falstaff* ("Wednesday night," 6 May 1953), *From the Opera* (14 June 1953), *Cosi fan tutte* (25 Nov. 1953), *Stratford Festival* (6 Aug. 1954; 6 Aug. 1955), *Eugene Onegin* (17 Nov. 1954), *Otello* ("Wednesday night," 4 May 1955), *Concert Hall* (5 July 1955; 20 Nov. 1956; 2 Apr. 1957), *CBC Symphony Orchestra* (19 Dec. 1955; 8 Oct. 1956; 15 Mar. 1959), *CBC Symphony Strings* (11 June 1956; 30 June 1961), Phèdre in *Hippolyte et Aricie* ("Wednesday night," 13 Feb. 1957; 8 May 1957; "Sunday night," 18 Oct. 1964), *Requiem by Verdi* ("Wednesday night," 10 Apr. 1957), *Pop concert* (14 Apr. 1957; 3 Apr. 1959; 26 Apr. 1966), *Jenufa* ("Wednesday night," 24 Apr. 1957), *Madrigal Singers* ("Wednesday night," 2 July 1958), *Baroque Ensemble* ("Wednesday night," 19 Feb. 1959), *Händel and Haydn* (1 June 1959; 6 June 1959), *English composers of the 12th century* ("Wednesday night," 16 Sept. 1959), *Sunday concert* (18 June 1961; 16 July 1961), *St.*

Matthew passion ("Wednesday night," 18 Apr. 1962), *Music for a new pair of ears* (11 Mar. 1962), "Celebrity concert" ("Wednesday night," 1962/63), *Choral concert* ("Wednesday night," 2 Jan. 1963), *Dido and Aeneas* ("Wednesday night," 17 July 1963), *Christmas Day* (25 Dec. 1963), *Cantata no. 51* by Bach (19 Jan. 1964), *Tenebrae for holy Saturday* ("Sunday night," 1 Mar. 1964), *Music diary* (22 Nov. 1964), *Hart House Orchestra* ("Sunday night," 31 Jan. 1965), *Solomon* (5 Sept. 1965), *Brahms lieder* ("Tuesday night," 30 Nov. 1965), *Les nuits d'été* by Berlioz (15 Dec. 1965), *Messiah* (24 Dec. 1965), "Encore" (26 Dec. 1965; part II, 2 June 1968), *Altenberg lieder* ("Concerts from two worlds," 9 Jan. 1966), "Tuesday night" (3 May 1966; 22 Aug. 1967; 30 Jan. 1968; 28 May 1968), *Les Jeunesses Musicales* ("Tuesday night," 16 Aug. 1966), "Canadian recitalist" (31 Mar. 1967), *Sam Slick* ("Tuesday night," 4 July 1967), *Concert in the style of 1867* ("Centenary concert," 21 Dec. 1967).

TELEVISION

Sang in several CBC productions, e.g. "Concert hour" (6 Jan. 1955; 10 Feb. 1955), *Art of fugue* ("Festival," 4 Mar. 1963).

GYE, Marie-Louise Émma Cécile Lajeunesse
see ALBANI, Marie-Louise Émma Cécile

HAGEN, Betty-Jean 1930–
(Betty-Jean Greicius)
Violinist; b. 17 Oct. 1930 in Edmonton, Alta.; daughter of Goskall Olson and Ada (Lancey) Hagen; m. Vincent Greicius 24 July 1954; children: Elaine Marian.

EDUCATION

Commenced piano lessons in Edmonton, 1933; Chicago Conservatory of Music, Ill., studied piano and violin, 1938, violin, 1939; studied with Clayton Hare, Calgary, Alta.; attended high school in Calgary, graduated 1948; studied with Geza de Kresz, Royal Conservatory of Music, Toronto, Ont., 1949-51; Ivan Galamian and at Juilliard School of Music, New York.

HOME

3103 Fairfield Ave., New York 63, NY, USA.

CAREER

Edmonton Philharmonic Orchestra, violinist c.1945-47; toured Canada, 1947; Calgary Symphony Orchestra, violin soloist 1947-49; singer in Calgary 1948-49; New York debut, Town Hall, 15 Nov. 1950; annual tours of Canada and USA 1950–, Europe 1951–.

MEMBER

Toronto Musicians' Association.

AWARDS, HONOURS

Alberta Music Festival, first prizes for violin,

piano, ear-test, sight-singing, 1937, 1938; Chicago Conservatory of Music, double scholarship for violin and piano, 1938; Royal Conservatory of Music, Toronto, scholarship, 1948; Toronto Women's Musical Club scholarship, 1950; Naumburg Musical Foundation award, New York, 1950; T. Eaton graduating scholarship of $1000, 1951; Pathé-Marconi prize, Paris, France, 1951; Harriet Cohen medal for the most outstanding woman musician of the British Commonwealth, London, England, 1952; Carl Flesch award, London, England, 1953; Leventritt Foundation award, New York, 1955.

CONCERT STAGE

Numerous appearances as violin soloist with New York Philharmonic Symphony Orchestra, London Philharmonic Orchestra, England, Concertgebouw Orchestra, Amsterdam, The Netherlands, orchestras in US at Cleveland, Ohio, Pittsburgh, Pa., Chicago, Buffalo, NY, and Denver, Colo.; London debut, Wigmore Hall, London, England, recital Jan. 1952; soloist with New York Philharmonic Symphony Orchestra (Carnegie Hall, New York, 4 Nov. 1956); soloist with Vancouver Festival Orchestra under Herbert von Karajan (Vancouver Civic Auditorium, BC, 13 July 1959).

RADIO

Violin recital with Leo Barkin, piano ("Sunday night," CBC, 1 Dec. 1963).

RECORDINGS

Recorded on Beaver Records.

HAIG, S. Colson-, pseud.
see GLASSCO, John

HAILEY, Arthur* 1920–
Author; b. 5 Apr. 1920 in Luton, England; son of George and Elsie (Wright) Hailey; came to Canada in 1947; m. Sheila Dunlop 28 July 1951; children: Jane b. 30 Apr. 1954, Steven b. 20 Mar. 1956, Diane b. 23 Feb. 1958.

EDUCATION

Attended school in Luton until 1934.

RELIGION

None.

HOME

Lyford Cay, New Providence, Bahamas.

OFFICE

Arthur Hailey Ltd., 7 Lyncroft Drive, West Hill, Ont.

CAREER

Office boy and clerk in London, England 1934-39; Royal Air Force, 1939-47, pilot, became flight-lieutenant; Maclean Hunter Publishing Company, Toronto, Ont., editor 1947-53; Trailmobile Canada Limited, Toronto, sales promotion manager 1953-56; mainly literary 1956–; resided in California, 1966–.

MEMBER

Authors League of America; Writers Guild of

America; NATAS; Canadian Council of Authors and Artists (honorary life member).

AWARDS, HONOURS

Canadian Council of Authors and Artists most distinguished creative achievement award, 1956; NATAS nomination for best teleplay writing, 1956; Doubleday Canadian prize novel award for *In high places*, 1962.

WRITINGS

(with J. Castle) *Runway zero-eight* (novel), Doubleday, 1959 (based on his TV play *Flight into danger*; serialized in *Ladies home journal*); *The final diagnosis* (novel), Doubleday, 1959 (Literary Guild and *Reader's digest* Condensed Book Club selection; published in England under title *The young doctors*, Transworld, 1962; based on his TV play *No deadly medicine*); *Close-up on writing for television* (non-fiction), Doubleday, 1960; *In high places* (novel), Doubleday, 1961 (Literary Guild selection); *Hotel* (novel), Doubleday, 1965 (Literary Guild, *Reader's digest* Condensed Book Club, and Dollar Book Club selection; filmed as *Hotel*, Warner Bros., 1967); *Airport* (novel), Doubleday, 1968 (Literary Guild and *Reader's digest* Book Club selection); numerous television plays, e.g. *Diary of a nurse* ("Playhouse 90"), *Shadow of suspicion* ("Drama theatre," CBC), *Flight into danger* (CBC, 1956), *Course for collision* ("GM theatre," CBC, Apr. 1957), *Death minus one* ("GM presents," CBC, 1959), *Time lock* (CBC, produced Romulus Films, 1959); several screenplays, e.g. *Zero hour* (based on his TV play *Flight into danger*; Paramount, 1957), *The young doctors* (based on his novel *The final diagnosis*; United Artists, 1961). Works have been extensively translated.

CONTRIBUTED: Plays and articles to *Four plays of our time*, edited by H.A. Voaden, Macmillan, 1960; *Maclean's, Saturday night*.

HAINES, Frederick Stanley 1879–1960

Artist; b. 31 Mar. 1879 in Meaford, Ont.; son of George and Martha (Smith) Haines; m. Bertha Annie May Morehouse 1900; children: Dorothy; d. 21 Nov. 1960 in Thornhill, Ont.

EDUCATION

Attended Meaford High School; studied under George A. Reid (*q.v.*) and William Cruikshank, Central Ontario School of Art, Toronto, Ont., 1896; studied under Juliaan de Vriendt, Académie Royale des Beaux-Arts, Antwerp, Belgium, 1913.

CAREER

Engaged in commercial art and painted in Toronto; Canadian National Exhibition, Toronto, secretary of the department of graphic art 1920-24, commissioner of fine arts 1924-51; Art Gallery of (now Ontario) Toronto, director 1927-32; Ontario College of Art, Toronto, principal 1932-51.

MEMBER

Little Billee Sketch Club, Toronto; Mahlstick

Club, Toronto; Canadian Society of Graphic Art; Society of Canadian Painter-Etchers (co-founder); Hungarian Society of Painter Etchers, Budapest, (honorary member); Society of Printer Engravers in Colour, London, England; Chicago Society of Etchers, Ill; Society of Print Makers of California; Ontario Society of Artists (elected, 1906; president, 1924-27); Royal Canadian Academy (Associate 1919; Academician 1933; president, 1939-42); Canadian Society of Painters in Water Colour (co-founder).

AWARDS, HONOURS

Gold medal for figure painting, Académie Royale des Beaux-Arts, Antwerp, Belgium, 1914.

EXHIBITIONS

ONE-MAN: Memorial Exhibition, Art Gallery of Toronto, Art Gallery of Hamilton, Ont., Willistead Art Gallery, Windsor, Ont., Sarnia Public Library and Art Gallery, Ont., 1961-62.

GROUP: Represented in group exhibitions held in Canada during his life time including annual exhibitions of Society of Canadian Painter-Etchers, Canadian Society of Graphic Art, Canadian Society of Painters in Water Colour, Ontario Society of Artists, Royal Canadian Academy and Canadian National Exhibitions; Canadian Section of Fine Arts, British Empire Exhibition, Wembley, England, 1925; *Exposition d'art canadien*, Musée du Jeu de Paume, Paris, 1927; Exhibition of Contemporary Canadian Painting Arranged ... for Circulation in the Southern Dominions of the British Empire, 1936; A Century of Canadian Art, Tate Gallery, London, 1938; World's Fair, New York, NY, 1939; An Exhibition of Canadian Paintings Held at Fortnum and Mason Ltd., London, 1955.

COLLECTIONS IN WHICH REPRESENTED

Art Gallery of Hamilton; Art Gallery of Ontario, Toronto; Glyndhurst Art Gallery, Brantford, Ont.; Hart House Permanent Collection, University of Toronto; Meaford High School; National Gallery of Canada, Ottawa, Ont.; Richview Collegiate Insitute, Toronto; Sarnia Public Library and Art Gallery, Ont.; Saskatoon Art Gallery, Sask.; Thornhill High School, Ont.; University Women's Club, Toronto; Willistead Art Gallery.

HAMBLETON, Jack

see HAMBLETON, John

HAMBLETON, John 1901–61

(Jack Hambleton)

Author; b. 6 July 1901 in Leek, Staffordshire, England; son of James and Mary (Hill) Hambleton; came to Canada in 1905 and settled in Valleyfield, PQ; m. Nora Nelson 28 July 1928; children: Jessie b. 15 Sept. 1932; d. 26 Oct. 1961.

EDUCATION

Attended school in Port Edward, Ont. till 1914.

CAREER

Employed on a Great Lakes freighter 1914; in a machine shop, London, Ont. and an automobile plant, Detroit, Mich.; US Army in Siberia 1917-18; Canadian Press, Toronto, Ont., teletype operator, editorial department reporter 1924, 1928-34; *Star*, Windsor, Ont., journalist 1928; Ontario Department of Travel and Publicity, publicity director; *Star*, Toronto, and *Globe and mail*, Toronto, reporter and outdoors columnist; freelance writer 1947-61.

WRITINGS

Fisherman's paradise (non-fiction), Longmans, Green, 1946; *Hunter's holiday* (non-fiction), Longmans, Green, 1947; *Forest ranger* (juvenile fiction), Longmans, Green, 1948; *Young bush pilot* (juvenile fiction), Longmans, Green, 1949; *Abitibi adventure* (juvenile fiction), Longmans, Green, 1950; *Cub reporter* (juvenile fiction), Longmans, Green, 1951; *Charter pilot* (juvenile fiction), Longmans, Green, 1952; *Wolverine* (juvenile fiction), Longmans, Green, 1954; *Temagami guide* (juvenile fiction), Longmans, Green, 1954; *Wings over Labrador* (juvenile fiction), Longmans, Green, 1957; *Fire in the valley* (novel), Longmans, Green, 1960; several radio scripts, e.g. "The sportsman's show" (series, CBC, 25 June 1947 to 8 Feb. 1951). Works have been translated into German, Dutch, and Swedish.

CONTRIBUTED: Articles to *Forest and outdoors*, *Saturday night, Rod and gun*.

HAMBLETON, Ronald* **1917—**
Author; b. 9 June 1917 in Preston, Lancashire, England; son of Gordon and Mary (Sharples) Hambleton; came to Canada in 1924; m. 1942; children: four sons and one daughter.

EDUCATION

Attended Penwortham Primary School, Preston, Tecumseh Public School and John Oliver High School, Vancouver, BC.

HOME

148 Collier St., Toronto 5, Ont.

CAREER

Theatre under the Stars, Vancouver, 1938; London, England, journalist and stage manager 1939-40; CBC, Toronto, continuity writer and broadcaster 1942, 1946-51 and 1953-62; CFPL, London, Ont. 1943; Maclean Publishing Company, Toronto editorial department 1944; freelance writer and broadcaster 1946—; *Reading*, co-founder 1946; resided in France and England 1951-53; *Mayfair*, monthly correspondent for BBC 1951-53; Granada Television, London, England, writer 1957.

MEMBER

ACTRA; Society of Authors, London, England.

AWARDS, HONOURS

Canada Council senior arts fellowship, 1959/60 and 1964/65.

RADIO

Participated in many CBC programs, e.g. wrote and narrated *Italy — in sun and shadow* ("Wednesday night," 14 June 1961); edited and hosted "Worth repeating" (series, 29 June 1961—).

WRITINGS

A tour of the city (poems), CBC, 1951; *Object and event* (poems), Ryerson, 1953; *Every man is an island* (novel), Hutchinson, 1959; *An evening of the year* (poems), CBC, 1959; *There goes MacGill* (novel), Hutchinson, 1962; *Mazo de la Roche of Jalna* (biography), Hawthorn, 1966; *The colonel and the lady* (TV play; produced CBC, 1953); *The lady and the tiger* (TV play; produced CBC, 1953); *The woman who came to stay* (TV play; produced CBC, 1953); libretto for *The luck of Ginger Coffey* (opera; commissioned by Canadian Opera Company, 1967); numerous radio scripts, e.g. *Five famous author journalists* (CBC, 2 June 1964), *Yukon discovery day* (CBC, 17 Aug. 1964), *The stately pen* ("The fourth estate," CBC, 29 Aug. 1966), *The world of Stephen Leacock* ("Venture," CBC, 13 Sept. 1964); many TV scripts, e.g. *Architecture for worship, learning, recreation* ("Explorations," CBC, 1, 8, and 15 Mar. 1961), *The face of God* (CBC, *31 Mar. 1961)*, *Stravinsky at 80* ("Festival," CBC, 11 June 1962), *The age of Howe* ("Tueday night, CBC, 18 Jan. 1966).

EDITED: *Unit of five*, Ryerson, 1944.

CONTRIBUTED: Articles, short stories, and poems to *Anthology of Canadian poetry*, compiled by R. Gustafson, Penguin, 1942; *The book of Canadian poetry*, edited by A.J.M. Smith, Gage, 1943; *Canadian poetry in English*, edited by B. Carman and others, rev. & enl. ed., Ryerson, 1954; *The Penguin book of Canadian verse*, edited by R. Gustafson, Penguin, 1958; *The Oxford book of Canadian verse in English and French*, edited by A.J.M. Smith, Oxford, 1960; *Poetry, Townsman, Voices, Rhode Island Sunday journal, Canadian poetry, Contemporary verse, First statement, Northern review, Canadian forum, Canadian home journal, Maclean's, National home monthly, Saturday night, Chatelaine, New statesman and nation*.

HAMBOURG, Boris 1884—1954
Cellist and teacher; b. 27 Dec. 1884 in Voronezh, USSR; son of Michael and Catherine Hambourg; came to Canada in 1910 and settled in Toronto, Ont.; m. Marie Bauchope 1923; d. 24 Nov. 1954 in Toronto.

EDUCATION

Studied cello with Herbert Whalen in London, England; studied composition with I. Knorr, Hoch Conservatorium, Frankfurt, Germany; studied cello with Hugo Becker in Berlin, Germany.

CAREER

Debut, Pyrmont, NSW, Australia 1903; toured Australia, New Zealand and S. Africa 1903-10, Europe 1913, 1914, 1921, 1929, England 1948, 1949; Hambourg Trio, cellist 1905-54, toured Europe with this group 1905-10; Hambourg Conservatory of Music, Toronto, co-founder and director 1914-16, principal 1916-54; Music Lovers' Club, Toronto, founder; Hart House String Quartet, Toronto, cellist 1924-45, toured Europe with this group 1930, 1934, 1937.

MEMBER
Arts and Letters Club, Toronto.

CONCERT STAGE
Cellist, debut in London, England (Aeolian Hall) 1904, in Berlin, 1906, in N. America, Pittsburgh, Pa., 1910; cellist with original Hambourg Trio, jubilee tour of Canada, USA, 1935; cellist, Wigmore Hall, London, Nov. 1950.

RECORDINGS
Several records, Victor, 1920s.

COMPOSITIONS
Cello pieces and songs.

HAMEL, Martine van
see VAN HAMEL, Martine

HAMILTON, Rosemary Deveson
see DEVESON, Rosemary

HARLOW, Robert G.* 1923–
Author; b. 19 Nov. 1923 in Prince Rupert, BC; son of Roland Alden and Kathleen Isobel (Grant) Harlow; m. Ruth Ann Mottelson 15 Mar. 1949 (marriage dissolved); m. Margaret Mary Mills 8 Feb. 1958; children: (first marriage) Gretchen b. 28 Dec. 1949; (second marriage) Genevieve b. 20 Dec. 1964, Kathleen b. 14 Dec. 1966.

EDUCATION
Attended King George Elementary School, 1929-36 and Baron Byng High School, Prince George, BC, 1936-40; University of British Columbia, BA, 1948; Iowa State University, MFA, 1951; Banff School of Advanced Management, Alta., certificate, 1962.

RELIGION
None.

HOME
4715 Caulfield Place, West Vancouver, BC.

OFFICE
Department of Creative Writing, University of British Columbia, Vancouver 8, BC.

CAREER
RCAF, 1941-45, became flying-officer, awarded DFC; CBC, Vancouver, regional talks producer 1951-53, CBU station manager 1953-55, director of radio BC region 1955-64; University of British Columbia, lecturer in creative writing 1964-65, associate professor and head 1965–.

AWARDS, HONOURS
Iowa State University teaching fellow, 1948-51.

RADIO
Produced *The mind of the poet – Milton Acorn* ("Saturday evening," CBC, 18 Jan. 1964).

WRITINGS
Royal Murdoch (novel), Macmillan, 1962; *A gift of echoes* (novel), Macmillan, 1965; *The eye* (radio play; produced CBC, Vancouver, Oct. 1959);

(with L.L. Kent) *When tomorrow dies* (screenplay; produced summer, 1965); *A chosen people* (TV script; produced "Heritage," CBC, 27 Mar. 1966).

CONTRIBUTED: Articles and book reviews to *Canadian literature*.

HARMER, Shirley 1930–
Singer and entertainer; b. 1930 in Oshawa, Ont.; m. (third marriage) Damiano Durinzi, Mar. 1968.

HOME
Resident in Italy.

CAREER

AWARDS, HONOURS
ACTRA S.W. Caldwell award for most promising television performer, 1953.

CONCERT STAGE
Numerous appearances in major night clubs across Canada; singer, Expo 67, Montreal, PQ, 3, 4 June 1967.

RADIO
Many appearances on radio, 1952-68; singer, Canada Day programs (CBC, 1 July 1962, 1963, 1964); star performer, "Shirley Harmer show" (series, CBC, 1963-64); guest artist, "Showcase" (series, CBC, 31 Jan. 1964); singer, "The Saturday set" (series, CBC, summer 1964).

TELEVISION
Numerous appearances on CBC series, e.g. "Four for the show" (1953), "Parade" (1962, 1963), "A summer night" (summer 1963), "A show from two cities" (1963), "Show of the week" (several programs, 1963, 1964); singer for series "Dave Garroway show" (NBC, New York, NY, 1953); many appearances as guest and star artist in features, e.g. *The big revue* (CBLT Toronto, 1953), *The best of Tommy Ambrose* (CBC, 30 Aug. 1962), *Timmy's Easter parade* (CBC, 15 Apr. 1962), *Canada day in the Middle East* (CBC, from United Nations base in the Middle East, 24 May 1963), *Timmy's Easter basket* (CBC, 22 Mar. 1964), program on Percy Faith ("Music Canada," Oct. 1966).

RECORDINGS
Recorded for MGM, c.1953.

HARRIS, Lawren Stewart 1885–1970
Artist; b. 23 Oct. 1885 in Brantford, Ont.; son of Thomas and Anna (Stewart) Harris; m. Beatrice Helen Phillips (deceased); m. Bess Larkin 29 Aug. 1934; children: (first marriage) Lawren Phillips b. 10 Oct. 1910, Margaret b. 12 Dec. 1913, Howard Kilbourne b. 10 Apr. 1919; d. 29 Jan. 1970 in Vancouver.

EDUCATION
Attended public schools in Toronto, Ont.; St. Andrew's College, Toronto; University of Toronto, 1903; studied under Adolph Schlabitz in Berlin and Munich, Germany, 1904-1907.

RELIGION
Baptist in childhood, student of Eastern philosophy in adulthood.

CAREER
Travelled in France, Italy, and England 1904-07; travelled in Palestine and Arabia preparing illustrations for *Going down from Jerusalem*, by Norman Duncan, Harper, 1909 and for *Harper's magazine* 1909; returned to Canada and settled in Toronto 1910; built the Studio Building (with Dr. MacCallum) at 25 Severn Street, Toronto, which was opened in 1914; painted in Toronto 1910-34 making sketching trips to Mattawa, Ont., and Timiskaming, Ont., 1912, to the Laurentians 1913, to Algoma annually 1918-20, to Nova Scotia and Newfoundland 1921, to the north shore of Lake Superior annually 1921-25, to Jasper Park and other Rocky Mountain parks annually 1925-28, to the Arctic 1930, to the Gaspé, PQ., 1932, to Pointe au Baril, Ont., 1933; Canadian Army, 1915-17; Dartmouth College, Hanover, NH, artist in residence 1934-38; painted in Santa Fé, NM, 1938-40; member of the board of the Vancouver Art Gallery, 1941—; assisted in the formation of the Western Canada Art Circuit 1943; trustee of the Emily Carr scholarship fund 1946—; trustee of the National Gallery of Canada, Ottawa, Ont. 1950-65; painter in Vancouver 1940—.

MEMBER
Artists' League (co-founder); Group of Seven (co-founder; member, 1918-33); Canadian Group of Painters (co-founder; president, 1933); Federation of Canadian Artists (co-founder, 1940; president, 1944-47); Ontario Society of Artists (elected, 1912; resigned, 1933); Arts and Letters Club, Toronto; American Foundation for Transcendental Painting (president, 1939); Transcendentalist Group of Painters, Santa Fé (member, *c.*1940).

AWARDS, HONOURS
Gold medal, Sesquicentennial Exposition, Philadelphia, Pa., 1926; Museum of Art prize, Pan American Exposition, Baltimore, Md., 1931; LLD from University of British Columbia, 1946; LLD from University of Toronto, 1951; LLD from University of Manitoba, 1953; Canada Council medal, 1962.

EXHIBITIONS
ONE-MAN: Vancouver Art Gallery, 1941, 1945 and 1963; Art Gallery of (now Ontario) Toronto, 1948; National Gallery of Canada, Ottawa, 1963.
GROUP: Represented in group exhibitions held in Canada since 1911 including annual exhibitions of Royal Canadian Academy, Ontario Society of Artists, Canadian Group of Painters, and Canadian National Exhibitions; represented in Group of Seven exhibitions; represented in exhibitions organized by National Art Gallery of Canada, Ottawa, including its Annual Exhibitions; paintings by Canadian Artists, City Art Museum, St. Louis, Mo., 1918; Société Anonyme, 1920; Canadian Section of Fine Arts, British Empire Exhibition, Wembley, England, 1924 and 1925; Annual Exhibition of Paintings in Oil, Carnegie Institute, Pittsburgh, Pa., 1925; Sesquicentennial Exposition, Philadelphia, Pa., 1926; *Exposition d'art canadien*, Musée du Jeu de Paume, Paris, France, 1927; Exhibition of Canadian Art at the British Empire Trade Exhibition, Buenos Aires, Argentina, 1931; Contemporary Canadian Painters, Roerich Museum, New York NY, 1932; Exhibition of Contemporary Canadian Painting Arranged ... for Circulation in the Southern Dominions of the British Empire, 1936; Exhibition of Paintings, Drawings and Sculpture by Artists of the British Empire Overseas, Royal Institute Galleries, London, England, 1937; A Century of Canadian Art, Tate Gallery, London, 1938; World's Fair, New York, 1939; Aspects of Contemporary Painting in Canada, Addison Gallery, Andover, Mass., 1942-43; University of Washington, Seattle, 1942; San Francisco Museum of Art, Calif., 1943; Canadian Art 1760-1943, Yale University Art Gallery, 1944; Exhibition of Canadian Painting and Folk Arts, São Paulo and Rio de Janeiro, Brazil, 1944-45; Painting in Canada, a Selective Historical Survey, Albany Institute of History and Art, Albany, NY, 1946; Forty Years of Canadian Painting, Museum of Fine Arts, Boston, Mass., 1949; Painters of Canada ... 1668-1948, Richmond, Va., 1949; Canadian Painting, National Gallery of Art, Washington, DC, 1950; Colombo Plan Exhibition, Colombo, 1951; University of Maine, Orono, 1951; German Industries Exhibition, Berlin, 1952; Coronation Exhibition, 1953; exhibition of Canadian painting shown in Pakistan, India, and Ceylon, 1954-55; An Exhibition of Canadian Paintings held at Fortnum and Mason Limited, London, England, 1955.

COLLECTIONS IN WHICH REPRESENTED
Art Gallery of Hamilton, Ont.; Art Gallery of Ontario, Toronto; Brock Hall, University of British Columbia; Dominion Galleries, Montreal, PQ; Detroit Institute of Art, Mich.; Hart House Permanent Collection, University of Toronto; National Gallery of Canada; McMichael Conservation Collection of Art, Kleinburg, Ont.; Montreal Museum of Fine Arts; Vancouver Art Gallery; Willistead Art Gallery, Windsor, Ont.; Winnipeg Art Gallery, Man.; Women's Union, University of Toronto; YWCA, Toronto; Yale University Art Gallery; London Public Library and Art Museum, Ont.; Owens Museum, Mount Allison University.

WRITINGS
Contrasts (poems), McClelland & Stewart, 1922; *A disquisition on abstract painting*, Rous &

Mann Press Limited, 1954.

CONTRIBUTED: Articles to *Canadian art, Journal of the Royal Architectural Institute of Canada, Canadian theosophist, Canadian bookman, Canadian forum, Vancouver Art Gallery bulletin, Yearbook of arts in Canada, 1928-29*, Macmillan, 1929.

HARVEY, Jean-Charles 1891-1967

Author; b. 10 Nov. 1891 in La Malbaie, PQ; son of John and Mina (Trudel) Harvey; m. Germaine Deschenes 1923; m. Evangeline Pelland; children: four sons, three daughters; d. 3 Jan. 1967 in Montreal, PQ.

EDUCATION

Attended Séminaire de Chicoutimi, PQ; Université Laval.

RELIGION

Roman Catholic.

CAREER

La patrie, La presse, Montreal, editorial staff; *Le soleil*, Quebec, PQ, editor-in-chief 1926-34; Quebec Bureau of Statistics, chief 1934-37; *Le jour*, editor and director 1937-46; CBC and CKAC, Montreal, commentator and scriptwriter 1946-52; *Le petit journal*, Montreal, editor 19?-66.

AWARDS, HONOURS

Prix David for *L'homme qui va*, 1929.

WRITINGS

Marcel Faure (novel), Marquis, 1922; *Pages de critique* (non-fiction) Soleil, 1926; *L'homme qui va* (short stories), 1929; *Les demi-civilisés* (novel) Totem, 1934 (translated into English); *Sébastien Pierre* (short stories), Quotidien, 1935; *Art et combat, mélanges*, Valiquette, 1938; *Les grenouilles demandent un roi* (non-fiction), Jour, 1942; *Les paradis de sable* (novel), Institut Littéraire de Québec, 1953; *La fille du silence* (poems), Orphée, 1958; *Pourquoi je suis antiséparatiste* (non-fiction), Homme, 1962; *Des bois, des champs, des bêtes* (essays), Homme, 1965; *Visages du Québec*, Cercle du Livre de France, 1965.

CONTRIBUTED: Articles, poetry, and short stories to *Delta, Liberté*.

HAWORTH, Peter 1889–

Artist; b. 28 Feb. 1889 in Oswaldtwistle, Lancashire, England; son of Peter and Helen (Taylor) Haworth; m. Zema Cogill 28 Feb. 1923; came to Canada Mar. 1923 and settled in Toronto.

EDUCATION

Attended New Lane School, Moscow Mill School and Accrington Grammar School in Accrington, Lancashire, England; studied at the Manchester School of Art, 1910-14; attended Victoria College, University of Manchester; studied under Sir William Rothenstein and R. Anning Bell, Royal College of Art, London, England, ARCA (degree granted by University of London) 1914-15, 1922.

RELIGION

Church of England.

HOME

111 Cluny Dr., Toronto, Ont.

CAREER

Royal Flying Corps, 1915-19, became flying officer, awarded DFC; painter in Toronto 1923–; Central Technical School, Toronto, art teacher 1923-29, director of art 1929-55; joint illustrator (with Bobs Cogill Haworth of *The Kingdom of the Saguenay*, by Marius Barbeau (*q.v.*), Macmillan, 1936; appointed war artist on special assignment with the RCN and RCAF on the west coast of Canada during World War II; University of Toronto, department of art and archaeology, lecturer 1946-56.

COMMISSIONS

Executed many liturgical commissions, both stained glass and murals, in churches in Toronto, Ottawa, and Hamilton, Ont., and Quebec, PQ.

MEMBER

Royal Society of Artists (elected fellow, 1950); Royal Canadian Academy (Associate 1946; Academician 1954); Canadian Society of Painters in Water Colour (elected, 1931; president, 1935-40); Canadian Group of Painters (elected, 1938); Ontario Society of Artists (elected, 1932); Federation of Canadian Artists (elected, 1942; president Ontario region, 1944-45); Arts and Letters Club, Toronto.

AWARDS, HONOURS

National Scholarship, Royal College of Art, London, England, 1914; Royal College of Art scholarship.

EXHIBITIONS

ONE-MAN: Art Gallery of (now Ontario) Toronto, 1950; Print Room, Winnipeg, Man., 1954; Eaton's Fine Art Gallery, Toronto, 1957; Roberts Gallery, Toronto, 1960 and 1964.

GROUP: Represented in group exhibitions held in Canada since 1923 including annual exhibitions of Royal Canadian Academy, Canadian Society of Graphic Art, Ontario Society of Artists, Canadian Society of Painters in Water Colour, Canadian Group of Painters, and Canadian National Exhbitions; represented in group exhibitions organized by National Gallery of Canada, Ottawa, including its Annual Exhibitions; Exhibition of Contemporary Canadian Painting Arranged ... for Circulation in the Southern Dominions of the British Empire, 1936; Exhibition of Paintings, Drawings and Sculpture by Artists of the British Empire Overseas, Royal Institute Galleries, London, 1937; A Century of Canadian Art, Tate Gallery, London, 1938; World's Fair, New York, NY, 1939; Exhibition of Water Colours By Canadian Artists, Gloucester, England, 1939; Canadian Water Colours, Arnot Art Gallery, Elmira, NY, 1946; group exhibitions in Australia, New Zealand, Brazil, and Scotland.

COLLECTIONS IN WHICH REPRESENTED
National Gallery of Canada, Ottawa; Art Gallery of Ontario, Toronto; London Public Library and Art Museum, Ont.; N.B.M. Gallery, New York; Art Gallery, Cambridge, New Zealand.

HAYNES, Elizabeth Sterling   ?—1957
Actress, director, and teacher; b. in county Durham, England; daughter of William Sterling; m. Nelson W. Haynes 1922; children: Shirley b. 1923, Sterling b. 1928; d. 26 Apr. 1957 in Toronto, Ont.

EDUCATION
University of Toronto, BA.

CAREER
Hart House Theatre, Toronto, actress; University of Alberta, director for University Dramatic Society 1923-30, director of dramatics for Department of Extension 1932-37, director and actress for Studio Theatre 1950-55; Alberta Drama League, co-founder and past president 1929; Edmonton Little Theatre, Alta., co-founder and first director 1929-32; Banff School of (now Fine Arts) the Theatre, Alta., co-founder and instructor 1933-36; Alberta Department of Education, teacher of acting 1936-37; New Brunswick Department of Education, 1937-c.1940; Allied Arts Council, Edmonton, director of School of Allied Arts 1944-45, chairman of Writing and Drama Committee.

AWARDS, HONOURS
Edmonton Junior Chamber of Commerce citizenship award, 1944; Canadian drama award for outstanding contribution to Canadian theatre, 1946.

THEATRE
Made debut as Portia in *Julius Caesar*; professional debut at Hart House Theatre; played title role in *The madwoman of Chaillot* (Edmonton), title role in *Elizabeth the Queen* (command performance for Governor General's visit, Edmonton, 30 Aug. 1932), *Riders to the sea* (Edmonton Little Theatre, 1934); directed numerous productions, e.g. *Dear Brutus* (University Dramatic Society, 1923), *He who gets slapped* (University Dramatic Society, 1927), *Aren't we all* (University Dramatic Society, 1927), *The farmer's wife* (Edmonton Little Theatre, 1929), *The adding machine* (Edmonton Little Theatre, 1929; University Dramatic Society, 1930), *Shall we join the ladies?* (University Dramatic Society, 1930), *The first Mrs. Fraser* (Edmonton Little Theatre, 1930/31), *Loyalties* (Edmonton Little Theatre, 1930/31), *Mary Rose* (Edmonton Little Theatre, 1930/31), *The young idea* (Edmonton Little Theatre, 1930/31), *Lilliom* (Edmonton Little Theatre, 1930/31), *Pageant of Empire* for silver jubilee (Arena, Edmonton, 24 May 1935), *Eve of St. Mark* (Edmonton Little Theatre, 1943), *Night must fall* (Edmonton, Little Theatre, 1944), *Macbeth* (Studio Theatre, 1950/51), *Androcles and the lion* (University Dramatic Society, 1951), *The glass menagerie* (University Dramatic Society, 1951), *Othello* (Studio Theatre, 1952/53; Dominion Drama Festival Calvert trophy, 1953), *The playboy of the western world* (Studio Theatre, 1955).

RADIO
Gave many talks on playwriting, directing, etc. (CKUA, University of Alberta, 1933-37).

WRITINGS
(with T. Cohen) *Complete elementary manual on the arts of the theatre,* 2v, Institute of Applied Art, 1935.
CONTRIBUTED: Articles on the theatre to bulletins published by the University of Alberta Department of Extension; *Alberta golden jubliee anthology,* edited by W.G. Hardy, McClelland & Stewart, 1955.

HÉBERT, Adrien   1890—
Artist; b. 12 Apr. 1890 in Paris, France; son of Louis Philippe and Maria (Roy) Hébert; came to Canada in infancy.

EDUCATION
Studied under Edmond Dyonnet (*q.v.*) and Joseph Saint-Charles (*q.v.*),   Monument National, Montréal, PQ, 1904-06; studied under William Brymner (*q.v.*), Art Association of Montreal; attended École des Beaux-Arts, Paris, 1912-14.

CAREER
Returned to Montreal, PQ, 1914; travelled to Paris, 1923.

MEMBER
Royal Canadian Academy (Associate 1932; Academician 1941); Arts Club (elected, 1918; president, 1938); Pen and Pencil Club (1940).

AWARDS, HONOURS
Jessie Dow prize, Art Association of Montreal, 1936 and 1940.

EXHIBITIONS
ONE-MAN: Watson Art Galleries, Montreal; T. Eaton Co. Gallery, Toronto; restaurant de L'Ile Sainte-Hélène, Montréal, 1956.
GROUP: Represented in group exhibitions held in Canada since 1920 including exhibitions of Royal Canadian Academy and Art Association of Montreal; World's Fair, New York, NY, 1939.

COLLECTIONS IN WHICH REPRESENTED
Musée du Québec, PQ; National Gallery of Canada, Ottawa, Ont.; Musée des Beaux-Arts, Montréal; Musée du Havre, France; Musée de Nîmes, France.

HÉBERT, Henri 1884-1950

Sculptor; b. 3 Apr. 1884 in Montreal, PQ; son
of Louis Philippe and Maria (Roy) Hébert; d. 11?
May 1950 in Montreal.

EDUCATION
Studied under Edmond Dyonnet, (q.v.), Monument National, Montréal, evening classes, 1896-
98; attended Écoles de la Ville de Paris, France,
evening classes, 1898-1900; studied under Corbel,
DeCorchemont, Genuys, and others, École des
Arts Décoratifs and Lycée Montaigne, Paris,
1900-02; studied under William Brymner (q.v.),
Art Association of Montreal, 1902-04; studied
under Gabriel-Jules Thomas and Antoine
Injalbert, École des Beaux-Arts, Paris, 1904-08.

RELIGION
Roman Catholic.

CAREER
Worked for a time under his father in Montreal
c.1909; McGill University, department of architecture, instructor in freehand drawing and clay
modelling 1909-20; Monument National,
Montréal, instructor in clay modelling 1923-25;
executed works of decoration, busts, monuments,
plaques, medals, and war memorials in Montreal
1909-50.

COMMISSIONS
Leight Gregor monument, Parc Jeanne Mance,
Montreal, 1913; Sir William Edmond Logan
plaque, Percé, PQ, Toronto, Ont., and Ottawa,
Ont., 1913; Reverend Father Lefebvre statue,
Memramcook, NB, 1914; Damien Rolland plaque,
Montreal; Tom Wilson plaque, Canadian Rockies;
medal, Selwyn House School, Montreal, 1917;
Evangeline statue, Grand Pré, NS, 1920; medal,
Amateur Skating Association of Canada, 1920;
J.P. Learmont plaque, Quebec House, Westerham,
Kent, England, 1920; Sir Louis Lafontaine statue,
Quebec, PQ, 1921; medal, Patriots of 1837,
Montreal; medal, École Polytechnique, Montreal;
Abraham Martin monument, Quebec, 1922; war
memorial plaque, Engineers Club, Montreal, 1922;
Sir Rodolphe Forge monument, Sainte Irénée,
PQ, 1923; war memorial, Yarmouth, NS, 1923;
Sacred Heart statue, Saint Henri, PQ, 1923;
war memorial, Outremont, PQ, 1925; decorations,
Moyse Hall, McGill University, 1926; Sir Lomer
Gouin medal, 1928; Sir Louis Hippolyte
Lafontaine monument, Montreal, 1930; De
Lesseps monument, Gaspé, PQ, 1932; decorations,
École des Hautes Études Commerciales,
Montreal; decorations, École Technique de
Montréal; decorations, Sainte-Marguerite-Marie
Church, Montreal; basreliefs, Saint-John-the-
Baptist Church, Pawtucket, RI; decorations,
Nurses' Home, Montreal General Hospital;
decorations, New Western General Hospital,
Montreal; decorations, St. Ambroise Church,
Montreal; decorations, McDougall and Cowans
Building, Montreal.

MEMBER
Royal Canadian Academy (Associate 1912;
Academician 1920); Sculptors' Society of
Canada (charter member); Royal Society of
Arts (elected fellow, 1939).

AWARDS, HONOURS
Medals for freehand drawing and architectural drawing, Écoles de la Ville de Paris; LL D
from University of Montreal, 1940.

EXHIBITIONS
ONE-MAN: Montreal Museum of Fine Arts,
1953.

GROUP: Represented in group exhibitions
held in Canada during his lifetime including
annual exhibitions of Royal Canadian Academy
and exhibitions of Art Association of Montreal;
represented in group exhibitions organized by
National Gallery of Canada, Ottawa, including
its Annual Exhibitions; Salon des Artistes
Français, Paris, on several occasions; *Exposition
d'art canadien,* Musée du Jeu de Paume, Paris,
1927; Exhibition of Paintings, Drawings and
Sculpture of the British Empire Overseas, Royal
Institute Galleries, London, England, 1937; A
Century of Canadian Art, Tate Gallery, London,
1938.

COLLECTIONS IN WHICH REPRESENTED
National Gallery of Canada, Ottawa; Art Gallery
of Ontario, Toronto; Musée du Québec, PQ.

HÉBERT, Marjolaine

Actress and director.

HOME
2162 Sherbrooke St. W., #22, Montreal 109, PQ.

CAREER
Théâtre de Marjolaine, Eastman, PQ, founder
and director 1960–.

MEMBER
Union des Artistes de Montréal; Canadian Theatre
Centre.

THEATRE
Played in many productions, e.g. *Liliom* (l'Équipe,
Montréal, 1946), Georgette in *L'école des femmes*
(l'Équipe, Montréal, 1947), *Trois garçons, une
fille* (Théâtre du Rideau Vert, Montréal, 1949),
On purge bébé (Théâtre Anjou, Montréal, 1954),
Le mari, la femme et la mort (Le Théâtre Club,
Montréal, 1961), Yvette in *Mère Courage*
(Théâtre du Nouveau Monde, Montréal, 20 Oct.
1965), *Retour des oies blanches* (La Comédie
Canadienne, Montréal, 19 Oct. 1966), *Encore
cinq minutes* (Théâtre du Rideau Vert, 15 Jan.
1967), *On n'aime qu'une fois* (Marjolaine,
24 June 1967), *... Et puis la neige vint* (La
Comédie Canadienne, 16 Nov. 1967), *Elle
tournera la terre* (La Comédie Canadienne,
17 Nov. 1967), *L'arche de Noë* (Marjolaine,
29 June 1968), *Le Tartuffe* (Théâtre du Nouveau
Monde, 8 Nov. 1968), *La nuit des rois* (Théâtre
du Nouveau Monde, 13 Dec. 1968).

HÉBERT, Paul   1924–
Actor and director; b. 28 May 1924 in Thetford
Mines, PQ; son of Alphonse and Mary (Camden)
Hébert; m. Huguette Lapierre 5 Feb. 1949;
children: Michel b. 1951, François b. 1953,
Stéphane b. 1955, Marc b. 1957.
EDUCATION
Attended Collège de Lévis, PQ; Université Laval;
Old Vic Theatre School, London, England,
1949-51.
RELIGION
Roman Catholic.
HOME
4154 Marlowe Ave., Montreal 28, PQ.
CAREER
Summer Theatre, Sainte-Adèle, PQ, founder 1936;
Théâtre Anjou, Montréal, founder and actor
1954–; Montreal International Theatre, actor
1966; Théâtre du Nouveau Monde, Montréal,
actor 1968–.
MEMBER
Union des Artistes de Montréal; National Arts
Centre, Ottawa (vice-chairman of the board of
trustees).
THEATRE
Played in many productions, e.g. Chicaneau in
Les plaideurs (Le Théâtre Club, Montréal,
1958), Capitaine in *L'effet Glapion* (Théâtre de
l'Égrégore, Montréal, 21 Oct. 1965), George in
Qui a peur de Virginia Woolf? (International
Theatre, 19 Jan. 1966), Mari in *Une femme douce*
(Théâtre de l'Égrégore, European tour 1966),
Macdonald in *Louis Riel* (J.L. Roux, Nouveau
Monde, 1968), *Pygmalion* (Nouveau Monde, 12
Jan. 1968), *Le chemin du roy* (Théâtre de
l'Égrégore, Montréal, 29 Apr. 1968), *Le
Tartuffe* (Nouveau Monde, 8 Nov. 1968), *La nuit
des rois* (Nouveau Monde, 13 Dec. 1968);
directed *La peur des coups* (Anjou, 1954), *On
purge bébé* (Anjou, 1954; Théâtre Populaire du
Québec, tour, 14 Oct. 1967), *Le printemps de
la Saint-Martin* (Anjou, 1954), *La mégère
apprivoisée* (Sainte-Adèle, 1956), *Six person-
nages en quête d'auteur* (Sainte-Adèle, 1956),
Le mariage forcé (Théatre Populaire du Québec,
tour, 14 Oct. 1967).
FILM
Played in several productions, e.g. *La vie heureuse
de Leopold Z, La vie de Georges Étienne, The
luck of Ginger Coffey.*
RADIO
Played in many productions, e.g. Archbishop of
Quebec in *Charbonneau et le chef* (CBC, 30 June
1968).
TELEVISION
Played in many productions, e.g. *Un mois à la
campagne, Les trois soeurs, L'Apollon de Bellac.*

HÉBERT, Pierre*   1944–
Film director and artist; b. 19 Jan. 1944 in

Montreal; son of Marcel and Carmel (Messier)
Hébert.
EDUCATION
Attended École St. Vincent Ferrier, Montréal,
1949-55; Collège St. Viateur, Montréal, BA,
1956-62; University of Montreal, B Sc, 1962-64,
post-graduate 1964-65, 1968-69; Polytechnic
Institute, Brooklyn, NY, 1967.
HOME
397 St. Joseph's Boul., W., Apt. #20, Montréal,
PQ.
OFFICE
c/o National Film Board of Canada, Box 6100,
Montréal 3, PQ.
CAREER
National Film Board, Montreal, animated film
director 1965–; La Commission Image Publique
et Festival, animator 1968.
MEMBER
Association Professionelle des Cinéastes du
Québec.
FILMS
Directed and produced *Histoire grise* (1962),
Histoire d'une bébite (1962), *Opus-1* (1964;
special prize, Evian Film Festival, France,
1965); animated *Le révolutionnaire* (Les Films,
J.P. Lefebvre, 1965); directed and animated
Une histoire de la communication (National
Film Board, 1965); co-directed *Mon oeil* (J.P.
Lefebvre, 1966); directed *Op hop* (National
Film Board, 1966; first prize, short films category,
Fifth Festival of Canadian Films, Montreal Inter-
national Film Festival, 1967); animated *Le
jeu des propositions* (National Film Board, 1966);
directed *Population explosion* (National Film
Board, 1967), *Opus 3* (National Film Board, 1967),
Around perception (National Film Board, 1968);
animated *Jusqu'au coeur* (National Film Board,
1968).
EXHIBITIONS
ONE-MAN: Galerie Claude Haefely, Montreal,
1964.
GROUP: Represented in group exhibitions held
in Canada since 1964 including annual exhibi-
tions of L'Atelier Libre de Recherche Graphique,
Montréal, Musée du Québec, PQ, Musée d'Art
Contemporain, Montreal; Paris Biennal, Musée
d'Art Moderne, France, 1967.
COLLECTIONS IN WHICH REPRESENTED
L'Atelier Libre de Recherche Graphique.
WRITINGS
CONTRIBUTED: Articles to *Objectif.*

HEDORE, Win
see BLOORE, Ronald L.

HEIDEN, Heino*   1923–
Dancer, teacher, and choreographer; b. 6 Oct.
1923 in Barmen, Westphalia, Germany; son of
Gerhard and Madeleine (Devreker) Heiden; m. Igna

Beth 15 Sept. 1952 (marriage dissolved Apr. 1954); came to Canada in 1952.

EDUCATION
Attended school in Hagen, Westphalia; studied ballet with Tatiana Gsovska and Victor Gsovsky in Berlin, Germany, 1940; Olga Preobrajenska, Paris, France, 1950; Royal Ballet School, London, England, 1963.

RELIGION
Roman Catholic.

HOME
Apt. 1410, 1280 St. Marc St., Montreal, PQ.

OFFICE
Ballettgemeinschaft Lübeck-Kiel, Bühnen der Hansestadt, 24 Lübeck, West Germany.

CAREER
Romantisches Ballet, Germany, dancer 1942; Staatsoper, Berlin, corps de ballet, 1945, soloist 1946; Staatsoper, Dresden, Germany, premier danseur, assistant ballet master and choreographer 1947; Opera Comique, Berlin, premier danseur 1948; Hamburg Ballet Theatre, Germany, ballet master and soloist 1950; Ballet of Janine Charrat, Paris, dancer 1950/51; Gärtnerplatz Theatre, Munich, Germany, premier danseur and assistant ballet master 1951/52; BC School of Dancing, Vancouver, teacher 1952-54; BC Ballet Company, Vancouver, choreographer 1953-54; Vancouver Ballet, director and choreographer c.1954; CBC, Montreal, choreographer 1954-60; National Theatre Ballet, Mannheim, West Germany, choreographer and director 1960-63; Koninklijke Vlaamse Opera, Antwerp, Belgium, director and choreographer 1965-66; Ballettgemeinschaft, Lübeck-Kiel, West Germany, choreographer and director 1967–.

AWARDS, HONOURS
BC Ballet Festival first prize for choreography for *Daphnis and Chloë*, 1953.

THEATRE
Made debut as Piccolo in *The White Horse Inn* (City Theatre, Hagen, c.1931); danced Snob in *La boutique fantasque* (Massine, Gartnerplatz, 1951); choreographed *Cinderella* (Vancouver Civic Ballet Society, Dec. 1952; excerpts Canadian Ballet Festival, Ottawa, Ont., May 1953); *Pygmalion* and *Daphnis and Chloë* (Vancouver Civic Ballet Society, 1953; Canadian Ballet Festival, Ottawa, May 1953), *Evocation to Apollo* (BC Ballet, 1954; Canadian Ballet Festival, Toronto, Ont., May 1954), *Magician's holiday* (BC Ballet, 1954; Canadian Ballet Festival, Toronto May 1954; 1961), *Mazurka* (Vancouver Ballet, 1954), *Petrouchka* excerpts (Vancouver Ballet, 1954), *Claire de lune* (Vancouver Ballet, 1954; Ottawa Ballet, 1957), *Fanny* (musical, European première, Gärtnerplatz, 1956), *Les ballons* (Ottawa Ballet, 1957), *The Chinese nightingale* (Washington Ballet, DC, 1957; 1964; Royal Winnipeg Ballet, Man., Playhouse, Winnipeg, 15 Jan. 1959), *Wry and ginger* (musical, Montreal, 1958); several operas and operettas 1960-63, e.g. *Aïda, Rigoletto, Falstaff, Dafne, Un ballo in maschera, Der Revisor, Neues vom Tage, Tannhäuser, Schwanda der Dudelsackpfeifer, The White Horse Inn, Boccaccio, The beggar student; Divertimento* (1960), *Le baiser de la fée* (1960), *Danza* (1960), *Valses nobles et sentimentales* (1961), *Liebermann jazz concerto* (1961), *Herodiade* (1961), *Nobilissima visione* (1961), *Agon* (1962), *La fille mal gardée* (1962; Washington Ballet, 1964; Vancouver Ballet Society, Queen Elizabeth Playhouse, 15 May 1966; Koninklijke Vlaamse Opera, 1965; Ballettgemeinschaft, 1967), *Straussiana* (1962), *Cassenoisette* (1963), *The unicorn, the gorgon and the manticore* (Washington Ballet, 1964), *The green flute* (Vancouver, 1964), *Monsieur de Croes inviteert* (Koninklijke Vlaamse Opera, 1965), *La prima ballerina* (National Ballet of Canada, Expo 67, Montreal, 26 Oct. 1967), *A la Rossini* (1967), *Vivaldi* (1967), *The comedians* (1967; Amsterdam, The Netherlands, 1969), *Le lac des cygnes* (1968), *Oberon* (Staatsoper, Munich, 1968).

TELEVISION
Choreographed many CBC productions, e.g. *Mephisto valse* ("Heure du concert," 1954), *Le manège* ("Heure du concert," 1954), *Menu à la Rossini* ("Heure du concert," 1954), *Holiday* ("Summer festival," 29 Aug. 1954), *Nobilissima visione* ("Heure du concert," 1955), *The Chinese nightingale* ("Heure du concert," 1955; Germany, The Netherlands, 1964), *Le voleur de lune* (1955), *Indian legend* (1955), *Le vieux mari* (1955), *Le veuve scandaleuse* (1955), *Goyescas* (1955), *La fontaine de Paris* (1955), *Stanley Park* ("Heure du concert," June 1955), "Feu de bois" (weekly series, 1956), *A l'auberge* (1956), "In the story book" (weekly children's series, 1956), *Les ballons* (1957), "Silhouette" (weekly series, 1957), "Porte ouverte" (weekly series, 1957-58), *Daphnis and Chloë* ("Heure du concert," 1957), "Couronne d'or" (weekly series, 1958), "Music hall" (weekly series, 1958-59).

HEIM, Emmy 1885-1954
(Emmy Heim Singer)
Singer (soprano); b. 1885 in Vienna, Austria; m. 1915; m. Franz Singer 1917; came to Canada in 1934 and became Canadian citizen in 1951; d. 13 Oct. 1954 in Toronto, Ont.

EDUCATION
Studied voice with Frances Mütter in Vienna for 13 years.

CAREER
Toured Germany, 1911–; sang for soldiers in Warsaw during World War I; toured Hungary and Czecho-Slovakia; sang in Montreal, 1934;

taught summer school in Salzburg, Austria;
Royal Conservatory of Music, Toronto, guest
lecturer and tutor 1938, teacher of singing 1947-
54; sang at Red Cross hospitals and military
camps in UK during World War II; Oxford and
Cambridge Universities, guest lecturer 1944.

THEATRE
Debut in Vienna, 1911; English debut, 1929;
Canadian debut in recital at Hart House
Theatre, Toronto, 1934; sang in numerous lieder
concerts and interpreted many contemporary lied
compositions.

HEMING, Arthur Henry Howard   1870-1940

Artist and author; b. 17 Jan. 1870 in Paris, Ont.;
son of George Edward and Frances Ann (Morgan)
Heming; d. 31 Oct. 1940 in Hamilton, Ont.

EDUCATION
Attended public schools in Paris; studied at the
Hamilton Art School; studied under Frank
Vincent DuMond, Art Students League, New
York, NY., c. 1899; studied under Frank Brangwyn
in London, England, 1904.

RELIGION
Anglican.

CAREER
Began travelling in the wilderness in 1886, making
forty-six trips to the north and west to paint wild-
life and scenery during his lifetime; sold drawings
to New York and London magazines from 1887
on contributing illustrations to fifty-eight magazines published in England, the United States,
France, Germany, Italy, Sweden, and Canada
during the period 1887-1939; Hamilton Art
School, teacher 1887-90; *Dominion illustrated*,
magazine illustrator in the 1890s; commissioned
by *Harper's magazine* to accompany the author
Casper Whitney to the barren grounds of Canada
as an illustrator; illustrated *Mooswa & others of
the boundaries* by W.A. Fraser, Scribner, 1900,
The outcasts by W.A. Fraser, Scribner, 1901,
The Sa'-zada tales, by W.A. Fraser, Scribner,
1905, *The three sapphires*, by W.A. Fraser, Doran,
1918; lived in New York and worked as an illustrator c.1905-10; painted, wrote, and worked as a
magazine illustrator in Toronto, Ont., 1910-40.

MEMBER
Ontario Society of Artists (elected, 1929); Royal
Canadian Academy (Associate 1934); Society of
Illustrators of New York (elected member);
Society of Authors, Playwrights and Composers,
London (elected member); Authors' League of
America (elected member).

EXHIBITIONS
ONE-MAN: Frost and Reed Galleries, London,
1934.
GROUP: Exhibition of Canadian Art at the British
Empire Trade Exhibition, Buenos Aires, Argentina,
1931; A Century of Canadian Art, Tate Gallery,
London, 1938.

COLLECTIONS IN WHICH REPRESENTED
National Gallery of Canada, Ottawa, Ont.; Royal
Ontario Museum, Toronto.

WRITINGS
Spirit Lake, Macmillan, 1907; *The drama of the
forests*, Doubleday, Page, 1921; *The living forest*,
Doubleday, Page, 1925.

HÉNAULT, Gilles*   1920–

Poet; b. 1 Aug. 1920 in Saint-Majorique, PQ; son
of Octavien and Edouardina (Joyal) Hénault; m.;
children: Claude b. 9 Feb. 1943, Jean-Yves b. 23
Mar. 1950.

EDUCATION
Attended University of Montreal.

RELIGION
Roman Catholic.

HOME
4853 Grosvenor, Montréal, PQ.

OFFICE
Musée d'Art Contemporain, 4040 Sherbrooke St.
E., Montréal, PQ.

CAREER
Le Canada, Le devoir, Le jour, La presse, Montreal,
journalist and art, theatre, and literary critic; CBC,
Montreal; International Film Festival, Montreal,
jury member 1964; Québec Concours Artistique,
judge 1965; Musée d'Art Contemporain, Montreal,
director 1966–.

MEMBER
Canadian Art Museum Directors Association.

AWARDS, HONOURS
Canada Council arts scholarship, 1960; Grand
jury des lettres, first prize, 1961; Concours
littéraire du Québec, second prize, 1961.

RADIO
"Le sel de la semaine" (series, CBC).

WRITINGS
Théâtre en plein air (poems and prose), Cahiers de
la File Indienne, 1946; *Totems*, Erta, 1953;
Voyages aux pays de mémoire (poems and prose),
Erta, 1959; *Sémaphore*, Hexagone, 1961.
CONTRIBUTED: Articles and poetry in English
and French to *Canadian art, Canadian forum,
Liberté, Magazine Maclean, Tamarack review,
Vie des arts.*

HENDERSON, George, pseud.
see GLASSCO, John

HENDERSON, James   1871-1951

Artist; b. 21 Aug. 1871 in Glasgow, Scotland; son
of James Henderson; m. Jean 1900; came to Canada 1909 and settled in Winnipeg, Man.; d. 5 July
1951 in Regina, Sask.

EDUCATION
Attended public schools in Glasgow; attended
evening classes, Glasgow School of Art c.1890;
studied in London, England, c.1895.

RELIGION
Anglican.

CAREER

Apprenticed to a Glasgow lithographer 1888-95; worked as an engraver becoming chief engraver for his firm, and made stage sets in London c.1895-1909; engaged in commercial art in Winnipeg, including designing covers for the publication *The trail;* engaged in commercial art and portrait commissions in Regina 1910-15; established a studio in Fort Qu'Appelle, Sask., 1915; painted Indians and landscapes in Fort Qu'Appelle, making painting trips to BC, Ont., and Scotland, 1915-51.

MEMBER

Ontario Society of Artists.

AWARDS, HONOURS

LLD from University of Saskatchewan, 1951.

EXHIBITIONS

GROUP: Represented in group exhibitions held in Canada during his lifetime including annual exhibitions of Ontario Society of Artists, Royal Canadian Academy and exhibitions of Art Association of Montreal; represented in group exhibitions organized by National Gallery of Canada, Ottawa, Ont., including its Annual Exhibitions; New English Art Club, London, 1908; Canadian Section of Fine Arts, British Empire Exhibition, Wembley, England, 1924; Exhibition of Contemporary Canadian Painting Arranged ... for Circulation in the Southern Dominions of the British Empire, 1936; A Century of Canadian Art, Tate Gallery, London, 1938.

COLLECTIONS IN WHICH REPRESENTED

Glenbow Foundation, Calgary, Alta.; Moose Jaw Public Library, Sask.; Norman Mackenzie Art Gallery, Regina; Nutana Collegiate, Saskatoon, Sask.; University of Saskatchewan.

HENDRY, Thomas Best* 1929–

Author and administrator; b. 7 June 1929 in Winnipeg, Man.; son of Donald and Martha (Best) Hendry; m. Irene Chick 1958 (marriage dissolved 1963); m. Judith Carr 1963; children: (first marriage) Thomas John b. 16 Sept. 1961; (second marriage) Christopher Stephan b. 9 Oct. 1967.

EDUCATION

Taché School, St. Boniface, Man., 1935-44; Norwood Collegiate Institute, St. Boniface, 1944-45; Kelvin High School, Winnipeg, 1945-47; attended University of Manitoba; Institute of Chartered Accountants of Manitoba, CA, 1955.

HOME

34 Elgin Ave., Toronto 5, Ont.

OFFICE

Festival Theatre, Stratford, Ont.

CAREER

Rainbow Stage, Winnipeg, manager and producer-co-ordinator; Theatre 77, Winnipeg, co-founder 1957-58; Manitoba Theatre Centre, Winnipeg co-founder and administrator 1958-63; Canadian

Players, Toronto, reorganizer 1964; Canadian Theatre Centre, Toronto, executive secretary 1964-67, general secretary 1967-69; Canadian National Commission for UNESCO, executive committee member 1966–; Stratford, Ont. Festival, literary manager, 1969–.

MEMBER

AEA; ACTRA; Canadian Theatre Centre; Institute of Chartered Accountants of Manitoba (1955); Winnipeg Press Club (1960); Arts and Letters Club of Toronto (1967).

AWARDS, HONOURS

Canada Council senior arts fellowship to study theatre centres in USA and Europe, 1963/64; Centennial medal, 1967.

THEATRE

Played in many productions of Rainbow Stage, Winnipeg Little Theatre, Children's Theatre of Greater Winnipeg, e.g. Randolph in *Pussy cat, pussy cat where have you been?*, Flunk, a polar bear, and Gregory, the snowman in *Peter and the snowman* (Muddiwater Puppets, Winnipeg, tour 1952).

FILM

Played Driving instructor in *Flagged for action* (National Film Board of Canada, 1952).

RADIO

Played in many CBC productions, e.g. "Prairie playhouse," Buddy Jackson in *The Jacksons and their neighbours* (serial, 1960-63).

TELEVISION

Played cornet player in *Cornet at midnight* (spring, 1954); *Manitoba Theatre Centre* ("Telescope," CBC, 21 Mar. 1968).

WRITINGS

(adapter with M. Charles Cohen) *Mateo Falcone* (radio play based on Mérimée's short story; produced CBC, 1952); *Fudge and the space pirates* (puppet play; produced Winnipeg Junior League Touring Puppet Theatre, 1953); *Summer theatre* (TV script; produced CBC, 1955); (adapter) *The anniversary* (TV play based on Chekhov's play; produced CBC, 1956); *A city in white* (TV script; produced CBC, 1957); *Filing cabinet* (TV script; produced CBC, 1957); *Trapped* (children's play; produced Manitoba Theatre Centre, Nov. 1961); (with Len Peterson) *All about us* (revue; produced Canadian Players, tour 1964; CTV, 1964); *Fifteen miles of broken glass* (play; produced "Festival," CBC TV, 21 Sept. 1966; "Stage," CBC radio, 15 Oct. 1967); and many scripts for radio series, e.g. "Anthology," "Wednesday night."

CONTRIBUTED: Articles and short stories to *The Canadians, 1867-1967*, edited by J.M.S. Careless, Macmillan, 1967; *Tulane drama review, Le théâtre dans le monde, Playbill, Star weekly, Winnipeg world, Architecture Canada, Performing arts, Canadian art*.

WORK IN PROGRESS: "Last man on horseback" (radio play); "The walking wounded" (play);

"Mooney" (pilot script for television series);
"Centre: a memoir of the founding of the MTC."

HENRY, Jeff* 1922–

Dancer, choreographer, and teacher; b. 10 Nov.
1922 in Port-of-Spain, Trinidad; son of
Valentine and Mathilda (Langton) Henry; m.
Frances Osterman 11 Nov. 1960; children:
Terrence b. 31 Jan. 1963; came to Canada in
1961 and settled in Montreal in 1963.

EDUCATION
Attended St. Thomas Private School and Lincoln
High School in Trinidad; studied at Sigurd
Leeder School and Laban Art of Movement
Studio in London, England; studied dance with
Martha Graham, Antony Tudor, and Charles
Weidman in New York, NY.

HOME
76 Somerville Ave., Westmount, Montreal, PQ.

OFFICE
National Theatre School of Canada, 407
St. Lawrence Boul., Montreal 1, PQ.

CAREER
Canadian National Exhibition, Toronto, soloist
1955; Little Carib Company, Trinidad, choreographer and assistant artistic director 1955-58;
Stratford, Ont. Festival, teacher of dance and
movement 1961-64; National Theatre School of
Canada, Montreal, teacher of dance and movement
1961–; Le Théâtre de Marjolaine, Eastman, PQ,
choreographer 1965-66; Les Feux Follets, Montréal,
dance master 1965; Detroit Art Institute, Mich.,
and Goodman Theatre, Chicago, Ill., consultant
on movement for actors and teaching methods
of dance and movement for actors 1965; Le
Théâtre du Nouveau Monde, Montréal, choreographer 1966-67; Wayne State University, Detroit,
consultant on movement for actors 1966; Expo 67,
Montreal, Trinidad and Tobago Pavilion consultant
1967.

MEMBER
AEA; Canadian Theatre Centre; Union des Artistes
de Montréal.

AWARDS, HONOURS
Jamaican Government citation for contribution
to Jamaican theatre, 1957; Canada Council grant,
1961; Rockefeller Foundation grant, 1962/63.

THEATRE
Choreographed Il est une saison (Marjolaine, 1965),
Les sorcières de Salem (Nouveau Monde, 9 Jan.
1966), Ne ratez pas l'espion (Marjolaine, 25 June
1966), Le soulier de satin (Nouveau Monde, 7
Jan. 1967), Canadian Pulp and Paper show and
Youth Pavilion show (Expo 67), Culture vivante
(Quebec Ministry of Culture, 1968); devised and
choreographed Africa in the Caribbean (Saidye
Bronfman Centre, Montreal, 1968).

TELEVISION
Choreographed several CBC productions, e.g.

Henrietta's wedding ("Wayne and Shuster show,"
1961), La boîte à surprise (1964), Jeunesse oblige
(1965), Âge tendre (1966), The abduction from
the seraglio ("Le beau dimanche," Sept. 1967;
"World of music," 17 Mar. 1968).

HEY, Betty
see FARRALLY, Betty

HIEBERT, Paul Gerhardt* 1892–

Author; b. 17 July 1892 in Pilot Mound, Man.;
son of John and Maria Hiebert; m. Dorothea
Cunningham 27 Feb. 1926.

EDUCATION
University of Manitoba, BA in philosophy,
1916; University of Toronto, MA in Gothic and
Teutonic philology, 1917; McGill University,
M Sc in physics and chemistry, 1922, Ph D in
chemistry, 1924.

RELIGION
Protestant.

HOME
118 Wilde Ave., Carman, Man.

CAREER
School teacher in Saskatchewan, 1914; University of Manitoba, professor of chemistry 1924-53.

MEMBER
Canadian Authors Association (Winnipeg, Man.,
branch, president, 1948-49; honorary president);
Canadian Institute of Chemistry (fellow).

AWARDS, HONOURS
University of Manitoba gold medal, 1916;
Governor General's medal for science, 1924;
Leacock medal for humour for Sarah Binks,
1947.

RADIO
Participated in programs, e.g. "Prairie talks"
(series, 1 Apr. 1965); As one of our selves (CBC,
24 Mar. 1967).

WRITINGS
Sarah Binks (novel), Oxford, 1947 (produced CBC
radio); Tower in Siloam (non-fiction), McClelland
& Stewart, 1966; Willows revisited (novel),
McClelland & Stewart, 1967.

CONTRIBUTED: Poems to Canadian poetry.

HIESTER, Mary Augusta
see REID, Mary Hiester

HILL, George William 1861-1934

Sculptor; b. 1861 in Shipton Township, Canada
East, PQ; m. Elsie Annette Kent; children: one
son, two daughters; d. 17 July 1934 in
Montreal, PQ.

EDUCATION
Attended St. Francis College, Richmond, PQ;
studied at Académie Julian and École des Beaux-
Arts in Paris, France, 1889-94.

CAREER
Sculptor in Montreal 1894-1934.

COMMISSIONS
South African War memorial, Montreal, 1904;
bust of W.H. Drummond, Carnegie Institute,
New York, NY, 1907; South African memorial,
London, Ont., 1908; George Brown group,
Ottawa, Ont., 1910; Thomas D'Arcy McGee
memorial, Ottawa, 1910; pediment for parlia-
ment buildings, Regina, Sask., c.1911; Georges
Étienne Cartier monument, Fletcher's Field,
Montreal; war memorial, Westmount, PQ; war
memorial, Magog, PQ; Nurse's National memorial,
Hall of Fame, Parliament Buildings, Ottawa.
    MEMBER
Royal Canadian Academy (Associate 1908;
Academician 1915); Pen & Pencil Club.
    EXHIBITIONS
GROUP: Represented in group exhibitions of
Royal Canadian Academy; Paris Salon, 1905.

HINE, Daryl*   1936–
(William Daryl Hine)
Poet; b. 24 Feb. 1936 in Burnaby, BC; son of
Robert Fraser and Elsie May (James) Hine.
    EDUCATION
Attended McGill University; University of
Chicago, MA, 1965, Ph D, 1967.
    HOME
5533 South Cornell St., Chicago, Ill. 60637, USA.
    CAREER
Mainly literary; Canadian Legation, Paris, France;
resided in France until 1962; travelled exten-
sively in Europe; University of Chicago, assistant
professor of English and humanities 1967–.
    AWARDS, HONOURS
Canada Foundation fellowship for poetry, 1958;
Canada Council arts scholarship, 1959/60;
Merrill award, 1962 and 1963; Borestone
Mountain prize, 1968.
    WRITINGS
Five poems, Emblem, 1954; *The carnal and the
crane,* Contact, 1957 *(McGill poetry series,* no.2);
The devil's picture book, Abelard-Schuman, 1960;
The Prince of Darkness & Co. (novel), Abelard-
Schuman, 1961; *Polish subtitles* (non-fiction),
Abelard-Schuman, 1962; *The wooden horse,*
Atheneum, 1965; *Minutes; poems,* Atheneum,
1968; many radio plays, e.g. *Defunctive music*
("Wednesday night," CBC, 28 Jun. 1961), *The
power failure* ("Summer stage," CBC, 13 Aug.
1961; "Saturday evening," CBC, 30 May 1964),
(adapter) *Alceste* (based on Euripides' play
Alcestis; "Stage," CBC, 1965/66).
CONTRIBUTED: Poetry to *The Penguin book
of Canadian verse,* edited by R. Gustafson,
Penguin, 1958; *The Oxford book of Canadian
verse in English and French,* edited by A.J.M.
Smith, Oxford, 1960; *Poet's choice,* edited by
P. Engle and J. Langland, Dial, 1962; *An anthology
of Commonwealth verse,* edited by J.J. O'Donnell,

Blackie, 1963; *Poems of our moment,* edited
by J. Hollander, Pegasus, 1968; numerous periodicals, e.g. *Alphabet, Canadian forum, Contemporary verse, Delta, Fiddlehead, Queen's
quarterly, Tamarack review.*
WORK IN PROGRESS: "The death of Seneca"
(play).

HINE, William Daryl
see HINE, Daryl

HIRSCH, John Stephen*   1930–
Director and author; b. 1 May 1930 in Siófok,
Hungary; son of Joseph and Ilona (Horvath)
Hirsch; came to Canada in 1948 and settled
in Winnipeg, Man.
    EDUCATION
Attended Zsido Gymnasium in Budapest,
Hungary; St. John Technical High School in
Winnipeg; University of Manitoba, BA honours
English, 1951; Central School of Speech and
Drama, London, England.
    OFFICE
Stratford Festival Theatre, Stratford, Ont.
    CAREER
Muddiwater Puppets, Winnipeg, founder
c.1952; Winnipeg Little Theatre, production
manager and director 1953-54; CBWT, Winnipeg,
TV producer 1954-57; Rainbow Stage,
Winnipeg, artistic director 1956; Theatre 77,
Winnipeg, co-founder 1957; Manitoba Theatre
Centre, Winnipeg, co-founder and artistic
director 1958-67, founding artistic director
1967–; National Theatre School of Canada,
Montreal, PQ, member of board of governors
and guest lecturer 1960–; National Arts
Centre, Ottawa, Ont., theatre adviser 1964–;
Stratford, Ont. Festival, associate director
1967, co-artistic director 1968-69.
    MEMBER
Canadian Theatre Centre; Association of
Stage Directors, USA; Royal Winnipeg Ballet
board of directors.
    AWARDS, HONOURS
McLean scholarship from University of
Manitoba; Chancellor's prize for fiction from
University of Manitoba; Golden boy award of
Manitoba; New Canadian of the year from
National Council of Jewish Women; Honorary
Fellow of University College, University of
Manitoba; LL D from University of Manitoba;
LL D from University of Toronto; Canada
Council grant to attend Theatre Conference
at Commonwealth Arts Festival, Glasgow,
Scotland, 1965/66; Medal of service of the
Order of Canada.
    THEATRE
Directed numerous productions, e.g. *A
streetcar named Desire* (Manitoba Theatre

Centre), *Cat on a hot tin roof* (Crest Theatre, Toronto, Ont., 1963), *Peter Pan* (Vancouver International Festival, BC, 1963), *Pygmalion* (Manitoba Theatre Centre, 1963/64), *The hostage* (Manitoba Theatre Centre, 1963/64), *A midsummer night's dream* (Manitoba Theatre Centre, 1963/64; Montreal, 13 Mar. 1968 and Stratford, Ont. Festival, 12 June 1968), *Names and nicknames* (Manitoba Theatre Centre, 1963/64), *All about us* (Canadian Players, tour 1964), *Mother Courage* (Manitoba Theatre Centre, fall 1964; Théâtre du Nouveau Monde, Montréal, 13 Feb. 1966), *The taming of the shrew* (Manitoba Theatre Centre, Dec. 1964), *Who's afraid of Virginia Woolf?* (Manitoba Theatre Centre, 1964/65), *The cherry orchard* (Stratford, Ont. Festival, 26 July 1965), *The importance of being earnest* (Manitoba Theatre Centre, 3 Nov. 1965), *Andorra* (Manitoba Theatre Centre, 1 Dec. 1965), *The threepenny opera* (Manitoba Theatre Centre, 9 Feb. 1966), *Henry VI* (Stratford, Ont. Festival, 7 June 1966), *A funny thing happened on the way to the Forum* (Manitoba Theatre Centre, 1966), *Yerma* (Lincoln Center Repertory Theater, New York, NY, 9 Dec. 1966), *Galileo* (Lincoln Center Repertory Theater, 13 Apr. 1967), *Richard III* (Stratford, Ont. Festival, 1967), *Colours in the dark* (Stratford, Ont. Festival, 1967), *Saint Joan* (Lincoln Center Repertory Theater, 4 Jan. 1968), *The three musketeers* (Stratford, Ont. Festival, 22 July 1968).

FILM
John Hirsch: a portrait of a man and a theatre (National Film Board of Canada 0165049; CBC, 31 Mar. 1965).

RADIO
Konstantin Stanislavsky ("Architects of modern thought," CBC, 14 Mar. 1962); panellist on *Problems and responsibilities of regional theatres* ("Soundings," CBC, 23 Dec. 1965).

TELEVISION
Directed *Fifteen miles of broken glass* ("Festival," CBC, 21 Sept. 1966).

WRITINGS
Several children's plays, e.g. *Box of smiles, Sour Kringle, Destination Planet D, Rupert the great;* puppet plays, e.g. *Peter the snowman,* 1952, *The dog who never learned.*
CONTRIBUTED: Articles and poems to *Architects of modern thought,* 5th and 6th series, CBC, 1962; *Alphabet, Northern review, Canadian art, Royal Architectural Institute of Canada journal.*

HOBDEN, Andrée Maillet
see MAILLET, Andrée

HODGSON, Thomas Sherlock*   1924–
Artist; b. 5 June 1924 in Toronto, Ont.; son of D.E. and Mary (Self) Hodgson; m. Wilma Stein

1947; children: Mark, Rand, Lise, Kara.
EDUCATION
Attended Central Technical School, Toronto, 1939-43; Ontario College of Art, Toronto, graduate in drawing and painting, 1946.
RELIGION
Agnostic.
HOME
274 Macpherson Ave., Toronto 5, Ont.
CAREER
RCAF, 1943-45, became sergeant; Telfer Paper Box Company, artist, six months 1946-47; E.W. Reynolds Advertising Company, assistant art director, six months 1948; John Adams Company, artist 1948-49; Photo Engravers, artist, six months 1949; Odeon Theatres, artist 1950; Art and Design Studios, artist 1951, 1952-54, part time 1954-56; Art Associates, artist, six months, 1952; CBC, artist, one month 1952; freelance commercial artist in Toronto 1956-58; Vickers and Benson, artist 1958-62; Ontario College of Art, teacher 1963; Foster Advertising Company, part-time idea consultant 1962-67; freelance artist in Toronto 1968–.
MEMBER
Ontario Society of Artists (elected, 1954); Canadian Society of Painters in Water Colour (elected, 1954); Canadian Group of Painters (elected, 1956); Painters Eleven (co-founder, 1953); Royal Canadian Academy (Associate 1962); Canadian Younger Artists Group (vice-president, 1948); Canadian Society of Painter-Etchers and Engravers (Associate 1947).
AWARDS, HONOURS
Toronto Art Directors' Club certificate, 1954; Toronto Art Directors' Club medal, 1955; award, Winnipeg Art Gallery exhibition, 1956/57; honour award and Windsor, Newton award, Canadian Society of Painters in Water Colour, 1957; award, Monsanto Art Competition, 1957; honour award, Canadian Society of Painters in Water Colour, 1959; Baxter award, Ontario Society of Artists, 1959; Canada Council senior arts fellowship, 1963.
EXHIBITIONS
ONE-MAN: Gallery of Contemporary Art, Toronto, 1954, 1956 and 1957; Dorothy Cameron Gallery, Toronto, 1962; Albert White Art Gallery, Toronto, 1965.
GROUP: Represented in annual exhibitions of Ontario Society of Artists, Canadian Society of Painter-Etchers and Engravers, Canadian Society of Graphic Art, Canadian Group of Painters, Royal Canadian Academy, Canadian Younger Artists Group, Canadian Society of Painters in Water Colour, and Painters Eleven; represented in exhibitions organized by National Gallery of Canada, Ottawa, Ont., including its first, second, third, fourth, and fifth Biennial Exhibitions of Canadian Painting, 1955, 1957, 1959, 1961 and

1963; International Exhibition at the Carnegie Institute, Pittsburgh, Pa., 1955; New Delhi International, India, 1956.

COLLECTIONS IN WHICH REPRESENTED
Art Gallery of Ontario, Toronto; Fairleigh Dickinson University, Rutherford, NJ; National Gallery of Canada; Sir George Williams University; University of British Columbia; Victoria College, University of Toronto; Owens Museum, Mount Allison University.

HOLMES, David Leonard* 1936—
Dancer; b. 1936 in Vancouver, BC; son of Howard and Cecil (Burtrum) Holmes; m. Anna-Marie Ellerbeck 13 Aug. 1960.

EDUCATION
Attended school in Vancouver; studied singing with Melchoire Luise, La Scala, Milan, Italy; studied ballet with Lydia Karpova, Vancouver, 1957-58; Royal Winnipeg Ballet, Man., 1958-59, 1960-62; Audrey de Vos and Errol Addison, London, England, 1959-60; Alexander Pushkin, Leningrad, USSR, 1962/63—; Karel Shook, Amsterdam, The Netherlands, 1966-67.

HOME
c/o Box 465, Mission City, BC; Egelantiers Straat 4''', Amsterdam, The Netherlands.

CAREER
Royal Winnipeg Ballet, soloist 1960-62; Leningrad Kirov Ballet, guest artist 1962/63—; London's Festival Ballet, principal, 1963/64; Les Grands Ballets Canadiens, Montréal, PQ, star 1964/65; Het Nationaal Ballet, Amsterdam, principal 1965-67; Chicago International Ballet, Ill., guest star 1968.

MEMBER
AEA.

AWARDS, HONOURS
Canada Council arts scholarship for study abroad.

THEATRE
Made debut in World of the wonderful dark (Vancouver International Festival, 1958); created Violin in A court occasion (Macdonald, Playhouse, Winnipeg, 26 Dec. 1961), Prothalamion (Macdonald, Banff School of Fine Arts, Alta., Aug. 1961); danced Albrecht in Giselle (Coralli-Perrot), Prince Siegfried in Le lac des cygnes (Petipa-Ivanov), Marseillais in The flames of Paris (Vainonen), Solar in La bayadère (Petipa), Sanguinic in The four temperaments (Balanchine), Romeo in Romeo and Juliet (Lavrosky), Le corsaire pas de deux (Petipa, opening of Playhouse, Fredericton, NB, 26 Sept. 1964), title role in Apollo (Apollon musagète, Balanchine), Spring waters pas de deux (Messerer), Taras Bulba pas de deux (Fenster), Diane and Acteon, Don Quixote pas de deux (Petipa), Casse-noisette pas de deux (Ivanov),

Gluck melody, Faust pas de deux (Perrot), Laurencia pas de deux (Chabukiana); created male role in La peri (Van Dantzig), Transfigured night (Corelli).

TELEVISION
Danced in several CBC productions, e.g. "World of music," "Music hall," "Festival," and in England, Portugal, The Netherlands, and France.

HOLMES, Robert 1862-1930
Artist; b. 25 June 1862 in Cannington, Ont.; son of John and Ann (Donald) Holmes; d. 14 May 1930 in Toronto, Ont.

EDUCATION
Attended schools in Port Perry and Hamilton, Ont.; studied under William Cruikshank, Central Ontario School of Art, Toronto, c.1881-84; Gerald Maira, W.R. Lethalay, and A.B. Pite, Royal College of Art, London, England for two years c.1885; University of New York.

CAREER
Itinerant art teacher in Ontario during the late 1880s; Upper Canada College, Toronto, drawing master 1891-1920, house master 1896-1901; St. Andrew's College, Toronto, drawing master for a number of years; Toronto Art School, teacher; Ontario College of Art, Toronto, head of department of design, later lecturer in art history and head of department of elementary art 1912-30; illustrated Rambles of a Canadian naturalist, by S.T. Wood, Dent, 1916; teacher and painter in Toronto c.1890-1930.

MEMBER
Toronto Art Students' League (co-founder, 1890; president, 1891-1904); Society of Graphic Art (president, 1909-11); Mahlstick Club, Toronto; Ontario Society of Artists (elected, 1909; president, 1919-23); Royal Canadian Academy (Associate 1909; Academician 1919); Canadian Society of Applied Art (vice-president, 1909); Arts and Letters Club, Toronto (elected, 1908).

EXHIBITIONS
GROUP: Represented in group exhibitions held in Canada during his lifetime including annual exhibitions of Ontario Society of Artists and Royal Canadian Academy; A Century of Canadian Art, Tate Gallery, London, 1938.

COLLECTIONS IN WHICH REPRESENTED
Art Gallery of Ontario, Toronto; National Gallery of Canada, Ottawa, Ont.

HOOD, Robert Allison 1880-1958
Novelist; b. 20 Mar. 1880 in Cupar, Fife, Scotland; son of John and Margaret (Bennet) Hood; came to Canada c.1906 and settled in Vancouver, BC; d. 1958.

EDUCATION
Attended Bell Baxter Academy, Cupar and Harris Academy, Dundee, Scotland; University of

California, Berkeley, BL, 1905, ML, 1914.
RELIGION
Presbyterian.
CAREER
Hood Brothers (real estate), Vancouver 1906-58.
MEMBER
Canadian Authors Association (past vice-president;
Vancouver branch, former chairman); Vancouver
City Library Board.
WRITINGS
The chivalry of Keith Leicester, McClelland &
Stewart, 1918; *The quest of Alistair,* McClelland
& Stewart, 1921; *By shore and trail in Stanley
Park* (non-fiction), McClelland & Stewart, 1929;
The case of Kinnear, Macmillan, 1942; *Ballads
of the Pacific North-West,* Ryerson, 1946;
Vignettes of Vancouver (poems), Education
Services, 1954.

HOORN, Carol Lucille
see FRASER, Carol Lucille

HOUSSER, Muriel Yvonne McKague
see HOUSSER, Yvonne McKague

HOUSSER, Yvonne McKague* 1898–
(Muriel Yvonne McKague Housser)
Artist; b. 4 Aug. 1898 in Toronto, Ont.;
daughter of Hugh Henry and Louise (Elliott)
McKague; m. Frederick Broughton Housser 1935.
EDUCATION
Studied under Robert Holmes (*q.v.*), G.A. Reid
(*q.v.*), and J.W. Beatty, Ontario College of
Art, Toronto, 1915-19, post-graduate course,
1920; Lucien Simon, René Prinet, and Maurice
Denis, Académie de la Grande Chaumière,
Académie Colarossi, and Académie Ranson, Paris
1921-22 and 1924; Cizek in Vienna, Austria,
summer 1930; Emil Bisttram, Taos, N. Mex.,
1939; Hans Hofmann, Provincetown, Mass., for
two summers in the 1950s.
RELIGION
Theosophical Society of Canada.
HOME
11 Marconi Court, Willowdale, Ont.
CAREER
Ontario College of Art, instructor *c.* 1923-46;
Doon School of Fine Arts, Ont., summer session
instructor; Ontario Department of Education
summer courses at the Art Gallery of Toronto,
instructor; Port Hope Summer School, Ont.,
instructor; Ryerson Institute, Toronto, instructor; Hart House Theatre, Toronto, set and
costume designer; worked as a illustrator and
designed covers for *Canadian home journal*;
painter in Toronto 1920–.
COMMISSIONS
Murals, CPR.
MEMBER
Royal Canadian Academy (Associate 1942;

Academician 1951; member of council, 1963-64);
Ontario Society of Artists (elected, 1928; some-
time member of executive); Canadian Group of
Painters (co-founder; former president); Feder-
ation of Canadian Artists; Heliconian Club,
Toronto.
AWARDS, HONOURS
Scholarships, Ontario College of Art, 1915-19;
purchase award, Canadian National Exhibition
1953; Baxter award, Ontario Society of Artists,
1965.
EXHIBITION
ONE-MAN: Victoria College, University of
Toronto; Heliconian Club, Toronto; Calverley
Gallery, Richmond Hill, Ont., 1965.
GROUP: Represented in group exhibitions held
in Canada from 1923 on including annual exhibi-
tions of Royal Canadian Academy, Ontario Society
of Artists, Canadian Society of Graphic Art,
Canadian Group of Painters, and Canadian National
Exhibitions; represented in exhibitions organized
by National Gallery of Canada, Ottawa, Ont.,
including its Annual Exhibitions and its first
Biennial Exhibition of Canadian Painting, 1955;
Canadian Section of Fine Arts, British Empire
Exhibition, Wembley, England, 1925; Paintings by
Contemporary Canadian Artists, an exhibition
circulated in the United States by the American
Federation of Arts, 1930; Exhibition of Contem-
porary Painting Arranged ... for Circulation in
the Southern Dominions of the British Empire,
1936; Exhibition of Paintings, Drawings and
Sculpture by Artists of the British Empire Over-
seas, Royal Institute Galleries, London, England,
1937; Great Lakes Exhibition Assembled by the
Albright-Knox Art Gallery, Buffalo, NY, 1939;
A Century of Canadian Art, Tate Gallery, London,
1938; World's Fair, New York, NY, 1939; *Pintura
Canadense Contemporanea,* Rio de Janeiro,
Brazil, 1944; Canadian Women Artists, Riverside
Museum, New York, 1947; Contemporary Cana-
dian Painting, Canadian Club, New York, 1948;
Painters of Canada ... 1668-1948, Virginia Museum
of Fine Arts, Richmond, Va., 1949; Canadian
Painting and Sculpture, American British Art
Gallery, New York, 1951.
COLLECTIONS IN WHICH REPRESENTED
Art Gallery of Ontario, Toronto; Hart House
Permanent Collection, University of Toronto;
London Public Library and Art Museum, Ont.;
National Gallery of Canada; Trinity College, Uni-
versity of Toronto; Victoria College, University
of Toronto; Peterborough Public Library, Ont.;
McMichael Conservation Collection of Art,
Kleinburg, Ont.

HUMPHREY, Jack Weldon 1901-67
Artist; b. 12 Jan. 1901 in Saint John, NB; son
of Charles Percy and Nellie Alberta (Weldon)
Humphrey; m. Jean Elizabeth Fowler 18 June

1942; d. 23 Mar. 1967 in Saint John.

EDUCATION

Attended Mount Allison University 1917-18; studied under Philip Hale, Boston Museum School of Fine Arts, Mass., 1920-24; attended National Academy of Design, New York, NY, winters 1924-29; studied under Charles Hawthorne at National Academy of Design, 1927-29; attended Cape Cod School of Art, Provincetown, Mass., summers 1925-29; studied under Charles Hawthorne at Cape Cod School of Art, summers 1925-27 and 1929; Hans Hofmann in Munich, Germany, spring 1930.

RELIGION

Protestant.

CAREER

Travelled and studied in Europe for nine months 1929/30; painted in Saint John 1930-52, 1954-67; painted in Mexico for two and a half months 1938; Queen's University Summer School, art teacher 1945; painted in France 1952-54; frequent visits to New York 1954-67.

MEMBER

Eastern Group (charter member; later resigned); Canadian Group of Painters; Canadian Society of Painters in Water Colour (director, 1944; vice-president, 1945); Canadian Society of Graphic Art (regional representative, 1946, 1956, and 1959; eastern vice-president, 1951); Contemporary Arts Society, Montreal, PQ, (until its dissolution); Canadian Arts Council Committee of the International Association of Plastic Arts; Royal Canadian Academy (declined nomination, 1950).

AWARDS, HONOURS

LLD from University of New Brunswick, 1951; Canadian Government Royal Society overseas fellowship, 1952; Canada Council short term grant, 1958; prize, Winnipeg Show, Winnipeg Art Gallery, Man., 1958; Canada Council senior arts fellowship, 1960; first purchase prize, First Atlantic Awards Exhibition of Dalhousie University, 1961.

EXHIBITIONS

ONE-MAN: Picture Loan Society, Toronto, Ont., 1938 and 1939; Montreal Museum of Fine Arts, 1943 and 1955; Vancouver Art Gallery, BC, 1945; Yacht Club, St. Andrews, NB, 1946; Cody Art Gallery, Saint John, 1946 and 1947; Commodore Hotel, St. Andrews, 1948; New Brunswick Museum, Saint John, 1949, 1954, and 1964; Mount Allison University, 1949 and 1954; University of New Brunswick, 1950, 1961, and 1965; Robertson Galleries, Ottawa, Ont., 1954; Walter Klinkhoff Gallery, Montreal, 1962 and 1965; Penthouse Gallery, Montreal, 1964; National Gallery of Canada, Ottawa, 1966 and later toured Canada 1966-67.

GROUP: Represented in group exhibitions held in Canada from 1929 on including annual exhibitions of Canadian Society of Painters in Water Colour, Canadian Group of Painters, and Canadian Society of Graphic Art; represented in group exhibitions organized by National Gallery of Canada, Ottawa, including its first, second, third, and fifth Biennial Exhibitions of Canadian Painting, 1955, 1957, 1959, and 1963; Philadelphia Water Color Society exhibition, 1929; New York Water Color Club exhibition, 1929; A Century of Canadian Art, Tate Gallery, London, England, 1938; Exhibition of Canadian Water Colours, toured cities in England and Scotland, 1939; World's Fair, New York, 1939; International Biennial Water Colour Exhibition, Brooklyn Museum, Brooklyn, NY, 1941; Aspects of Contemporary Painting in Canada, Addison Gallery, Andover, Mass., 1942-43; Exhibition of Prints by Artists of the United Nations, Philadelphia, Pa., 1943; Exhibition of Canadian Art, Smith College, Northampton, Mass., 1943; *Pintura Canadense Contemporanea*, Rio de Janeiro, Brazil, 1944; Canadian Art 1760-1943, Yale University Art Gallery, 1944; Canadian Water Colors, Grand Central Galleries, New York, 1945; Exhibition of Canadian Graphic Arts, São Paulo, Brazil, and Rio de Janeiro, 1946; Exhibition of Canadian Water Colours, Philadelphia, 1946; *UNESCO ... Exposition internationale d'art moderne, peinture, graphique et décoratif, architecture*, Musée d'Art Moderne, Paris, France, 1946; Exhibition of Canadian Art, Canadian Club, New York, 1948; Painters of Canada ... 1668-1948, Virginia Museum of Fine Arts, Richmond, Va., 1949; Exhibition of Canadian Art, London, 1949; Canadian Painting, National Gallery of Art, Washington, DC, 1950; Seattle Art Museum exhibition, Wash., 1950; University of Maine exhibition, Orono, Me., U.S.A. 1951; Canadian Painting, Legion Grounds, San Francisco, Calif., 1951; Pennsylvania Academy exhibition, Philadelphia, 1952; International Exhibition, New Delhi, India, 1953; Canadian section of the *Salon de l'Art Libre*, Musée d'Art Moderne, Paris, 1953; National Arts Club exhibition, New York, 1954; An Exhibition of Canadian Paintings held at Fortnum and Mason Limited, London, 1955; Portfolio of Canadian Art, Dallas, Tex., 1958; Canadian Water Colours and Prints, American Federation of Arts tour, 1959-60; Canadian Art, Instituto National de Bellas Artes, Mexico City, Mexico, 1960-61; *Art au Canada*, Musée de Bordeaux, France, 1962; Commonwealth Art Today, London, 1962 and Edinburgh, Scotland, 1963; New York artists exhibition, Brussels, Belgium, 1964; Canadian Drawings and Prints, Commonwealth Arts Festival, Cardiff, Wales, 1965.

COLLECTIONS IN WHICH REPRESENTED
Atlantic House, London; Art Gallery of Ontario, Toronto; Canadian Industries Ltd. Collection, Montreal; Canadian Embassies in Washington, Moscow, USSR, The Hague, The Netherlands, Oslo, Norway, Caracas, Venezuela, Colombo, Ceylon, and Tokyo, Japan; Confederation Art Gallery and Museum, Charlottetown, PEI; Dalhousie University; Edmonton Art Gallery, Alta.; Hart House Permanent Collection, University of Toronto; London Public Library and Art Museum, Ont.; Beaverbrook Art Gallery, Fredericton, NB; Memorial University of Newfoundland; National Gallery of Canada; New Brunswick Museum, Saint John; Royal Victoria College, McGill University; Saint John Art Club; Seagram Collection, Montreal; Sir George Williams University; University of New Brunswick; Winnipeg Art Gallery; Department of Transport, Ottawa; Mount Allison University; University of Moncton.

HURRY, Leslie 1909–
Designer and artist; b. 10 Feb. 1909 in London, England; son of Alfred George and Edith Louise Perry (Butcher) Hurry.
EDUCATION
Attended St. John's Wood Art School, London; Royal Academy Schools of Painting and Sculpture, London.
HOME
"The Bunting's," Hundon, nr. Clare, Suffolk, England.
OFFICE
c/o Festival Theatre, Stratford, Ont.
CAREER
Sadler's Wells (now Royal) Ballet Company, London, designer 1942–; Old Vic Theatre Company, London, designer 1944, 1951, 1954-61; Covent Garden Opera Company, Royal Opera House, London, designer 1947, 1954, 1958, 1960; Shakespeare Memorial (now Royal Shakespeare) Theatre Company, Stratford-upon-Avon, England, designer 1949, 1950, 1960; Sadler's Wells Opera Company, London, designer 1957–; illustrated *David Copperfield*, by Charles Dickens, Macmillan 1952.
THEATRE
Designed décor for *Hamlet* (ballet; Sadler's Wells Ballet, New, 19 May 1942; Royal Opera House, Covent Garden, 2 Apr. 1964), *Le lac des cygnes* (Sadler's Wells Ballet, New, 7 Sept. 1943; Royal Opera House, Covent Garden, 14 Dec. 1952; 1965), *Hamlet* (Old Vic, Apr. 1944; Royal Shakespeare Theatre, 1963), *Turandot* (Covent Garden, May 1947), *Medea* (Globe, London, 29 Sept. 1948), *Cymbeline* (Shakespeare Memorial Theatre, May 1949), *King Lear* (Shakespeare Memorial Theatre, July 1950; Old Vic, 19 Feb. 1958; Stratford, Ont. Festival, 1964), *Tamburlaine the great*

(Old Vic, 24 Sept. 1951; Winter Garden, New York, NY, 19 Jan. 1956), *La scherzi della sortie* (Ballet Rambert, London, 1952), *The living room* (Wyndham's, London, 16 Apr. 1953), *Venice preserv'd* (Lyric, Hammersmith, London, 15 May 1953), *La forza del destino* (Edinburgh Festival, Scotland, 1952), *Der Ring der Nibelungen* (Covent Garden Opera, 1954), *The tempest* (Old Vic, 13 Apr. 1954; 29 May 1962), *Richard II* (Old Vic, 1955), *Timon of Athens* (Old Vic, 5 Sept. 1956), *The gates of summer* (UK tour, 1956), *The moon and sixpence* (Sadler's Wells Opera, 24 May 1957), *Richard III* (Old Vic, 29 May 1957), *The hidden king* (Edinburgh Festival, 1957), *Henry VI*, parts I, II, III (Old Vic, 1957), *Cat on a hot tin roof* (Comedy, London, 30 Jan. 1958), *Mary Stuart* (Old Vic, 17 Sept. 1958), *Tristan und Isolde* (Covent Garden Opera, 4 June 1958), *The Cenci* (Old Vic, 29 Apr. 1959), *Andrea Chénier* (Sadler's Wells Opera, 13 Oct. 1959), *Saint Joan* (Old Vic, 9 Feb. 1960), *Troilus and Cressida* (Shakespeare Memorial Theatre, 26 July 1960; Aldwych, London, 15 Oct. 1962), *Das Rheingold* (Covent Garden Opera, 1960), *The duchess of Malfi* (Aldwych, London, 15 Dec. 1960), *Becket* (Royal Shakespeare Theatre, Aldwych, London, 11 July 1961), *Mourning becomes Electra* (Old Vic, 21 Nov. 1961); costumes for *The beggar's opera* (Royal Shakespeare Theatre, Aldwych, London, 16 July 1963); designed *John Gabriel Borkman* (Duchess, London, 4 Dec. 1963); costumes for *Maggie May* (Adelphi, London, 22 Sept. 1964); designed *Julius Caesar* (Stratford, Ont. Festival, 16 June 1965), *Fidelio* (Sadler's Wells Opera Company, 1965), *Nicholas Romanov* (Manitoba Theatre Centre, Winnipeg, Man., 9 Mar. 1966), *The last of the tsars* (Stratford, Ont. Festival, 12 July 1966), *Queen of spades* (Sadler's Wells Opera, 1966), *The government inspector* (Stratford, Ont. Festival, 1967), *Albert Herring* (Stratford, Ont. Festival, 1967), *A midsummer night's dream* (Stratford, Ont. Festival, 12 June 1968), *Cinderella* (opera; Stratford, Ont. Festival, 6 July 1968).
WRITINGS
Leslie Hurry: settings and costumes, edited by Lillian Browse, Faber & Faber, 1946; *Paintings and drawings*, Grey Walls Press, 1950 [1952].
EXHIBITIONS
ONE-MAN: Wertheim Gallery, 1937; Redfern Gallery, London, 1941, 1942, 1945; Roland, Browse & Delbanco, London, 1946-50.
GROUP: Paintings and theatre designs in National Gallery of Canada, Ottawa, Ont.; theatre designs in Arts Council, UK, 1964.
COLLECTIONS IN WHICH REPRESENTED
Victoria and Albert Museum, London; Birmingham City Art Gallery, England; Whitworth Art Gallery, Manchester, England; Brighton Art Gallery, England; Melbourne Art Gallery, Australia.

HURTUBISE, Jacques* 1939–
Artist; b. 28 Feb. 1939 in Montreal; son of Paul and Clotilde (Savoie) Hurtubise; m. Monique Colangelo June 1961; children: Nathalie b. 12 Dec. 1963.

EDUCATION
Attended École des Beaux-Arts, Montréal, 1956-60.

HOME
10221-52 Ave., Rivières des Prairies, Montréal 39, PQ.

CAREER
Travelled in Quebec, the Maritimes, and Newfoundland, summers 1959 and 1960; painted in New York, NY, 1960-61; Dartmouth College, Hanover, NH, artist in residence 1967; painter in Montreal 1961–.

AWARDS, HONOURS
Purchase prize, Spring Exhibition, Montreal Museum of Fine Arts, 1958; Max Beckman scholarship, 1960-61; grand prize for painting, Concours Artistique de la Province de Québec, 1965; Canada Council scholarships 1965 and 1966; Canada Council arts bursary, 1966/67.

EXHIBITIONS
ONE-MAN: Montreal Museum of Fine Arts, 1961; Galerie Denyse Delrue, Montréal, 1962 and 1963; Galerie du Siècle, Montreal, 1964, 1965, and 1966; Galerie Nova et Vetera, Montréal, 1965; East Hampton Gallery, New York, 1966 and 1967; Travelling Exhibition, Eastern Canada Art Circuit, 1966; Hopkins Center Art Galleries, Dartmouth College, 1967; Isaacs Gallery, Toronto, Ont., 1967; Dunkelman Gallery, Toronto, 1967.
GROUP: Represented in group exhibitions held in Canada since 1958 including Spring Exhibitions of Montreal Museum of Fine Arts; represented in group exhibitions organized by National Gallery of Canada, Ottawa, Ont., including its fifth and sixth Biennial Exhibitions of Canadian Painting, 1963 and 1965; eighth and ninth International Biennial Exhibitions of São Paulo, Brazil, 1965 and 1967; Nine Canadians, Institute of Contemporary Art, Boston, Mass., 1967; Seven Canadians, Massachusetts Institute of Technology, Cambridge, 1968; Art d'Aujourd'hui, Paris, France, Rome, Italy, and Lausanne, Switzerland, 1968.

COLLECTIONS IN WHICH REPRESENTED
Musée du Québec, PQ; Sir George Williams University; Musée d'Art Contemporain, Montréal; Saskatoon Art Centre, Sask.; National Gallery of Canada; Department of External Affairs, Ottawa; Department of Education, Quebec; Pirelli International Ltd.; Dartmouth College; Canada Council, Ottawa; Toronto Dominion Bank, Toronto; Massachusetts Institute of Technology; Art Gallery of Ontario, Toronto; Vancouver Art Gallery, BC; Memorial University of Newfoundland.

HUTCHISON, Margaret
Author; b. in Salmon Arm, BC.

CAREER
School teacher in BC.

WRITINGS
Tamarac (novel), Macmillan, 1957; radio scripts and plays for school broadcasts.
CONTRIBUTED: Poetry to magazines, e.g. Canadian poetry.

HYLAND, Frances 1927–
(Frances Hyland McCowan)
Actress; b. 25 Apr. 1927 in Shaunavon, Sask.; daughter of Thomas and Jessie (Worden) Hyland; m. George McCowan; children: Evan.

EDUCATION
University of Saskatchewan, BA in English, 1948; Royal Academy of Dramatic Art, London, England, 1948-50.

HOME
84 Poplar Plains Crescent, Toronto 7, Ont.

CAREER
H.M. Tennent, London, actress 1950-54; Stratford, Ont. Festival, actress 1954-55, 1957-59, 1964–; Canadian Players, Toronto, actress 1955- ?; Crest Theatre, Toronto, actress 1954-65; Manitoba Theatre Centre, Winnipeg, actress 1966–; Playhouse Theatre Company, Vancouver, BC, actress 1966–.

MEMBER
AEA; ACTRA.

AWARDS, HONOURS
Scholarship from IODE, Regina Little Theatre, and Princess Patricia Club, Regina, Sask., 1948; scholarship from Royal Academy of Dramatic Art, 1949; silver medal from Royal Academy of Dramatic Art.

THEATRE
Played Stella Kowalsky in A streetcar named Desire (Aldwych, London, June 1950), Perdita in The winter's tale (Edinburgh Festival, Scotland, 1950; Stratford, Ont. Festival, 1958), Caroline in The guilty party, Jackie Fuller in The gentle rain, Esther Brodsky in The same sky (Lyric, Hammersmith, London, Jan. 1952; Duke of York's, London, 18 Mar. 1952), Mary Silver in The step forward (Strand, London, July 1952), Hester Worsley in A woman of no importance (Savoy, London, 12 Feb. 1953), Gertie in The little idiot ("Q," Kew, London, Nov. 1953), Gelda in The dark is light enough (Lyceum, Edinburgh, Feb. 1954), Isabella in Measure for measure (Stratford, Ont. Festival, 1954), Bianca in The taming of the shrew (Stratford, Ont. Festival, 1954), The living room (Crest, 1954/55), The confidential clerk (Crest, 1954/55), Portia in The merchant of Venice (Stratford, Ont. Festival, 1955), title role in Saint Joan (Canadian Players, tour 1955/56), Second witch and Lady Macbeth in Macbeth (Canadian Players, tour 1955/56), Ophelia in Hamlet (Cana-

dian Players, tour 1956/57; Stratford, Ont. Festival, 1957), Solveig and Anitra in *Peer Gynt* (Canadian Players, tour 1956/57), Olivia in *Twelfth night* (Stratford, Ont. Festival, 1957), Laura James in *Look homeward, angel* (Ethel Barrymore, New York, NY, 28 Nov. 1957), Eliza Doolittle in *Pygmalion* (Crest, 1958/59), *The good woman of Setzuan* (Goodman, Chicago, Ill., 1958/59), Desdemona in *Othello* (Stratford, Ont. Festival, 1959), Phebe in *As you like it* (Stratford, Ont. Festival, 1959), Fleur-Therese Haugabrook in *A time to laugh* (Piccadilly, London, 24 Apr. 1962), Pip in *Moby Dick* (Ethel Barrymore, New York, 28 Nov. 1962) *Masterpieces of comedy* (Canadian Players, Canadian and American tour 1962/63), Princess in *Love's labour's lost* (Stratford, Ont. Festival Company, Chichester, England, Apr. 1964), Lucile in *The bourgeois gentleman* (Stratford, Ont. Festival Company, Chichester, Apr. 1964; Stratford, Ont. Festival, 1964), Guest in *Timon of Athens* (Stratford, Ont. Festival Company, Chichester, Apr. 1964), Goneril in *King Lear* (Stratford, Ont. Festival, 1964), Mrs. Dainty Fidget in *The country wife* (Stratford, Ont. Festival, 1964), Cleopatra in *Caesar and Cleopatra* (Crest, 1964), Cathrine in *Mother Courage* (Manitoba Theatre Centre, 1964), Doll Tearsheet in *Henry IV,* part II (Stratford, Ont. Festival, 15 June 1965), Calpurnia in *Julius Caesar* (Stratford, Ont. Festival, 16 June 1965), Varya in *The cherry orchard* (Stratford, Ont. Festival, 26 July 1965), Doreen in *The private ear* and Belinda Sidley in *The public eye* (Crest, 17 Oct. 1965), Ariel in *The tempest* (Manitoba Theatre Centre, 12 Jan. 1966), Tsarina in *Nicholas Romanoff* (Manitoba Theatre Centre, 9 Mar. 1966), Margaret of Anjou in *Henry VI* (Stratford, Ont. Festival, 7 June 1966), Anya Vyroubova in *The last of the tsars* (Stratford, Ont. Festival, 12 July 1966), Queen Margaret in *Richard III* (Stratford, Ont. Festival, 1967), Mistress Ford in *The merry wives of Windsor* (Stratford, Ont. Festival, 1967), Blanche DuBois in *A streetcar named Desire* (Playhouse, 29 Feb. 1968), Lady Utterword in *Heartbreak House* (Shaw Festival, Niagara-on-the-Lake, Ont., 27 June 1968), Francine in *The chemmy circle* (Shaw Festival, Niagara-on-the-Lake, 8 Aug. 1968).

FILM

Played in *The performer*, part II (National Film Board of Canada 0159050), narrator in *Cattle ranch* (National Film Board of Canada 0161068), *The drylanders* (National Film Board of Canada 0164044), *Each day that comes* (National Film Board of Canada 0166008).

RADIO

Played in several CBC productions, e.g. title role in *The lady of the camelias* ("Stage," 12 Feb. 1967), Helen in *The soldiers* ("Stage," 26 May 1968).

TELEVISION

Played in many CBC productions, e.g. *The heiress* (1958/59), *Not made in heaven* (1958/59), guest star on "RCMP," (series, 1959), Sybil in *Desire* ("The unforeseen," 10 Feb. 1960), *The old ladies* ("Festival," 31 Oct. 1960), Queen Victoria in *Durham's Canada* ("Explorations," 14, 21, 28 Dec. 1960), Calpurnia in *Julius Caesar* ("Festival," 19 Dec. 1960), voice in *Full of grace* (24 Dec. 1960), *The vigilante* ("GM presents," 29 Jan. 1961), *The three sisters* ("Festival," 13 Feb. 1961), teacher in *The test* ("Explorations," 28 Feb. 1962), title role in *The Duchess of Malfi* ("Festival," 19 Mar. 1962), *Bedtime story* ("Quest," 19 Mar. 1962), Wife in *Grand exits* ("Festival," 16 Apr. 1962), Rachel in *Question of fact* ("Playdate," 15 Nov. 1962), title role in *Major Barbara* ("Festival," 8 Jan. 1964), Katherine in *Silent night, lonely night* ("Festival," 1 Dec. 1965; 14 Dec. 1966).

ILIAL, Léo

Actor.

HOME

4650 Earnscliffe Ave., Montreal 248, PQ.

CAREER

Théâtre du Nouveau Monde, Montréal, actor 19?- ? [1965−].

MEMBER

Union des Artistes de Montréal; Canadian Theatre Centre.

THEATRE

Played in many productions, e.g. Chrysalde in *L'école des femmes* (Nouveau Monde, 20 Oct. 1965), Cibo in *Lorenzaccio* (Nouveau Monde, 21 Nov. 1965), Mikhail Lvovitch Astrov in *L'oncle Vania* (Théâtre de l'Égrégore, Montréal, 4 Jan. 1966), John Hale in *Les sorcières de Salem* (Nouveau Monde, 9 Jan. 1966), Kurt in *The dance of death* (Manitoba Theatre Centre, Winnipeg, 6 Apr. 1966), *Du vent dans les branches de Sassafras* (Théâtre du Rideau Vert, Montréal, 15 Nov. 1966), *Le soulier de satin* (Nouveau Monde, 7 Jan. 1967), *On n'a pas tué Joe Hill* (Nouveau Monde, 18 Feb. 1967), *Été* (Montreal International Theatre, 10 July 1967), *Bois-brûlés* (Nouveau Monde, 3 Nov. 1967), *Pygmalion* (Nouveau Monde, 12 Jan. 1968), *Le rhinoceros* (Nouveau Monde, 22 Mar. 1968), *Bilan* (Nouveau Monde, 4 Oct. 1968), *La nuit des rois* (Nouveau Monde, 13 Dec. 1968).

RADIO

Played in many productions, e.g. *Milmort* (CBC, Vancouver, 28 Oct. 1968).

IRWIN, Grace Lilian* 1907−

Novelist; b. 14 July 1907 in Toronto; daughter of John and Martha (Fortune) Irwin.

EDUCATION
Attended Howard School and Parkdale Collegiate
Institute, Toronto; University of Toronto, BA in
classics and English, 1929, MA in Greek, 1932;
Ontario College of Education, specialist's certifi-
cate.
RELIGION
Christian.
HOME
33 Glenwood Avenue, Toronto, Ont.
CAREER
Humberside Collegiate Institute, Toronto, teacher
of Latin, English, and history 1931-42, head of
Latin and Greek department 1942–; University of
Toronto, Senate member 1952-56; travelled ex-
tensively in Britain and Europe.
MEMBER
Toronto Classical Club (past president); Ontario
Classical Association (executive committee);
Canadian Classical Association.
AWARDS, HONOURS
Centennial medal.
WRITINGS
Least of all saints, McClelland & Stewart, 1952
(translated into German and Norwegian);
Andrew Connington, McClelland & Stewart,
1954 (translated into German); *In little place,*
Ryerson, 1959; *Servant of slaves,* McClelland
& Stewart, 1961 (translated into German and
Chinese); *Contend with horses,* Eerdmans,
1968.
CONTRIBUTED: Poems and articles to *Little
songs for little people,* edited by B.L. Kurth
and M. McManns, Clarke, Irwin, 1943; *Saturday
night, The family herald, His.*

JABEZ, pseud.
see NICOL, Eric Patrick

JACKSON, Alexander Young* 1882–
Artist; b. 3 Oct. 1882 in Montreal, PQ; son of
Henry A. and Georgina (Young) Jackson.
EDUCATION
Attended Prince Albert Public School, Montreal,
until 1894; studied under William Brymner (*q.v.*),
Royal Canadian Academy night classes in Mont-
real *c.*1900-05; Walter M. Clute and Frederick
Richardson, Art Institute of Chicago, Ill.,
evening classes, 1906-07; Jean-Paul Laurens,
Académie Julian, Paris, France, 1907-08.
RELIGION
Anglican.
HOME
McMichael Conservation Collection of Art,
Kleinburg, Ont.
CAREER
Employed first briefly as an office boy, later as
an apprentice in lithography by a lithographing

company in Montreal 1894-1900; Adam Beck's
printing house, designer 1900-05; travelled in
Europe, two months in 1905; Lammers
Schilling Co., Chicago, designer 1906; studied in
Europe 1907-09; employed by a photo-engraving
firm in Montreal as an artist 1910-11; painted in
Ontario 1913-14; painted near Jasper Park, Alta.,
summer 1914; Canadian Army 1915-1918,
official war artist 1917-19; painted in Toronto,
making painting trips to northern Ontario, Quebec,
Jasper Park, British Columbia, the Arctic, Great
Bear Lake, Alaska Highway, and elsewhere in
Canada 1919-55; illustrated *Chez nous (Our old
Quebec home),* by Adjutor Rivard, McClelland
& Stewart, 1924; appointed member of the
Canadian War Artists Committee 1942; Banff
Summer School of Fine Arts, Alta., teacher
1943-47 and 1949; painted in Manotick, Ont.,
1955-61; painter in Ottawa 1961–.
MEMBER
Group of Seven (co-founder, 1920); Canadian
Group of Painters (co-founder); Royal Canadian
Academy (Associate 1914, Academician 1919;
resigned, 1932; reinstated, 1953); Ontario Society
of Artists (elected, 1914); Arts and Letters Club,
Toronto (elected, 1913).
AWARDS, HONOURS
LL D from Queen's University, 1941; CMG, 1946;
LL D from McMaster University, 1953; LL D from
Carleton University, 1957; Canada Council medal,
1961/62; LL D from University of Saskatche-
wan, 1963; LL D from University of British
Columbia, 1966; D LITT from McGill University,
1967; Companion of the Order of Canada, 1967.
EXHIBITIONS
ONE-MAN: Art Gallery of Toronto, 1953;
National Gallery of Canada, Ottawa, 1953; Art
Gallery of Hamilton, Ont., 1960.
GROUP: Represented in group exhibitions held
in Canada including annual exhibitions of
Ontario Society of Artists, Royal Canadian
Academy, and Canadian Group of Painters and
exhibitions of Group of Seven; represented in
group exhibitions organized by National Gallery
of Canada, Ottawa; Paintings by Canadian Artists,
City Art Museum, St. Louis, Mo., 1918; Canadian
Section of Fine Arts, British Empire Exhibition,
Wembley, England, 1924; Sesqui-Centennial
International Exposition, Philadelphia, Pa.,
1926; *Exposition d'art canadien,* Musée du Jeu
de Paume, Paris, 1927; Fine Arts Academy,
Buffalo, NY, 1928; Museum of Fine Arts,
Boston, Mass., 1932; Contemporary Canadian
Painters, Roerich Museum, New York, NY,
1932; Exhibition of Contemporary Canadian
Painting Arranged ... for Circulation in the
Southern Dominions of the British Empire, 1936;
Exhibition of Paintings, Drawings and Sculpture
by Artists of the British Empire Overseas, Royal

Institute Galleries, London, England, 1937; A Century of Canadian Art, Tate Gallery, London, 1938; World's Fair, New York, 1939; University of Washington, 1942; Aspects of Contemporary Painting in Canada, Addison Gallery, Andover, Mass., 1942-43; *Pintura Canadense Contemporanea,* Rio de Janeiro, Brazil, 1944; Canadian Art 1760-1943, Yale University Art Gallery, 1944; Painting in Canada, a Selective Survey, Albany Institute of History and Art, Albany, NY, 1946; *UNESCO ... Exposition internationale d'art moderne, peinture, graphique et décoratif, architecture,* Musée d'Art Moderne, Paris, 1946; Canadian Painting, National Gallery of Art, Washington, DC, 1950; Colombo Plan Exhibition, Colombo, Ceylon, 1951; University of Maine, 1951; Florida State Fair, Tampa, 1952; International Exhibition, New Delhi, India, 1953; exhibition of Canadian painting shown in Pakistan, India and Ceylon, 1954-55; An Exhibition of Canadian Paintings Held at Fortnum and Mason Limited, London, 1955; *Art et Travail,* Musée d'Art, Geneva, Switzerland, 1957.

COLLECTIONS IN WHICH REPRESENTED
Art Gallery, Wellington, New Zealand; Art Gallery of Hamilton, Ont.; Art Gallery of Ontario, Toronto; Hart House Permanent Collection, University of Toronto; Montreal Museum of Fine Arts; Musée du Québec, PQ; National Gallery of Canada; Sarnia Public Library and Art Museum, Ont.; Springfield Gallery, Springfield, Ill.; Tate Gallery; Vancouver Art Gallery, BC; Sir George Williams University; Art Gallery of Greater Victoria, BC; McMichael Conservation Collection of Art, Kleinburg, Ont.; Owens Museum, Mount Allison University.

WRITINGS
The far north, Rous and Mann, 1928; *Banting as an artist,* Ryerson, 1943; *A painter's country,* Clarke, Irwin, 1958.
CONTRIBUTED: Articles to *Canadian art.*

JACQUELIN, pseud.
see DESILETS, Alphonse

JAMIESON, Edna Jaques
see JAQUES, Edna

JAQUES, Edna* 1891–
(Edna Jaques Jamieson)
Poet; b. 17 Jan. 1891 in Collingwood, Ont.; daughter of Charles A. and Ellen (Donohue) Jaques; m. William E. Jamieson 30 Nov. 1921 (deceased); children: Joyce b. 6 Jan. 1923.
EDUCATION
Attended public schools in Collingwood and Briercrest, Sask.; business college in Victoria, BC.
RELIGION
United Church.

HOME
7 Honeywell Place, Willowdale, Ont.
CAREER
Lecture tours across Canada; Wartime Prices and Trade Board, Ottawa, Ont., feature writer 1941-47; lecturer in New England states, 1947-48.
MEMBER
Canadian Authors Association; Canadian Press Club; Canadian Club.
WRITINGS
Drifting soil, Times Herald, 1934; *Wide horizons,* Times Herald, 1934; *My kitchen window,* Allen, 1935; *Dreams in your heart,* Allen, 1937; *Beside still waters,* Allen, 1939; *Britons awake,* Allen, 1940; *Aunt Hattie's place,* Allen, 1941; *Roses in December,* Allen, 1944; *Back door neighbors,* Allen, 1946; *Hills of home,* 1948; *Fireside poems,* Allen, 1950; *The golden road,* Alleln, 1953; *The best of Edna Jaques,* Modern Press, 1966.
CONTRIBUTED: Poetry to *The desk drawer anthology,* compiled by A.R. Longworth and T. Roosevelt, Doubleday, Doran, 1937; *Flying colours,* edited by C.G.D. Roberts, Ryerson, 1942; *Masterpieces of religious verse,* edited by G.D. Morrison, Harper, 1948; *Poems for red letter days,* compiled by E.H. Sechrist, Macrae Smith, 1951; *Canadian poetry in English,* edited by B. Carman and others, rev. & enl. ed., Ryerson, 1954; many periodicals, e.g. *Canadian home journal, Canadian author and bookman, Country guide, Maclean's, National home monthly.*

JARVIS, Lilian 1931–
Dancer and teacher; b. 1931 in Toronto, Ont.
EDUCATION
Studied ballet with Mildred Wickson and Boris Volkoff in Toronto; modern dance with Martha Graham, New York, NY.
CAREER
National Ballet of Canada, Toronto (charter member), corps de ballet 1951/52, soloist 1952-60, 1961-63; National Ballet School of Canada, Toronto, teacher 196?- ? .
MEMBER
AEA.
AWARDS, HONOURS
Canada Council arts scholarship, 1962/63 and general award 1964/65.
THEATRE
Danced in *Carousel* (Drury Lane, London, England, 1950), Swanhilda in *Coppelia* (St. Leon), Sugar Plum Fairy and Snow Queen in *Cassenoisette* (Franca after Ivanov), title role in *Giselle* (Coralli-Perrot), Odette in *Le lac des cygnes,* act II (Petipa-Ivanov), *Le jardin aux lilas* (Tudor); created Mermaid in *The fisherman and his soul* (Strate, Palace, Hamilton, Ont., 5 Nov. 1956), Rose in *Ballad* (Strate, Capitol, Ottawa, Ont., 29 Oct. 1958); danced title role in *Pineapple Poll* (Cranko,

Hamilton, 3 Nov. 1959); created Fourth song in *Time cycle* (Strate, Stratford, Ont. Festival, 13 July 1962).

TELEVISION
Danced title role in *Pineapple Poll* (Cranko, "Ford startime," CBC, 22 Dec. 1959).

JASMIN, André 1922–

Artist; b. 7 Dec. 1922 in Montreal, PQ.

EDUCATION
Attended Collège de Joliette and Collège André-Grasset, Montréal; studied under Paul Émile Borduas, École du Meuble, Montréal.

CAREER
Designed sets and costumes for play by Molière 1945, for La Compagnie du Masque in Montreal, for Ruth Sorel's ballets *La Gaspésienne* and *Papatages;* designed and made marionnettes for Micheline Legendre 1948-49; gave lecture course in art history in his studio in Montreal; lecture series at the National Gallery of Canada, Ottawa, Ont. 1966; École des Beaux-Arts, Montréal, professor.

MEMBER
Association des Artistes non-figuratifs de Montréal (elected, 1956); Société d'Art Contemporain (elected, 1943).

AWARDS, HONOURS
Prize for painting, Concours Artistique de la Province de Québec, 1955.

EXHIBITIONS
ONE-MAN: Collège St. Laurent, Montréal, 1947; Librairie Tranquille, Montréal, 1948; Galerie Agnès Lefort, Montréal, 1951, 1952, 1953, 1954, and 1955; Collector's Gallery, New York, NY, 1956; Musée du Collège de Joliette, Montréal, 1957; Restaurant Hélène de Champlain, Montréal, 1957; Galerie Denyse Delrue, Montreal, 1958; Montreal Museum of Fine Arts, 1960; Galerie Libre, Montréal, 1960; Centre d'Art d'Alma, Montréal, 1960; Galerie Delisle, Chicoutimi, PQ, 1960; Centrale de l'Association des Architectes de la Province de Québec, Montréal, 1962; Galerie Nova et Vetera, Montréal, 1963; Galerie Claude Haeffely, Montréal, 1963; Galerie Penthouse, Montréal, 1963; Centre d'Art d'Argenteuil, Lachute, PQ, 1964; Centre d'Art du Mont-Royal, Montréal, 1965.
GROUP: Represented in group exhibitions held in Canada since 1944 including annual exhibitions of Société d'Art Contemporain, Association des Artistes non-figuratifs de Montréal, Montreal Museum of Fine Arts; *Exposition itinérante de décors et costumes de théâtre* on tour in Canada and at the Museum of Modern Art, New York, 1949; *Arts contemporains du Canada* on tour in Europe, 1958-59; Aspects of Canadian Painting, Canada House, New York, 1959.

COLLECTIONS IN WHICH REPRESENTED
Canadian Industries Ltd. Collection, Montreal; Musée du Collège du Joliette; Musée du Québec, PQ, National Gallery of Canada, Ottawa, Ont.; Sir George Williams University.

JASMIN, Claude* 1930–

Playwright and novelist; b. 10 Nov. 1930 in Montreal, PQ; son of Edouard and Germaine (Lefebvre) Jasmin.

EDUCATION
Attended Collège André Grasset and Institut des Arts Appliqués, Montréal, diploma in ceramics, 1951.

HOME
11870 rue Zotique-Racicot, Montréal, PQ.

CAREER
Art teacher; *La presse*, Montréal, art critic 1961-66; *Sept jours,* Montréal, art critic 1967–; CBC, Montreal, television set designer and writer.

AWARDS, HONOURS
Cercle du Livre de France second prize for *Et puis tout est silence*, 1959, and first prize for *La corde au cou*, 1960; France-Québec prize for *Ethel et le terroriste*, 1965.

WRITINGS
Et puis tout est silence (novel), Écrits du Canada français, 1960; *La corde au cou* (novel), Cercle du Livre de France, 1960 (produced Cooperatio Film, 1965); *Délivrez-nous du mal* (novel), Page, 1961 (produced Cooperatio Film, 1966); *Ethel et le terroriste* (novel), Déom, 1964 (translated into English); *Pleure pas, Germaine* (novel), Parti Pris, 1965; *Les artisans créateurs* (non-fiction), Lidec, 1967; *Les coeurs empaillés: nouvelles,* Parti Pris, 1967; *La nouvelle gigue* (play; produced Dominion Drama Festival, 1955); several radio plays for CBC series "Les nouveautés dramatiques," 1951-56; *La rue de la liberté* (TV play; produced CBC, 1960); *La mort dans l'âme* (TV play; produced CBC, 1962); *Blues pour un homme averti* (play), Parti Pris, 1964 (produced CBC TV, 1963; L'Estoc, Québec, PQ, 1966); *Le veau d'or* (play; all trophies from Dominion Drama Festival, 1963); *Les mains vides* (TV play; produced CBC, 1965); *Pour vivre au portage* (centennial play; produced L'Assomption, PQ, 1967); *Tuer-kill* (play; produced Pavillon de la Jeunesse, Expo 67, Montréal); *Pour manger son père* (play; produced CBC, 1968); *L'escalier de l'oratoire* (play), 1968.
CONTRIBUTED: Articles to *Manifeste*, edited by R. Roussil, Jour, 1965; *Canadian art, Commerce, Liberté, Magazine Maclean, Vie des arts.*

JEFFERYS, Charles William 1869-1951

Artist; b. 25 Aug. 1869 in Rochester, Kent, England; son of Charles Thomas and Ellen (Kennard) Jefferys; m. Jane M.F. Adams 1894 (d. 1899); m. Clara Ada Beatrice West 1907; children: Katharine, Elizabeth, Margaret, Barbara,

Mrs. C.A. Thompson; d. Oct. 1951.

EDUCATION

Attended Dufferin Street school and Winchester Street school in Toronto, Ont.; studied under George A. Reid (*q.v.*) in Toronto in the 1880s; studied under Charles M. Manly (*q.v.*) in Toronto *c.*1890.

CAREER

Toronto Lithographing Company, apprentice for five years in the 1880s; *New York Herald,* NY, artist 1893-1900; contributed illustrations to the *Calendars* of Toronto Art Students League 1893-1904; returned to Canada 1900; illustrated books and magazines in Toronto; *Toronto daily star* and the *Globe*, Toronto, illustrator on commission in the early 1900s; co-founder and publisher (with Knox Magee) of *The moon* 1902-03; illustrated *Makers of Canada*, Morang & Co., 1911; University of Toronto, School of Architecture, instructor in drawing and painting 1912-29; illustrated *Chronicles of Canada*, Glasgow, Brook, 1915; artist for Canadian War Memorials 1916-18; illustrated *Old Man Savarin stories*, by E.W. Thompson, Doran, 1917; assistant editor and illustrator of *Chronicles of America*, edited by Allen Johnson, Yale, 1921; commissioned by Ontario Department of Education to illustrate school histories written by George M. Wrong 1921; illustrated *Pageant of America*, edited by R.H. Gabriel, Yale, 1925-29; historical consultant for reconstruction of Habitation of Port Royal by Canadian Government 1938; his painting "Founding of Halifax" reproduced on Canadian four-cent stamp issue 1949.

COMMISSIONS

Design for medal commemorating Jubilee of Canadian Confederation, 1927; design for J.B. Tyrrel medal, Royal Society of Canada, 1928; murals, Manoir Richelieu, Murray Bay, PQ, 1928; murals, Chateau Laurier, Ottawa, Ont., 1930; murals, Royal Ontario Museum, Toronto; design for bas-relief panels on Memorial Arch, Niagara Falls, Ont., 1937.

MEMBER

Royal Canadian Academy (Associate 1912; Academician 1927); Ontario Society of Art (elected, 1902; vice president and treasurer, 1908-11; president, 1913-19); Graphic Arts Club, Toronto (president, 1903-04); Canadian Society of Applied Art; Ontario Historical Society (honorary life member; president, 1942-43); Canadian Society of Painters in Water Colour (co-founder; president, 1929-31); Arts and Letters Club, Toronto (co-founder; president, 1924-26); Canadian Authors Association (co-founder); Champlain Society (council member); Faculty Club of the University of Toronto (honorary life member); Canadian Society of Graphic Art; Toronto Art Students League; Guild of Canadian Commercial Artists.

AWARDS, HONOURS

LLD from Queen's University, 1931.

EXHIBITIONS

ONE-MAN: Art Gallery of Toronto, 1927 and 1942; Mellors Art Gallery, Toronto, 1934; Little Gallery, Toronto, 1948; Ontario Society of Artists, Toronto and London, 1952.

GROUP: Represented in group exhibitions held in Canada from the 1890s on including exhibitions of Toronto Art Students League, Ontario Society of Artists, Royal Canadian Academy, Canadian Society of Graphic Art, and Canadian Society of Painters in Water Colour; represented in group exhibitions organized by National Gallery of Canada, Ottawa, including its Annual Exhibitions; exhibitions of the New York Water Colour Club, American Water Color Society, and Pennsylvania Academy of Arts, Philadelphia, Pa.; Pan-American Exposition, Buffalo, NY, 1901; Louisiana Purchase Exposition, St. Louis, Mo., 1904; Canadian Art Exhibition, Walker Art Gallery, Liverpool, England, 1910; Canadian Section of Fine Arts, British Empire Exhibition, Wembley, England, 1924 and 1925; *Exposition d'art canadien*, Musée du Jeu de Paume, Paris, France, 1927; Exhibition of Contemporary Canadian Painting Arranged ... for Circulation in the Southern Dominions of the British Empire, 1936; A Century of Canadian Art, Tate Gallery, London, England, 1938; World's Fair, New York, 1939; Painters of Canada ... 1668-1948, Virginia Museum of Fine Arts, Richmond Va., 1949.

COLLECTIONS IN WHICH REPRESENTED

Art Gallery of Ontario, Toronto; Arts and Letters Club, Toronto; Hart House Permanent Collection, University of Toronto; National Gallery of Canada; Nutana Collegiate Institute, Saskatoon, Sask.; Ottawa Teachers College; Agnes Etherington Art Centre, Queen's University; Royal Ontario Museum, Toronto; Sarnia Public Library and Art Museum, Ont.

WRITINGS

Dramatic episodes in Canada's history, Star Printing and Publishing Co., 1930; *Canada's past in pictures*, Ryerson, 1934; *The picture gallery of Canadian history*, Ryerson, 1942-45.

CONTRIBUTED: Articles to *Canadian historical review, Canadian geographical journal.*

JOACHIM, Walter 1912—

(Walter Joachimsthal)

Cellist; b. 1912 in Düsseldorf, Germany; son of Emil and Rosa (Bähr) Joachimsthal; came to Canada in 1952 and settled in Montreal.

EDUCATION

Studied singing with his father; studied music with Hermann Zitzman, cello with Karl Maria Schwamberger in Cologne, Germany; attended State Academy of Music, Cologne.

HOME
2050 rue St. Luc, Montréal, PQ.

CAREER
Cologne Chamber Orchestra, principal cello; Rhenische Kammerorchester, cellist 1929-30; Quartetto d'Italia on tour in Europe, India, Middle East, and Far East, cellist 1930-33; returned to Germany 1933; worked in Prague, Czecho-Slovakia, as concert soloist, chamber music ensemble player, cinema musician 1934-38; in Malaya 1938-40; went to Shanghai, China, 1940; principal cellist in refugees' orchestra; interned by Japanese, released 1945; Shanghai Conservatory of Music, teacher of master class in cello 1945-50; repatriated to Germany; worked in Montreal as store clerk and packer 1952; Montreal Symphony Orchestra, principal cellist 1952–; Conservatoire de Musique de la Province de Québec, Montréal, professor of cello; Montreal String Quartet, cellist; Jeunesses Musicales du Canada summer camp, Mount Orford, PQ, cello instructor; National Youth Orchestra of Canada, cello instructor; John Newmark Trio, cellist.

AWARDS, HONOURS
State Academy of Music, Cologne, scholarship, 1916.

CONCERT STAGE
Numerous appearances in recitals and concerts in Germany 1920-33, 1950-52, the Orient 1930-50, North America 1952–; cellist in concerts by Musica Antica e Nueva, Montreal; cello recitals, Expo 67, Montreal, 17, 18 June 1967.

RADIO
Many appearances on CBC series in recitals, e.g. "Distinguished artists," "Distinguished Canadian artists," "Tuesday night"; with instrumental groups in programs of chamber music and in "Wednesday night" series; double-bass in *Jazz concert* ("Wednesday night," 12 Aug. 1959).

TELEVISION
Appearances on CBC in "Concert" and "Festival" series.

JOBIN, Louis 1845-1928
Sculptor; b. 1845 in St. Raymond, PQ; d. Mar. 1928 in Ste. Anne de Beaupré, PQ.

EDUCATION
Studied under François-Xavier Berlinquet, Québec, PQ, *c.* 1855; studied woodcarving at Quebec and New York, NY.

CAREER
Spent boyhood at Point aux Trembles, PQ; made figureheads for sailing ships; moved to New York, carved wooden figures of Indians for cigar store decoration; moved to Quebec, made religious figures for churches and wayside shrines; lived and worked in Montreal, PQ, 1870-75; spent last years at Ste. Anne de Beaupré, PQ, made carvings for pilgrims and churches.

COMMISSIONS
Figure of the Blessed Virgin, Cape Trinity on the Saguenay River, PQ, 1880; figure of Neptune, Neptune Hotel, Mountain Street, Quebec; roadside figures at Beaumont and Lévis, PQ.

EXHIBITIONS
GROUP: Represented in group exhibitions held in Canada; A Century of Canadian Art, Tate Galler London, England, 1938.

COLLECTIONS IN WHICH REPRESENTED
National Gallery of Canada, Ottawa, Ont.; Art Gallery of Ontario, Toronto; Musée du Québec, PQ

JOHNSON, Edward 1881-1959
(Edoardo di Giovanni, pseud.)
Singer (tenor); b. 22 Aug. 1881 in Guelph, Ont.; son of James Evans and Margaret (O'Connell) Johnson; m. Countess Beatrice d'Arneiro 2 Aug. 1909 (d. 1919); children: Fiorenza; became US citizen, 1922; d. 20 Apr. 1959 in Guelph.

EDUCATION
Attended Collegiate Institute, Guelph; University of Toronto, law course for 1 year; studied voice with von Feilitsch, New York, NY; in Paris, France, 1906; with Vincenzo Lombardi, Florence, Italy, 1909-12.

RELIGION
Anglican.

CAREER
Choir boy in Guelph; Newark synagogue, NJ, singer *c.* 1902; Washington Avenue Baptist Church, Brooklyn, NY, singer *c.* 1902; Brick Presbyterian Church, New York, soloist *c.* 1902; La Scala, Milan, Italy, leading tenor 1914-19; toured England South America, 1916, Portugal, 1917; Chicago Opera Company, Ill., leading tenor 1919-21; Metropolitan Opera Company, New York, leading tenor 1921-35, director 1935, general director 1935-50, Metropolitan Opera Auditions of the Air, founder; associated with Chicago Musical College and Juilliard School of Music, New York; Naumburg Foundation, board member; Martha Baird Rockefeller Fund for Music, board member; Toronto Opera Festival Company, board chairman, Royal Conservatory of Music, chairman of the board 1945-58.

AWARDS, HONOURS
CBE; Cavaliere Ufficiale della Corona d'Italia; Légion d'Honneur; distinguished medals from Sweden, Brazil, and other countries; National Ballet of Canada, honorary patron; New York Canadian Club award for his contribution as singer, impresario, and leader in the field of musical education; MusD from University of Toronto; LLD from University of Western Ontario, 1929; DLitt from Union College, NY, 1943; namesake of Edward Johnson Building, University of Toronto, 1962.

THEATRE
Operatic debut in *Andrea Chénier* (Verdi Theatre, Padua, Italy, Jan. 1912); sang in numerous productions, e.g. general understudy in *Maid Marion* (Boston, Mass., 1902), Samson in *Samson and Delilah* (concert version, Worcester, Mass., 1904), *The apostles* (Oratorio Society, New York, 1907), Niki in *A waltz dream* (Broadway, New York, 27 Jan. 1908), *Carmen* (concert version, Boston Orchestra tour, c.1909), *Aïda* (concert version, Boston Orchestra tour, c.1909), *The flying Dutchman* (concert version, Boston Orchestra tour, c.1909), leading role in *L'ombra di Don Giovanni* (La Scala, 1914), title role in *Parsifal* (Italian première, Toscanini conducting, La Scala, c.1914), *Fedra* (La Scala, 1915), *La nave* (La Scala, 1918), *Il tabarro* (La Scala, c.1918), *Gianni Schicchi* (La Scala, c.1919), Avito in *L'amore dei tre re* (Chicago Opera Company, New York, c.1920; Metropolitan Opera Company, 16 Nov. 1922), leading role in *La vestale* (Metropolitan Opera, c.1922), Dimitri in *Boris Godunov* (Metropolitan Opera, 1922), Caravadossi in *Tosca* (Metropolitan Opera, 1922), Des Grieux in *Manon Lescaut* (Metropolitan Opera, 1922), Aethelwold in *The king's henchman* (Metropolitan Opera, c.1923), Pelléas in *Pelléas et Mélisande* (Metropolitan Opera, c.1924), title role in *Fra Gherardo* (Metropolitan Opera, c.1934), title role in *Sadko* (Metropolitan Opera, c.1934), Sir Gower Lackland in *Merry Mount* (Metropolitan Opera).
RECORDINGS
Pre-electric records of opera arias with RCA Victor.

JOHNSON, Emily Pauline
see JOHNSON, Pauline

JOHNSON, Pauline   1862?-1913
(Emily Pauline Johnson; Tekahionwake)
Poet; b. 10 Mar. 1862? at Six Nations Indian Reserve, Brant County, Upper Canada (now Ont.); daughter of George Henry Martin and Emily (Howells) Johnson; d. 7 Mar. 1913 in Vancouver, BC.
EDUCATION
Privately educated and attended Brantford Collegiate School, Ont.
CAREER
Mainly literary; recital tours of Canada, USA, and England 1892-1908.
WRITINGS
The white wampum, Lane, 1895; *In the shadows*, p.p., 1898; *Canadian born*, Morang, 1903; *When George was king and other poems*, Times (Brockville, Ont.), 1908; *Legends of Vancouver*, McClelland & Stewart, 1911; *Ojiston*, Werner, 1911; *Flint and feather*, Musson, 1912; *The Shagganappi* (novel), Briggs, 1912; *The moccasin maker* (novel), Briggs, 1913; *Legend of Siwash*

Rock, Vancouver Business and Professional Women's Club, 1952.
CONTRIBUTED: Poetry and articles to numerous periodicals, e.g. *Gems of poetry, The week, Saturday night, Athenaeum, Harper's weekly, Canadian magazine*.

JOHNSTON, James*   1915–
Director and actor; b. 4 June 1915 in Coleman, Alta.; son of John and Jane (Mounsey) Johnston; m. Cathryn Graham 2 Oct. 1942; children: Janice Graham b. 13 June 1944, Julie Elspeth b. 4 Feb. 1952.
EDUCATION
Attended Britannia High School in Vancouver; Edda Edson Theatre Workshop, Hollywood, Calif., 1939; Academy of Dramatic Arts, New York, NY, 1946-47.
HOME
6430 Elm St., Vancouver 13, BC.
CAREER
RCAF, 1942-45; Theatre Under the Stars, Vancouver, actor 1946-49, stage director 1949-63; University of British Columbia, Musical Society stage director 1955-66, Frederic Wood Theatre actor; CBC, Vancouver, sketch director on TV series 1968–.
MEMBER
ACTRA; AEA.
THEATRE
Played in many productions, e.g. *Trial of a city* (opening of Frederic Wood), *Salad days* (opening of new Frederic Wood, 1963), *The fantasticks, In the rough, In the rough II, Thurber carnival* (Playhouse Theatre Company, Vancouver, 5 Dec. 1968); directed c.50 musicals (Theatre Under the Stars, 1949-63), 11 musicals (University of British Columbia Musical Society, 1955-66).
FILM
Played in *The 49th parallel* (J. Arthur Rank, 1938).
RADIO
Played in numerous CBC productions, e.g. Bill in *The Carson family* ("BC farm broadcast," 1947-66), *The other and I* ("Vancouver Theatre," 18 Mar. 1961), Brutus in *Coriolanus* (26 Sept. 1964), guest on "Over the edge" (series, 1967), *The inspector general* ("Midweek theatre," 15 Feb. 1967), Jim Sturges in *Welcome Island* ("BC farm broadcast," 14 Oct. 1968–).
TELEVISION
Played in several CBC productions e.g. *The Florentine cherub* ("Studio Pacific," 23 Sept. 1959), Hawthorne in *Circles of power*, part II ("Camera west," 9 Sept. 1964), *A second look* ("Gallery," 16 Nov. 1968); directed "People in conflict" (series, CTV, 1963-68), "Magistrate's court," (series, CTV, 1966-68).

JOHNSTONE, Elizabeth Leese
see LEESE, Elizabeth

JONES, Lynn Berta Springbett
see SEYMOUR, Lynn

JOUDRY, Patricia 1921–
(Patricia Joudry Dinsdale; Patricia Joudry Steele)
Playwright; b. 1921 in Spirit River, Alta.; m.
Delmar Dinsdale (marriage dissolved); m. John
Steele; children: (first marriage) daughter, and Gay
b. *c.*1944; (second marriage) daughter, and Steph-
anie b. *c.*1955, Melanie b. *c.*1958.
HOME
Shornhill, Withington, Gloucestershire, England;
2266 Clifton Ave., Montreal, PQ.
CAREER
Resided and worked as actress and radio writer in
Montreal, PQ; spent three years in New York, NY,
as alternate radio writer for *The Aldrich family*
series; CBC, Toronto, Ont., radio writer for
Affectionately Jenny series until 1957; resided in
England, 1957–.
WRITINGS
Teach me how to cry (play), Dramatists Play
Service, 1955 (Dominion Drama Festival best
play award, 1956; produced Theatre De Lys, New
York, 1955; produced under title *Noon has no
shadows*, Arts Theatre, London, England, July
1958; produced under title *The restless years*,
Universal-International Films, 1958); *Walk alone
together* (play; second prize in Stratford, Ont.
Festival-*Globe and mail* playwriting competition;
produced London, England, 1959); *Semi-detached*
(play; produced Martin Beck Theater, New York,
10 Mar. 1960); *Three rings for Michelle* (play),
Dramatists Play Service, 1960; *The man with the
perfect wife* (play; produced Palm Beach, Fla.,
1965?); numerous radio and television plays.
CONTRIBUTED: Short story to *Canadian home
journal.*

JULIEN, Octave-Henri 1852-1908
Artist; b. 14 May 1852 in Faubourg St. Roch,
Québec, PQ; son of Henri and Zoé (Julien) Julien;
m. Marie-Louise Legault *dit* Deslauriers; children:
Jeanne and seventeen other children; d. 17 Sept.
1908 in Montreal, PQ.
EDUCATION
Attended schools in Quebec; attended the Univer-
sity of Ottawa, Ont.; largely self-taught as an
artist.
CAREER
Lived in Toronto, Ont., 1854-60; lived in Quebec,
1860-67; lived in Ottawa, 1867-68 or 1869; Leggo
& Cie, later Desbarats' and afterwards Burland's,
engraving firm, Montreal, apprentice, later
engraver and printer 1869-88; contributed illustrations to *Canadian illustrated news, Favorite,
L'Alamach du peuple, Le farceur, Le canard, Le
grelot, Vrai canard, Le violon, Le franc parleur,
Canadian magazine, Grit, Harper's, Century Magazine, L'illustration, Le monde illustré, Graphic,*

L'opinion publique, 1873-88; illustrated *Les
anciens Canadiens,* by Phillippe-Aubert de Gaspé,
A. Coté, 1877; illustrated legends and stories pub-
lished by his contemporaries; *Star,* Montreal,
cartoonist and head of art department 1888-1908.
EXHIBITIONS
ONE-MAN: Art Club of Montreal, 1936; National
Gallery of Canada, Ottawa, 1938.
GROUP: A Century of Canadian Art, Tate Gallery,
London, England, 1938.
COLLECTIONS IN WHICH REPRESENTED
Montreal Museum of Fine Arts; Musée du Québec.

JULIETTE 1927–
(Juliette Augustina Sysak Cavazzi; Juliette Augus-
tina Sysak)
Singer; b. 1927 in Winnipeg, Man.; m. Toni
Cavazzi *c.*1948.
HOME
16 Rosedale Rd., Apt. 716, Toronto 5, Ont.
CAREER
Dal Richards Orchestra, Hotel Vancouver, BC,
singer 1940; CBC, singer on radio 1942–, TV 1954-
66, judge for *Song market* competition 1968;
nightclub and dance hall singer in Vancouver 1944-
54.
MEMBER
ACTRA.
RADIO
Many appearances in CBC series, e.g. "Sophisti-
cated strings" (1942), "Here's Juliette" (1942-
43), Alan Young's show (1943-44); feature programs 1967–, e.g. *Timmy's Easter parade of
stars* (7 Apr. 1968).
TELEVISION
Featured singer in CBC series, e.g. "The Billy
O'Connor show" (1954-56), "Twenty minutes of
music and song," "The Juliette show," and
"Juliette" (1956-66); guest on CBC variety programs, e.g. "Showcase," "Parade," "Show of the
week," and feature programs, e.g. *A hatful of music*
(24 July 1960), *A Christmas greeting* (25 Dec.
1966).

KALLMANN, Helmut* 1922–
Music historian; b. 7 Aug. 1922 in Berlin, Ger-
many; son of Arthur and Fanny (Paradies) Kall-
mann; came to Canada in 1940; m. Ruth Singer
31 Dec. 1955; children: stepdaughter Lynn
Procter b. 27 Sept. 1941.
EDUCATION
Attended Elementary School No. 12, Berlin-
Schöneberg 1928-32; Hohenzollern-Gymnasium,
Berlin, 1932-39; University of Toronto, BMus, 1946-
49; Royal Conservatory of Music, Toronto, piano
grade X certificate, 1948; studied piano with

Margery Moore, London, England, c.1939 and Naomi Adaskin, Greta Kraus (q.v.), and Florence Steinhauer, Toronto.

HOME
9 Pulford Cres., Ottawa, Ont. K2B 6L6.

OFFICE
Music Division, National Library, 395 Wellington St., Ottawa, Ont.

CAREER
Audit clerk, Toronto, c.1943/44; bookstore assistant, Toronto, 1944-46; CBC Music Library, Toronto, music clerk 1950, music librarian 1951, senior music librarian 1961, supervisor 1962-70; *Canadian music journal*, member of editorial board c.1956–; Canadian Music Library Association, co-founder 1956, chairman 1957/58, 1967/68; National Library, Ottawa, chief of Music Division 1970–.

MEMBER
Canadian Music Council (1952); Bibliographical Society of Canada (1958); International Association of Music Libraries (Canadian delegate, c.1958–); University of Toronto Faculty of Music Alumni Association (president, 1963/64); Canadian Folk Music Society.

AWARDS, HONOURS
Humanities Research Council of Canada grant, 1955; Canada Council grant, 1961/62.

WRITINGS
A history of music in Canada, 1534-1914, University of Toronto, 1960; (with James Bannerman) "Music in Canada" (radio scripts; produced CBC, May-Aug. 1965); program notes for several recordings, e.g. *The widow* by Calixa Lavallée, RCA Victor LSC 2981, 1967, *Light Canadian orchestral classics*, Capitol, 1967, *Colas et Colinette* by Joseph Quesnel, Select SSC 24160.
EDITED: *Catalogue of Canadian composers*, CBC, 1951.
CONTRIBUTED: "Historical background" in *Music in Canada*, edited by E. MacMillan, University of Toronto, 1955; "Music composition" in *Encyclopedia Canadiana*, Grolier, 1966; "François Dangé" and "André-Louis de Merlac" in *Dictionary of Canadian biography*, University of Toronto, 1966; "Historical background" in *Aspects of music in Canada*, edited by A. Walter, University of Toronto, 1969; articles to *Harvard dictionary of music, Die Musik in Geschichte und Gegenwart, Canadian music journal, Canadian composer, Canadian annual review, Canadian Library Association bulletin, Musicanada, Toronto telegram, Fontes artis musicae*.
WORK IN PROGRESS: "Canadian music publications to 1921"; "Bibliography of folk music in Canada."

KASH, Eugene 1912–
Violinist and conductor; b. 1 May 1912 in Toronto,

Ont.; son of Joseph and Gertrude Kash; m. Maureen Katherine Stewart Forrester (q.v.) July 1954; children: Paula b. c.1956, Gina Deborah b. c.1959, Daniel Joshua b. c.1960, Linda b. 17 Jan. 1962, daughter b. 18 Dec. 1965.

EDUCATION
Studied with Luigi von Kunitz, 1917- ?; Curtis Institute of Music, Philadelphia; Vienna State Academy, Austria.

RELIGION
Jewish.

OFFICE
Preparatory School, Philadelphia Academy of Music, Philadelphia, Pa., USA.

CAREER
Toronto Promenade Symphony Concerts, concert master 1941-42; National Film Board of Canada, music editor, director of music 1942-50; Ottawa Philharmonic Orchestra, Ont., conductor 1950-57; National Youth Orchestra of Canada, conductor, administrator 1957-64; Fairfield County Symphony Orchestra, Conn., conductor 1961-63; Montreal Symphony Orchestra, PQ, conductor of youth concerts 1964-67; Academy of Music, Philadelphia, dean of preparatory school 1967?–.

MEMBER
Toronto Musicians Association.

FILM
Conductor in *Children's concert* (National Film Board of Canada, 1967); *String instruments* (National Film Board of Canada, 1967).

RADIO
Appearances on CBC, as violinist on "Wednesday night" (23 May 1962), "Tuesday night" (19 July 1966), "Canadian recitalist" (23 Oct. 1967); conductor of CBC String Orchestra (27 Sept. 1965), "Summer concert" (26 Aug. 1966) and CBC Symphony Orchestra "Sunday concerts" (24 Nov. 1964); music commentator on "Records in review" (7 Aug. 1965).

KASH, Maureen Kathleen Stewart Forrester
see FORRESTER, Maureen

KELLY, Ron* 1929–
Film director and writer; b. 11 June 1929 in Vancouver, BC; son of Arthur Robinson and Anita (Bergére) Kelly; m. Cynthia Von Rhau 19 Dec. 1952; children: Caitlin b. 6 June 1957.

EDUCATION
Attended Pauline Johnson School in West Vancouver; West Vancouver High School; University of British Columbia, 1948-53; studied with Ray Boulting, Shepparton Studios, England, 1959-60.

RELIGION
Atheist.

HOME
Apt. #423, 11 Elm Ave., Toronto, Ont.

CAREER
CBC, Vancouver, 1953-55, freelance film
director 1956-59, 1962-65, and 1967-68; BBC,
London, England, freelance film director
1960-61; National Film Board of Canada, Montreal, PQ, freelance film director 1966-67; Twentieth Century Fox, Hollywood, Calif., freelance
film director 1967; UNESCO Film Seminar,
Buenos Aires, Argentina, Canadian representative
Sept.-Oct. 1968; Walt Disney Studios, Hollywood, freelance film director 1968; travelled and
filmed extensively in the United Kingdom, France,
Spain, North Africa, Japan, and Mexico.

MEMBER
Directors Guild of America; Directors Guild of
Canada.

AWARDS, HONOURS
Canada Council fellowship, 1959/60; Centennial
medal, 1967; Canada Council travel grant,
1967/68.

FILMS
Produced and directed *The quality of the act*;
wrote, photographed, directed, produced, and
edited *Spanish village, Dark gods*; produced and
directed *A bit of bark*; wrote, produced, directed,
and edited *The tearaways* (BBC; golden palm,
Eurovision Television Festival, Cannes, France,
1962); directed and produced *Pelly Bay* ("Camera
Canada," CBC, 31 Mar. 1961); wrote, directed,
and produced *Montreal* (National Film Board),
Caio Maria, The open grave ("Horizon," CBC,
Mar. 1963; City of Genoa prize, Italia Prize Competition, Genoa, Italy, 1964; award, Canadian
Film Awards, Toronto, 1965); produced *The
Fraser* ("Canada 98," CBC, 25 Nov. 1964);
directed and produced *The thirties — a glimpse
of a decade* (CBC, 1964; Wilderness award, CBC,
1964); wrote, produced, directed, and edited
The gift (CBC, 11 Nov. 1965; best director
award, Canadian Film Awards, Toronto, 1966;
participation, Edinburgh Film Festival, Scotland,
1966; participation, London Film Festival,
England, 1967); directed *The long dream*
("Telescope," CBC, 12 Oct. 1967), *Birthplace of
a nation* ("Telescope," CBC, 7 Dec. 1967), *The
last man in the world* ("Wojeck," CBC; Wilderness
award, CBC, 1966; best Canadian director award,
Canadian Film Awards, Toronto, 1967; golden
nymph award, Monte Carlo Film Festival,
Monaco, 1967); directed and joint author of
Waiting for Caroline (CBC and National Film
Board for "Festival," CBC, 29 Nov. 1967;
best colour cinematography [ex aequo],
Canadian Film Awards, Toronto, 1968).

WORK IN PROGRESS
Directing "Biography of a grizzly" (Walt Disney
Studios, Hollywood, now in production);
writing script and directing "The Megantic out-
law" (now in production).

**KENDERDINE, Augustus Frederick Lafosse
1870-1947**
Artist; b. 31 Mar. 1870 in Manchester, England;
came to Canada 1907 and settled in Lashburn,
Sask.; m.; children: Richard and two daughters;
d. 4 Aug. 1947 in Saskatoon, Sask.

EDUCATION
Studied at the Manchester School of Art, England;
studied under Jules Lefebvre, Académie Julian,
Paris, France, c. 1890.

CAREER
Apprenticed to a fine art dealer in England
c. 1884; Duke of Lancaster's Cavalry Regiment,
trooper and instructor in equitation; owned an
art shop and painted portraits in Blackpool,
England; visited Japan 1904; ranched at Lashburn,
Sask., 1908-20; established a studio on the University of Saskatchewan campus 1920; University
of Saskatchewan, instructor in art 1920-36;
Regina College, professor of art and director of
the School of Fine Arts 1936-47; founded summer
art school at Emma Lake, Sask., 1936, director
1936-47; painted in Saskatchewan 1920-47.

EXHIBITIONS
ONE-MAN: Saskatoon Art Centre, and on tour
to a number of Saskatchewan centres, 1959;
Mendel Art Gallery, Saskatoon, 1967.
GROUP: Represented in group exhibitions held
in Canada from 1920 on including Canadian
National Exhibitions; represented in group
exhibitions organized by National Gallery of
Canada, Ottawa, Ont., including its Annual
Exhibitions; Royal Academy, London, England,
1901.

COLLECTIONS IN WHICH REPRESENTED
Glenbow Foundation, Calgary, Alta.; Norman
Mackenzie Art Gallery, Regina, Sask.; Mendel
Art Gallery; Nutana Collegiate Collection,
Saskatoon.

WRITINGS
Twelve views of Saskatchewan, Stovel, 1933.

KING, Allan Winton* 1930—
Film maker; b. 6 Feb. 1930 in Vancouver, BC;
son of John Owen and Kathleen Mary (Keegan)
Winton, foster father Earl C. King; m. Phyllis
April Leiterman 2 May 1952; children: Anna
Augusta b. 28 Aug. 1961.

EDUCATION
Attended Stratford House, Vancouver, 1934-36;
Maple Grove primary school, Vancouver, 1936-37;
Prince of Wales primary school, Vancouver,
1937-38; Kerrisdale primary school, Vancouver,
1938-39 and 1940; Bayview primary school,
Vancouver, 1939-40; Henry Hudson primary
school, Vancouver, 1941; Kitsilano High School,
Vancouver, 1941-46; Magee High School,
Vancouver, 1946-47; University of British
Columbia, BA in honours philosophy, 1954.

RELIGION
None.
HOME
23 Belsize Dr., Toronto, Ont.
OFFICE
Allan King Associates (Canada) Ltd., 241
Bedford Rd., Toronto 5, Ont.
CAREER
CBC, producer and director 1954-58; self-
employed 1958-61; Allan King Associates Ltd.,
Canada, England, and America, president and
chairman 1962—; Browndale Residential School,
chairman 1968—; has travelled extensively through-
out Europe, Asia, Africa, and America on filming
trips.
MEMBER
Association of Cinema and Television Technicians;
Directors Guild of Canada; Society of Film
Makers (vice-president).
FILMS
Produced and directed *Skid row* ("Explorations,"
CBC; award, Canadian Film Awards, Toronto,
1957), *The Yukoners, Portrait of a harbour,
Gyppo loggers, The Pemberton Valley* (CBC,
1958), *Dreams, Three Yugoslavian portraits, The
field day, Rickshaw boy* ("Closeup," CBC; first
prize, Vancouver International Film Festival,
1961; first prize, International Documentary and
Short Film Festival, Leipzig, Germany, 1966),
Joseph Drenters ("Quest," CBC), *Lynn Seymour*
("Telescope," CBC; first prize, Festival Inter-
nationale del Cinema Formato Ridotto, Salerno,
Italy, 1965), *Bjorn's inferno* ("Document," CBC,
20 Apr. 1967; participation, Ninth Annual San
Francisco International Film Festival, Calif.,
1965), *Running away backwards* (Allan King
Associates for "The human camera," CBC, 6
June 1965; participation, La Biennale de Venezia
Film Festival, Italy; participation, Montreal Film
Festival, PQ; participation, Vancouver Film
Festival; participation, Mannheim International
Film Week, Germany; silver boomerang, Mel-
bourne Film Festival, Australia; honourable
mention, Ninth Annual San Francisco Inter-
national Film Festival, 1965), *Warrendale*
(Allan King Associates and CBC, 1967; best
film, La Semaine de la Critique, Cannes, France,
1967; diploma of merit, International Federation
of Film Societies; grand prize, Fifth Festival of
Canadian Films, Montreal International Film
Festival, 1967; film of the year, best feature,
best direction, Canadian Film Awards, Toronto,
1967; best foreign film, British Film Awards,
London, England; participation, New York
Film Festival, NY, 1967; participation, San
Francisco International Film Festival, 1967;
Fifteenth Sydney Film Festival, Australia,
1968), "Creative persons"(series, National
Educational Television, USA, 1968; BBC, London,

England, 1968; Norddeuscher Rundfunk,
West Germany, 1968; CBC, 1968), *The new
woman* (CTV).
WORK IN PROGRESS
Producing and directing "A married couple,"
Allan King Associates for Aquarius Films
Limited.

KIRBY, William   1817-1906
(Britannicus, pseud.)
Author; b. 13 Oct. 1817 in Kingston-upon-Hull,
Yorkshire, England; son of John and Charlotte
(Parker) Kirby; came to Canada in 1839 and
settled in Niagara-on-the-Lake, Upper Canada
(now Ont.); m. Eliza Madeline Whitmore 1847;
children: John Colborne (deceased), Eugene
Guildford (deceased); d. 23 June 1906 in
Niagara.
EDUCATION
Attended school in Newby Wiske, Yorkshire.
RELIGION
Anglican.
CAREER
Journeyman tanner, Cincinnati, Ohio, 1832-39;
tanner, Niagara-on-the-Lake 1839-46, 1847-50;
Mail, Niagara, editor 1850-71; collector of
customs, Niagara 1871-95.
MEMBER
Royal Society of Canada (charter member,
1882-94); Niagara Historical Society (president,
1891).
WRITINGS
*Counter manifesto to the annexationists of
Montreal* (non-fiction), Davidson, 1849; *The
U.E.: a tale of Upper Canada* (poem), the author,
1859; *The golden dog* (novel), Lovell, 1877
(translated into French); *The United Empire
Loyalists of Canada* (biography), Briggs, 1884;
Canadian idylls (poems), Welland, Ont., 1884;
Annals of Niagara, Tribune, 1896; *Sir James Le
Moine* (biography), the author, 1898; *Reminis-
cences of a visit to Quebec, July 1839*, the
author, 1903.
CONTRIBUTED: Articles and poems to *Canadian
Methodist magazine* and *Rose-Belford's Canadian
and national review* (formerly *Belford's monthly*).

KIRKCONNELL, Watson*   1895—
Author; b. 16 May 1895 in Port Hope, Ont.;
son of Thomas Allison and Bertha Gertrude
(Watson) Kirkconnell; m. Isabel Peel 1924 (d.
1925); m. Hope Kitchener 1930; children: (first
marriage) two sons; (second marriage) three
daughters.
EDUCATION
Attended Collegiate Institute, Lindsay, Ont.;
Queen's University, MA, 1916; attended Toronto
Conservatory of Music, Ont., 1919-20; Lincoln
College, University of Oxford, 1921-22; Univer-
sity of Debrecen, Hungary, Ph D, 1940.

RELIGION
Baptist.

HOME
101 Main St., Wolfville, NS.

CAREER
Canadian Army, 1916-19, became captain; Wesley College (now University of Winnipeg), professor of English 1922-30, professor of classics 1930-40; McMaster University, head of English department 1940-48; Writers' War Committee for Canada, chairman 1942-44; Acadia University, president 1948-64, president emeritus 1964–, professor of English and head of department 1966–; University of Debrecen, University of Pittsburgh, and University of Iceland, visiting lecturer; travelled in Europe, Asia, and Africa.

MEMBER
Canadian Authors Association (national president, 1942-44, 1956-58); Humanities Research Council of Canada (co-founder; first chairman, 1944-48); Royal Society of Canada (elected fellow, 1936; president, Section II, 1967-68); member of several learned societies in many countries.

AWARDS, HONOURS
Queen's University medals for Latin and Greek, 1916; IODE overseas scholarship, 1921; knight officer of the Order of Polonia Restituta, 1935; Polish Academy of Literature silver laurel, 1937; Lorne Pierce medal, 1942; Nova Scotia Drama League trophy for *The mod at Grand Pré,* 1956; knight commander of the Order of the Falcon, Iceland, 1963; Shevchenko medal and plaque, 1964; Humanities Research Council of Canada medal, 1964; Hungarian Freedom Fighters gold medal of freedom, 1964; George Washington medal from American Hungarian Studies Foundation, 1967; University of Winnipeg honorary fellow, 1968; LL D from University of Ottawa, 1945 and University of New Brunswick, 1950; DP Ec from Ukrainian Free University, 1950; D Litt from McMaster University, 1952, Assumption College, 1955, and University of Manitoba, 1957; D-ès-Let from Laval University, 1962; DCL from St. Mary's University, 1964; D Litt from Acadia University, 1964 and St. Francis Xavier University, 1966.

WRITINGS
Kapuskasing, an historical sketch, Queen's University, 1921; *Victoria county centennial history,* Watchman-Warder, 1921; *International aspects of unemployment,* Holt, 1923; *Botanical survey of South Victoria,* Warder, 1926; *The tide of life and other poems,* Ariston, 1930; *The European heritage* (non-fiction), Dent, 1930; *Canada to Iceland* (poems), Warder, 1930; *The eternal quest* (poems), Columbia, 1934; *A Canadian headmaster* (biography), Clarke, Irwin, 1935; *Manitoba symphony* (poems), 1937?;

Golden jubilee of Wesley College, Winnipeg (non-fiction), Columbia, 1938; *Titus the toad* (juvenile fiction), Oxford, 1939; *Lyra sacra* (poems), the author, 1939; *Canada, Europe and Hitler* (non-fiction), Oxford, 1939; *The flying bull and other tales* (poems), Oxford, 1940; *Western idyll* (poems), the author, 1940; *Ukrainian Canadians and the war* (non-fiction), Oxford, 1940; *Twilight of liberty* (non-fiction), Oxford, 1941; *Canadians all* (non-fiction), Director Public Information (Ottawa, Ont.), 1941; *Our Ukrainian loyalists* (non-fiction), Ukrainian Canadian Committee, 1943; *Seven pillars of freedom* (non-fiction), Oxford, 1944; (with A.S.P. Woodhouse) *The humanities in Canada,* Humanities Research Council, 1947; *The celestial cycle* (non-fiction), University of Toronto, 1952; *Totalitarian education,* Prince of Wales College, 1952; *Common English loan words in east European languages,* Ukrainian Free Academy of Sciences, 1952; *The Acadia record, 1838-1953,* Acadia University, 1953; *Canadian toponomy and the cultural stratification of Canada,* Ukrainian Free Academy of Sciences, 1954; *The place of Slavic studies in Canada,* Ukrainian Free Academy of Sciences, 1958; *The Baptists of Canada,* Baptist Federation of Canada, 1958; *Acadia University and the town of Wolfville,* Wolfville, 1962; *The primordial church of Horton,* Wolfville, 1963; *That invincible Samson* (non-fiction), University of Toronto, 1964; *Sixteen decades of parsonages, a series of dramatic dialogues,* Davidson Brothers, 1964; *Centennial tales and selected poems,* University of Toronto, 1965; *A slice of Canada: memoirs,* University of Toronto, 1967; *The celestial cycle, the theme of Paradise Lost in world literature,* Gordian, 1967; *The mod at Grand Pré* (opera), p.p., 1955.

EDITED: *Manitoba poetry chapbook,* Canadian Authors Association, 1933.

TRANSLATED: *European elegies,* Graphic, 1928; *North American book of Icelandic verse,* Carrier and Isles, 1930; *Magyar muse,* Kanadai Magyar Ujság Press, 1933; *Canadian overtones,* Columbia, 1935; *A golden treasury of Polish lyrics,* Polish Press, 1936; *The Quebec tradition,* selected by S. Marion, Lumen, 1946; *A little treasury of Hungarian verse,* American Hungarian Federation, 1947; Adam Mickiewicz's *Pan tadeusz,* Polish Institute of Arts and Sciences in America, 1962; (with C.H. Andrusyshen) *The Ukrainian poets, 1189-1962,* University of Toronto, 1963; (with C.H. Andrusyshen) *The poetical works of Taras Shevshenko,* University of Toronto, 1964.

CONTRIBUTED: Poetry and articles to many anthologies, e.g. *Anthology of Canadian poetry,* compiled by R. Gustafson, Penguin, 1942; *Icelandic poems and stories,* edited by R. Beck,

Princeton, 1943; *A pageant of old Scandinavia*, edited by H.G. Leach, Princeton, 1946; *Masterpieces of religious verse*, edited by J.D. Morrison, Harper, 1948; *Poems to remember*, edited by E.F. Kingston, Dent, 1951; *A little treasury of world poetry*, edited by H. Creekmore, Scribner, 1952; *Poetry for senior students; an anthology of shorter poems*, edited by J.L. Gill and L.H. Newell, Macmillan, 1953; *Twentieth century Canadian poetry*, edited by E. Birney, Ryerson, 1953; *Canadian poetry in English*, edited by B. Carman and others, rev. and enl. ed., Ryerson, 1954; *Old poems and new*, edited by E.F. Kingston, Dent, 1954; *A treasury of Jewish poetry*, edited by N. Ausubel and M. Ausubel, Crown, 1957; *The singing and the gold; poems translated from world literature*, compiled by E. Parker, Crowell, 1962; *Atlantic advance, Dalhousie review, Canadian author and bookman, Canadian music journal, Canadian poetry, Public affairs, Royal Society of Canada transactions, Saturday night.*

WORK IN PROGRESS

"Acadia University, 1938-1963"; "The third Canadian muse"; "The Hungarian helicon"; "Two temptations: analogues of *Comus* and *Paradise regained.*"

KIYOOKA, Harry Mitsuo* 1928—

Artist; b. 18 Feb. 1928 in Calgary; son of Harry Shigekiyo and Kiyo (Oye) Kiyooka.

EDUCATION

Attended Victoria High School, Edmonton, Alta., 1946-47; University of Alberta, BEd in art education, 1947-48, 1950-52; studied under Edward Bawden, Banff School of Fine Arts, Alta., 1949; University of Manitoba, BFA in painting and art history, 1952-54; Michigan State University, MA in painting and art history, 1955-56; University of Colorado, MFA in painting and art history, 1957.

HOME

123 Waterloo Dr. SW, Calgary, Alta.

OFFICE

Dept. of Art, Faculty of Fine Arts, University of Calgary, Calgary, Alta.

CAREER

Sullivan Lake School District No. 9, Alta., teacher 1948-50; Alberta Department of Water Resources, surveyor, summers 1951-56; University of Manitoba Saturday morning art classes, teacher 1953-54; Prince George School District, BC, high school art teacher 1954-55; Michigan State University, graduate assistant 1955-56; University of Colorado, graduate assistant 1956-57; travelled and painted in Europe 1958-61; University of Calgary, assistant professor of art 1961—.

MEMBER

Alberta Society of Artists (elected, 1962; president, 1967-68).

AWARDS, HONOURS

Bursary, Province of Alberta, 1947; summer school bursary, Sullivan Lake School District No. 9, 1949; Birks scholarship in painting for Alberta, 1950; Fuller Brush Company art scholarship, 1952; foreign tuition scholarship in art, Michigan State University, 1956; Canada Council scholarship 1958/59 and 1959/60; honorable mention, Winnipeg Biennial, Winnipeg Art Gallery, Man., 1962; Jacox award (joint prize), All Alberta Exhibition of Paintings, Edmonton Art Gallery, Alta., 1966; first prize, Winnipeg Show, Winnipeg Art Gallery, 1966; Canada Council senior fellowship, 1966.

EXHIBITIONS

ONE-MAN: Richardson Art Gallery, Winnipeg, 1954; Coste House, Calgary, 1955; Calgary Allied Arts Centre, 1963; New Design Gallery, Vancouver, BC, 1966.

GROUP: Represented in group exhibitions held in Canada since 1953 including exhibitions of Royal Canadian Academy, Alberta Society of Artists, and All Alberta Exhibitions of Paintings; sixth Biennial Exhibition of Canadian Painting, National Gallery of Canada, Ottawa, Ont., 1965; Canadian Prints and Drawings, Cardiff Commonwealth Arts Festival, Cardiff, Wales, 1965.

COLLECTIONS IN WHICH REPRESENTED

Winnipeg Art Gallery.

KLAMPFER, John Walker* 1945—

Dancer; b. 22 Aug. 1945 in Edmonton, Alta.; son of Frank and Marion (Hook) Klampfer; m. Amanda Vaughan 28 May 1966.

EDUCATION

Attended school in Vancouver, BC; studied ballet with Kay Armstrong (*q.v.*), Vancouver Ballet School; National Ballet School of Canada, Toronto, Cecchetti examinations grade 1, 2, and elementary, 1962-64; De Vry Technical Institute of Canada, Toronto, electronics diploma, 1967.

HOME

Apt. 204, 199 Roehampton Ave., Toronto 12, Ont.

CAREER

National Ballet of Canada, Toronto, corps de ballet 1964-67, soloist 1967-68.

MEMBER

AEA.

AWARDS, HONOURS

Koerner Foundation grant, Vancouver, 1961/62; Canada Council arts scholarship, 1962/63, 1963/64.

THEATRE

First danced Russian dance in *Casse-noisette* (Franca after Ivanov, 1964), King of the mice in *Casse-noisette* (Franca after Ivanov, 1965), Soloist boy in *Adagio cantabile* (Poll, 1965), Carnival divertissement in *Romeo and Juliet* (Cranko, 1966), Guest in *Le jardin aux lilas* (Tudor, 1966), Pas de deux boy in *One in five* (Powell, 1967), Lead boy in *Les rendez-vous* (Ashton, 1967), Spanish dance in *Le lac des cygnes* (Bruhn, 1967), Solo bandit in *La prima ballerina* (Heiden, 1967), Prince's companion in *Cinderella* (Franca, 1968).

TELEVISION
Danced in *Romeo and Juliet* (Cranko, "Festival," CBC, 15 Sept. 1965; 2 Mar. 1966), *Le lac des cygnes* (Bruhn, "Festival," CBC, 27 Dec. 1967).

KNAPP, Budd* 1915–
(Wilfrid Arthur Knapp)
Actor; b. 9 Jan. 1913 in Ottawa, Ont.; son of Wilfrid Arthur and Frances (Carpenter) Knapp; m. Ede Patricia Arthurs 7 Mar. 1942; children: Linda Penelope b. 18 Jan. 1943.

EDUCATION
Attended primary and secondary school in Ottawa and Toronto, Ont.

HOME
Apt. 508, 3635 Ridgewood Ave., Montreal 26, PQ.

CAREER
Ottawa Little Theatre, actor 1934-35; John Holden Players, Bala, Muskoka, Ont. and Winnipeg, Man., actor 1936-38; CBC, Toronto and Montreal, actor 1940–.

MEMBER
ACTRA (life member); AEA; Canadian Theatre Centre.

THEATRE
Played in *The gimmick* (Grand, Leeds, England, Mar. 1959), Peter Croslyn in *Roger the sixth* (Westminster, London, England, 24 May 1960), Willy Loman in *Death of a salesman* (Theatre-on-the-Mountain, Montreal, 9 Feb. 1961), John Cleary in *The subject was roses* (Ottawa, Nov. 1966; Toronto, Dec. 1966; Edmonton, Alta., Apr. 1967), Tobias in *A delicate balance* (Winnipeg, Apr. 1968); directed *Antigone* (Anouilh, Ottawa, Feb. 1968).

FILM
Played in *Johnny Concho* (Kent Productions, 1956), *The great American pastime* (Metro Goldwyn Mayer, 1956), *Never take sweets from a stranger* (Hammer Films).

RADIO
Played in numerous CBC productions, e.g. *The monkey's paw* (1940), Uncle George in *John and Judy* (serial, 1942-54), Benet in *Western star* ("Wednesday night," 9 Nov. 1960), Narrator in *Great eastern* ("Wednesday night," Feb. 1961), *Uncle Vanya* ("Summer stage," 16 July 1961), *Emile and the devil* ("Sunday night," 20 Sept. 1964), Narrator in *The fate of a poet* ("Sunday night," 31 Jan. 1965), Becket in *Murder in the Cathedral* ("Stage," 5 Feb. 1965; "Sunday night," 4 Apr. 1965), Sexton in *The black spider* ("Sunday night," 2 May 1965), Deke in *Pastures*

of plenty ("Midweek theatre," 9 June 1965), *The changing of the gods* ("Summer stage," 23 July 1965), Burleigh MacDuff in *The old man's house* ("Sunday night," 29 Aug. 1965), title role in *The old man said no* ("Midweek theatre," 1 Dec. 1965), Narrator in *Big Geordie* ("Tuesday night," 8 Mar. 1966), Edouard de la Cour in *A new dialogue on two world systems* ("Tuesday night," 30 Aug. 1966), Walker Evans in *Let us now praise famous men* ("Tuesday night," 6 Dec. 1966), Narrator in *Century* (1 Jan. 1967), Narrator in *The life of Joseph Howe* ("Tuesday night," 6, 13 June 1967), *Bravo, Billy Brown* ("Midweek theatre," 4 Oct. 1967).

TELEVISION
Played in numerous CBC productions, e.g. *Collision* ("GM presents," 27 Nov. 1960), *The town that didn't care* ("GM presents," 21 May 1961), *Standard of dying* ("Q for quest," 23 May 1961), *Power by proxy* ("GM presents," 25 June 1961), *The gambler* ("Festival," 29 Oct. 1962), Narrator in "A place for everything" (12 week series, 3 July 1964), Gogo in *Waiting for Godot* ("Festival," 2 Dec. 1964), Heel in *The golden bull of boredom* ("Eye opener", 16 Mar. 1965), *Whisper into my good ear* ("Festival," 22 Dec. 1965), Narrator in *Rivers to the sea: Margaree* ("Canada 99," 6 Feb. 1966), Marmeladov in *The murderer* ("Festival," 23 Feb. 1966), title role in *Julius Caesar* ("Canadian school telecasts," 1966; 2 May 1967), guest star on "Wojeck" (series), "Quentin Durgens, MP" (series).

KNAPP, Wilfrid Arthur
see KNAPP, Budd

KOENIG, Wolf
Film maker; b. in Germany.

OFFICE
c/o National Film Board of Canada, PO Box 6100, Montreal, PQ.

FILMS
Animated *The romance of transportation* (National Film Board, 1952); photographed *Corral* (National Film Board, 1954); photographed and edited *Gold* (National Film Board, 1955); co-directed *City of gold* (National Film Board, 1957; first prize, documentary short features class, Tenth International Film Festival, Cannes, France, 1957; first prize, general interest category, Second International Irish Film Festival, Cork, Ireland, c.1957; award of merit, non-theatrical arts and experimental category and film of the year award, Tenth Annual Canadian Film Awards, Toronto, Ont., 1957; honourable mention, Ninth Annual Robert J. Flaherty Film Awards, New York, NY, 1957; first prize, documentary category, International Exhibition of Electronics, Nuclear Energy, Radio and Television, Rome, Italy, 1958; honour-

able mention, Third International Festival of Documentary and Experimental Films, Montevideo, Uraguay, 1958; gold medal, Trento Film Festival, Italy, 1958; first prize, documentary films category, Vancouver Film Festival, BC, 1958; best film, general category, Yorkton Film Festival, Sask., 1958; purchase prize, Festival of Contemporary Arts, University of Illinois, 1959; blue ribbon award, American Film Festival, New York; first prize, First Festival de Cine Documental Ibero-Americano y Filipino, Bilbao, Spain; first prize, Eighth Annual Film Festival, Columbus, Ohio, c.1960; honourable mention, First Festival of Experimental and Documentary Films, Santiago, Chile, c.1960; gold medal, Chamber of Deputies, Florence, Italy; gold medal, Festival of the People, Florence); produced *The great toy robbery* (National Film Board, 1963; St. Finbarr trophy, animated film and cartoon category, Eighth Cork Film Festival, Ireland, c.1963; diploma, Eleventh Yugoslav Festival of Documentary and Short Films, Belgrade, Yugoslavia, c.1964); co-directed and photographed *Steel town* (National Film Board; special, CBC, 30 Apr. 1967).

KOERNER, John Michael Anthony
see KORNER, John

KORNER, John*   1913–
(John Michael Anthony Koerner)
Artist; b. 29 Sept. 1913 in Novy Jicin, Czecho-Slovakia; son of Theodore and Bertha Koerner; came to Canada in 1939 and settled in Vancouver; m. Eileen Newby; children: Sidney Joan, Diane Louise.

EDUCATION
Studied law at Charles University of Prague and University of Geneva, 1934-38; studied painting and design under Fritz Kausek in Prague, Czecho-Slovakia; studied history and philosophy of art at Sorbonne, 1937-38; studied art under Victor Tischler, Othon Friesz, and Paul Colin in Paris, France.

HOME
5816 Kingston Rd., Vancouver 8, BC.

CAREER
Alaska Pine Co. Ltd., Vancouver, public relations and personnel officer 1939-50; Vancouver School of Art, instructor in painting and drawing 1953-58; Vancouver Art Gallery, member of Council 1955-60; Vancouver Community Arts Council, member of board 1957-59; University of British Columbia, art instructor 1958-62; painter in Vancouver 1939–.

COMMISSIONS
Mural, R.J. Young residence, Vancouver; mural, D.H. Simpson residence, Vancouver; mural, A.B. Cliff office, Vancouver; mural, CHQM, Vancouver; mural, King's Daughters Hospital, Duncan, BC.

MEMBER
Canadian Group of Painters (vice-president, 1959-60); BC Society of Artists (president, 1956-58); Royal Canadian Academy (Associate 1960; resigned, 1965).

AWARDS, HONOURS
Prizes, Winnipeg Show, Winnipeg Art Gallery, Man., 1955, 1957, and 1961; prize, Burnaby Show, BC, 1958; British Columbia centennial award, 1958; purchase award, Vancouver Art Gallery, 1960; Centennial medal, 1967.

EXHIBITIONS
ONE-MAN: Vancouver Art Gallery, 1940, 1952, and 1956; Art Gallery of Greater Victoria, BC, 1954; New Design Gallery, Vancouver, 1956, 1957, 1959, 1961, 1962, and 1963; Art Gallery of Toronto, (now of Ontario), 1958; Galerie Agnès Lefort, Montréal, PQ, 1958, 1960, 1963, and 1965; Laing Gallery, Toronto, 1959, 1960, 1961, and 1962; Seligman Gallery, Seattle, Wash., 1959, 1962, 1964, and 1967; Hart House, University of Toronto, 1960; Morris International Gallery, Toronto, 1963 and 1965; Alex Fraser Gallery, Vancouver, 1964 and 1965; Studio Gallery, Vancouver, 1966; Galerie Dresdnere, Montréal, 1966.
GROUP: Represented in group exhibitions held in Canada since 1954; first, second, fourth, and fifth Biennial Exhibitions of Canadian Painting, National Gallery of Canada, Ottawa, Ont., 1955, 1957, 1961, and 1963; represented in international exhibitions held in South Africa, Australia, and India, 1956; Seattle Art Museum, 1957 and 1960; San Francisco Civic Center, Calif., 1959; Portland Art Museum, Oreg., 1959; Time and Life Building, New York, NY, 1960; World's Fair, Seattle, 1962; Commonwealth Centre, London, England, 1961.

COLLECTIONS IN WHICH REPRESENTED
Art Gallery of Greater Victoria; Art Gallery of Ontario, Toronto; Beaverbrook Art Gallery, Fredericton, NB; British Columbia Government House, Victoria; Burnaby Art Gallery; Canadian Industries Ltd. Collection, Montreal; Department of External Affairs, Ottawa; Edmonton Art Gallery, Alta.; Hart House Permanent Collection, University of Toronto; Kelowna Centennial Museum, BC; London Public Library and Art Museum, Ont.; Musée d'Art Contemporain, Montréal; Montreal Museum of Fine Arts; National Gallery of Canada; Reader's Digest, Toronto; Royal Bank of Canada, Toronto; Smithsonian Institution, Washington, DC; Brock Collection, Maclean Collection, Graduate Centre Collection, and Faculty Club Collection, University of British Columbia; University of Victoria; Vancouver Art Gallery; Winnipeg Art Gallery; Queen's University; Seattle Art Museum.

WRITINGS
CONTRIBUTED: To *Canadian art*.

KOROL, Taras
see KOROL, Ted

KOROL, Ted
(Taras Korol)
Designer.
HOME
34B-27 Balmoral, Winnipeg, Man.
OFFICE
c/o Rainbow Stage Theatre, 508 Lindsay Building, 228 Notre Dame Ave., Winnipeg 2, Man.
CAREER
Sisler High School, Winnipeg, teacher in English and art, producer and director of musical comedies; Rainbow Stage Theatre, Winnipeg, costume and set designer; Royal Winnipeg Ballet, costume and set designer; Manitoba Theatre Centre, Winnipeg, costume and set designer; Actor's Showcase, Winnipeg, costume and set designer; Contemporary Dancers, Winnipeg, costume and set designer.
THEATRE
Designed costumes and sets for many productions, e.g. *My fair lady* (Rainbow Stage), *Oliver* (Rainbow Stage), *Anerca* (Contemporary Dancers, Apr. 1966), *Carnival* (Rainbow Stage, 3 July 1968).

KRAUS, Greta   1907–
Harpsichordist and teacher; b. 1907 in Vienna, Austria; came to Canada in 1938.
EDUCATION
Attended Academy of Music, Vienna.
CAREER
RADIO
Harpsichordist in numerous CBC programs, e.g. *Music by composers of royal birth* (16 Sept. 1959), with Douglas Bodle (18 June 1961), *St. Matthew passion* (18 Apr. 1962), *Dido and Aeneas* (17 July 1963), 3 recitals (Sept. 1964), "Distinguished artists" (series, 27 July 1966), "Harp and harpsichord soloists of today" (series, July 1967).
RECORDINGS
Recorded with Hallmark.

KRISH, Tanya Moiseiwitsch
see MOISEIWITSCH, Tanya

LA FLECHE, Marie Marguerite Louise Gisèle
see MACKENZIE, Gisèle

LALIBERTÉ, Alfred   1878-1953
Sculptor; b. 18 May 1878 in Ste. Élizabeth de Warwick, Arthabaska, PQ; son of Joseph and Marie (Richard) Laliberté; m. Jeanne Lavallée 22 June 1940; d. 13 Jan. 1953 in Montreal, PQ.
EDUCATION
Attended village school, Ste. Élizabeth de War-

wick, until *c*.1891; attended evening classes at Council of Arts and Manufacturers, Monument National, Montreal, *c*.1898; studied under Gabriel Jules Thomas and Antoine Injabert, École Nationale des Beaux-Arts, Paris, France, for two years *c*.1904.
RELIGION
Roman Catholic.
CAREER
Employed in carding mill *c*.1891-98; engaged in various occupations in Montreal 1898-1903; lived in Paris 1903-07; returned to Canada 1907; appointed professor at the Arts Council, Montreal 1907; lived in Paris 1910-11; École des Beaux-Arts, Montréal, professor 1922-53; reproductions of 122 bronzes published in an album by La Librairie Beauchemin, 1934; executed historical and religious monuments, statues, busts, medallions, and medals in Montreal 1907-53.
COMMISSIONS
Sculpture, St. Joseph's Oratory, Montreal and Sacré Coeur de Charlesbourg, PQ; sculpture of Father Marquette, Parliament Buildings, Quebec, PQ, 1910-11; sculpture of Father Brébeuf, Parliament Buildings, Quebec, 1910-11; sculpture of fountain in Maisonneuve, PQ, 1914; sculpture of Intendant Talon, Parliament Buildings, Quebec, 1916; sculpture of Lord Dorchester, Parliament Buildings, Quebec, 1916; statue of Robert Borden, Quebec; sculpture of Louis Hébert, Parliament Buildings, Quebec, 1917; Dollard des Ormeaux monument, Lafontaine Park, Montreal, 1918; sculpture of Pierre Boucher de Grosbais, Parliament Buildings, Quebec, 1922; sculpture of Pierre Gauthier de Varennes de la Vérendrye, Parliament Buildings, Quebec, 1922; Sir Wilfrid Laurier monument, Ottawa, Ont., 1926.
MEMBER
Canadian Sculptors' Society (co-founder, 1928); Royal Canadian Academy (Associate 1912; Academician 1919); Académie des Beaux-Arts de l'Institut de France (membre correspondant pour le section de sculpture, 1948).
AWARDS, HONOURS
First prize for sculpture, provincial exhibition in Quebec, 1898; honourable mention, Paris *Salon*, 1905; first prize for sculpture, Paris *Salon*, 1917; LLD from University of Montreal, 1940.
EXHIBITIONS
ONE-MAN: Arts Council, Montreal, 1907; Johnson & Copping Gallery, Montreal, 1912; Montreal Gallery of Fine Arts, 1943; Simpson Gallery, Montreal, 1966.
GROUP: Represented in group exhibitions held in Canada during his lifetime including annual exhibitions of Royal Canadian Academy and Spring Exhibitions of Art Association of Montreal; Paris *Salon*, 1904, 1905, 1906, and 1917.

COLLECTIONS IN WHICH REPRESENTED
Musée du Québec, PQ; National Gallery of
Canada, Ottawa.

LAJEUNESSE, Marie-Louise Émma Cécile
see ALBANI, Marie-Louise Émma Cécile

LAMB, Molly
see BOBAK, Molly

LAMBERT, Margery* 1939—
(Margery Lambert Nunes)
Dancer and teacher; b. 3 May 1939 in New
Westminster, BC; daughter of Alan Martin and
Alice (Bogue) Lambert; m. Armando Da
Silva Nunes 3 Mar. 1964.
EDUCATION
Attended school in New Westminster, and
Bellingham and Tacoma, Wash.; studied ballet
with Josephine Slater, New Westminster; Jan
Collum, Tacoma; Robert Joffrey, Valentina
Perejaslavec, and Olga Tavolga (formerly of
Leningrad Kirov Ballet) in New York, NY;
Russian character dancing with Yurek Lawoski,
Valentina Perejaslavec, and Casimir Kokich,
New York; modern jazz with Matt Mattox,
New York, beginner and intermediate courses,
1961.
RELIGION
Espiscopalian.
OFFICE
c/o Bailado Gulbenkian Foundation, Avenida de
Berna, Lisbon, Portugal.
CAREER
Pilgrim Productions Children's Theatre, New
York, dancer and actress 1957-59; Yurek Lawoski
Character Dance Company, New York, 1959;
Ballet Russe de Monte Carlo, corps de ballet
1960-61, Concert company summer 1961,
soloist 1961-62; Les Grands Ballets Canadiens,
Montréal, soloist 1962-66, leading dramatic
1966—; Gulbenkian Music Festival, Portugal,
guest artist summer 1965; San Carlos Opera,
Lisbon, Portugal, guest artist summer 1965;
Académie des Grands Ballets Canadiens,
Montréal, teacher 1967—.
MEMBER
AGMA; Union des Artistes de Montréal.
AWARDS, HONOURS
Honorary citizen of Mobile, Ala.
THEATRE
First danced Queen of the Wilis in *Giselle*
(Coralli-Perrot, 1961), Gypsy in *La fille mal
gardée* (Caton, 1961/63), Young girl in *Le
spectre de la rose* (Fokine, 1962/63), Grahn in
Pas de quatre (Dolin, 1963/64), Fouetté girl
in *Graduation ball* (Lichine, 1963/64); created
title role in *Medea* (Paige, 1964/65); first
danced Oriental dance in *Casse-noisette* (Nault,

1964/65), La sylphide pas de deux in *Graduation
ball* (Lichine, 1964/65), Black Swan pas de deux
from *Le lac des cygnes* (Petipa-Ivanov, Gulbenkian Music Festival, 1965), *Don Quixote* pas
de deux (Petipa, Gulbenkian Music Festival,
1965), dancer in *La spinalda* (San Carlos Opera
House, 1965), Delilah in *Dark vision* (Paige,
1965/66), Young girl in *Sea gallows* (Hyrst,
1965/66); created title role in *La corriveau*
(Paige, 1966/67), Mother in *The brood* (Kuch,
1968/69); choreographed *Aspiration* (Les
Grands Ballets Canadiens Workshop, 1964),
Rumanian rhapsody (Les Grands Ballets Can-
adiens Workshop, 1966).
TELEVISION
Danced in *Stillpoint* (Bolender, CBC, 1962),
Graduation ball (Lichine, CBC, 1963), *Hommage*
(Hyrst, CBC, 1963), Beauty in *Beauty and the
beast* (Seillier, CBC, 1964), *Hungarian rhapsody*
(Chiriaeff, CBC, 1964), title role in *Medea* (Paige,
Lisbon, 1965), Black Swan pas de deux from *Le
lac des cygnes* (Petipa-Ivanov, Lisbon, 1965),
La sylphide pas de deux from *Graduation ball*
(Lichine, Lisbon, 1965), Chosen maiden in *Le
sacre du printemps* (Nault, CBC, 1967), title role
in *La corriveau* (Paige, CBC, 1967).

LAMOTHE, Arthur* 1928—
Film maker; b. 7 Dec. 1928 in Saint-Mont, France;
came to Canada in June 1963 and settled in
Montreal.
EDUCATION
Attended University of Montreal, 1954-61.
HOME
1143 Laurier Ave., W., Montreal, PQ.
CAREER
Image, Montréal, founder and staff-member
1954-55; La commission royale d'enquête sur
les perspectives économiques du Canada, re-
searcher 1955; CBC, 1957-59; Collège Sainte-
Marie, Montréal, lecturer 1960-61; École
Normale Secondaire, University of Montreal,
lecturer 1961; National Film Board of Canada,
Montreal 1962-65; Le Conseil d'Orientation
économique du Québec, researcher 1963;
Société générale cinématographique, Montréal,
founder and president 1965; École Normale
Jacques-Cartier, Montréal, lecturer 1968; Festival
international du film de Montréal, founder and
member.
MEMBER
Association des Producteurs de Films du Québec
(secretary-treasurer); Association Professionnelle
des Cinéastes du Québec (founder and member);
Cinémathèque Canadienne.
FILMS
Produced "Ce soir" (series, CBC, 1959-60),
"Premier plan" (series, CBC, 1960-61),
"L'événement" (series, CBC, 1961), "Ciné-club"

(series, CBC, 1961); photographed *Manger* (National Film Board, 1961; gold medal, Mostra Conserve, Parma, Italy, 1964-65), *Dimanche d'Amérique* (National Film Board, 1961); narrated *Pour quelques arpents de neige* (National Film Board, 1962); directed and produced *Bûcherons de la Manouane* (National Film Board, 1962; voile d'argent, Locarno Film Festival, Switzerland, 1963; first prize, short films category, Canadian Film Festival, Montreal, 1963; critic's prize, Evian Festival, 1964; special mention, Ann Arbor Film Festival, Mich., 1964); directed and co-produced *De Montréal à Manicouagan* (National Film Board, 1963); co-directed *La beauté même* (National Film Board, 1964); directed, produced, and photographed *La neige a fondu sur la Manicouagan* (National Film Board, 1965); directed and produced *Poussière sur la ville* (Société générale cinématographique-Cooperatio, 1965), *Bilan 66* (Société générale cinématographique, 1966); directed *Ce soir-là, Gilles Vigneault* (Société générale cinématographique, 1966), *La moisson* (National Film Board, 1967), *Mon pays* (Société générale cinématographique, 1967), *Le chemin de fer du Labrador* (Société générale cinématographique for Gaumont Télévision, Paris, France, 1967); adapted *Buster Keaton rides again* (National Film Board, 1967; special prize for best biographical documentary, Melbourne International Film Festival, Australia, 1967-68; first prize [ex aequo], medium length films, Festival of Canadian Films, Montreal International Film Festival, 1966-67; best general information film, Canadian Film Awards, Montreal, 1966-67; first prize, music, literature, and films category, American Film Festival, New York, NY, 1967-68; silver trophy, documentary category, Tenth San Francisco International Film Festival, Calif., 1966-67; special prize - CIDALC, Seventeenth International Exhibition of the Documentary Film, Venice, Italy, 1966-67; gold medal - MIFED, International Contest of Public Relations Films, Milan, Italy, c.1968); directed, produced, and photographed *L'intégration du malade mental dans la société* (Société générale cinématographique for National Film Board, 1968); directed and produced *Conflit scolaire à Saint-Léonard* (Société générale cinématographique, 1968); produced *La semaine syndicale de L'U.G.E.Q.* (Société générale cinématographique, 1968), *L'occupation de Collège Saint-Ignace* (Société générale cinématographique, 1968), *La marche de la F.T.Q.* (Société général cinématographique, 1968); *Tévec 4* (1968); *Actualités cinématographiques* (1968).

LANDSLEY, Patrick Alfred* 1926—
Artist; b. 13 Aug. 1926 in Winnipeg, Man.; son of Walter Patrick and Winnifred (Stanier) Landsley; m. Carol Margaret Wilson 31 Oct. 1953; children:

Sean David b. 17 Aug. 1962, Liam Peter b. 13 Sept. 1964, Tracy Valida b. 8 Dec. 1967.
EDUCATION
Attended Taché School, St. Boniface, Man., 1932-40; attended Norwood Collegiate, St. Boniface, 1941-43; studied under L.L. Fitzgerald and Joseph Plaskett (*q.v.*), Winnipeg School of Art, 1947-49; Arthur Lismer (*q.v.*), Jacques de Tonnancour (*q.v.*), and Gordon Webber, (*q.v.*) Montreal Museum of Fine Arts School, 1950-51; Fernand Léger, Académie Montmartre, Paris, France, 1951; Gustave Singier, Académie Ranson, Paris, 1952.
RELIGION
Roman Catholic.
HOME
3614 Ontario Ave., Montreal, PQ.
CAREER
RCNVR, 1944-46; studied and painted in Paris 1951-53; Lower Canada College, Montreal, art teacher 1955-58; Montreal YWCA art department, teacher 1954-58 and 1962-64; Montreal Museum of Fine Arts School, teacher 1954-67; Macdonald College, PQ, teacher for one term 1957; Snowdon YM - YWHA, Montreal, teacher 1960-63; McGill University, fine arts department, lecturer 1960—; Sir George Williams University, lecturer 1967—.
COMMISSIONS
Mural, Beth-El Synagogue, Montreal, 1968 (with George Tondino and Ghitta Caiserman-Roth).
MEMBER
Canadian Group of Painters; Association des Artistes Non-figuratifs de Montréal (elected, 1956).
AWARDS, HONOURS
Scholarship, Montreal Museum of Fine Arts, 1950-51; scholarship, Canada Foundation, 1951; prize winner, Winnipeg Show, Winnipeg Art Gallery, Man., 1955; Canada Council grant, 1966 and 1967.
EXHIBITIONS
ONE-MAN: Galerie Denyse Delrue, Montréal, 1958; McGill University, 1961; Penthouse Gallery, Montreal, 1963.
GROUP: Represented in group exhibitions held in Canada since 1954 including Spring Exhibitions of Montreal Museum of Fine Arts, Winnipeg Shows at Winnipeg Art Gallery, Winter Exhibitions at Art Gallery of Hamilton, Ont., annual exhibitions of Ontario Society of Artists and Canadian Group of Painters; represented in group exhibitions organized by National Gallery of Canada, Ottawa, Ont., including its fourth Biennial Exhibition of Canadian Painting, 1961; Galerie Craven, Paris, 1952; *Salon de Mai*, Musée d'Art Moderne, Paris, 1952; Artists of the Commonwealth, Imperial Institute, London, England, 1953; *Association des Artistes Non-*

figuratifs de Montréal exhibition, Canada House, New York, NY, 1959.

COLLECTIONS IN WHICH REPRESENTED
Musée du Québec, PQ; Loyola University; Sir George Williams University.

WRITINGS
CONTRIBUTED: Articles to *Montreal star.*

LANGEVIN, André   1927–

Novelist and playwright; b. 1927 in Montreal, PQ.

HOME
RR3, St. Hilaire, PQ.

CAREER
Journalist; CBC, Montreal, producer.

AWARDS, HONOURS
Cercle du Livre de France award for *Évadé de la nuit*, 1951 and *Poussière sur la ville*, 1953; first prize of Concours d'Oeuvres Théâtrales du Théâtre du Nouveau Monde, 1957; Canada Council senior arts fellowship, 1959/60; Prix Liberté, 1967.

WRITINGS
Évadé de la nuit (novel), Cercle du Livre de France, 1951; *Poussière sur la ville* (novel), Cercle du Livre de France, 1953 (translated into English); *Le temps des hommes* (novel), Cercle du Livre de France, 1956; *Une nuit d'amour* (play; produced Théâtre du Nouveau Monde, Montreal, 1954); *L'oeil du peuple* (play; produced Théâtre du Nouveau Monde, 1 Nov. 1957).
CONTRIBUTED: Articles to *Liberté, Magazine Maclean.*

LAPIERRE, Eugène   1899–

(Joseph Eugène Lapierre)
Composer and organist; b. 8 June 1899 in Montreal; son of David and Virginie (Papineau) Lapierre; m. Rose Lilianne Sansfaçon 15 Aug. 1922; children: Hermine, Marie, Emmanuel, Monique, Évangéline, Jean.

EDUCATION
Attended Académie de Ste.-Brigitte in Montreal, 1906-13; Collège de St.-Jean d'Iberville, PQ; studied music with Frères des Écoles Chrétiennes and Lucien Perreault; University of Montreal, 1919-22, D Mus, 1930; Conservatoire National de Musique, Montréal, 1920-24; Institut Grégorien, Paris, France, diploma, 1927; studied with Marcel Dupré, Georges Caussade, and Vincent d'Indy, Conservatoire de Paris, 1927-28.

RELIGION
Roman Catholic. ,

HOME
3425 rue St.-Denis, Montréal, PQ.

CAREER
Académie de Ste.-Brigitte, Montréal, boy soprano 1904-12; Ste.-Philomène de Rosemont, Montréal, organist; St.-Denis, Montréal, organist; St.-Jacques, Montréal, organist 1922-24; Conservatoire Nationale de Musique, Montréal,

secretary 1922-24, re-organizer 1927, director, choirmaster, and teacher of organ, solfège, and liturgical music 1928-35; Diocesan Commission for Sacred Music, Montreal, president; Gregorian Institute of America, Toldeo, Ohio, professor of organ and accompaniment; St.-Alphonse de Youville, Montréal, organist; *Radiomonde*, music critic; Congrès de la Langue Française, Québec, lecturer 1935; Music Educators National Conference, Cleveland, Ohio, delegate for Quebec 1946; University of Montreal, Superior Board of the Faculty of Music, member 1950–; Provincial Commission for the Advancement of Musical Training, member 1960.

MEMBER
CPAC; Société des Artistes Musiciens de Montréal (past president).

AWARDS, HONOURS
Quebec government scholarship, 1924; Prix David for literature for *Calixa Lavallée*, 1937.

COMPOSITIONS
Ecce fidelis, motet, 1926, Herelle, Paris; *Passacaille*, organ, 1929; *St.-Jean de Dieu*, choral hymn, 1935, Boucher; *Alma*, organ, 1937; *Le vieil arbre*, song, 1940, Fassio Lachute; *Gavotte in A*, piano, 1941; *Le tinton*, song, 1941, Bonne Chanson; *Le père des amours*, opera, 1942; *Minuet*, choir, 1942; *Villanelle*, song, 1942, Bonne Chanson; *Romance du soir*, song, 1942, Fassio Lachute; *Alma mater*, choir, 1943, University of Montreal; *Noël canadien*, song, 1943; *Adeste*, organ, 1944, Boucher; *Tantum ergo*, choir, 1944; *Pastorale*, organ, 1945, Boucher; *La luciole*, song, 1946; *Dis-moi, Lina*, song, 1946; *Prière nuptiale*, song, 1947, Bonne Chanson, also under title *Wedding prayer*, Bonne Chanson; *Ava admirabile*, motet, 1948, Bonne Chanson; *Trio*, flute, oboe, and bassoon, 1950; *Qui ad justitiam*, motet, 1950; *Marche solennelle*, organ, 1951; *Les clochers canadiens*, cantata; *Canadien, souviens-toi*, choir; *Gavotte et musette*, piano, Archambault; *Chanson de Charlemagne*, song; *Postlude sur "Alma redemptoris,"* organ, 1953, Fassio; *Mes plus beaux noëls*, juvenile songbook, 1961, Archambault; *Mes plus beaux airs*, juvenile songbook, 1963, Archambault; *Hymns for morning and evening devotions*, Gregorian Institute of America, 1964.

WRITINGS
La musique au sanctuaire, 1932; *Pourqoui la musique*, 1933; *Calixa Lavallée, musicien national de Canada*, A. Levesque, 1937; *Un style canadien de musique*, Éditions du "Cap diamant," 1942; *Gregorian chant accompaniment*, Gregorian Institute of America, 1949.
CONTRIBUTED: Articles to *La revue trimestrielle, Le semeur, La quinzaine musicale, L'action musicale.*

LAPIERRE, Joseph Eugène

see LAPIERRE, Eugène

LAPOINTE, Gatien* 1931–
Poet; b. 18 Dec. 1931 in Sainte-Justine de Dorchester, PQ; son of Evangéliste and Elise (Lessard) Lapointe.
EDUCATION
Attended Petit Séminaire, Québec, PQ and École des Arts Graphiques, Montréal, PQ; Université de Montréal, MA; Collège de France, Paris, Université de Paris, D.-ès-Let.
HOME
Chemin des Bouleaux, L'Acadie, PQ.
OFFICE
Collège Militaire Royal, Saint-Jean-sur-le-Richelieu, PQ.
CAREER
Travelled extensively in Europe, 1956-62; Collège Militaire de Saint-Jean and Université de Montréal, teacher; McGill University and Carleton University, vitising professor; CBC and National Film Board of Canada, Montreal, freelance writer.
AWARDS, HONOURS
Royal Society of Canada fellowships, 1956/57 and 1957/58; Prix du Club des Poètes de Paris for *Lumière du monde*, 1959; Canada Council grant, 1963; Troisième Prix of the Quebec government, Prix du Maurier, and Governor General's literary award for *Ode au Saint-Laurent*, 1963; Quebec government fellowship, 1966/67; Premier Prix of the Quebec government, 1967.
WRITINGS
Jour malaisé, the author, 1953; *Otages de la joie*, the author, 1955; *Le temps premier; Lumière du monde*, Grassin, 1962; *Ode au Saint-Laurent; J'appartiens à la terre*, Jour, 1963; *Le premier mot; Le pari de ne pas mourir*, Jour, 1967.
CONTRIBUTED: Poetry to *Anthologie de la poésie canadienne-française*, edited by G. Sylvestre, Beauchemin, 1958; *Oxford book of Canadian verse*, edited by A.J.M. Smith, Oxford, 1960; *La poésie canadienne*, edited by A. Bosquet, Seghers, 1962; *Littérature du Québec*, edited by G. Robert, Déom, 1964; *Un siècle de littérature canadienne*, edited by G. Sylvestre, HMH, 1967; poetry and articles to *L'action, Le devoir, Liberté, Poetry-Australia, Soleil, Cité libre*.

LAPOINTE, Paul-Marie* 1929–
Poet; b. 22 Sept. 1929 in Saint-Félicien, PQ; son of Antoine and Antoinette (Rousseau) Lapointe; m. Gisèle Verreault 1952; children: Michèle, Frédéric.
EDUCATION
Attended Séminaire de Chicoutimi, PQ; Collège de Saint-Laurent, PQ; studied architecture at École des Beaux-Arts, Montréal.
RELIGION
Roman Catholic.
HOME
912 Dunlop, Outremont, Montréal 8, PQ.

CAREER
L'événement journal, Le nouveau journal, La presse, Montréal, journalist; CBC, Montreal, scriptwriter; *Magazine Maclean*, editor-in-chief 1964-69.
AWARDS, HONOURS
Quebec government first prize in poetry, 1965.
WRITINGS
Le vierge incendié, Mithra-Mythe, 1948; *Six poems; with versions in English*, Contact, 1955; *Choix de poèmes:Arbres*, Hexagone, 1960; *Pour les âmes*, Hexagone, 1964.
CONTRIBUTED: Poetry to several anthologies, e.g. *La poésie canadienne*, edited by A. Bosquet, Seghers, 1962; *Anthologie de la poésie canadienne française*, edited by G. Sylvestre, Beauchemin, 1963; poetry and articles to *Liberté, Magazine Maclean*.

LAROCHE, Roland* 1927–
Actor and director; b. 27 Dec. 1927 in Cap de la Madeleine, PQ; son of Émile and Cécile (Paquet) Laroche.
EDUCATION
Collège Bourget, Rigaud, PQ, diploma 1945; studied drama with professor Henri Poitras, 1948-49; Conservatoire Lasalle, 2nd year certificate, 1949-50; National Academy of Theatre Arts, Pleasantville, NY, 1950; Artist Theatre School, New York, NY, 1951-52; studied drama with Jean Dalmain and Jean Gascon, Théâtre du Nouveau Monde, Montréal, 1954-56; with Jean Doat and Jean Valcourt, Conservatoire d'Art Dramatique de la Province, Montréal 1954-55, 1957; with Pierre Valde, Théâtre de l'Oeuvre, Paris, France, 1960; École de Mime Jacques Lecoq, Paris, 1960-61; Université du Théâtre des Nations, Paris, 1961.
RELIGION
Roman Catholic.
HOME
1850 Lincoln Ave., Apt. 804, Montreal 25, PQ.
CAREER
L'Association des Artistes de St. Hyacinthe, PQ, director and amateur actor 1945-50; Old Town Theatre, Smithtown, NY, actor 1951-52; Theatre Artists Inc., New York, actor and stage-manager 1952-53; La Compagnie de Montréal, actor and administrator 1954–; Le Théâtre Club, Montréal, actor 1954–; Théâtre de Dix Heures, Montréal, actor 1954–; Théâtre du Nouveau Monde, Montréal, actor and stage-manager 1955–; Théâtre du Rideau Vert, Montréal, actor 1958–; Théâtre de l'Égrégore, Montréal, co-founder and stage-director 1959–; La Boutique d'Opéra, Montréal, instructor 1962-63; National Theatre School, Montreal, teacher 1964–; Canadian Players Foundation and Montreal Symphony Orchestra, production manager 1964-65; Expo 67, Montreal, production manager of national

days at Place des Nations 1967; Dominion Drama Festival, Theatre Clinics teacher, Kingston, Ont. 1967, Winnipeg, Man. 1968; Quebec Music Festival, summer course teacher 1968.

MEMBER
Canadian Theatre Centre; Centre d'essai des auteurs dramatiques inc., Montréal; Quebec Music Festival Inc.; Union des Artistes de Montréal.

AWARDS, HONOURS
Prix Eugène Jousse for best stage manager from Dominion Drama Festival for *Les insolites*, 1956; Ministère de la Jeunesse de la province grant for studies in Europe, 1959; Canada Council arts scholarship, 1960, 1961; Trophy Louis Jovet for best direction from Dominion Drama Festival for *Le pendu*, 1967.

THEATRE
Played in *Cocktail d'Yvette* (Artistes de St. Hyacinthe), *Ces dames aux chapeaux verts* (Artistes de St. Hyacinthe), *Mon oncle et mon curé* (Artistes de St. Hyacinthe), *La rhumba* (Artistes de St. Hyacinthe), *Altitude 3200* (Artistes de St. Hyacinthe), *Le président Haudecoeur* (Artistes de St. Hyacinthe), *Épousez-nous, Monsieur* (Artistes de St. Hyacinthe), *Nous irons à Valparaiso* (Artistes de St. Hyacinthe), *La petite hutte* (Artistes de St. Hyacinthe), *L'empereur de Chine* (Artistes de St. Hyacinthe), Politician in *Rip van Winkel* (Children's Theatre of New York, American tour 1950, 1951), Grandfather in *Happy time* (Old Town, 1951), Monk in *Le roi ivre* (Dix Heures, Sept. 1956), Interpreter in *Le journal de Jules Renard* (Dix Heures, Jan. 1957), Léon in *Edmée* (Dix Heures, Jan. 1957), Tibia in *Les caprices de Marianne* (Rideau Vert, May 1958), Mouftan in *Le Dodu* (Théâtre Club, June 1958), title role in *Qui est Dupressin?* (l'Egrégore, 1961), Yvan Yvanovitch Triletzki in *Ce fou de Platonov* (l'Égrégore, 1961), King Venceslav in *Ubu-roi* (l'Égrégore, 1962), Pompier in *La cantatrice chauve* (l'Égrégore, 1962); stage-managed *Auto-da-fé* (Theatre Artists, 1952), *Presenting Jane* (Theatre Artists, 1952), *Try! try!* (Theatre Artists, 1952), *Red Riding Hood* (Theatre Artists, 1952), *The screen* (Theatre Artists, 1953), *Down in the valley* (Theatre Artists, 1953), *The love of Dom Perlinplim* (Theatre Artists, 1953); stage-managed and played Richard in *The lady's choice* (Theatre Artists, 1953), Hector in *The heroes* (Theatre Artists, 1953), Marin in *The bait* (Theatre Artists, 1953), Belisa in *The garden* (Theatre Artists, 1953), Valère in *Le médecin malgré lui* (La Compagnie, Festival régional d'art dramatique, 1954), Cook in *La mouette* (Nouveau Monde, 1955); stage-managed *Le chandelier* (Théâtre Club, 1955), *Le barrage* (Théâtre Club, 1955), *La nuit des rois* (Théâtre Club, 1956), *La mégère apprivoisée* (Théâtre d'été Chanteclerc, Ste. Adèle, PQ, July

1956); stage-managed and played Laborne in *Némo* (Nouveau Monde, Jan. 1956), Radiesthéiste in *Les insolites* (La Compagnie, Mar. 1956; Festival national d'art dramatique, Sherbrooke, PQ, May 1956), Dr. Balzoni in *Le menteur* (La Compagnie, Mar. 1958), *Le malade imaginaire* (Nouveau Monde, Stratford, Ont. Festival, Aug. 1958); stage-managed *Les trois farces* (Nouveau Monde, 1958/59), *Le temps des lilas* (Nouveau Monde, 1958/59), *Venise sauvée* (Nouveau Monde, 1958/59), *Clérambard* (Nouveau Monde, 1958/59), *Long day's journey into night* (Nouveau Monde, 1958/59), *Les taupes* (Nouveau Monde, Nov. 1959); stage-managed and played Colombo in *Les violettes* (L'Égrégore, 1962); directed *Une femme douce* (l'Égrégore, Nov. 1959; European tour 1966), *Le licou* (Maison du Canada, Paris, France, Jan. 1960), *Magie rouge* (l'Égrégore, 1961), *Rimbaud recital* (l'Égrégore, 1962), *The great god Brown* (l'Égrégore, 1962), *Une saison en enfer* (l'Égrégore, 1963), *Le medium* (Boutique d'Opéra, 1964), *La balançoire* (l'Égrégore, 1966), *Le barbier de Séville* (Théâtre Lyrique de Québec, 1967), *Le pendu* (Dominion Drama Festival, St. John's, Nfld., 1967), *Api 2967* (l'Égrégore 1967), *Amédée* (Domino Theatre, Kingston, 1967), *Hamlet, prince du Québec* (Théâtre de l'Escale, Montréal, 17 Jan. 1968).

RADIO
Directed *Le château de Barbe Bleue* ("Heure du concert," CBC, 1962), *Suor Angelica* ("Heure du concert," CBC, 1965).

TELEVISION
Played in numerous productions, e.g. *Le survenant, Histoire du Canada, Radisson, Roman de la science, Première, Les petits pains de Sainte Geneviève*, Stage-manager in *Quatuor* (CBC, Nov. 1955), *Dans sa candeur naïve* (Nov. 1955), le Soldat in *Rivemale* (Mar. 1956), *L'enfant de noël* (1956), *Les Plouffes* (serial, CBC, 1956-57), Greffier in *Une lettre perdue* (1957), le Père in *Profil d'adolescent* (1957), *La dette* (May 1957), *Défense de stationner* (June 1957), *Le trèfle à quatre feuilles* (Sept. 1957), *La boîte à surprise* (CBC, 1958); adapted *Mister Sleeman is coming* ("Shoestring-theatre," Dec. 1959), *Monsieur mon voisin* (serial, CBC, 1961-67), *Les belles histoires* (CBC, 1967-68).

LAROSE, Ludger   1868-1915
Artist; b. 1868 in Montreal, PQ; d. 1915 in Montreal.

EDUCATION
Studied under Abbé Chabert, École des Arts et Manufactures, Montréal; studied under Gustav Moreau and Jean-Paul Laurens, École des Beaux-Arts, Paris, France, 1887.

CAREER
Sent by church authorities to work on a chapel in

Europe; travelled to Rome, Italy to copy masters; taught art in Montreal, 1894-1910; Westmount schools, PQ, teacher, 1912-15.

EXHIBITIONS
ONE-MAN: National Gallery of Canada, Ottawa, Ont., 1953.
GROUP: Inter-American Biennial of Painting and Graphic Art Exhibition, Museum of Fine Arts, Mexico City, Mexico, 1960.
COLLECTIONS IN WHICH REPRESENTED
Musée du Québec, PQ; National Gallery of Canada.

LAURENDEAU, André 1912-68
Author; b. 21 Mar. 1912 in Montreal, PQ; son of Arthur and Blanche (Hardy) Laurendeau; m. Ghislaine Perrault 4 June 1935; children: Francine, Jean, Yves, Olivier, Geneviève, Sylvie; d. 1 June 1968.

EDUCATION
Université de Montréal, BA, graduate studies 1934-36; Université de Paris, 1935-37; Institut Catholique, Paris, France.

RELIGION
Roman Catholic.

CAREER
Action nationale, Montréal, director 1937-43, 1948-54; Quebec government, member of Legislative Assembly 1944-48; *Le devoir*, Montréal, joint editor-in-chief 1947-56, editor-in-chief 1957; Royal Commission on Bilingualism and Biculturalism, co-chairman 1963.

AWARDS, HONOURS
National Newspaper award, 1957 and 1963; Prix du Théâtre du Nouveau Monde for *Deux femmes terribles*, 1960.

TELEVISION
Produced *Pays et merveille* (1953-61), news broadcasts (1961-62).

WRITINGS
Voyages au pays de l'enfance (non-fiction), Beauchemin, 1960; *La crise de la conscription 1942* (non-fiction), Jour, 1962; *Une vie d'enfer* (novel) HMH, 1965; *La vertu des chattes* (play), Écrits du Canada français, 1956 (produced CBC TV, 1957; Théâtre d'été de Percé, PQ); *Deux femmes terribles* (play), Écrits du Canada français, 1961 (produced Théâtre du Nouveau Monde, Montréal, 1961; translated into English; "Festival," CBC TV 1965); *Marie Emma* (play), Écrits du Canada français, 1963 (produced on TV).
CONTRIBUTED: Articles to *Action nationale, Canadian business, Canadian forum, Liberté, Maclean's, Saturday night, World affairs*.

LAWRENCE, Leslie* 1934–
Designer; b. 30 July 1934 in Toronto; son of Leslie Arthur and Gertrude Maud Aileen (Fitzsimons) Lawrence; m. Wendy Roland Michener, Sept. 1957 (deceased); children: Caitlin Erica, Miranda Elizabeth.

EDUCATION
Attended Allenby Public School, Norway Public School, Toronto; University of Toronto Schools; University of Toronto, BA, 1956; studied with Abd'el Kadar Farah at École Supérieure de l'Art Dramatique, Strasbourg, France, 1959-60.

HOME
44 Summerhill Gdns., Toronto 7, Ont.

OFFICE
Canadian Broadcasting Corporation, 90 Sumach St., Toronto, Ont.

CAREER
Hart House Theatre, Toronto, actor 1953; *U.C. undergrad*, literary magazine, editor *c.*1953-56; Red Barn Theatre, Jackson's Point, Muskoka, Ont., actor 1955; Prud'hommes Garden Centre Theatre, Vineland, Ont., actor 1956; Straw Hat Players, Port Carling, Muskoka, Ont., actor 1957; Crest Theatre, Toronto, actor 1956-57, resident designer 1961-62; CBC, Toronto, actor 1956-57, special effects department 1960-61, design department 1964; travelled in USSR and Scandinavia 1958; LRM Productions, Toronto, co-founder 1959; freelance set designer, Toronto, 1961; Neptune Theatre, Halifax, consultant designer of stage and auditorium 1963, designer 1963–; National Theatre School, Montreal, head of design section 1964; Canadian Opera Company, Toronto, designer 1966; Crest Hour Company, Toronto, designer 1967.

MEMBER
Canadian Theatre Centre; Associated Designers of Canada (secretary-treasurer, 1966; corresponding secretary, 1968).

AWARDS, HONOURS
E.A. Dale award for contribution to undergraduate theatre, *c.*1956; Canada Council fellowship for study at Centre Dramatique de l'Est, Strasbourg, France, 1959-60.

THEATRE
Played leading role and co-designed *Teach me how to cry* (Women's Alumnae Dramatic Society, Toronto, 1956; Dominion Drama Festival, best production award); designed sets and costumes for *The cocktail party* (Valetta, Malta, 1959), *Dark of the moon* (Camp Manitowabing, Ont., 1959), *Hamlet of Stepney Green* (Radio City, Toronto, 1959); sets for *The mother* (Royal Conservatory of Music, Opera School, Toronto, 1961), *I Pagliacci* (Canadian Opera Company, Toronto, 1961), *Spring thaw* (Crest, 1962; Royal Alexandra Theatre, Toronto, 1963), *Caesar and Cleopatra* (Vancouver International Festival, 1962), *Madama Butterfly* (Canadian Opera Company, Toronto, 1962; 26 Sept. 1967), *Cosi fan tutte* (Canadian Opera Company, tour 1963), *Major Barbara* (Neptune, 1963), *Mary Mary* (Neptune, 1963), *The fourposter* (Neptune, 1963), *Antigone* (Neptune, 1963), *The sleeping beauty* (Neptune, 1963), *The fantasticks* (Neptune, 17

Dec. 1963), *Diary of a scoundrel* (Neptune, 15 Jan. 1964), *Louisbourg* (Neptune, 17 Mar. 1964), *Twelfth night* (Neptune, 1964), *Two for the seesaw* (Neptune, 1965), *The school for wives* (Neptune, 1965), *As you like it* (Neptune, 1965), *The crucible* (Neptune, 4 May 1966), *Henry IV*, part I (Neptune, 14 June 1966), *Faust* (Canadian Opera Company, 1966), sets for *The taming of the shrew* (Neptune, 1967), *Brouart* (Hart House Theatre, Toronto, 2 Feb. 1968), *Marat/Sade* (Trinity Square Theatre, Toronto, 1968), *Jacques Brel is alive and well and living in Paris* (Bayview Playhouse, Toronto, 1968), *3 acts for an evening* (Jonas Malcolm Productions, Toronto, 6 Nov. 1968).

FILM
Designed sets for several productions, e.g. *Carstairs tell the people* (Crawley Films, 1967).

TELEVISION
Designed sets for several productions, e.g. *A threepenny profile* ("Sunday show," CBC, 1966), "Quentin Durgens, MP" (series, CBC, 1967).

WRITINGS
CONTRIBUTED: Articles to *Globe & mail* (Toronto).

LAWSON, Ernest 1873-1939
Artist; b. 22 Mar. 1873 in Windsor, NS; son of Archibald Lawson; d. 18 Dec. 1939 in Miami Beach, Fla.

EDUCATION
Attended school in Halifax, NS; Kingston Collegiate Institute, Ont. until *c.*1888; Art Students League, New York, NY; studied under John Henry Twatchman and J. Alden Weir, Cos Cob, Conn.; Jean-Pierre Laurens and B. Constant, Académie Julian, Paris, France, 1893-96.

CAREER
Lived in Kansas City, Mo., for a year and a half *c.*1889; lived in Mexico for a year *c.*1890; lived in Toronto, Ont., 1896-97; landscape painter in New York 1898-1936; painted in Spain 1916; painted in Newfoundland and Nova Scotia 1924; Broadmoor Art Academy, Colorado Springs, Colo., teacher 1926; Kansas City Art Institute and School of Design, Mo., teacher 1928; painted in New York 1929-36; painted in Florida 1936-39.

MEMBER
National Academy (Associate 1908; Academician 1917); American Painters and Sculptors, New York; National Institute of Arts and Letters.

AWARDS, HONOURS
Silver medal, Louisiana Purchase Exposition, 1904; Jennie Sesnan gold medal, Pennsylvania Academy of Fine Arts, 1907; gold medal, American Academy of Arts and Sciences, 1907; gold medal, Panama-Pacific Exposition, San Francisco, Calif., 1915; Corcoran silver medal, Corcoran Gallery of Art, Washington, DC, 1916; Innes gold medal, National Academy of Design, 1917; Joseph E.

Temple gold medal, Pennsylvania Academy of Fine Arts, Philadelphia, 1920; Saltus gold medal for merit, National Academy of Design, 1930; Hallgarten prize, National Academy of Design, 1908; Benjamin Altman prize, National Academy of Design, 1916, 1921, and 1928; William A. Clark prize, Corcoran Gallery of Art, Washington, 1916; first prize, Carnegie Institute, Pittsburgh, Pa., 1921.

EXHIBITIONS
ONE-MAN: Milch Gallery, Ferargil Galleries, New York; Babcock Gallery, National Gallery of Canada, Ottawa, Ont., 1967.
GROUP: Represented in Canadian Art Club exhibitions in Toronto, 1911-15; represented in group exhibitions in Whitney Museum of American Art, New York, Metropolitan Museum of Art, New York, National Academy of Design, New York, Corcoran Gallery of Art, Brooklyn Museum, NY, Carnegie Institute, and Pennsylvania Academy of Fine Arts, during his lifetime; Paintings by Canadian Artists, City Art Museum, St. Louis, Mo., 1918; British Empire Exhibition, Wembley, England, 1924; International Exposition, Ghent, Belgium, 1925; *Exposition d'art canadien*, Musée du Jeu de Paume, Paris, 1927.

COLLECTIONS IN WHICH REPRESENTED
Art Gallery of Ontario, Toronto; Barnes Foundation, Merion, Pa.; Brooklyn Museum; Carnegie Institute; Chicago Art Institute, Ill.; Columbus Gallery of Fine Arts, Ohio; Corcoran Gallery of Art; Detroit Institute of Arts, Mich.; William Rockhill Nelson Gallery of Art, Kansas City; Metropolitan Museum of Art; Monclair Museum, NJ; National Gallery, Washington; National Gallery of Canada, Ottawa, Ont.; Newark Museum, NJ; City Art Museum, St. Louis; Fine Arts Gallery of San Diego, Calif.; Telfair Academy of Arts and Sciences, Inc., Savannah, Ga.; Whitney Museum of American Art, New York; Worcester Art Museum, Mass.; Butler Institute of American Art, Youngstown, Ohio.

LAYTON, Irving Peter* 1912—
Poet; b. 12 Mar. 1912 in Neamtz, Rumania; son of Moses and Keine (Moscovitch) Lazarovitch; came to Canada in 1913 and settled in Montreal; m. (second marriage) Frances Sutherland 13 Sept. 1946; m. Aviva Cantor 13 Sept. 1958; children: (second marriage) Max Rubin b. 7 Apr. 1946, Naomi Parker b. 1 June 1950; (third marriage) David Herschel b. 24 July 1964.

EDUCATION
Attended Alexandra Public School and Baron Byng High School, Montreal; Macdonald College, PQ, BSc, 1939; McGill University, MA in economics and political science, 1946.

HOME
5731 Somerled Ave., Montreal, PQ.

CAREER

Canadian Army, 1942-43, lieutenant; Jewish Public Library, Montreal, lecturer 1943-58; high school teacher, Montreal 1945-60; Junior Immigrant Aid Society, Montreal, teacher 1945-50; Junior Teacher's Seminary, Montreal, lecturer 1946-48; Sir George Williams University, lecturer 1949-65, poet-in-residence 1965 and 1966; McGill University, teaching fellow, 1949; YM-YWHA, Montreal, lecturer 1964-67; *First statement* and *Northern review*, editorial board member; *Black mountain review*, contributing editor; travelled in Europe, Israel, India, and Nepal; toured Ontario and Quebec with Leonard Cohen, Earle Birney, and Phyllis Gotlieb 1965; has given readings in almost all major Canadian and American universities; University of Guelph, poet-in-residence 1969.

AWARDS, HONOURS

Canada Foundation fellowship, 1959; Canada Council senior arts fellowship, 1959; Governor General's literary award for poetry, 1959; Governor General's literary award for *A red carpet for the sun*, 1960; University of Western Ontario President's medal for "Keine Lazarovitch," 1961; Centennial medal, 1967; Canada Council special arts award, 1968.

MEMBER

PEN Club.

WRITINGS

Here and now, First Statement, 1945; *Now is the place* (stories and poems), First Statement, 1948; *The black huntsmen*, Contact, 1951; (with Louis Dudek and Raymond Souster) *Cerberus*, Contact, 1952; *Love the conqueror worm*, Contact, 1953; *In the midst of my fever*, Divers, 1954; *The long peashooter*, Laocoon, 1954; *The blue propeller*, Contact, 1955; *The cold green element*, Contact, 1955; *The bull calf and other poems*, Contact, 1956; *Music on a kazoo*, Contact, 1956; *The improved binoculars, selected poems*, Contact, 1956; *A laughter in the mind*, J. Williams, 1958; *A red carpet for the sun*, McClelland & Stewart, 1959; *The swinging flesh* (poems and stories), McClelland & Stewart, 1961; *A hasty selection from Irving Layton's 16 volumes of poetry*, 1962?; *The laughing rooster*, McClelland & Stewart, 1964; *Periods of the moon*, McClelland & Stewart, 1967; *The shattered plinths*, McClelland & Stewart, 1968.

EDITED: (with L. Dudek) *Canadian poems, 1850-1952*, rev. 2nd ed., Contact, 1953; *Origin; a quarterly for the creative*, v.18, winter-spring, 1956; *Pan-ic; a selection of contemporary Canadian poems*, 1958; *Poems for 27 cents by Lorna Chaisson and others*, 1961; *Love where the nights are long; Canadian love poems*, McClelland & Stewart, c.1962; *Anvil; a selection of work shop poems*, 1966.

CONTRIBUTED: Poems and short stories to *Canadian poetry in English*, edited by B. Carmen and others, rev. and enl. ed., Ryerson, 1954; *A treasury of Jewish poetry*, edited by Nathan and Marynn Ausubel, Crown, 1957; *The book of Canadian poetry*, edited by A.J.M. Smith, 3rd ed. rev. and enl., W.J. Gage, 1957; *The Penguin book of Canadian verse*, edited by R. Gustafson, Penguin Books, 1958; *The Oxford book of Canadian verse in English and French*, edited by A.J.M. Smith, Oxford, 1960; *Canadian short stories*, edited by Robert Weaver, Oxford, 1960; *Poet's choice*, edited by P. Engle and others, Dial, 1962; *An anthology of Commonwealth verse*, edited by M.J. O'Donnell, Blackie & Son, 1963; *Erotic poetry; the lyrics, ballads, idyls, and epics of love – classical to contemporary*, edited by W. Cole, Random, 1963; *Sprints and distances; sports in poetry and poetry in sport*, compiled by L. Morrison, Crowell, 1965; *Modern Canadian verse in English and French*, edited by A.J.M. Smith, Oxford, 1967; *Queen's quarterly, Encounter, Black mountain review, Canadian forum, Tamarack review, Fiddlehead, Northern review, Maclean's, Liberté, Delta, Saturday night, Origin, Free lance*.

WORK IN PROGRESS: "Selected poems," McClelland & Stewart, 1969; "The whole bloody bird," McClelland & Stewart, 1969.

LEACOCK, Stephen   1869-1944

Author; b. 30 Dec. 1869 in Swanmore, Hampshire, England; son of Walter Peter and Agnes Emma (Butler) Leacock; came to Canada in 1876 and settled in Georgina County, Ont.; m. Beatrix Maude Hamilton 7 Aug. 1900 (d. in 1925); children: Stephen Lushington; d. 28 Mar. 1944 in Toronto, Ont.

EDUCATION

Attended Upper Canada College, Toronto, until 1887; University of Toronto, BA in modern languages, 1887–91; Strathroy Collegiate Institute, Ont., high school teacher's certificate, 1888; University of Chicago, Ph D in political economy, 1903.

RELIGION

Anglican.

CAREER

Uxbridge High School, Ont., member of the staff 1889; Upper Canada College, Toronto, teacher 1891-99; McGill University, special lecturer 1901-03, associate professor 1905, William Dow professor of political economy and head of the department of political science and economics 1908-36; toured the Empire for Rhodes Trust 1907-08; lectured frequently in Canada and the USA.

MEMBER

Royal Society of Canada (elected fellow, 1919);

Political Science Association of America (member of the council); Canadian Authors' Association.

AWARDS, HONOURS

D Litt from Brown University, 1917; LL D from Queen's University, 1919; D Hu L from Dartmouth College, NH, 1920; D Litt from University of Toronto; DCL from Bishop's College (now University); LL D from McGill University; Lorne Pierce medal, 1937.

WRITINGS

Economic prosperity in the British Empire ... (non-fiction), Houghton, 1906; *Elements of political science* (non-fiction), Houghton, 1906; *Baldwin, Lafontaine and Hincks* (biography), Morang, 1907; *Greater Canada; an appeal* (essays), Montreal News, 1907; *Literary lapses; a book of sketches*, Gazette Printers, 1910; *Nonsense novels* (fiction), Lane, 1911; *Sunshine sketches of a little town*, Lane, 1912; *Behind the beyond* (fiction), Lane, 1913; *Adventures of the far north; a chronicle of the frozen seas*, Glasgow Brook, 1914; *The dawn of Canadian history; a chronicle of aboriginal Canada and the coming of the white man*, Glasgow Brook, 1914; *The mariner of St. Malo; a chronicle of the voyages of Jacques Cartier*, Glasgow Brook, 1914; *Arcadian adventures with the idle rich* (non-fiction), Lane, 1914; *The methods of Mr. Sellyer; a book store study* (non-fiction), Lane, 1914; *Moonbeams from the larger lunacy* (fiction), Lane, 1915; (with Basil Macdonald Hastings) *"Q." A farce in one act* (play), French, 1915; *Greatest pages of American humor* (non-fiction), Doubleday, 1916; *Further foolishness; sketches and satires on the follies of the day*, Lane, 1916; *Essays and literary studies*, Lane, 1916; *Frenzied fiction*, Lane, 1918; *The Hohenzollerns in America with the Bolsheviks in Berlin and other impossibilities* (fiction), Lane, 1919; *Winsome Winnie and other new nonsense novels*, Lane, 1920; *The unsolved riddle of social justice* (non-fiction), Lane, 1920; *My discovery of England* (essays), Lane, 1922; *Over the footlights* (essays), Dodd, Mead, 1923; *College days* (fiction), Dodd, Mead, 1923; *Short circuits* (fiction), Macmillan, 1924; *The garden of folly* (fiction), Gundy, 1924; *The proper limitations of state interference* (essays), 1924; *Winnowed wisdom: a new book of humour*, Dodd, Mead, 1926; *Mackenzie, Baldwin, Lafontaine and Hincks* (biography), Oxford, 1926; *My memories and miseries as a school master*, 19 ?; *The iron man and the tin woman; with other such futurities; a book of little sketches of to-day and tomorrow*, Dodd, Mead, 1929; *The Leacock book* (fiction), Lane, 1930; *Laugh with Leacock*, Dodd, Mead, 1930; *Wet wit and dry humour*, Dodd, Mead, 1931; *Back to prosperity; the great opportunity of the Empire conference ...* (non-fiction), Macmillan, 1932; *Afternoons in Utopia* (fiction), Dodd,

Mead, 1932; *The dry Pickwick and other incongruities* (fiction), Lane, 1932; *Mark Twain* (non-fiction), Davies, 1932; *Lahontan's voyages* (non-fiction), Graphic, 1932; *Stephen Leacock's plan to relieve the depression in 6 days, to remove it in 6 months, to eradicate it in 6 years* (essays), Macmillan, 1933; *Charles Dickens, his life and work* (non-fiction), Davies, 1933; *Lincoln frees the slaves* (essays), Putnam, 1934; *Greatest pages of Charles Dickens* (non-fiction), Doubleday, 1934; *The perfect salesman* (fiction), edited by E.V. Knox, McBride, 1934 (published in England under title *Stephen Leacock*, Methuen, 1934); *The pursuit of knowledge: a discussion of freedom and compulsion in education* (essays), Liverwright, 1934; *Too much college; or education eating up life: with kindred essays in education in humour*, Dodd, Mead, 1934; *Humor: its theory and technique* (non-fiction), Dodd Mead, 1935; *The restoration of the finances of McGill University*, the author, 1935; *Helliments of hickonomics, in hiccoughs of verse done in our social planning mill*, Dodd, Mead, 1936; *Funny pieces: a book of random sketches*, Dodd, Mead, 1936; *Humour and humanity: an introduction to the study of humour*, Butterworth, 1937; *Here are my lectures and stories*, Dodd, Mead, 1937; *My discovery of the west: a discussion of east and west in Canada*, Allen, 1937; *Model memoirs and other sketches from simple to serious*, Dodd, Mead, 1938; *All right, Mr. Roosevelt (Canada and the United States)* (essays), Oxford, 1939; *Stephen Leacock's laugh parade*, Dodd, Mead, 1940; *Our British Empire, its structure, its history, its strength* (non-fiction), Lane, 1940; *Canada: the foundations of its future* (non-fiction), Distillers Corp. Ltd., 1941; *Montreal: seaport and city* (non-fiction), Doubleday, 1942; *Our heritage of liberty; its origin, its achievement, its crisis* (essays), Dodd, Mead, 1942; *My remarkable uncle and other sketches*, Dodd, Mead, 1942; *Memories of Christmas* (fiction), Bush, 1943; *"My old college" 1843-1943* (essays), the author, 1943; *Happy stories just to laugh at*, Dodd, Mead, 1943; *How to write* (essays), Dodd, Mead, 1943; *Canada and the sea* (non-fiction), Beatty, 1944; *Last leaves* (fiction), McClelland & Stewart, 1945; *While there is time: the case against social catastrophe* (non-fiction), McClelland & Stewart, 1945; *Leacock roundabout: a treasury of the best works of Stephen Leacock*, Dodd, Mead, 1946; *The boy I left behind me* (autobiography), Doubleday, 1946.

CONTRIBUTED: Short stories and essays to numerous anthologies, e.g. *Copeland reader: an anthology of English poetry and prose*, edited by C.T. Copeland, Scribner, 1926; *28 humorous stories old and new*, edited by E. Rhys and C.A.D. Scott, Appleton, 1926; *Canadian short stories*, edited by R. Knister, Macmillan, 1928; *Golden tales of Canada*, edited by M.L. Becker, Dodd, Mead, 1938; *Second century of detective stories*, edited by E.C. Bentley, Hutchison, 1938; *Great American parade*, Doubleday, 1939; *Novel and story*, edited by E. Sedgewick and H.A. Domincovich, Little, 1939; *Literature for interpretation*, edited by G.S. Bates and H. Kay, Expression, 1939; *All in fun; an omnibus of humor*, edited by A. Churchill, McBride, 1940; *Home book of Christmas*, edited by M.L. Becker, Dodd, 1941; *Comic relief; an omnibus of modern American humor*, compiled by R.N. Linscott, Blue Ribbon Books, 1942; *World's greatest spy stories*, edited by V. Starrett, World Publications, 1944; *Misadventures of Sherlock Holmes*, edited by E. Queen, Little, 1944; *World's great humorous stories*, World Publications, 1944; *Chucklebait*, edited by M.C. Scoggin, Knopf, 1945; *Desert island decameron,* edited by H.A. Smith, Doubleday, 1945; *Murder without tears*, edited by W.J. Cuppy, Sheridan, 1946; *Treasury of golf humour*, edited by D. Dacks, Lantern, 1949; *World's greatest Christmas stories*, edited by E. Posselt, Ziff-Davies, 1949; short stories, essays, and articles to *Queen's quarterly, Saturday night, Canadian home journal, Maclean's, Canadian banker, Western business and industry, Truth, Life, Puck,* and *Canadian magazine.*

LEDUC, Fernand* 1916–
Artist; b. 4 July 1916 in Montreal, PQ; son of Rosaire Leduc; m. Thérèse Renaud 17 May 1947; children: Isabelle b. 19 Aug. 1949.

EDUCATION
Attended Normal School, Montreal; École des Beaux-Arts, Montréal, 1939-44; studied with P.-E. Borduas, Montreal, 1942-47; studied in Paris, 1947-53.

RELIGION
Roman Catholic.

HOME
14, rue Rodier, Paris 9e, France.

CAREER
Worked with Automatistes, Montréal, 1942-47; École des Beaux-Arts, Montréal, 1944-47; travelled to France 1947-53; returned to Montreal 1953-59; returned to Paris, 1959.

MEMBER
Association des Artistes non-figuratifs de Montréal (founder; president, 1956); Salon des Réalités Nouvelles à Paris; Fédération Française des Sociétés d'Art Graphique et Plastique, Paris; Société d'Art Contemporain; Automatistes (founding member).

AWARDS, HONOURS
Lauréat du concours artistique de la Province de Québec, 1957; Canada Council senior arts fellowship, 1959; Canada Council arts award, 1967.

EXHIBITIONS
ONE-MAN: Club Canadien, Paris, 1951; Musée de Granby, PQ, 1955; Galerie l'Actuelle, Montréal, 1956; Art Gallery of (now of Ontario) Toronto, 1957; Galerie Denyse Delrue, Montréal, 1958; Galerie Lycée Pierre Corneille, Montréal, 1959; Galerie Artek, Montréal, 1959; Galerie Hautefeuille, Paris, 1962; Délégation du Québec à Paris, 1962; Galerie Soixante, Montréal, 1963 and 1965; Musée du Québec, PQ, 1966; Musée d'Art Contemporain, Montréal, 1966.

GROUP: Represented in Canadian group exhibitions since 1943 including exhibitions of Société d'Art Contemporain, La Matière Chante group of Montreal, Les Sagittaires, Canadian National Exhibition; represented in group exhibitions organized by National Gallery of Canada, Ottawa, Ont., including the fourth, fifth, sixth, and seventh Biennial of Canadian Painting, 1961, 1963, 1965, and 1967; Galerie du Luxembourg, Paris, 1947; Salon des Surintendépendants, Paris, 1948; Galerie Creuze, Paris, 1951; *Salon de Mai,* Paris, 1952; L'APIAW, Brussels, Belgium, 1954; *Phases de l'Art Contemporain*, Paris, 1955; Parma Gallery, New York, NY, 1956; *Art Abstrait Formel*, Galerie Hautefeuille, Paris, 1962; *Art Abstrait International*, Musée de Ceret, France, 1962; *Festival des Deux Mondes*, Spoleto, Italy, 1962; *Mouvement Automatiste Canadien*, Rome, Italy, 1962; Salon des Réalités Nouvelles, Paris, 1965 and subsequent years.

COLLECTIONS IN WHICH REPRESENTED
National Gallery of Canada; Musée des Beaux-Arts de Montréal; Musée d'Art Contemporain, Montréal; Musée du Québec; Delégation du Québec à Paris; Musée de Céret, France; Musée d'Alès, France; Art Gallery of Ontario, Toronto; Musée d'Israel.

LEDUC, Roland 1907–
Conductor and cellist; b. 25 July 1907 in Montreal; son of Adélard and Laetitia (Rolland) Leduc; m. Annette Lasalle; children: Lise b. 1948, Yves b. 1950.

EDUCATION
Attended Collège Ste.-Thérèse, Montréal; studied piano with his father, cello with J.B. Dubois in Montreal, to 1927; studied with Mary Loevensohn, P. Gilson, and A. de Boeck, Conservatoire Royale, Brussels, Belgium, 1927-31; studied conducting with Pierre Monteux in Hancock, Me., 1948.

HOME
5, rue Villeneuve, Hull, PQ.

OFFICE
Conservatoire de Musique et d'Art Dramatique de la Province de Québec, 1700 rue Berri, Montréal 24, PQ.

CAREER
Orchestre du Conservatoire Royal de Bruxelles,

cellist 1927-31; Orchestre Philharmonique de Bruxelles, cellist; Concerts Défaunn, Brussels, cellist; Concerts Populaires, Brussels, cellist; École de Musique de Québec, teacher of cello 1931–; Institut Pédagogique de Montréal, teacher; Montreal Symphony Orchestra, first cellist; CBC Little Symphonies Orchestra, conductor 1948–; Conservatoire de Musique et d'Art Dramatique de la Province de Québec, teacher of cello 1942, director 1960–.

MEMBER
Union des Artistes de Montréal.

AWARDS, HONOURS
Quebec government scholarship for study in Belgium, 1927; Conservatoire Royal, Brussels, first and second prizes; Prix Van Cutsem, 1931.

THEATRE
Directed *King David* by Honegger (Notre-Dame de Montréal, 1954).

CONCERT STAGE
Guest conductor of many symphony orchestras, e.g. Quebec, Edmonton, Alta., Winnipeg, Man., Toronto, Ont.

RADIO
Conducted and narrated "Radio college" (CBC series, c.1950); guest conductor of orchestras on CBC, e.g. CBC String Orchestra in première of *Concerto for flute and strings* by Graham George (23 Sept. 1964), Quebec Symphony Orchestra ("Symphony hall," 23 Mar. 1965), CBC Montreal Orchestra (6 June 1966; 29 May 1968), Montreal Chamber Orchestra ("Encore," 24 July 1966).

TELEVISION
Conducted on CBC series, e.g. "Showcase" (6 Nov., 25 Dec. 1960), "Concert" (27 Aug. 1962).

RECORDINGS
Recorded by CBC IS: *Concerto, Images,* and *Paysana* by Claude Champagne; *Suite for orchestra no. 2* by Gabriel Cusson; *Prélude* by J. Papineau-Couture; *Cassation* by François Morel; *Concertino* by George Fiala; recorded by RCA Victor: *Le rituel de l'espace* by F. Morel, and *Symphony no. 2* by Clermont Pépin, both with Little Symphonies Orchestra, CC 1007, 1967.

LEESE, Elizabeth   ?-1962
(Elizabeth Leese Johnstone)
Dancer, choreographer, and teacher; b. in Germany; came to Canada c.1937; m. Kenneth Johnstone c.1938; d. 1962.

EDUCATION
Studied modern dance at Jooss-Leeder School; ballet with Lubov Egorova in Paris, France; acting and dance in London, England; English diction with Eleanor Stuart in Montreal, PQ.

CAREER
Trudi Schoop Company, tour of USA 1937; Volkoff Canadian Ballet, Toronto, Ont., soloist 1939-42; Canadian Government Recreational Dance Project, director 1942-45; founded school in Montreal, 1945; founded and directed company in Montreal, 1945-58.

THEATRE
Choreographed many works, e.g. *Lady from the sea*; played title role in *I remember Mama* (Montreal Repertory Theatre), title role in *Anna Christie* (Montreal Repertory Theatre, 1953).

FILM
Forbidden journey (Selkirk Productions).

LEIGH, Angela*   1927–
(Angela Firmin)
Dancer and teacher; b. 24 Apr. 1927 in Kampala, Uganda, East Africa; daughter of Stanley and Betty (Esherwood) Firmin; came to Canada in Mar. 1946; m.; children: Stephanie b. 26 July 1949.

OFFICE
National Ballet School of Canada, 111 Maitland St., Toronto 5, Ont.

CAREER
National Ballet of Canada, Toronto (charter member), corps de ballet 1951-52, soloist 1952-66; Western Theatre Ballet, England, guest artist 1964; National Ballet School of Canada, Toronto, teacher and choreographer 1968-69.

MEMBER
AEA.

THEATRE
First danced Prelude in *Les sylphides* (Fokine, 1951/52), *Gala performance* (Tudor, Capitol, Ottawa, Ont., 18 Nov. 1953), Woman in his past in *Le jardin aux lilas* (Tudor, 1953/54), Operetta star and Queen of the carriage trade in *Offenbach in the underworld* (Tudor, 1954/55), Odette-Odile in *Le lac des cygnes* (Petipa-Ivanov, 1954/55), Snow Queen and Sugar Plum Fairy in *Casse-noisette* (Franca after Ivanov, 1955/56), First solo in *Dark elegies* (Tudor, 1955/56), Lead girl in *Les rendez-vous* (Ashton, 1956/57), *Pas de chance* (Adams, 1956/57); created Witch in *The fisherman and his soul* (Strate, Palace, Hamilton, Ont., 5 Nov. 1956); first danced Felice in *Winter night* (Gore, 1957/58), Elder sister in *Ballad* (Strate, 1958/59), Dawn in *Coppélia* (St. Leon, Capitol, Ottawa, 30 Oct. 1958); created role in *Pas de six* (Adams, St. Catharines, Ont., 6 Nov. 1959), *Antic spring* (Strate, Palace, Hamilton, 24 Oct. 1960); first danced Blue bird in *Princess Aurora* (Petipa, Palace, Hamilton, 24 Oct. 1960); created role in *Barbara Allen* (Adams, Palace, Hamilton, 26 Oct. 1960); first danced in *Concerto barocco* (Balanchine, Capitol, Ottawa, 21 Nov. 1961), *One in five* (Powell, Ottawa, 22 Nov. 1961), *Serenade* (Balanchine, 1962/63); created role in *Sequel* and First song in *Time cycle* (Strate, Stratford, Ont. Festival, 13 July 1962); first danced Nurse in *Romeo and Juliet* (Cranko,

1963/64), *Triptych* (Strate, 1964/65), Dancer in *The rake's progress* (de Valois, 1965/66), Pimpinella in *Pulcinella* (Strate, 1965/66).

TELEVISION

Danced in several CBC productions, e.g. Queen of the Wilis in *Giselle* (Coralli-Perrot, "Festival," 17 Dec. 1962), *Mother and daughter* ("Telescope," 14 Feb. 1964), Nurse in *Romeo and Juliet* (Cranko, "Festival," 15 Sept. 1965; 2 Mar. 1966).

LEIGHTON, A.C. 1901-65

Artist; b. 1901 in Hastings, Sussex, England; came to Canada in 1929 and settled in Calgary, Alta.; d. *c.*May 1965 in Calgary.

EDUCATION

Attended Hastings School of Art and Hornsey School of Art, London, England; studied in Paris, France.

CAREER

Dartford School of Art, London, instructor *c.*1920; visited Canada 1925 and 1927; Provincial Institute of Technology and Art, Calgary, instructor and head of art department 1929- ?; Province of Alberta, art director 1929-37; illustrated *Far horizons* by B. Carman, McClelland & Stewart, 1926 and *Victoria, B.C.* by M. Willison, Empress Hotel, 1933; Banff School of Fine Arts, Alta., co-founder 1935.

COMMISSIONS

Paintings, British Railways; paintings, CPR; paintings, Vickers Ltd., London.

MEMBER

Ridley Art Club; East Sussex Art Club; Jasper Arts League; Royal Society of British Artists (elected, 1929); Royal Canadian Academy (Associate 1935); Canadian Society of Painters in Water Colour; Alberta Society of Artists (founder, 1931; honorary president); International Institute of Arts and Letters.

EXHIBITIONS

GROUP: Represented in group exhibitions held in Canada during his lifetime including annual exhibitions of Canadian Society of Painters, Canadian National Exhibition, and Royal Canadian Academy; exhibited with Royal Academy, London, 1934; Paris *Salon*; Hull Museum Art Gallery, England; Royal Institute, London; World's Fair, New York, NY, 1939.

COLLECTIONS IN WHICH REPRESENTED

Galleries in Eastbourne, Hastings, Brighton, and Hull, England; Glasgow, Scotland; Vancouver Art Gallery, BC; Winnipeg Art Gallery, Man.; Edmonton Art Gallery, Alta.; New York Central Reference Library; Glenbow Foundation, Calgary.

WRITINGS

CONTRIBUTED: Articles to *Studio, Sphere* (London), *Revue moderne* (Paris).

LEMELIN, Roger* 1919-

Novelist; b. 7 Apr. 1919 in St. Sauveur de Québec; son of Joseph and Florida (Dumontier) Lemelin; m. Valeda Lavigueur 27 Oct. 1945; children: Pierre, Jacques, Diane, André, Sylvie.

EDUCATION

Attended Académie Commerciale, Québec.

RELIGION

Roman Catholic.

HOME

1080 Ave. des Braves, Québec, PQ.

OFFICE

South Shore Forest Products Co., Ltd., 71 St. Pierre St., Quebec 2, PQ.

CAREER

Time reporter, Quebec, 1948-; South Shore Forest Products Co., accountant, manager.

MEMBER

Royal Society of Canada (elected fellow, 1949); Canadian Authors Association.

AWARDS, HONOURS

Prix de la Langue Française de l'Académie Française, and Prix David for *Au pied de la pente douce*, 1946; Guggenheim fellowships, 1946 and 1947; *Liberty* trophy for best TV dramatist for *The Plouffe family*, 1955; Prix de Paris for *Pierre le magnifique*; medal of the Académie Française, 1965.

WRITINGS

Au pied de la pente douce, Arbre, 1944 (translated into English); *Les Plouffe*, Belisle, 1948 (translated into English; produced as TV serial); *Fantaisies sur les péchés capitaux* (short stories), Beauchemin, 1949; *Pierre le magnifique,* Institut Littéraire du Québec, 1952 (translated into English); *L'homme aux oiseaux* (film script; National Film Board of Canada, 1951; Canadian film award).

CONTRIBUTED: Articles to *Maclean's, Queen's quarterly, Transactions of the Royal Society of Canada, Saturday night.*

LESIEUR-DÉSAULNIERS, Gonzalve

see DÉSAULNIERS, Gonzalve

LESLIE, Kenneth 1892-

Poet; b. 1 Nov. 1892 in Pictou, NS; son of Robert Jamieson and Rebecca (Starratt) Leslie; m. Beth Moir (deceased); m. Nora S. Totten 1960; children: (first marriage) Gloria, Kathleen, Rosaleen, and Alexander.

EDUCATION

Dalhousie University, BA, 1912; Nebraska University, MA, 1914; attended Harvard University.

RELIGION

Baptist.

HOME
1074 Wellington St., Halifax, NS.
CAREER
Protestant, New York, editor 1938; *Newman*,
editor 1968.
AWARDS, HONOURS
Governor General's literary award for *By stubborn
stars and other poems*, 1938.
WRITINGS
Windward rock, Macmillan, 1934; *Such a din*,
1935; *Lowlands low*, the author, 1936; *By
stubborn stars and other poems*, Ryerson, 1938;
Songs of Nova Scotia, A. Pelletier, 1962? ; *Christ,
church and communism*, Northern Bookhouse,
1962.
CONTRIBUTED: Poems to several anthologies,
e.g. *Anthology of Canadian poetry*, edited by
R. Gustafson, Penguin Books, 1942; *The book
of Canadian poetry*, edited by A.J.M. Smith,
University of Chicago, 1943; *The eternal sea,
an anthology of sea poetry*, edited by W.M.
Williamson, Coward-McCann, 1946; *Twentieth
century Canadian poetry*, edited by E. Birney,
Ryerson, 1953; *Canadian poems 1850-1952*,
edited by L. Dudek and I. Layton, rev., Contact,
1953; *Canadian poetry in English*, edited by
B. Carman and others, rev. and enl., 1954; *The
Penguin book of Canadian verse*, edited by
R. Gustafson, Penguin Books, 1958; *Erotic
poetry; the lyrics, ballads, idyls and epics of
love - classical to contemporary*, edited by
W. Cole, Random, 1963; *The Oxford book of
Canadian verse in English and French*, edited
by A.J.M. Smith, Oxford, 1964; *Canadian
poetry*.
WORK IN PROGRESS: Collected verse.

LETENDRE, Rita*   1929–
(Rita Letendre Eloul)
Artist; b. 1 Nov. 1929 in Drummondville, PQ;
daughter of Héliddore and Anna Marie Letendre;
m. Kosso Eloul 1964.
EDUCATION
Studied with Jacques de Tonnancour (*q.v.*), École
des Beaux-Arts, Montréal, 1949; later studied with
P.-E. Borduas.
RELIGION
None.
HOME
Apt. 1802, 45 Balliol St., Toronto 7, Ont.
CAREER
Worked at odd jobs till *c.*1959; travelled and
worked in Europe 1962-63; participated in the
California International Symposium of Sculpture,
created an epoxy mural "Sunforces."
COMMISSIONS
Epoxy mural, Long Beach State College Sym-
posium 1965; plastic and glass mural, Arts and
Trade School of Drummondville, *c.*1966.

MEMBER
La Guilde Graphique, Montréal (elected, 1967);
Aesthetic Research Centre, Los Angeles (1966).
AWARDS, HONOURS
Prix de la Jeune Peinture, 1959; prix Rodolphe
de Repentigny, Montréal, 1960; prix de la pro-
vince de Québec, 1961; Canada Council travel
grant, 1962; Canada Council grant, 1963; prize,
Piccola Europa Competition, Spoleto, Italy,
1962; Bourse d'Aide du Ministère des Affaires
Culturelles du Québec, 1967.
EXHIBITIONS
ONE-MAN: Galerie L'Échourie, Montréal,
1955; Galerie L'Actuelle, Montréal, 1956; Galerie
Artek, Montréal, 1958; Galerie Denyse Delrue,
Montréal, 1959 and 1961; Montreal Museum
of Fine Arts 1961; Dorothy Cameron Gallery,
Toronto, Ont., 1961 and 1963; Here and Now
Gallery, Toronto, 1962; University of Ottawa
Gallery, 1963; Galerie Camille Herbert, Montréal,
1963 and 1965; Galerie Agnès Lefort, Montréal,
1966; Gallery Pascal, Toronto, 1967.
GROUP: Represented in group exhibitions
held in Canada since 1952 including exhibitions
of Automatistes, Montreal Museum of Fine
Arts Spring Show; represented in group exhibi-
tions organized by National Gallery of Canada,
Ottawa, Ont., including third and fourth Bien-
nial of Canadian Painting, 1959 and 1961;
Gallery Parma, New York, NY, 1957; Aspects of
Canadian Painting, Canada House, New York,
1959; Modern Painting of Canada, organized by
the Ministry of Cultural Affairs of PQ; Spoleto,
Italy, 1962; Galerie Arnaud, Paris, France, 1964;
Guest Printing, Tamarind Lithography Workshop,
1965; Guest Printing, Gemini Ltd., Los Angeles,
1966.
COLLECTIONS IN WHICH REPRESENTED
Montreal Museum of Fine Arts; Musée d'Art
Contemporain, Montréal; Musée du Québec, PQ;
Art Gallery of Vancouver, BC; Speed Museum,
Ky.; Representative Collection of the Ministry
of Foreign Affairs in Ottawa; Long Beach Museum
of Fine Arts, Calif.; Art Gallery of Ontario,
Toronto; Brandeis University Museum of Art.

LETOURNEAU, Jacques
Actor and director.
HOME
Saint-Denis-sur-Richelieu, PQ.
CAREER
Le Théâtre Club, Montréal, co-founder and actor
1954.
MEMBER
Union des Artistes de Montréal; Canadian
Theatre Centre.
AWARDS, HONOURS
Canada Council senior arts fellowship,
1960/61.

THEATRE

Played in many productions, e.g. Chevalier in *Meurtre dans la cathédrale* (Les Compagnons de Saint-Laurent, Montréal, 1950), *Voulez-vous jouer avec moâ?* (Théâtre Marist, Montréal, 1952), Raskolnikov in *Crime et châtiment* (Théâtre Marist, 1952), *Cécé* (Théâtre Club, 1958), Poet in *La quadrature du cercle* (Théâtre Club, 1958), Dandin in *Les plaideurs* (Théâtre Club, 1958), *Les violons de l'automne* (Théâtre Club, 1960); directed *Celles qu'on prend dans ses bras* (Théâtre Club), *Sébastien* (Théâtre Club, 1954); directed and played in *Virage dangereux* (Théâtre Club, 1954); directed *Le barrage* (Théâtre Club, Oct. 1955), *Les trois mousquetaires* (Théâtre Club, 1956), *Le mal court* (Théâtre Club, fall 1959), *L'heure éblouissante* (Théâtre Club, 1961), *La femme et la mort* (Théâtre Club, Feb. 1961), *Le mari* (Théâtre Club, 1961), *Le marchand de Venise* (Théâtre Club, 1963); directed and played Bogdanovitch in *La veuve joyeuse* (Théâtre Lyrique de Nouvelle France, Québec, 6 Feb. 1966); directed *La périchole* (Théâtre Lyrique de Nouvelle France, 29 Jan. 1967), *La belle Hélène* (Théâtre Lyrique de Montréal, 19 Apr. 1967), *Monsieur Beaucaire* (Théâtre Lyrique de Nouvelle France, 10 Feb. 1968).

LEVINE, Les 1936–
Does not wish to be included.

LEYRAC, Monique c.1932–
(Monique Tremblay; Monique Tremblay Dalmain) Singer and actress; b. c. 1932 in Montreal; m. Jean Dalmain (*q.v.*) 1952; children: Sophie b. 1954.

EDUCATION
Studied theatre with Jeanne Maubourg in Montreal.

HOME
3570 ave. Ridgewood, #303, Montréal 247, PQ.

CAREER
First public appearance c. 1945; CBC, actress c. 1946, hostess for variety series 1961-64; Le Faisan Doré, Montréal, nightclub singer c. 1949; went to Paris, France 1950; sang in cabarets; toured Switzerland, Lebanon, and Belgium 1951; returned to Canada 1951; lived in France 1952-56; Théâtre d'Anjou, Montréal, actress; Théâtre du Nouveau Monde, Montréal, actress 1956-60; Jeunesses Musicales du Canada, actress 1962; worked with Gilles Vigneault (*q.v.*) and Claude Léveillée 1963; folk singer 1963–; toured Quebec 1965, USSR 1967; Festival of Canada, singer on tour 1968.

MEMBER
Union des Artistes de Montréal.

AWARDS, HONOURS
International Song Festival, Sopot, Poland, prize and grand prize, 1965; Charme de la Chanson contest, Ostend, Belgium, first prize, 1965; Companion of the Order of Canada, 1967.

THEATRE
Played in *Le mariage forcé, Sganarelle, La jalousie du Barbouillé, Richard II, Le dindon* (Théâtre du Nouveau Monde, 1960), Polly Peachum in *L'opéra de quat' sous* (Orpheum, Montreal, 1962), *Georges Dandin, Monsieur Masure, Le malade imaginaire* (Théâtre du Nouveau Monde, 1959), *Le médecin malgré lui, L'idiote* (Théâtre du Rideau Vert, 1962), *Le fils d'Achille, La peur des coups, Les boulingrins*, title role in *Bérénice* (Jeunesses Musicales du Canada, 1962), *The threepenny opera* (Toronto, 1962), *Les dialogues des Carmélites, Oscar*.

CONCERT STAGE
Folk singer, Comédie Canadienne, Montréal, Oct. 1964, Dec. 1965; Place des Arts, Montreal, (with Swingle Singers) 1965, 1968; Olympia, Paris, 1965; Town Hall, New York, NY, Mar. 1966; Massey Hall, Toronto, Ont., 25 Feb. 1967; Expo 67, Montreal, 1967; University of Toronto, 1967; O'Keefe Centre, Toronto, 1968.

RADIO
Played title role in *Song of Bernadette*, ("Lux radio-theatre," c. 1945), hostess on "Plein soleil" (series, CBC, 1961-63), folk singer on "Ralph Harris show" (BBC, 1968); numerous appearances on CBC, French, and Belgian radio.

TELEVISION
Featured artist in series, e.g. "Anne-Marie," "Ciel de lit," "Boîte à surprise," "Ce soir ou jamais," "Bonsoir chérie," "Festival" (CBC, 1967); hostess on "Pleins feux" (series, CBC, 1964); played in several productions, e.g. *Le malade imaginaire* (CBC, 1960); sang in several feature programs e.g. *Deux villes se rencontrent* (CBC, 17 Nov. 1963), *Musique aux Champs-Élysées* (Warsaw, Poland, 1967); *O'Keefe Centre presents Canada's loveliest stars* (CBC, 16 Jan. 1968).

RECORDINGS
All long-play recorded by Columbia: *Monique Leyrac*, FS 601; *Monique Leyrac en concert*, FS 644; *Monique Leyrac à Paris*, FS 657; several others.

LIGHTFOOT, Gordon Meredith* 1939–
Folksinger and composer; b. 17 Nov. 1939 in Orillia, Ont.; son of Gordon and Jess Victoria (Trill) Lightfoot; m. Brita Olaisson 6 Apr. 1963; children: Fred b. 1 Feb. 1964, Ingrid b. 31 Dec. 1965.

EDUCATION
Completed high school in Orillia, 1957; studied piano to Grade 8; taught himself drums and guitar; Westlake School of Modern Music, Los Angeles, Calif., 1957-58.

HOME
94 Farnham Ave., Toronto, Ont.

CAREER

Sang in church choir as boy soprano; sang and played drums in high school; bank clerk in Toronto 1957; CBC, singer, dancer, and drummer in series "Country hoedown" 1958-61; went to Europe; appeared in coffeehouses in Canada and USA 1963- ; gave concerts in all principal cities of Canada and USA and many Canadian small towns 1965- ; toured British Isles 1966.

AWARDS, HONOURS

US national top 20 reached by *For lovin' me*, 1964; American Society of Composers, Authors and Publishers award as writer composer for *Ribbon of darkness*, 1965; Gold Record award for 100,000 copies of *Lightfoot*, 1968.

CONCERT STAGE

Best known in North America for personal appearances; in coffeehouses, e.g. Odyssey, Boston, Mass., Second Fret and The Inn, Philadelphia, Pa., The Living End, Cleveland, Ohio, Gaslight South, Miami, Fla., L'Hibou, Ottawa, Ont., Riverboat, Toronto; in concerts in principal halls, e.g. Varsity Stadium (Feb. 1965) and City Hall (1967), Toronto, Ont., Town Hall, New York, NY (Nov. 1965), and Place des Arts, Montréal, PQ (1968); concert, Newport Folk Festival, RI (1965).

FILM

Narrated *Movin'* (Peterson Productions, Toronto, 1968).

RADIO

Appeared in musical shows (CBC, 1958-61, 1964-).

TELEVISION

Host-singer for "Country and western show" (series, BBC, 1963); many appearances on CBC series, e.g. "Music Canada" (19 Oct. 1966), "Showcase" (30 July 1967); featured in *Lightfoot forward* ("Telescope 67," 14 Sept. 1967), *Wherefore and why* ("Show of the week," 18 Mar. 1968).

RECORDINGS

Issued by Compo, Lachine, PQ: *Just like Tom Thumb's blues* with *Ribbon of darkness*, UA 929; *Spin, spin* with *For lovin' me*, UA 50055; *Go-go round* with *I'll be alright*, UA 50114; *Lightfoot*, UAL 3487, UAS 6487; *The way I feel*, UAL 3587, UAS 6587; *Did she mention my name?*, UAS 6649.

COMPOSITIONS

Many folk-music style songs, e.g. *Early morning rain*, 1964; *For lovin' me*, 1964; *I'm not sayin'*, 1965; *Ribbon of darkness*, 1965; recorded by folk-singers and groups, e.g. Harry Belafonte, Joan Baez, Peter, Paul and Mary, Ian and Sylvia.

LIGHTHALL, William Douw 1857-1954
(Wilfred Chateauclair, pseud.)
Author; b. 27 Dec. 1857 in Hamilton, Ont.; son of William Francis and Margaret Lighthall; m. Cybel Wilkes 1890; children: W.W.S. Lighthall and two daughters; d. 3 Aug. 1954 in Westmount, PQ.

EDUCATION

Attended Montreal High School, PQ; McGill University, BA, 1879, BCL, 1881; MA, 1889.

CAREER

Canadian Army, College Company; Prince of Wales Regiment 1877-78, Victoria Rifles 1881-83, Reserves of the Victoria Rifles; called to the bar in Montreal 1881; travelled in Europe 1881; Town of Westmount, commissioner 1899, mayor 1900-02; Union of Canadian Municipalities, founder 1901; made King's Counsel 1906; School Commission of Montreal, president 1908-09; Royal Metropolitan Parks Commission of Montreal, member; McGill University, representative fellow in arts 1911-13; Château de Ramezay Historical Museum, founder; Great War Veterans' Association (now Canadian Legion) founder 1915; Committee of Friends of the Canadian Association of Returned Soldiers, member; Montreal public library, trustee 1922-27; practised law till 1944.

MEMBER

Royal Society of Canada (elected fellow, 1902; president, 1918-19); Antiquarian Society of Montreal (president, 1912; honorary president); Canadian Authors Association (past president; charter member); Society of Canadian Literature (originator); St. James Literary Society (honorary president); Royal Society of Literature of Great Britain; Literary and Historical Society of Quebec (corresponding member).

AWARDS, HONOURS

Dux of Montreal High School; gold medal, Montreal High School; Shakespeare gold medal, McGill University; DCL from McGill University, 1921; medal of City Improvement League of Montreal, 1939.

WRITINGS

Thoughts, moods and ideals (poems), Witness, 1887; *Sketch of the new utilitarianism, including a criticism of the ordinary argument from design and other matter* (non-fiction), Witness, 1887; *The young seigneur, or nation making* (fiction), Drysdale, 1888; *Songs of the great dominion* (poems), Scott, 1889; *An account of the battle of Chateauguay* (non-fiction), Drysdale, 1889; *Spiritualized happiness-theory, or new utilitarianism* (non-fiction), Witness, 1890; *Montreal after 250 years* (non-fiction), Grafton, 1892 (also published under title *Sights and shrines of Montreal*, Grafton, 1907); *The false chevalier, or The lifeguard of Marie Antoinette* (fiction), E. Arnold, 1898; *The glorious enterprise*, C.A. Marchand, 1902; *Canada, a modern nation* (non-fiction), Witness, 1904; *Thomas Pownall: his part in the conquest of Canada* (biography), Hope, 1904; *Hiawatha the Hochelagan, an aboriginal romance*, 1906; *La Corne*

St. Luc: the "General of the Indians" (biography), 1908; *The master of life, a romance of the five nations,* Musson, 1908; *The governance of empire,* the author, 1910; *The land of Manitou* (poems), Desbarats, 1916; *The philosophy of purpose* (non-fiction), the author, 1920; *Old measures, collected verse,* Chapman, 1922; *The teleology of the outer consciousne* (non-fiction), the author, 1924; *The outer consciousness; a biological entity ...,* Witness, 1926; *Superpersonalism* (non-fiction), Witness, 1926; *The person of evolution; the outer consciousness ...* , Macmillan, 1930; *The cosmic aspect of outer consciousness; the outer knowledge; the directive power* (non-fiction), Kennedy, 1930; *The origin of the Maya civilization, can China contribute to its solution,* Printed for the Royal Society of Canada, 1933.
EDITED: *Songs of the great dominion,* Scott, 1889; *Canadian poems and lays,* Scott, 1893.
CONTRIBUTED: Poems to several anthologies, e.g. *A Victorian anthology,* edited by C. Stedman, Houghton, Mifflin, 1895; *The Oxford book of Canadian verse,* edited by W. Campbell, Oxford, 1912; *Poems of American history,* edited by B.E. Stevenson, rev. ed., Houghton, Mifflin, 1922; *Canadian poets,* edited by J.W. Garvin, rev., McClelland & Stewart, 1926; *My country,* edited by B.E. Stevenson, Houghton, Mifflin, 1932; *Our Canadian literature,* edited by B. Carman and L. Pierce, rev., Ryerson, 1935; *Flying colours,* edited by Sir C.G.D. Roberts, Ryerson, 1942; *Canadian poetry in English,* edited by B. Carman and others, rev. and enl., Ryerson, 1954; *Transactions of the Royal Society of Literature of the United Kingdom, Transactions of the Royal Society of Canada, The week.*

LIPSETT, Arthur
Film director.
OFFICE
c/o National Film Board of Canada, Box 6100, Montreal 3, PQ.
FILMS
Directed *Very nice, very nice* (National Film Board, 1961; special prize of the jury, Septième Journées Internationales du Film de Court-Métrage, Festival de Tours, France, *c.*1961; Chris certificate award, experimental category, Tenth Annual Columbus Film Festival, Ohio, *c.*1963; nomination for academy award, Academy of Motion Picture Arts and Sciences, Hollywood, Calif.), *The experimental film* (National Film Board, 1962), *Free fall* (National Film Board, 1964; award, Montreal; award, San Francisco, Calif.), *21-87* (National Film Board, 1964; first prize, Ann Arbor Film Festival, Mich.; most popular film, Midwest Film Festival, Chicago, Ill.; second prize, Third Annual Film Makers Festival, Palo Alto, Calif., *c.*1964), *A trip down*

Memory Lane (National Film Board, 1965; award, Venice, Italy; award, San Francisco).

LISMER, Arthur   1885-1969
Artist; b. 27 June 1885 in Sheffield, England; came to Canada in 1911; m. Esther Mawson 1912; children: Marjorie b. May 1913; d. 23 Mar. 1969 in Montreal, PQ.
EDUCATION
Attended Sheffield School of Art, 1898-1905, certified with distinction; attended Académie Royale des Beaux-Arts, Antwerp, Belgium, 1906.
CAREER
David Smith and Co., Toronto, Ont., lithographer 1911; Grip Engraving Co., Toronto, commercial artist 1912; Ontario College of Art, Toronto, teacher 1913-16, vice-principal 1919-27; Nova Scotia School of Art, Halifax, principal 1916-19; Canadian War Memorials, offical war artist 1917-18; Hart House, Toronto, art director 1924-26; Art Gallery of Toronto, educational supervisor 1929-36; travelled to South Africa to organize children's art classes 1936-37; Columbia University Teacher's College, professor 1938-39; Montreal Museum of Fine Arts, PQ., educational supervisor 1940; Ontario Department of Education, teacher; University of Toronto, Department of Extension, sometime lecturer; McGill University, assistant professor of fine arts 1948-54.
MEMBER
Heeley Art Club, Sheffield, England (secretary, 1921); Arts and Letters Club, Toronto; Ontario Society of Artists (elected, 1913); Royal Canadian Academy (Associate 1919; Academician 1946); Group of Seven (founding member, 1919); Canadian Group of Painters (elected, 1933; charter member); Canadian Society of Painters in Water Colour; Federation of Canadian Artists.
AWARDS, HONOURS
Honorary diploma from Nova Scotia College of Art, 1940; LL D from Dalhousie University, 1942; Canada Council medal, 1962; Companion of the Order of Canada, 1967.
EXHIBITIONS
ONE-MAN: Victoria School of Art and Design, Halifax, 1919; National Gallery of Canada, Ottawa, Ont., 1950; Galerie Agnès Lefort, Montréal, 1963.
GROUP: Represented in group exhibitions held in Canada since 1911 including exhibitions of Ontario Society of Artists, Canadian National Exhibition, Royal Canadian Academy, Canadian Group of Painters; represented in group exhibitions organized by National Gallery of Canada; City Art Museum, St. Louis, Mo., 1919; British Empire Exhibition, London, England 1924; *Exposition d'Art canadien,* Paris, France, 1927; Sesquicentennial Exposition, Philadelphia, Pa., 1927; Fine Arts Academy, Buffalo, NY, 1928;

Exhibition of Canadian Art, British Empire Trade Exhibition, Buenos Aires, Argentina, 1931; Contemporary Canadian Painters, Roerich Museum, New York, 1932; Carnegie International, Pittsburgh, Pa., 1935; A Century of Canadian Art, Tate Gallery, London, England, 1938; Addison Gallery of Fine Arts, Andover, Mass., 1942; University of Washington, 1942; Yale University, 1944; Musée d'Art Moderne, Paris, 1946; Exhibition of Canadian Graphic Arts, Sâo Paulo, Rio de Janeiro, Brazil, 1946; Museum of Fine Arts, Boston, Mass., 1946; University of Delaware, 1952; Florida State Fair, 1952; New Delhi International, India, 1953.

COLLECTIONS IN WHICH REPRESENTED
National Gallery of Canada; Vancouver Art Gallery, BC; Art Gallery of Ontario, Toronto; Montreal Museum of Fine Arts; Musée du Québec, PQ; Norman Mackenzie Art Gallery, University of Saskatchewan, Regina; Hart House, University of Toronto; McMichael Conservation Collection of Art, Kleinburg, Ont.

LIVESAY, Dorothy*   1909–
(Dorothy Kathleen Livesay Macnair)
Poet; b. 12 Oct. 1909 in Winnipeg, Man.; daughter of John Frederick Bligh and Florence (Randal) Livesay; m. Duncan Cameron Macnair 14 Aug. 1937 (d. 12 Feb. 1959); children: Peter Livesay b. 19 Apr. 1940, Helen Marcia b. 10 July 1942.

EDUCATION
Attended Laura Secord School, Winnipeg, 1915-16; Glen Mawr School, Toronto, Ont., senior matriculation, 1922-27; Trinity College, University of Toronto, BA, 1931, social work diploma, 1934; La Sorbonne, Diplôme d'études supérieures, 1932; University of British Columbia, secondary teacher's diploma, 1956, M Ed, 1966.

RELIGION
Unitarian.

HOME
c/o Peter Macnair, 349 Linden Ave., Victoria, BC.

CAREER
Freelance author; *Tribune*, Winnipeg, reporter; *Star*, Toronto, reporter; social worker in Montreal, PQ, 1934, USA 1934-35, Vancouver, BC, 1936-38; *Contemporary verse*, founding committee member 1941; University of British Columbia, extension department lecturer 1949/50, supervisor of correspondence course and part-time lecturer in creative writing 1951-53, teaching assistant in English 1955/56, teaching assistant 1964/65, lecturer in creative writing 1965/66; YWCA, Vancouver, young adult education director 1953-55; secondary school teacher of English, Vancouver, 1956-58; UNESCO, education program specialist in Paris 1959-60. English specialist in Northern Rhodesia (now Zambia) 1960-63; University of New Brunswick, writer-in-residence 1966/67, assistant professor of English 1967/68; University of Alberta, assistant professor of English 1968/69.

MEMBER
ACUTE; Canadian Authors Association (chairman of committee for books for Germany, 1947; national executive member and vice-president of Vancouver branch, 1947/48); United Nations Association; World Federalists; Humanities Association of Canada; Canadian Federation of University Women; Canadian Poets Guild; League of Canadian Poets (regional representative. 1966/67).

AWARDS, HONOURS
Jardine memorial prize for English verse from University of Toronto, 1929; Governor General's literary award for *Day and night*, 1944 and *Poems for people*, 1947; Lorne Pierce medal, 1947; Canada Council award for study, 1958, 1963/64.

WRITINGS
Green pitcher, Macmillan, 1928; *Signpost*, Macmillan, 1932; *Day and night*, Ryerson, 1944; *Poems for people*, Ryerson, 1947; *Call my people home*, Ryerson, 1950 (*Ryerson poetry chapbooks*, 143; produced CBC radio, *c*.Mar. 1949); *New poems*, Emblem Books, 1955; *Selected poems <1926-1956>*, Ryerson, 1957; *The colour of God's face*, Unitarian Service Committee, 1964; *The unquiet bed*, Ryerson, 1967; *The documentaries*, Ryerson, 1968; several CBC radio scripts, e.g. *Momatkum* (*c*.1950), *Edith Sitwell anthology* ("Wednesday night," 17 Mar. 1954; "Tuesday night," 14 Dec. 1964), *The story of Emily Dickinson* (*c*.1955); libretto for *Susan Allison* and *The lake* (produced CBC, *c*.1955).
CONTRIBUTED: Poetry, short stories, and articles to *New harvesting*, edited by E.H. Bennett, Macmillan, 1938; *The book of Canadian poetry*, edited by A.J.M. Smith, University of Chicago, 1943; *Twentieth century verse*, edited by I. Dilworth, Clarke, Irwin, 1945; *Best American short stories*, edited by M. Foley, Houghton, Mifflin, 1951; *Twentieth century Canadian verse*, edited by E. Birney, Ryerson, 1953; *Canadian anthology*, edited by C.F. Klinck and R.E. Watters, Gage, 1955; *The clear spirit*, edited by M.Q. Innis, University of Toronto, 1966; *The Penguin book of Canadian verse*, edited by R. Gustafson, rev. ed., Penguin, 1967; *Poets between the wars*, edited by M. Wilson, McClelland & Stewart, 1967; *Canadian forum, Canadian bookman, Canadian poetry, Contemporary verse, Saturday night, Star weekly, Prism, Tamarack review, Queen's quarterly, Atlantic advocate, Fiddlehead, Delta, Canadian literature*.

WORK IN PROGRESS
Novelette; autobiographical sketches.

LOCHHEAD, Douglas Grant* 1922–
Poet and artist; b. 25 Mar. 1922 in Guelph, Ont.;
son of Allan Grant and Helen Louise (Van Wart)
Lochhead; m. Jean St. Clair Beckwith 17 Sept.
1949; children: Sara Louise b. 22 Dec. 1953, Mary
Elizabeth b. 12 Dec. 1957.

EDUCATION
Attended primary schools in Ottawa, Ont., 1928-
35; Glebe Collegiate Institute, Ottawa, 1935-
40; McGill University, 1940-43, 1950-51; studied
with Carl Schaefer (q.v.), University of Toronto,
1945/47; Kenneth Evett, Cornell University,
1952/53; Kenneth Lochhead.

RELIGION
Presbyterian.

HOME
315 Rosewell Ave., Toronto 12, Ont.

OFFICE
Massey College, 4 Devonshire Place, Toronto 5,
Ont.

CAREER
Canadian Army, 1943-45; Muter and Culiner,
Toronto, advertising copywriter 1948; *Journal*,
Ottawa, reporter 1949; Central Mortgage and
Housing Corporation, Ottawa, information
officer 1949-50; Victoria College (now
University of Victoria), BC, librarian and lecturer
in sociology 1951-52; Cornell University
cataloguer 1952-53; Dalhousie University,
librarian and professor 1953-60; York University, librarian and assistant professor of English
1960-63; Massey College, University of Toronto,
librarian 1963–, senior fellow 1964–; University of Toronto, special lecturer in graduate
department of English 1964, professor in
graduate department of English 1965–, special
lecturer in School of Library Science 1965–.

MEMBER
ACUTE; Canadian Library Association (former
executive member, 1952-63); Bibliographical
Society of Canada (former publications committee
chairman); Bibliographical Society, London,
England; Bibliographical Society of University
of Virginia; Society of Graphic Designers of
Canada; Guild of Handprinters; Oxford
Bibliographical Society; League of Canadian
Poets; The Quadrats, Toronto.

AWARDS, HONOURS
Canada Council grants in aid of research, 1964,
1967, and 1968.

EXHIBITIONS
GROUP: Represented in group exhibitions held
in Canada.

WRITINGS
The heart is fire, Ryerson, 1959 (Ryerson poetry
chapbooks, 184); *An old woman looks out on*

Gabarus Bay remembering history, June 8, 1958,
Three Fathom Press, 1959; *It is all around*,
1960 (Ryerson poetry chapbook, 191); *Shepherds
before kings*, Three Fathom Press, 1963; *Singles*,
Three Fathom Press, 1968.
EDITED: (with S.B. Elliott) *Atlantic provinces
checklist*, V.1-2, Atlantic Provinces Economic
Council, 1957-59; (with H.N. Frye and J.A.
Irving) Thomas McCulloch's *The Stepsure
letters*, McClelland & Stewart, 1960; David
Silverberg's *The song of songs*, Upstairs Gallery,
1961; Saul Field's *Themes from the old
testament*, Upstairs Gallery, 1964; Carl Dair's
*First proof of Cartier, Roman and italic, the first
Canadian type for text composition...*, Cape,
1967; Alexander Glen Gilbert's *From Montreal
to the Maritime provinces and back*, Bibliographical Society of Canada, 1967.
CONTRIBUTED: "Nova Scotia" in *Collier's
encyclopedia yearbook*, Crowell-Collier, 1955-56;
articles and poetry to *Papers of the Bibliographical Society of Canada*, *Saturday night*,
Canadian poetry, *Canadian forum*, *Queen's
quarterly*, *Dalhousie review*, *Contemporary
verse*, *CLA bulletin*, *Canadian art*, *Apollo*.
WORK IN PROGRESS
Editing "Bibliography of Canadian bibliographies,"
2nd ed., rev. and enl., Bibliographical Society of
Canada and University of Toronto Press; "Con-
cordance to poetry of E.J. Pratt," to be published
c.1970; "Wisdoms" (poems), to be published
1968; (with Kenneth Lochhead) book on Manitoba.

LOISELLE, Hélène* 1928–
Actress; b. 17 Mar. 1928 in Montreal; daughter of
Jean-Baptiste and Odile (Dubreuil) Loiselle;
m. Lionel Villeneuve 5 Nov. 1949; children:
Anne b. 1951, Pierre b. 1952, Catherine b. 1957,
Isabelle b. 1959, Christine b. 1961.

EDUCATION
Attended La Commission Scolaire, Montréal;
studied drama with Charlotte Boisjoli and
François Rozet, Montréal; Bernard Bimont, Paris,
France.

HOME
4818 Victoria Ave., Montreal 29, PQ.

CAREER
Les Compagnons de Saint-Laurent, Montréal,
actress 1946–.

THEATRE
Played in many productions, e.g. Esther in *Deux
sur une balançoire* (Théâtre de Percé, PQ);
Yolande Donadieu in *Les maxibules* (Théâtre
de l'Égrégore, Montréal), Pauline in *Polyeucte*
(Théâtre Universitaire Canadien), title role in
Andromaque (Théâtre Universitaire Canadien),
Henriette in *Les femmes savantes* (Théâtre
Universitaire Canadien), Alexandra in *Si jamais
je te pince* (Théâtre Universitaire Canadien),
Cassandre in *La guerre de Troie n'aura pas lieu*

(Théâtre du Rideau Vert, Montréal), Rosette in
On ne badine pas avec l'amour (Compagnons,
1945), Sylvette in *Les romanesques* (Compagnons, 1946/47), *Le diable s'en mêle* (l'Équipe,
Montréal, summer 1949), *La dame de l'aube*
(Compagnons, 1949/50), Juliette in *Roméo et
Juliette* (Compagnons, 1949/50), Hyacinthe in
Les fourberies de Scapin (Compagnons, 1951),
Chambres à louer (La jeune scène, 1954), *La
nuit des rois* (Le Théâtre Club, Montréal, 15 Feb.
1956), *Le cri de l'engoulevent* (La Comédie Canadienne, Montréal, 1960), Mme. Malingear in *La
poudre aux yeux* (Théâtre du Rideau Vert, 18
May 1967), *Le chemin du roy* (l'Égrégore, Montréal, 29 Apr. 1968), *Ce soir on improvise* (Théâtre
du Rideau Vert, 16 Oct. 1968), *Les belles soeurs*
(Théâtre du Rideau Vert, 28 Aug. 1968).

FILM
Played in documentaries of the National Film
Board of Canada.

RADIO
Played leading roles in many productions.

TELEVISION
Played in many productions, e.g. title role in
L'éventail de Lady Windermere, Edith in *L'ombre*,
Tatiana in *Les petits bourgeois*, Madeleine in
Victime du devoir, Sonia in *Uncle Vania*, *Chemin
privé* (1960).

LORING, Frances Norma 1887-1968
Sculptor; b. 14 Oct. 1887 in Wardner, Idaho;
daughter of Frank and Charlotte (Moore) Loring;
came to Canada in 1912 and became Canadian
citizen in 1920; d. 5 Feb. 1968 in Newmarket,
Ont.

EDUCATION
Educated in Switzerland, Germany, and at Sorbonne, Paris, France; attended École des Beaux-Arts, Geneva, Switzerland, 1901; studied with
Güttner, Munich, Germany, winter of 1903/04;
attended Académie Colorassi, Paris, 1904-07;
studied under George Milligan, Art Institute,
Chicago, Ill., 1907; Belo Pratt, Boston Academy
of Fine Arts, Mass., 1908; attended Art Students
League, New York, NY, 1910.

CAREER
Worked and travelled in Canada, summer 1908;
met Florence Wyle (*q.v.*), Art Institute Chicago,
1910, and shared studio with her in Toronto
from 1913; Ontario College of Art, Toronto,
guest teacher; lectured and gave demonstrations;
taught privately; travelled to western Canada
with A.Y. Jackson (*q.v.*), 1952.

COMMISSIONS
Canadian War Memorials, National Gallery of
Canada, Ottawa, Ont.; monument, Galt, Ont.;
St. Stephen, Osgoode Hall, Toronto; sculpture,
St. Michael's Hospital, Toronto; sculpture, Bank
of Montreal, Toronto; sculpture, Rainbow Bridge,
Niagara Falls, Ont.; lions, eastern entrance to

Queen Elizabeth Highway, Toronto; Sculpture,
Henry Oakes Theatre, Niagara Falls; sculpture,
Customs and Immigration Building, Niagara
Falls; statue of Sir Robert Borden, Parliament
Hill, Ottawa, 1957.

MEMBER
Ontario Society of Artists (1919; resigned, 1933);
Royal Canadian Academy (Associate 1920;
Academician 1947); Sculptor's Society of Canada
(founder member, 1928; secretary-treasurer,
1928-42; vice-president, 1942; past president);
Federation of Canadian Artists (co-founder);
Women's Art Association of Canada (president,
1939); National Arts Council (founder).

AWARDS, HONOURS
Medal, University of Alberta, 1954; LL D from
University of Toronto.

EXHIBITIONS
ONE-MAN (Wyle and Loring), Pollock Gallery,
Toronto, 1965.
GROUP: Represented in group exhibitions
held in Canada since 1908 including annual
exhibitions of Ontario Society of Artists, Royal
Canadian Academy, Canadian National Exhibition, Women's Art Association, Toronto,
Sculptor's Society of Canada; represented in
annual exhibitions organized by National Gallery
of Canada; Canadian Section of Fine Arts,
British Empire Exhibition, Wembley, England,
1924-25; *Exposition d'Art canadien*, Musée du
Jeu de Paume, Paris, 1927; Coronation Exhibitions, 1937; A Quarter Century of Canadian Art,
Tate Gallery, London, England, 1938; World's
Fair, New York, NY, 1939.

COLLECTIONS IN WHICH REPRESENTED
Edmonton Art Gallery, Alta.; Art Gallery of
Ontario, Toronto; National Gallery of Canada;
London Public Library and Museum, Ont.

LOVEROFF, Frédéric Nicholas 1894—
Artist; b. 8 June 1894 in Tiflis, Russia; came
to Canada with his parents in 1900 and settled
in Saskatchewan.

EDUCATION
Studied under J.W. Beatty, G.A. Reid (*q.v.*),
and J.E.H. MacDonald (*q.v.*), Ontario College of
Art, Toronto, Ont., 1913.

CAREER
Travelled and painted in Manitoba; painter in
Toronto.

MEMBER
Royal Canadian Academy (Associate 1920;
retired, 1934); Ontario Society of Artists
(elected, 1922; retired, 1934).

EXHIBITIONS
GROUP: Represented in group exhibitions held
in Canada including annual exhibitions of Ontario
Society of Artists and Royal Canadian Academy.

COLLECTIONS IN WHICH REPRESENTED
Leicester Gallery, England; National Gallery of

Canada, Ottawa, Ont.; Saskatoon Art Gallery, Sask.; Norman Mackenzie Art Gallery, Regina, Sask.

LOW, Colin Archibald* 1926–
Film director and producer; b. 24 July 1926 in Cardston, Alta.; son of Gerald and Marian (Campbell) Low; m. Eugenia Exilda St. Germain; children: Ben Gerald, Stephen, Garth Alexander.
EDUCATION
Attended Old Chief School in Twin Lakes, Alta.; secondary school in Jefferson, Alta.; Calgary Institute of Technology and Art, Alta.
HOME
4844 Grosvenor, Montreal, PQ.
OFFICE
3255 Côte de Liesse Rd., Montréal, PQ.
CAREER
National Film Board of Canada, Montreal 1945–, head of animation department 1950-63, designer and co-director of Labyrinthe for Expo 67, Montreal 1964-67; Anders Beckman Advertising Studio, Sweden, exhibition designer 1948-49; travelled extensively in Europe and Asia.
AWARDS, HONOURS
LL D from Memorial University, 1968.
FILMS
Directed *Age of the beaver* (National Film Board, 1952; special award, non-theatrical open class, Fifth Annual Canadian Film Awards, Toronto, Ont., 1952-53); co-directed *The romance of transportation in Canada* (National Film Board, 1953; nomination for best short subject, Academy of Motion Picture Arts and Sciences, Hollywood, Calif., 1952-53; honourable mention, non-theatrical open class, Fifth Annual Canadian Film Awards, Toronto, 1952-53; best animated travel and transportation film, Third International Week of Travel and Folklore Films, Brussels, Belgium, 1953-54; first prize, animated short subjects class, Sixth International Film Festival, Cannes, France, 1953-54; diploma of merit, experimental category, Seventh Annual International Film Festival, Edinburgh, Scotland, 1953-54; special award, British Film Academy Awards, London, England, 1953-54; silver medal [first prize], animated section, First Annual International Film Festival, Durban, South Africa, 1954-55; cup of the Cortina Industry of Transports, Twelfth Annual International Competition of Films on Sports, Cortina d'Ampezzo, Italy, 1955-56; grand prize for short films, "Inter-action" Prize, Paris, France, 1955-56; first prize, documentary and educational category, Midwest Film Festival, Chicago, Ill., 1964-65); directed *Corral* (National Film Board, 1954; bronze medal [second prize], documentary category, First Annual International Film Festival, Durban, 1954-55; diploma of merit, art category, Eighth

Annual International Film Festival, Edinburgh, 1954-55; special mention, theatrical short class, Seventh Annual Canadian Film Awards, Toronto, 1954-55; first prize, documentary films category, Fifth International Exhibition of Documentary and Short Films, Venice, Italy, 1954-55; recognition of merit, cultural value shorts and feature category, Second Annual Golden Reel Film Festival, Chicago, 1955-56); co-directed *Riches of the earth* (National Film Board, 1954; first prize, non-theatrical open class, Seventh Annual Canadian Film Awards, Toronto, 1954-55; first prize, First International Survey of Scientific and Didactic Films, Padua, Italy, 1956-57); directed *Gold* (National Film Board, 1955; diploma of merit, Ninth Annual International Film Festival, Edinburgh, 1955-56; first prize, theatrical short class, Eighth Annual Canadian Film Festival, Toronto, 1955-56), *The Jolifou Inn* (National Film Board, 1955; selected for screening, Ninth Annual International Film Festival, Edinburgh, 1955-56; special mention, theatrical short class, Eighth Annual Canadian Film Awards, Toronto, 1955-56; first prize, creative arts category, Fourth International Documentary Film Festival, Yorkton, Sask., 1956-57; first prize, art category, Third Annual Kootenay Film Festival, BC, 1957-58; first prize, First Spanish, American and Philippines Film Festival, Bilbao, Spain, 1959-60); co-directed *City of gold* (National Film Board, 1957; first prize, documentary short features class, Tenth International Film Festival, Cannes, France, 1957-58; St. Finbarr trophy [first prize], general interest category, Second International Irish Film Festival, Cork, Ireland, 1957-58; selected for screening, Eleventh Annual International Film Festival, Edinburgh, 1957-58; nominated for best short subject, Academy of Motion Picture Arts and Sciences, Hollywood, 1957-58; nominated for best documentary, British Film Academy Awards, London, England, 1957-58; honourable mention, Ninth Annual Robert J. Flaherty Film Awards, City College Institute of Film Techniques, New York, NY, 1957-58; award of merit, non-theatrical arts and experimental category, Tenth Annual Canadian Film Awards, Toronto, 1957-58; purchase prize, Festival of Contemporary Arts, University of Illinois, 1958-59; honourable mention, Third Festival of Documentary and Experimental Films, Montevideo, Uruguay, 1958-59; first prize, documentary category, International Exhibition of Electronics, Nuclear Energy, Radio and Television, Rome, Italy, 1958-59; film of the year award and award of merit, arts and experimental category, Tenth Annual Canadian Film Awards, Toronto, 1958-59; gold medal, Trento Film Festival, Italy, 1958-59; first prize, documentary films category,

Vancouver International Film Festival, BC, 1958-59; best film, general category, Yorkton Film Festival, 1958-59; first prize, First Spanish, American and Philippines Film Festival, Bilbao, 1959-60; blue ribbon award, history and biography category, American Film Festival, New York, 1959-60; honourable mention, First Festival of Experimental and Documentary Films, Santiago, Chile, 1960-61; first prize, Eighth Annual Film Festival, Columbus, Ohio, 1960-61; gold medal, Festival of the Peoples, Florence, Italy, 1961-62); designed *It's a crime* (National Film Board, 1957; selected for screening, Eleventh Annual International Film Festival, Edinburgh, 1957-58; diploma of honour, Locarno Film Festival, Switzerland, 1958-59; diploma, Third International Industrial and Labour Film Festival, Antwerp, Belgium, 1960-61); animated *The living stone* (National Film Board, 1958; nominated for best documentary, Academy of Motion Picture Arts and Sciences, Hollywood, 1959-60; diploma of honour, Twelfth International Film Festival, Locarno, 1959-60; honourable mention, Cultural and Documentary Film Week, Mannheim, Germany, 1959-60; honourable mention, Robert Flaherty Awards, New York 1959-60; best Canadian-made short subject award, Winnipeg Film Festival, Man., 1959-60; award of merit, Eleventh Annual Canadian Film Awards, Toronto, 1959-60; medal of honour of the CIDALC, Tenth International Film Week on Tourism and Folklore, Brussels, 1960-61; mention, Fourth International Festival of Documentary and Experimental Film, Montevideo, 1960-61; blue ribbon award, graphic arts category, American Film Festival, New York, 1960-61; cup of the Minister of Tourism and Entertainment, Rapallo, Italy, 1960-61; silver cup of the Province of Genoa, Rapallo, 1960-61); co-produced *A is for architecture* (National Film Board, 1959; silver cup and medal [third prize], Sixth Rapallo Film Festival, 1959-60; silver medal [special CIDALC prize], Second Ibero-American-Filipino Documentary Film Contest, Bilbao, 1960-61; silver cup, International Exhibition of Electronics, Nuclear Energy, Radio, Television and Cinema, Rome, 1960-61; certificate of merit, Canadian Film Awards, Toronto, 1960-61; first prize, Sixth Biennial International Documentary Film Festival, Yorkton, 1960-61; Chris certificate award, arts and crafts category, Tenth Annual Columbus Film Festival, 1962-63); directed *City out of time* (Ntaional Film Board, 1959; special diploma, Third Annual International Film Festival, Vancouver, 1960-61); co-directed *Universe* (National Film Board, 1960; diploma of honour, Second International Festival of Scientific and Technical Films, Belgrade, Yugoslavia, 1960-61; jury's prize, Thirteenth International Film Festival, Cannes, 1960-61;

technical mention, Commission Supérieure Technique du Cinéma Français, Cannes, 1960-61; Chris certificate award, information-education category, Columbus Film Festival, 1960-61; diploma of merit, Edinburgh Film Festival, 1960-61; best animated film, British Film Academy Awards, London, 1960-61; blue ribbon award, science and mathematics category, American Film Festival, New York, 1960-61; award, Scholastic Teachers' Annual National Film and Filmstrip Awards, New York, 1960-61; cup of the minister of tourism and entertainment, Rapallo Film Festival, 1960-61; special commendation, Stratford Film Festival Critics' Circle, Ont., 1960-61; films of the year award and award of merit, theatrical films category, Thirteenth Annual Canadian Film Awards, Toronto, 1960-61; major award, documentary films category, Third Annual Vancouver International Film Festival, 1960-61; golden sheaf trophy, Sixth Biennial Documentary Film Festival, Yorkton, 1960-61; best documentary film and grand prix, First International Festival of Educational Films, Buenos Aires, Argentina, 1961-62; nominated for best documentary short, Academy of Motion Picture Arts and Sciences, Hollywood, 1961-62; first prize, documentary category, Salerno Film Festival, Italy, 1961-62; scientific silver oak leaf [first prize], Third International Festival of Children's Films, La Plata, Argentina, 1962-63; award of merit, First Scientific Film Festival, Caracas, Venezuela, 1963-64; golden delfan [first prize], scientific films category, Second International Film Festival on Arts and Education, Tehran, Iran, 1964-65); directed *Circle of the sun* (National Film Board, 1961; honourable mention, Festival of the Peoples, Florence, 1961-62; one of the outstanding films of the year, London Film Festival, 1961-62; best film on folklore, Twelfth International Tourist and Folklore Film Week, Brussels, 1962-63; documentary silver oak leaf [first prize], Third International Festival of Children's Films, La Plata, 1962-63; award of merit, general information category, Fourteenth Annual Canadian Film Awards, Toronto, 1962-63; first prize, general category, International Documentary Film Festival, Yorkton, 1962-63; best film, Victoria Film Festival, BC, 1963-64; diploma of honour and trophy, First International Festival of Tourism Films, Tarbes, France, 1967-68), *The days of Whisky Gap* (National Film Board, 1961; grand prix "Eurovision" for TV films, Cannes, 1961-62; honourable mention, sociology category, Vancouver Film Festival, 1961-62; certificate of merit, Canadian Historical Association, Toronto, 1964-65); co-produced *Very nice, very nice* (National Film Board, 1961; nominated for best live action short, Academy of Motion Picture Arts and Sciences, Hollywood, 1961-62; special prize

of the jury, Seventh International Days of Short
Films, Tours, France, 1961-62; Chris certificate
award, experimental category, Tenth Annual
Columbus Film Festival, 1962-63), *My financial
career* (National Film Board, 1962; first prize,
animated film category, San Francisco International Film Festival, Calif., 1962-63; nominated
for best cartoon, Thirty-Sixth Annual Awards,
Academy of Motion Picture Arts and Sciences,
Hollywood, 1963-64; blue ribbon award, literature in films category, Sixth American Film
Festival, New York, 1964-65), *Pot-pourri*
(National Film Board, 1962); co-produced and
co-directed *The ride* (National Film Board,
1963); co-produced *The world of David Milne*
(National Film Board, 1963; blue ribbon award,
graphic arts category, American Film Festival,
New York, 1963-64); directed *The Hutterites*
(National Film Board, 1964; Chris certificate
award, religion category, Twelfth Annual
Columbus Film Festival, 1964-65; second
prize, Festival dei Popoli, Florence, 1964-65;
honourable mention, Melbourne Film Festival,
Australia, 1964-65; first prize, shorts category,
Festival of Canadian Films, Montreal International
Film Festival, 1964-65; best black and white cinematography, Canadian Cinematography Awards,
Toronto, 1964-65; first prize, human relations
category, Eighth Biennial International Documentary Film Festival, Yorkton, 1964-65;
Landers Associates award of merit, Review of
16 mm Non-theatrical Films, Los Angeles,
1965-66; blue ribbon award, doctrinal and
denominational topics category, American Film
Festival, New York, 1965-66); co-produced *I
know an old lady who swallowed a fly* (National
Film Board, 1964; certificate of merit, cartoon
category, International Film Festival, Chicago,
Ill., 1965-66; diploma of merit, International
Festival of Films for Children, Gottwaldov,
Czecho-Slovakia, 1965-66; second satellite award,
First Annual Children's Film Festival, Santa
Barbara, Calif., 1966-67), *21-87* (National Film
Board, 1964; first prize, Ann Arbor Film Festival,
Mich., 1964-65; most popular film, Midwest Film
Festival, Chicago, 1964-65; second prize, Third
Annual Film Makers Festival, Palo Alto, Calif.,
1964-65); animated *Labyrinthe* (National Film
Board for Expo 67, Montreal, 1967; award for
technical development and innovation, Canadian
Film Awards, Toronto, 1968).

LUND, Alan*
Choreographer, director, and dancer; b. in
Toronto, Ont.; son of Benjamin and Ellen (Oaten)
Lund; m. Blanche Harris 3 May 1944; children:
Brian b. 3 June 1953, Raymond b. 22 Mar. 1958,
Kevin b. 19 Nov. 1961, Jeffrey b. 1 Apr. 1965.

EDUCATION
Attended Pape Ave. School and Danforth Tech-
nical School in Toronto; studied dance with
Virginia Virge in Toronto; Pauline Grant, London,
England; Anatole Vilzak, New York, NY.

HOME
52 Bannatyne Dr., Willowdale, Ont.

OFFICE
Alan and Blanche Lund School of Dance, 2
Floor, 5385 Yonge St., Willowdale, Ont.

CAREER
RCNVR, special services 1943-45; sub-lieutenant;
Alan and Blanche Lund School of Dance,
Toronto, co-founder and director; Canadian
National Exhibition Grandstand Show, Toronto,
director; *Spring thaw*, choreographer 1957-59,
1962-, director 1966-68; Stratford, Ont. Festival,
choreographer 1960-65; Charlottetown Festival,
PEI, director and choreographer 1965-, artistic
director 1968-.

MEMBER
ACTRA; AEA; Canadian Theatre Centre.

AWARDS, HONOURS
Liberty dance award runner-up 1961.

THEATRE
Danced in *Meet the Navy* (1943-45), *Piccadilly
hayride* (Prince of Wales, London, 11 Oct. 1946),
Fancy free (Prince of Wales, London, 15 May
1951), *Fun and the fair* (Palladium, London),
Royal Command Performances (Hippodrome,
Palladium, and Victoria Palace, London); choreo-
graphed *Irene* (His Majesty's, London, 21 Mar.
1945), *Together again* (Victoria Palace, London,
17 Apr. 1947), *Salad days, A midsummer night's
dream* (Stratford, Ont. Festival, 1960), *Romeo
and Juliet* (Stratford, Ont. Festival, 1960),
Coriolanus (Stratford, Ont. Festival, 1961),
Henry VIII (Stratford, Ont. Festival, 1961),
Love's labour's lost (Stratford, Ont. Festival,
1961), *The canvas barricade* (Stratford, Ont.
Festival, 1961), *The tempest* (Stratford, Ont.
Festival, 1962), Cadets' song in *Cyrano de
Bergerac* (Stratford, Ont. Festival, 1962-63),
The gondoliers (Stratford, Ont. Festival, 1962),
Timon of Athens (Stratford, Ont. Festival,
1963), *The mikado* (Stratford, Ont. Festival,
1963), *That Hamilton Woman* (Crest Theatre,
Toronto, 1963), *Le bourgeois gentilhomme*
(Stratford, Ont. Festival, 1964), *The country
wife* (Stratford, Ont. Festival, 1964), *The
rise and fall of the city of Mahagonny*
(Stratford, Ont. Festival, 1965), *The marriage
of Figaro* (Stratford, Ont. Festival, 1965);
directed and choreographed *Anne of Green
Gables* (Charlottetown Festival, 1965),
The adventures of Private Turvey (Charlottetown
Festival, 1966), *Katimavik revue* (Canada
Pavilion, Expo 67, Montreal, PQ, 1967),
Paradise Hill (Charlottetown Festival,

3 July 1967), *Elle tournera la terre* (La Comédie Canadienne, Montréal, 17 Nov. 1967), *Johnny Belinda* (Charlottetown Festival, 1 July 1968), *Sunshine town* (Charlottetown Festival, 29 July 1968).

FILM
Danced in *Meet the Navy* (Elstree Studios, 1945).

TELEVISION
Choreographed and/or danced in many CBC series, e.g. "Show time," "Hit parade," "Mr. Showbusiness," "World of music," "Parade," "Joan Fairfax show," *Timmy's Easter parade of stars* (15 Apr. 1962), *Spring thaw* ("Parade," 13 July 1961), *Wayne and Shuster hour* ("Show of the week," 29 Nov. 1965), *Tom Jones* ("O'Keefe Centre presents," 13 Feb. 1968), *In the Klondike* ("Show of the week," 6 May 1968).

LUSCOMBE, George*   1926–
Actor, producer, and director; b. 17 Nov. 1926 in Toronto; son of Edward and Anne (O'Donnell) Luscombe; m. Mary Mona Walton 8 Aug. 1958; children: Glenda Elizabeth Newham (step-daughter) b. 25 May 1954, Nadine-Anne b. 11 Sept. 1962, Daren Mae b. 11 Jan. 1966.

EDUCATION
Chester Public School, Toronto, 1931-39; East York Collegiate, Toronto, 1940; Danforth Technical School, Toronto, industrial course 1941, art course 1942-46.

RELIGION
Atheist.

HOME
27 Humewood Dr., Toronto 10, Ont.

OFFICE
Toronto Workshop Productions, 12 Alexander St., Toronto 3, Ont.

CAREER
People's Repertory Theatre, Ont., actor 1948-49; Midland Repertory Company, England, actor 1950-52; Joan Littlewood's Theatre Workshop Productions, Stratford, East, London, England, actor 1952-56; CBC, Toronto, actor 1956-66; National Film Board of Canada, Montreal, PQ, actor 1956-66; Toronto Workshop Productions, founder, producer, and director 1959–.

MEMBER
ACTRA; AEA (UK, 1952-56; Canada, 1956–); Canadian Theatre Centre (member of board, 1968).

THEATRE
Played in many productions, e.g. *Lysistrata* (Edinburgh Festival, Scotland, 1954), *Mother Courage* (Devon Festival, England, 1955), *Arden of Faversham* (Paris Festival, France, 1956), *Volpone* (Paris Festival, 1956), *A ballad opera* (Warsaw Festival, Poland, 1956); directed numerous productions, e.g. *Burlap bags*; directed and co-authored *Hey, Rube* (1961), *Before Compiègne* (1963); directed *Wozzeck* (1963); directed and co-authored *The mechanic* (16 July 1966); directed *The Golem of Venice* (16 July 1966), *The*

Captain of Kopenick (1967/68); directed and co-authored *Gentlemen be seated* (31 Dec. 1967); directed *The alchemist* (Jan. 1968), *The travellers* (1 May 1968); directed and co-authored *Faces* (world première, 28 May 1968); directed *Flood* (Canadian première, 5 Nov. 1968), *Che Guevara* (12 Dec. 1968).

TELEVISION
Played in many CBC productions, e.g. Billy Pierce in *Man with a rope* ("Playdate," 2 Mar. 1964), title role in *The songs of Joe Hill* ("Other voices," 20 Oct. 1964; 4 May 1965), *Toronto Workshop Productions* ("Show of shows," 22 Nov. 1964).

LYMAN, John 1886-1967
(John Goodwin Lyman)
Artist; b. 29 Sept. 1886 in Biddeford, Me.; son of Frederick Gold and Mary Isabel (Goodwin) Lyman; came to Canada in 1886; m. Corinne St. Pierre 8 Apr. 1911; d. 26 May 1967 in Barbados.

EDUCATION
Attended Abingdon School, Montreal, PQ, and Montreal High School till 1900; attended Hotchkiss School, Lakeville, Conn. 1901-05; McGill University, 1905-07; studied under Marcel Béronneau, Paris, France, 1907; Royal College of Art, South Kensington, London, England, 1907 (autumn); Jean-Paul Laurens, Académie Julian, Paris, 1908-09; Henri Matisse, Académie Henri Matisse, Paris, 1909-10.

RELIGION
Protestant.

CAREER
Travelled and studied in Europe 1907-13, 1915-17, 1919-29; spent winters in Bermuda 1912/13, 1914/15, 1917/18; served in Red Cross, France 1915-17, awarded Médaille de la Reconnaissance Française 1917; travelled in USA 1918-19; spent winters in Hammamet, Tunisia and summers in Paris, 1919-22; returned to Canada 1910, 1911, 1913, 1914, 1917, and 1926; settled in Canada 1931; The Atelier, established in co-operation with Hazen Sise, Georgie Holt, and André Biéler (*q.v.*) 1931; wrote reviews for *The Montrealer* 1936-40; McGill University, department of fine arts, assistant professor 1948-49, associate professor 1949-57, chairman of department 1951-55; spent summers in USA 1958-62; spent winters in West Indies 1958-65; settled in Barbados 1966.

MEMBER
Société d'art contemporain (founder, 1939; president, 1939-45); Eastern Group of Painters (founder, 1939); Fellow of the Royal Society of Art, London, 1954; Humanities Society of Canada.

EXHIBITIONS
ONE-MAN   Art Association of Montreal, PQ, 1913; Johnson Art Galleries, Montreal, 1927; W. Scott and Sons, Montreal, 1931 and 1937; Valentine Gallery, New York, NY, 1936; McGill University Faculty Club, 1939; Dominion

Gallery, Montreal, 1944, 1947, and 1955; Lycée Pierre Corneille, Montréal, 1954; Art Gallery of Hamilton, Ont., 1963; Montreal Museum of Fine Arts, 1936; Musée du Québec, PQ, 1966; Musée d'Art Contemporain, Montréal, 1967.

GROUP: Represented in group exhibitions held in Canada since 1913 including annual exhibitions of Montreal Museum of Fine Arts Spring show, Contemporary Art Society, Eastern Group of Painters; represented in group shows organized by National Gallery of Canada, Ottawa, Ont.; Armory Show, New York, 1913; Salon des Indépendants, Paris, 1925-27; Salon d'Automne, Paris, 1925-27; Salon des Tuileries, 1927; Dallas, Tex., 1937; A Century of Canadian Art, Tate Gallery, London, 1938; World's Fair, New York, 1939; Aspects of Contemporary Canadian Painting in Canada, 1942-43, Detroit, Mich., 1943; San Francisco Museum of Art, Calif., 1943; Oregon Art Museum, Portland, 1944; University of Vermont, 1944; Canadian Art 1760-1943, Yale University Art Gallery, 1944; Exhibition of Canadian Painting and Folk Arts, São Paulo and Rio de Janeiro, Brazil, 1944 and 1946; Painting in Canada, a Selective Historical Survey, Albany Institute of History and Art, NY, 1946; Santiago, Chile, 1946; Exhibition of International Modern Art at Musée d'Art Moderne in Paris originated by UNESCO 1946; Canadian Painting, National Gallery of Art, Washington, DC, 1950; Coronation, 1953.

COLLECTIONS IN WHICH REPRESENTED
National Gallery of Canada; Musée du Québec; Montreal Museum of Fine Arts; University of Manitoba; McGill University; Art Gallery of Hamilton; Beaverbrook Art Gallery, Fredericton, NB; Musée d'Art Contemporain, Montréal.

WRITINGS
J.W. Morrice (biography), Éditions de l'Arbre, 1945.
CONTRIBUTED: Articles to several periodicals.

McARTHUR, Peter 1866-1924
Author; b. 10 Mar. 1866 in Ekfrid Township, Middlesex, Ont.; son of Peter and Catherine (McLennan) McArthur; m. Mabel C. Haywood-Waters; children: Daniel Carman b. 12 Aug. 1897, Peter McKellar b. 28 June 1900, Catherine Elizabeth b. 13 Mar. 1903, James Frederick b. 24 Aug. 1905, Ian Stewart b. 11 Aug. 1907; d. 28 Oct. 1924 in London, Ont.

EDUCATION
Attended Wardsville High School, Ont.; Strathroy High School and Model School, Ont., third class teacher's certificate, 1885-87; University of Toronto, 1888/89.

CAREER
Mainly literary; taught school in Caradoc, Ont., 1888; *Mail*, Toronto, Ont., 1889-90; freelance journalist in New York, NY, 1890-95; *Truth*, assistant editor and drama critic 1895, editor-in-chief and art manager 1895-97; freelance work in New York and London, England 1897-1904; McArthur & Ryder, New York, advertising agency 1904-08; *Globe*, Toronto, columnist 1908-24; *Ourselves*, founder and editor 1910-12; *Farmer's advocate*, feature writer 1911-17.

WRITINGS
Five sonnets, p.p., 1899; *Lines* (poems), p.p., 1901; *To be taken with salt: being an essay on teaching one's grandmother to suck eggs*, Limpus Baker, 1903; *The ghost and the burglar* (short story), McArthur & Ryder, 1905; *The peacemakers* (short story), McArthur & Ryder, 1905; *The sufficient life*, Long Island Loan and Trust Co., 1906; *The prodigal and other poems*, Mitchell Kennerley, 1907; *In pastures green* (essays), Dent, 1915; *The red cow and her friends* (essays), Lane, 1919; *Sir Wilfrid Laurier* (non-fiction), Dent, 1919; *The affable stranger* (essays), Allen, 1920; *The last law - brotherhood* (essays), Allen, 1921; *Stephen Leacock* (non-fiction), Ryerson, 1923; *Unselfish money* (non-fiction), Reinsurance Co., n.d.; *The deep waters. Lighthouse flashes* (non-fiction), Ontario Equitable Life and Accident Insurance Co., n.d.; *A chant of mammonism* (non-fiction), Ontario Equitable Life and Accident Insurance Co., n.d.; *The anchor post* (non-fiction), Ontario Equitable Life and Accident Insurance Co., n.d.; *The river of gold* (non-fiction), Ontario Equitable Life and Accident Insurance Co., n.d.; *Around home* (essays), Musson, 1925; *Familiar fields* (essays), Dent, 1925; *Friendly acres* (essays), Musson, 1927.
CONTRIBUTED: Poetry, articles, and essays to *The Oxford book of Canadian verse*, compiled by W. Campbell, Oxford, 1914; *Canadian poets*, edited by J.W. Garvin, McClelland & Stewart, 1916; *The new era in Canada*, edited by J.O. Miller, Dent, 1917; *Canadian poems of the great war*, edited by J.W. Garvin, McClelland & Stewart, 1918; *Our Canadian literature*, edited by A.D. Watson and L.A. Pierce, Ryerson, 1922; *Saturday night, Puck, Chatter, Harper's weekly, Atlantic monthly, Review of reviews, Punch, Farmer's advocate, Forum, Canadian magazine, Judge, Life, Town topics, Current literature, Everbody's.*

McCANCE, Larry* 1917-70
Actor, director, and producer; b. 4 Feb. 1917 in Vancouver, BC; son of John Alexander and Mary Theresa (McHugh) McCance; m. Ursula Alice Lucas 8 Sept. 1941; children: Linda Rose b. 13

Nov. 1943, Edward Alexander b. 25 July 1948;
d. 3 Jan. 1970.

EDUCATION

Attended Lonsdale primary school in North
Vancouver and North Vancouver High School.

RELIGION

Protestant.

CAREER

Made professional acting and singing debut on
radio station in Vancouver 1933; freelance
actor, singer, and stage manager in Vancouver
1933-41; Theatre Under the Stars, Vancouver,
founding member 1936; CJOR, Vancouver,
announcer 1939-41, announcer-actor 1945-47;
CBC, freelance actor Vancouver 1939-41,
leading actor Toronto 1947-56; RCAF, 1941-45;
National Film Board of Canada, Montreal,
actor 1947-56; Jupiter Theatre, Toronto, actor
1947-56; Melody Fair Musical Stock Company,
Toronto, general manager, 1954; BC Centennial
Commission, Victoria, executive secretary 1956-
58; Actors' Equity Association, Toronto,
Canadian representative 1958-69; American
Guild of Musical Artists; Toronto, Canadian
representative 1958-69.

MEMBER

ACTRA; AEA; Canadian Theatre Centre.

THEATRE

Played in many productions, e.g. Quince in *A
midsummer night's dream* (Theatre Under the
Stars), Prince in *Death takes a holiday* (Island
Theatre), Messer Schmann in *Ring round the moon*
(Jupiter); wrote and directed centennial spectac-
ulars for Waterloo and Elgin counties, Ont.
1952 and *Dominion of destiny* (Maple Leaf
Gardens, Toronto, 1953).

RADIO

Played in many CBC productions.

McCOURT, Edward Alexander* 1907-72

Novelist and teacher; b. 10 Oct. 1907 in
Mullingar, Westmeath, Ireland; son of William
Alexander and Elizabeth (Gillespie) McCourt;
came to Canada in 1909 and settled in Alberta;
m. Anna Margaret Mackay 12 Sept. 1938;
children: Michael b. 29 Mar. 1942; d. 6 Jan. 1972
in Saskatoon, Sask.

EDUCATION

Attended rural primary schools in Alberta completed secondary school by correspondence;
University of Alberta, BA honours in English,
1932; Merton College, University of Oxford, BA,
1934, MA, 1937.

RELIGION

United Church.

CAREER

Ridley College, St. Catharines, Ont., teacher
1935-36; Upper Canada College, Toronto, Ont.
teacher 1936-38; Queen's University, lecturer
1938-39; University of New Brunswick, lecturer
1939-44; University of Saskatchewan, professor
of English 1944-72; travelled extensively in
Europe.

AWARDS, HONOURS

Rhodes scholarship, 1932; joint winner of
Ryerson All Canada fiction award for *Music at
the close*, 1947.

WRITINGS

The flaming hour, Ryerson, 1947; *Music at the
close*, Ryerson, 1947 (produced CBC radio,
"Winnipeg drama," 16, 23, 30 May 1957; translated into Swedish); *The Canadian west in
fiction*, Ryerson, 1949; *Home to the stranger*,
Macmillan, 1950; *Buckskin brigadier, the story
of the Alberta field force*, Macmillan, 1955; *The
wooden sword*, McClelland & Stewart, 1956;
Revolt in the west, the story of the Riel rebellion,
Macmillan, 1958; *Walk through the valley*,
McClelland & Stewart, 1958; *Fasting friar*,
McClelland & Stewart, 1963 (published in England under title *The Ettinger affair*, Macdonald,
1963; produced CBC radio, 1967 and "Midweek
theatre," 3 Apr. 1968; CBC TV, "The serial,"
3, 10, 17, 24 June 1965); *The road across
Canada* (non-fiction), Macmillan, 1965;
Remember Butler, the story of William Butler,
McClelland & Stewart, 1967; *Saskatchewan* (non-
fiction), Macmillan, 1968; several CBC radio plays,
e.g. *The white mustang* (17 Feb. 1957; "Prairie
playhouse," 15 May 1958), *Songs my mother
taught me* ("Prairie playhouse," 19 Mar. 1959),
Cranes fly south ("Prairie playhouse," 16 Apr.
1959), *Godless man* (17 Mar. 1960), *Where
there's a will* ("Prairie playhouse," 4 Nov. 1960),
The uprooting ("Prairie playhouse," 8 Sept.
1961), *The trumpet shall sound* ("Prairie playhouse," 24 Sept. 1962).

EDITED: Joseph Conrad's *Youth*, Ryerson,
1958.

CONTRIBUTED: "Canadian literature in
English" in *Collier's encyclopedia*, Crowell-
Collier, 1947; short stories and articles to
Saturday evening post stories, Random House,
1952; *Canadian short stories*, edited by R.
Weaver and H. James, Oxford, 1952; *Adventures
in reading*, edited by J.M. Ross and others,
Harcourt, Brace, 1952; *Cavalcade of the north*,
edited by G.E. Nelson, Doubleday, 1958; *Masks
of fiction*, edited by A.J.M. Smith, McClelland
& Stewart, 1961; *Wide horizons*, edited by H.H.
Wagenheim, Holt, Rinehart & Winston, 1963; *A
world of events*, American Book, 1963; *Our*

century in prose, edited by E.H. Winter, Macmillan, 1966; *Saturday night, Queen's quarterly, Maclean's, Dalhousie review, United Church observer, Saturday review of literature, Saskatchewan history, Imperial Oil review, Northern review, Saturday evening post.*

WORK IN PROGRESS
"Yukon-Northwest Territories," to be published by Macmillan; biography of William Kinglake.

McCOWAN, Frances Hyland
see HYLAND, Frances

McCRAE, John 1872-1918
Poet; b. 30 Nov. 1872 in Guelph, Ont.; son of David and Janet Simpson (Eckford) McCrae; d. 28 Jan. 1918 in Boulogne, France.

EDUCATION
Attended Guelph Collegiate and Vocational Institute, 1883-88; University of Toronto, BA in biology, 1894, MB, 1898; Member of Royal College of Physicians, London, England.

CAREER
General Hospital, Toronto, Ont.; resident house officer 1898; Johns Hopkins Hospital, Baltimore, Md., resident house officer 1899; South African Field Force, 1899-1900, lieutenant of artillery, awarded Queen's medal; McGill University, fellow in pathology 1900–?, lecturer in medicine; General Hospital, Montreal, PQ, pathologist 1900–?; Alexandra Hospital, Montreal, physician; Royal Victoria Hospital, Montreal, assistant physician; First Canadian Artillery Brigade, 1914-18, became lieutenant-colonel, awarded DSO and mentioned in dispatches three times; First British Army, consulting physician 1918.

MEMBER
Pen and Pencil Club; Association of American Physicians (elected member, 1914).

WRITINGS
A text-book of pathology, Lea & Febiger, 1914; *In Flanders fields and other poems*, W. Briggs, 1919.
CONTRIBUTED: Poetry to *University magazine, Punch, Spectator, Canadian magazine, Massey's magazine, Varsity, Westminster.*

MACDONALD, Brian 1928–
Choreographer and director; b. 14 May 1928 in Montreal, PQ; son of Ian Ronald and Mabel (Lee) Macdonald; m. Olivia Wyatt (d. 8 Aug. 1959); m. Annette Weidersheim-Paul 20 Dec. 1964; children: (first marriage) Brian Justin Wyatt.

EDUCATION
Attended Westmount High School, Montreal; McGill University, BA honours in English, 1953; studied ballet with Gérald Crevier and Elizabeth Leese (*q.v.*) in Montreal; Martha Graham School, New York; studied with Françoise Sullivan, Montreal.

OFFICE
Royal Winnipeg Ballet, 322 Smith St., Winnipeg 2, Man.; Harkness Ballet, 4 E. 75th Ave., New York, NY 10021, USA.

CAREER
Herald, Montreal, music critic 1949-51; National Ballet of Canada, Toronto (charter member), corps de ballet 1951-53; CBC, Montreal, choreographer 1954–?; Montreal Theatre Ballet, co-founder 1956; Royal Winnipeg Ballet, visiting choreographer 1958; official choreographer 1959–; Royal Swedish Ballet, Stockholm, Sweden, director 1964-66; Norwegian Ballet, Oslo, Norway, director 1964-66; Royal Swedish Ballet Festival, founder 1965–; Harkness Ballet, New York, artistic director 1967–.

MEMBER
Canadian Theatre Centre.

AWARDS, HONOURS
Canada Council senior arts fellowship, 1958, 1960/61; King's scholarship, Stockholm; 2nd Paris International Festival of the Dance, France, gold star for best abstract ballet for *Aimez-vous Bach?*, Nov. 1964; Medal of service of the Order of Canada, 1967.

THEATRE
Choreographed *L'ouest, L'Acadie* and *Kébec* (with Michel Cartier, Les Feux-Follets, Montréal), *Post script* (National Ballet of Canada, 1956), *The darkling* (Playhouse, Winnipeg, 17 Oct. 1958), *Aimez-vous Bach?* (Berlin, Germany, 1958), *Les whoops-de-doo* (Flin Flon Community Centre, Man., 3 Oct. 1959), *A court occasion* (Playhouse, Winnipeg, 26 Dec. 1961), *Prothalamion* (Banff School of Fine Arts, Alta., Aug. 1961; restaged for Norwegian Ballet under title *Hymn*, 1962/63), *Time out of mind* (Robert Joffrey Ballet, New York, 28 Sept. 1962), *Capers* (Robert Joffrey Ballet, New York, 1963), *Pas d'action* (c.1965), *Octet* (Royal Swedish Ballet, c.1965), *While the spider slept* (Royal Swedish Ballet, June 1965), *Cucurucu* (Royal Swedish Ballet Festival, 5 June 1966), *L'oiseau de feu* (Royal Swedish Ballet, 1966), *The threepenny opera* (Manitoba Theatre Centre, Winnipeg, 9 Feb. 1966), *Rose Latulippe* (Stratford, Ont. Festival, 16 Aug. 1966), *Songs without words* (Royal Winnipeg Ballet, 1967), *Tschaikovsky* (Harkness Ballet, Chicago, Ill., Mar. 1967), *Zealous variations* (Harkness Ballet, 1967), *Canto indio* (Harkness Ballet, 1967).

TELEVISION
Choreographed many CBC productions, e.g. "Heure du concert" (series, 1954–?), "Dancing storybook" (13-week children's series, 1961), *The darkling* (Royal Winnipeg Ballet, 14 Aug. 1961), *Les whoops-de-doo* (Royal Winnipeg Ballet, 26 Aug. 1962), *Rose Latulippe* ("Music Canada," 12 Apr. 1967).

MacDONALD James Edward Hervey 1873-1932
Artist; b. 12 May 1873 in Durham, England; son
of William Henry MacDonald; came to Canada in
Apr. 1887 and settled in Hamilton, Ont.; m. Har-
riet Joan Lavis, 1899; children: Thoreau b. 21
Apr. 1901; d. 26 Nov. 1932 in Toronto, Ont.

EDUCATION
Attended Durham Model School; studied under
John Ireland and Arthur Heming (q.v.), Hamilton
Art School night classes, 1887-88; G.A. Reid
(q.v.) and William Cruikshank, Central Ontario
School of Art and Design, Toronto, night and
Saturday afternoon classes, c.1893.

CAREER
Toronto Lithography Co., apprentice c.1889-95;
Grip Limited, Toronto, artist in the design department c.1895-1903; Carlton Studios, London, England, designer 1903-07; Grip Limited, artist 1907-
11; painter and freelance designer in Toronto
making sketching trips to Quebec and northern
Ontario 1911-21; Ontario College of Art, Toronto,
instructor in decorative and commercial design
1921-27, head of department of graphic and commercial art 1927-32, acting principal 1928-29,
principal 1929-32; Canadian forum, art editor
1923; made sketching trips in Ontario and annual
summer trips to the Rockies, 1924-30.

COMMISSIONS
Ceiling paintings, St. Anne's Church, Toronto,
1923; decorations for foyer, Claridge Apartments,
Toronto, 1928; mosaic decorations, Concourse
Building, Toronto, 1929.

MEMBER
Group of Seven (co-founder, 1920); Ontario So-
ciety of Artists (elected, 1909); Royal Canadian
Academy (Associate 1912; Academician 1931).

EXHIBITIONS
ONE-MAN: Art Gallery of Toronto, 1933; National
Gallery of Canada, Ottawa, Ont., 1933; Mellors Gal-
leries, Toronto, 1937; Dominion Gallery, Montreal,
PQ, 1947; Art Gallery of Hamilton, 1957.
GROUP: Represented in group exhibitions held
in Canada including annual exhibitions of Ontario
Society of Artists, Royal Canadian Academy, and
Canadian National Exhibitions; represented in
group exhibitions organized by National Gallery
of Canada including its Annual Exhibitions; Canadian Art Exhibition, Walker Art Gallery, Liverpool, England, 1910; Exhibition of Canadian Art,
Crystal Palace, Festival of the Empire, London,
England, 1910; ... Paintings by the Group of
Seven Canadian Artists, Buffalo Fine Arts Academy and Albright-Knox Art Gallery, Buffalo, NY,
1921; British Empire Exhibition, Wembley, England, 1924 and 1925; Exhibition of Paintings
by Canadian Artists, Worcester Art Museum,
Mass., 1924; Sesqui-Centennial International Exposition, Philadelphia, Pa., 1926; Exposition
d'Art canadien, Musée du Jeu de Paume, Paris,
France, 1927; An Exhibition of Paintings by

Contemporary Canadian Artists, City Art Museum, St. Louis, Mo., 1930; Contemporary Canadian Painters, Roerich Museum, New York, NY,
1932; A Century of Canadian Art, Tate Gallery,
London, 1938; Golden Gate International Exposition, San Francisco, Calif., 1939; Canadian
Art 1760-1943, Yale University Art Gallery,
1944; Painting in Canada, a Selective Historical
Survey, Albany Institute of History and Art,
Albany, NY, 1946; Forty Years of Canadian
Painting, Museum of Fine Arts, Boston, Mass.,
1949; Canadian Painting, National Gallery of
Art, Washington, DC, 1950; exhibition of Cana-
dian painting shown in Pakistan, India, and
Ceylon, 1954-55; Canadian Group of Seven and
Eskimo Folk Art, Chautauqua Art Association
and Chautauqua Institution, NY, 1963.

COLLECTIONS IN WHICH REPRESENTED
Agnes Etherington Art Centre, Queen's University;
Art Gallery of Hamilton; Art Gallery of Ontario,
Toronto; Beaverbrook Art Gallery, Fredericton,
NB; Hamilton Teacher's College; Hart House Perm-
anent Collection and Faculty Club, University of
Toronto; London Public Library and Art Museum,
Ont.; McMichael Conservation Collection of Art,
Kleinburg, Ont.; Montreal Museum of Fine Arts;
National Gallery of Canada; Ontario Department
of Public Works; Vancouver Art Gallery, BC; Owens
Museum, Mount Allison University.

WRITINGS
Village & fields; a few country poems, Woodchuck Press, 1933; My high horse; a mountain
memory (poems), Woodchuck Press, c.1933;
West by east and other poems, Ryerson, 1933;
A word to us all (poems), Ryerson, 1945.
CONTRIBUTED: To Globe, Rebel, Lamps, Statesman, Canadian forum, Canadian bookman, Journal
of the Royal Architectural Institute of Canada.

MACDONALD, James Williamson Galloway
1897-1960
(Jock Macdonald)
Artist; b. 31 May 1897 in Thurso, Caithness-
shire, Scotland; son of Sinclair and Marion (Galloway) Macdonald; m. Barbara Elinor Nice 4 Jan.
1926; came to Canada in 1926 and settled in Vancouver, BC; children: Fiona Elinor b. 1 July;
d. 3 Dec. 1960 in Toronto, Ont.

EDUCATION
Attended Miller Institute, Thurso, 1902-11; attended George Watson's Boys' College, Edinburgh,
Scotland, 1915-19; studied under Charles Paine
and John Platt, Edinburgh College of Art, design
diploma, 1920-22; Scottish Education Authority,
art specialist teachers' certificate, 1922.

RELIGION
Presbyterian.

CAREER
Argyll and Sutherland Highlanders, 1915-19;
Sundour Fabrics, Carlisle, England, textile de-

signer 1922-25; Lincoln School of Art, England, teacher of design; Vancouver School of Art, head of design department 1926-33; School of Decorative and Applied Art (BC College of Art), Vancouver, co-founder and co-director 1933-35; Vancouver Art Gallery, council member 1933-35 and 1937-45; Vancouver Art Gallery, director of children's art classes 1943-46; Banff School of Fine Arts, Alta., instructor in landscape painting 1940-46; Provincial Institute of Technology and Art, Calgary, Alta., director of school of art 1945-46; Ontario College of Art, Toronto, professor of painting 1946-60; International Students' Seminar sponsored by UNESCO, Breda, The Netherlands, special lecturer summer 1949; International Students' Seminar sponsored by UNESCO, France, special lecturer summer 1950; travelled to France on a fellowship, 1954.

MEMBER
BC Society of Fine Arts (president, 1933; life member, 1946); Canadian Society of Painters in Water Colour (president, 1952-54); Ontario Society of Artists (elected, 1948); Painters Eleven; Canadian Group of Painters (charter member); Royal Canadian Academy (Associate 1959); International Arts and Letters Society (elected life member, 1960).

AWARDS, HONOURS
Honorable mention in landscape division, Lord Willingdon competition, 1933; Queen's Coronation medal, 1953; Royal Society of Canada fellowship overseas award, 1954.

EXHIBITIONS
ONE-MAN: Hart House, University of Toronto, 1957; Park Gallery, Toronto, 1958; Westdale Gallery, Hamilton, Ont., 1959; Art Gallery of Toronto, 1960; Here and Now Gallery, Toronto, 1960; Roberts Gallery, Toronto, 1962.
GROUP: Represented in group exhibitions held in Canada including exhibitions of Royal Canadian Academy, Canadian Group of Painters, Ontario Society of Artists, Canadian Society of Painters in Water Colour, and Painters Eleven; represented in group exhibitions organized by National Gallery of Canada, Ottawa, Ont., including its second Biennial Exhibition of Canadian Painting, 1959; Exhibition of Contemporary Canadian Painting Arranged ... for Circulation in the Southern Dominions of the British Empire, 1936; Exhibition of Paintings, Drawings and Sculpture by Artists of the British Empire Overseas, Royal Institute Galleries, London, England, 1937; A Century of Canadian Art, Tate Gallery, London, 1938; World's Fair, New York, NY, 1939; Detroit Museum of Fine Art, Mich., 1958.

COLLECTIONS IN WHICH REPRESENTED
Art Gallery of Ontario, Toronto; Hamilton Art Gallery; Hart House Permanent Collection, University of Toronto; Imperial Oil Ltd. Collection, Toronto; London Public Library and Art Museum, Ont.; National Gallery of Canada; University of British Columbia; Vancouver Art Gallery; Owens Museum, Mount Allison University; Canadian Industries Ltd. Collection, Montreal; Montreal Museum of Fine Arts; Beaverbrook Art Gallery, Fredericton, NB; Regina Art Gallery, Sask.

MACDONALD, Jock
see MACDONALD, James Williamson Galloway

MACDONALD, Lucy Maud Montgomery
see MONTGOMERY, Lucy Maud

MacDONALD, Manly Edward 1889—
Artist; b. 15 Aug. 1889 in Point Anne, Ont.; son of William Charles and Sarah MacDonald; m. Beverly Lambe 1918; children: Sarah Beverly, Francis Duncan.

EDUCATION
Studied under Ernest Fosbery, Albright Art School, Buffalo, NY; William M. Panton and Philip Hale, School of the Boston Museum of Fine Arts, Mass., 1912-13; G.A. Reid (q.v.) and J.W. Beatty, Ontario College of Art, Toronto, Ont., 1914-16.

CAREER
Painted for Canadian War Memorials, 1918; travelled and painted in Europe 1921; painting presented to Queen Elizabeth by the city of Toronto; painting presented to the city of Tokyo, Japan, by the city of Toronto.

MEMBER
Royal Canadian Academy (Associate 1919; Academician 1948); Ontario Society of Artists (elected, 1919; resigned, 1951).

AWARDS, HONOURS
Travelling scholarship, Royal Canadian Academy, 1918.

EXHIBITIONS
GROUP: Represented in group exhibitions held in Canada including annual exhibitions of Royal Canadian Academy and Ontario Society of Artists; British Empire Exhibition, Wembley, England, 1924; World's Fair, New York, NY, 1939; *Pintura Canadense Contemporanea*, Rio de Janeiro, Brazil, 1944; Colombo Plan Exhibition, Colombo, Ceylon, 1951; New Delhi International, India, 1953; An Exhibition of Canadian Painting held at Fortnum and Mason, Ltd., London, England, 1955.

COLLECTIONS IN WHICH REPRESENTED
National Gallery of Canada, Ottawa, Ont.; London Public Library and Art Museum, Ont.; Union Carbide Co., Toronto; Abitibi Power and Paper Co., Ont.; Agnes Etherington Art Centre, Queen's University.

McDOWELL, Franklin Edgar Davey 1888-1965
Novelist; b. 1888 in Bowmanville, Ont.; m. Kathleen 1920; d. 19 July 1965 in Toronto, Ont.

RELIGION
Protestant.

CAREER
World, Toronto, 1909- ?; *Manitoba free press,* Winnipeg; *Mail and empire,* Toronto; *News,* Toronto; *The sailor,* editor; CNR, Toronto, central region public relations representative 1923-53; Governor General's Awards Board, chairman 1949-51.

MEMBER
Canadian Authors Association (Ont. vice-president, 1944-45; honorary life member, 1958); Huronia Historical Sites Association (honorary director); Society of Authors, UK; Ontario Historical Association.

AWARDS, HONOURS
Governor General's literary award for *The Champlain road,* 1939; LL D from University of Western Ontario, 1955.

WRITINGS
The Champlain Road, Macmillan, 1939; *Forges of freedom,* Macmillan, 1943.
CONTRIBUTED: Short stories and articles to *Saturday night, Echoes, Canadian home journal, Canadian magazine.*

McKAY, Arthur Fortescue* 1926–
Artist; b. 11 Sept. 1926 in Nipawin, Sask.; son of Joseph Fortescue and Georgina Agnes McKay; m. Lorelli June; children: Valori b. 1955, Alysoun b. 1956, Daniel b. 1962.

EDUCATION
Studied under J.W.G. Macdonald (*q.v.*), Provincial Institute of Technology and Art, Calgary, Alta., 1946-48; Académie de la Grande Chaumière, Paris, France, 1949-50; School of Painting and Sculpture, Columbia University; Barnes Foundation, Merion, Pa., 1956-57; studied under Barnett Newman, Emma Lake Workshop, Sask., 1959.

RELIGION
None.

HOME
5489 Spring Garden Rd., Halifax, NS.

CAREER
University of Saskatchewan School of Art, Regina Campus, part-time instructor 1950-52, special lecturer in art 1952-61, associate professor 1963, director 1964–; Nova Scotia College of Art, professor of art 1967-68.

AWARDS, HONOURS
Purchase award, Spring Exhibition, Montreal Museum of Fine Arts, 1962; Humanities Research Council grant, 1956/57; Canada Council senior arts fellowship, 1963/64.

EXHIBITIONS
ONE-MAN: Norman Mackenzie Art Gallery, Regina, Sask., 1953; Western Canada Art Circuit, 1961; Regina Public Library, 1965.

GROUP: Represented in group exhibitions held in Canada since 1954; represented in group exhibitions organized by National Gallery of Canada, Ottawa, Ont., including its second, third, fourth, fifth, and sixth Biennial Exhibitions of Canadian Painting, 1957, 1959, 1961, 1963, and 1965; Fifteen Canadian Painters, Museum of Modern Art, New York, NY, 1961; Contemporary Canadian Art, toured Africa, 1962; International Exhibition, Albright-Knox Museum, Buffalo, NY, 1963; Post Painterly Abstraction, Los Angeles County Museum, Calif., 1964.

COLLECTIONS IN WHICH REPRESENTED
Art Gallery of Ontario, Toronto; Brock Hall Collection, University of British Columbia; Montreal Museum of Fine Arts, PQ; Norman Mackenzie Art Gallery, Regina; Vancouver Art Gallery, BC.

MacKAY, Louis Alexander 1901–
(John Smalacombe, pseud.)
Poet; b. 27 Feb. 1901 in Hensall, Ont.; son of William and Martha Elma (Smallacombe) MacKay; m. Constance C. Charlesworth 29 June 1928; children: Pierre Anthony b. 19 Feb. 1933, Katherine Camilla Ann b. 2 Nov. 1935.

EDUCATION
Attended Hensall Public School, 1907-14; Clinton Collegiate Institute, Ont., 1914-19, and Guelph Collegiate Institute, Ont., 1918; University of Toronto, BA, 1923, MA, 1924; Balliol College, University of Oxford, BA, 1929, MA, 1948.

RELIGION
Anglican.

HOME
36 Ardmore Road, Berkeley 7, Calif., USA.

CAREER
Victoria College, University of Toronto, lecturer in classics 1923-25; University College, University of Toronto, lecturer in classics 1928-32, assistant professor of Latin 1932-41; *Canadian forum,* editorial board 1932-35; University of British Columbia, associate professor of classics 1941-48; University of California, Berkeley, professor of Latin 1948-68, professor emeritus 1968–; travelled in Europe and USA.

MEMBER
Archaelogical Institute of America; Philological Association of the Pacific Coast; Classical Association of Canada; American Philological Association (president, 1960).

AWARDS, HONOURS
McCaul gold medal in classics, 1923; Rhodes scholarship, 1925; Guggenheim fellowship, 1945.

WRITINGS
Viper's bugloss, Ryerson, 1938; *The ill-tempered lover and other poems,* Macmillan, 1948; *The wrath of Homer* (non-fiction), University of Toronto, 1948; *Notes on Lucretius* (non-fiction), University of California, 1950; *Janus* (non-fiction), University of California, 1956.

CONTRIBUTED: Plays, poetry, and articles to Canadian plays from Hart House Theatre, v.2, edited by V. Massey, Macmillan, 1927; Anthology of Canadian poetry, compiled by R. Gustafson, Penguin, 1942; The book of Canadian poetry, edited by A.J.M. Smith, University of Chicago, 1943; Twentieth century verse, edited by I. Dilworth, Clarke, Irwin, 1945; The wordly muse; an anthology of serious light verse, edited by A.J.M. Smith, Abelard, 1951; One thousand and one poems of mankind, edited by H.W. Wells, Tupper & Love, 1953; Canadian poetry in English, chosen by B. Carman and others, rev, & enl. ed., Ryerson, 1954; The silver treasury of light verse, edited by O. Williams, New American Library, 1957; The blasted pine, edited by F.R. Scott and A.J.M. Smith, Macmillan, 1957; The Oxford book of Canadian verse in English and French, chosen by A.J.M. Smith, Oxford, 1960; The Penguin book of Canadian verse, edited by R. Gustafson, rev. ed., Penguin, 1967; Saturday night, Canadian forum, Canadian poetry, Poetry, Contemporary verse, Northern review, Canadian review of music and art.

MacKENZIE, Gisèle 1927–
(Marie Marguerite Louise Gisèle La Fleche; Gisèle Shuttleworth)
Singer, violinist, and entertainer; b. 10 Jan. 1927 in Winnipeg, Man.; daughter of Georges MacKenzie and Gabrielle Celine Oliva Marietta (Manseau) La Fleche; m. Robert J. Shuttleworth 24 Feb. 1958 (marriage dissolved 1966); children: MacKenzie Duffy, Gisèle Melissa.

EDUCATION
Attended Sacred Heart School in Winnipeg; studied violin with Taras Hubichi 1936-41; Toronto (now Royal) Conservatory of Music, Ont., studied with Kathleen Parlow, (q.v.), 1941-45; Jarvis Collegiate School, Toronto; Harbord Collegiate School, Toronto.

RELIGION
Roman Catholic.

HOME
15824 Woodvale Rd., Encino, Calif., USA.

CAREER
Glenmount Hotel, Muskoka, Ont., violinist 1945; CBC, entertainer 1946-50; radio and TV entertainer in USA 1950-60, 1962–; toured USA and Canada 1953; worked with Jack Benny 1953; Gisèle MacKenzie show, star entertainer 1957-58.

AWARDS, HONOURS
Toronto Conservatory of Music, scholarship; Critics' award for most popular female singer in Canada, 1949; Canadian National Sportsman's Show award of silver tray for outstanding achievements in radio and television, 1954; Disk jockeys' top Canadian artist award, 1955.

MEMBER
Academy of Television Arts and Sciences (director, 1956-57).

THEATRE
Played leading role in South Pacific (Dallas, Tex.; summer 1955), title role in Annie get your gun (Kansas City, Kans.; summer 1956), Anna in The King and I (tour of USA, summer 1957).

RADIO
Appeared in many series, e.g. "Meet Gisèle" (CBC 1946-49), "London by lamplight" (CBC, 1949), "Let's start an argument," "Morgantime" (1949-51).

TELEVISION
Appeared in many series, e.g. "Club 15" (CBS, Hollywood, Calif., 1951-63), "Your hit parade" (NBC, New York, NY, 1953-57), "Kraft Theatre," "General Electric Theatre," "Studio One," Jack Benny show, Jack Paar show.

RECORDINGS
Numerous recordings by Capitol Records, e.g. Hard to get.

McKENZIE, Robert Tait 1867-1938
Sculptor; b. 26 May 1867 in Almonte, Ont.; son of William and Catherine (Shiels) McKenzie; m. Ethel O'Neil Aug. 1907; d. 28 Apr. 1938 in Philadelphia, Pa.

EDUCATION
Attended Almonte High School; Collegiate Institute, Ottawa, Ont., McGill University, BA, 1889, MD, CM, 1892; Springfield College, Mass., MPE, 1914.

RELIGION
Presbyterian.

CAREER
Montreal General Hospital, PQ, house surgeon 1893; ship's surgeon 1894; McGill University, medical director of physical education and demonstrator, later lecturer, in anatomy 1894-1904; orthopaedic surgeon in private practice in Montreal 1894-1904; house physician to the Earl and Countess of Aberdeen, Rideau Hall, Ottawa, Ont., 1895-96; Montreal Art Association, lecturer on artistic anatomy 1901; Harvard University summer school, lecturer 1904; Olympic games lecture course, St. Louis, Mo., lecturer 1904; University of Pennsylvania, professor and director of the department of physical education 1904-31, J. William White Research professor of physical education 1931-38; Royal Army Medical Corps, became temporary major 1915; inspector of physical therapy and remedial surgery in military hospitals in Great Britain and Canada 1915-18; sculptor in Montreal and later in Philadelphia c.1900-38.

COMMISSIONS
War memorial, Cambridge, England, 1922; Baker Memorial, House of Commons Lobby, Ottawa,

Ont.; memorial, Almonte; Scottish American War
Memorial, Princes Street Gardens, Edinburgh, Scot-
land, 1923; General James Wolfe monument,
Greenwich Park, London, England; Dominion
Confederation Memorial, Parliament Buildings,
Ottawa; Radmor Memorial, Pennsylvania; war
memorial, Girard College, Philadelphia; Spirit of
Nursing monument, Red Cross Gardens, Washington, DC; Delano Memorial, Washington, 1933.
MEMBER
American Physical Education Association (president, 1913-15); Society of Directors of Physical
Education in Colleges (president, 1912); American Academy of Physical Education (co-founder;
president, 1927-38); American Medical Association; Philadelphia College of Physicians and Sur-
geons (elected fellow); Royal Canadian Academy
(honorary Academician 1928).

AWARDS, HONOURS
Silver medal, St. Louis, 1904; King Gustavus IV's
medal, Stockholm, Sweden, 1912; honourable
mention, Panama Pacific Exhibition, 1915; LL D
from McGill University, 1919.

EXHIBITIONS
ONE-MAN: London, c.1918.
GROUP: Represented in group exhibitions held
in Canada from c.1902 on including annual exhibitions of Royal Canadian Academy; exhibitions
of Royal Academy, England; exhibitions of American Society of Artists; A Century of Canadian
Art, Tate Gallery, London, 1938.

COLLECTIONS IN WHICH REPRESENTED
Metropolitan Museum, New York, NY; Fitzwil-
liam Museum, University of Cambridge; Ashmol-
ean Museum, University of Oxford; Montreal Museum of Fine Arts, PQ; Newark Art Museum, NJ;
National Gallery of Canada, Ottawa; Yale University Art Gallery; City Art Museum, St. Louis;
Princeton University; Balmoral Castle, Scotland;
University of Pennsylvania; Harvard University.

WRITINGS
The Barnjum barbell drill, American Sports Publishing Co., 1906; *Exercise in education and medicine*, Saunders, 1909; *Reclaiming the maimed: a
handbook of physical therapy*, Macmillan, 1918.
CONTRIBUTED: Articles to medical and educational journals.

MacKINNON, Sheila* 1937—
Dancer; b. 23 Sept. 1937 in Medicine Hat, Alta;
daughter of Douglas and Ann Geneveve (Whelan)
MacKinnon.
EDUCATION
Attended St. Ann's Academy in Victoria; studied
ballet with Wynne Shaw in Victoria, Royal Academy of Dancing, elementary and intermediate
examinations; Audrey de Vos, Maria Fay, and
Andrew Hardy in London, England; Rosella Hightower and José Ferran in Cannes, France.

RELIGION
Roman Catholic.
HOME
c/o D. MacKinnon, 4853 Townsend Dr., RR 3
Victoria, BC.
OFFICE
Royal Winnipeg Ballet, 322 Smith St., Winnipeg
2, Man.
CAREER
Royal Winnipeg Ballet, corps de ballet 1959-64,
soloist 1964-66, principal 1966—.
MEMBER
ACTRA; AEA; Royal Academy of Dancing.
THEATRE
Danced *Don Quixote* pas de deux (Petipa), Pas de
trois in *Roundelay* (Boris), Gretel in *Hansel and
Gretel* (Spohr), *Variations* (Conte), *Un et un font
deux* (Conte), Violin in *A court occasion* (Mac-
donald), Maiden in *The bitter weird* (deMille),
Pas dix (Balanchine), Nightingale in *The little em-
peror and the mechanical court* (Clouser), *Protha-
lamion* (Macdonald), White girl in *The darkling*
(Macdonald), *Intermede* (Spohr), *Ballet premier*
(Spohr), Pink girl in *The comedians* (Boris), *The
Chinese nightingale* (Heiden), Pas de trois and
Black Swan pas de deux from *Le lac des cygnes*
(Petipa), Leftover swan in *Les whoops-de-doo*
(Macdonald), Little girl and ballerina in *Aimez-
vous Bach?* (Macdonald), Jenny Diver in *The beg-
gar's ballet* (Moulton), *Chiaroscuro* (Darrell), *May-
erling* (Darrell), *Tribute* (Clouser), *Napoli*, act III
(Bournonville), *Flower festival in Genzano* pas de
deux (Bournonville), *Sylvia variations* (Clouser),
Young girl and Mother in *While the spider slept*
(Macdonald), Young girl in *The still point* (Bolender), *Spring waters* pas de deux (Messerer),
Sappho in *Out of Lesbos* (Clouser), *Le corsaire*
pas de deux (Gorsky), Riel's wife in *Riel* (Clou-
ser), *Song without words* (Macdonald), White
couple in *Les patineurs* (Ashton), title role in
Rose Latulippe (Macdonald), *Pastiche* (Dolin),
Daydream (Ahonen), *Le jazz hot* (Boris, 1960);
created Oboe in *A court occasion* (Macdonald,
Playhouse, Winnipeg, 26 Dec. 1961), Pierrette in
Rose Latulippe (Macdonald, Stratford, Ont. Fes-
tival, 16 Aug. 1966).
TELEVISION
Played Sue in "Dancing storybook" (13-week
children's series, CBC); danced Pierrette in *Rose
Latulippe* ("Music Canada," CBC, 12 Apr. 1967).

MacLEAN, Quentin Stuart Morvaren 1896-1962
Organist and composer; b. 4 May 1896 in London,
England; son of Alexander Morvaren MacLean;
m.; came to Canada and settled in Toronto, Ont.;
d. 9 July 1962 in Toronto.
EDUCATION
Studied organ with Harold Osmund in Broad-
stairs, England, 1905; F.G. Shuttleworth in Lon-

don, 1907; H. Graedener, Vienna Conservatory of Music, Austria, 1907-09; Karl Straube and composition with Max Reger, Leipzig Conservatory, Germany, 1912-14.

RELIGION
Roman Catholic.

CAREER
Westminster Cathedral, London, assistant organist 1919-20; Grand Cinema, Fulham, England, organist 1920; Globe Cinema, Acton, England, organist; Regent Cinema, Brighton, England, organist early 1920s; Pavilion Theatre, Shepherds Bush, London, organist; Regal Cinema, Marble Arch, London, organist; Trocadero Theatre, Elephant and Castle, London, organist 1931-39; BBC, theatre organist to 1939; CBC, theatre organist 1939-62; Shea's Hippodrome, Toronto, organist 1939-47; Church of the Holy Rosary, Toronto, organist 1942-62; Shea's Victoria, Toronto, organist 1947-49.

MEMBER
CAPAC; Royal Canadian College of Organists.

CONCERT STAGE
Organ soloist, Leipzig Bach Festival, 1918; recitalist in London at Royal Albert Hall, St. Mark's, N. Audley St., and Broadcasting House; organ soloist under Herman Scherchen in first English performance of *Organ concerto* by Hindemith; organist, opening of BBC theatre organ, Broadcasting House, London, 1936; organist, recital of test pieces, Royal College of Organists, London; recitalist, Convocation Hall, University of Toronto, 1960, Mar. 1961; St. Agathe-des-Monts, 1960.

RADIO
Theatre organist in recitals (CBC, 1941-62).

TELEVISION
Organ accompanist and soloist, "Great hymns of all time" from organ of St. Cuthbert's, Toronto (1961).

RECORDINGS
Many recordings in England before 1939; recordings by CBC IS.

COMPOSITIONS
Principal works: *Sonata*, organ, 1932; *Concerto for organ*, 1935; *String quartet*, 1936; *Trio*, violin, cello, and piano, 1937; *Trio*, guitar, flute, and viola, 1937; *Rhapsody on two English folk tunes*, harp and orchestra, 1938; *Babbling*, orchestra, K. Prowse; *Rondelet*, orchestra, K. Prowse; *Parade of the sunbeams*, orchestra or band, K. Prowse; *Stabat mater*, tenor, choir, and orchestra, 1941; *Algonquin legend*, violin and piano or strings, 1942; *Variations*, orchestra, 1943; *Postlude on "Victimae Paschali,"* organ, 1944; *Concerto for electric organ*, organ and orchestra, 1945; *Mass for four voices*, choir and organ, 1946; *Mass on Easter themes*, choir and organ, 1947; *Terra tremuit*, offertory motet, choir and

organ, 1948; *Mass, Jesu redemptor omnium*, choir and organ, 1949; *The three rivers*, vocal, 1949; *Violin concerto; Prelude and fugue on a tuning formula; Harpsichord concerto.*

MacLENNAN, Hugh* 1907–

(John Hugh MacLennan)
Novelist and teacher; b. 20 Mar. 1907 in Glace Bay, NS; son of Samuel J. and Katherine (McQuarrie) MacLennan; m. Dorothy Duncan 22 June 1936 (d. 1957); m. Aline Frances Walker May 1959.

EDUCATION
Attended Tower Road School in Halifax, NS; Halifax Academy; Dalhousie University, BA, 1928; Oriel College, University of Oxford, BA, 1932; Princeton University, MA, Ph D, 1935.

RELIGION
Presbyterian.

OFFICE
Department of English, McGill University, Montreal, PQ.

CAREER
Lower Canada College, Montreal, PQ, head of classics department 1935-45; McGill University, part-time associate professor of English 1951-64, full-time associate professor 1966, professor 1967–; travelled extensively.

MEMBER
Royal Society of Canada (elected fellow, 1953); Royal Society of Literature; North Hatley Club; Canadian Club.

AWARDS, HONOURS
Rhodes scholarship, 1928; Governor General's gold medal from Dalhousie University, 1929; Guggenheim fellowship, 1943; Governor General's literary award for *Two solitudes*, 1945, for *The precipice*, 1948, for *Cross country*, 1949, for *Thirty and three*, 1954, for *The watch that ends the night*, 1959; D Litt from University of Western Ontario, 1952; Lorne Pierce medal, 1952; D Litt from University of Manitoba, 1953; LLD from Dalhousie University, 1955; D Litt from Waterloo Lutheran University, 1961; Canada Council senior arts fellowship, 1962/63; Molson prize, 1966; Companion of the Order of Canada.

WRITINGS
Oxyrhyncus, an economic and social study, Princeton, 1935; *Barometer rising*, Duell, Sloan & Pearce, 1941 (translated into German, French, and Rumanian); (with E. Vaillancourt and J.P. Humphrey) *Canadian unity and Quebec*, Montreal, 1942; *Two solitudes*, Duell, Sloan & Pearce, 1945 (translated into Dutch, Swedish, Spanish, French, Japanese, Estonian, and Czech); *The precipice*, Collins, 1948; *Cross country* (essays), Collins, 1949; *Each man's son*, Macmillan, 1951 (excerpt produced National Film Board of Canada 106B

0154 016); *The present world as seen in its literature*, University of New Brunswick, 1952; *Thirty
and three* (essays), edited by D. Duncan, Macmillan, 1954; *The future of the novel as an art form*,
University of Toronto, 1959; *The watch that ends
the night*, Macmillan, 1959 (translated into
Swedish, German, French, and Spanish); *Scotch-
man's return, and other essays*, Macmillan, 1960;
Seven rivers of Canada, Macmillan, 1961; *An
orange from Portugal* (autobiography), Village
Press, 1964; *The colour of Canada*, McClelland &
Stewart, 1967; *Return of the sphinx*, Macmillan,
1967 (translated into German); *The world when
we were born* (TV script; CBC, 1 July 1967).
EDITED: *McGill: the story of a university*,
Allen & Unwin, 1960.
CONTRIBUTED: Articles to *Saturday review of
literature, Maclean's, Canadian author and bookman, Canadian literature, Vogue, Montreal standard, Canadian library, Montrealer, Holiday,
Chatelaine, Foreign affairs, National home
monthly*.

MacLENNAN, John Hugh
see MacLENNAN, Hugh

MacMILLAN, Andrew 1914-67
Singer (bass baritone) and stage director; b. 1914
in Glasgow, Scotland; son of William and Johanna
(McCrindle) MacMillan; came to Canada as a boy;
m. Elsie Pearce; children: Melissa; d. 7 Feb. 1967
in Toronto, Ont.
EDUCATION
Musical training in Montreal, PQ, and at Royal
Conservatory of Music Opera School, Toronto.
CAREER
Royal Canadian Engineers, Canadian Army Show,
toured Europe for 3 years during World War II;
Royal Conservatory of Music Opera School,
Toronto, assistant stage director *c*.1948, dramatic
coach, stage director 1961-67; toured Central
America.
THEATRE
Sang in numerous productions, e.g. title role,
Count, and Dr. Bartolo in *The marriage of Figaro*
(Canadian Opera Company), Papageno in *The
magic flute* (Canadian Opera Company), Alfonso
in *Cosi fan tutte* (Canadian Opera Company),
Police in *The consul* (Canadian Opera Company),
Lunardo in *School for fathers* (Canadian Opera
Company), Eisenstein and Frank in *Die Fleder-
maus* (Canadian Opera Company), Father in
Hansel and Gretel (Canadian Opera Company),
Popoff in *The merry widow* (Canadian Opera
Company), Dr. Bartolo in *The barber of Seville*
(Canadian Opera Company), Sam in *A masked
ball* (Canadian Opera Company), Del Aqua in *A
night in Venice* (Canadian Opera Company),

Falstaff in *The merry wives of Windsor* (Canadian
Opera Company, tour), Leporello in *Don Giovanni*
(Canadian Opera Company), Schaunard in *La
bohème* (Canadian Opera Company, tour), Zuniga
in *Carmen* (Canadian Opera Company), *I Pagliacci*
(Canadian Opera Company, tour 1961), Jupiter
in *Orpheus in the underworld* (Canadian Opera
Company, 1961), *Spring thaw*; directed and sang
Bob in *The old maid and the thief* (Royal Conser-
vatory of Music Opera School), Uberto in *La
serva padrona* (Royal Conservatory of Music
Opera School), Ketzel in *The bartered bride*
(Royal Conservatory of Music Opera School);
directed *Madama Butterfly* (Canadian Opera
Company, 1962), *La bohème* (Canadian Opera
Company, 1963; 23 Sept. 1965), *Falstaff* (Banff
School of Fine Arts, Alta., 1963), *L'elisir d'amore*
(Banff School of Fine Arts, 1964), *Die Fleder-
maus* (Canadian Opera Company, 15 Sept. 1964),
Amahl and the night visitors (Banff School of
Fine Arts, Dec. 1964).
RADIO
Sang in many CBC productions, e.g. Dr. Bartolo
in *The marriage of Figaro* (19 Oct. 1960).
TELEVISION
Sang in many CBC productions.

MACNAIR, Dorothy Kathleen Livesay
see LIVESAY, Dorothy

MAILLARD, Nellie
see DAVID, Nellie Maillard

MAILLET, Andrée
(Andrée Maillet Hobden)
Author; b. in Montreal; daughter of Roger and
Corinne (Dupuis) Maillet; m. L. Hamlyn Hobden;
children: three.
HOME
28 Arlington, Westmount, Montreal 6, PQ.
CAREER
Journalist and European correspondent; *Petit
journal* and *Photo-journal*, Montréal, reporter;
Amérique Française, Montréal, publisher-director;
TV lecturer and panelist.
MEMBER
Anglo-American Press Association.
AWARDS, HONOURS
Quebec government first prize and Book-of-the-
year medal of Canadian Association of Children's
Librarians for *Le chêne des tempêtes*, 1965.
WRITINGS
Contes pour enfants, Variétés, 1943; *Ristontac*
(juvenile fiction), Parizeau, 1945; *Profil de
l'original* (novel), Amérique Française, 1952; *Les
Montréalais* (novel), Jour, 1963; *Le lendemain
n'est pas sans amour* (short stories), Beauchemin,
1963; *Le paradigme de l'idole* (prose poem),

Amérique Française, 1964; Élémentaires (poems), Déom, 1964; Le marquiset têtu (prose poem), Casterman, 1965; Le chêne des tempêtes (juvenile fiction), Fides, 1965; Les remparts de Québec (novel), Jour, 1965; Nouvelles Montréalaises (short stories), Beauchemin, 1966; Le chant de l'Iroquoise (poems), Jour, 1967; Le meurtre d'Igouille (play), Ecrits du Canada français, 1967 (produced Théâtre de l'Estoc, Québec, PQ, 1965); Souvenirs en accords brisés (play; produced CBC TV, Nov. 1965); La Montréalaise (play), Écrits du Canada français, 1967 (produced Théâtre de l'Estoc, 1967).

CONTRIBUTED: Articles and short stories to Le devoir, Liberté.

MAJOR, Leon* 1933—

Director; b. 3 Jan. 1933 in Toronto; son of Samuel and Sara (Sobolaff) Major; m. Judith Strand 25 Feb. 1961; children: Joshua b. 17 Dec. 1961, Rebecca b. 21 Jan. 1963, Rachel b. 19 Feb. 1966, Naomi b. 6 July 1967.

EDUCATION
University of Toronto, BA; studied at Royal Conservatory of Music, Toronto; theatre with Robert Gill, Hart House Theatre, and John Blatchley and Pierre LeFevre Crest Theatre, Toronto, and with various European companies.

RELIGION
Jewish.

HOME
56 Rathnelly Ave., Toronto 7, Ont.

OFFICE
Hart House Theatre, University of Toronto, Toronto, Ont.

CAREER
Crest Theatre, Toronto, actor 1954, director 1959-61, resident director 1961/62; Straw Hat Players, Port Carling, Muskoka, Ont., stage manager 1954; Stratford, Ont. Festival, director 1960, 1962, assistant artistic director 1961; Canadian Opera Company, Toronto, stage director 1960-68; Spring thaw, director 1962-63; Neptune Theatre, Halifax, NS, founder and artistic director 1962-68; artistic adviser 1968—; University of Toronto Centre for the Study of Drama, director of production 1968—.

MEMBER
AEA; Canadian Theatre Centre (president, 1969).

AWARDS, HONOURS
Four awards from Central Ontario Drama League and Calvert trophy from Dominion Drama Festival for production of Teach me how to cry, 1956; Canada Council research fellowship, 1958, grant, 1968.

THEATRE
Stage manager for Speaking of murder (St. Martin's, London, England, 4 June 1958); directed Noon has no shadows (Arts, London, 18 July 1958), The Ham let of Stephney Green (Toronto, 1959), The hollow (Crest, 1959), My three angels (Crest, 1959), Two for the seesaw (Crest, 1959); staged The telephone (Toronto Symphony Orchestra); directed The teacher (Stratford, Ont. Festival, 1960), I Pagliacci (Canadian Opera Company, 1961, 1966), The zoo story (Crest, 1961), The madwoman of Chaillot (Crest, 1961), Caesar and Cleopatra (Crest, 1962; Vancouver International Festival, 1962), The gondoliers (Stratford, Ont. Festival, 1962), Rigoletto (Canadian Opera Company, Oct. 1962; 20 Sept. 1965), Hansel and Gretel (Canadian Opera Company, 1962, 1963), Spring thaw (1962-63), Antigone (Neptune, 1963), The fantasticks (Neptune, 17 Dec. 1963), Carmen (Canadian Opera Company, 1964), Diary of a scoundrel (Neptune, 15 Jan. 1964), Desire under the elms (Neptune, 4 Feb. 1964), Bus stop (Neptune, 25 Feb. 1964), Louisbourg (Neptune, 17 Mar. 1964), Twelfth night (Neptune, 1964), As you like it (Neptune, 1965), Turandot (Canadian Opera Company, 17 Sept. 1965), Please don't sneeze (Museum Children's Theatre, Toronto, 10 Jan. 1966), A shot in the dark (Neptune, 6 May 1966), Henry IV, part I (Neptune, 14 June 1966), The sleeping bag (Neptune, 19 July 1966; 1967); Faust (Canadian Opera Company, 1966), The wooden world (Neptune, 1967; 1968), Barefoot in the park (Neptune, 1967), The taming of the shrew (Neptune, 1967), Louis Riel (Canadian Opera Company, O'Keefe Centre, Toronto, 23 Sept. 1967; 16 Sept. 1968), Patience (City Center Gilbert and Sullivan Company, New York, NY, 15 May 1968), The rainmaker (Neptune, 1 July 1968), Tosca (Canadian Opera Company, 21 Sept. 1968), The changling (Hart House, 21 Oct. 1968), The fan (Hart House, 28 Oct. 1968).

RADIO
Narrator in School for wives ("Midweek theatre," CBC, 2 June 1965), guest on Excerpts from Peter Grimes ("Opera time," CBC, 16 Oct. 1965), Excerpts from Macbeth ("Opera time," CBC, 17 Sept. 1966).

TELEVISION
Guest on Festival (CBC Vancouver, 2 Aug. 1962); directed The gondoliers ("Festival," CBC, 19 Nov. 1962); produced The suitcase ("Quest," CBC, 13 Jan. 1963).

MANDEL, Eli 1922—

(Elias Wolf Mandel)
Poet and teacher; b. 1922 in Estevan, Sask.

EDUCATION
University of Saskatchewan, BA, MA; University of Toronto, PhD.

OFFICE
Department of English, York University, Toronto, Ont.

CAREER
Collège Militaire Royal de Saint-Jean, PQ, teacher

of English; University of Alberta, associate professor of English 1957-63?, professor 1965-68?; York University, 1963-65, professor 1968? –.

WRITINGS
(with G. Turnbull and P. Webb) *Trio*, Contact, 1954; *Fuseli poems*, Contact, 1960; *Black and secret man*, Ryerson, 1964; *Criticism: the silent-speaking words* (radio scripts), CBC, 1966 ("Ideas," 23 Mar. -4 May 1966); *An idiot joy*, M.G. Hurtig, 1967.
EDITED: (with J.G. Pilon) *Poetry 62*, Ryerson, 1961.
CONTRIBUTED: Poetry and articles to *The book of Canadian poetry*, edited by A.J.M. Smith, 3rd ed., rev. & enl., Gage, 1957; *The Penguin book of Canadian verse*, edited by R. Gustafson, Penguin, 1958; *The Oxford book of Canadian verse in English and French*, edited by A.J.M. Smith, Oxford, 1960; *An anthology of Commonwealth verse*, edited by M.J. O'Donnell, Blackie, 1963; *Modern Canadian verse in English and French*, edited by A.J.M. Smith, Oxford 1967; *Queen's quarterly, Alphabet, Canadian forum, Canadian literature, Northern review, Contact, CIV/n, Fiddlehead, Tamarack review, Edge, Literary review*.

MANLY, Charles Macdonald   1855-1924
Artist; b. Sept. 1855 in Englefield Green, Surrey, England; son of John G. Manly; came to Canada with his parents 1866 and settled in Toronto, Ont.; d. 4 Apr. 1924 in Toronto.
EDUCATION
Studied at Heatherly School, London, England; Metropolitan School of Art, Dublin, Ireland, 1879.
CAREER
Ontario College of Art, Toronto, instructor 1890- ?; lived for a time at Conestoga, Ont.; organized composition classes of Art Students' League, Toronto; contributed illustrations to Toronto Art Students' League *Calendars*; commercial artist, teacher, and painter in Toronto.
MEMBER
Ontario Society of Artists (elected, 1876; president, 1902-05); Royal Canadian Academy (Associate 1890); Toronto Art Students' League (co-founder, 1886); Graphic Arts Club (co-founder); Art and Letters Club, Toronto.
AWARDS, HONOURS
Honourable mention, Pan-American Exposition, Buffalo, NY, 1901; Jessie Dow award, Art Association of Montreal, PQ, 1911.
EXHIBITIONS
GROUP: Represented in group exhibitions held in Canada during his lifetime including annual exhibitions of Ontario Society of Artists and Royal Canadian Academy, exhibitions of Art

Association of Montreal and Canadian National Exhibitions; Pan-American Exposition, Buffalo, 1901.
COLLECTIONS IN WHICH REPRESENTED
National Gallery of Canada, Ottawa, Ont.; Toronto Teachers College.

MARSHALL, Joyce   1913–
Novelist; b. 28 Nov. 1913 in Montreal, PQ; daughter of William Wallace and Ruth Winnifred (Chambers) Marshall.
EDUCATION
Attended Westmount High School in Montreal; St. Helen's College in Dunham, PQ; McGill University, honours BA, 1935; MA.
HOME
105 Isabella St., Toronto 285, Ont.
CAREER
Mainly literary; resided in Scandinavia 1961-63.
MEMBER
Canadian Authors Association; Authors' League of America.
AWARDS, HONOURS
Writers' Club first prize for short story "Come ye apart," 1936; Canadian Women's Press Club first prize for short story "And the hill-top was Elizabeth"; *New liberty* short story prize, 1953; Canada Council senior arts fellowship, 1960/61.
WRITINGS
Presently tomorrow, McClelland & Stewart, 1946; *Lovers and strangers*, Longmans, Green, 1957.
TRANSLATED: Gabrielle Roy's *The road past Altamont*, Harcourt, Brace & World, 1966; Mère Marie de l'Incarnation's *Word from New France*, Oxford, 1967.
CONTRIBUTED: Short stories and articles to *Canadian short stories*, edited by R. Weaver and H. James, Oxford, 1952; *Family herald, Canadian poetry magazine, Saturday night, Dalhousie review, Queen's quarterly, Tamarack review, Montrealer*.

MARSHALL, Lois   1924–
Singer (soprano); b. 1924 in Toronto, Ont.; daughter of David and Florence Marshall.
EDUCATION
Attended Wellesley School and studied with Elsie Hutchinson, Toronto; Royal Conservatory of Music, Toronto; studied with Emmy Heim, Toronto; Weldon Kilburn, Toronto, 1938–.
HOME
32 Golfhaven Dr., Scarborough, Ont.
OFFICE
c/o Columbia Artists Management Inc., 165 W. 57th St., New York, NY 10019, USA.
CAREER
Columbia Artists Management, New York, 1953–; Philadelphia, Pa., Boston, Mass., Cincinnati, Ohio,

Chicago, Ill., Washington, DC, Vancouver, BC, Symphony Orchestras, guest soloist; Harrogate Festival, England, National Eisteddfod of Wales Festival, Edinburgh Festival, Scotland, guest soloist; Bach Aria Group, New York, 1965-66; Tchaikovsky International Competition for Vocalists, Moscow, USSR, judge June 1966; toured extensively in North America, Europe, and USSR.

AWARDS, HONOURS

Toronto Public School singing contest winner, 1938; "Singing stars of tomorrow" first prize, 1950; Eaton Graduate award, 1950; Canadian representative at the Sesquicentennial in Washington, 1950; Walter W. Naumburg Musical Foundation award, New York, 1952; University of Alberta national award from Banff School of Fine Arts, 1962; LL D from University of Toronto, 1965; Companion of the Order of Canada, Jan. 1968.

CONCERT STAGE

Sang in numerous productions, e.g. *St. Matthew passion* (St. Paul's Cathedral, Toronto, annually 1947-50; with Mendelssohn Choir and Toronto Symphony Orchestra under Sir Ernest MacMillan, *c*.1953-54), *Mass in B minor* by Bach (St. Paul's Cathedral, Toronto, *c*.1950), *Magnificat* (St. Paul's Cathedral, Toronto, *c*.1950), *Manzoni requiem* (Mendelssohn Choir, Toronto, under Sir Ernest MacMillan, 15 Nov. 1950), soloist (Toronto Symphony Orchestra, 21 Nov. 1950), *Messiah* (Ottawa, 1952; Mendelssohn Choir and Toronto Symphony Orchestra under Sir Ernest MacMillan, 1953/54, 1956; National Symphony Orchestra, Washington, 1955), New York debut (Town Hall, 2 Dec. 1952), *Missa solemnis* (NBC Symphony Orchestra and Robert Shaw Chorale under Arturo Toscanini, Carnegie Hall, New York, spring 1953; San Francisco, Calif. 1955), *Symphony no. 9* by Beethoven (Minneapolis, Minn., 1955), *2 songs by Geoffrey Ridout* (Carnegie Hall, New York, under Leopold Stokowski, 16 Oct. 1953), *Festival concert* (Stratford, Ont. Festival, 1955, 1957, 31 July 1958, 6 and 13 Aug. 1961, 1962, 1964, 1965), *Don Giovanni* (National Symphony Orchestra, Washington, 1955-56), *The abduction from the seraglio* (Royal Philharmonic Orchestra under Sir Thomas Beecham, London, England, May 1956), soloist (York Concert Society, Apr. 1957), soloist (Eaton Auditorium, Toronto, 17 Jan. 1958), soloist (Cleveland Orchestra, Ohio; Edinburgh Festival, *c*.1958), Mimi in *La bohème* (Boston Opera Company, 29 Jan. 1959), *Solomon* oratorio (Stratford, Ont. Festival, 27 Aug. 1965).

RADIO

Sang in many European and North American productions, e.g. *Christmas eve concert* (CBS, Dec. 1953), *Music from the festivals* ("Wednesday night," CBC, 5 Aug. 1959), *Symphony no. 9* by Beethoven (20 Dec. 1959), *The damnation of*

Faust ("Wednesday night," CBC, 22 Nov. 1961), *Celebrity recital* (CBC, 16 May 1962), *University celebrity recital* (CBC, 23 May 1964), *Messiah* (24 Dec. 1966), *Liebeslieder Walzer* ("Tuesday night," CBC, 1968), "Thursday music" (series, CBC, 6 June 1968), *Mass in B minor* by Bach ("Tuesday night," CBC, 18 June 1968), *The Great Lakes suite* (12 Sept. 1968).

TELEVISION

Sang in several productions, e.g. BBC TV *c*.1956, *West side story* (CBC, Dec. 1967).

RECORDINGS

Made many recordings, e.g. *Solomon*, Angel 3546 B (35340-35341) 1956. *Messiah* selections, RCA Victor, LM 2088, 1957; RCA Victor, LM 6134, 1957. *Missa solemnis*, RCA Victor LM 6013. *Spanische Liebeslieder*, Columbia ML 5861, 1963. *Mass in B minor* by Bach, 2 Epic SC-6027; 3-BSC-102. *The abduction from the seraglio*, 2 Ang. 3555-B/L; S-3555-B/L.

MARSHALL, Marilyn Young
see YOUNG, Marilyn

MARTIN, Thomas Mower   1838-1934

Artist; b. 5 Oct. 1838 in London, England; son of Edward H. and Susannah Martin; m. Emma Nichols 1861; came to Canada in June 1862 and settled in Muskoka, Ont.; children: four sons and five daughters; d. 16 Mar. 1934 in Toronto, Ont.

EDUCATION

Attended Military College, Enfield, England; studied at South Kensington Galleries, London; studied water colours under Humphreys in London; mainly self-taught as an artist.

RELIGION

Swedenborgian.

CAREER

Homesteaded in Muskoka 1862; moved to Toronto 1863 and later opened a studio there; founded Ontario School of Art, Toronto, 1876, director 1877-79; painted in Lake Superior area 1881; painted in Rocky Mountains and British Columbia 1887 and subsequent years; painted in England 1906 and 1907; illustrated *Canada* by Wilfred W. Campbell, A.&C. Black, 1907; art teacher and painter in Toronto 1863-1934.

MEMBER

Ontario Art Union (co-founder, 1870); Ontario Society of Artists (co-founder and charter member, 1872); Royal Canadian Academy (charter Academician 1880); Royal British Colonial Society of Artists (elected, 1908); Toronto Etching Society; British Northern Academy of Arts (elected, 1912); Royal Society of Arts (elected, 1912).

EXHIBITIONS

ONE-MAN: Art Association of Montreal, PQ, 1935; Art Gallery of Toronto, 1936.

GROUP: Represented in group exhibitions held

in Canada during his lifetime including annual exhibitions of Ontario Society of Artists and Royal Canadian Academy; Centennial Exhibition, Philadelphia, Pa.; Colonial and Indian Exhibition, London; World's Columbian Exposition, Chicago, Ill., 1893.

COLLECTIONS IN WHICH REPRESENTED
Glenbow Foundation, Calgary, Alta.; Hunt Club, Pittsburgh, Pa.; National Gallery of Canada, Ottawa, Ont.; Windsor Castle, England.

WRITINGS
A number of pamphlets on Swedenborgian doctrine.
CONTRIBUTED: To *The week* and several Swedenborgian journals.

MARTIN-VISCOUNT, Bill* 1940—
(William Martin-Viscount)
Dancer; b. 29 Sept. 1940 in Libau, Man.

EDUCATION
Attended school in Manitoba; studied ballet with Arnold Spohr at Royal Winnipeg Ballet School, 1956-58; Harold Turner and Errol Addison at Royal Ballet School, London, England, 1958-59, 1961; Royal Academy of Dancing honours graduate certificate; Kirsten Ralov and Hans Brenaa at Royal Danish Ballet, Copenhagen, Denmark, 1963; Asaf Messerer and Alexei Yermolayev at Bolshoi Ballet, Moscow, USSR, 1966-67.

HOME
298 Maddock Ave., RR 1, Winnipeg, Man.

CAREER
Royal Opera Ballet, London, dancer 1958-59; Royal Winnipeg Ballet, corps de ballet 1959-61, principal 1962-67; London's Festival Ballet, soloist 1961-62; Radio City Music Hall, New York, NY, guest artist 1967, 1968; Bolshoi Ballet, Moscow, guest artist 1966; taught in USA, 1967—; Banff School of Fine Arts, Alta., guest artist and teacher 1967—; Dallas Civic Ballet, Tex., guest teacher and associate ballet master 1967—; City Center Joffrey Ballet, New York, principal 1968—.

MEMBER
AEA.

AWARDS, HONOURS
Royal Winnipeg Ballet School scholarship; Canada Council arts scholarship for study abroad, 1961, 1963, 1966; Koerner Foundation scholarship, 1966.

MARTIN-VISCOUNT, William
see MARTIN-VISCOUNT, Bill

MASSON, Henri Leopold* 1907—
Artist; b. 10 Jan. 1907 in Namur, Belgium; son of Armand and Bertha (Bournonville) Masson; came to Canada with his mother in 1921 and settled in Ottawa; m. Germaine Saint Denis 29

Aug. 1929; children: Armande b. 31 May 1930, Carl b. 29 July 1937, Jacques b. 15 Aug. 1939.

EDUCATION
Attended St. Jean Baptiste School, Ottawa, 1921-23; studied under George Rowles, Ottawa Art Association evening classes, 1924-28; studied at the Athenée Royale, Brussels, Belgium, 1919-21; mainly self-taught as an artist.

HOME
70 Spruce St., Ottawa, Ont.

CAREER
A.W. Whitcomb Co., apprentice metal engraver 1923-32, master engraver 1932-45; visited USA 1938; National Gallery of Canada, Ottawa, instructor in children's classes 1948-50; Queen's University summer school, instructor 1948-52; Banff School of Fine Arts, Alta., instructor 1954; Doon School of Fine Arts, Ont., instructor 1960-64; genre and landscape painter in Ottawa, painting chiefly in Hull and Gatineau Valley, PQ, 1934—.

COMMISSIONS
Illustrations for article "The Revolt of French Canada" by Philip Siekman in *Fortune magazine*, 1965.

MEMBER
Canadian Group of Painters (elected, 1942); Canadian Society of Painters in Water Colour (elected, 1942); Canadian Society of Graphic Art (elected, 1942); Ontario Society of Artists (elected, 1938); Federation of Canadian Artists (president of the Ottawa branch, 1945).

AWARDS, HONOURS
LL D from Assumption College, Windsor, Ont., 1955.

EXHIBITIONS
ONE-MAN: Picture Loan Society, Toronto, Ont., 1938 and 1940; Le Caveau, Ottawa, 1940; Contemporary Art Studios, Ottawa, 1942; Laing Fine Art Galleries, Toronto, 1942; L'Art Français, Montréal, PQ, 1942, 1943, 1944, 1946, and 1962; Little Gallery, Ottawa, 1944-49; T. Eaton Fine Art Galleries, Toronto, 1945; Montreal Museum of Fine Arts, 1953; Robertson Galleries, Ottawa, 1955; Le Foyer de l'Art, Ottawa, 1958; Westmount Public Library, Montreal, 1963; Walter Klinkhoff Gallery, Montreal, 1963; Galerie Martin, Montréal, 1966; Art Lenders, Montreal, 1967; Wallack Art Gallery, Ottawa, 1967.
GROUP: Represented in group exhibitions held in Canada including annual exhibitions of Canadian Group of Painters, Canadian Society of Painters in Water Colour, Canadian Society of Graphic Art, and Ontario Society of Artists; represented in exhibitions organized by National Gallery of Canada, Ottawa, including its first Biennial Exhibition of Canadian Painting, 1955; World's Fair, New York, NY, 1939; Aspects of

Contemporary Painting in Canada, Addison Gallery, Andover, Mass., 1942-43; International Water Colour Exhibition, Brooklyn Museum, NY, 1942 and 1944; Morse Gallery, Winter Park, Fla., 1942; Canadian Art 1760-1943, Yale University Art Gallery, 1944; Pintura Canadense Contemporanea, Rio de Janeiro, Brazil, 1944; Philadelphia Water Colour Club, Pa., 1946; UNESCO ... Exposition internationale d'art moderne, peinture, graphique et décoratif, architecture, Musée d'Art Moderne, Paris, France, 1946; Six Canadian Painters, West Palm Beach, Fla., 1947; Canadian Painting, National Gallery of Art, Washington, DC, 1950; University of Maine, 1951; São Paulo Biennial exhibition, Museo de Arte Moderna, Brazil, 1951; Florida State Fair, Tampa, 1952; Colombo International Exhibition of Modern Art, New Delhi, India, 1953; exhibition of Canadian painting shown in Pakistan, India, and Ceylon, 1954-55; An Exhibition of Canadian Paintings held at Fortnum and Mason Ltd., London, England, 1955.

COLLECTIONS IN WHICH REPRESENTED
Art Gallery of Ontario, Toronto; Bezalel Museum, Israel; Calgary Allied Arts Centre, Alta.; Caracas Museum, Venezuela; Edmonton Art Gallery, Alta.; Hamilton Art Gallery, Ont.; Hart House Permanent Collection, University of Toronto; Beaverbrook Art Gallery, Fredericton, NB; Musée du Québec, PQ.; Musée Vinadelmar, Chile; National Gallery of Canada; Seminary, Joliette, PQ; Vancouver Art Gallery, BC.; Winnipeg Art Gallery, Man.; London Public Library and Art Museum, Ont.; Sarnia Public Library and Art Museum, Ont.; Willistead Art Gallery, Windsor, Ont.; Dalhousie University; Agnes Etherington Art Centre, Queen's University.

MATHIEU, Rodolphe 1894-1962
Composer and pianist; b. 10 July 1894 in Grondines, PQ; d. 1962.

EDUCATION
Attended Schola Cantorum, Paris, France; studied composition with Vincent d'Indy and orchestration with Louis Aubert and Albert Roussel, Paris, c.1918-25; studied with Alexis Contant (q.v.) Montreal, PQ.

CAREER
L'Institut Pédagogique de Montréal, teacher of harmony, counterpoint, and fugue; Couvent des Soeurs de Ste-Anne, Lachine, PQ, teacher of harmony, counterpoint, and fugue; Canadian Institute of Music, founder and director.

AWARDS, HONOURS
Quebec government scholarship for study in Paris, c.1918.

COMPOSITIONS
Saisons, voice, piano; Quand tu pleures, voice and string quartet; Après ton appel, voice and string quartet; Symphony for voice; Lied, violin, paino, Hérelle; Debout, Canadiens, choir, piano or orchestra; 12 Monologues, violin and cello; Symphony-ballet, with choir; Sonata no. 2, cello; piano; Trois préludes, timpanon, percussion, harp, strings, 1912-15; Un peu d'ombre, timpanon, harp celesta, strings, 1913, first performed by Lamoureux Orchestra under Paul Paray, Paris, Nov. 1925; Harmonie du soir, voice, violin, orchestra, 1918, first performed by Lamoureux Orchestra under Paul Paray, Paris; Quintet, piano, strings, performed by Montreal Quartet with Charles Reiner and taped by CBC IS, 1956; Sonata no. 1, piano, performed by Guy Bourassa and taped by CBC IS, 1956; Trois préludes (Sur un nom, Vague, Une muse), piano, first performed by Josephte Dufresne, taped by CBC IS, 1956; Quartet, strings, first performed by Quartet Krettly, at la Société Pro Musica, Paris, 1961; Trio, piano, violin, cello, first performed by la Société Pro Musica, Paris, 1964.

MATTICE, Hortense Crompton
see GORDON, Hortense

MAXWELL, Victor, pseud.
see BRAITHWAITE, Max

MAZZOLENI, Ettore* 1905-68
Conductor and music educator; b. 18 June 1905 in Brusio, Switzerland; son of Frederico and Catherina (Monigatti) Mazzoleni; came to Canada in 1929 and settled in Toronto, Ont.; m. Winifred Macmillan 26 June 1932 (d. 1952); m. Edith Joanne Ivey 11 July 1953; children: (first marriage) Andrea R. b. 1 June 1940, Elena C. b. 5 Sept. 1946; (second marriage) Gina b. 27 Dec. 1959; d. 1 June 1968.

EDUCATION
Attended elementary schools in England; Keble College, University of Oxford, BA, 1924-27; studied piano and composition, Royal College of Music, London, England.

RELIGION
Anglican.

CAREER
Royal College of Music, London, opera coach and conductor 1927-29; Upper Canada College, Toronto, teacher of music and English 1929-44; Toronto (now Royal) Conservatory of Music, lecturer in music history and conductor of orchestra 1930, principal 1945-68; Toronto Symphony Orchestra, associate conductor 1943-48; Toronto Opera Festival Association, director 1951-53, general director 1954-56; Toronto Opera School, director 1952-66; Canadian Opera Company, Toronto conductor c.1957-66.

MEMBER
Arts and Letters Club of Toronto (past president); Toronto Musicians Association.

AWARDS, HONOURS

University of Rochester, NY, hon. D Mus, 1949; University of Alberta national award in music, 1954; Royal College of Music, hon. fellow, 1961.

THEATRE

Conducted Don Giovanni (Toronto Opera Festival, 1956), Die Fledermaus (Canadian Opera Company, Toronto Opera Festival, 1957, 1964), Tales of Hoffmann (Toronto Opera Festival, 1958), Barber of Seville (Toronto Opera Festival, 1959), Nights in Venice (Toronto Opera Festival, 1960), Gallantry and Riders to the sea (Toronto Opera School, 1960), The bartered bride (Canadian Opera Company, Toronto Opera Festival, 1961), The mother (Toronto Opera School, 1961), A dinner engagement (Toronto Opera School, 1962), Hansel and Gretel (Toronto Opera Festival, 1963, 1964), Deirdre (Toronto Opera School, 1965; Toronto Opera Festival, 1966), Die Kluge (Toronto Opera School, 1966).

CONCERT STAGE

Guest conductor, Hart House Orchestra, Toronto; CBC Symphony Orchestra; Halifax Symphony Orchestra, NS; Pro Arte Orchestra, Vancouver Symphony Orchestra, BC; Victoria Symphony Orchestra, BC; L'Orchestre Symphonique de Québec; Toronto Summer Symphony; York Symphony Orchestra, Pa.; Toronto Philharmonic Orchestra.

RADIO

Conducted numerous CBC programs, e.g. "Wednesday night," "Concerts from two worlds," Deirdre of the sorrows (1946), Peter Grimes (1949), Esther (1952), Tale of two cities (1954), Five Tudor portraits (1957), Night blooming Cereus (1959, 1960); conducted CBC Symphony Orchestra and CBC Halifax Chamber Orchestra on numerous programs.

COMPOSITIONS

Songs, incidental music for plays, arrangements of folk songs, and orchestral transcriptions.

WRITINGS

CONTRIBUTED: "Solo artists" in Music in Canada, edited by E. MacMillan, University of Toronto, 1955; articles to Opera Canada.

MEAGHER, Aileen Alethea* 1910–

Artist; b. 26 Nov. 1910 in Edmonton, Alta.; daughter of Arthur Thomas and Mary Frances (Mulcahy) Meagher.

EDUCATION

Attended Oxford Street School in Halifax; Convent Sacred Heart, Halifax, graduate, 1931; Dalhousie University, BA and diploma in education, 1931-33; studied art, Ontario Department of Education Arts and Crafts classes, Toronto, Ont., four summers 1948-53; studied under Hans Hofmann, Provincetown, Mass., summers 1954-57; Ruth Wainwright (q.v.), night classes in Halifax,

1951-56; Gentile Tondino (q.v.) Tatamagouche, NS, 1956-57.

RELIGION

Roman Catholic.

HOME

1461 Seymour St., Halifax, NS.

CAREER

Represented Canada in Olympic Games in Los Angeles, Calif., 1932 and Berlin, Germany, 1936; represented Canada in British Empire Games in England 1934 and Australia 1938; St. Patrick's Boys' School and St. Mary's Boys' School, Halifax, teacher 1934-67; travelled in Spain and Italy 1958; travelled in Ireland 1960, 1963, 1965, and 1967; Halifax City schools art staff, teacher 1967–.

AWARDS, HONOURS

Second in 220-yard race, second in 440 yard relay race, and first in 660-yard relay, British Empire Games, England, 1934; third in 400-metre relay, Olympic Games, Berlin, 1936; second in 440-yard relay and third in 660-yard relay, British Empire Games, Australia, 1938; Norton H. Crowe award, Amateur Athletic Union of Canada, 1935; Velma Springstead trophy, 1935; water colour prize, Nova Scotia Amateur Show, 1950; first prize, Maritime Art Exhibition, 1962; admitted to Amateur Athletic Union of Canada's Hall of Fame, 1965.

EXHIBITIONS

ONE-MAN: Zwicker's Granville Gallery, Halifax, 1958.

GROUP: Represented in group exhibitions held in Halifax and elsewhere in Atlantic provinces.

COLLECTIONS IN WHICH REPRESENTED

Owens Museum, Mount Allison University; Dalhousie University; St. Mary's University; Centennial Gallery, Halifax.

MERCURE, Pierre 1927-66

Composer; b. 21 Feb. 1927 in Montreal, PQ; son of Louis-Philippe and Eva-Marie (Dupré) Mercure; m.; children: Michèle b. 1952, Christian and Daniel b. 1954, Patrick b. 1962; d. Jan. 1966 in Avallon, France.

EDUCATION

Attended St. Antonin of Snowdon primary school and Jean de Brébeuf Classical College in Montreal, graduated 1946; studied composition with Claude Champagne, Conservatoire de Montréal, 1947; studied with Nadia Boulanger, orchestration with Arthur Hoérée, conducting with Jean Fournet, Paris, France, 1949-51; studied serial technique with Luigi Dallapiccola, Berkshire Music Center, Tanglewood, Lenox, Mass. summer 1951; studied electronic music with Richard Mayfield in New York, NY; studied synthetic sounds and electronic engineering.

RELIGION
Roman Catholic.

CAREER
Montreal Symphony Orchestra, bassoonist 1946-50; CBC, Montreal, co-ordinator of musical programs 1952-66; Semaine Internationale de Musique Actuelle, organizer 1961; Montreal Festival, music director 1961; toured France, Belgium, Germany, and Austria; lectured on actual changes in music with soloists at Ligue de la Jeunesse Féminine, Montréal; International Music Council, Paris, Canadian delegate 1964.

MEMBER
CAPAC.

AWARDS, HONOURS
Prize of $100 for *Kaleidoscope*, 1948; Quebec government scholarship for studies in Paris, 1949, at Tanglewood, Lenox, 1951; Montreal Symphony Orchestra annual award, 1964; International Competition of Contemporary Music, Cava dei Tirreni, Italy, first prize for *Triptyque*, Aug. 1965; Canada Council grant, 1965/66.

FILM
Music director of *Walls of memory* (National Film Board of Canada, 1963).

TELEVISION
Originated and produced "Heure du concert" (series, CBC) including productions of *Orphée* (1961), *La bohème* (1965), *Wozzeck, Le roi David, Oedipus Rex, Pelléas et Mélisande, Lac des cygnes*, etc.; produced programs in "Festival" (series, CBC, with celebrities, e.g. Elisabeth Schwarzkopf, Claudio Arrau (1964), Pierrette Alarie (1966).

COMPOSITIONS
Alice in Wonderland, incidental music, 1947; *Kaleidoscope*, orchestra, 1948, G. Ricordi, first performed 1948 in Montreal by CBC Orchestra under Jean-Marie Beaudet, recorded on air-check tape with CBC Orchestra under Eric Wild; *Pantomime*, ballet suite, 1948, score from Canadian Music Centre, first performed 1949 in Montreal by CBC Orchestra under Jean-Marie Beaudet, recorded by CBC IS with CBC Orchestra under Geoffrey Waddington; *Colloque*, low voice and piano, 1949, BMI Canada; *Lucretia Borgia*, trumpet, harpsichord, and percussion, 1949; *Emprise*, clarinet, bassoon, cello, and piano, 1950; *Dissidence*, three songs, soprano and piano, 1955, G. Ricordi; *Cantata pour une joie*, soprano, choir, and orchestra, 1956, G. Ricordi, first performed 1956 in Montreal at the Canadian League of Composers concert by Marguerite Lavergne, soprano, and CBC Chorus and Orchestra under Jean Beaudet, recorded by CBC IS with same performers; *Divertissement* or *Divertimento*, string quartet and string orchestra, 1957, first performed 1957 in Montreal by McGill Chamber Orchestra under Alexander Brott, recorded by CBC IS with the same performers, commissioned by Lapitsky Foundation; *Triptyque*, orchestra, 1959, G. Ricordi, first performed 1959 in Vancouver, BC, by orchestra under Walter Susskind, commissioned by Vancouver Festival, recorded by Columbia with Toronto Symphony Orchestra under Seiji Ozawa; *Incandescence*, ballet suite, synthetic sound, 1961; *Structures métalliques no. 1*, four-channel magnetic tape, 1961; *Structures métalliques no. 2*, four-channel magnetic tape, 1961; *Répercussions*, three channels of Japanese carillon sound on magnetic tape, 1961; *Improvisations*, one channel of piano sound on magnetic tape, 1961; *Psaume pour abri*, cantata, narrator, two choirs, strings, brass, percussion, and electronic sound, 1963, first performed 15 May 1963 on CBC "Wednesday night," commissioned by CBC and composed for radio performance; *Tétrachromie*, electronic sound, 1964, recorded by Columbia; *Lignes et pointes*, orchestra and electronic sound, 1964, played by Montreal Symphony Orchestra, recorded by RCA Victor; also composed music for films produced by National Film Board.

MEREDITH, John 1933–
(John Meredith Smith)
Artist; b. 1933 in Fergus, Ont.; son of William Stanley and Lillian May (Plant) Smith.

EDUCATION
Attended Ontario College of Art, Toronto.

OFFICE
c/o Isaacs Gallery, 832 Yonge St., Toronto 5, Ont.

CAREER
Painter in Toronto.

EXHIBITIONS
ONE-MAN: Gallery of Contemporary Art, Toronto, 1958 and 1959; Isaacs Gallery, Toronto, 1961, 1963, 1965, and 1967; Blue Barn Gallery, Ottawa, Ont., 1965.

GROUP: Represented in group exhibitions held in Canada; represented in group exhibitions organized by National Gallery of Canada, Ottawa, including its sixth Biennial Exhibition of Canadian Painting, 1965; Detroit Cultural Center, Mich., 1963; Albright-Knox Art Gallery, Buffalo, NY, 1963 and 1964; International Biennial, Paris, France, 1965; Canadian prints at the Edinburgh Festival, Scotland, 1968; *Art d'Aujourd'hui*, Paris, France, 1968.

COLLECTIONS IN WHICH REPRESENTED
Art Gallery of Ontario, Toronto; Agnes Etherington Art Centre, Queen's University; National Gallery of Canada; Confederation Art Gallery and Museum, Charlottetown, PEI; Vancouver Art Gallery, BC; Willistead Art Gallery, Windsor, Ont.; Montreal Museum of Fine Arts; University of Waterloo; Philadelphia Museum of Art; Norman Mackenzie Art Gallery, Regina, Sask.

MERTINS, Christa* 1936–
(Christa Mertins Spatz)
Dancer; b. 17 Mar. 1936 in Guatemala City,
Guatemala; daughter of Heinz and Maria (Hammer)
Mertins; m. Peter Spatz 5 Feb. 1960 (d. June 1963).

EDUCATION
Attended American School, Ecuador, 1953; stu-
died dance with Inge Brueckmann, Sabine Nauen-
dorff, and Kitty Sakailardis at Casa de la Cultura,
Guayaquil, Ecuador, 1950-53; Ernst Uthoff, Lola
Botka, Elena Poliakowa, and Heinz Poll at
Extensión de Musica de la Universidad de Chile,
Santiago, 1953-55; Antony Tudor and Margaret
Craske at Metropolitan Operà Ballet School, and
Merce Cunningham and Mary Hinkson in New
York, NY, 1957; Harkness Ballet, New York,
1964.

HOME
4636 rue Jeanne-Mance, Montréal 152, PQ.

OFFICE
Les Grands Ballets Canadiens, 5415 Chemin de la
Reine Marie, Montréal 248, PQ.

CAREER
Ballet Nacional de Guatemala, Guatemala City,
first soloist 1955-59, prima ballerina and teacher,
1960-63, guest artist 1965, 1966; Ballet de Cuba,
soloist for South American tour 1959; Les Grands
Ballets Canadiens, Montréal, soloist 1964/65, leading dancer 1965–; Jacob's Pillow Dance Festival,
Lee, Mass., 1965; Baltimore Ballet, Md., guest
artist 1968.

MEMBER
AEA; Union des Artistes de Montréal.

AWARDS, HONOURS
US State Department exchange student scholarship
to Metropolitan Opera Ballet School, New York,
1957; Gold medal of merit Bellas Artes Republic
Guatamala, 1963; Harkness Foundation scholarship, summer 1964.

THEATRE
First danced Black Swan pas de deux from *Le lac
des cygnes* (Petipa-Ivanov, 1960-63), *The sleeping
beauty* pas de deux (Petipa, 1960-63), Taglione in
Pas de quatre (Lester, 1960-63), Young girl in *Le
spectre de la rose* (Fokine, 1960-63), Odette-
Odile in *Le lac des cygnes* (Petipa-Ivanov, 1960-63);
created role in *La espagnola* (Paige, 1964), *Swan of
Tuonela* (Dolin, Jacob's Pillow Dance Festival,
1965); first danced Nocturne and Valse in *Les
sylphides* (Fokine, 1964-66), *Pas de quatre* (Dolin,
1964-66), Sugar Plum Fairy in *Casse-noisette*
(Nault, 1964-66), *Dark vision* (Paige, 1964-66),
title role in *L'oiseau de feu* (Nault, 1964-66), title
role in *Giselle* (Dolin after Coralli, 1964-66),
Allegro brillante (Balanchine, 1964-66).

MESS, Suzanne
Costume designer; daughter of James Mess.

EDUCATION
Studied at Helene Pons Studio, New York, NY;
Royal College of Art, Toronto.

HOME
1 Warren Rd., Toronto 7, Ont.

OFFICE
Canadian Opera Company, 129 Adelaide St. W.,
Suite 517, Toronto 1A, Ont.

CAREER
CBC, costume designer 1955–; Vancouver Opera
Association, BC, costume designer; Edmonton Opera
Association, Alta., costume designer; Central City,
Colo., resident costume designer; Canadian Opera
Company, Toronto, costume designer.

MEMBER
Canadian Theatre Centre.

THEATRE
Designed costumes for numerous productions, e.g.
Die Fledermaus (Metropolitan Opera Company,
New York), *Les sylphides* (National Ballet of
Canada, 1951/52), *Salomé* (Canadian Opera Com-
pany, 1952; 25 Sept. 1965; Sept. 1968), *Ballet
behind us* (National Ballet of Canada, 1952/53),
Carousel (Opera Festival, Toronto, Oct. 1957),
Mavra (Canadian Opera Company, 25 Sept. 1965),
La traviata (Théâtre Lyrique de Nouvelle France,
Québec, PQ, 23 Oct. 1965; Canadian Opera Com-
pany, 20 Sept. 1966), *Rigoletto* (Canadian Opera
Company, 20 Sept. 1965; Vancouver Opera Assoc-
iation, 21 Oct. 1967), *The barber of Seville*
(Canadian Opera Company, 18 Sept. 1965; Vancouver Opera Association, 14 Nov. 1967), *Madama
Butterfly* (Vancouver Opera Association, 28 Oct.
1965; Canadian Opera Company, Toronto, 1967),
Il trovatore (Vancouver Opera Association, 17 Feb.
1966), *The crucible* (Neptune Theatre, Halifax, NS,
4 May 1966), *Henry IV* (Neptune Theatre, summer
1966), *Hansel and Gretel* (Vancouver Opera Assoc-
iation, 29 June 1966), *Faust* by Gounod (Canadian
Opera Company, 15 Sept. 1966; Montreal Symphony Orchestra, Expo 67), *I Pagliacci* and *Cavalleria rusticana* (Vancouver Opera Association, 13
Oct. 1966), *Lucia di Lammermoor* (Vancouver
Opera Association, 11 Mar. 1967), *Otello* (Montreal
Symphony Orchestra, Expo 67, Montreal, PQ, July
1967), *The tales of Hoffmann* (Canadian Opera
Company, 18 Oct. 1967), *The flying dutchman*
(Vancouver Opera Association, 3 Feb. 1968;
Théâtre Lyrique du Québec, 13 Feb. 1968), *The
dandy lion* (Young People's Theatre, Toronto, Mar.
1968), *Tosca* (Vancouver Opera Association, 1 May
1968; Canadian Opera Company, 21 Sept. 1968).

RADIO
Designed costumes for many CBC productions, e.g.
"Showtime" (series, 1955-57).

TELEVISION
Designed costumes for numerous CBC operas, e.g.
Salomé (1952), *Otello, Rigoletto, The magic flute.*

MILLAIRE, Albert* 1935—
Actor and director; b. 18 Jan. 1935 in Montreal; son of Albert and Laura (Rollet) Millaire; m. Rita Imbeault 2 May 1959; children: Anne b. 20 Mar. 1960, Catherine b. 14 Aug. 1961.

EDUCATION
Attended École de Lévis, PQ, 1941-48; Collège de l'Assomption, 1948-55; Conservatory of Music and Dramatic Art, Montreal, 1955-57.

HOME
4065 Marcil Ave., Montreal 260, PQ.

OFFICE
Place des Arts, Montréal, PQ.

CAREER
CBC, Montreal, actor 1956—; Le Théâtre Club, Montréal, actor 1959-62; Théâtre du Nouveau Monde, Montréal, actor 1960—, associate artistic director 1966—; Les Jeunesses Musicales, Mt. Orford, PQ, lecturer in history of theatre; travelled extensively in Europe, 1963/64 and in USA and Canada.

MEMBER
Union des Artistes de Montréal; Canadian Theatre Centre.

AWARDS, HONOURS
Two intercollegiate trophies for oratory, 1955; second prizes in classic comedy and in modern drama, first prize in classic tragedy from Conservatory of Music and Dramatic Art, Montreal, 1957; trophy for best actor from Le congrès du spectacle de Montréal, 1963; Canada Council scholarship, 1964; Le ministère de la jeunesse de la province de Québec scholarship, 1964.

THEATRE
Played in many productions, e.g. Vladimir in *Waiting for Godot* (Théâtre de Dix Heures, Montréal, 1957), *Ouragan sur le caine* (Gamma-Phi-Théâtre, Montréal, 1958), Mr. F. in *Le mal court* (Théâtre Club, 1959), title role in *Cinna* (Théâtre Club, 1959), *Oreste* (Nouveau Monde, 1960), *L'heure éblouissante* (Théâtre Club, 1961), Bassanio in *Le marchand de Venise* (Théâtre Club, 1962), title role in *Système Fabrizzi* (Nouveau Monde, 1964), Preacher in *Klondyke* (Nouveau Monde, 1964), Lorenz in *Lorenzaccio* (Nouveau Monde, 1965), Eilif in *Mère Courage* (Nouveau Monde, 20 Oct. 1965), *Il est une saison* (Théâtre de Marjolaine, Eastman, PQ, 1965), Gildore in *La dalle des morts* (Nouveau Monde, 20 Mar. 1966), *Bois-brûlés* (Nouveau Monde, 3 Nov. 1967), *Soulier de satin* (Nouveau Monde, 7 Jan. 1967), *Homme pour homme* (Nouveau Monde, 31 May 1968), *Le Tartuffe* (Nouveau Monde, 8 Nov. 1968), *La nuit des rois* (Nouveau Monde, 13 Dec. 1968); directed *Tueur sans gage* (Centre Theatre, Montreal, 1961), *Les sorcières de Salem* (Nouveau Monde, 9 Jan. 1966), *Le rhinoceros* (Nouveau Monde, 22 Mar. 1968); directed and played in *Les grands soleils* (Nouveau Monde, 25

Apr. 1968); directed *Bilan* (Nouveau Monde, 4 Oct. 1968).

FILM
Played in several National Film Board of Canada productions and in many others of private companies.

RADIO
Played in many CBC productions and on CKAC, Montreal and CKVL, Verdun, PQ.

TELEVISION
Played in many CBC productions, e.g. Pierre Lemoyne in "D'Iberville" (series, CBC, 7 Aug. 1967).

MILLER, Albert
see MILLS, Alan

MILLER, Monique*
Actress; b. 9 Dec.; daughter of Arthur and Noëlla (Villeneuve) Miller; m. (marriage dissolved); children: Patrice Gascon b. 10 Sept. 1955.

EDUCATION
Attended St. Gabriel L'Allemand and École Supérieure Ste. Croix, Montreal; studied diction and phonetics with Mme. I.L. Audet; drama with Jean Gascon and Jean-Louis Roux (q.v.), École du Théâtre du Nouveau Monde, Montreal.

HOME
715 Stuart Ave., Montreal 154, PQ.

CAREER
Théâtre du Gesù, Montréal, actress 1952-54; Théâtre du Nouveau Monde, Montréal, actress 1952—; Théâtre du Rideau Vert, Montréal, actress 1964—; La Nouvelle Compagnie Théâtrale, Montréal, actress 1964—.

MEMBER
Union des Artistes de Montréal.

AWARDS, HONOURS
Dominion Drama Festival, Montreal, best actress award for *Zone*, 1953; best TV actress for *Tit-coq*, *Yerma*, *Grouchenka*, *Comme tu me veux*; radio awards.

THEATRE
Played in many productions, e.g. *De l'autre côté du mur* (Gesù, 1952), Marianne in *L'avare* (Nouveau Monde, 1952), Ciboulette in *Zone* (Gesù, 1953), Isabelle in *La cuisine des anges* (Nouveau Monde, 1953), Francine in *Chambre à louer* (La Jeune Scène, Montréal, 1954), *Three farces* (Nouveau Monde, 1954), *Une nuit d'amour* (Nouveau Monde, 1954), Constance in *Les trois mousquetaires* (Le Théâtre Club, Montréal, 1957); title role in *Florence* (La Comédie Canadienne, Montréal, 1960), Sichel in *Le pain dur* (Nouveau Monde, 1963), Camille in *On ne badine pas avec l'amour* (Rideau Vert, 1964), Silvia in *Le jeu de l'amour et du hasard* (La Nouvelle Compagnie Théâtrale, Montréal, 1964), Catherine in *Une maison un jour* (Rideau Vert, 1965; Paris, France, Moscow and Leningrad, USSR, 1965), Chimène in *Le Cid* (La Nouvelle Compagnie Théâtrale, 1965),

Elvire in *Don Juan* (La Nouvelle Compagnie Théâtrale, 1966), Prouhèze in *Le soulier de satin* (Nouveau Monde, 1967), title role in *La putain respectueuse* (Rideau Vert, 1967), Illona in *Anatole* (Nouveau Monde, 1967?), Eliza in *Pygmalion* (Nouveau Monde, 1968), Daisy in *Rhinoceros* (Nouveau Monde, 1968), Suzie in *Bilan* (Nouveau Monde, 1968), Pintari in *La collection* et *L'amant* (Rideau Vert, 1968), Viola in *La nuit des rois* (Nouveau Monde, 1968/69).

FILM
Played in several productions, e.g. Marie-Ange in *Tit-coq* (1952).

RADIO
Played in many productions, e.g. *Anna Christie, Delicate balance, Vêtir ceux qui sont nus, Les mouches, Inès de Castro, Se trouver, Tout pour le mieux, La greffe, L'orage, Les exilés.*

TELEVISION
Played in many serials and title role in *Florence* (1957), title role in *Yerma*, title role in *La savetière prodigieuse* (1957), Grouchenka in *The brothers Karamazov* (1960), Colette in *Bousille et les justes* ("Festival," CBC, 26 Feb. 1962), Fiancée in *Noces de sang* (1960/61), *Comme tu me veux* (1962), Belle in *L'amour des 4 colonels* (1962), Masha in *Three sisters* (1963), *L'indiscret* (1963), Tatiana in *La pensée* (1963), Mrs. Cheveley in *Un mari idéal* (1965), Mme. de Lery in *Un caprice* (1966), *La collection* and *L'amant* (1966-69).

MILLIGAN, James 1928-61
Singer (baritone); b. 1928 in Halifax, NS; son of Francis Millidge and Josephine (MacDonald) Milligan; m. Edith Scott June 1951; children: Scott b. 1 Apr. 1958; d. 28 Nov. 1961 in Basel, Switzerland.

EDUCATION
Royal Conservatory of Music, Toronto, Ont. 1948-55; studied with Emmy Heim (*q.v.*), Toronto; Ernesto Barbini, New York, NY, USA.

CAREER
Royal Conservatory of Music Opera School, Toronto, soloist; Canadian Opera Festival (now Canadian Opera Company), Toronto, soloist; Glyndebourne Opera Company, England, soloist 1956; Covent Garden Opera Company, London, England, soloist 1956/57; Basel City Theatre, staff member and principal; toured Switzerland and southern France with l'Orchestre de la Suisse Romande; travelled extensively in Europe and USA.

AWARDS, HONOURS
Grand award from "Singing stars of tomorrow," 1954; first award from International Music Festival Geneva, Switzerland, 23 Sept. 1955; Canada Council senior arts fellowship, 1960/61.

THEATRE
Sang in many productions, e.g. *Manon, Rigoletto, La forza del destino, School for fathers, La bohème, La traviata, Hiawatha, The kingdom, The apostles, Belshazzar's feast, Dream of Gerontius, Five Tudor portraits, A sea symphony, Sea drift, Dona nobis pacem, Missa solemnis, Requiem* by Verdi, New York debut (Carnegie Hall, 1954), *Messiah* (Toronto Mendelssohn Choir, 27 Dec. 1955), *Pop concert* (Toronto Symphony Orchestra, 20 Jan. 1956), Escamillo in *Carmen* (Covent Garden, c. 1956), soloist (Toronto Symphony Orchestra, Nov. 1960), Wanderer in *Siegfried* (Bayreuth Festival, Aug. 1961).

RADIO
Sang in many European and North American productions, e.g. solo recitals (BBC), *Messiah* (CBC), 24 Dec. 1966).

RECORDINGS
Messiah, RCA Victor LM 6134, 1957; RCA Victor LM 2088, 1957; Angel Records album 3598 C (Ang 35807-35809) 1959. *The gondoliers*, 2 Angel 3570; S-3570. *H.M.S. Pinafore*, 2 Angel 3589; S-3589. *Pirates of Penzance*, 2 Angel 3609; S-3609. *Idomeneo*, 3 Angel 3574.

MILLS, Alan 1914-
(Albert Miller)
Folk singer and actor; b. 1914 in Montreal; m.

HOME
4948 Grosvenor Ave., Montreal 29, PQ.

CAREER
Montreal evening journal, reporter 1929; *Montreal herald*, newspaper work, 1930-35, 1937-47; Goss London Singers, bass 1935-37; CBC, actor and singer 1947-; toured N. America many times, Europe twice.

MEMBER
Union des Artistes de Montréal; CAPAC.

AWARDS, HONOURS
Canadian Radio Awards, first prize, 1951; Canada Council travel grant, 1960.

CONCERT STAGE
Numerous appearances in Canada and USA, e.g. Newport Folk Festival, RI, 1960; University Hall, Acadia University, 1962.

FILM
Sang in *The voyageurs* (National Film Board of Canada, 1967), *I know an old lady who swallowed a fly* (National Film Board, 1967).

RADIO
Sang and played in numerous CBC productions, e.g. "Folk songs for young folks" (1947-53), "Songs de chez nous," "The happy time" (series, 1952), *Men of the mountain* ("Wednesday night," 23 Mar. 1966).

TELEVISION
Over 2000 appearances on Canadian and American

networks as folk singer; played in *Laura Limited* (serial, CBC); *A matter of principle* ("Explorations," 10 May 1961), *Songs of praise* ("Heritage," 23 Dec. 1962).

RECORDINGS
Over 24 records, RCA Victor and Folkways.

COMPOSITIONS
Numerous folk song and ballad arrangements; *I know an old lady*, folk song, 1951, Southern Music.

WRITINGS
Alan Mills book of folk songs and ballads, Canadian Music Sales, 1949 (also published under title *Folk songs for young folk*, 1957); *Favourite songs of Newfoundland,* BMI Canada, 1958; (with E. Fowke) *Canada's story in song*, W.J. Gage, 1960; *Chantons un peu*, BMI Canada, 1961; *Favourite French folk songs*, Oak, 1963; *The hungry goat*, Rand, McNally, 1964.

MITCHELL, Janet   1915–
Artist; b. 24 Nov. 1915 in Medicine Hat, Alta.

EDUCATION
Attended Crescent Heights High School, Calgary, Alta.; Banff School of Fine Arts, Alta., 1942; studied at Alberta Institute of Technology and Art, Calgary, night classes; studied under Gordon Smith at Jasper, Alta., 1959; University of Saskatchewan Emma Lake Workshop, 1961; Heatherly Art School and Camden Art Centre, Hampstead Artists Council, London, England.

HOME
RR 3, Salmon Arm, BC.

CAREER
Employed as a clerk in the Income Tax Office in Calgary for some years; travelled in Europe 1967-68; painter in Calgary and later in Salmon Arm.

COMMISSIONS
Painting for Rose Festival at Expo 67, Montreal, Reader's Digest of Canada, 1966.

MEMBER
Alberta Society of Artists; Canadian Society of Painters in Water Colour.

AWARDS, HONOURS
Banff School of Fine Arts scholarship, 1942; award winner for water colour, Winnipeg Biennial, Winnipeg Art Gallery, Man., 1960; honourable mention, All Alberta Show, 1963; planned sales award and medal, Canadian Society of Painters in Water Colour, 1964.

EXHIBITIONS
ONE-MAN: Breithaupt Galleries, Toronto, Ont., 1949; Robertson Galleries, Ottawa, Ont., 1956 and 1959; Calgary, 1959; Calgary Allied Arts Centre, 1963; Western Canada Art Circuit, 1964; Canadian Art Galleries, Calgary, 1964; Fleet Galleries, Winnipeg, 1965; Jacox Galleries, Edmonton, Alta., 1965; Sobot Galleries, Toronto, 1965; Bonli Gallery, Toronto, 1967.

GROUP: Represented in group exhibitions held in Canada including exhibitions of Alberta Society of Artists and Canadian Society of Painters in Water Colour; first Biennial Exhibition of Canadian Painting, National Gallery of Canada, Ottawa, 1955.

COLLECTIONS IN WHICH REPRESENTED
National Gallery of Canada; Calgary Allied Arts Centre; University of Alberta; University of Calgary; London Public Library and Art Museum, Ont.; Sarnia Public Library and Art Gallery, Ont.; Willistead Art Gallery, Windsor, Ont.

MOISEIWITSCH, Tanya*   1914–
(Tanya Moiseiwitsch Krish)
Designer; b. 3 Dec. 1914 in London, England; daughter of Benno and Daisy (Kennedy) Moiseiwitsch; m. Felix Krish Dec. 1942 (d. 1942).

EDUCATION
Attended Central School of Arts and Crafts, London; studied scenic painting at Old Vic Theatre, London.

HOME
c/o Westminster Bank Ltd., 185 Sloane St., London, SW1, England.

OFFICE
c/o Tyrone Guthrie Theatre, 725 Vineland Place, Minneapolis, Minn. 55403, USA.

CAREER
Abbey Theatre, Dublin, Ireland, designer 1935-39; "Q" Theatre, Kew, London, designer 1940; Oxford Playhouse, England, designer 1941-44; Old Vic Theatre, Liverpool, England, designer 1944/45; Old Vic Theatre, Bristol, England, designer 1945/46; Old Vic Theatre, London, designer 1945/46; Shakespeare Memorial (now Royal Shakespeare) Theatre Company, Stratford-upon-Avon, England, designer 1949–, Australian tour 1952; Stratford, Ont. Festival, designer 1953-58, 1960-63, 1967, designed stage 1953, 1957; Minnesota Theatre Company, Tyrone Guthrie Theatre, Minneapolis, principal designer 1963–, re-designed stage with Brian Jackson 1963.

AWARDS, HONOURS
D Litt from University of Birmingham, England, 1964.

THEATRE
Designed many productions for Abbey Theatre, e.g. *Deuce o' Jacks* (Sept. 1935); designed *The golden cuckoo* (Duchess, London, 2 Jan. 1940), *Dr. Faustus* (Old Vic, Liverpool, 1944/45), *John Gabriel Borkman* (Old Vic, Liverpool, 1944/45), *School for scandal* (Old Vic, Liverpool, 1944/45), *Point Valaine* (Old Vic, Liverpool, 1944/45), *The beaux-stratagem* (Old Vic, Bristol, 1945/46), *Twelfth night* (Old Vic, Bristol, 1945/46; Stratford, Ont. Festival, 1957), *Uncle Vanya* (Old Vic, New, London, 16 Jan. 1945), *The critic* (Old Vic, New, Oct. 1945), *Cyrano de Bergerac* (Old Vic, New, 1945/46; co-designer at Stratford, Ont.

Festival, 1962); designed *The time of your life* (Lyric, Hammersmith, London, 14 Feb. 1946), *Peter Grimes* (Royal Opera House, Covent Garden, London, 1947; New York, NY, Jan. 1967), *Bless the bride* (Adelphi, London, 26 Apr. 1947), *The beggar's opera* (Sadler's Wells, London, 6 Sept. 1948), *The cherry orchard* (Old Vic Theatre Company, New, 25 Nov. 1948; Piccolo Teatro, Milan, Italy, 1955; Minnesota Theatre Company, 15 June 1965), *A month in the country* (Old Vic Theatre Company, New, 30 Nov. 1949), *Henry VIII* (Shakespeare Memorial Theatre, 1949; Old Vic, 6 May 1953), *Treasure hunt* (Apollo, London, 14 Sept. 1949), *Home at seven* (Wyndham's, London, 7 Mar. 1950), *The holly and the ivy* (Lyric, Hammersmith, 28 Mar. 1950; Duchess, London, 10 May 1950), *Captain Carvallo* (St. James's, London, 9 Aug. 1950); co-designed *Richard II* (Shakespeare Memorial Theatre, 1951); designed *The passing day* (Lyric, Hammersmith, 20 Mar. 1951; Ambassadors, London, 3 July 1951); co-designed *Henry IV,* parts I and II (Shakespeare Memorial Theatre, 3 Apr., 8 May 1951; co-designed part I, Stratford, Ont. Festival, 1958), *Henry V* (Shakespeare Memorial Theatre, 31 July 1951; Stratford, Ont. Festival, 1956); designed *Figure of fun* (Aldwych, London, 16 Oct. 1951), *A midsummer night's dream* (Old Vic, 26 Dec. 1951), *The deep blue sea* (Duchess, London, 6 Mar. 1952), *Timon of Athens* (Old Vic, 28 May 1952), *Othello* (Shakespeare Memorial Theatre, Australian and New Zealand tour, 1952); sets for *Julius Caesar* (Old Vic, London, 24 Feb. 1953; Stratford, Ont. Festival, 1955); co-designed *The glorious days* (Palace, London, 28 Feb. 1953); designed *Richard III* (Stratford, Ont. Festival, 1953), *All's well that ends well* (Stratford, Ont. Festival, 1953; Shakespeare Memorial Theatre, 21 Apr. 1959), *The taming of the shrew* (Stratford, Ont. Festival, 1954, 1962), *Oedipus rex* (Stratford, Ont. Festival, 1954), *The matchmaker* (Edinburgh Festival, Scotland, Aug. 1954; Haymarket, London, 4 Nov. 1954; Royale, New York, 5 Dec. 1955), *The merchant of Venice* (Stratford, Ont. Festival, 1955; Habimah Theatre, Tel-Aviv, Israel, 1958/59), *A life in the sun* (Edinburgh Festival, 1955), *Merry wives of Windsor* (Stratford, Ont. Festival, 1956), *Two gentlemen of Verona* (Old Vic, London, 22 Jan. 1957; Stratford, Ont. Festival Company, Phoenix, New York, 18 Mar. 1958), *The broken jug* (Stratford, Ont. Festival Company, Phoenix, 1 Apr. 1958), *The winter's tale* (Stratford, Ont. Festival, 1958); settings for *Much ado about nothing* (Shakespeare Memorial Theatre, 26 Aug. 1958), *The bright one* (Winter Garden, London, 10 Dec. 1958), *Don Giovanni* (Sadler's Wells, London, 1959), *The wrong side of the park* (Cambridge, London, 3 Feb. 1960), *Romeo and Juliet* (Stratford, Ont. Festival, 1960), *King John* (Stratford, Ont. Festival, 1960), *Ondine* (Aldwych, London, 12 June 1961), *Coriolanus* (Stratford, Ont. Festival,

1961), *Love's labour's lost* (Startford, Ont. Festival, 1961); *The alchemist* (Old Vic, London, 28 Oct. 1962), *Hamlet* (Minnesota Theater Company, 7 May 1963), *The miser* (Minnesota Theater Company, 8 May 1963), *The three sisters* (Minnesota Theater Company, 18 June 1963), *Volpone* (Minnesota Theater Company, 1964; National Theatre, London, 1968), *Saint Joan* (Minnesota Theater Company, 1964), *The way of the world* (Minnesota Theater Company, 11 May 1965), *As you like it* (Minnesota Theater Company, 1966); co-designed *The skin of our teeth* (Minnesota Theater Company, 1966), *Antony and Cleopatra* (Stratford, Ont. Festival, 1967), *The house of Atreus* (Minnesota Theater Company, 1967).

MOLINARI, Guido*   1933–
Artist; b. 12 Oct. 1933 in Montreal; son of Joseph Charles and Marie Mathilda Evelyn (Dini) Molinari; m. Fernande Saint-Martin 19 July 1958; children: Guy b. 19 Jan. 1960, Claire b. 4 Apr. 1962.
EDUCATION
Attended Sisters of Providence kindergarten in Montreal 1939-41; Our Lady of Mt. Carmel elementary school, 1942-47; St. Stanislas high school 1948-49 in Montreal; privately tutored 1950; attended evening classes, École des Beaux-Arts, Montréal, 1948-50; studied under Marion Scott and Gordon Webber (*q.v.*), School of Art and Design, Montreal Museum of Fine Arts, Mar.-Apr. and Oct.-Nov. 1951.
RELIGION
Roman Catholic (non-practising).
HOME
1611 rue de la Visitation, Montréal, PQ.
CAREER
Galerie l'Actuelle, Montréal, founder, director 1955-57; School of Art and Design, Montreal Museum of Fine Arts, professor of design 1963-65; painter in Montreal.
MEMBER
Association des Artistes non-figuratifs (co-founder); Association des Arts plastiques; Royal Canadian Academy (Associate 1964); Société d'Éducation par l'Art; Association des Artistes Professionels du Québec (vice-president).
COMMISSIONS
Mural, Vancouver International Airport, BC, 1968.
AWARDS, HONOURS
Prize, *Salon de la Jeune Peinture*, 1959; fourth prize for painting, Concours artistique de la province de Québec, 1961; Jessie Dow prize, Spring Exhibition, Montreal Museum of Fine Arts, 1962; purchase award, Spring Exhibition, Montreal Museum of Fine Arts, 1962; purchase award, First Biennial, Winnipeg Art Gallery, Man., 1962; purchase award, fourth International Award Exhibition, Solomon R. Guggenheim Museum, New York, NY, 1964; purchase award, exhibition at the Rose Art Museum, Brandeis University, 1964; Zacks purchase prize, Royal Canadian

Academy, 1964; grand award (shared with Jack Bush), Spring Exhibition, Montreal Museum of Fine Arts, 1965; purchase award, Concours artistique de la province de Québec, 1966; third prize, Winnipeg Show, Winnipeg Art Gallery, 1966; John Simon Guggenheim Memorial Foundation fellowship, 1967; Canada Council grant, 1968.

EXHIBITIONS

ONE-MAN: Galerie de l'Échourie, Montréal, 1954; Galerie l'Actuelle, Montréal, 1956 and 1957; Parma Gallery, New York, 1956; Galerie Artek, Montréal, 1958; Montreal Museum of Fine Arts, 1961; Galerie Nova et Vetera, Collège St. Laurent, PQ, 1962 and 1967; Penthouse Gallery, Montreal, 1962 and 1963; Jerrold Morris International Art Gallery, Toronto, 1963; East Hampton Gallery, New York, 1963, 1964, 1965, 1966, and 1967; Galerie Libre, Montréal, 1963; Norman Mackenzie Art Gallery, Regina, Sask., 1964; Vancouver Art Gallery, 1964; Galerie du Siècle, Montréal, 1964, 1965, and 1966; Edmonton Art Gallery, Alta., 1966; 20-20 Gallery, London, Ont., 1967.

GROUP: Represented in group exhibitions held in Canada since 1953 including Spring Exhibitions of Montreal Museum of Fine Arts and exhibitions of Association des Artistes non-figuratifs; represented in group exhibitions organized by National Gallery of Canada, Ottawa, Ont., including its third, fourth, fifth, and sixth Biennial Exhibitions of Canadian Painting, 1959, 1961, 1963, and 1965; Parma Gallery, 1956; *Aspects de la peinture canadienne*, Canada House, New York, 1959; Paris Biennial, Paris, France, 1962; *Festival des Deux Mondes*, Spoleto, Italy, 1962; Geometric Abstractions in Canada, Camino Gallery and Bleeker Gallery, New York, 1962; Twelve Canadian Painters, toured Africa, 1962; Canadian Painting, Speed Museum, Louisville, Ky., 1962; Contemporary Canadian Painters and Sculptors, Rochester Memorial Art Gallery, NY, 1963; Rental Collection exhibition, Staten Island Museum, NY, 1963; IV International Awards exhibition, Guggenheim Museum, New York, Berlin, Germany, Buenos Aires, Argentina, and elsewhere, 1964; The Responsive Eye, Museum of Modern Art, New York, St. Louis, Mo., Seattle, Wash., Baltimore, Md., and Pasadena, Calif., 1965; Retinal Painting, University of Texas, Austin and Houston, Tex., 1965; Optical Painting, Ohio State University and Southern Illinois University, 1965; OP from Montreal, University of Vermont, 1965; Optical Art, Fordham University, 1965; Purity and Vision, Southampton College, NY, 1965; Color Dynamism: Now and Then, East Hampton Gallery, New York, 1965; Color Motion, Brookhaven National Laboratories, Upton, NY, 1965; The Deceived Eye, Fort Worth Art Center, Tex., 1965; Perceptions in OP ART, University of Southern Florida, 1965-66; Op Art and its Antecedents, American Federation of Arts travelling Show, 1966; Optical travelling show, Museum of Modern Art, New York, 1966-67; Recent Acquisitions Show, Museum of Modern Art, New York, 1966; September Exhibition, Southampton College, NY, 1966; International Art Festival, New York, 1966; Seven Decades, Guggenheim Museum, 1967; Canadian Art Today, Union Carbide Building, New York, 1967; Canadian Prints Exhibition, Museum of Modern Art, New York, 1967; 19 Canadian Painters, Musée d'Art Moderne, Paris, 1968; Seven Montreal Painters, Massachusetts Institute of Technology, Cambridge, Mass., and Museum of Modern Art, Washington, DC, 1968; *Biennale*, Venice, Italy, 1968; Peter Stuyvesant Collection Exhibition, 1968.

COLLECTIONS IN WHICH REPRESENTED

Kunstmuseum, Basel, Switzerland; Solomon R. Guggenheim Museum; Museum of Modern Art, New York; Walter P. Chrysler Museum, Provincetown, Mass.; Rose Art Museum, Brandeis University, Boston, Mass.; Vancouver Art Gallery; Norman Mackenzie Art Gallery, Regina; Winnipeg Art Gallery; Art Gallery of Ontario, Toronto; National Gallery of Canada; Montreal Museum of Fine Arts; Sir George Williams University; Canadian Industries Ltd. Collection, Montreal; Hart House, University of Toronto; Department of External Affairs, Ottawa; Musée d'Art Contemporain, Montréal; Musée du Québec, PQ; Edmonton Art Gallery; Chase Manhattan Bank Collection, New York; Carleton University; York University; Toronto-Dominion Bank, Toronto; Peter Stuyvesant Foundation Collection, Amsterdam, Holland.

MONTGOMERY, Lucy Maud 1874-1942
(Lucy Maud Montgomery Macdonald)
Novelist; b. 30 Nov. 1874 in Clifton, PEI; daughter of Hugh John and Clara Woolner (Macneill) Montgomery; m. Ewan Macdonald 5 July 1911; children: Chester Cameron b. 7 July 1912, Hugh b. 13 Aug. 1914 (d. 14 Aug. 1914), Stuart b. 7 Oct. 1915; d. 24 Apr. in Toronto, Ont.

EDUCATION

Attended school in Cavendish, PEI and Prince Albert, Sask.; Prince of Wales College, Charlottetown, PEI, teacher's licence, 1893/94; Dalhousie College (now University), 1895/96.

CAREER

Mainly literary; school teacher in Bideford, PEI 1894/95, 1896-98; *Daily echo*, Halifax, NS, reporter 1901-02; freelance author.

MEMBER

Artists' Institute of France; Canadian Women's Press Club; Canadian Authors Association; Royal Society of Arts (elected fellow, 1935).

AWARDS, HONOURS
OBE, 1935.
WRITINGS
Anne of Green Gables, Page, 1908; *Anne of Avonlea*, Page, 1909; *Kilmeny of the orchard*, Page, 1910; *The story girl* (short stories), Page, 1911; *Chronicles of Avonlea* (short stories), Page, 1912; *The golden road*, Page, 1913; *Anne of the Island*, Page, 1915; *The watchman and other poems*, McClelland & Stewart, 1916; *Anne's house of dreams*, Stokes, 1917; *Rainbow valley*, McClelland & Stewart, 1919; *Further chronicles of Avonlea* (short stories), Page, 1920; *Rilla of Ingleside*, McClelland & Stewart, 1921; *Emily of New Moon*, Stokes, 1923; *Emily climbs*, Stokes, 1925; *The blue castle*, McClelland & Stewart, 1926; *Emily's quest*, Stokes, 1927; *Magic for Marigold*, McClelland & Stewart, 1929; *A tangled web*, Stokes, 1931 (published in England under title *Aunt Becky began it*, Hodder & Stoughton, 1931); *Pat of Silver Bush*, Stokes, 1933; (with A.M. Keith and M.B. McKinley) *Courageous women* (non-fiction), McClelland & Stewart, 1934; *Mistress Pat*, Stokes, 1935; *Anne of Windy Poplars*, Stokes, 1936; *Jane of Lantern Hill*, McClelland & Stewart, 1937; *Anne of Ingleside*, Stokes, 1939. Works have been extensively translated.
CONTRIBUTED: Short stories and poetry to *Canadian poets*, edited by J.W. Garvin, rev. ed., McClelland & Stewart, 1926; *Youth's companion, Saturday night, Family herald and weekly star, Sunday school times, Everywoman's world, Ladies home journal, Current literature.*

MOORE, Brian 1921–
Novelist; b. 25 Aug. 1921 in Belfast, Northern Ireland; son of James Bernard and Eileen (McFadden) Moore; came to Canada in 1948 and became Canadian citizen; m. Jacqueline Scully 28 Feb. 1951; m. *c.*1965; children: (first marriage) Michael.
EDUCATION
Attended school in Northern Ireland.
CAREER
Mainly literary; British Ministry of War Transport, 1943-45; UNRRA, mission to Warsaw, Poland, *c.*1946-48; *Gazette*, Montreal, PQ, proofreader, reporter, and re-write man *c.*1949–?; freelance author.
AWARDS, HONOURS
Author's Club of Great Britain award for *Judith Hearne*, 1956; Quebec government literary award for *Judith Hearne*, 1956; Beta Sigma Phi award for *Judith Hearne*, 1956; Guggenheim fellowship, 1959; Canada Council arts fellowship, 1960/61; Governor General's literary award for *The luck of Ginger Coffey*, 1960; National Institute of Arts and Letters award, 1961.
WRITINGS
Judith Hearne, Deutsch, 1955 (published in USA

under title *The lonely passion of Judith Hearne*, Little, Brown, 1956); *The feast of Lupercal*, Little, Brown, 1957 (produced on TV, "Festival," CBC, 7 Oct. 1964); *The luck of Ginger Coffey*, Little, Brown, 1960 (produced on TV, "Festival," CBC, 19 June 1961; on film Continental Distributing Inc., 1964); *An answer from limbo*, Little, Brown, 1962; (with editors of *Life*) *Canada*, Time, 1963; *The emperor of ice cream*, Viking, 1965; *I am Mary Dunne*, Viking, 1968.
CONTRIBUTED: Short stories and articles to *Atlantic monthly, Tamarack review, Cornhill, Weekend, Northern review.*

MOORE, Dora Mavor* 1888–
Director, producer, actress, and teacher; b. 1888; daughter of James and Christina Gordon (Watt) Mavor; m. Francis John Moore (deceased); children: James Mavor b. 8 Mar. 1919, two other sons.
EDUCATION
Attended Havergal College and Margaret Eaton School in Toronto; University of Toronto; École Superieure des Demoiselles in Brussels, Belgium; Royal Academy of Dramatic Art in London, England.
HOME
8 Ridelle Ave., Toronto 19, Ont.
CAREER
Colonial Theatre Stock Company, actress *c.*1910; stock companies in New York, NY, and Chicago, Ill., actress *c.*1911; Ben Greet Pastoral Players, New York, actress 1912; Ben Greet Repertory Company, actress; Old Vic Theatre Company, London, actress *c.*1914-16; Margaret Eaton School and Forest Hill Village School, Toronto, lecturer in dramatic expression; University Extension Players, Toronto, founder and lecturer in dramatic expression 1930; Hart House Touring Players, Toronto, founder and director; Village Players, Toronto, founder 1938; New Play Society, Toronto, founder and director 1946–?; New Play Society School, Toronto, managing director and director of education *c.*1953–; Ontario Hospital, Whitby, drama teacher; First Panamerican Theatre Congress, Mexico City, Mexico, Canadian delegate and third vice-president 12-18 Oct. 1957.
MEMBER
Canadian Theatre Centre.
AWARDS, HONOURS
Scholarship to Royal Academy of Dramatic Art; B'nai B'rith woman of the year, Toronto; Heliconian Club, Toronto, silver ladle, 1958; Canada Council arts fellowship, 1965/66; Canadian drama award, 1967; Centennial medal.
THEATRE
Made acting debut (Colonial Theatre Stock Company, Ottawa, 1910); played in *Romance* (Maxine Elliott's, New York, 10 Feb. 1913), *Julius Caesar* (Lyric, New York, *c.*1913), *Poor little thing*

(Bandbox, New York, 22 Dec. 1914), *Everyman* (Ben Greet Pastoral Players, tour), Kate Hardcastle in *The school for scandal* (Ben Greet Pastoral Players), Viola in *Twelfth night* (Old Vic, London, 1916); directed *The bluebird* (Central Neighbourhood House, Toronto, c.1906).

MOREL, François 1926–
Composer, pianist, and teacher; b. 14 Mar. 1926 in Montreal, PQ; son of Charles Edouard and Marie-Anne (Lavigne) Morel.

EDUCATION
Studied piano with Germaine Malépart, fugue and counterpoint with Isabelle Delorme, composition with Claude Champagne, (*q.v.*) Conservatory of Music of the Province of Quebec, Montreal, 1944-47, member 1947.

HOME
1425 boul. d'Auteuil, Duvernay ouest, Laval, PQ.

CAREER
Taught piano privately 1947–; Institute Nazareth, Montreal, professor of composition c.1961–; CBC, freelance arranger of music 1964–.

MEMBER
BMI Canada.

COMPOSITIONS
Esquisse pour orchestre, Op. 1, 1947, BMI Canada, first performed 7 Oct. 1947 on CBC by CBC Orchestra under Alexander Brott, recorded by CBC IS, no. 129 with Toronto Symphony Orchestra under Sir Ernest MacMillan; *Suite de deux pièces*, orchestra, 1948, first performed 11 Mar. 1949 by Orchestre Symphonique des Jeunes under Fernand Graton; *Ronde enfantine*, piano, 1949, BMI Canada; *Quatre chants japonais*, voice and piano, 1949; *Quatuor à cordes no. 1*, 1952; *Deux études de sonorité*, piano, 1952-54, F. Harris; *Antiphonie*, orchestra, 1953, BMI Canada, first performed 1953 at Carnegie Hall, New York, NY, by orchestra under Leopold Stokowski; *Prière*, organ, 1954, BMI Canada; *Cassation*, wind ensemble, 1954, recorded by CBC IS; *Les rivages perdus*, voice and piano, 1954; *Symphonie pour cuivre*, brass, 1956; *Spirale*, chamber orchestra, 1956; *Rythmologie*, percussion ensemble, 1957; *Rituel de l'espace*, winds, brasses, percussion, cellos, basses, 1958-59, commissioned by Montreal Symphony Orchestra; *Boréal*, orchestra, 1959, commissioned by Montreal Symphony Orchestra; *Beatnik*, jazz band, 1959; *Conflit*, jazz band, 1960; *Joie de cuivres*, jazz band, 1960; *Solo for Nick*, saxophone and jazz band, 1960; *Jazz for background*, jazz band, 1960; *Jazz baroque suite*, jazz band, 1960; *Le mythe de la roche percée*, orchestra, 1960-61, Peters; *L'étoile noire*, orchestra, 1961-62, BMI Canada; *Invention in F*, jazz band, 1961; *Quintette pour cuivres no. 1*, 1962, recorded by Montreal Brass Quintet; *Le fugue du chat*, winds, 1963; *Quatuor à cordes*

no. 2, 1963, first performed 10 July 1963 by Canadian String Quartet, commissioned by CBC; *Osmonde*, women's voices à capella, 1963; *Symphonies pour jazz-band*, 1963; *Prismes-anamorphoses*, orchestra, 1968, first performed 29 Nov. 1968 by CBC Festival Orchestra under Jean Deslauriers, commissioned by CBC.

MORRICE, James Wilson 1865-1924
Artist; b. 10 Aug. 1865 in Montreal, PQ; son of David Morrice; d. 23 Jan. 1924 in Tunis, Tunisia.

EDUCATION
University of Toronto, BA, 1886; Osgoode Hall, Toronto, LL B, 1889; attended Académie Julian, Paris, France, for short time; studied with Henri Harpignies; worked with Whistler, 1892; worked with Matisse in Paris and North Africa.

CAREER
Called to the Ontario bar, 1899; travelled to Europe (Wales, The Netherlands, and France) 1890; painted mainly in Paris, other European cities, Africa, and West Indies from 1890 with frequent winter visits to Canada till 1914; member of Salon d'Automne, Paris; painted for the Canadian War Memorials in France, 1918; visited Canada in 1920.

COMMISSIONS
Mural, Canadian War Memorials Collection, Ottawa, Ont., 1918.

MEMBER
Royal Canadian Academy (Academician; honorary non-resident member); Société Nationale des Beaux-Arts (vice-president); La Société Nouvelle (1908-14); International Society of Painters, London, England; International Society of Painters, Paris; Canadian Art Club (charter member, 1907).

AWARDS, HONOURS
Silver medal, Pan American Exhibition, Buffalo, NY, 1901; Jessie Dow first prize for oil painting, Montreal Art Association, 1919.

EXHIBITIONS
ONE-MAN: *Salon d'Automne*, Paris, 1924; Art Association of Montreal, 1925 and 1937; Galerie Simonson, Paris, 1926; Musée du Jeu de Paume, Paris, 1933; Art Gallery of (now of Ontario) Toronto, 1937; National Gallery of Canada, Ottawa, 1937 and 1965; Royal Canadian Academy, 1953; Montreal Museum of Fine Arts, 1965.
GROUP: Represented in group exhibitions held in Canada since 1888 including annual exhibitions of Canadian Art Club, Toronto, Royal Canadian Academy, Art Association of Montreal Spring Show, Canadian National Exhibition; represented in group shows organized by National Gallery of Canada since 1932; *Salon*, Société Nationale des Beaux-Arts, Paris, 1896 and 1902; International Society of Sculptors, Painters and Gravers, 1901 and 1914; Pan American Exhibition, Buffalo,

1901; Carnegie Institute, Pittsburgh, Pa., 1906, 1914, and 1921; Société Nouvelle, Paris, 1910; Goupil Gallery, Paris, 1914; Goupil Gallery, London, 1921; *Salon d'Automne*, Paris, 1923; Galerie Simonson, Paris, 1926; *Exposition d'Art canadien*, Musée du Jeu de Paume, Paris, 1927; A Century of Canadian Art, Tate Gallery, London, 1938; An Exhibition of Canadian Paintings held at Fortnum and Mason Ltd., London, 1955; Biennial Exhibition, Venice, Italy, 1958.

COLLECTIONS IN WHICH REPRESENTED
National Gallery of Canada; Montreal Museum of Fine Arts; Musée du Jeu de Paume, Paris; Tate Gallery, London; Luxembourg Gallery, Paris; Louvre, Paris; Musée des Beaux-Arts, Lyons, France; Moscow, USSR; Philadelphia Art Gallery, Pa.; National Gallery, London; National Gallery of Art, Washington, DC; Nantes, France; Museum of Modern Western Art, Odessa, USSR; Pennsylvania Academy of Fine Art, Philadelphia; Laing Galleries, Toronto; Art Gallery of Ontario, Toronto; Musée National d'Art Moderne, Paris; Beaverbrook Art Gallery, Fredericton, NB; Winnipeg Art Gallery, Man.; London Public Library and Art Museum, Ont.; Vancouver Art Gallery, BC; Musée du Québec, PQ; Art Gallery of Hamilton, Ont.

MORRIS, Kathleen Moir*   1893–
Artist; b. 2 Dec. 1893 in Montreal; daughter of Montague John and Eliza Howard (Bell) Morris.

EDUCATION
Attended Miss Gardiner's Private School, Montreal; studied under William Brymner, (*q.v.*) Art Association of Montreal, *c.*1910-18; Maurice Cullen in Montreal (*q.v.*), 1912-13.

RELIGION
Anglican.

HOME
79 Windsor Ave., Westmount, Montreal 6, PQ.

CAREER
Painted in Montreal until 1922; painted in Ottawa, Ont. 1922-29; painted in Montreal 1929-65.

MEMBER
Royal Canadian Academy (Associate 1929); Canadian Group of Painters (elected, 1940).

AWARDS, HONOURS
Honourable mention, Willingdon Arts Competition, 1930.

EXHIBITIONS
ONE-MAN: Art Association of Montreal, 1939; Montreal Arts Club, 1956 and 1962.
GROUP: Represented in group exhibitions held in Canada including annual exhibitions of Royal Canadian Academy and Ontario Society of Artists; Spring Exhibitions, Montreal Museum of Fine Arts; Canadian Section of Fine Arts, British Empire Exhibition, Wembley, England, 1924 and 1925; First Pan-American Exhibition, 1925; *Exposition d'Art canadien*, Musée du Jeu de Paume,

Paris, France, 1927; exhibition of Canadian art at the British Empire Trade Exhibition, Buenos Aires, Argentina, 1931; Exhibition of Contemporary Canadian Painting Arranged ... for Circulation in the Southern Dominions of the British Empire, 1936; Exhibition of Paintings, Drawings and Sculpture by Artists of the British Empire Overseas, Royal Institute Galleries, London, England, 1937; A Century of Canadian Art, Tate Gallery, London, 1938; World's Fair, New York, NY, 1939; *Pintura Canadense Contemporanea*, Rio de Janeiro, Brazil, 1944; Canadian Women Artists, Riverside Museum, New York, 1947; Contemporary Canadian Painting, Canadian Club, New York, 1948; Festival of Britain, London, 1951.

COLLECTIONS IN WHICH REPRESENTED
Art Gallery of Greater Victoria, BC; Art Gallery of Hamilton, Ont.; Canadian Legation, Paris; Hart House Permanent Collection, University of Toronto; Mackenzie King Museum, Kitchener, Ont.; Montreal Museum of Fine Arts; National Gallery of Canada, Ottawa.

MORRISON, Mary*   1926–
(Mary Morrison Freedman)
Singer (soprano); b. 9 Nov. 1926 in Winnipeg, Man.; daughter of Donald and Louise (Macleod) Morrison; m. Harry Freedman (*q.v.*) 15 Sept. 1951; children: Karen Liese b. 21 Oct. 1953, Cynthia Jane b. 27 Sept. 1956, Lori Ann b. 19 Mar. 1958.

EDUCATION
Attended Lord Roberts High School and Kelvin Technical High School in Winnipeg; studied voice and piano with Doris Mills, Winnipeg; Royal Conservatory of Music, Toronto, 1945-50, ARCT and artists diploma, studied with Ernesto Vinci and Emmy Heim (*q.v.*), 1945-52, with Weldon Kilburn, 1945–.

HOME and OFFICE
35 St. Andrew's Gdns., Toronto 5, Ont.

CAREER
Royal Conservatory of Music Opera School, Toronto, teacher; Hart House Orchestra, Toronto, guest soloist; Opera Festival Association (now Canadian Opera Company), Toronto, founding member and soloist 1946-55, 1960, 1967; CBC Opera Company, founding member and soloist 1947–; CBC Symphony Orchestra, guest soloist; Mendelssohn Choir, Toronto, guest soloist 1950; toured western Canada, 1952; Festival Singers, Toronto, soloist 1954-67; Winnipeg Philharmonic Choir, guest soloist 1954; toured Japan, 1961; Lyric Arts Trio, Toronto, 1964–; Bach Elgar Choir, Hamilton, Ont., guest soloist 1965-67; La Société de Musique Contemporaine du Québec, soloist 1966-68; Women's Musical Club, Toronto, soloist 1967; Expo 67, Canadian Pavilion, Montreal, soloist summer 1967; Guelph Light Opera

Society, Ont., guest soloist 1967; toured European festivals of contemporary music, 1968.

MEMBER

ACTRA.

AWARDS, HONOURS

"Singing stars of tomorrow" semi-finalist; Rose bowl and Tudor bowl from Manitoba Music Festival, 1944; scholarship from Royal Conservatory of Music, Toronto, 1946; Senior School scholarships from Gaelic Society of Winnipeg, 1946; Kiwanis scholarship, 1946; Miss Opera Star, 1950; Canada Music Citation award, 14 Jan. 1969.

THEATRE

Debut with Toronto Symphony Orchestra (Massey Hall, Toronto, 1947); sang in numerous productions, e.g. soloist in *Nelson Mass* (Toronto), *Mass in C minor* (Toronto), *Mass in B minor* by Bach (Toronto), *Magnificat* (Toronto), *St. Matthew passion* (Toronto; New York, NY), *St. John passion* (Hamilton), *Christmas oratorio* (Ottawa, Ont.), *Elijah* (Toronto), *Gloria* (Stratford, Ont.; Toronto), *Cantatas* by Bach (Toronto), *Requiem* by Verdi (Winnipeg), *Spring symphony* (Toronto), *Rejoice in the lamb* (Hamilton), *Cantata academica* (Toronto), *King David* (Toronto), *Mass* and *Cantata* by Stravinsky (Stratford, Ont.), *Cantata pour une joie* (Toronto), *The children's crusade* (Toronto), *The sea symphony* (Winnipeg), *Antarctica symphony* (Toronto), Euridice in *Orfeo ed Euridice* (1949), *Naughty Marietta* (Winnipeg, 1949), Mimi in *La bohème* (Royal Conservatory of Music Opera School, Eaton Auditorium, Toronto, 5 May 1949), *Vagabond king* (Winnipeg, 1950), Marguerite in *Faust* (1951), Pamina in *The magic flute* (1952), Marie in *The bartered bride* (1952), Fiordiligi in *Cosi fan tutte* (1953), Felice in *The school for fathers* (1954), soloist (Montreal Bach Choir, Osaka Festival, Japan, 1961), *Anerca* (première, Festival of Contemporary Music, Montreal, 1962), Sara in *Louis Riel* (world première, Canadian Opera Company, Toronto, 23 Sept. 1967), Marguerite in *Jeanne d'Arc au bûcher* (Ozawa conducting, Philharmonic Hall, Lincoln Center, New York, 1967).

FILM

Sang in several productions, e.g. *A city sings* (National Film Board of Canada, 1944), *The roots of madness* (Wolper Productions, USA, 1966), *Isabel* (Paramount, 1967).

RADIO

Sang in many CBC productions, e.g. "Star time" (series), "The Northern Electric hour" (series), "Gilbert & Sullivan" (series), *Just a song* (1942), *Sweet hearts* (1943-44), Euridice in *Orfeo ed Euridice* (1948), Micaela in *Carmen* (1948; 1949) Liù in *Turandot* (1950), Mimi in *La bohème* (1948; 1951), Lucy in *Tale of two cities* (1954), Countess in *The marriage of Figaro* (1956; 19 Oct. 1960), Nella in *Gianni Schicchi* (1957),

Fiordiligi in *Cosi fan tutte* (1958), *Opera for six voices* (1961), "Distinguished artists" (series, 4 Mar. 1963), *The ascension* (13 June 1963), "Ten centuries concerts" (series, 1962-66), *Japanese lyrics* (10 June 1964), "CBC strings" (series, 22 July 1964; 14 July 1966), *Anerca* (13 Sept. 1964), *New Canadian music* (20 Sept. 1964), *In memoriam Anne Frank* (1965), "Tuesday night" (series, 23 Nov. 1965; 14 Dec. 1965; 25 Jan. 1966; 8 Mar. 1966; 14 Feb. 1967; 7 May 1968), Lady-in-waiting in *The fool* (1966), "Concerts from two worlds" (series, 20 Feb. 1966; 4 Mar. 1966; 1 Dec. 1966; 12 Dec. 1966), *The human condition* (10 June 1966), *Summer concert*, part I (22 July 1966), *Music 1967* (10 Jan. 1967), "Encore," part I (series, 19 Feb. 1967; 26 Mar. 1967; 12 May 1968), Sara in *Louis Riel* (19 Oct. 1967), *Canada dash, Canada dot* ("Encore," part I, 3 Dec. 1967), "Chamber music" (series, 28 June 1968; 2, 5 Jan. 1969), *The age of bel canto* ("Tuesday night," 5 Sept. 1968).

TELEVISION

Sang in many CBC productions, e.g. Nella in *Gianni Schicchi* ("Showtime," 1955/56), Countess in *The marriage of Figaro* (1956), "World of music" (series, 1960), *The Place of the Skull* (20 Apr. 1962), *700 million* (documentary, 1964), *Festival of miniatures* ("Festival," 10 June 1964).

RECORDINGS

Centennial project, RCA Victor, volumes II and V. *St. Matthew passion*, Beaver Recordings. *The children's crusade*, Beaver Recordings.

MOUSSEAU, Jean Paul* 1927–

Artist, designer; b. 1 Jan. 1927 in Montreal; son of Benjamin and Aurore (Dequoy) Mousseau; m. Denise Guilbault; children: Katerine b. 9 Mar. 1950.

EDUCATION

Studied under Jérôme, Collège Notre-Dame, Montréal, 1940-45; studied interior decoration at École du Meuble, Montréal, 1945-46; studied under Paul-Émile Borduas, Montréal, 1944-50.

RELIGION

None.

HOME

1467 Crescent, Montréal, PQ.

CAREER

Member of Group Automatiste in Montreal 1944-51; travelled to Europe and represented young Canadian painters in Prague, Czecho-Slovakia, 1947; illustrated *Les sables du rêve* (poem) by Thérèse Renaud, 1946; co-signer of the manifesto *Refus global*, Mithra-Mythe, 1948; decorated the restaurant L'Échourie, Montréal, 1953; designed program cover for "Jeunesses Musicales," 1955; designed posters and program covers for *The trial* (Théâtre du Nouveau Monde, Montreal,

1955); Centre d'Art de Ste. Adèle, PQ, professor of painting 1955-57; illustrated poems by Claude Gauvreau, Éditions Erta, 1956; drawings for Éditions Erta, 1956; decorations for a book and art fair, Ste. Adèle, 1956-57; decorations for the window of Librairie Tranquille, Montréal; five Christmas card designs for Artistica, Montreal, 1958; worked on the execution of murals in collaboration with Mariette Rousseau-Vermette in Montreal 1958-59; decorations for one hundredth anniversary of Granby, PQ, 1959; École des Beaux-Arts, Montréal, teacher 1959-60; colourist with Gérard Notebaert, architect, 1958-60; stained glass windows Séminaire de Joliette, PQ, 1960; illustrated the cover of a book of poetry by Yves Préfontaine, 1960; production consultant, *Barbe bleue* ("Heure du concert," CBC, 1961); completely redecorated Théâtre de l'Égrégore, Montréal, 1961; decorated the restaurant Chez-Son-Père, 1963; designed program covers for Théâtre de l'Égrégore, season 1963/64; decorated three discothèques in Montreal and one in Quebec, PQ 1966-67; theatre designer, illustrator, muralist, and painter in Montreal 1949—.

COMMISSIONS
Mural, Collège Notre-Dame, 1958; (with Vermette) five murals, Chalet du Lac aux Castors, Montréal, 1958; five murals (with Vermette), Dorval Airport, Montreal, 1959; mural (with Vermette), Ciba Co., Montreal, 1959; mural (with Vermette), Caisse Populaire du Lac St. Jean, PQ, 1959; mural (with Vermette), École Ville St. Laurent, PQ, 1959; two stained plastic windows, Centre d'Achat Rockland, Ville Mont Royal, PQ, 1959; three sculptures, concert hall of Jeunesses Musicales, Mont Orford, PQ, 1960; thirty-two luminous objects, Dorval Airport, Montreal, 1960; plastic panel, Chapelle Catholique de Shawbridge, PQ, 1960; panel, for Maurice Roux, Lachine, PQ, 1961; mural, Montreal Star building, 1961; mural, l'Hydro-Québec building, 1961; mural, Palais de Justice, Drummondville, PQ, 1961; mural, Peel Station, Montreal Metro, 1966.

MEMBER
Société d'Art Contemporain; Association des Artistes non-figuratifs de Montréal (co-founder).

AWARDS, HONOURS
First prize, Winnipeg Show, Winnipeg Art Gallery, Man., 1946 and 1954; trophy for best scenery for *Une femme douce*, Gala du Spectacle, 1959; Canada Council senior arts fellowship, 1960/61; first prize, Section Esthétique Industriel, concours provincial, PQ, 1960.

THEATRE
Designed costumes and posters for *Les deux arts* (1949); scenery for *La leçon* (Théâtre Amphitryon, 1955), *La fleur à la bouche* (Théâtre Amphitryon, 1955), *La demande en mariage* (Théâtre Amphitryon, 1955), *Georges Dandin* (Théâtre

Amphitryon, 1955), *L'Échange* (Nouveau Monde, 1955), *Une femme douce* (Égrégore, 1959), *Le pélican* (Égrégore, 1960), *Fin de partie* (Égrégore, 1960), *Été et fumée* (Égrégore, 1960); scenery, costumes, and lighting for *François Riopelle* (Festivals de Montréal, 1961); scenery and lighting for *Magie rouge* (Égrégore, 1961), *Ce fou de Platonov* (Égrégore, 1961); scenery for *Les jeux d'Arlequin* (Les Grands Ballets Canadiens, Montréal, 1963); scenery and lighting for *Monsieur Bonhomme et les incendiaires* (Égrégore, 1964), *Fin de partie* (Égrégore, 1964).

EXHIBITIONS
ONE-MAN: Librairie Tranquille, Montréal, 1949; Galerie l'Actuelle, Montréal 1955 and 1956; Galerie Denyse Delrue, Montréal, 1958 and 1960; Montreal Museum of Fine Arts, 1961; Galerie 60, Montréal, 1964.
GROUP: Represented in group exhibitions held in Canada since 1944 including Automatiste exhibitions, annual exhibitions of Montreal Museum of Fine Arts Spring Show, Winnipeg Show, and Association des Artistes Non-Figuratifs; represented in group exhibitions organized by National Gallery of Canada, Ottawa, Ont., including the first Biennial of Canadian Painting, 1955; Prague, 1947; *Automatistes à Paris*, Galerie Luxembourg, Paris, France, 1947; Young Canadian Painters, Belgium, 1954; Canadian Abstract Paintings, circulated by the Smithsonian Institute, Washington, DC, 1956-57; exhibition of Canadian Art, Canadian Pavilion, Brussels International Exposition, Belgium, 1958; *Festival des Deux Mondes*, Spoleto, Italy, 1962; Galerie Toninelli, Milan, Italy, 1964.

COLLECTIONS IN WHICH REPRESENTED
National Gallery of Canada; Musée d'Art Contemporain, Montréal.

MOWAT, Farley McGill* 1921—
(Bunje, pseud.)
Author; b. 12 May 1921 in Belleville, Ont.; son of Angus McGill and Helen Elizabeth (Thomson) Mowat; m. Frances Elizabeth Thornhill 20 Dec. 1947; m. Claire Angel Wheeler; children: (first marriage) Robert Alexander b. 4 Apr. 1954, David Peter b. 10 June 1957.

EDUCATION
Attended primary schools in Belleville, Trenton, and Windsor, Ont.; Victoria School and Nutana Collegiate Institute in Saskatoon, Sask., 1933-37; North Toronto Collegiate and Richmond Hill High School, Ont., 1937-39; University College, University of Toronto, 1946-49.

HOME
25 John St., Port Hope, Ont.

CAREER
Mainly literary; Canadian Army, 1939-45, became captain; *The chat*, editor; Beaver Club of Canada, co-founder.

AWARDS, HONOURS
University of Western Ontario President's medal for short story "Lost in the barren lands," 1952; Anisfield-Wolf award for *People of the deer*, 1953; Women's Canadian Club of Toronto award for *The regiment*, 1956; Governor General's literary award for *Lost in the barrens*, 1956; Book-of-the-year medal from Canadian Library Association for *Lost in the barrens*, 1956; Hans Christian Andersen award honours list for *Lost in the barrens*, 1956.

WRITINGS
People of the deer (non-fiction), Little, Brown, 1952; *The regiment* (non-fiction), McClelland & Stewart, 1955; *Lost in the barrens* (juvenile fiction), Little, Brown, 1956 (also published under title *Two against the north*); *The dog who wouldn't be* (non-fiction), Little, Brown, 1957 (produced CBC radio, "Stage," 14 Nov. 1965); *The grey seas under* (non-fiction), Little, Brown, 1958; *The desperate people* (non-fiction), Little, Brown, 1959; *The serpent's coil* (non-fiction), McClelland & Stewart, 1961; *Owls in the family* (non-fiction), Little, Brown, 1961; *The black joke* (fiction), McClelland & Stewart, 1962; *Never cry wolf* (non-fiction), McClelland & Stewart, 1963; *Westviking* (non-fiction), McClelland & Stewart, 1965; *The curse of the Viking grave* (juvenile fiction), McClelland & Stewart, 1966; *Canada north* (non-fiction), McClelland & Stewart, 1967; (with John de Visser) *This rock within the sea*, McClelland & Stewart, 1968; many CBC TV scripts, e.g. *Sea fare* ("Telescope," 17 Jan. 1964), *Diary of a boy on vacation* (15 Aug. 1964). Works have been extensively translated.

EDITED
S. Hearne's *Coppermine journey*, Little, Brown, 1958; *Ordeal by ice*, McClelland & Stewart, 1960; *Polar passion*, McClelland & Stewart, 1967. CONTRIBUTED: Stories and articles to *The Saturday evening post stories*, Random House, 1951; *Stop, look and laugh*, edited by W.B. Coates, Nelson, 1960; *The Faber book of stories*, edited by K. Lines, Faber & Faber, 1960; *Northern lights*, selected by G.E. Nelson, Doubleday, 1960; *Atlantic monthly, Saturday evening post, Maclean's, Saturday night, Atlantic advocate, Argosy, Bluebook, The chat*.

WORK IN PROGRESS
"Water dog" (about Newfoundland); book on seals and sealing; "Man and the sea" (TV scripts).

MURRAY, Eva von Gencsy
see VON GENCSY, Eva

MUSGROVE, Alexander Johnston 1882-1952
Artist; b. 22 Nov. 1882 in Edinburgh, Scotland; son of Alexander and Elizabeth (Bruce) Musgrove; came to Canada in June 1913 and settled in Winnipeg, Man.; m. Vera Young 1925; children: Maurice French Bruce b. 26 July 1926, Alexander Young b. 19 Aug. 1933; d. Jan. 1952 in Winnipeg.

EDUCATION
Attended Edinburgh University; Glasgow School of Art, Scotland, diploma, in the early 1900s, Doctor of Art 1925.

RELIGION
United Church.

CAREER
Glasgow School of Art, teacher; London, England, Board of Education, teacher prior to 1913; organized and judged art exhibitions and painted in Great Britain; Winnipeg Art School and Winnipeg Art Gallery, director 1913-21, curator 1932-49; one of his paintings chosen for a collection given to Russia by Canada; founded his own art school, The Studio, in Winnipeg *c*.1921; art teacher in Winnipeg 1913-52.

MEMBER
Winnipeg Art Students Sketch Club (founder, 1914); Manitoba Society of Artists (co-founder, 1925; life member, 1951).

AWARDS, HONOURS
Bronze medallion, International Business Machines exhibition at Canadian National Exhibition, Toronto, Ont., 1940.

EXHIBITIONS
ONE-MAN: Winnipeg Art Gallery, 1964.
GROUP: Represented in group exhibitions held in Great Britain including exhibitions of Royal Academy and Royal Scottish Academy and in exhibitions held elsewhere in Europe; represented in group exhibitions held in Canada from 1913 on; Los Angeles Printmakers Association exhibition, Calif., 1940.

COLLECTIONS IN WHICH REPRESENTED
International Business Machines Permanent Collection; Winnipeg Art Gallery.

NAKAMURA, Kazuo* 1926—
Artist, sculptor; b. 13 Oct. 1926 in Vancouver, BC; son of Toichi and Yoshiyo (Uyemoto) Nakamura; m. Lillian Yuriko Kobayakawa 15 Sept. 1967.

EDUCATION
Attended Central Technical School, Toronto, 1948-51.

HOME
30 Old Mill Dr., Toronto 9, Ont.

CAREER

MEMBER
Painters Eleven, Toronto.

AWARDS, HONOURS
Prize, Fourth International Exhibition of Drawings

and Engravings, Lugano, Switzerland, 1956; purchase award, fifth International Hallmark Art Award Exhibition, New York, NY, 1960.

EXHIBITIONS

ONE-MAN: Picture Loan Society, 1952; Hart House, University of Toronto, 1953; Gallery of Contemporary Art, Toronto, 1956 and 1958; Jerrold Morris Gallery, Toronto, 1962 and 1965.

GROUP: Represented in group exhibitions held in Canada since 1952 including annual exhibitions of Canadian Society of Painters in Water Colour, Canadian Society of Graphic Art, Ontario Society of Artists, and Royal Canadian Academy; represented in group exhibitions organized by National Gallery of Canada, Ottawa, Ont., including the First Biennial of Canadian Painting, 1955; Painters Eleven, American Abstract Artists Exhibition, Riverside Museum, New York, 1957; Fourth International Exhibition of Drawings and Engravings, Lugano, 1956; Canadian Abstract, Smithsonian Tour, USA, 1957; Canadian Contemporary Painting, Australian Tour, 1958; First International American Biennial, Mexico City, Mexico, 1958; Contemporary Canadian Art, Central Museum, Utrecht, Groningen Museum, The Netherlands, 1958, Musée Rath, Geneva, Switzerland, 1959; Walraf-Richartz Museum, Cologne, Germany, 1959; Canadian Graphics and Drawings, Yugoslavian Tour, 1959; Twentieth Biennial International Watercolor Exhibition, Brooklyn Museum, New York, 1959; Fifth International Hallmark Art Award Exhibition, New York, 1960; Canadian Prints, Drawings and Watercolor, American Federation of Arts Tour, USA 1960; Seconde Biennale, Musée d'Art Moderne, Paris, France, 1961; Canadian Painting, Polish Tour, 1962; Canadian Painting, Central Africa, 1962; Nineteen Canadian Painters, Louisville, Ky., 1962; Commonwealth Painting, London, England, 1962; Recent Acquisitions, Museum of Modern Art, New York, 1963; Canadian Painting, London, 1963; Member's Loan Gallery Acquisitions, Albright-Knox Gallery , Buffalo, NY, 1963; World Show, Washington Square Gallery, New York, 1964; Cardiff Commonwealth Exhibition of Drawings, Wales, 1965; Centennial Exhibition of Canadian Prints and Drawings, Australian Tour, 1967.

COLLECTIONS IN WHICH REPRESENTED

National Gallery of Canada; Museum of Modern Art, New York; Art Gallery of Ontario, Toronto; Winnipeg Art Gallery, Man.; Beaverbrook Art Gallery, Fredericton, NB; Willistead Art Gallery, Windsor, Ont.; Lugano Collection; Hart House, University of Toronto; Victoria College, University of Toronto; University of Western Ontario; University of Guelph; Sir George Williams University; University Club of Montreal, PQ; York University; Hallmark Collection, USA; David Thompson Collection, Pittsburgh, Pa.; Toronto Dominion Centre; Northern and Central Gas Collection, Toronto; Canadian Imperial Bank of Commerce, Montreal; Imperial Oil Collection, Toronto; Canadian Industries Ltd. Collection, Montreal; Department of External Affairs, Ottawa; Hirshhorn Collection, New York; Philip Johnson Collection, New York; Pirelli Collection, Montreal.

NARRACHE, Jean, pseud.
see CODERRE, Émile

NELSON, Sarah
See NELSOVA, Zara

NELSOVA, Zara   1918—
(Sarah Nelson)
Cellist; b. 1918 in Winnipeg, Man.; m. Grant Johannesen 1968 (?).

EDUCATION

Educated privately and in London, England; studied music with Herbert Walenn, London Violoncello School, and Emanuel Fevermann and Pablo Casals.

HOME

300 Central Park W., New York 29, NY.

OFFICE

Violoncello Faculty, Juilliard School of Music, 120 Claremont Ave., New York, NY 10027, USA.

CAREER

Winnipeg debut c. 1923; concerts in London c. 1929; London Symphony Orchestra under Sir Malcolm Sargent, London debut as soloist c. 1931; Canadian Trio, with Kathleen Parlow (q.v.) and Sir Ernest MacMillan, c. 1941-44; soloist with many orchestras, e.g. New York Philharmonic, Buffalo, NY, Philharmonic, Chicago, Ill., Pittsburgh, Pa., Detroit, Mich., Vancouver, BC, Symphonies, CBC Vancouver Concert; played in several music festivals, e.g. International Casals, Prague, Czecho-Slovakia, Aspen, Colo.; toured extensively, e.g. Australia, Africa, North America, Europe; Juilliard School of Music, New York, violoncello faculty 1962—.

CONCERT STAGE

Commissioned and played *Sonata for cello and piano* by Alexei Haieff, 2nd in Ford Foundation program for concert soloists series (Grace Rainey Rogers Auditorium, 8 Nov. 1963); played with Pittsburgh Symphony Orchestra (Carnegie Hall, New York, 13 Nov. 1963), London Symphony Orchestra-Bach Choir Concert (Festival Hall, London, 25 Sept. 1968), concert (Grace Rainey Rogers Auditorium, 16 Oct. 1968).

RADIO

Soloist in numerous CBC programs, e.g. *Cycle of Beethoven sonatas* ("Distinguished artists,"

1945-46), "Heure du concert" (series, c.1954-55), "Recital" (series, 1959-62), *Drama and music* ("Wednesday night," 8 June 1960), *University celebrity recital* ("Sunday night," 25 Oct. 1964), "Symphony hall" (series, 31 Mar. 1966), *Concerts from two worlds* ("Centenary concerts," 6, 21 July 1967), "Canadian chamber music concerts" (series, 22, 28 Aug. 1967), "Distinguished Canadian artists" (series, 3 Sept. 1967), *Friday concert* (13 Oct. 1967), *Part 1 – CBC Celebrity Recital* ("Music," 12 July 1968).

TELEVISION
Soloist in several CBC programs, e.g. "Concert" (series, 4 Dec. 1960).

RECORDINGS
Concerto for violoncello and orchestra by S. Barber, London LPS 332, 1951. *Voice in the wilderness* by E. Bloch, London LL 1232, 1956. *Schelomo* by E. Bloch, Hebrew rhapsody for cello and orchestra, Vanguard Cardinal Series VCS 10007, 1967. Several recordings by CBC IS and London records.

NEWMAN, Gerald Miller* 1926–
Producer and director; b.14 Mar. 1926 in Vancouver; son of Jacob and Eva (Miller) Newman; m. Joyce Agnes Bishop 20 May 1946; children: Geoffrey b. 13 June 1948, Timothy b. 1 Aug. 1955.

EDUCATION
Maple Grove Elementary School, Vancouver, 1931-37; Point Grey Junior High School, Vancouver, 1937-40; Magee High School, Vancouver, 1940-43; University of British Columbia, BA, 1943-45, 1949-51.

HOME
1293 Jefferson Ave., West Vancouver, BC.

OFFICE
Department of English, Simon Fraser University, Burnaby 2, BC.

CAREER
CBC, Vancouver, TV co-ordinating producer 1956, radio producer 1956-67, senior producer in charge of radio drama for Pacific region 1959-67, co-supervisor "Saturday evening" 1965-67, executive producer of "The human condition" 1966; Simon Fraser University, lecturer in English 1967–.

MEMBER
ACUTE.

RADIO
Produced numerous CBC programs, e.g. *The playboy of the western world* ("Sunday night," 3 May 1959), *Richard II* ("Sunday night," 24 May 1959), *The white devil* ("Sunday night," 5 July 1959), *The shoemaker's holiday* ("Wednesday night," 8 July 1959), *The plaindealer* ("Sunday night," 2 Aug. 1959), *Venice preserved* ("Sunday night," 22 Nov. 1959), *Twelfth night* ("Sunday night," 3 Jan. 1960), *Phèdre* ("Sunday night," 28 Feb. 1960), *Richard III* ("Sunday night," 24 Apr.

1960), *The seagull* ("Sunday night," 22 May 1960), *Love for love* ("Sunday night," 24 July 1960), *The stranger* ("Summer stage," 14 Aug. 1960), *The good of the sun* ("Summer stage," 21 Aug. 1960), *Hamlet* ("Wednesday night," 11 Jan. 1961), *The beaux' stratagem* ("Sunday night," 26 Feb. 1961), *Break of noon* ("Sunday night," 26 Mar. 1961), *Crucifixion* (based on York cycle of mystery plays, 31 Mar. 1961), *The summer people* ("Wednesday night," 24 May 1961; "Saturday evening," 22 Feb. 1964), *Comus* ("Sunday night," 18 June 1961), *The burning city* ("Sunday night," 29 Oct. 1961), *A new way to pay old debts* ("Sunday night," 26 Nov. 1961), *The school for scandal* ("Sunday night," 25 Feb. 1962), *The doctor's dilemma* ("Sunday night," 1 Apr. 1962), *The third day* ("Wednesday night," 25 Apr. 1962; "The human condition," 17 June 1966), *A slight ache* ("Wednesday night," 2 May 1962), *The benefactor* ("Wednesday night," 17 Oct. 1962), *Much ado about nothing* ("Saturday evening," 29 Dec. 1962), *The bourgeois gentleman* ("Wednesday night," 9 Jan. 1963), *Dangerous corner* ("Saturday evening," 23 Feb. 1963; 12 Dec. 1964), *The misanthrope* ("Saturday evening," 30 Mar. 1963), *The wild duck* ("Saturday evening," 27 Apr. 1963), *The Indian queen* ("Saturday evening," 15 June 1963), *The three sisters* ("Saturday evening," 5 Oct. 1963), *Oedipus rex* ("Saturday evening," 14 Dec. 1963; 29 May 1965), *The dance of death* ("Saturday evening," 25 Jan. 1964), *Penny for dreadful* ("Saturday evening," 21 Mar. 1964), *Antony and Cleopatra* ("Sunday night," 26 Apr. 1964), *A penny for a song* ("Saturday evening," 9 May 1964), *The power failure* ("Saturday evening," 30 May 1964), *A midsummer night's dream* ("Saturday evening," 4 July 1964), *Coriolanus* ("Saturday evening," 26 Sept. 1964), *The electric tree* ("Midweek theatre," 9 Dec. 1964), *The man who ate the popomack* ("Midweek theatre," 6 Jan. 1965), *The photograph* ("Sunday night," 14 Mar. 1965), *The changeling* ("Saturday evening," 27 Mar. 1965), *I spy* ("Saturday evening," 31 Mar. 1965), *A tidy end* ("Midweek theatre," 28 Apr. 1965), *The physicists* ("Sunday night," 16 May 1965), *The family reunion* ("Saturday evening," 26 June 1965), *Once burnt, twice shy* ("Sunday night," 18 July 1965), *The floor of night* ("Midweek theatre," 21 July 1965), *The enterprise of England* ("Sunday night," 12 Sept. 1965), "A man at Westminster" (26-week series, 27 Oct. 1965), *Le Tartuffe* ("Midweek theatre," 17 Nov. 1965), Interrogation sequence in *Edith Cavell* ... ("Project 66," 12 Dec. 1965), *An inspector calls* ("Midweek theatre," 12 Jan. 1966), *The lady from the sea* ("Saturday evening," 29 Jan. 1966), *Tin* ("Midweek theatre," 9 Feb. 1966), *Benito Cereno* ("The human condition," 5 Apr. 1966), *The rehearsal* ("Tuesday night," 21 June 1966), *The devil's disciple* ("Saturday evening," 25 June 1966; 23 July 1966), *Death stalked the olive trees* ("Saturday evening," 9 July 1966), *Lease of love* ("Summer stage," 10 July 1966), *The killer* ("Tuesday night," 12 July 1966), *The owl is a heretic* ("Midweek theatre," 27 July 1966), *The magistrate* ("Summer stage," 4 Sept. 1966), *Death of a salesman* ("Saturday evening," 24 Sept. 1966), *The Scarlatti affair* ("Mystery theatre," 5 episodes, 6 Jan. 1967–), *The importance of being earnest* ("Saturday evening," 21 Jan. 1967), *Friedhof* ("Saturday evening," FM, 8 July 1967), *Defender of the past* ("Summer stage," 12 July 1967), *The death of Brock* ("Summer stage," 16 July 1967), *The best room in the house* ("Saturday evening," FM, 30 Nov. 1968).

NEWMAN, Sidney
see NEWMAN, Sydney

NEWMAN, Sydney* 1917–
(Sidney Newman)
Producer; b. 1 Apr. 1917 in Toronto, Ont.; m. Margaret Elizabeth McRae 20 May 1944; children: Deirdre, Jennifer, Gillian.
EDUCATION
Attended Central Technical School, Toronto, 1931-35; studied under Carl Schaeffer (*q.v.*), Elizabeth Wynn Wood and Charles Goldhammer.
OFFICE
National Film Board of Canada, PO Box 6100, Montreal 101, PQ.
CAREER
National Film Board of Canada, splicer-boy 1941, executive producer 1947-52, researched TV at NBC, New York, NY, 1949-50, commissioner 1970–; director and editor of Armed Forces training and war information shorts 1942; CBC, Toronto, director and supervisor of features and outside broadcasts 1952, producer and national drama supervisor 1954-58; Associated British Cinema, London, England, producer and supervisor of drama for TV 1958; BBC, London, head of drama group 1962-68; Associated British Productions Limited, Elstree, England, feature film producer.
MEMBER
Society of Film and Television Arts (fellow).
AWARDS, HONOURS
Ohio State University award for religious drama; *Liberty* award for best drama series; President's award of the Writers Guild of Great Britain; Desmond Davis award of the Society of Film and Television Arts.
THEATRE
Co-presented *Progress to the park* (Saville, London, 3 May 1961).
TELEVISION
Produced numerous programs, e.g. *Flight into*

danger (CBC), *Course for collision* (CBC), "General Motors theatre" (series, CBC, 1954-58), "On camera" (series, CBC, 1954-58), "Ford theatre" (series, CBC, 1955), "Graphic" (series, CBC, 1957), "Armchair theatre" (series, ABC, 1958), *No trams to Lime Street* (ABC, 1959), *A night out* (ABC, 1960), *Stephen D* (BBC, 1963), *The tea party* (BBC, 1965), *The rise and fall of the city of Mahagonney* (BBC, 1967).
FILMS
Produced "Canada carries on" (series, National Film Board, 1945), *Suffer little children* (National Film Board), *It's fun to sing* (National Film Board, *c.*1949; silver medal, Tenth International Film Festival, Venice, Italy, 1949-50), *After prison, what?* (National Film Board, *c.*1950; first award, theatrical category, Third Annual Canadian Film Awards, Toronto, 1950-51), *Ski skill* (National Film Board, *c.*1951; medal, International Competition of Films on Sports, Cortina d'Ampezzo, Italy, 1951-52; ski club cup [first prize], Sestrieres Ski Club Festival, Italy, 1951-52).
WORK IN PROGRESS
Five feature films.

NICHOLS, Jack 1921–
Artist; b. 16 Mar. 1921 in Montreal, PQ.
EDUCATION
Mainly self-taught; studied with F.H. Varley and Louis Muhlstock; studied under W. Stanley Hayter, New York, NY; attended California School of Fine Art; attended National Polytechnical School, Mexico City, Mexico.
OFFICE
Ontario College of Art, 100 McCaul St., Toronto, Ont.
CAREER
Northern Vocational School, Toronto, teacher; University of Toronto, teacher; Art Gallery of Toronto, teacher; RCN *c.*1940-42, ordinary seaman 1944-46, sub-lieutenant, official war artist; painted and studied in the southwestern USA, 1947; Vancouver School of Art, BC, teacher 1948; painted in Paris, France 1956-58; Ontario College of Art, Toronto, teacher.
COMMISSIONS
Mural, Salvation Army Building, Toronto, 1955.
MEMBER
Canadian Group of Painters; Canadian Society of Graphic Art; Royal Canadian Academy (Associate; Academician).
AWARDS, HONOURS
Guggenheim fellowship, 1947; prize, Canadian Group of Painters exhibition, 1945; purchase prize, International Exhibition of Black and White, Lugano, Switzerland, 1952; Coronation medal, 1953; purchase prize, National Annual Exhibition, Hamilton, Ont., 1954; Canadian Government overseas award, 1956-57; Canada Council

fellowship 1956, 1960/61; Royal Society of Canada fellowship.

EXHIBITIONS
ONE-MAN: Picture Loan Society, Toronto, 1941, 1950, 1953, 1956, and 1963; Art Gallery of Ontario, Toronto, 1942; Hart House, University of Toronto, 1942 and 1954; Art Gallery, Springfield, Mass., 1952; London Public Library and Art Museum, Ont., 1952; University of Massachusetts, 1952; Montreal Museum of Fine Arts, PQ, 1952; Victoria College, University of Toronto, 1955; exhibition touring art galleries of western Canada, 1955-56; Contemporary Art Associates, Ottawa, Ont., 1958.
GROUP: Represented in group exhibitions held in Canada including annual exhibitions of Canadian Group of Painters, Canadian Society of Painters in Water Colour, Ontario Society of Artists, Royal Canadian Academy, Canadian Society of Graphic Art, Canadian National Exhibition; represented in group exhibitions organized by National Gallery of Canada, Ottawa, including the first Biennial of Canadian Painting, 1955; Aspects of Contemporary Painting in Canada, Addison Gallery, Andover, Mass., 1942-43; Canadian Art 1760-1943, Yale University Art Gallery, 1944; Philadelphia Water Colour Society, Pa., 1945; National Gallery, London, England, 1946; Canadian Graphic Arts, Rio de Janeiro, Brazil, 1946; Exhibition of International Modern Art, Musée d'Art Moderne, Paris, originated by UNESCO, 1946; Forty Years of Canadian Painting, Museum of Fine Arts, Boston, Mass., 1949; Canadian Painting, National Gallery of Art, Washington, DC, 1950; International Exhibition of Black and White, Lugano, 1952; International Graphic Art Show, Cincinnati Art Museum, Ohio, 1956; International Graphic Art Show, Yugoslavia, 1955; Paris, 1958; Venice Biennial, Italy, 1958; Exhibitions of Canadian Art held in the Canadian pavilion, Brussels International Exposition, Belgium, 1958.

COLLECTIONS IN WHICH REPRESENTED
Agnes Etherington Art Centre, Queen's University; National Gallery of Canada; Art Gallery of Ontario; Vancouver Art Gallery, BC; Art Gallery of Hamilton, Ont.; London Public Library.and Art Museum.

NICOL, Eric Patrick* 1919—
(Jabez, pseud.)
Author; b. 28 Dec. 1919 in Kingston, Ont.; son of William and Amelia Camille (Mannock) Nicol; m. Myrl M. Heselton 13 Sept. 1955; children: Catherine Suzanne, Claire Melinda, Christopher Patrick b. Aug. 1963.
EDUCATION
Attended Langara Elementary School and Lord Byng High School in Vancouver; University of British Columbia, BA, 1941, MA, 1948; attended Sorbonne, 1949/50.

RELIGION
Agnostic.
HOME
3993 W. 36th Ave., Vancouver, BC.
OFFICE
c/o Vancouver Daily Province, 2250 Granville St., Vancouver, BC.
CAREER
RCAF, 1942-45; News herald, Vancouver, columnist 1942-43; B.C. digest, associate editor 1945-47; University of British Columbia, lecturer in English 1946-48, member of the senate 1960-66, instructor in creative writing 1964—; BBC, London, England, scriptwriter 1950-51; Province, Vancouver, columnist 1951—; travelled extensively.
MEMBER
Honorary Literature and Science Society of University of British Columbia (elected, 1941); Civil Liberties Union (Vancouver branch corresponding secretary, 1946-47).
AWARDS, HONOURS
University graduate scholarship, 1941; French government silver medal, 1949; French government scholarship; Leacock award for humour for The roving I, 1950, Shall we join the ladies?, 1955, and Girdle me a globe, 1957.
WRITINGS
(with J. Scott) Sez we (fiction), News Herald, 1943; Sense and nonsense (essays), Ryerson, 1947; The roving I (essays), Ryerson, 1950; Twice over lightly (essays), Ryerson, 1953; Shall we join the ladies? (essays), Ryerson, 1955; Girdle me a globe, Ryerson, 1957; A history of Canada, D. Hackett, 1959; In darkest domestica (essays), Ryerson, 1959; (with P. Whalley) Say, uncle; a completely uncalled for history of the US, Ryerson, 1961 (produced CBC radio, 4 July 1962); A herd of yaks, the best of Eric Nicol, Ryerson, 1962; (with P. Whalley) Russia, anyone? a completely uncalled for history of the USSR, Harper & Row, 1963; Space age, go home (fiction), Ryerson, 1964; 100 years of what?, Ryerson, 1966; A scar is born, Ryerson, 1968; Beware the quickly who (play); Her science man lover (play; produced University of British Columbia Player's Club, 1942); Like father, like fun (play; produced Playhouse Theatre, Vancouver, 24 Mar. 1966); The fourth monkey (play; produced Playhouse Theatre, Vancouver, 10 Oct. 1968); Borderline (TV play; produced CBC 1968); numerous CBC radio scripts and plays, e.g. "Laughing matter" (series), Single gentlemen preferred ("Vancouver Theatre," 16 Aug. 1946), Fifteen men ("Vancouver Theatre," 2 July 1947), Hail fellow, well met ("Vancouver Theatre," 27 Sept. 1947), Once upon a moon ("Vancouver Theatre," 23 Oct. 1947; "Vancouver Theatre," 26 Jan. 1962), (with N. Campbell), O please, Louise ("Vancouver Theatre," 7 Dec. 1947), My views on the news (8, 9, 12 Nov. 1954; published under

title *Man's future and who needs it?*, CBC, 1954), *The giant beyond the Rockies* ("National school broadcast," 18 Nov. 1966); many CBC TV scripts and plays, e.g. *The other cheek* (21 Jan. 1960), *The bathroom* ("Quest," 14 Jan. 1964), "Chorus anyone" (series, 28 June 1964–?), "x" (series, 31 Jan. 1966–?), *Spud Murphy's hill* ("Where the action was," 16 June 1967), *Borderline* (1968).

CONTRIBUTED: Essays and articles to *Ubyssey, B.C. digest, Torch, Wings, New liberty, Saturday night, Maclean's, Food for thought, New world, Beaver, Industrial Canada, B.C. library quarterly, Canadian author and bookman, Habitat.*

NIMMONS, Phil* 1923–
(Phillip Rista Nimmons)
Composer, clarinetist, and teacher; b. 3 June 1923 in Kamloops, BC; son of George Rista and Hilda Louise (McCrum) Nimmons; m. Noreen Liese Spencer 5 July 1950; children: Holly Jane b. 23 Dec. 1954, Carey Jocelyn b. 18 Oct. 1956, Phillip Rista Spencer b. 9 May 1963.

EDUCATION
Attended Queen Mary Public School, 1930-36 and Lord Byng High School, 1936-40, Vancouver, BC; University of British Columbia, BA, 1940-44; studied clarinet with Arthur Christman, choral music with Igor Buketoff, and general music at Juilliard School of Music, New York, NY, 1945-47; composition with Arnold Walter, John Weinzweig (*q.v.*), Richard Johnston, and general music at Royal Conservatory of Music, Toronto, Ont., 1947-50.

RELIGION
Christian.

HOME
114 Babcombe Dr., Thornhill, Ont.

CAREER
Ray Norris Quintet, Toronto, member 1943-45; CBC, Toronto, composer 1943–; Phil Nimmons Jazz Group, Toronto, founder and director 1953-58; Nimmons 'N' Nine, founder and director 1958–; Advanced School of Contemporary Music, Toronto, co-founder and teacher with Oscar Peterson and Ray Brown 1960-64; Nimmons 'N' Nine Plus Six, Toronto, founder and director 1965–.

MEMBER
Canadian League of Composers (founding member); Toronto Musicians' Union.

AWARDS, HONOURS
Juilliard School of Music clarinet scholarship; Royal Conservatory of Music composition scholarship; nomination for Playboy Jazz Award from Playboy Jazz Festival, Chicago, Ill.; BMI (Canada) certificate of honour for contribution to music in Canada and jazz composition *Watch out for the little people.*

CONCERT STAGE
Performed in festivals and concerts at University of Toronto, York University, Lakehead University, University of Western Ontario, University of New Brunswick, St. Mary's University; Stratford, Ont. Festival, 1957; Toronto Symphony Orchestra, 1958, 1967; Toronto Jazz Festival, 1959; Canadian pavilion, Expo 67, Montreal, 1967; tours of Canadian Armed Forces in Europe 1962, 1967, Canada 1965, Middle East 1965, 1966, Cyprus 1965, 1967, Greenland 1967, Africa, India, and Pakistan 1967.

RADIO
Played on several CBC series, e.g. "Jazz Canadiana," "Nimmons 'N' Nine," "On Stage," "Jazz workshop," "Jazz club."

TELEVISION
Played on numerous CBC programs, e.g. "The Barris beat" (series, 1958/59), "Folio" (series, 1959-61), "Show Time" (series, 1959), "Festival" (series, 1960-62), "Parade" (series, 1961), *All-Canadian jazz show* (4 Nov. 1960), *The Canadian jazz show* (10 May 1961).

COMPOSITIONS
Chamber music, for small woodwind ensemble. *Songs*, for female voice. *Summer rain*, vocal, 1948. *Parting*, vocal, 1948. *A little black man*, vocal, 1948. *Sonatina*, flute and string quartet, 1948. *Toccata*, for piano, 1949. *Scherzo*, for orchestra, 1950. *String quartet*, 1951. *Suite for spring*, for orchestra, 1950. *Interlude*, for viola and piano, 1951. Many unpublished jazz compositions registered with BMI (Canada). Several film scores, e.g. *A dangerous age*, S.J. Furie Productions, 1957; *A cool sound from hell* (originally *The young and the beat*), S.J. Furie Productions, 1959. Many drama scores for CBC programs, e.g. *The fantastic emperor, Affectionately Jenny, Dr. Dogbody's leg, High adventurers*, "Stage" (series), "Sunday night" (series, 1950–), "Tuesday night" (series, 1950–), "Wednesday night" (series, 1950–), *Century* (1 Jan. 1967).

RECORDINGS
The Canadian scene, Verve, 1957. *Nimmons 'N' Nine*, Verve MGVS 6153, 1959. *Take ten*, RCA Victor, 1964. *Mary Poppins swings*, RCA Victor, 1964. *Strictly Nimmons*, RCA Victor, 1965.
WORK IN PROGRESS: Jazz compositions for Nimmons 'N' Nine Plus Six; work for solo accordion; work for violin and piano; jazz composition for string quartet, piano and jazz quartet.

NISBET, Joanne* 1931–
(Joanne Nisbet Scott)
Dancer; b. 15 July 1931 in Karachi, Pakistan; daughter of James Maltman Wilson and Victoria Agnes Alexander (Dickie) Nisbet; m. David Robert Scott (*q.v.*) 15 Apr. 1957; came to Canada in 1959.

EDUCATION
No formal schooling; studied ballet with Ballet
Rambert, London, England, 1945-46; with Lubov
Egorova, Paris, France, 1946-48; Anna Ivanova,
London.

RELIGION
Church of Scotland.

HOME
7 Playter Boul., Toronto 6, Ont.

OFFICE
National Ballet of Canada, 157 King St. E.,
Toronto 1, Ont.

CAREER
Ballet Rambert, London, corps de ballet 1945-46;
Palladium Theatre, London, dancer 1949; Sadler's
Wells Theatre (now Royal) Ballet, London, corps
de ballet 1950-55; London's Festival Ballet,
corps de ballet 1955-59; National Ballet of Canada, Toronto, corps de ballet 1959-61, assistant
ballet mistress 1961-62, ballet mistress 1962—.

MEMBER
AEA; Imperial Society of Teachers of Dancing
(Cecchetti Society Branch), London.

TELEVISION
Danced Lady Montague in *Romeo and Juliet*
(Cranko, "Festival," CBC, 15 Sept. 1965; 2 Mar.
1966).

NOWLAN, Alden A.* 1933—
Author; b. 25 Jan. 1933 in Windsor, NS; son of
Freeman and Grace (Reese) Nowlan; m. Claudine
Orser; children: John Alden.

HOME
Mitchell Apts., Parks St., Saint John, NB.

OFFICE
Telegraph-Journal, Saint John, NB.

CAREER
The observer, Hartland, NB, reporter and news
editor 1952-63; *Telegraph journal*, Saint John,
1963—, news editor 1965—; University of New
Brunswick, writer in residence 1968/69.

AWARDS, HONOURS
Canada Council arts scholarship, 1961, arts
award, 1966; Guggenheim fellowship, 1967; Governor General's literary award for *Bread, wine
and salt*, 1967.

WRITINGS
The rose and the Puritan (poems), University of
New Brunswick, 1958; *A darkness in the earth*
(poems), Hearse, 1959; *Under the ice* (poems),
Ryerson, 1961; *Wind in a rocky country* (poems),
Emblem Books, 1961; *The things which are*
(poems), Contact, 1962; *Bread, wine and salt*
(poems), Clarke, Irwin, 1967; *Miracle at Indian
River/stories*, Clarke, Irwin, 1968.
CONTRIBUTED: Short stories, poetry, and arti-
cles to *A book of Canadian stories*, edited by D.
Pacey, rev. ed., Ryerson, 1962; *Five New Bruns-
wick poets*, Fiddlehead, 1962; *Poetry of mid-
century, 1940-1960*, edited by M. Wilson, Mc-
Clelland & Stewart, 1964; *Modern Canadian
stories*, edited by G. Rimanelli and R. Ruberto,
Ryerson, 1966; *The Penguin book of Canadian
verse*, edited by R. Gustafson, rev. ed., Penguin,
1967; *Modern Canadian verse in English and
French*, edited by A.J.M. Smith, Oxford, 1967;
*Atlantic advocate, Fiddlehead, Canadian forum,
Queen's quarterly, Tamarack review, Canadian
poetry, Dalhousie review, Waterloo review, Alphabet, Canadian commentator, Forest and outdoors,
Canadian author and bookman, Delta, Canadian
literature.*

NUDLEMAN, Nordyk, pseud.
see GLASSCO, John

NUNES, Margery Lambert
see LAMBERT, Margery

OGILVIE, Will* 1901—
(William Abernethy Ogilvie)
Artist; b. 30 Mar. 1901 in Stutterheim, Cape
Province, South Africa; son of Walter and Bertha
(Frachét) Ogilvie; settled in Toronto in 1925; m.
Sheelah Rita 21 Apr. 1958.

EDUCATION
Attended Public School, Stutterheim, 1910-14;
Queens College, Queenstown, Cape Province,
1915-20; studied with Erich Mayer, Johannesburg,
South Africa, 1921-24; attended Art Students
League, New York, NY, 1928-30; studied with
Kimon Nicoliades.

RELIGION
Protestant.

HOME
PO Palgrave, Ont.

OFFICE
Department of Fine Art, University of Toronto,
Toronto, Ont.

CAREER
Travelled in South Africa in 1931, 1954, and
1963; School of Art Association of Montreal, PQ,
director 1938-41; Canadian Army, 1941-46, official war artist, 1942-46, became major, awarded
MBE; Ontario College of Art, Toronto, instructor
1947-57; Banff School of Fine Arts, Alta., instructor, summer 1947; Queen's University, instructor
summer 1948; Mount Allison University, instructor summer 1958; travelled in France, Italy,
Greece, and Mexico.

COMMISSIONS
Mural, commissioned by Honorable Vincent Massey and Mrs. Massey, Chapel of Hart House, University of Toronto, 1936.

MEMBER
Canadian Group of Painters (charter member, 1933; president, 1948); Canadian Society of Painters in Water Colour (elected, 1934).

AWARDS, HONOURS
Royal Society fellowship for travel in Italy, 1957/58.

EXHIBITIONS
ONE-MAN: Picture Loan Society, Toronto, annually 1934-66; Gainsborough Galleries, Johannesburg, 1954; Hart House, University of Toronto, Toronto, 1957 and 1962; Adler Fielding Gallery, Johannesburg, 1963; Victoria College, University of Toronto, 1964; Wells Gallery, Ottawa, Ont., 1966; Fleet Gallery, Winnipeg, Man., 1966; Roberts Art Gallery, Toronto, 1967.
GROUP: Represented in group exhibitions held in Canada since 1933 including annual exhibitions of Canadian Group of Painters, Canadian Society of Painters in Water Colour; Exhibition of Contemporary Canadian Painting Arranged ... for Circulation in the Southern Dominions of the British Empire, 1936; A Quarter Century of Canadian Art, Tate Gallery, London, England, 1938; World's Fair, New York, 1939; Exhibition of Water Colours by Canadian Artists, Gloucester, England, 1939; War Art, National Gallery, London, 1943; Brussels War Art, Belgium, 1944; Rio de Janeiro, Brazil, 1946; Exhibition of International Modern Art, Musée d'Art Moderne, Paris, France, originated by UNESCO, 1946.

COLLECTIONS IN WHICH REPRESENTED
National Gallery of Canada, Ottawa; Art Gallery of Ontario, Toronto; London Public Library and Art Museum, Ont.; Art Gallery of Hamilton, Ont.; Sarnia Art Gallery, Ont.; Art Gallery of Winnipeg, Man.; Edmonton Art Gallery, Alta.; Roberts Art Gallery, Toronto; Hart House, University of Toronto.

O'HARA, Geoffrey 1882-1967

Composer and pianist; b. 2 Feb. 1882 in Chatham, Ont.; son of Robert Murray and Maria Sophia (Dobbs) O'Hara; m. Constance M. Dougherty 7 June 1919; children: Hamilton Murray b. 31 Dec. 1920, Nancy Jackson b. 31 Dec. 1925; d. 31 Jan. 1967 in St. Petersburg, Fla.

EDUCATION
Attended Chatham Collegiate Institute; studied music with private teachers in Toronto, Ont., and New York, NY.

RELIGION
Episcopalian.

CAREER
Chatham Episcopal church, organist 1894—?; vaudeville pianist in Canada and USA; wrote songs and operettas early 1900s-67; studied folk songs and dances of Canadian Indian tribes; US Secretary of the Interior's Dept., research on the music of Indians of Oklahoma, Arizona, and New Mexico to 1913, instructor in American Indian music 1913-17; recorded Navajo music for Smithsonian Institution, Washington, DC; songs featured by Caruso and Al Jolson 1913; US Army 1917-18, songleader in army camps; Columbia University Teachers' College, instructor in community music 1936-37; Huron College, S. Dak., instructor in music and song-writing 1947-48.

MEMBER
ASCAP (director, 1942-45); American Guild of Composers and Artists (council member, 1943); Composers-Authors Guild (president, 1945); Society for the Preservation of Barber Shop Quartet Singing in America (founder, president of Manhattan chapter, and composer of theme song *The old songs*); Song Writers Protective Association (president, 1922).

AWARDS, HONOURS
Hon. D Mus from Huron College, 1947; Henry Hadley award for services to American music, 1947.

COMPOSITIONS
Over 150 popular songs and religious choruses, e.g. *K-K-K Katy, Give a man a horse he can ride, I love a little cottage, Wreck of the "Julie Plante", Little Bateese, There is no death, The living God, One world, Christmas means thinking of Jesus, I walked today where Jesus walked*, 1937, *He smiled on me, God lives in my heart, The four chaplains; Peggy and the pirate*, operetta, 1927; *Riding down the sky*, operetta, 1928; *The count and the co-ed*, operetta, 1929; *The smiling sixpence*, operetta, 1930; *Lantern land*, operetta, 1931; *Harmony hall*, operetta, 1933; *The princess runs away*, operetta, 1934; *Our America*, operetta, 1934; *Puddinhead the first*, operetta, 1936; *Little women*, operetta, 1940, S. French; *The Christmas thieves*, operetta, 1943.

WRITINGS
(with J. Murray Gibbon) *Canadian folk songs, old and new*, Dutton, 1927.

OKADA, Hideki, pseud.
see GLASSCO, John

O'NEILL, Charles 1882-1964
Bandmaster and composer; b. 31 Aug. 1882 in Duntocher, Scotland; came to Canada in 1906 and settled in Ontario; d. Sept. 1964.

EDUCATION
Attended secondary schools in Glasgow, Scotland and London, England; studied conducting and orchestration, Royal Military School, Kneller Hall, England; studied organ with A.L. Peace, harmony with A. Evans in England, composition with Herbert Sanders in Ottawa, Ont.; McGill Conservatorium, Mus B 1914, Mus D, 1924.

CAREER

Organist in Scotland and England c.1896-1906; Royal Canadian Artillery Band, Kingston, Ont., cornettist 1906; Royal Canadian Artillery, Quebec, PQ, bandmaster and director of music; Royal 22nd Regiment, Quebec, director of music; CBC Little Symphony Orchestra, Quebec, associate conductor; University of Wisconsin, acting director of music department; State Teachers' College, Potsdam, NY, professor of composition and conducting 1937-47; Royal Conservatory of Music, Toronto, Ont., teacher of theory and composition 1947-64.

MEMBER

CAPAC; Canadian Bandmasters Association.

COMPOSITIONS

Nobility, overture, band, 1943, Remick; *Majesty*, overture, 1945, Remick; *Prelude and fugue in G*, orchestra, 1945-46; *Fidelity*, overture, band, 1947, Remick; *Suite of four numbers*, orchestra, 1948; *Sovereignty*, overture, band, 1949, Remick; *Air de ballet "La ballerina"*, orchestra, 1950; *The ancient mariner*, cantata; *A day in June*, orchestra; *Remembrance*, orchestra, also for band, C. Fischer; *The land of the maple and the beaver*, orchestra, Boosey & Hawkes; *Souvenir de Québec*, band, C. Fischer; *Mademoiselle Coquette*, band, C. Fischer; *Sunshine and flowers*, band; *Andalusia*, band; *The knight errant*, band, Waterloo Music; *The silver cord*, band, G. Schirmer; *Builders of youth*, band, C. Fischer; *Aladdin's lamp*, C. Fischer; *The three graces*, band, S. Fox; *Festival*, band; *Prince Charming*, band; *Concert overture in F minor*, band; *Mon ami*, band, Waterloo Music; *Nulli secundus*, band, Waterloo Music; *The emblem*, band, Waterloo Music; *Royal 22nd Regiment*, band; *Autumn glory*, band; *Greghmount*, band; *Trumpet tune in the old style*, four cornets and band; *I will extol thee*, choir, C. Fischer; *Say thou dost love me*, choir, C. Fischer; *Sweet echo*, choir; *Nunc dimittis*, choir.

OPTHOF, Cornelis* 1930—

Singer (baritone); b. 10 Feb. 1930 in Rotterdam, The Netherlands; son of Johannes Adrianus and Cornelia (Lops) Opthof; came to Canada in 1949; m. Natalie Ann Landyga 15 Aug. 1959; children: Natalie Ann b. 14 Sept. 1960, Tamara Roxan b. 25 Dec. 1964, Nicholas b. 21 Jan. 1968.

EDUCATION

Attended secondary school and technical school in Rotterdam; studied voice with Catherine Hendrikse, Vancouver, BC; Royal Conservatory of Music Opera School, Toronto, 1957-59.

RELIGION

Roman Catholic.

HOME

106 Lake Promenade, Toronto 14, Ont.

CAREER

Canadian Opera Company, Toronto, soloist; Philadelphia Opera Company, Pa., soloist; Vancouver Opera Association, soloist; Vancouver International Festival, 1963; toured Canada; Australian tour with Joan Sutherland, 1965.

MEMBER

ACTRA; AEA.

AWARDS, HONOURS

Royal Conservatory of Music Opera School scholarship, 1957-59; CBC Classical Talent Festival first prize, 1960; Canada Council general award, 1964/65.

THEATRE

Sang in numerous productions, e.g. Dr. Caius in *The merry wives of Windsor, The pirates of Penzance* (Stratford, Ont. Festival, 1961), *The gondoliers* (Stratford, Ont. Festival, 1962), Marcello and Schaunard in *La bohème* (Canadian Opera Company, Toronto, 1962; tour, 1963), Father in *Hansel and Gretel* (Canadian Opera Company, tour, 1963; Vancouver Opera Association, 1966), Guglielmo and Alfonso in *Cosi fan tutte* (Canadian Opera Company, tour, 1963; Stratford, Ont. Festival, 1967), Eisenstein in *Die Fledermaus* (Canadian Opera Company, tour, 1963); Count Almaviva in *The marriage of Figaro* (Stratford, Ont. Festival, 1964; Canadian Opera Company, Montreal, 1964; Place des Arts, Montréal, 1967), Valentine in *Faust* (Australia, 1965; Edmonton Opera Association, 1966), Germont in *La traviata* (Australia, 1965; Sadler's Wells Opera Company, London, England, 1966), Belcore in *L'elisir d'amore* (Australia, 1965), Enrico Ashton in *Lucia di Lammermoor* (Australia, 1965; Edmonton Opera Association, 24 Jan. 1968), title role in *Don Giovanni* (Stratford, Ont. Festival, 8 July 1966), Frederik in *Lakmé* (Seattle Opera Association, Wash., 1967), *Albert Herring* (Stratford, Ont. Festival, 1967), Malatesta in *Don Pasquale* (Canadian Opera Company, Feb. 1967), Sir John A. Macdonald in *Louis Riel* (world première, Canadian Opera Company, Toronto, 19 Oct. 1967), Figaro in *The barber of Seville* (Canadian Opera Company, tour, 1968).

RADIO

Sang in many CBC productions, e.g. *Brébeuf* ("Distinguished artists"), *Songs of the wayfarer* (1960), Count in *The marriage of Figaro* ("Sunday night," 9 Aug. 1964), title role in *Don Giovanni* ("Opera time," 28 May 1966; 23 Aug. 1966), "Concerts from two worlds" (series, 17 Nov. 1966), Sir John A. Macdonald in *Louis Riel* (19 Oct. 1967), "Thursday music" (series, 3 Oct. 1968).

TELEVISION

Sang in many CBC productions, e.g. "Parade" (series, 26 July 1960), Count of Monterone in *Rigoletto* ("Festival," 3 Feb. 1965).

RECORDINGS

Filippo in *Beatrice di Tenda*, London and Decca, 1966.

OSBORNE, Gwendolyn
Dancer and teacher; daughter of John R. and
Mary (Burpee) Osborne; d. in Boston, Mass.

EDUCATION
Attended Model School and Lisgar Collegiate in
Ottawa, Ont.; studied dancing with Konstantin
Kobeleff in New York, NY.

CAREER
Taught ballet, interpretative, and Spanish dancing
in Ottawa.

OXENHAM, Andrew William* 1945–
Dancer; b. 12 Oct. 1945 in London, England; son
of Lawrence William and Marjorie Cecelia Oxen-
ham; came to Canada in 1957 and became Canadian citizen in 1963.

EDUCATION
Attended school in England and Canada; studied
ballet at Bristol School of Ballet, England, British
Ballet Organization Grade 1-4 with honours,
1956; with Gweneth Lloyd at Canadian
School of Ballet, 1957-60; National Ballet School
of Canada, Toronto, Grades 3,4,5 with honours,
Royal Academy of Dancing elementary diploma,
Cecchetti Society elementary diploma, 1960-64.

RELIGION
Anglican.

HOME
100A Avenue Rd., Toronto 5, Ont.

OFFICE
National Ballet of Canada, 157 King St. E., Toronto 1, Ont.

CAREER
National Ballet of Canada, Toronto, corps de ballet, 1964-66, soloist 1966–.

MEMBER
AEA; Royal Academy of Dancing, London
(1960–); Cecchetti Society of Dancing, London
(1963–).

AWARDS, HONOURS
Scholarship to Bristol School of Ballet, 1956;
Peter Cheetam scholarship of Royal Academy of
Dancing, Canada, 1960; Canada Council arts
scholarship, 1962/63.

THEATRE
First danced leading Scottish lad in *La sylphide*
(Bruhn, Washington, DC, Aug. 1965), *Solitaire*
(MacMillan, Washington, Aug. 1965), Dancing
Master in *The rake's progress* (de Valois, Jan.
1966), Benvolio in *Romeo and Juliet* (Cranko,
Apr. 1967), Clown in *Le lac des cygnes* (Bruhn,
1967), *Cinderella* (Franca, 1968), *Cyclus* (Strate,
1968).

TELEVISION
Danced in Chinese dance in *Music in the night*
("Festival," CBC, 25 Dec. 1964), *Solitaire* (Mac-
Millan, "Prom programme," CTV), Clown in *Le
lac des cygnes* (Bruhn, "Festival," CBC, 27 Dec.
1967).

PACKARD, Frank Lucius 1877-1942
Novelist; b. 2 Feb. 1877 in Montreal, PQ; son of
Lucius Henry and Mary Frances (Joslin) Packard;
m. Marguerite Pearl MacIntyre 31 Aug. 1910;
children: Lucius Henry, Robert Joslin, Horace
Frank, Marguerite Pearl; d. 17 Feb. 1942 in Lachine, PQ.

EDUCATION
Attended Montreal High School and Woodstock
College; McGill College, B Sc, 1897; L'Institute
Montefiore, L'Université de Liège, Belgium,
1897/98.

CAREER
Mainly literary; civil engineer in USA, 1898–?;
travelled extensively.

MEMBER
Canadian Authors Association; Authors Club,
London, England.

WRITINGS
On the iron at Big Cloud (short stories), Crowell,
1911; *Greater love hath no man*, Copp Clark,
1913 (produced as silent movie and play); *The
miracle man*, Copp Clark, 1914; *The beloved
traitor*, Copp Clark, 1915; *The adventures of
Jimmy Dale*, Copp Clark, 1917; *The sin that was
his*, Copp Clark, 1917; *The wire devils*, Copp
Clark, 1918; *From now on*, Copp Clark, 1919;
The further adventures of Jimmy Dale, Burt,
1919; *The night operator* (short stories), Copp
Clark, 1919; *The white moll*, Copp Clark, 1920;
Pawned, Copp Clark, 1921; *Doors of the night*,
Copp Clark, 1922; *Jimmy Dale and the phantom
clue*, Copp Clark, 1922; *The four stragglers*, Copp
Clark, 1923; *The locked book*, Copp Clark, 1924;
Broken waters, Copp Clark, 1925; *The running
special* (short stories), Copp Clark, 1925; *The
red ledger*, Doran, 1926; *The devil's mantle*,
Doran, 1927; *Two stolen idols*, Burt, 1927;
Shanghai Jim (short stories), Doubleday, Doran,
1928; *Tiger claws*, Doubleday, Doran, 1928;
The big shot, Copp Clark, 1929; *Jimmy Dale and
the blue envelope murder*, Copp Clark, 1930;
The gold skull murder, Doubleday, Doran, 1931;
The hidden door, Doubleday, Doran, 1933; *The
purple ball*, Doubleday, Doran, 1933; *Jimmy
Dale and the missing hour*, Doubleday, Doran,
1935; *The dragon's jaws*, Doubleday, Doran,
1937; *More knaves than one* (short stories),
Hodder & Stoughton, 1938.
CONTRIBUTED: Stories and articles to *Crafts-
man, Century, Outing magazine, Canadian magazine, Cosmopolitan, Publisher's weekly*.

PALMER, Frank* 1921–
(Herbert Franklin Palmer)
Artist; b. 24 Nov. 1921 in Calgary; son of George
Henry and Grace Elizabeth (Barager) Palmer; m.
Georgina Alexandra Drowley 5 Feb. 1955.

EDUCATION
Attended Rideau Park School and Western
Canada High School in Calgary; studied part time
at the Ontario College of Art, Toronto, Ont.,
1942; studied under Jack L. Shadbolt (*q.v.*)
part time at the Vancouver School of Art, BC,
1945; studied at the Art Center School, Los
Angeles, Calif., 1948.

RELIGION
Protestant.

HOME
1444 28th St. SW, Calgary, Alta.

OFFICE
Alberta College of Art, 13th Ave. and 10th St.
NW, Calgary, Alta.

CAREER
Served in the RCAF during World War II; employed by Cleland-Kent Engraving Co., Vancouver, 1945-48; freelance artist in Calgary 1949-58;
Alberta College of Art, Calgary, instructor in
commercial and fine arts 1958—.

MEMBER
Royal Canadian Academy (Associate 1959; Academician 1966); Canadian Society of Painters in
Water Colour (elected, 1954; second vice-president, 1958); Alberta Society of Artists (elected,
1950; chairman Calgary group, 1949).

AWARDS, HONOURS
Jessie Dow prize for watercolour, Spring Exhibition, Montreal Museum of Fine Arts, 1954.

EXHIBITIONS
GROUP: Represented in group exhibitions held
in Canada including exhibitions of Canadian So-
ciety of Painters in Watercolour; second, third,
fourth, fifth, and sixth Biennial Exhibitions of
Canadian Painting, National Gallery of Canada,
Ottawa, Ont., 1957, 1959, 1961, 1963, and 1965;
California Watercolor Society exhibition, 1955.

COLLECTIONS IN WHICH REPRESENTED
Art Gallery of Hamilton, Ont.; Art Gallery of
Ontario, Toronto; Beaverbrook Art Gallery,
Fredericton, NB; Calgary Allied Arts Centre; De-
partment of External Affairs, Ottawa; London
Public Library and Art Museum, Ont.; McMaster
University; National Gallery of Canada; Univer-
sity of Calgary; University of New Brunswick;
Imperial Oil Canadian Collection, Toronto; Metro-
politan Life Insurance Co. Collection, Ottawa.

PALMER, Herbert Franklin
see PALMER, Frank

PALMER, Herbert Sydney   1881—
Artist; b. 15 June 1881 in Toronto; son of
Charles and Frances (Baldwin) Palmer; m. Mar-
garet Elizabeth Jamieson 19 Oct. 1921.

EDUCATION
Attended primary and secondary school in Toronto; attended Central Ontario School of Art,

Toronto, *c.*1901-05; studied with F.S. Challener
and J.W. Beatty *c.*1901-05.

RELIGION
United Church.

HOME
170 St. Clements Ave., Toronto, Ont.

CAREER
Worked on Canadian War Memorials, 1917; Canadian National Exhibition, Fine Arts Department
curator 1926-41; retired.

COMMISSIONS
Sarnia Public Library, Ont.; Collegiate Institute,
Saskatoon, Sask.; Department of Education of
Ontario.

MEMBER
Royal Canadian Academy (Associate 1915; Academician 1934; secretary, 1948-53); Canadian
Society of Graphic Art (elected, 1919); Arts and
Letters Club, Toronto; Ontario Society of Artists (elected, 1909; vice-president, treasurer,
1919-20; secretary, 1926-56; honorary secretary,
1956—).

AWARDS, HONOURS
Baxter Art Foundation award for distinguished
service to the arts, 1960; Centennial medal, 1967.

EXHIBITIONS
ONE-MAN: T. Eaton Co. Fine Art Gallery, Toronto, annually *c.*1925-50.

GROUP: Represented in group exhibitions held
in Canada since 1905 including annual exhibitions
of Royal Canadian Academy, Ontario Society of
Artists, Canadian National Exhibition; Canadian
Section of Fine Arts, British Empire Exhibition,
Wembley, England, 1925; *Exposition d'art cana-
dien*, Musée du Jeu de Paume, Paris, France,
1927; Exhibition of Contemporary Canadian
Painting arranged ... for circulation in the Sou-
thern Dominions of the British Empire, 1936; A
Century of Canada Art, Tate Gallery, London,
England, 1938.

COLLECTIONS IN WHICH REPRESENTED
National Gallery of Canada, Ottawa; Art Gallery
of Ontario, Toronto; Hart House, University of
Toronto; Sarnia Public Library; Emmanuel Collection, Toronto.

PANNETON, Philippe   1895-1960
(Ringuet, pseud.)
Novelist; b. 30 Apr. 1895 in Trois Rivières, PQ;
son of Ephrem François and Eva (Ringuet) Panneton; m. France de Laplante; d. 29 Dec. 1960
in Lisbon, Portugal.

EDUCATION
Attended Université Laval; Université de Montréal, MD, 1920; graduate studies in Paris, France,
1920-23.

CAREER
Montreal, PQ, medical practice; Université de
Montréal, professor of medicine; Notre Dame

Hospital, Montreal and Crèche d'Youville, PQ, chief of department of ophtalmology and oto-rhino-laryngology; Canadian ambassador to Portugal, 1956-60; lectured and travelled extensively.

MEMBER
Académie Canadienne-Française (founding member and past president); Association Canadienne-Française pour l'Avancement des Sciences; American Anthropological Association; American Association for the Advancement of Science; National Geographic Society; Société Canadienne d'Histoire Naturelle; Société Canadienne de Géographie; National Film Society of Canada (honorary vice-president, Montreal branch).

AWARDS, HONOURS
Prix David, 1924 and 1940; Prix de l'Académie Française, Governor General's literary award, and Prix des Vikings, Paris, for *Trente arpents*, 1940; Prix Duvernay, 1955; Lorne Pierce medal, 1959.

WRITINGS
(with L. Francoeur) *Littératures* (non-fiction), 1924; *Trente arpents*, Flammarion, 1938 (translated into English, German, Dutch); *Un monde était leur empire* (non-fiction), 1943; *L'héritage et autres contes* (short stories), Variétés, 1946; *Fausse monnaie*, Variétés, 1947; *Le poids du jour*, Variétés, 1949; *L'amiral et le facteur* (non-fiction), Dussault, 1954; *Confidences* (non-fiction), Fides, 1965.

CONTRIBUTED: Short stories and articles to *Tamarack review, L'ordre, Idées*.

PANTON, Lawrence Arthur Colley   1894-1954
Artist; b. 15 June 1894 in Egremont, Cheshire, England; son of Charles William and Caroline (Colley) Panton; came to Canada in 1911 and settled in Toronto, Ont.; m. Marion Pye 27 Jan. 1920; children: Charles Laurence (killed in action in World War II); d. 22 Nov. 1954 in Toronto.

EDUCATION
Attended Lincoln Grammar School in England; Central Secondary School, Sheffield, England; studied under C.M. Manly (*q.v.*) and F.S. Challener, Ontario College of Art, Toronto; studied art at Central Technical School, Toronto.

RELIGION
Anglican.

CAREER
Grand Trunk Railway, office assistant sometime before 1915; *Evening telegram*, Toronto, bookkeeper 1915 and 1920-22; Canadian Army, 1916-19; Rous and Mann Ltd., Toronto, designer; Central Technical School, Toronto, art teacher 1924; Western Technical School, Toronto, director of art 1926-37; Northern Vocational School, Toronto, director of art, 1937-51; Ontario College of Art, Toronto, principal 1951-54; revised the constitution of Royal Canadian Academy; painter in Toronto, making painting trips to northern Ontario and Nova Scotia.

MEMBER
Graphic Arts Club, Toronto; Canadian Society of Graphic Art (sometime secretary); Canadian Society of Painters in Water Colour (founding member, 1926; president, 1929-33; secretary for three years); Ontario Society of Artists (elected, 1925; president, 1932-36); Royal Canadian Academy (Associate 1934; Academician 1943; vice-president, 1952-53); Federation of Canadian Artists (elected, 1942; chairman Ontario section, 1945); Canadian Group of Painters (elected, 1949); Arts and Letters Club, Toronto, (president, 1954); Society of Canadian Painter-Etchers (elected, 1924).

AWARDS, HONOURS
Second prize for design for victory bonds in World War II; Taber Dulmage Feheley award, Ontario Society of Artists, 1949.

EXHIBITIONS
ONE-MAN: Laing Galleries, Toronto, 1949; Art Gallery of Toronto, 1955.

GROUP: Represented in group exhibitions held in Canada from 1922 on including annual exhibitions of Ontario Society of Artists, Canadian Society of Graphic Art, Canadian Society of Painters in Water Colour, Royal Canadian Academy, and Canadian National Exhibitions; Annual Exhibitions of Canadian Art, National Gallery of Canada, Ottawa, Ont.; British Empire Exhibition, Wembley, England, 1924; Exhibition of Contemporary Canadian Painting Arranged ... for Circulation in the Southern Dominions of the British Empire, 1936; Exhibition of Paintings, Drawings and Sculpture by Artists of the British Empire Overseas, Royal Institute Galleries, London, England, 1937; A Century of Canadian Art, Tate Gallery, London, 1938; World's Fair, New York, NY, 1939; *Pintura Canadense Contemporanea*, Rio de Janeiro, Brazil, 1944; *UNESCO ... Exposition internationale d'art moderne, peinture graphique et décoratif, architecture*, Musée d'Art Moderne, Paris, France, 1946; Contemporary Canadian Painting, Canadian Club, New York, 1948.

COLLECTIONS IN WHICH REPRESENTED
Art Gallery of Ontario, Toronto; London Public Library and Art Museum, Ont.; National Gallery of Canada; National Gallery of South Australia, Adelaide, Australia; Winnipeg Art Gallery, Man.; Owens Museum, Mount Allison University.

WRITINGS
CONTRIBUTED: To publications of the Ontario Society of Artists.

PARLOW, Kathleen   1890-1963
Violinist; b. 1890 in Calgary, Alta.; d. 1963 in Oakville, Ont.

EDUCATION
Privately educated; studied violin with Henry

Holmes, San Francisco, Calif., 1895–?; violin and chamber music with Leopold Auer, Imperial Conservatory, St. Petersburg (now Leningrad), Russia, 1906.

CAREER
First command performance before Queen Alexandra, London, England, 1905; Festival of Russian Music, Belgium, guest soloist 1906; formal debut, Berlin, Germany, 1908; guest soloist with numerous orchestras, e.g. Berlin Philharmonic, London Symphony, Sir Henry Woods Queen's Hall in London, Colonne in Paris, Vienna Philharmonic, Scandinavian Symphony, St. Petersburg and Moscow Symphony, Toronto Symphony, Boston Symphony; toured extensively in Europe, the Far East, and North America; directed several chamber music groups 1929–?; Royal Conservatory of Music, Toronto, teacher 194? –?, annual lecture recitals; University of Western Ontario, annual lecture recitals; McGill Conservatorium of Music, Montreal, PQ, lecture recitals, Feb. 1940; South Mountain String Quartet, Pittsfield, Mass., first violinist summer 1941; Canadian Trio, co-founder with Sir Ernest MacMillan and Zara Nelsova (q.v.) 1941; Canadian Concert Series, Toronto, soloist 1942-43; Parlow String Quartet, founder c.1943, recitalist until 1959; played the Guarnerius del Gesù violin.

AWARDS, HONOURS
Gifts from the royal families of Great Britain, Norway, Rumania, Russia, China, Japan; University of Alberta National award in music, 1956.

PATRY, Pierre* 1933–
Film director and producer; b. 2 Nov. 1933 in Hull, PQ; son of Joseph and Alda (Lamoureux) Patry; m. Agathe Guitor 28 Aug. 1954; children: Johanne b. 16 Aug. 1955, Marc b. 26 May 1957, Stéphanne b. 30 May 1960, Sylvain b. 1 Apr. 1963.

EDUCATION
Attended St. Paul primary school, Aylmer, PQ, 1940-48; Collège St. Laurent, Montréal, PQ, 1948-49; Collège Marie-Médiatrice, Hull, 1949-54; University of Ottawa, 1954-55.

RELIGION
Roman Catholic.

HOME
6th Ave., Vaudreuil sur le Lac, PQ.

OFFICE
Cultural Centre, Cité des Jeunes, Vaudreuil, PQ.

CAREER
CKCH Radio, Hull, actor, director, and announcer 1951-53; CBC, Ottawa, Ont. and Montreal, actor, scriptwriter, and announcer 1953-68; National Film Board of Canada, Montreal, director and producer 1957-65; toured and lectured on film throughout eastern Canada since 1959; travelled extensively in Europe 1962–; Cooperatio Film Company Inc., Montreal, co-founder, director, producer, and manager 1963–; Dominion Drama Festival, governor 1967; Cultural Centre, Cité des Jeunes, Vaudreuil, director 1967–.

MEMBER
Association Canadienne des Producteurs de Films du Québec; Association Professionnelle des Cinéastes (administrator, 1968); Canadian Amateur Theatre Association (founder and president, 1966-68); Canadian Film-Library; Cinémathèque Canadienne; FCCQ (Montreal region, president); Society of Artists; Society of Film Makers; Syndicat Général du Cinéma et de la Télévision; Union des Artistes de Montréal.

AWARDS, HONOURS
St. Jean-Baptiste award, 1953; honorary medal of the city of Ottawa, 1957; Conseil des Arts, 1965, 1966, and 1967; Canada Council grant, 1966/67.

FILMS
Co-directed *Panoramique* (National Film Board, 1957), *Le monde du travail* (National Film Board, 1957); wrote and directed *La roulette* (National Film Board, 1957), *Germaine Guèvremont, écrivain* (National Film Board, 1958), *Les petites soeurs* (National Film Board, 1959), *Collège contemporain* (National Film Board, 1960); *La main* (National Film Board, 1960); directed, produced, and co-authored *Louis-Hyppolite Lafontaine* (National Film Board, 1961); co-directed *Centres de loisir* (National Film Board, 1961); wrote and directed *Petit discours de la méthode* (National Film Board, 1962); directed *Luciano* (National Film Board, 1962); directed and produced *Il y eut un soir, il y eut un matin* (National Film Board, 1963); directed, produced, and co-authored *Trouble-fête* (Cooperatio, 1963; award, Cannes Film Festival, France, 1964; honourable mention, Montreal International Film Festival, 1964); wrote and directed *Une femme pour les autres* (National Film Board, 1964); wrote, directed, and produced *La corde au cou* (Cooperatio, 1964; trophée meritas, Gala des Artistes, 1966); directed, produced, and co-authored *Cain* (Cooperatio, 1964; trophée meritas, Gala des Artistes, 1965); wrote and directed *Trois hommes au mille carre* (National Film Board, 1965; special mention, Montreal International Film Festival, 1966; prix du sous-secrétariat au tourisme espagnol, 1966; first prize, Seizième Semaine Internationale du Film Touristique, Brussels, Belgium, 1966; first prize, Canadian Tourist Association, Toronto, Ont., 1966); directed and produced *Délivrez-nous du mal* (Cooperatio, 1965), *Poussière sur la ville* (Cooperatio, 1965); directed *Entre la mer et l'eau douce* (Cooperatio, 1966); co-directed *Candidat-gouverneur Milton Shapp* (Cooperatio, 1966); directed and co-produced *A great big thing* (Cooperatio, 1966).

WRITINGS
L'imperatore si Roma, Rome, Italy; *La poste* (screenplay, produced National Film Board, 1960); *Le grand duc* (radio play; produced Radio Canada, 1962); *Rue de l'Anse* (radio play; produced Radio Canada, 1963-64).

PATTERSON, Harry Thomas
see PATTERSON, Tom

PATTERSON, Tom* 1920–
(Harry Thomas Patterson)
Director public relations; b. 11 June 1920 in Stratford, Ont.; son of Harry and Lucinda (Whyte) Patterson; m. Dorothy W. Hoyle 25 Mar. 1948 (marriage dissolved); m. Patricia Scott; children: (first marriage) Robert, Penelope Margot, Timothy John Cecil; (second marriage) Lucy Ann, Lyle.
EDUCATION
Attended Avon School and Collegiate Vocational School in Stratford; Trinity College, University of Toronto, BA, 1948.
RELIGION
Presbyterian.
HOME:
140 Norman St., Stratford, Ont.
CAREER
Canadian Dental Corps, 1939-45, sergeant; *Civic administration magazine*, associate editor; Stratford, Ont. Festival, founder and general manager 1952, director of planning 1954-66, director of public relations 1966-69, consultant 1969–; Canadian Players, Toronto, Ont., co-founder 1954; West Indian Festival of the Arts, co-ordinator 1958; Canadian Theatre Exchange, founder 1960; National Theatre School of Canada, Montreal, PQ, founder, director, and first chairman of board of governors 1960-61; Dawson City Festival Foundation, Yukon, consultant 1961-62; Canada Council Centennial Committee, 1964-65.
MEMBER
Canadian Theatre Centre.
AWARDS, HONOURS
Canadian drama award; Canada Arts Council 2nd annual award; Canadian Council of Authors and Artists president's award, 1955; Canada Council grant for travel to and preparation of the West Indian Festival of the Arts, 1958; Medal of service of the Order of Canada, 1967.

PEDDIE, Francis Grove
see PEDDIE, Frank

PEDDIE, Frank 1897-1959
(Francis Grove Peddie)
Actor; b. 18 Feb. 1897 in Springfield, Fifeshire, Scotland; son of Francis Grove and Elizabeth (Wallace) Peddie; came to Canada in 1927 and settled in Toronto, Ont.; m. Lillian McNish 17 Aug. 1928; children: David b. 1 Feb. 1930, James b. 24 Nov. 1935; d. 20 July 1959 in Toronto.
EDUCATION
Attended Springfield Board School and Cupar secondary school in Scotland; St. Andrews University; Osgoode Hall Law School, Toronto, graduated 1932.
RELIGION
United Church.
CAREER
British Army, 1914-18, awarded MC; Indian Police Force; practised law in Toronto 1932-52; freelance actor 1927-58.
MEMBER
Arts and Letters Club.
THEATRE
Played in numerous productions, e.g. Mitrich in *Power of darkness* (Hart House Theatre, Toronto, 1934), Nicola in *Arms and the man* (Hart House, 1934), Casalonga in *His widow's husband* (Hart House, 1935), Dr. Paddy Cullen in *The doctor's dilemma* (1936), Captain Boyle in *Juno and the paycock* (New Play Society, Toronto, c.1947), *Salad days*, title role in *Socrates* (Jupiter Theatre, Toronto, 1952), Father in *The blood is strong* (Ryerson Polytechnic Institute, Toronto, 1954), David McBane in *The glass cage* (Crest Theatre, Toronto, 1957; Piccadilly, London, England, 26 Apr. 1957).
FILM
Narrator in *Newfoundland scene* (Crawley Films, 1950; Canadian film of the year, 1951).
RADIO
Played in numerous CBC productions, e.g. *Down dairy lane*, Lord Steyne in *Vanity Fair*, Ebenezer in *Kidnapped*, title role in *The black bonspiel of Wullie MacCrimmon* ("Stage"), title role in *Dr. Dogbody's leg*, title role in *Macbeth*, Parson Manders in *Ghosts* ("Wednesday night"), "The family doctor" (series, 1934), *Forgotten footsteps* (serial, 1936-37), Thomas Craig in *The Craigs* ("Farm forum," 1939-58), "Stage" (series, 1944-58), Old Man Gatenby in "Jake and the kid" (series, 1944-46), Wardle in *Pickwick papers* ("Stage," 1948/49), Colin Glencannon in *Duggan's dew* (1950), title role in *Socrates* (1953), *The ancient mariner* (1955).
TELEVISION
Played in several CBC productions, e.g. Mr. McGarrity in *Maggie Muggins* (serial), Captain Boyle in *Juno and the paycock*, Father in *The blood is strong* (1954).

PEGASUS, pseud.
see BENSON, Nathaniel Anketell Michael

PELLAN, Alfred* 1906–
(Alfred Pelland)
Artist; b. 16 May 1906 in Quebec, PQ; son of

Alfred and Maria-Regina (Damphousse) Pelland;
m. Madeleine Poliseno 23 July 1949.

EDUCATION
Attended École de Limoilou (Frères du Sacré-
Coeur), Québec; École des Beaux-Arts, Montréal,
PQ, 1920-25; studied under Lucien Simon,
École Supérieure des Beaux-Arts de Paris, France,
1926-c.1930; attended Grande Chaumière and
Académie Colarossi, Paris, 1927-28.

HOME
649 Boul. des Mille Iles, Ville Auteuil, Laval, PQ.

CAREER
Travelled to Paris on a scholarship 1926, studied
for four years, and remained in France to work on
his own; visited Quebec in 1936; travelled to Italy
in 1929 and Greece in 1936; returned to Canada
1940; took a studio in Montreal, 1941; École des
Beaux-Arts, Montréal, teacher 1943-52; illustrated
Iles de la nuit (poems), by Alain de Grandbois, L.
Parizeau, 1944; official representative of Canada
at the Chicago Art Institute, Ill., 1945; designed
costumes, sets, and properties for Madeleine et Pierre, Monument National, Montréal, 1944-45; illustrated Voyage d'Arlequin, by E. de Grandmount,
Les Cahiers de la File Indienne, 1946; designed costumes, sets, properties, and make-up for Twelfth
night, Théâtre du Gesù, Montréal, 1946; moved
to Sainte-Rose, Laval, 1950; travelled to Paris 1952
and worked there till 1955; returned to Sainte-Rose
in 1956; Arts Centre, Ste. Adèle, PQ, teacher, summer 1957; designed curtain for the Montreal theatre
Ballet, 1957; Canada Council conference, Kingston,
Ont., visual art panel member, 1957; Quebec Arts
Council member 1961, resigned in 1962; lectured
at the National Gallery of Canada, Ottawa, Ont.,
1960 and Montreal Museum of Fine Arts, 1961;
illustrates for advertising, etc.; International Jury,
Paris Fourth Biennial Exhibition, member, 1965;
designed costumes and decors for Twelfth night,
(Stratford, Ont. Festival, 1967).

COMMISSIONS
Painting, Canadian Embassy in Rio de Janeiro,
Brazil; painting, Tétrault Shoe Ltd., Montreal;
fluorescent painting, late M. Jean Désy, Canada;
painting, Musée National d'Art Moderne, Paris;
mosaic, City Centre Building, Montreal, 1957;
mosaic, École Saint-Patrice, Granby, PQ, 1958;
ceramic and mosaic, three murals for the Mirons,
Montreal, 1962; painting, Winnipeg Airport, Man.,
1963; stained glass, Place des Arts, Montréal, 1963;
stained glass, Church of Saint-Théophile, Laval-
Ouest, 1964; painting, National Library & Archives, Ottawa, 1967.

MEMBER
Société d'Art Contemporain; Prisme d'Yeux.

AWARDS, HONOURS
First prizes with medals for painting, design,
sculpture, sketching, advertising, anatomy, École
des Beaux-Arts, Québec, 1920-25; first Province

of Quebec bursary to Paris, 1926-30; first prize for
painting, École des Beaux-Arts de Paris, Atelier
Simon, 1926; first prize in poster competition for
"Kiwanis Frolics Program," Quebec, 1926; first
prize at First Great Exhibition of Mural Art in
Paris, 1935; first prize for painting at the 65th
Annual Spring Exhibition, Montreal Museum of
Fine Arts, 1948; first prize at Province of Quebec
competition, 1948; Royal Society of Canada
bursary, 1952-53; first prize, Canadian mural competition for the City Centre Building, Montreal,
1957; Canada Council senior fellowship, 1958;
National Award in Painting and Related Arts from
University of Alberta, 1959; Canada Council
medal, 1965; Companion of the Order of Canada,
1967; Centennial medal, 1967.

EXHIBITIONS
ONE-MAN: Académie Ranson, Paris, 1935;
Galerie Jeanne Bûcher, Paris, 1939; Musée du
Québec, PQ, 1940; Montreal Museum of Fine
Arts, 1940; Galerie Bignou, New York, NY, 1942;
Galerie Municipale, Québec, 1942; Galerie l'Atel-
ier, Ottawa, 1952; Art Gallery of Toronto, Ont.,
(Archambault and Pellan), 1952; Coq Liban, Paris,
1954; Cercle Paul Valery, Paris, 1954; Musée
National d'Art Moderne, Paris, 1955; Hall of
Honour of the City Hall, Montreal, 1956; Laing
Galleries, Toronto, 1957; Galerie Denyse Delrue,
Montréal, 1958 and 1960; Robertson Galleries,
Ottawa, 1960; National Gallery of Canada;
Montreal Museum of Fine Arts; Art Gallery of
Toronto, 1960-1961; Roberts Gallery, Toronto,
1961 and 1964; Galerie Libre, Montréal, 1963;
Kitchener-Waterloo Art Gallery, Ont., 1964; Sher-
brooke-Art, Domaine Howard, Sherbrooke, PQ,
1964; Rodman Hall, St. Catharines and District
Arts Council, Ont., 1964; Winnipeg Art Gallery,
1968.
GROUP: Represented in group exhibitions held
in Canada including group exhibitions of Indépendants, Société d'Art Contemporain, Canadian
Group of Painters, Canadian National Exhibition,
Montreal Museum of Fine Arts Spring Show,
Winnipeg Show; represented in group exhibitions
organized by National Gallery of Canada, including
second, third, and sixth Biennial of Canadian Painting, 1957, 1959, and 1965; Galerie Beaux-Arts,
Paris, 1933; Salon d'Automne, Paris, 1934; Salon
des Tuileries, Paris, 1935; Galerie des Quatre-Che-
mins, Paris, 1935; Galerie Bernheim, Paris, 1936;
Galerie de Paris, 1936; Galerie de l'Équipe, Paris,
1936; Galerie Joseph Barra, Paris, 1936; Exposition des Surindépendants, Paris, 1937 and subsequent years; Galerie "Au Carrefour," Paris, 1937;
Galerie Gilliet Pierre Worms, Paris, 1938; Galerie
SV, Prague, Czecho-Slovakia, 1938; Galerie Montaigne, Paris, 1938; Group exhibition, The Hague,
The Netherlands, 1938; Group exhibition at 41
Grosvenor Square, London, England, 1938; Group

exhibition at 9 boul. Montparnasse, Paris, 1938; Galerie No. 14, rue des Beaux-Arts, Paris, 1939; Museum of Modern Art, Washington, DC, 1939; Contemporary Painting in Canada, Addison Gallery of American Art, Andover, Mass., 1942; 1942; Pan-American exhibition, Boston, Mass., 1942; Pan-Canadian exhibition of the Contemporary Art Society, Morse Gallery of Art, Winter Park, Fla., 1942; Group of Canadian painters, Rio de Janeiro, 1944; Canadian Art Group, Yale University Art Gallery, 1944; *La Province de Québec*, Women's International Exhibition of Arts and Industries, Madison Square Garden, New York, 1945; *Premier Salon des Réalités Nouvelles*, Palais de New York, Paris, 1946; UNESCO, *Exposition Internationale d'Art Moderne*, Musée d'Art Moderne, Paris, 1946; *Exposition Internationale de la XXVIe Biennale*, Venice, Italy, 1952; *IIe Mostra Inernazionele de Bianco e Nero*, Lugano, Switzerland, 1952; Canadian Art for Israel, Bezalel Museum, Jerusalem, 1953; *Dixième Salon de Mai*, Musée Municipal d'Art Moderne, Paris, 1954; *Art Contemporain au Canada*, Palais des Beaux-Arts, Brussels, Belgium, 1958; *Primera Bienal Interamericana de Pintura y Grabado*, Instituto Nacional de Bellas Artes, Secreteria de Educacion Publica, Mexico, 1958; Dallas Museum for Contemporary Arts, A Canadian Portfolio, 1958, Tex.; *Moderne Canadese Schilderkunst*, Utrecht Central Museum, The Netherlands, 1958; *Moderne Canadese Schilderkunst*, Groningen Museum, The Netherlands, 1958; *Art Contemporain au Canada*, Musée Rath, Geneva, Switzerland; *Zeitgenossische Kunst in Kanada,* Walraf-Richartz Museum, Cologne, Germany; 1959; *Nowoczesne Malarstwo Kanadyjskie*, Muzeum Narodowe w Warszawie, Poland, 1963; *Festival des Deux Mondes*, Spoleto, Italy, 1963; Fifteen Canadian Artists, organized by Canadian Advisory Committee, Canada Council, Museum of Modern Art, New York, for circulation in USA, 1963; *5 Peintres Canadiens*, Musée Galliera, Paris, 1963-64; Canadian Painting 1939-63, Tate Gallery, London, England, 1964.

COLLECTIONS IN WHICH REPRESENTED
Musée National d'Art Moderne, Paris; Musée de Grenoble, France; Musée du Québec; National Gallery of Canada; Montreal Museum of Fine Arts; Art Gallery of Ontario, Toronto; Lord Beaverbrook Art Gallery, Fredericton, NB; Hamilton Art Gallery, Ont.; Edmonton Art Gallery, Alta.; Kitchener-Waterloo Art Gallery, Ont.; Dalhousie Art Gallery, Halifax, NS; Musée d'Art Contemporain, Montréal; Willistead Art Gallery, Windsor, Ont.; Galerie Jeanne Bûcher, Paris.

PELLAND, Alfred
see PELLAN, Alfred

PELLETIER, Denise* 1928–
Actress; b. 22 May 1928 in St. Jovite, Terrebonne, PQ; daughter of Albert and Reine (Vaugeois) Pelletier; m. Basil Zarov 25 Jan. 1958; children: Stéphane b. 29 Nov. 1959.

HOME
9779 boul. Lasalle, Ville Lasalle, PQ.

CAREER
Started acting in radio plays; L'Équipe, Les Compagnons de Saint-Laurent, Théâtre du Nouveau Monde, Théâtre du Rideau Vert, Théâtre de l'Égrégore, Montréal, actress; Manitoba Theatre Centre, Winnipeg, actress; travelled for one year in the Congo.

MEMBER
Union des Artistes de Montréal.

AWARDS, HONOURS
Radio and television Queen, 1955; Best Television Actress, 1956.

THEATRE
Played in numerous productions, e.g. title role in *Saint Joan, Un caprice* (Compagnons), *Iphigénie* (Théâtre Gesù, Montréal), Duchesse in *Leocadia* (Compagnons, 1946), *Les parents terribles* (Monument National, Montréal, 1947), Agrippine in *Britannicus* (Compagnons, Jan. 1949), *La cathédrale* (Monument National, 1950), *Polichinelle* (Montreal, 1950), *Célimare le bien-aimé* (Nouveau Monde, 1951), Germaine in *Tit-coq* (North American tour, 1951), *L'avare* (Nouveau Monde, 1951), *La folle* (Montreal Repertory Theatre, 1953), *Philippe et Jonas* (Nouveau Monde, 1953/54), *La fontaine de Paris* (Nouveau Monde, 1953/54), *Le printemps de la Saint-Martin* (Théâtre Anjou, Montréal, 1954), title role in *Athalie* (Nouveau Monde, Montreal Festival, 1956), *L'échange* (Nouveau Monde, 1957), *L'oeil du peuple* (Nouveau Monde, 1957), *Balmareda* (Théâtre de Percé, PQ, 1958?), *Florence* (La Comédie Canadienne, Montréal, 1960), Béline in *Le malade imaginaire* (Nouveau Monde, Stratford, Ont. Festival, 18 Aug. 1958), *Les trois farces* (Nouveau Monde, Stratford, Ont. Festival, 1958), *La danse de mort* (Nouveau Monde, 1964), Madame Rosepettle in *Le placard* (l'Égrégore, 30 Nov. 1965), title role in *Mère Courage* (Nouveau Monde, Jan. 1966), Alice in *Dance of death* (Stratford, Ont. Festival, 1966), Queen Isabel in *Henry V* (Stratford, Ont. Festival, 1966), Duchess of Gloucester in *Henry VI* (Stratford, Ont. Festival, 1966), *O Dad, poor Dad* (l'Égrégore, 1966), *The blue bird* (Rideau Vert, 1967), Nicole in *Le bourgeois gentilhomme* (Nouveau Monde, National Centennial Tour, 1967; Expo 67, Montreal), Arkadina in *The seagull* (Stratford, Ont. Festival, 23 July 1968), *Ce soir on improvise* (Rideau Vert, 16 Oct. 1968).

RADIO
Played in several productions, e.g. Annie Green-

wood in *Un homme et son péché* (CBC, 1950), title role in *Medea*.

TELEVISION

Played in many productions, e.g. Cécile in *La famille Plouffe* (serial, CBC, 1956-57), Alice in *La danse de mort, L'échange* (1960).

PELLETIER, Wilfrid 1896—

Conductor; b. 20 June 1896 in Montreal, PQ; son of Elzear and Zelire Pelletier; m. Queena Mario 1925 (marriage dissolved 1936); m. Rose Bampton 24 May 1937; children: Camille, François.

EDUCATION

Studied music with his father, 1903-14; piano with Isidore Philipp, harmony with Rousseau, harmony with Widor, opera tradition with Bellaique in Paris, France, 1914-17.

HOME

322 E. 57th St., New York NY, USA.

OFFICE

Ministère des Affaires Culturelles, Québec, PQ.

CAREER

Montreal Opera, assistant conductor 1913-14; Metropolitan Opera Association, New York, accompanist and coach 1917, assistant conductor 1922-32, principal conductor 1932—; Ravinia Opera Company, Chicago, Ill., conductor summers 1921-31; San Francisco Opera Company, Calif., conductor 1921-31; Les Concerts Symphoniques de Montréal, founder and conductor 1934-38; Societé des Festivals de Montréal, founder and conductor 1936; toured S. Africa 1939; Montreal Symphony Orchestra, conductor; Conservatoire de Musique et d'Art Dramatique, Montréal, director 1942-61; Quebec Symphony Orchestra, conductor 1951—; New York Philharmonic children's concerts, conductor 1953-57; Ministère des Affaires Culturelles, Québec, director of music 1961—; Jeunesses Musicales du Canada, national president 1968—.

AWARDS, HONOURS

Quebec government scholarship for study in Europe, 1914; DMus from University of Montreal, 1936; DMus from Laval University; DMus from New York College of Music; Legion of Honour, France; Companion of the Order of St. Michael and St. George; Christian den Tiendes Friheds Meds, Denmark; Canada Council medal, 1961-62; Companion of the Order of Canada, 1967; DMus from University of Ottawa, 1967.

THEATRE

Conductor of all major operas especially by French and Italian composers (Metropolitan Opera Company, 1922–).

FILM

Conducted *Big broadcast of 1938* (Paramount, 1938); documentary film on his work (National Film Board of Canada, 1960).

RADIO

Numerous appearances on North American networks in series, e.g. "Simmons hour," "Packard hour," "Firestone program"; founded and conducted Metropolitan Opera series "Auditions of the air" (1934-46); conducted "Talent festival" (CBC, 1966-67); numerous appearances as guest conductor on CBC.

RECORDINGS

Many recordings, e.g. *Otello* by Verdi with Metropolitan Opera Company, Victor; *Requiem* by Gabriel Fauré with Montreal Festivals Orchestra and choir of Les Disciples de Massenet, Victor.

WRITINGS

CONTRIBUTED: "Orchestras" in *Music in Canada*, edited by E. MacMillan, University of Toronto, 1955.

PÉPIN, Clermont 1926—

(Jean Joseph Clermont Pépin)

Composer and music educator; b. 15 May 1926 in Saint-Georges-de-Beauce, PQ.

EDUCATION

Studied piano and harmony with Georgette Dionne in Quebec; Académie de Musique de Québec, diploma in piano, 1935; studied with Claude Champagne (*q.v.*) and Arthur Letondal in Montréal, PQ; Laval University, diploma, 1938, MusB; studied with Rosario Scalero and Jeanne Behrend, Curtis Institute, Philadelphia, Pa.; with Arnold Walter and Lubka Kalessa, Royal Conservatory of Music, Toronto, Ont., artist's diploma, 1949; studied composition with A. Honegger in Paris, France, 1949-51.

HOME

205A, Chemin de la Côte-Ste.-Catherine, Montréal, PQ.

CAREER

Formal debut, 1941; Conservatoire de Musique et d'Art Dramatique de la Province de Québec, teacher, director of studies 1952—.

MEMBER

CAPAC.

AWARDS, HONOURS

CAPAC special prize, 1937, three scholarships; Curtis Institute, scholarship, 1941; Quebec government scholarship, Prix d'Europe, 1949; Canadian Amateur Hockey Association scholarship, 1951; Laval University Centenary Composition Contest, first prize for *Guernica*, 1953; Radio Luxembourg, second prize for *Le rite du soleil noir*, 1955.

COMPOSITIONS

Andante, piano, 1939; *Petite étude no. 1*, piano, 1940, Western Music; *Thème et variations*, piano, 1940; *Pièce*, piano, 1943; *Concerto pour piano et orchestre no. 1*, 1946; *Petite étude no. 2*, piano, 1946, Western Music; *Toccato no. 1*, piano, 1946; *Variations symphoniques*, orchestra, 1947;

Petite étude no. 3, piano, 1947, Western Music; *Thème et variations no. 2*, piano, 1947; *Sonate*, piano, 1947; *Adagio*, string orchestra, 1947-56; *Symphonie no. 1*, 1948; *Quatuor à cordes no. 1*, 1948, first performed 1948 in Rochester, NY, recorded by Kathleen Parlow String Quartet; *Concerto pour piano et orchestre no. 2*, 1949; *Cycle Éluard*, song cycle, soprano and piano, 1949; *Nocturne*, piano and strings, 1950; *Petite étude no. 4*, piano, 1950; *Passacaille*, organ, 1950; *Suite pour piano*, 1950; *Étude Atlantique*, piano, 1950; *Nocturne pour piano*, 1950; *Le cantique des cantiques*, cantata, choir, and string orchestra, 1950; *Guernica*, orchestra, 1952, Canadian Music Centre, first performed 1953 in Quebec under Wilfrid Pelletier; *Les portes de l'enfer*, ballet suite, 1953; *Petite étude no. 5*, piano, 1954; *Deux pièces*, piano, 1956; *L'oiseau-phoénix*, ballet, 1956; *Le malade imaginaire*, incidental music, 1956; *Suite pour "La légende dorée,"* piano, 1956; *Musique pour Athalie*, woodwinds and brass, 1956; *Quatuor à cordes no. 2*, or *Variations*, 1956, first performed 1957 in Montreal by Montreal String Quartet; *Symphonie no. 2*, chamber orchestra, 1957, recorded by RCA Victor CC 1007 with Orchestre des Petites Symphonies; *Fantaisie*, string orchestra, 1957, also for tenor solo, choir, and orchestra, 1957; *Le porte-rêve*, ballet suite, 1957; *Mouvement*, choir and orchestra, 1958; *Quatuor à cordes no. 3*, or *Adagio et fugue*, 1959, first performed 1959 at Saskatoon Music Festival, Sask., recorded by Columbia ML 5764 with Canadian String Quartet; *Trio*, violin, cello, and piano, 1959; *Quatuor à cordes no. 4*, or *Hyperboles*, 1960, first performed 1960 in Montreal by Montreal String Quartet; *Hymn to the north wind*, cantata, tenor and orchestra, 1960; *Monologue*, orchestra, 1961, first performed in Montreal by Orchestre des Petites Symphonies under Roland Leduc, recorded by CBC Symphony Orchestra under Alexander Brott; *L'heure éblouissante*, incidental music, 1961; *Toccata no. 3*, piano, 1961; *Nombres pour deux pianos et orchestre*, 1962, recorded; *Three miniatures*, school orchestra, 1963; *Chants de Buchenwald*, contralto, 1964; *Danse frénétique*, piano, 1966, recorded by RCA Victor CC 1022 with Malcolm Troup; *Symphonie no. 3*, or *Quasars*, orchestra, 1967, first performed 7 Feb. 1967 in Montreal by Orchestre Symphonique de Montréal, commissioned by Orchestre Symphonique de Montréal for Canada's centennial; *Pièces de circonstance*, i.e. *Fanfare*, tenor and winds, and *L'oiseau gai*, school choir and winds, 1967.

PÉPIN, Jean Joseph Clermont
see PÉPIN, Clermont

PERRAULT, Pierre
Author. Does not wish to be included.

PERRÉARD, Suzanne Louise Butler
see BUTLER, Suzanne Louise

PETER, John Desmond* 1921–
Author; b. 8 Oct. 1921 in Queenstown, Cape Province, South Africa; son of Edward Frederick and Leila Hedwig (Lehman) Peter; m. Barbara Mary Girdwood 6 Dec. 1946; came to Canada in 1950 and settled in Winnipeg, Man.; children: Jonathan William b. 11 Aug. 1948, Christopher Justin b. 6 Feb. 1950, Katherine Mary b. 24 May 1953, Nicholas Michael b. 16 Sept. 1955, Stephanie Joan Louise b. 28 Nov. 1960.
EDUCATION
Attended Queen's College, Queenstown, 1929-38; Rhodes University, South Africa, BA, 1939-42, LL B 1944, D Litt; Gonville and Caius College, University of Cambridge, MA, 1952.
RELIGION:
Agnostic.
HOME
3950 Telegraph Bay, Victoria, BC.
OFFICE
English Department, University of Victoria, Victoria, BC.
CAREER
South African Artillery, 1943, gunner; University of Manitoba, associate professor and professor of English 1950-61; University of Victoria, associate professor of English 1961-62, professor 1962–; University of Wisconsin, visiting professor 1964/65, University of Oxford, Commonwealth visiting professor 1966/67; *Malahat review*, co-founder and co-editor, 1967–.
AWARDS, HONOURS
Hugh LeMay Fellow at Rhodes University, 1957/58; $10,000 Doubleday Canadian prize novel award for *Along that coast*, 1964.
WRITINGS
Complaint and satire in early English literature, Clarendon, 1956; *A critique of Paradise lost*, Columbia, 1960; *Along that coast* (novel) Doubleday, 1964; *Take hands at winter* (novel) Doubleday, 1967.
CONTRIBUTED: Poetry and articles to *A book of South African verse*, Oxford, 1959; *Tamarack review, Maclean's, London magazine, Encounter.*
WORK IN PROGRESS: Novels, short stories.

PETERSON, Margaret* 1902–
Artist; b. 3 June 1902 in Seattle, Wash.; daughter of Edwin R. and Ellen Charlotte (Larson) Peterson; m. Howard O'Hagan 6 Jan. 1937; came to Canada in 1952 and settled on Vancouver Island, BC.
EDUCATION
Attended Seward Grammar School, Seattle, 1908-16; attended Broadway High School, Seattle, 1916-20; studied under Hans Hoffman and Worth

Ryder, University of California, Berkeley, AB, 1923-26, MA, 1929-32; studied with Vaclau Vytlacil and André Lhôte, Paris, France, 1931-32; studied mosaic with Professor Renato Signorini, Academie de Bella Arte, Ravenna, Italy, 1964.

HOME
Victoria, BC.

OFFICE
(temporary) Lingua (per Messina) Isole Eolie, Italy.

CAREER
University of California, Berkeley, instructor 1928-37, assistant professor of art 1937-47, associate professor 1947-50; travelled and worked in Mexico and Central America, 1934, 1943, 1949, 1951, and 1958; illustrated "The man on the flying trapeze" (song), *Vanity Fair*, 1935; travelled and worked in BC summers of 1935-39, 1943, 1946, and 1947-48; lived summer of 1946, 1947-48 and 1951 at Green Point, Cowichan Bay, BC, settled at Green Point 1953-56; lived in Emily Carr's studio, Victoria, BC; travelled from Sweden to Egypt, 1963-68; did research in Egypt, 1967; temporarily in Sicily, Italy.

COMMISSIONS
Mosaic panel, McPherson Library, University of Victoria, 1964.

MEMBER
San Francisco Art Association, 1935-55; British Columbia Society of Artists (elected, 196?; resigned, 1965).

AWARDS, HONOURS
Tansig travelling fellowship, University of California, 1931-32; first prize, San Francisco Women Artists, 1936; purchase prize, San Francisco Art Association, 1942 and 1947; blue ribbon, Pacific Arts Festival, 1952; first prize, San Francisco Women Artists, 1952; Canada Council senior grant, 1963.

EXHIBITIONS
ONE-MAN: California Palace of the Legion of Honour, San Francisco, Calif., 1933 and 1960; Bibliotheca Nationale, Mexico, 1934; Henry Museum, Seattle, 1934; Paul Elder Gallery, San Francisco, 1934; Raymond and Raymond, San Francisco, 1945; San Francisco Art Museum, Civic Center, 1950 and 1958; New Gallery, Algonquin Hotel, New York, NY, 1951; Art Gallery of Greater Victoria, 1953, 1959, and 1962; Du Casse Studio, San Francisco, 1958; University of California, San Jose, 1958; The Point, Victoria, 1960; Art Gallery of the University of British Columbia, 1961; Monterey Peninsula Chapter, American Federation of Arts, Carmel, Calif., 1965.
GROUP: Represented in group exhibitions organized by National Gallery of Canada, Ottawa, Ont. including the fourth and fifth Biennial of Canadian Painting, 1961 and 1963; São Paulo Bienniale, Brazil, 1963.

COLLECTIONS IN WHICH REPRESENTED
San Francisco Art Museum; California Palace of the Legion of Honour, San Francisco; San Francisco California Art Institute; University of California, Berkeley; Art Gallery of Greater Victoria; Oakland Art Museum, Calif.; National Gallery of Canada; University of California, Cowell College and Stevenson College, Santa Cruz; Fathers of Confederation Memorial Building, Charlottetown, PEI; University of Victoria; McPherson Library, University of Victoria.

PEZZETTI, Emilia Cundari
see CUNDARI, Emilia

PHARIS, Gwen
see RINGWOOD, Gwendolyn Margaret Pharis

PICHER, Claude* 1927—
Artist; b. 30 May 1927 in Québec, PQ; son of Edouard Boisseau and Clémence Mathieu Picher.

EDUCATION
Attended Séminaire de Québec, PQ, 1939-43; Séminaire Joliette, Québec, 1943-45; studied with Jean Paul Lemieux, École des Beaux-Arts, Québec, 1945-46; studied on his own, 1946-47; studied with Julian Levi, New School of Social Research, New York, NY, 1948; studied with Coche de la Ferté, Philippe Stern, Jean Cassou, and Mme. Bouchot-Saupique, École du Louvre, Paris, France, 1948-49; studied with Déméter Galanis, École Nationale Supérieure des Beaux-Arts de Paris, 1948-49; studied with Albert Gleizes, St-Rémy de Province, 1949-50.

HOME
33, des Épinettes, Matane, PQ.

CAREER
Toured principal museums and art centres in France 1949; Musée du Québec, moniteur, helped with presentation of exhibitions 1950-54, director of exhibitions, surveyed department of restoration for sculpture and painting 1954-55, liaison officer with the Montreal Museum of Fine Arts, PQ, Hamilton Art Gallery, Ont., London Public Library and Art Museum, Ont., Willistead Library and Art Gallery, Windsor, Ont., Detroit Institute of Arts, Mich., and National Gallery of Canada, Ottawa, Ont., assistant curator 1963-64, editor of *Bulletin du Musée du Québec*; Concours Artistiques de la Province, secretary 1955-58; restoration work on historic sites and monuments for Commission des monuments et sites historiques de la Province and Musée du Québec; Conseil Canadien des Arts, secretary 1957-58; organized conferences in Québec, Montréal, and Toronto, Ont.; studied in Mexico and the Yucatan 1958; art critic for *Arts et pensée, Vie des arts, Revue des arts et lettres,* and on TV programs, e.g. *Idées en marche, Choc des idées,* and *Carrefour;* regular columns in

l'Événement-journal and *Soleil; Vie des arts* secrétaire de rédaction; *Canadian art,* correspondent for Québec; National Gallery of Canada, liaison officer, 1958-61; visited London, England, 1961; travelled to Italy and Greece; has devoted time solely to painting since 1964.

MEMBER
Royal Canadian Academy (Associate 1960); Société des Arts Plastiques de la Province de Québec (founder, 1955); Association des Anciens Boursiers du Gouvernement Français.

AWARDS, HONOURS
First prize for design, children's section, Exposition provinciale de Québec, 1941; first prize for design, adult section, Exposition provinciale de Québec, 1942; first prize for painting, second prize for design, Exposition provinciale de Québec, 1943; first and second prize for painting, Exposition provinciale de Québec, 1945; first prize for painting, Exposition provinciale de Québec, 1946; Québec government bursary for study in Europe, 1948/49 and 1949/50; Government of France bursary for study in France, 1948/49; Elisabeth T. Greenshields Memorial Foundation bursary, 1955/56; first prize for painting, Montreal Museum of Fine Arts Spring Show, 1956; Catherwood Foundation of Bryn Mawr College, Pa., for research in Mexico and Yucatan, 1958; Canada Council grants, 1961 and 1965.

EXHIBITION
ONE-MAN: Palais Montcalm (Galerie Municipale), Québec 1947; L'Atelier, Québec, 1952; Galerie Agnès Lefort, Montréal, 1955; Galerie La Boutique, Québec, 1957 and 1959; Montreal Museum of Fine Arts, 1958; Here & Now Gallery, Toronto, 1960; Roberts Gallery, Toronto, 1962 and 1964; Galerie Zannetin, Québec, 1964 and 1967; Musée du Québec, 1967.
GROUP: Represented in group exhibitions held in Canada since 1945 including annual exhibitions of Montreal Museum of Fine Arts; represented in group exhibitions organized by National Gallery of Canada, including the second Biennial of Canadian Painting, 1957; Second Paris International Biennial, Paris, 1962; Fifth Canadian Biennial of Painting, Commonwealth Institute, London, England, 1963.

COLLECTIONS IN WHICH REPRESENTED
Agnes Etherington Art Centre, Queen's University; National Gallery of Canada; Musée du Québec; Musée du Petit Séminaire de Québec, PQ; Art Gallery of Ontario, Toronto; Laval University; Beaverbrook Art Gallery, Fredericton, NB.

WRITINGS
CONTRIBUTED: Articles to *Arts et pensée, Vie des arts, Canadian art, Revue des arts et lettres, L'autorité* and *Le devoir.*

PILON, Jean-Guy* 1930—
Poet; b. 12 Nov. 1930 in Saint Polycarpe, PQ; son of Arthur and Alida (Besner) Pilon; m. Céline Chartier 1955; children: François b. 1956, Daniel b. 1957.

EDUCATION
Université de Montréal, LL L, 1954.
HOME
4222 Northcliffe, Montreal, PQ.
OFFICE
Canadian Broadcasting Corporation, PO Box 6000, Montreal, PQ.

CAREER
CBC, producer 1954, supervisor of cultural programs 1961—; Éditions de l'Hexagone, Montréal, 1953-60; Liberté, Montréal, founder 1959, board of directors 1959—; Rencontres des Écrivains du Canada, founder; Conseil des Arts du Québec 1961-67; travelled extensively.

MEMBER
PEN Club; Royal Society of Canada; Société des Écrivains canadiens.

AWARDS, HONOURS
Prix David for *Les cloîtres de l'été,* 1956; Canada Council grants, 1958, 1965/66, 1966/67, senior arts fellowship, 1960/61.

WRITINGS
La fiancée du matin, Amicitia, 1953; *Les cloîtres de l'été,* Hexagone, 1957; *La mouette et le large,* Hexagone, 1960; *Recours au pays,* Hexagone, 1961; *Pour saluer une ville,* Seghers, 1963; *Solange* (novel), Jour, 1966; *Comme eau retenue,* Hexagone, 1968.
CONTRIBUTED: Poetry to several anthologies, e.g. *Anthologie de la poésie canadienne-française,* edited by G. Sylvestre, Beauchemin, 1958; *Oxford book of Canadian verse in English and French,* edited by A.J.M. Smith, Oxford, 1960; articles, poems, and stories to *Canadian forum, Canadian literature, Culture, Liberté, Revue de l'Université Laval, Tamarack review.*

PILTCH, Bernie
Saxophonist; b. in Montreal, PQ.
EDUCATION
Attended school in Toronto.
HOME
19 Park Rd., Toronto 5, Ont.
CAREER
Benny Louis, Bert Niosi, and Bobby Gimby Bands, leading alto-saxophonist, 1930s and 1940s; CBC, studio musician; Norm Symonds Octet, saxophonist in 1956; Ron Collier Quintet, saxophonist c.1957—; Ron Collier Jazz Ensemble, alto-saxophonist in 1967.
MEMBER
Toronto Musicians Association.
CONCERT STAGE
Appeared with Norm Symonds Octet at Stratford,

Ont. Festival, 1956; with Ron Collier Jazz
Ensemble at Expo 67, Montreal, 18-21 July
1967.

TELEVISION
Featured artist "Cal Jackson show."

PLASKETT, Joseph Francis*   1918–
Artist; b. 12 July 1918 in New Westminster, BC;
son of Frank and Mary (Draper) Plaskett.

EDUCATION
Attended Sir Richard McBride primary school,
Sapperton, New Westminster; Duke of Con-
naught secondary school, New Westminster;
University of British Columbia, BA, 1939;
studied under P.V. Ustinov, F.A. Amess (*q.v.*),
J.L. Shadbolt (*q.v.*) and B.C. Binning,
Vancouver School of Art, BC, night school,
1940-42; studied under David Park, Clifford
Still, California School of Fine Arts, San
Francisco, 1946; studied under Hans Hofmann,
New York, NY, and Provincetown, Mass., 1947
and 1948; studied under Fernand Léger and
Jean Lombard, Paris, 1949 and 1950; attended
Slade School, London, England, 1951; studied
under William Stanley Hayter, Paris, 1953-54.

HOME
2 rue Pecquay, Paris 4, France.

CAREER
North Shore College, North Vancouver, BC,
teacher 1940-45; Coquitlam High School, BC,
teacher 1945-46; Winnipeg School of Art, Man.,
principal 1947-49; Vancouver School of Art,
night school teacher 1951-53 and 1956-57;
University of British Columbia, extension
division teacher 1955-57; has travelled extensively including Spain, Portugal, Morocco,
Tunisia, Italy, Ireland, Yugoslavia, Greece,
Turkey, Switzerland, and Austria; since 1949
has alternated residence between Paris and
British Columbia.

COMMISSIONS
Ballet decor for Winnipeg Ballet, 1949;
commissions for *Maclean's*; BC Centennial
painting.

MEMBER
British Columbia Society of Artists (elected,
*c.*1944); Canadian Group of Painters (elected,
*c.*1950).

AWARDS, HONOURS
Honourable mention for watercolor, BC Artists'
Exhibition, 1941; Winnipeg Art Gallery, 1952;
bronze medal, Vancouver Art Gallery Association, 1944; Emily Carr scholarship, 1946;
Canadian government overseas scholarship,
1953; Canadian Council award, 1967-68.

EXHIBITIONS
ONE-MAN: Vancouver Art Gallery, 1940,
1943, 1945, 1952, and 1956; Kamloops, BC,
1945; Saskatoon, Sask., 1945; Picture Loan
Society, Toronto, Ont., several shows between
1952 and 1960; New Design Gallery, Vancouver,
1955, 1957, 1960, 1963, and 1965; University
of British Columbia, 1960; Waddington Gallery,
Montreal, PQ, 1961 and 1964; Robertson
Gallery, Ottawa, Ont., 1962 and 1967; Little
Gallery, New Westminster, 1965; Griffiths
Gallery, Vancouver, 1968.

GROUP: Represented in group exhibitions
held in Canada since 1940; exhibitions
organized by National Gallery of Canada,
Ottawa, including the second, third, and
fourth Biennial of Canadian Painting, 1957,
1959, and 1961; Biennial of Graphic Art,
Bergamo, Italy, 1952; São Paulo Biennial,
Brazil, 1954; Five Canadian Painters, Galliera
Museum, Paris, 1963.

COLLECTIONS IN WHICH REPRESENTED
National Gallery of Canada; Vancouver Art
Gallery; Edmonton Art Gallery, Alta.; London
Public Library and Art Museum, Ont.; Beaver-
brook Gallery, Fredericton, NB; Winnipeg
Art Gallery; Art Gallery of Ontario, Toronto;
Sir George Williams University.

WRITINGS
CONTRIBUTED: Articles to *Canadian art*.

PLUMMER, Arthur Christopher Orme
see PLUMMER, Christopher

PLUMMER, Christopher*   1929–
(Arthur Christopher Orme Plummer)
Actor; b. 13 Dec. 1929 in Toronto, Ont.; son
of John and Isabella Mary (Abbott) Plummer;
m. Tammy Lee Grimes 19 Aug. 1956 (marriage
dissolved 1960); m. Patricia Audrey Lewis 4
May 1962; children: (first marriage) Amanda
Michael b. 23 Mar. 1957.

EDUCATION
Attended Montreal High School and Jennings
Private School in Montreal, PQ; studied
speech with Iris Warren and voice with C.
Herbert Caesari in London, England, 1964.

OFFICE
c/o Jane Broder, 40 E. 49th St., New York,
NY, 10017, USA.

CAREER
Open Air Playhouse, Shakesperian Society,
and Montreal Repertory Theatre, actor; Brae
Manor Theatre, Knowlton, PQ, actor; Stage
Society and Canadian Repertory Theatre,
Ottawa, Ont., actor 1950; Bermuda Repertory
Theatre, actor 1952; Jupiter Theatre, Toronto,
actor 1952/53; American Shakespeare Festival,
Stratford, Conn., actor 1955; Stratford, Ont.
Festival, actor 1956-58, 1960, 1962, 1967;
Royal Shakespeare (formerly Shakespeare
Memorial) Theatre Company, Stratford-upon-
Avon, England, actor 1961.

MEMBER
AEA; AFTRA; SAG; The Players; Garrick Club.

AWARDS, HONOURS

Theatre world award for Count Peter Zichy in *The dark is light enough*, 1954/55; *Evening standard* award for best actor as Henry II in *Beckett*, London, England, 1961.

THEATRE

Made professional debut as Lieut. Victor O'Leary in *John loves Mary* (Canadian Repertory Theatre, 1950); played in *The corn is green* (Canadian Repertory Theatre, 1950), *The Browning version* (Canadian Repertory Theatre, 1950), *Murder without crime* (Canadian Repertory Theatre, 1950), Old Mahon in *The playboy of the western world* (Bermuda Repertory Theatre, 1952), Gerard in *Nina* (Bermuda Repertory Theatre, 1952; American tour, 1953), Anthony Cavendish in *The royal family* (Bermuda Repertory Theatre, 1952), Ben in *The little foxes* (Bermuda Repertory Theatre, 1952), Duke Mantia in *The petrified forest* (Bermuda Repertory Theatre, 1952), Bernard Kersal in *The constant wife* (Bermuda Repertory Theatre, 1952), *Socrates* (Jupiter Theatre, 1952/53), *The lady's not for burning* (Jupiter Theatre, Jan. 1953), George Phillips in *The Starcross story* (Royale, New York, 13 Jan. 1954), Manchester Monaghan in *Home is the hero* (Booth, New York, 22 Sept. 1954), Count Peter Zichy in *The dark is light enough* (ANTA, New York, 23 Feb. 1955), Jason in *Medea* (ANTA, Théâtre Sarah Bernhardt, Paris, France, June 1955), Mark Antony in *Julius Caesar* (American Shakespeare Festival, 12 July 1955), Ferdinand in *The tempest* (American Shakespeare Festival, 1 Aug. 1955), Earl of Warwick in *The lark* (Longacre, New York, 17 Nov. 1955), title role in *Henry V* (Stratford, Ont. Festival, 1956; Stratford, Ont. Festival Company, Edinburgh Festival, Scotland, 1956), Narrator in *A soldier's tale* (New York City Center Opera Company, 16 Oct. 1956), Louis Rohen in *The night of the auk* (Playhouse, New York, 3 Dec. 1957), title role in *Hamlet* (Stratford, Ont. Festival, 1957), Sir Andrew Aguecheek in *Twelfth night* (Stratford, Ont. Festival, 1957), Bardolph in *Henry IV*, part I (Stratford, Ont. Festival, 1958), Benedick in *Much ado about nothing* (Stratford, Ont. Festival, 1958; Royal Shakespeare Company, 1961), Leontes in *The winter's tale* (Stratford, Ont. Festival, 1958), Nickles in *J.B.* (ANTA, New York, 11 Dec. 1958), Philip the bastard in *King John* (Stratford, Ont. Festival, 1960), Mercutio in *Romeo and Juliet* (Stratford, Ont. Festival, 1960), title role in *Richard III* (Royal Shakespeare Company, 1961), Henry II in *Beckett* (Aldwych, London, 11 July 1961), title role in *Macbeth* (Stratford, Ont. Festival, 1962), title role in

Cyrano de Bergerac (Stratford, Ont. Festival, 1962), title role in *Arturo Ui* (Lunt-Fontane, New York, 11 Nov. 1963), Pizzaro in *Royal hunt of the sun* (ANTA, New York, 26 Oct. 1965), Antony in *Antony and Cleopatra* (Stratford, Ont. Festival, 1967).

FILM

Played the Playwright in *Stage struck* (Buena Vista, 1958), Walt Murdoch in *Wind across the Everglades* (Warner Brothers, 1958), *The performer*, part II (National Film Board of Canada 0159050), *Mister Plummer* (National Film Board of Canada 0163013), Commodus in *The fall of the Roman Empire* (Paramount, 1964), Captain Von Trapp in *The sound of music* (Fox, 1964), Raymond Swann in *Inside Daisy Clover* (Warner Brothers, 1966), Field Marshall Rommel in *The night of the generals* (Horizon Pictures, 1966), Eddie Chapman in *Triple cross* (Cineurop, 1967); co-produced and played title role in *Oedipus rex* (Paramount, 1967).

TELEVISION

Played Montano in *Othello* (CBC, 1952), *The light that failed* ("Studio I," 1953), title role in *Oedipus rex* ("Omnibus," CBS, 1956), Miles Hendon in *The prince and the pauper* ("Dupont show of the month," NBC, 1957), Soldier in *Little moon of Alban* ("Hallmark hall of fame," NBC, 1958), Doctor in *Johnny Belinda* ("Hallmark hall of fame," NBC, 1958), Thomas Mendip in *The lady's not for burning* ("Omnibus," CBS, 1958), Agamemnon and Orestes in *Oresteia* ("Omnibus," CBS, 1959), Helmer in *A doll's house* ("Hallmark hall of fame," NBC, 1959), Mike in *The Philadelphia story* ("Dupont show of the month," NBC, 1959), *Autocrat and son* ("American heritage," NBC, 1960), title role in *Captain Brassbound's conversion* ("Hallmark hall of fame," NBC, 1960), Rassendyl in *The prisoner of Zenda* ("Dupont show of the month," NBC, 18 Jan. 1961), Prince in *Time remembered* ("Hallmark hall of fame," NBC, 1961), *Accent* ("British Shakespeare Festival," CBS, 1961), title role in *Cyrano de Bergerac* ("Hallmark hall of fame," NBC, 1962), title role in *Hamlet* (BBC and Danish World Television; "Festival," CBC, 15 Apr. 1964), *Christopher Plummer* ("Telescope," CBC, 25 Sept., 2 Oct. 1964).

POIRIER, Gérard*   1930–

Actor; b. 5 Feb. 1930 in Montreal; son of Henri and Elzire (Cassivi) Poirier; m. Francine Montpetit 11 May 1957; children: Anne-Marie b. 24 May 1958, Catherine b. 1 Jan. 1961.

EDUCATION

Attended Saint-Paul-de-la-Croix, Montréal,

1937-45; École Supérieure Saint Viateur, Montréal, 1945-47; Séminaire Marie-Médiatrice, Montréal, 1947-50; Collège André Grasset, Montréal, 1950-51; École Normale Jacques Cartier, Montréal, 1951-52; BA, B Paed; studied French literature at Institut Alexandre and University of Montreal.

RELIGION
Roman Catholic.

HOME
3488 Marcil Ave., Montreal 28, PQ.

CAREER
Théâtre du Rideau Vert, Montréal, actor and permanent member; CBC, Montreal, actor; travelled extensively in Europe.

MEMBER
Union des Artistes de Montréal.

AWARDS, HONOURS
Trophée Méritas, best actor of the year, 1967.

THEATRE
Played Romeo in *Romeo and Juliet*, Sigismond in *La vie est un songe*, Pedro in *La reine morte*, *Dona Rosita* (Rideau Vert, 1957), *La magicienne en pantouffle* (Rideau Vert, 1957), Buckingham in *Les trois mousquetaires* (Théâtre Club, Montréal, 1958), Dorante in *Heureux stratagème* (Théâtre des Nations, Paris, France, 1963), Michel in *Une maison ... un jour* (Rideau Vert, 11 Sept. 1965), Thésée in *Le songe d'une nuit d'été* (Rideau Vert, 15 Sept. 1965), Romeo Daddi in *On ne sait comment* (Rideau Vert, 15 Nov. 1965), Dufausset in *Chat en poche* (Rideau Vert, 15 Feb. 1966), Verchinine in *Les trois soeurs* (Rideau Vert, 15 Apr. 1966); directed *Les portes claquent, Pas d'âge pour l'amour, L'ami de la famille, Chat en poche* (Rideau Vert, 15 Feb 1966), *La poudre aux yeux* (15 May 1967), *Partage de midi* (Rideau Vert, 15 Apr. 1968), *Ce soir on improvise* (Rideau Vert, 16 Oct. 1968).

RADIO
Played in numerous drama serials.

PRATT, Edwin John 1883-1964
(Ned Pratt)
Poet and teacher; b. 4 Feb. 1883 in Western Bay, Nfld.; son of John and Fanny Pitts (Knight) Pratt; m. Viola Leone Whitney 20 Aug. 1919; children: Mildred Claire, b. 18 Mar. 1921; d. 26 Apr. 1964 in Toronto, Ont.

EDUCATION
Methodist College, St. John's, Nfld., London matriculation, 1901-03; Victoria College, University of Toronto, BA, 1907-11, BD, 1913, Ph D, 1917.

RELIGION
United Church.

CAREER
Draper's apprentice, St. John's, 1898-1901; school teacher and student preacher in Moreton's Harbour, Clarke's Beach, Bell Island, and Portugal Cove, Nfld., 1903-07; University of Toronto, demonstrator and lecturer in psychology at University College 1911-17, associate professor of English at Victoria College 1919-33, professor 1933-53, head, professor emeritus 1953-64; *Canadian poetry magazine*, editor 1936-42; *Saturday night*, editorial board 1952.

MEMBER
Royal Society of Canada (elected fellow, 1930); Canadian Authors Association (honorary president, 1955-64).

AWARDS, HONOURS
Toronto award of merit; Governor General's literary award, 1937, 1949, 1952; Lorne Pierce medal, 1940; D Litt from University of Manitoba, 1945; Companion of the Order of St. Michael and St. George, 1946; D Litt from McGill University, 1949; LL D from Queen's University, 1949; DCL from Bishop's University, 1949; University of Alberta gold medal for literature, 1951; D Litt from University of Toronto, 1953; D Litt from Assumption University, 1957; D Litt from University of Western Ontario, 1957; Canada Council grant in recognition of 75th birthday, 1958, medal, 1961/62; D Litt from Memorial University, 1961.

WRITINGS
Studies of Pauline eschatology and its background (non-fiction), W. Briggs, 1917; *Rachel; a story of the sea in verse*, p.p., 1917; *Newfoundland verse*, Ryerson, 1923; *The witches' brew*, Selwyn & Blount, 1925; *Titans*, Macmillan, 1926; *The iron door, an ode*, Macmillan, 1927; *The Roosevelt and the Antinoe*, Macmillan, 1930; *Verses of the sea*, Macmillan, 1930; *Many moods*, Macmillan, 1932; *The Titanic*, Macmillan, 1935; *The fable of the goats and other poems*, Macmillan, 1937; *Brébeuf and his brethren*, Macmillan, 1940; *Dunkirk*, Macmillan, 1941; *Still life and other verse*, Macmillan, 1943; *Collected poems*, Macmillan, 1944; *They are returning*, Macmillan, 1945; *Behind the log*, Macmillan, 1947; *Ten selected poems*, Macmillan, 1947; *Towards the last spike*, Macmillan, 1952; *Here the tides flow*, Macmillan, 1962.

EDITED
Thomas Hardy's *Under the greenwood tree*, Macmillan, 1937; *Heroic tales in verse*, Macmillan, 1941.

CONTRIBUTED: Poetry and articles to many anthologies, e.g. *New harvesting; contemporary Canadian poetry, 1918-1938*, chosen by E.H. Bennett, Macmillan, 1938; *The book of*

Canadian poetry, edited by A.J.M. Smith, University of Chicago, 1943; *Twentieth century Canadian poetry*, edited by E. Birney, Ryerson, 1953; *Canadian poetry in English*, chosen by B. Carman and others, rev. & enl. ed., Ryerson, 1954; *The Penguin book of Canadian verse*, edited by R. Gustafson, Penguin, 1958; *The Oxford book of Canadian verse in English and French*, edited by A.J.M. Smith, Oxford, 1960; *Atlantic advocate, Canadian poetry magazine, Saturday night, Maclean's, Canadian author and bookman, University of Toronto quarterly, Contemporary verse, Queen's quarterly, Here and now.*

PRATT, Ned
see PRATT, Edwin John

PRÉFONTAINE, Claude
Actor and director.
HOME
5195 Brillon Ave., Montreal 260, PQ.
CAREER
MEMBER
Union des Artistes de Montréal.
THEATRE
Played in many productions, e.g. Baron Touzenbach in *Les trois soeurs* (Théâtre du Rideau Vert, Montréal, 15 Apr. 1966), *Retour des oies blanches* (La Comédie Canadienne, Montréal, 19 Oct. 1966), *Il est une saison* (La Comédie Canadienne, 18 Jan. 1967), *Le pendu* (Théâtre de l'Égrégore, Montréal, 10 Feb. 1968); directed *Jeanne et les juges* (La Nouvelle Compagnie Théâtrale, Montréal, Jan. 1966), *Don Juan* (La Nouvelle Compagnie Théâtrale, Mar. 1966).
RADIO
Played in several productions, e.g. Roger Morin in *Nineteen ninety-nine* (CBC, 7 June 1967).
TELEVISION
Played in several productions, e.g. *Les frères Karamazov* (CBC, 1960).

PRESSNELL, Constance Elizabeth
see BERESFORD-HOWE, Constance Elizabeth

PRÉVOST, André*   1934–
Composer; b. 1934 in Saint-Jérôme, PQ.
EDUCATION
Studied with Clermont Pépin (*q.v.*) and Jean Papineau-Couture, Conservatoire de Musique de la Province de Québec, to 1960; studied composition with Oliver Messiaen, Conservatoire de Paris, France, 1960–?; Henri Dutilleux, École Normale de Musique, Paris; Michel Philippot in Paris, June 1964.
HOME
234 Ave. Querbes, Outremont, Montréal 8, PQ.

CAREER
University of Montreal, professor of music in 1967.
MEMBER
BMI Canada; CAPAC.
AWARDS, HONOURS
Conservatoire de Musique de la Province de Québec, first prize in composition 1960; Quebec government scholarship, 1960; Canada Council arts scholarship, 1960/61; Prix d'Europe, for composition, 1963; Fondation Les Amis d'Art prize for *Fantasmes*, Nov. 1963; Montreal Symphony Orchestra prize for *Fantasmes*, Mar. 1964.
COMPOSITIONS
Musiques peintes, soprano and piano, 1955; *Quatuor no. 1*, 1958, first performed 1959 in Montreal at Sarah Fischer Concerts; *Mobiles*, flute, violin, viola, and cello, 1959, first performed 1962 in Paris on RTF broadcast, recorded on air-check tape; *Poème de l'infini*, percussion and strings, 1959-60; *Scherzo*, string orchestra, 1960; *Sonate pour violin et piano*, 1960-61, BMI Canada, first performed 1962 on CBC Montreal with Jacques Verdon and Gilles Manny, recorded by Baroque JA 19002 with the same performers; *Sonate pour violoncelle et piano*, 1962, first performed 1962 in Paris at Maison du Québec concert by Pierre Morin and Rachel Martel, recorded 1966 on air-check tape with Audrey Piggott and Robert Rogers; *Triptyque*, flute, oboe, and piano, 1962, first performed 1962 on Jeunesses Musicales du Canada tour by Gail Grimstead, Jacques Simard, and Gilles Manny, recorded on air-check tape with the same performers; *Fantasmes*, percussion and strings, 1963, recorded 1967 by RCA Victor LSC 2980 with Montreal Symphony Orchestra, commissioned by Montreal Symphony Orchestra; *Mouvement*, brass quintet, 1963, first performed 1964 in Quebec by Montreal Brass Quintet; *Terre des hommes*, three choirs, two narrators, and orchestra, 1967, first performed 29 Apr. 1967 in Montreal at the grand opening of Expo 67 by orchestra under Pierre Hétu, commissioned by Expo 67 for Canada's centennial; *Soleils couchants*, choir; *Diallèle*, orchestra, 1968, first performed 5 Dec. 1968 on CBC "Thursday music" with Toronto Symphony Orchestra, commissioned by CBC.

PURDY, Alfred Wellington*   1918–
Poet; b. 30 Dec. 1918 in Wooler, Ont.; son of Alfred W. and Eleanor Louise (Ross) Purdy; m. Eurithe M.J. Parkhurst 1 Nov. 1941; children: Alfred A. b. 1945.
EDUCATION
Attended Dufferin Public School in Trenton;

Albert College in Belleville, Ont.; Trenton Collegiate Institute.

HOME
134 Front St., Trenton, Ont.

CAREER
Mainly literary; RCAF, 1940-45.

AWARDS, HONOURS
Canada Council arts scholarship, 1960, senior arts fellowship, 1964/65, award, 1967/68; University of Western Ontario President's medal for poem "The country north of Belleville," 1964; Governor General's literary award for *The Cariboo horses* 1965; Centennial medal, 1967.

WRITINGS
The enchanted echo, Clarke & Stuart, 1944; *Pressed on sand*, Ryerson, 1955 (Ryerson Poetry chapbook, 157); *Emu, Remember!*, University of New Brunswick, 1956; *The crafte so longe to lerne*, Ryerson, 1959; *Poems for all the Annettes*, Contact, 1962; *The blur in between, poems 1960-61*, Emblem, 1963; *The Cariboo horses*, McClelland & Stewart, 1965; *North of summer, poems from Baffin Island*, McClelland & Stewart, 1967; *Wild grape wine*, McClelland & Stewart, 1968; *Point of transfer* (play; produced Theatre-in-the-Dell, Toronto, Ont., 1962); many radio plays, e.g. (adapter) *The woman of Andros* (based on Thornton Wilder's novel), (adapter) *The lost sea* (based on Jan de Hartog's play), *The gathering of days* ("Sunday night," CBC, 1955; 1959) *Dormez-vous? – a poem for D-Day* ("Sunday night," CBC, 7 June 1964); several TV plays, e.g. *Point of transfer* ("Shoestring theatre," CBC, 1962), *The fall of Troy* ("Shoestring theatre," CBC, 1962).

EDITED: *The new Romans*, Hurtig, 1968.

CONTRIBUTED: Poetry and short stories to *Modern Canadian verse in English and French*, edited by A.J.M. Smith, Oxford, 1967; *Penguin book of Canadian verse*, edited by R. Gustafson, rev. ed., Penguin, 1967; *The blasted pine*, edited by F.R. Scott, and A.J.M. Smith, rev. & enl. ed., Macmillan, 1967; *The blue guitar*, edited by D. Rutledge and J.M. Bassett, McClelland & Stewart, 1968; *Tamarack review, Canadian forum, Montrealer, Prism, Delta, Fiddlehead, Outsider, Canadian poetry*.

QUILICO, Louis 1926–

Singer (baritone); b. 1926 in Montreal, PQ; m. Lina Pizzolongo.

EDUCATION
Attended St. Cecilia Academy, Rome, Italy, 1949; Conservatory of Music and Dramatic Art, Montreal, 1953; David Mannes School, New York, NY; studied with Martial Singher and Lina Pizzolongo.

OFFICE
Théâtre National de l'Opéra, Paris, France.

CAREER
St. Jacques Church, Montreal, choir boy; Vancouver Opera Association, BC; Theatre Colon, Buenos Aires, Argentina, guest soloist; New York City Center Opera Company, soloist 1955; San Francisco Opera Company, Calif., guest soloist *c*.1956; Spoleto Festival, Italy, guest soloist 1960; Covent Garden Opera Company, London, England, soloist 1960-63; Vienna State Opera, Austria, guest soloist *c*.1962/63; Philadelphia Academy of Music, Pa., guest artist 1963; Canadian Opera Company, Toronto, Ont., soloist 1963, 1966–; Paris Opera, France, soloist 1963-65, 1968/69; Opéra-Comique, Paris, soloist 1968/69; toured North America, Russia, and Europe.

MEMBER
Union des Artistes de Montréal.

AWARDS, HONOURS
St. Jean Baptiste Contest winner, 1947; "Stars of tomorrow" first prize, 1953; Metropolitan Opera Audition of the Air, New York, winner, 1955; Canada Council senior arts fellowship, 1960.

THEATRE
Sang in numerous productions, e.g. *Hop signor!*, 4 roles in *The tales of Hoffmann*, Sharpless in *Madama Butterfly* (Vancouver International Festival, BC, Queen Elizabeth Theatre, 22 July 1960), title role in *Rigoletto* (Canadian Opera Company, Oct. 1962; Bolshoi Theatre, Moscow, USSR, 1962; Paris Opera; Teatro Colon, Buenos Aires; Vancouver Opera Association, 21 Oct. 1967; Toronto Symphony Orchestra, Jan. 1968), Amonasro in *Aïda* (Vienna State Opera, *c*.1963; Canadian Opera Company, 13 Sept. 1968), Germont in *La traviata* (Vienna State Opera, *c*.1963; Bolshoi Theatre; Canadian Opera Company, 20 Sept. 1966; Baltimore Civic Opera, Md.; New York, Mar. 1968), *A masked ball* (Bath of Caracalla, Rome, 1964), Recital (Moncton, NB, 1964), Recital (Rimouski, PQ, 1964), *Macbeth* (Canadian Opera Company, 16 Sept. 1966), *Deirdre* (Canadian Opera Company, 24 Sept. 1966), *I Pagliacci* (Canadian Opera Company, 1966), *Cavalleria rusticana* (Canadian Opera Company, 17 Sept. 1966), *Oedipus rex* (Toronto Festival Singers and Toronto Symphony Orchestra under Elmer Iseler, 17 May 1967), Iago in *Otello* (Montreal Symphony Orchestra, Expo 67, Montreal, summer 1967), *Festival concert* (Stratford, Ont. Festival, 1967), *Messiah* (Toronto Mendelssohn Choir, Dec. 1967), *Alzira* concert version (American Opera Society, Carnegie Hall, New York, 24 Jan. 1968), *Celebrity recital* (University of Manitoba, 1 Mar. 1968), *Annual Freedom Festival* (Windsor Symphony Orchestra, Ont., summer 1968), *Summer concert series* (Montreal Symphony Orchestra, 1968), Scarpia in *Tosca* (Canadian Opera Company, 21 Sept. 1968; Bolshoi Theatre, Feb. 1969).

RADIO
Sang in numerous CBC productions, e.g. Sharpless in *Madama Butterfly* (Vancouver International Festival, 27 July 1960), "Tuesday night," (series, 1965), *University celebrity recital* ("Tuesday night," 4 Jan. 1966; 19 May 1967); *Friday concert* (13 Jan. 1967), *Music from Europe* (3 Sept. 1967), *Rigoletto* (21 Oct. 1967), *Messiah* (24 Dec. 1967), *Celebrity recital* ("Thursday music," 15 Feb. 1968; 23 Feb. 1968; 7 Nov. 1968), *Hercules* ("Saturday evening," 9 Mar. 1968).

TELEVISION
Sang in many CBC productions, e.g. Sharpless in *Madama Butterfly* (1958), Lescaut in *Manon* ("Heure du concert," 11 Feb. 1960), "Showcase for music" (20 Nov. 1960), title role in *The barber of Seville* ("Festival," 15 May 1961), *Opera highlights* ("Parade," 24 Oct. 1962), Iago in *Otello* ("Festival," 22 Apr. 1963), title role in *Rigoletto* ("Festival," 28 Oct. 1964; 3 Feb. 1965), *Concert, Italian style* ("Festival," 31 Mar. 1965), *Oedipus rex* (1968).

RECORDINGS
Pacem in terris, Vanguard, VRS 1134, 1965; Vanguard 1134, 71134. *Iphigénie en Tauride*, Angel 35632; S35632. *Aïda*, London 5798; 25798.

RAKINE, Marthe
Artist; b. 20 Nov. in Moscow, Russia; came to Canada in 1948 and settled in Toronto, Ont.; m. Boris Rakine.

EDUCATION
Attended École des Arts Décoratifs, Paris, France, 1926; studied under Othon Friesz, Académie de la Grand Chaumière, Paris, 1937; attended Ontario College of Art, Toronto, 1949-50.

CAREER
Painted in Paris, Toronto, and Lausanne, Switzerland.

MEMBER
Ontario Society of Artists.

AWARDS, HONOURS
Drakenfeld Co. prize, Canadian National Exhibition, 1950.

EXHIBITIONS
ONE-MAN: Hart House, University of Toronto, 1951; Eaton's College Street Art Gallery, Toronto, 1951.
GROUP: Represented in group exhibitions held in Canada since 1932 including annual exhibitions of Ontario Society of Artists, Canadian National Exhibition, and Royal Canadian Academy; represented in group exhibitions organized by National Gallery of Canada, Ottawa, Ont. including the second Biennial of Canadian Painting, 1957; *Salon des Indépendants*, Paris; Pittsburgh International Exhibition, Pa., 1952.

COLLECTIONS IN WHICH REPRESENTED
Agnes Etherington Art Centre, Queen's University; London Public Library and Art Museum, Ont.; Art Gallery of Ontario, Toronto; Hart House Permanent Collection, University of Toronto.

READE, Hamish, pseud.
see GRAY, Simon James Holliday

REID, Daphne Kate
see REID, Kate

REID, George Agnew   1860-1947
Artist; b. 25 July 1860 near Wingham, Ont.; son of Adam and Eliza (Agnew) Reid; m. Mary Augusta Hiester (*q.v.*) 1885 (d. 4 Oct. 1921 in Toronto, Ont.); m. Mary Evelyn Werinck 1922; d. 23 Aug. 1947 in Toronto.

EDUCATION
Studied with Robert Harris, J. Fraser, H. Perré, and M. Matthews, Central Ontario School of Art, Toronto, 1879-82; studied with Thomas Eakins, Pennsylvania Academy of Fine Arts, Philadelphia, Pa., 1883-85; studied with Benjamin Constant, Jean Paul Laurens and P. Dagnan-Bouveret, Julian and Colarossi academies, Paris, France, 1888-89; Prado Museum, Madrid, Spain, 1896.

CAREER
Ontario College of Art, Toronto, teacher 1890-1928, principal, 1912-29; Canadian representative Jury of Awards, Pan American Exposition, Buffalo, NY, 1901; Canadian War Memorials, official war artist, 1918.

COMMISSIONS
Mural, Jarvis Street Collegiate Institute, Toronto, 1895; mural, Royal Ontario Museum, Toronto; design and decorations, church, Ontario; six panels, Toronto City Hall; mural, Sir Edmund Walker's library, Toronto; mural, Professor Short's study, Ottawa, Ont.; mural, Queen's University Library; pastel studies, Pageants of Quebec, 1908; mural, Earlscourt Public Library, Toronto, 1926.

MEMBER
Royal Canadian Academy (Associate 1885; Academician 1890; president, 1906-09); Ontario Society of Artists (elected, 1885; president, 1897-1902); Canadian Society of Applied Art (elected, 1903; vice-president, 1903-04).

AWARDS, HONOURS
Medal, Ontario School of Art, 1880; medal, World's Fair, Chicago, Ill., 1893; medal, San Francisco Fair, Calif., 1894; combined Académie Julian prize for painted figures, 1889.

EXHIBITIONS
ONE-MAN: City Hall, Owen Sound, Ont., 1897; Toronto Public Library, 1948.
GROUP: Represented in group exhibitions held in Canada since 1882 including annual exhibitions of Ontario Society of Artists, Royal Canadian Academy, Canadian National Exhibition;

represented in exhibitions organized by National Gallery of Canada, Ottawa, since 1927; *Salon*, Paris, 1889; Royal Academy, London, England, 1913; Canadian Section of Fine Arts, British Empire Exhibition, London, 1924; *Exposition d'art canadien*, Musée du Jeu de Paume, Paris, 1927; A Century of Canadian Art, Tate Gallery, London, 1938; Art Gallery of Ontario, Toronto, 1945; Painting in Canada a Selective Survey, Institute of History and Art, Albany, NY, 1946.

COLLECTIONS IN WHICH REPRESENTED
National Gallery of Canada; Victoria College, University of Toronto; Art Gallery of Ontario, Toronto.

REID, Kate   1930–
(Daphne Kate Reid)
Actress; b. 4 Nov. 1930 in London, England; daughter of Walter Clarke and Helen Isabelle (Moore) Reid; m. Michael Sadlier 1952 (marriage dissolved); m. Austin Willis 13 July 1953 (marriage dissolved 1962); children: (second marriage) Reid b. 1956, Robin b. 1959.

EDUCATION
Attended Havergal College, Toronto; studied drama at Royal Conservatory of Music, Toronto; University of Toronto; studied acting with Uta Hagen and Herbert Berghof at HB Studio, New York, 1951.

HOME
14 Binscarth Rd., Toronto 5, Ont.

OFFICE
c/o Peter Witt, 37 W. 57th St., New York, NY, 10019, USA.

CAREER
Bermuda Repertory Theatre, actress 1952; Crest Theatre, Toronto, actress 1956–?; Stratford, Ont. Festival, actress 1959-65; Charlottetown Festival, PEI, actress 1966.

MEMBER
ACTRA (life member); AFTRA; AEA; Canadian Theatre Centre.

AWARDS, HONOURS
Dominion Drama Festival best actress 1946; Maurice Rosenfeld award as most promising radio newcomer, 1953; shared ACTRA bronze medal for artistic achievement, 1955; *Liberty* award for best television actress, 1956, 1961; Emmy award nominee for Queen Victoria in *The invincible Mr. Disraeli*, 1963; Tony award nominee for Caitlin Thomas in *Dylan*, 1965.

THEATRE
Played Nina in *The seagull* (Hart House Theatre, Toronto), Ruth in *Years ago* (Straw Hat Players, Port Carling, Muskoka, Ont., summer 1948), *Life with father* (Peterborough, Ont., summer 1949), Gaby in *The petrified forest* (Bermuda, 1952), *The little foxes* (Bermuda, 1952), Lizzie Currie in *The rainmaker* (Prud'Hommes Garden Centre

Theatre, Vineland, Ont., summer 1955; Crest, Feb. 1956), *The three sisters* (Crest, 1956), Catherine Ashland in *The stepmother* (St. Martin's, London, 5 Nov. 1958), Celia in *As you like it* (Stratford, Ont. Festival, 1959), Emilia in *Othello* (Stratford, Ont. Festival, 1959), *The cherry orchard* (Canadian Players, Toronto, 1959), title role in *The taming of the shrew* (Canadian Players, Toronto, 1959; Stratford, Ont. Festival, 1962), Nurse in *Romeo and Juliet* (Stratford, Ont. Festival, 1960), Helena in *A midsummer night's dream* (Stratford, Ont. Festival, 1960), Queen Katherine in *Henry VIII* (Stratford, Ont. Festival, 1961), Jaquenette in *Love's labour's lost* (Stratford, Ont. Festival, 1961), *The madwoman of Chaillot* (Crest), *Two programs of Shakespearian comedy* (Canadian Players, Toronto), Lady Macbeth in *Macbeth* (Stratford, Ont. Festival, 1962), Martha in *Who's afraid of Virginia Woolf?* (matinee company, Billy Rose, New York, 13 Oct. 1962; Manitoba Theatre Centre, Winnipeg, 1965), Adriana in *The comedy of errors* (Stratford, Ont. Festival, 1963), Cassandra in *Troilus and Cressida* (Stratford, Ont. Festival, 1963), Lisa and Sister Marthe in *Cyrano de Bergerac* (Stratford, Ont. Festival, 1963), Caitlin Thomas in *Dylan* (Plymouth, New York, 18 Jan. 1964), Portia in *Julius Caesar* (Stratford, Ont. Festival, 16 June 1965), Mme. Ranevskaya in *The cherry orchard* (Stratford, Ont. Festival, 26 July 1965), Celeste in *The mutilated* and Molly in *The gnadiges fräulein* in *Slapstick tragedy* (Longacre, New York, 22 Feb. 1966), Anna in *The Ottawa man* (Charlottetown Festival, 7 July 1966), Captain Crashaw and Air Raid Warden in *The adventures of Private Turvey* (Charlottetown Festival, 26 July 1966), *The subject was roses* (Playhouse Theatre, Toronto, Dec. 1960), Writer's wife in *What do you really know about your husband?* (Shubert, New Haven, Conn., 9 Mar. 1967), Esther Franz in *The price* (Morosco, New York, 7 Feb. 1968).

FILM
Played Hazel Starr in *This property is condemned* (Seven Arts, 1966), *A friend to his country* (National Film Board of Canada; "Explorations," CBC, 3 May 1961).

RADIO
Played in several CBC productions, e.g. Millamant in *The way of the world* ("Wednesday night," 6 July 1960), *The loved and the lost* ("Stage," 1 Oct. 1967), *The loves of Belle de Zouy-Ian alias Zelide* ("Age of elegance," FM, 19 Oct. 1967).

TELEVISION
Played in numerous CBC productions, e.g. *Unburied dead, Hamlet, Candide, Little women, A month in the country, Queen after death, Tiger at the gates* ("Ford startime," 9 Feb. 1960), title role in

Candida ("Ford startime," 15 Mar. 1960), Portia in *Julius Caesar* ("Festival," 19 Dec. 1960), Mother in *A matter of some importance* ("First person," 21 Dec. 1960), *The three sisters* ("Festival," 13 Feb. 1961), Anne of Cleves in *The royal gambit* ("Festival," 3 Apr. 1961), *Breaking point* ("GM presents," 16 Apr. 1961), guest on *Wayne and Shuster hour* (29 Apr. 1961), *The killdeer* ("Festival," 12 June 1961), *The prizewinner* ("Playdate," 1 Nov. 1961), *The day of the dodo* ("Festival," 8 Jan. 1962), Reporter's assistant in *The most beautiful girl in the world* ("Playdate," 4 Apr. 1962), Lady Macbeth in scene from *Macbeth* (1st telstar broadcast, 23 July 1962), Queen Victoria in *The invincible Mr. Disraeli* ("Hallmark hall of fame," NBC, 3 Apr. 1963), Grace in *Pastures of plenty* ("Playdate," 3 Feb. 1964), Mary Todd Lincoln in *Abe Lincoln in Illinois* ("Hallmark hall of fame," NBC, 1964), *The holy terror* ("Hallmark hall of fame," NBC, 1964/65, *The trial of Dr. Fancy* (1964/65), title role in *Mother Courage* ("Festival," 20 Jan. 1965), *A portrait of Kate Reid* ("Show on shows," 18 Apr. 1965), Rose Hunter in *All aboard for candyland* ("Wojeck," 27 Sept. 1966), *A Christmas greeting* (25 Dec. 1966), *Easter poetry and music* ("Man alive," 14 Apr. 1968).

REID, Mary Hiester   1854-1921
(Mary Augusta Hiester Reid)
Artist; b. 1854 in Reading, Pa.; daughter of Dr. John P. Hiester; m. George Agnew Reid (*q.v.*) 1885; came to Canada 1886 and settled in Toronto, Ont.; d. 4 Oct. 1921 in Toronto.

EDUCATION
Studied at School of Design, Philadelphia, Pa.; studied under Thomas Eakins at the Pennsylvania Academy of Fine Arts, Philadelphia, 1883-85; studied under P. Dagnan-Bouveret, Jean André Rixens, Blanc, and Gustave Courtois, and at the Académie Colarossi in Paris, France, 1888-89.

CAREER
Travelled in Europe 1885; still life and flower painter in Toronto 1886-1921.

MEMBER
Ontario Society of Artists (elected, 1887); Royal Canadian Academy (Associate 1893); Canadian Society of Applied Art (elected, 1904).

EXHIBITIONS
ONE-MAN: Art Gallery of (now of Ontario) Toronto, 1922.
GROUP: Represented in group exhibitions held in Canada from 1887 on including annual exhibitions of Ontario Society of Artists, Royal Canadian Academy, Spring Exhibitions of the Montreal Art Association and Canadian National Exhibitions; World's Columbian Exposition, Chicago, Ill., 1893.

COLLECTIONS IN WHICH REPRESENTED
Art Gallery of Ontario, Toronto; National Gallery of Canada, Ottawa, Ont.

RENAUD, Emiliano   1875-1932
Composer, organist, and pianist; b. 26 June 1875 in St. Jean de Matha, PQ; d. 3 Oct. 1932 in Montreal, PQ.

EDUCATION
Studied piano with Mme. Renaud; with Paul Letondal for 2 years; with Dominique Ducharme, c.1893-96; with Mme. Stepanoff, Berlin, Germany, c.1900-04.

CAREER
Collège Sainte Marie, Montréal, organist 1890; Les Eudistes de Church Point, NS, teacher of piano and choir master 1892; Sainte Marie, Oswego, NY, church organist 1896-97; McGill Conservatory of Music, professor of piano 1904-05; concert tours in USA, Canada, and England; accompanied Mme. Calve on USA tour 1912; resided in Boston, Mass., and New York, NY, 1915-21; returned to Montreal in 1921; taught, composed, and performed as pianist on radio programs, 1921-32.

REPPEN, Jack   1933-64
(John Richard Reppen)
Artist; b. 17 July 1933 in Toronto, Ont.; son of John Reppen; m. Claire; children: Christine b. c.1958, Michael b. c.1960; d. 2 June 1964 in Toronto.

EDUCATION
Attended Northern Vocational High School, Toronto; studied advertising design and illustration, Ontario College of Art, Toronto, evening classes; studied in Mexico.

CAREER
Traffic light repairman in Toronto; *Toronto daily star*, freelance cartoonist 1952-64; Prudential Insurance Company of America, Toronto, art director; painted in Mexico 1961; travelled in Europe 1962; painted in Yucatan, Mexico, 1963; painter, cartoonist, and commercial artist in Toronto 1952-64.

COMMISSIONS
Mural, Prudential Insurance Company of America, Toronto, 1960; mural, Tip Top Tailors, Toronto, 1960; mural, Constellation Hotel, Malton, Ont., 1962; mural, Little Long Lac Gold Mines Ltd., Toronto, 1963.

MEMBER
Ontario Society of Artists (elected, 1962).

AWARDS, HONOURS
Baxter award, Ontario Society of Artists, 1962; purchase award, Spring Exhibition, Montreal Museum of Fine Arts, 1962; prize, Winnipeg Biennial, Winnipeg Art Gallery, Man., 1962.

EXHIBITIONS
ONE-MAN: Gallery Moos, Toronto, 1959, 1960, 1961, and 1963; Galerie Agnès Lefort, Montréal, PQ, 1962 and 1963.
GROUP: Represented in group exhibitions held in Canada during his lifetime including exhibitions of Ontario Society of Artists, Royal Canadian Academy, and Spring Exhibitions of Montreal Museum of Fine Arts; fifth Biennial Exhibition of Canadian Painting, National Gallery of Canada, Ottawa, Ont., 1963; Canadian Painting, Rochester Art Gallery, Rochester, NY, 1962; 26 Canadians, Albright-Knox Art Gallery, Buffalo, NY, 1962.

COLLECTIONS IN WHICH REPRESENTED
Agnes Etherington Art Centre, Queen's University; Canadian Imperial Bank of Commerce, Montreal; Canadian Industries Limited Collection, Montreal; Hart House Permanent Collection, University of Toronto; London Public Library and Art Museum, Ont.; Montreal Museum of Fine Arts; Kensington Industries collection, Montreal; Musée d'Art Contemporain, Montréal.

REPPEN, John Richard
see REPPEN, Jack

RICHARDSON, Evelyn May Fox* 1902–
Author; b. 16 May 1902 in Emerald Isle, NS; daughter of Arthur Douglas and Hattie Belle (Larkin) Fox; m. Charles Laurie Morrill Richardson 14 Aug. 1926; children: Anne Gordon b. 1928, Laurie Morrill b. 17 July 1929 (d. 1947), Betty June b. c.1933.
EDUCATION
Attended Common School in Clark's Harbour, NS; Halifax County Academy, NS; Dalhousie University.
RELIGION
Baptist.
HOME
Barrington, NS.
CAREER
Mainly literary; taught school c.1921-26.
MEMBER
Canadian Authors Association; Cape Sable Historical Society (president).
AWARDS, HONOURS
Governor General's literary award for *We keep a light*, 1945; Ryerson fiction award for *Desired haven*, 1953; Diploma de honor de La Mujer de México y de America en la Cultura, 1960.
WRITINGS
We keep a light (non-fiction), Ryerson, 1945 (published in USA under title *We bought an island*, Macrae-Smith, 1954); *Desired haven* (novel), Ryerson, 1953 (Sears Roebuck People's Book Club selection; produced on radio "Ford theatre," CBC, 8 Jan. 1954); *No small tempest*

(novel), Ryerson, 1957; *My other islands* (non-fiction), Ryerson, 1960; *Living island* (non-fiction), Ryerson, 1965.
CONTRIBUTED: Short stories and articles to *Dalhousie review, Atlantic advocate, Saturday night, Down east, Yankee.*

RIDEOUT, Patricia* 1931–
(Patricia Rideout Dissmann)
Singer (contralto); b. 16 Mar. 1931 in Saint John, NB; daughter of Eric Aubrey and Florence May (Chase) Rideout; m. Rolf Edmund Dissmann 3 Sept. 1955.
EDUCATION
Attended Lorne Public School, Saint John, 1938-40; Victoria Public School, Saint John, 1941-45; Saint John High School, 1946-48, first class honours; Saint John Vocational School, honours graduate, 1949; studied piano with Beatrice Price, Saint John, 1941-43; studied voice with Agnes Forbes, Saint John, 1946-48; Royal Conservatory of Music, Toronto, Ont., 1949, Opera School, 1952-55; studied with Ernesto Vinci, Toronto, 1949-68.
RELIGION
Unitarian.
HOME
8 Fallingbrook Drive, Scarborough, Ont.
CAREER
Saint John Theatre Guild, student soloist 1947-48; Canadian Electrical Manufacturers, European Industrial Products and Disco Ltd., Toronto, secretary 1950-55; Red Barn Theatre, Jackson's Point, Muskoka, Ont., lead singer-dancer, 1950; University Settlement, Toronto, singing teacher 1954; Banff School of Fine Arts, Alta., soloist 1954, 1955; Festival Singers, Toronto, soloist 1956-68; Canadian Opera Company, Toronto, soloist 1956–; Toronto Mendelssohn Choir, soloist 1961, 1965-68; Toronto Symphony Orchestra, soloist.
MEMBER
ACTRA; AEA (executive committee, 1959-65); Heliconian Club.
AWARDS, HONOURS
Business and Professional Women's Club scholarship, 1947; Royal Conservatory of Music scholarship, 1949; Kiwanis Music Festival scholarship, 1952.
THEATRE
Formal debut at Toronto Art Gallery, 1956; sang in numerous productions and concerts, e.g. Baba in *The medium* (Royal Conservatory of Music Opera School, Hart House Theatre, Toronto, 1955), Bianca in *The rape of Lucretia* (Canadian première, Stratford, Ont. Festival, 1956), *Alto rhapsodie* (Hart House Glee Club, Toronto, 1957; Kingston, Ont., 1958; Toronto Men Teachers Choir, Kingston and Toronto, 1964), *King David*

(Festival Singers, Stratford, Ont. Festival, 1958), Maurya in *Riders to the sea* (Hart House Theatre, 1958; 1960), Berta in *The barber of Seville* (Canadian Opera Company, tour, 1958/59; Toronto, 1959; 18 Sept. 1965; 1967), Mrs. Brown in *Night blooming cereus* (Hart House Theatre, 1959), Smeraldina in *Love for three oranges* (Canadian Opera Company, 1959), Marcellina in *The marriage of Figaro* (Canadian Opera Company, 1960), *Operatic arias* (Kitchener-Waterloo Symphony Orchestra, Ont., 1960), *Messiah* (Winnipeg Symphony and Chorus, Man., 1960; Toronto Mendelssohn Choir and Toronto Symphony Orchestra, 1961; 1965; 1966), Suzuki in *Madama Butterfly* (Vancouver International Festival, 22 July 1960; Canadian Opera Company, Toronto, 1962), Mama Lucia in *Cavalleria rusticana* (Canadian Opera Company, 1961; 17 Sept. 1966), *Kindertotenlieder* (National Ballet of Canada, 1961), *Pierrot lunaire* (première, Toronto, 1962), *Dido and Aeneas* (Stratford, Ont. Festival, 1963; 14 July 1964), Annina in *Der Rosenkavalier* (Canadian Opera Company, 1963), *Symphony no. 9* by Beethoven (Calgary Philharmonic Orchestra, Alta., 1964; Toronto Mendelssohn Choir and Toronto Symphony Orchestra, 1966), *Stabat mater* (Ottawa Choral Society, Ont., 1964), *Trois poèmes de Mallarmé* (1964), *Magnificat* (Festival Singers, Stratford, Ont. Festival, 1964), Mother of Parasha in *Mavra* (Canadian Opera Company, 25 Sept. 1965), *Serenade to music* (Toronto Mendelssohn Choir, Toronto and Boston, Mass., 1965), *Mass* by Stravinsky (Festival Singers, Stratford, Ont. Festival, 31 July 1966), *In the beginning* (Festival Singers, Hanover, NH, Toronto, Waterloo, and Guelph, Ont., 1966), *Deirdre* (Canadian Opera Company, 24 Sept. 1966), *I Pagliacci* (Canadian Opera Company, 1966), *La traviata* (Canadian Opera Company, 20 Sept. 1966), Florence Pike in *Albert Herring* (Stratford, Ont. Festival, 1967), Julie Riel in *Louis Riel* (première, Canadian Opera Company, 23 Sept. 1967; Expo 67; 13 Sept. 1968), *Evocations* (Expo 67, Montreal, 1967), *Canada dash, Canada dot* (Expo 67, Montreal, 1967), *Cantata academica* (Toronto Mendelssohn Choir and Toronto Symphony Orchestra, 1967), *Nelson mass* (Toronto Mendelssohn Choir and Toronto Symphony Orchestra, 1967), *Il Tramonto* (Hamilton Philharmonic Orchestra, Ont., 1968), *Requiem canticles* (Canadian première, 1968).

RADIO

Sang in numerous CBC productions, e.g. *Hansel and Gretel* ("Opera festival," 1956), *Sunday morning recital* (1959, 1960, 1962, 1964), Mrs. Brown in *Night blooming cereus* ("Wednesday night," 16 Mar. 1960), *Madama Butterfly* (27 July 1960), Marcellina in *The marriage of Figaro* ("Wednesday night," 19 Oct. 1960), *Let's make*

an opera ("National music," 1961), *Pierrot lunaire* (première, "Wednesday night," 1962), *Riders to the sea* (4 Feb. 1962), *Jubilate Deo in D* ("Wednesday night," 1963), Sorceress in *Dido and Aeneas* ("Wednesday night," 17 July 1963), *Ten centuries concert* ("Sunday night," 12 Apr. 1964; "Tuesday night," 8 Mar. 1966), *Mavra* ("Sunday night," 10 May 1964), *Jonah* ("Sunday night," 1 Nov. 1964), *Kindertotenlieder* ("Concerts from two worlds," 1965), *Sea pictures* ("Concerts from two worlds," 1965), Giofanna in *Rigoletto* (3 Feb. 1965), *Schoenberg, Mahler and Brahms songs* ("Distinguished artists," 21 June 1965), *Mavra* excerpts ("Opera time," 25 Sept. 1965), *The line across* ("Tuesday night," 23 Nov. 1965), *Messiah* (24 Dec. 1965, "Encore," 26 Dec. 1965; 24 Dec. 1966), *Cantata academica* ("Concerts from two worlds," 1966), "Choirs in concert" (series, 31 Mar. 1966; "Thursday music," 24 Oct. 1968; 1 Nov. 1968), *Five songs for dark voice* ("Concerts from two worlds," 7 Nov. 1966; 14 Nov. 1966), *Bach cantata and Mozart aria* (30 Nov. 1966), *Evocations* (29 Nov. 1966; "Wednesday night," 25 Jan. 1967; "Distinguished Canadian artists," 13 Oct. 1967), *Hebrew songs and Mozart aria* (1967), *Sam Slick* (4 July 1967; "Tuesday night," 5 Sept. 1967), Florence Pike in *Albert Herring* ("Tuesday night," 8 Aug. 1967), Julie Riel in *Louis Riel* (19 Oct. 1967), *Canada dash, Canada dot* (3 Dec. 1967), Violet in *The brideship* (12 Dec. 1967), *Mass in B minor* by Bach ("Encore," 16 June 1968; "Tuesday night," 18 June 1968), *Port Royal concert* ("Encore," part I, 18 Aug. 1968).

TELEVISION

Sang in numerous CBC productions, e.g. *Hansel and Gretel* (1956), *Lord Byron's love letter* ("Heure du concert," 1957), Fidalma in *Il matrimonio segreto* (1958), Mrs. Sedley in *Peter Grimes* ("Festival," 1959), *Brahms lieder and folk songs* ("Music in miniature," 1960), Maurya in *Riders to the sea* ("Festival," 1962), *The art of the fugue* ("Festival," 4 Mar. 1963), Giovanna in *Rigoletto* ("Festival," 1964), *Festival of miniatures* ("Festival," 10 June 1964), Third lady in *The magic flute* ("Festival," 1965), Nurse in *Eugene Onegin* ("Festival," 1966).

RECORDINGS

Mavra, Columbia Records, Stereo MS 6991; Mono ML 6391. *Evocations*, 1966. *Five songs for dark voice*, 1966.

RIDOUT, Godfrey* 1918–
Composer and conductor; b. 6 May 1918 in Toronto; son of Douglas Kay and Amy Phyllis (Bird) Ridout; m. Freda Antrobus 5 Aug. 1944; children: Naomi b. 14 Dec. 1948, Victoria b. 26 May 1951, Michael b. 22 Mar. 1957.

EDUCATION

Attended Rosedale and Brown public schools in Toronto, 1923-26; Lakefield Preparatory School, Ont., 1927-32; Upper Canada College, Toronto, 1932-36; North Toronto Collegiate Institute, 1936-37; studied piano with Richard Tattersall, harmony, orchestration, and conducting with Ettore Mazzoleni (*q.v.*); studied counterpoint and organ with Charles Pealier, piano with Weldon Kilburn, composition with Healey Willan (*q.v.*), Toronto (now Royal) Conservatory of Music, associate (composition), 1938; University of Toronto, Faculty of Music, 1938.

RELIGION

Anglican.

HOME

71 Rowanwood Ave., Toronto 5, Ont.

OFFICE

Faculty of Music, University of Toronto, Toronto 5, Ont.

CAREER

Canadian Militia, second lieutenant 1938; Toronto (now Royal) Conservatory of Music, teacher of theory 1939–?; National Film Board of Canada, guest composer; *Canadian music*, assistant editor 1940-41; *Canadian review of music and art*, assistant editor 1942-43; CBC, guest composer, conductor, and commentator; Victoria College Music Club, Toronto, musical director 1944-57; University of Toronto, Faculty of Music, lecturer 1948-61, assistant professor 1961-65, associate professor 1965–; guest conductor of various orchestras; Eaton Operatic Society, Toronto, musical director 1949-59.

MEMBER

CAPAC (director, 1966–); Canadian League of Composers; Gilbert and Sullivan Society, Toronto branch (hon. vice-president).

AWARDS, HONOURS

Scholarship for study of composition, for *Ballade*, 1938; LLD from Queen's University, 1967; Centennial medal, 1967.

COMPOSITIONS

Ballade, viola and string orchestra, 1938, Canadian Music Centre, first performed 1939 in Toronto by Melodic Strings under Alexander Chuhaldin; *Festal overture*, orchestra, 1939, Canadian Music Centre, first performed 1943 in Toronto by CBC Symphony Orchestra under Sir Ernest MacMillan, recorded by CBC IS no. 41 with the same performers; *Two songs for soprano and oboe*, 1939; *Two études*, string orchestra, 1946, Chappell, first performed 1946 in Toronto by CBC Orchestra under Harold Sumberg, recorded on air-check tape by International String Congress Orchestra under Roy Harris; *Esther*, dramatic symphony, 1951; *Two mystical songs*, 1953, F. Harris, also revised under title *Cantiones mysticae*, soprano and orchestra; *Four*

sonnets, choir, 1953, G.V. Thompson, first performed in Carnegie Hall, New York, NY, under Leopold Stokowski, commissioned by Toronto Mendelssohn Choir for Lois Marshall; *A coronation ode*, choir and orchestra, 1953, commissioned by CBC for coronation of Queen Elizabeth II; *Music for a young prince*, orchestra, 1959, Canadian Music Centre, first performed 1959 by CBC Symphony Orchestra under Geoffrey Waddington, recorded on air-check tape by the same performers, commissioned by CBC for the opening of St. Lawrence Seaway by Queen Elizabeth II; *Three preludes on Scottish tunes*, organ, 1960, G.V. Thompson, Novello; *The dance*, choir and orchestra, 1960, Novello, commissioned by CBC; *Pange lingua*, choir and orchestra, 1960, Waterloo Music, first performed 1961 in Buffalo, NY, at Three Choir Hymn Festival, commissioned by Three Choir Hymn Festival; *Fall fair*, orchestra, 1961, G.V. Thompson, commissioned by CBC; *Cantiones mysticae no. 2, the Ascension*, choir and orchestra, 1962, commissioned by Lois Marshall; *Colas et Colinette*, reconstruction of comic opera by Joseph Quesnel, 1963, commissioned by Ten Centuries Concerts; *The country wife*, incidental music, 1964, first performed 1964 at Stratford, Ont. Festival; fanfares and accompanying music for the enthronement of the Bishop of Toronto, Oct. 1966; *In memoriam Anne Frank*, voice and orchestra, 1965, first performed 14 Mar. 1965 on CBC by Toronto Symphony Orchestra under Victor Feldbrill, commissioned by CBC; *When youth and age unite*, choir and orchestra, 1966, G.V. Thompson, commissioned by Canadian Music Educators Association; *La prima ballerina*, ballet suite, 1967, first performed Oct. 1967 at Expo 67, Montreal, PQ, by National Ballet Orchestra under George Crum, commissioned by National Ballet of Canada for Canada's centennial; *Folk songs of eastern Canada*, soprano and harp or strings, 1967, first performed 11 July 1967 at Toronto Festival by Lois Marshall and orchestra under Mario Bernardi, commissioned by CBC for Canada's centennial; *The homage of the wise*, three-part songs, 1968, first performed 14 May 1969 on CBC, commissioned by CBC; anthems, songs, part songs, and folk song arrangements, some published.

WRITINGS

CONTRIBUTED: Articles to *Canadian music, Canadian review of music and art*.

RINFRET, Jean-Claude* 1929–

Designer; b. 3 Sept. 1929 in Shawinigan, PQ; son of Antonio and Florida (Lafrenière) Rinfret; m. Estelle Madeleine Michaud 27 Dec. 1954; children: Marie-Josée b. 5 Dec. 1955, Martine b. 30 Jan. 1959.

EDUCATION

Attended École St-Maurice, Shawinigan; École Supérieure Immaculée-Conception, Shawinigan; École des Arts et Métiers, Montréal?, 1950-51; École des Beaux-Arts, Montréal, graduated 1953; École Supérieure des Arts Décoratifs, Paris, France, 1953; Institut du Panthéon, Paris, 1953-54.

RELIGION

Roman Catholic.

HOME

367 Ave. Querbes, Outremont, Montréal 8, PQ.

OFFICE

Canadian Broadcasting Corporation, 1625 Boul. de Maisonneuve, Montréal, PQ.

CAREER

Conservatoire de Musique, Les Jeunesses Musicales, Montreal Opera Guild, Montreal Symphony, Les Grands Ballets Canadiens, Montreal Festival Society, La Comédie Canadienne, Théâtre National Populaire, Théâtre du Rideau Vert, Théâtre du Nouveau Monde, Théâtre des Dix Heures, and Théâtre Amphytrion, Montréal, designer; Vancouver Opera Association, BC, Canadian Opera Company, Toronto, Ont., Théâtre de Percé, PQ, Théâtre d'Été, Eastman, PQ, and Théâtre Lyrique de Nouvelle France, Québec, PQ, designer; Les Compagnons de Saint-Laurent, Montréal, designer 1948-50; Central City Summer Festival, Colo., resident scenic designer; CBC, Montreal, designer 1954-66, design director 1967–; Le Théâtre Club, Montréal, designer 1956-63; École des Beaux-Arts, Montréal, teacher, designer 1959–; École des Beaux-Arts, Québec, teacher, designer 1960-62; Théâtre Lyrique de Nouvelle France, Québec, designer 1964; travelled extensively in Europe; Quadriennale de Prague, Czecho-Slovakia, delegate of the Province of Quebec 1967.

MEMBER

Canadian Theatre Centre; Associated Designers of Canada; International Theatre Institute.

AWARDS, HONOURS

Quebec government scholarship, 1953; Canada Council senior arts fellowship, 1964; Trophée Meilleur Décor for television, Montreal, 1960; Centennial medal 1967.

THEATRE

Designed sets for numerous productions, e.g. *Boubouroche* (Conservatoire), *La demande en mariage* (Conservatoire), *Un caprice* (Conservatoire), *Arlequin poli par l'amour* (Conservatoire), *Le médecin malgré lui* (Conservatoire), *A quoi rêvent les jeunes filles* (Conservatoire), *L'Arlésienne* (Conservatoire), *Voulez-vous jouer avec moâ?* (Théâtre de Percé), *En attendant Godot* (Théâtre de Percé), *Diogène* (Théâtre de Percé), *Les grands départs* (Théâtre de Percé), *Barberine* (Théâtre de Percé), *Les amants novices* (Théâtre de Percé), *Fridolinades* (Comédie Canadienne, 1956), *Humulus le muet* (Amphytrion, 1956), *Un imbécile* (Amphytrion, 1956), *L'éternel mari* (Amphytrion, 1956), *La Marguerite* (Amphytrion, Mar. 1956), *Les insolites* (Dix Heures, Mar. 1956), *La quadrature du cercle* (Théâtre Club, Apr. 1956), *La mégère apprivoisée* (Théâtre Sainte-Adèle, PQ, July 1956), *Le roi ivre* (Dix Heures, Nov. 1956), *On demande un souvenir* (Dix Heures, 1957), *The glass menagerie* (Nouveau Monde, Feb. 1957; Théâtre de Percé), *Edmée* (Dix Heures, Mar. 1957), *La fleur à la bouche* (Théâtre Club, Apr. 1957), *Pirouette* (Jeunesses Musicales, 1958), *The fool* (Jeunesses Musicales, 1958), *Au petit bonheur* (Atelier Georges Groulx, 1958), *Cécé* (Théâtre Club, Apr. 1958), *Quand la moisson sera courbée* (Comédie Canadienne, Nov. 1958), *Une mesure de silence* (Jeunesses Musicales, Aug. 1958), *Le gibet* (Comédie Canadienne, Nov. 1958), *La bagatelle* (Mountain Playhouse, Montreal, 1959), *Les plaideurs* (Théâtre Club, Feb. 1959), *The consul* (Mountain Playhouse, July 1959), *Cinna* (Théâtre Club, Aug. 1959), *Le mal court* (Théâtre Club, Oct. 1959), *Morts sans sépulture* (McGill University, Nov. 1959), *Première classique* (Grands Ballets, 1960), *Les violons de l'automne* (Théâtre Club, 1960; Paris, France, 1962), *Le cri de l'engoulevent* (Comédie Canadienne, Jan. 1960), *Le séducteur* (Théâtre Club, Mar. 1960), *Celles qu'on prend dans ses bras* (Théâtre Club, Nov. 1960), *L'heure espagnole* (Montreal Festival, 1961), *La serva padrona* (Montreal Festival, 1961), *Roméo et Juliette* (Opera Guild, 1961), *Nouveau ballet* (Grands Ballets, 1961), *Le mari, la femme et la mort* (Théâtre Club, Feb. 1961), *Cosi fan tutte* (Montreal Festival, 1962), *Faust* (Opera Guild, 1962), *L'heure éblouissante* (Théâtre Club, 1962), *Le mouton blanc de la famille* (Théâtre d'Été, Eastman, 1962), *Meurtre en fa dièse* (Théâtre d'Été, Eastman, 1962), *Werther* (Montreal Festival, 1963), *L'amour des quatre colonels* (Théâtre d'Été, Eastman, 1963), *La traviata* (Opera Guild, 1963), *Requiem pour une nonne* (Théâtre Club, 1963), *Le marchand de Venise* (Théâtre Club, Mar. 1963), *Britannicus* (Conservatoire, Mar. 1963), *Mascotte* (Théâtre du Parc Lafontaine, July 1963), *Le système Ribardier* (Théâtre d'Été, Estérel, PQ, July 1963), *Cocatier* (Théâtre d'Été, Estérel, July 1963), *Don Giovanni* (Place des Arts, Montréal, 1964), *Tosca* (Place des Arts, 1964; Feb. 1966), *Les monstres sacrés* (Théâtre d'Été, Eastman, 1964), *M. Chasse* (Théâtre d'Été, Eastman, 1964), *La cuisine des anges* (Théâtre des Prairies, Joliette, PQ, 1964), *Un otage* (Rideau Vert, May 1964), *Madama Butterfly* (Place des Arts, Jan. 1965), *La répétition ou l'amour puni* (Rideau Vert, Jan. 1965), *La traviata* (Canadian Opera Company, Feb. 1965), *Les beaux dimanches* (Comédie Canadienne, Feb. 1965), *Une maison ... un jour*

(Rideau Vert, Feb. 1965), *Lakmé* (Central City Opera House, July 1965), *Manon* (Central City Opera House, July 1965; Théâtre Lyrique, Nov. 1967), *Le barbier de Séville* (Central City Opera House, July 1965), *La locandiera* (Théâtre du Gesù, Montréal, Nov. 1965), *La belle Hélène* (Place des Arts, 1966), *La veuve joyeuse* (Théâtre Lyrique, Feb. 1966), *La bohème* (Place des Arts, Apr. 1966), *Hier les enfants dansaient* (Comédie Canadienne, Apr. 1966), *Vue du pont* (Théâtre de Percé; Montreal International Theatre, May 1966), *Mignon* (Théâtre Lyrique, Oct. 1966), *Au retour des oies blanches* (Comédie Canadienne, Oct. 1966), *Margoton* (Place des Arts, Nov. 1966), *On purge bébé* (Théâtre Populaire du Québec, Montréal, 1967), *Le mariage forcé* (Théâtre Populaire du Québec, 1967), *Le mariage de Figaro* (Opera Guild, Jan. 1967), *Valses de Vienne* (Place des Arts, Mar. 1967), *Lucia di Lammermoor* (Vancouver Opera, Mar. 1967), *Un simple soldat* (Comédie Canadienne, Apr. 1967), *Othello* (Place des Arts, Aug. 1967).

TELEVISION
Designed sets for numerous CBC productions, e.g. *Oedipus rex* (1956), *Roméo et Juliette* (1957), *Daphnis et Chloé* (1957), *Chopin* (1958), *Le paria* (1958), *Catarina* (1958), *Pagliacci* (1958), *La grande duchesse de Gérolstein* (1958), *The medium* (1959), *Marie Stuart* (1959), *Un mois à la campagne* (1959), *Prima Donna* (1960), *The old maid and the thief* (1960), *El retablo de Maese Pedro* (1961), *Dialogues des Carmélites* (1961), *La bohème* (1962), *Orfeo ed Euridice* (1963), *Bluebeard's castle* (1964), *Hansel and Gretel* (1965), excerpts from *Faust, La traviata, Boris Goudounov, Pagliacci* (1967).

WRITINGS
Rapport sur la télévision européenne, Radio Canada, 19?.
WORK IN PROGRESS: (with Jan Doat) "La mise en scène et le décor au théâtre."

RINGUET, pseud.
see PANNETON, Philippe

RINGWOOD, Gwen Pharis*   1910–
(Gwendolyn Margaret Pharis Ringwood; Gwen Pharis)
Author; b. 13 Aug. 1910 in Anatone, Wash.; came to Canada in 1913; m. John Brian Ringwood 1939; children: Stephen Michael, Susan Frances Leslie b. 19 Nov. 1942, Carol Blaine, Patrick Brian.

EDUCATION
Attended primary school in Magrath, Alta., and secondary school in Calgary, Alta.; University of Alberta, BA, 1934; University of North Carolina, MA, 1939.

HOME
PO Box 8, Williams Lake, BC.

CAREER
Mainly literary; University of Alberta, Department of Extension, secretary to Elizabeth Sterling Haynes (*q.v.*) c.1935; adjudicated drama and speech festivals; taught speech and creative writing courses.

MEMBER
Canadian Theatre Centre.

AWARDS, HONOURS
Canadian drama award; Ottawa Little Theatre Workshop annual Canadian playwriting competition prize for *Lament for harmonica (Maya)*, 1958.

WRITINGS
Younger brother (juvenile novel), Longmans, Green, 1959; *Still stands the house* (one-act play, 1938), French, 1957?; *Dark harvest* (play), Nelson, 1945 (produced BC regional drama festival, 1958); *The courting of Marie Jenvrin* (one-act play), French, 1951; *Lament for harmonica (Maya)* (play), Ottawa Little Theatre, 1960; *Chris Axelson* (one-act play; produced University of North Carolina); *The drowning of Wasyl Nemitchuk* (one-act play; produced Banff School of Fine Arts, Alta. under title *A fine coloured Easter egg*); *The rainmaker* (play; produced Banff School of Fine Arts); *Widger* (play; produced University of Alberta, 1950); *Stampede* (play; produced New Glasgow, NS, 1956); *Jana* (one-act play, 1966); *The deep has many voices* (one-act play, 1966); libretto for *Look behind you neighbour* (musical; produced Edson, Alta. 50th anniversary, 2 Nov. 1961); libretto for *The road runs north* (musical; produced Williams Lake, 1968); several radio and TV plays for CBC.
CONTRIBUTED: Plays and stories to *Best one act plays of 1939*, edited by J.W. Marriott, Harrap, 1940?; *American folk plays*, edited by F.H. Koch, Appleton-Century, 1939; *International folk plays*, edited by S. Selden, University of North Carolina, 1949; *Canadian short stories*, edited by R. Weaver and H. James, Oxford, 1952; *Cavalcade of the north*, edited by G.E. Nelson, Doubleday, 1958; *Canada on stage*, edited by S. Richards, Clarke, Irwin, 1960; *Stories from across Canada*, edited by B.L. McEvoy, McClelland & Stewart, 1966.
WORK IN PROGRESS: "You walk a narrow bridge" (novel).

ROBERTS, Charles George Douglas   1860-1943
Author; b. 10 Jan. 1860 in Douglas, York County, NB; son of George Goodridge and Emma Wetmore (Bliss) Roberts; m. Mary Isabel Fenety 29 Dec. 1880 (d. May 1930); m. Joan Montgomery Oct. 1943; children: (first marriage) Athelstan b. 1882, Lloyd b. 1884, Edith b. 1886, Douglas b. 1888; d. 26 Nov. 1943 in Toronto, Ont.

EDUCATION
Collegiate School, Fredericton, NB, 1874-76;

University of New Brunswick, BA with honours in mental and moral science and political economy, 1879, MA, 1881.

RELIGION

Anglican.

CAREER

Grammar school, Chatham, NB, headmaster 1879-81; York Street School, Fredericton, headmaster 1881-83; *The week*, editor 1883-84; freelance journalist 1884-85; King's College, Windsor, NS, professor of English and French literature 1885-88, professor of English literature and economics 1888-95; World's Fair, Chicago, Ill., literary arbiter 1893; freelance writer in Fredericton 1895; *The illustrated American*, New York, NY, assistant editor 1896; freelance writer 1896-1907; travelled extensively in Europe and North Africa; settled in England 1911; British Army, Legion of Frontiersmen, Aug. 1914 private, 16th Battalion of the King's Liverpool Regiment, Dec. 1914 commander, 1915, became captain; transferred to the Canadian Expeditionary forces, 1917, became major; subsequently associated with Sir Max Aiken on The Canadian War Records; returned to Canada 1925; *Canadian who was who*, volumes I and II, editor-in-chief 1934 and 1938; *The Canadian who's who*, volumes II and III, editor-in-chief, 1936-39; made extensive lecture tours in Canada.

MEMBER

Royal Society of Canada (elected fellow, 1890; president of section II, 1933); Canadian Authors Association (elected president, 1927 and 1928); Authors' Club, London, England; American National Institute of Arts and Letters (charter member; sole non-American member); PEN Club, Toronto, Ont.; Royal Society of Literature (elected, 1892).

AWARDS, HONOURS

Douglas silver medal in Latin and Greek, University of New Brunswick; medal in Latin prose composition, University of New Brunswick; LL D from University of New Brunswick, 1906; first Lorne Pierce medal for outstanding achievements in imaginative literature, 1926; knighted for his services to Canadian letters, 1935.

WRITINGS

Orion and other poems, Lippincott, 1880; *Later poems*, the author, 1881; *Later poems*, Crockett, 1882; *In divers tones* (poems), Lothrop 1887; *Poems of wild life*, Scott, 1888; *Autotochthon* (poems), the author, 1889; *Ave, an ode for the centenary of the birth of P.B. Shelley*, Williamson, 1892; *Songs of the common day and Ave*, Briggs, 1893; *The land of Evangeline and the gateway thither ...*, Dominion Atlantic Railway, 1894?; *The raid from Beauséjour, and how the Carter boys lifted the mortgage* (fiction), Hunt and Eaton, 1894; *The Canadian guide book* (non-fiction), Appleton, 1895; *Reube Dare's shad boat, a tale of the tide country* (fiction), Hunt and Eaton, 1895; *Earth's enigmas; a volume of stories*, Lamson, Wolffe, 1896; *Around the camp fire* (novel), Crowell, 1896; *The book of the native* (poems), Copp Clark, 1896; *The forge in the forest* (novel), Lamson, Wolffe, 1896; *A history of Canada for high schools and academies*, Lamson, Wolffe, 1897; *New York nocturnes and other poems*, Lothrop, 1898; *A sister to Evangeline, being the story of Yvonne de Lamouric* (novel), Lamson, Wolffe, 1898 (also published in England under title *Lovers in Acadie*); *By the marshes of Minas* (short stories), Page, 1900; *Heart of the ancient wood* (novel), Page, 1900; *Poems*, Silver Burdett, 1901; *Barbara Ladd* (novel), Page, 1902; *Kindred of the wild, a book of animal life* (short stories), Page, 1902; *The book of the rose* (poems), Page, 1903; *Discoveries and explorations in the century*, Linscott, 1904; *The watchers of the trails; a book of animal life* (fiction), Page, 1904; *The prisoner of mademoiselle; a love story*, Page 1904; *The watchers of the camp fire* (novel), Page, 1904; *The haunters of the pine gloom* (fiction), Page, 1905; *The little people of the Sycamore*, Page, 1905; *The king of Mamozekel* (fiction), Page, 1905; *Red fox* (fiction), Page, 1905; *The lord of the air* (fiction), Page, 1905; *The cruise of the yacht "Dido"* (fiction), Page, 1906; *The heart that knows* (novel), Page, 1906; *The return to the trails* (fiction), Page, 1906; *Poems*, Page, 1907; *The haunters of the silences, a book of animal life* (fiction), Page, 1907; *In the deep of the snow* (fiction), Crowell, 1907; *The young Acadian* (fiction), Page, 1907; *The house in the water; a book of animal life* (fiction), Page, 1908; *Red oxen of Bonval* (fiction), Dodd, 1909; *The backwoodsmen* (short stories), Macmillan, 1909; *Kings in exile: stories of captive animals*, Macmillan, 1910; *Neighbours unknown* (fiction), Ward, Lock, 1910; *More kindred of the wild* (fiction), Ward, Lock, 1911; *Babes of the wild* (fiction), Cassell, 1912; *A Balkan prince* (fiction), Everett, 1913; *Children of the wild* (short stories), Macmillan, 1913; *Feet of the furtive* (fiction), Macmillan, 1913; *Hoof and claw* (fiction), Ward, Lock, 1913; *The secret trails* (fiction), Macmillan, 1916; *Cock-crow* (fiction), Federal Printers, 1916; *The morning of the silver frost* (fiction), Federal Printers, 1916; *Canada in Flanders*, v. 3, Hodder, 1918; *The ledge on Bald Face* (novel), Ward, Lock, 1918 (also published in USA under title *Jim, the story of the backwoods police dog*); *New poems*, Constable, 1919; *In the morning of time* (short stories), Hutchison, 1919; *Some animal stories* (fiction), Dent, 1921; *Wisdom of the wilderness* (fiction), Dent, 1922; *More animal stories* (fiction), Dent, 1922; *They who walk in the wilds* (fiction), Macmillan, 1924;

The sweet o' the year and other poems, Ryerson, 1925; *The vagrant of time* (poems), Ryerson, 1927; *Be quiet wind; Unsaid* (two poems), the author, 1929; *Eyes of the wilderness* (fiction), Macmillan, 1933; *Further animal stories* (fiction), Dent, 1936; *The iceberg and three other poems*, Ryerson, 1937, *Canada speaks of Britain* (poems), Ryerson, 1941. Several works have been translated into German.

EDITED: *Poems of wild life*, Scott, 1888; (with William Carman Roberts and others) *Northland lyrics*, Small, Maynard, 1899; *The Alastor and Adonais of Shelley*, Silver Burdett, 1902; *Flying colours* (anthology), Ryerson, 1942.

TRANSLATED: Philippe Aubert de Gaspé's *The Canadians of old*, Appleton, 1890.

CONTRIBUTED: Poems to numerous anthologies, e.g. *A Victorian anthology, 1837-1895*, edited by E.C. Stedman, Houghton Mifflin, 1895; *Songs of nature*, compiled by John Burroughs, Garden City, 1901; *Poems of American history*, edited by Burton Egbert Stevenson, rev. ed., Houghton Mifflin, 1922; *The poetry cure*, compiled by Robert Haven Schauffer, Dodd, Mead, 1925; *Canadian poets*, edited by John W. Garvin, rev. ed., McClelland & Stewart, 1926; *The home book of verse*, edited by Burton Egbert Stevenson, 6th ed. and 8th ed., Henry Holt, 1926 & 1928; *The nature lover's knapsack*, edited by Osgood Grover, enl. ed., T.Y. Crowell, 1927; *Great Americans, as seen by the poets*, edited by Burton Egbert Stevenson, J.B. Lippincott, 1933; *Our Canadian literature*, edited by Bliss Carman and Lorne Pierce, rev. ed., Ryerson, 1935; *Poems worth knowing*, compiled by Claude E. Lewis, Copp Clark, 1941; *Anthology of Canadian poetry*, compiled by Ralph Gustafson, Penguin, 1942; short stories to numerous anthologies, e.g. *One of those coincidences and ten other stories*, edited by J. Hawthorne and others, Funk, 1899; *English short stories*, Dutton, 1921; *Canadian short stories*, edited by R. Knister, Macmillan, 1928; *Best bird stories I know*, compiled by J.C. Minot, Wilde, 1929; *Mainly horses*, edited by E. Rhys and C.A. D. Scott, Appleton, 1929; *Century of nature stories*, Hutchison, 1937; poems and short stories to *Maclean's, Saturday night, Canadian .bookman, Queen's quarterly, Canadian poetry, National home monthly, Country guide*, and *Canadian magazine, 1938-1939*.

ROBERTS, Goodridge* 1904—

(William Goodridge Roberts)
Artist; b. 24 Sept. 1904 in Barbados, British West Indies; son of George Edward Theodore and Frances Seymour (Allen) Roberts; came to Canada with his parents in 1905 and settled in Fredericton, NB; m. Marion Susan Willson 1933 (marriage dissolved); m. Joan Carruthers Carter 1954; children: Timothy b. 1962.

EDUCATION
Attended Ottawa Collegiate Institute, Ont., 1920-21; Fredericton High School, graduate, 1922; studied at École des Beaux-Arts, Montréal, 1923-25; studied under John Sloan, Max Weber, and Boardman Robinson, Art Students League, New York, NY, 1926-28.

RELIGION
Protestant.

HOME
355 Lansdowne Ave., Montreal, PQ.

CAREER
New Brunswick Forestry Department, Fredericton, draftsman 1929-31; Ottawa Art Association, instructor 1931-33; Queen's University, resident artist 1933-36; painted, lectured, and taught art privately in Montreal 1936-39; Art Association of Montreal Art School, instructor in drawing and painting 1939-43, 1945-50, 1952-53; RCAF, 1943-44, became flying officer; appointed Official War Artist with the RCAF in England; painted in France 1953-54; painted in Montreal 1954-59, 1960—; University of New Brunswick, resident artist, 1959-60.

COMMISSIONS
Painting of Saskatoon, Sask., Seagram's Collection of Canadian Cities, 1953.

MEMBER
Eastern Group (co-founder, 1938); Contemporary Arts Society (charter member); Canadian Group of Painters; Canadian Society of Painters in Water Colour; Canadian Society of Graphic Art; Royal Canadian Academy (Associate 1952; Academician 1956); International Association of Plastic Arts.

AWARDS, HONOURS
Jessie Dow prize for water colour painting, Montreal Museum of Fine Arts, 1939, 1947, and 1958; purchase award, Musée du Québec, PQ, 1948; RCAF Association purchase award for presentation to Queen Elizabeth, 1952; Canadian Government overseas fellowship, 1953; Junior League award, Winnipeg Art Gallery, Man., 1957; Glazebrook award, third Biennial Exhibition of Canadian Painting, National Gallery of Canada, Ottawa, 1959; L L D from University of New Brunswick, 1960; purchase award, Art Gallery of Hamilton, Ont., 1963; Canada Council art award, 1966/67.

EXHIBITIONS
ONE-MAN: Art Club of Montreal, 1932, 1939, and 1941; James Wilson Galleries, Ottawa, 1933 and 1938; Hart House, University of Toronto, 1933, 1938, and 1951; Queen's University, 1934 and 1935; Scott Gallery, Montreal, 1938; Montreal Museum of Fine Arts, 1940, 1942, and 1950; Beaux-Arts, Montréal, 1940 and 1942; Contempo Art Studios, Ottawa, 1941; McGill University 1942 and 1945; Dominion Gallery, Montreal, 1943, 1945, 1948, 1949, 1950, 1952, 1953, 1955, and 1962; Vancouver Art Gallery, BC,

1943; Collège Brébeuf, Montréal, 1943; Western Canada Art Circuit, 1944 and 1954; L'Atelier, Québec, 1951 and 1957; New Brunswick Museum, Saint John, NB, 1954; Galerie Creuze, Paris, France, 1954; University of New Brunswick Art Centre, 1954 and 1963; Vancouver Art Gallery, 1954; Robertson Galleries, Ottawa, 1958 and 1963; Beaverbrook Art Gallery, Fredericton, 1960; Waddington Galleries, Montreal, 1961; Penthouse Gallery, Montreal, 1961; Kitchener-Waterloo, Ont., 1963.

GROUP: Represented in group exhibitions held in Canada including annual exhibitions of Montreal Museum of Fine Arts, Royal Canadian Academy, and Canadian Society of Painters in Water Colour; represented in exhibitions organized by National Gallery of Canada, Ottawa, including its third, fifth, and sixth Biennial Exhibitions of Canadian Painting 1959, 1963, and 1965; World's Fair, New York, 1939; Aspects of Contemporary Painting in Canada, Addison Gallery, Andover, Mass., 1942-43; UNESCO ... *Exposition internationale d'art moderne, peinture, graphique et décoratif, architecture*, Musée d'Art Moderne, Paris, 1946; Painters of Canada ... 1668-1948, Virginia Museum of Fine Arts, Richmond, 1949; Forty Years of Canadian Painting, Museum of Fine Arts, Boston, Mass., 1949; Canadian Painting, National Gallery of Art, Washington, DC, 1950; University of Maine, 1951; São Paulo Biennial exhibition, Brazil, Museo de Arte Moderno, 1951 and 1953; XXVI Biennale, Venice, Italy, 1952; Pennsylvania Academy, Philadelphia, Pa., 1952; International Exhibition, Carnegie Institute, Pittsburgh, Pa., 1952 and 1955; Florida State Fair, Tampa, 1952; German Industries Exhibition, Berlin, 1953; Coronation Exhibition, London, England, 1953; exhibition of Canadian painting shown in Pakistan, India, and Ceylon, 1954-55; An Exhibition of Canadian Paintings held at Fortnum and Mason, Ltd., London, 1955; International Exhibition of Paintings held at the Athenee of Valencia, Venezuela, 1955; Contemporary Canadian Painters, an Exhibition ... for Circulation in Australia, 1957; Inter-American Biennial of Painting and Graphic Art, Museum of Fine Arts, Mexico City, Mexico, 1958; Exhibition of Canadian Art, Canadian Pavilion, Brussels International Exposition, Belgium, 1958; *L'Art du Canada*, Musée de Bordeaux, France, 1962; Canadian Art, Warsaw Museum, Poland, 1962; A Quarter Century of Canadian Art, Tate Gallery, London, 1964; Tokyo International Trade Fair, Japan, 1965.

COLLECTIONS IN WHICH REPRESENTED
Art Gallery of Hamilton, Ont.; Art Gallery of Ontario, Toronto; Bezalel Museum, Israel; Dalhousie University; Edmonton Art Gallery, Alta.; Hart House, University of Toronto; Lord Beaverbrook Art Gallery, Fredericton; McGill University; Montreal Museum of Fine Arts; Mount Allison University; Musée du Québec; National Gallery of Canada; Queen's University; University of British Columbia; University of New Brunswick; Vancouver Art Gallery; Winnipeg Art Gallery; Willistead Art Gallery, Windsor, Ont., Musée d' Art Contemporain, Montréal.

ROBERTS, Lloyd 1884-1966
(William Harris Lloyd Roberts)
Author; b. 31 Oct. 1884 in Fredericton, NB; son of Charles George Douglas (*q.v.*) and Mary Isabel (Fenety) Roberts; m. Hope Balmain 1 Jan. 1908 (d.1912); m. Leila White 15 Aug. 1914; m. Julia Bristow 1943; children: (first marriage) Patricia Bliss, (third marriage) Thaia Bliss and Mary Carman; d. 25 Jan. 1966 in Toronto, Ont.

EDUCATION
Educated by private tutors; attended King's College Collegiate, Windsor, NS; attended public and high schools in Fredericton.

RELIGION
Christian Science.

CAREER
Daily news, Nelson, BC, reporter 1911; *Citizen*, Ottawa, Ont., reporter; *Outing*, New York, NY, assistant editor 1904-07; Government of Canada, editor of immigration literature 1913-20; full-time writer 1920–; *The Christian Science monitor*, parliamentary correspondent 1925-39; correspondent for several other Canadian newspapers including the *Sun*, Vancouver, BC, and *Albertan*, Calgary, Alta.; official historian of annual trip of Dominion government supply ship *Nascopie* to Arctic 1936; RCMP liaison and public relations officer 1939-43; lectured from coast to coast.

MEMBER
Canadian Authors Association.

WRITINGS
England overseas (poems), Matthews, 1914; *Book of poems*, Goodchild, 1919; *The book of Roberts* (biography), Ryerson, 1923; *Along the Ottawa* (poems), Dent, 1927; *I sing of life; selected poems*, Ryerson, 1937; *Mother Doneby* (play); *Let's pretend* (play); *The bishop of St. Kitt's* (play).
CONTRIBUTED: Poems to several anthologies, e.g. *Canadian poets*, edited by J.W. Garvin, rev. ed., McClelland & Stewart, 1926; *Our Canadian literature*, edited by B. Carman and L. Pierce, rev. ed., Ryerson, 1935; *Days and deeds; a book of verse*, edited by B.E. Stevenson and E.B. Stevenson, Doubleday, Doran, 1938; *Flying colours*, edited by Sir C.G.D. Roberts, Ryerson, 1942; *Anthology of Canadian poetry*, edited by R. Gustafson, Penguin, 1942; *Canadian poetry in English*, edited by B. Carman and others, rev. and enl. ed., Ryerson, 1954; *Canadian poetry, Saturday night, Canadian geographical journal.*

ROBERTS, William Goodridge
see ROBERTS, Goodridge

ROBERTS, William Harris Lloyd
see ROBERTS, Lloyd

ROBINS, John Daniel   1884-1952
Author and teacher; b. 8 Sept. 1884 in Windsor,
Ont.; son of Thomas Brackbill and Elizabeth
Snelson (Plant) Robins; m. Leila Isabel Douglas
1917; d. 18 Dec. 1952 in Toronto, Ont.
EDUCATION
Albert College, Belleville, Ont., matriculation;
Victoria College, University of Toronto, BA,
1913, MA, 1922; attended University of Marburg,
Germany, 1914; University of Chicago, Ph D,
1927.
CAREER
Victoria College, University of Toronto, instruct-
or in German 1914, lecturer in German 1919-25,
associate professor of English 1925-33, professor
1933-52, head of English department 1938-52,
professor emeritus 1952; travelled extensively in
Europe.
AWARDS, HONOURS
Governor General's literary award for *The incom-
plete anglers*, 1943.
WRITINGS
The incomplete anglers (non-fiction), Collins,
1943; *Cottage cheese* (essays), Collins, 1951.
EDITED: *A pocketful of Canada*, Collins, 1946;
(with M.V. Ray) *A book of Canadian humour*,
Ryerson, 1951.
CONTRIBUTED: Short stories and articles to
Rebel, Canadian forum.

ROGERS, Otto Donald   1935—
Painter and sculptor; b. 19 Nov. 1935 in Kerro-
bert, Sask.
EDUCATION
Studied under Winona Mulcaster, Saskatoon
Teachers' College, 1952-53; University of Wis-
consin, B Sc in art education, 1953-58, M Sc in
fine art, 1959; studied in New York, NY, for three
months.
RELIGION
Baha'i.
HOME
827 University Dr., Saskatoon, Sask.
OFFICE
Fine Arts Department, University of Saskatchewan,
Saskatoon, Sask.
CAREER
University of Wisconsin, graduate assistant 1959;
produced a film *Working in watercolor*, distributed
by International Film Board, Chicago, Ill., *c.*1958;
Art journal, editor; University of Saskatchewan,
assistant professor of art 1959—.

COMMISSIONS
Sculpture, Prince Albert Regional Library, Sask.;
sculpture, Elks Club, Saskatoon, 1962; sculpture,
Bedford Road Collegiate, Saskatoon, 1962.
MEMBER
Society for Education through Art (president of
the Saskatchewan branch, 1962-63).
AWARDS, HONOURS
Purchase awards, Saskatchewan Arts Board for
Junior Collection, 1953 and 1954; Rothko award
in graphic art, 1956; purchase award, Wisconsin
Salon of Art, 1958; awards for painting, Milwaukee
Art Center, Wis., 1958 and 1959; Gimbels award
for oil painting, Milwaukee Art Center, 1959;
scholarship for painting class at the University of
Saskatchewan, Saskatchewan Arts Board, 1954;
scholarship, Emma Lake Workshop, Sask., 1954;
scholarships from the University of Wisconsin,
1956, 1957, and 1958; Canada Council art award,
1966/67.
EXHIBITIONS
ONE-MAN: Wisconsin; James Art Studio Gallery,
Saskatoon, 1962; Saskatoon Art Centre, 1963.
GROUP: Represented in group exhibitions held in
Canada from 1960 on; represented in exhibitions
organized by National Gallery of Canada, Ottawa,
Ont., including its fifth and sixth Biennial Exhibi-
tions of Canadian Painting, 1963 and 1965.
COLLECTIONS IN WHICH REPRESENTED
Bedford Road Collegiate; Department of External
Affairs, Ottawa; Lord Beaverbrook Art Gallery,
Fredericton, NB; Memorial Union Building, Uni-
versity of Saskatchewan; National Gallery of
Canada; Saskatchewan Arts Board Collection,
Regina; Saskatoon Teachers' College; Wisconsin
Union Collection, Madison, Wis.

RONEY, Irene Salemka
see SALEMKA, Irene

ROSS, James Sinclair
see ROSS, Sinclair

ROSS, Sinclair*   1908—
(James Sinclair Ross)
Novelist; b. 22 Jan. 1908 in Prince Albert, Sask.;
son of Peter and Catherine (Foster Fraser) Ross.
EDUCATION
Attended school in Prince Albert.
HOME
Apt. 16, 20 Spetson St., Athens, Greece.
CAREER
Royal Bank of Canada, clerk in Saskatchewan
1924-*c.*1941, Montreal, PQ *c.*1947-6?; Royal
Canadian Ordnance Corps 1942-*c.*1946; retired
to Athens.
WRITINGS
As for me and my house, Reynal & Hitchcock,

1941 (adapted for radio and produced "Stage," CBC, 10 Apr. 1964); *The well*, Macmillan, 1958; *The lamp at noon and other stories*, McClelland & Stewart, 1968 (title story adapted for TV and produced CBC, Jan. 1968); *Cornet at night* (short story; filmed National Film Board of Canada 105B 0163 017).

CONTRIBUTED: Short stories to *Canadian accent*, edited by R. Gustafson, Penguin, 1944; *Book of Canadian short stories*, edited by D. Pacey, Ryerson, 1950; *Canadian short stories*, edited by R. Weaver and H. James, Oxford, 1952; *Canadian short stories*, selected by R. Weaver, Oxford, 1960; *31 stories*, edited by M. Booth and C. Burhans, Prentice-Hall, 1960; *Modern Canadian stories*, edited by G. Rimanelli and R. Ruberto, Ryerson, 1966; Canadian high school anthologies; *Country guide, Nash's magazine, Queen's quarterly*.

ROUX, Jean-Louis* 1923—

Actor, director, and playwright; b. 18 May 1923 in Montreal; son of Louis and Berthe (Leclerc) Roux; m. Monique Oligny 25 Oct. 1950; children: Stéphane b. 2 Aug. 1961.

EDUCATION
Attended Couvent d'Hochelaga, Montréal, 1929-31; Mont Jésus-Marie, Montréal, 1931-33; Collège Sainte Marie, Montréal, 1933-42; Université de Montréal, BA cum laude, 1942, medical course, 1942-46, certificate d'études physiques, chimiques et biologiques, 1942.

HOME
2168 Sherbrooke St. W., Apt. 7, Montreal 25, PQ.

CAREER
Les Compagnons de Saint-Laurent, Montréal, 1939-44; La Compagnie de Ludmilla Pitoëff, Montréal and Europe, 1942-49; toured and studied in Paris, France and other European cities and in Tunis, 1946-50; Le Théâtre d'Essai, Montréal, co-founder, 1949; Le Théâtre du Nouveau Monde, Montréal, co-founder 1951, secretary general 1953-63, artistic director 1966—; CBC, Montreal, actor 1949—; École du Théâtre du Nouveau Monde, Montréal, instructor in history of theatre 1952-54; National Theatre School of Canada, Montreal, guest director; Canada Council Arts Panel, vice-president 1966; National Film Board of Canada, member of board of governors; Canadian Conference of the Arts, president 1967.

MEMBER
AEA; Union des Artistes de Montréal (vice-president, 1956); La Société des Auteurs et Compositeurs (president, 1956-65); Canadian Theatre Centre (honorary member, 1965; president, 1966).

AWARDS, HONOURS
French Government scholarship 1947-48; Le Congrès du Spectacle, best actor award, 1959; Canada Council grant for writing *Bois-brûlés*,

1963; Canada Council grant 1966/67; Centennial medal, 1967.

THEATRE
Played Jacques Hury in *L'annonce faite à Marie* (Pitoëff, 1942), Hippolyte in *Phèdre* (Pitoëff, 1946), Krogstadt in *Maison de poupée* (Pitoëff, Comédie des Champs-Elysées, Paris, France, 1947), Récitant in *Le vrai procès de Jeanne d'Arc* (Pitoëff, Théâtre Sarah Bernhardt, Paris, 1949), *La cathédrale* (Théâtre du Monument National, Montréal, 1950), Valère in *L'avare* (Nouveau Monde, 9 Oct. 1951), *Un inspecteur vous demande* (Nouveau Monde, 1951), Don Carlos in *Don Juan* (Nouveau Monde, 1954), Soria in *Le maître de Santiago* (Nouveau Monde, 1955), Kostia in *La mouette* (Nouveau Monde, 1955), Louis Laine in *L'échange* (Nouveau Monde, 1956), Orléans in *Henry V* (Stratford, Ont. Festival, 1956), Géronimo in *Le mariage forcé* (Nouveau Monde, 1958), Thomas Diafoirus in *Le malade imaginaire* (Nouveau Monde, 1958), Vézinet in *Un chapeau de paille d'Italie* (Nouveau Monde, 1958), Lucien in *Le temps des lilas* (Nouveau Monde, 1958), Malipiero in *Venise sauvée* (Nouveau Monde, 1959), Trissotin in *Les femmes savantes* (Nouveau Monde, 1960), *Histoire de rire* (Nouveau Monde, 1960), *Le dindon* (Nouveau Monde, 1960), Ponza in *Chacun sa vérité* (Nouveau Monde, 1961), Davoren in *L'ombre d'un franc-tireur* (Nouveau Monde, 1962), Burgundy in *Henry V* and *Henry VI* (Stratford, Ont. Festival, 6 and 7 June 1966), Kurt in *The dance of death* (Stratford, Ont. Festival, 19 July 1966), Dudard in *Le rhinoceros* (Nouveau Monde, 22 Mar. 1968); directed and played title role in *Orphée* (Montreal, 1943); directed *Il faut qu'une porte* ... (Montreal, 1946), *Un fils à tuer* (Théâtre d'Essai, Montréal, 1949), *Rose Latulippe* (Montreal, 1951); directed and played Gerald Croft in *Un inspecteur vous demande* (Nouveau Monde, 1951); directed *La nuit du 16 janvier* (Nouveau Monde, 1952), *La fontaine de Paris* (Nouveau Monde, 1954), *L'oeil du peuple* (Nouveau Monde, 1957), *Les taupes* (Nouveau Monde, 1959), *Pantagleize* (Nouveau Monde, 1960), *Deux femmes terribles* (Nouveau Monde, 1961); directed and played Louis in *Le pain dur* (Nouveau Monde, 1963), title role in *On n'a pas tué Joe Hill* (Nouveau Monde, 1967); directed *Le soulier de satin* (Nouveau Monde, 1967), *Bois-brûlés* (Nouveau Monde, 1967), *Anatole* (Nouveau Monde, 1967); directed and played Higgins in *Pygmalion* (Nouveau Monde, 12 Jan. 1968), Titus in *Bérénice* (Nouveau Monde, 15 Feb. 1968); directed *Le Tartuffe* (Nouveau Monde, 8 Nov. 1968), *La nuit des rois* (Nouveau Monde, 13 Dec. 1968).

FILM
Played in *Docteur Louise*, Jean-Louis Gauthier in *The thirteenth letter*.

RADIO
Played on numerous CBC programs and Néoptolème in *Philoctète* (Organisation radio télévision française, 1949).

TELEVISION
Played in numerous CBC productions, e.g. Le Choeur in *Oedipe roi* (Cocteau, official opening of Canadian TV, 1952), Ovide in *The Plouffe family* (serial, 1952-59), Père Charles in *Il est minuit, Dr. Schweitzer*, Blaise Couture in *Asmodée*, Pierre de Craon in *L'annonce faite à Marie*, Père provincial in *Sur la terre et au ciel*, Gletkin in *Les ténèbres sur la terre*, Sir Robert in *Un mari idéal*, Jean in *Yerma*, Verchinine in *Les trois soeurs*, Grégoire in *Le canard sauvage*, Forget in *The road to Chaldea* (27 Mar. 1968), Jules Paneau in *Nothing but a long goodbye*, Georges in *Pas d'amour*, Veltchaniniov in *l'éternel mari*, Henri Girard in *Monsieur Vernet*, Philippe de Silleranges in *L'ennemi*, Coelho in *La reine morte*.

WRITINGS
Rose Latulippe (play; produced in Montreal, 1951); *En grève* (essay), Éditions du Jour, 1963; *Bois-brûlés* (play), Éditions du Jour, 1968.

TRANSLATED: Barrie Stavis's *The man who never died* into French *On n'a pas tué Joe Hill*, 1967.

WORK IN PROGRESS: *... De mes canons* (play on Mgr. de Laval and Frontenac); French adaptation of Shakespeare's *Twelfth night*.

ROY, Gabrielle* 1909—
(Gabrielle Roy Carbotte)
Novelist; b. 22 Mar. 1909 in St. Boniface, Man.; daughter of Leon and Melina (Landry) Roy; m. Marcel Carbotte 1947.

EDUCATION
Attended Saint-Joseph Academy, St. Boniface; Teachers Training School, Winnipeg, Man., diploma; studied drama in London, England.

RELIGION
Roman Catholic.

HOME
Apt. 302, 135 W., Grande Allée, Quebec, PQ.

CAREER
Taught school in Cardinal and St. Boniface, Man. for seven years; travelled extensively in Europe 1937-39; Montreal, PQ, freelance journalist.

MEMBER
Cercle Molière; Royal Society of Canada (elected fellow, 1947); Grand Jury des Lettres canadiennes, 1961.

AWARDS, HONOURS
Académie Canadienne-Française medal, 1946; Académie Française award; Prix Femina for *Bonheur d'occasion*, 1947; Governor General's literary award for *Bonheur d'occasion*, 1947, and *Rue Deschambault*, 1957; "Femma de l'Année," 1951; Prix Duvernay, 1961; Companion of the Order of Canada, 1967; Canada Council medal, 1968.

WRITINGS
Bonheur d'occasion, Pascal, 1945 (translated into English, Norwegian); *La petite poule d'eau*, Beauchemin, 1950 (translated into English, German); *Alexandre Chenevert, caissier*, Beauchemin, 1954 (translated into English); *Rue Deschambault*, Beauchemin, 1955 (translated into English, Italian); *La montagne secrète*, Beauchemin, 1961; *La route d'Altamont*, HMH, 1966 (translated into English).

CONTRIBUTED: Short stories and articles to *Ten for Wednesday night*, edited by R. Weaver, McClelland & Stewart, 1961; *A book of Canada*, edited by W.E. Toye, Collins, 1962; *Adventures in appreciation*, edited by W. Loban and R. Olmstead, Harcourt, 1963; *Amérique française*, *Bulletin des agriculteurs*, *Le Canada*, *Châtelaine*, *Maclean's*, *Mademoiselle*, *La nouvelle revue canadienne*, *Oeuvres libres*, *Revue de Paris*, *Revue moderne*, *Vie des arts*.

ROZET, François
Actor.

EDUCATION
Studied in Lyon, France and at the Conservatoire de Paris, France.

HOME
4335 Western Ave., Montreal 215, PQ.

CAREER
Odéon Theatre, Paris, actor for 7 years; Le Vieux Colombier, Paris, actor; USA, South America, and Canada tour 1940; France-Film, Montreal, actor 1940; l'Académie Bourget, PQ, teacher c.1940; Théâtre du Nouveau Monde, Montréal, actor 1952—.

MEMBER
Union des Artistes de Montréal.

THEATRE
Played in many productions, e.g. *Côte de sable*, *De 9 à 5*, title role in *Le marchand de Venise* (Vieux Colombier, tour), title role in *Le mariage de Figaro* (Vieux Colombier, tour), title role in *Faust* (Vieux Colombier), *Les mal aimés* (Les Compagnons de Saint-Laurent, Montréal, 1941), *L'aiglon* (La Comédie de Montréal, 1941/42), *La nuit du 16 janvier* (Nouveau Monde, 1952/53), *Poil de carotte* (Théâtre du Gesù, Montréal, 1953?), Sorine in *La mouette* (Nouveau Monde, 1955/56), Adolphe and Charles Bellanger in *Mon père avait raison* (Nouveau Monde, Nov. 1957), Ferrante in *La reine morte* (Théâtre du Rideau Vert, Montréal, 1958), *Clérambard* (Nouveau Monde, spring 1959), Forlipopoli in *La locandiera* (La Nouvelle Compagnie Théâtrale, Montréal, Nov. 1965), Alexandre in *L'oncle Vania* (Théâtre de l'Égrégore, Montréal, 4 Jan. 1966), docteur Flache in *Une folie* (Théâtre de l'Égrégore, 17

Apr. 1966), *La mégère apprivoisée* (La Nouvelle Compagnie Théâtrale, 20 Nov. 1966), *Le soulier de satin* (Nouveau Monde, 7 Jan. 1967), *Bois-brûlés* (Nouveau Monde, 3 Nov. 1967), *Le rhinoceros* (Nouveau Monde, 22 Mar. 1968).

FILM
Played in several productions, e.g. *La guerre des valses* (Berlin, 19 ?), *La première légion* (Paris, 19 ?).

TELEVISION
Played in many productions, e.g. *Les frères Karamasov* (CBC, 1961), *La première légion* (1960).

RUSSELL, George Horne   1861-1933
Artist; b. 18 Apr. 1861 in Banff, Scotland; son of George and Susan (Conn) Russell; came to Canada in 1889 and settled in Montreal, PQ; m. Elizabeth Morrison 14 Dec. 1889; children: Norman Wells, one daughter; d. 25 June 1933 in St. Stephen, NB.

EDUCATION
Attended school in Banff; studied at the Aberdeen School of Art, Scotland; studied under A. Legros and Sir George Reid, South Kensington Art School, London, England.

RELIGION
United Church of Canada.

CAREER
Established a studio in Montreal 1889; painted portraits of numerous eminent Canadians of the day on commission; painted in Montreal, spending summers in St. Andrews, NB, 1889-1933.

COMMISSIONS
Paintings of the Rockies and Skeena River district in BC, Grand Trunk Railway, 1909.

MEMBER
Royal Canadian Academy (Associate 1910; Academician 1918; president, 1922-26); Montreal Arts Club (sometime president); Pen and Pencil Club, Montreal (sometime president).

EXHIBITIONS
GROUP: Represented in group exhibitions held in Canada during his lifetime including annual exhibitions of Royal Canadian Academy and exhibitions of Art Association of Montreal; International Exposition, Brussels, Belgium; exhibition of Canadian art at the British Empire Trade Exhibition Buenos Aires, Argentina, 1931; A Century of Canadian Art, Tate Gallery, London, 1938.

COLLECTIONS IN WHICH REPRESENTED
Art Gallery of Ontario, Toronto; Montreal Museum of Fine Arts; National Gallery of Canada, Ottawa, Ont.

RUTHERFORD, Richard
Dancer; b. in Norfolk, Va.; came to Canada in 1957 and settled in Winnipeg.

EDUCATION
(now American) Ballet Theater School, New York, NY; studied ballet with Edward Caton, Fernand Nault, Robert Joffrey, and Benjamin Harkvary in New York.

OFFICE
Royal Winnipeg Ballet, 322 Smith St., Winnipeg 2, Man.

CAREER
Westchester Ballet, USA, soloist; Royal Winnipeg Ballet, corps de ballet 1957–?, soloist, principal, régisseur; Rainbow Stage, Winnipeg, dancer.

MEMBER
AEA.

THEATRE
Danced in *The bitter weird* (de Mille), Green boy in *The comedians* (Boris), *Pas d'action* (Macdonald), *Aimez-vous Bach?* (Macdonald), Pas de trois in *Le lac des cygnes*, act I (Petipa-Ivanov), Bluebird in *The sleeping beauty*, act III (Petipa), Dancing master in *The finishing school* (Lloyd), *Grasslands* (Moulton), *Le jazz hot* (Boris), title role in *The Chinese nightingale* (Heiden); created Hansel in *Hansel and Gretel* (Spohr), Medicine Man in *Brave song* (Moulton, Playhouse, Winnipeg, 28 Dec. 1959), Flute in *A court occasion* (Macdonald, Playhouse, Winnipeg, 26 Dec. 1961), *Recurrence* (Clouser, 27 Dec. 1961), title role in *The little emperor and the mechanical court* (Clouser, Children's Theatre, Winnipeg, 8 Feb. 1962), Anselme in *Rose Latullipe* (Macdonald, Stratford, Ont. Festival, 16 Aug. 1966).

TELEVISION
Danced in several CBC productions, e.g. "Toes in tempo" (series), *Recurrence* (Royal Winnipeg Ballet, 26 Aug. 1962), Anselme in *Rose Latullipe* ("Music Canada," 12 Apr. 1967).

SAINT-CHARLES, Joseph   1868-1956
Artist; b. 10 July 1868 in Montreal, PQ; son of Adolphe and B. (Pupart) Saint-Charles; m. Anna St. Denis Dec. 1904; children: one child; d. 26 Oct. 1956 in Montreal.

EDUCATION
Attended primary and secondary schools in Montreal; studied art under M. Chabert in Montreal; studied under Gérôme, École des Beaux-Arts, Paris, France, 1888; studied under Benjamin Constant and Jules Lefebvre, Académie Julian, Paris; studied in Italy for two years.

RELIGION
Roman Catholic.

CAREER
Painted and studied in Paris and Italy 1888-1900; painted pictures for Sacré-Coeur Chapel, Mont-

réal, in Paris 1892; returned to Canada 1900; Monument National, Montréal, teacher of drawing; École des Beaux-Arts, Montréal, teacher, and University of Montreal, teacher from 1900 on; Commission des Écoles Catholiques, Montréal, professor; retired from teaching 1942; portrait and landscape painter in Montreal 1900-56.

MEMBER

Royal Canadian Academy (Associate 1909).

AWARDS, HONOURS

Gold medal and declared *hors concours*, École des Beaux-Arts, Paris, 1891; medal, École des Beaux-Arts, Paris, 1894; bronze medal, Pan-American Exposition, Buffalo, NY, 1901.

EXHIBITIONS

ONE-MAN: Centre d'Art du Mont-Royal, 1966.
GROUP: Represented in group exhibitions held in Canada during his lifetime including exhibitions held at Art Association of Montreal, Musée du Québec, PQ, and annual exhibitions of Royal Canadian Academy; Paris *Salon* during the 1890's; Pan Pacific Exposition, Buffalo, 1901.

COLLECTIONS IN WHICH REPRESENTED

Montreal Museum of Fine Arts.

SAINT-LUC, Jean de, pseud.

see GLASSCO, John

SAINT-PIERRE, Denyse

Actress.

HOME

15 rue Jean Boulogne, Paris, France.

CAREER

La Comédie de Montréal, actress 1943-44; l'Équipe, Monument National and various other theatrical companies, Montréal, actress *c*.1944—; Théâtre du Nouveau Monde, Montréal, actress 1952—; Film Festival Mar del Plata, Argentina, member of Canadian delegation 1953.

MEMBER

Union des Artistes de Montréal.

AWARDS, HONOURS

Miss Radio and TV, 1953; Best television actress, 1954.

THEATRE

Played in many productions, e.g. *La paix chez soi* (South and Central American tour, 194?), *Jeanne d'Arc* (South and Central American tour, 194?), *Poil de carotte* (South and Central American tour, 194?), *Marius* (Équipe, 194?), *L'homme qui se donnait la comédie* (Équipe, 194?), *Le grand poucet* (Équipe, fall 1946), *Les mains sales* (Mexico, 1950), *Asmodée* (Mexico, 1950), *Le corsaire* (Nouveau Monde, 1952/53), leading role in *Nemo* (Nouveau Monde, 1955/56), *Les trois farces* (Nouveau Monde, Stratford, Ont. Festival, 1956), *Mon père avait raison* (Nouveau Monde, Nov. 1957), *L'illusion comique* (Nouveau Monde, Montreal Festival, 1957), Angélique in *Le malade*

imaginaire (Nouveau Monde, Stratford, Ont. Festival, 1958), Anaïs in *Un chapeau de paille d'Italie* (Nouveau Monde, 1958), *Histoire de rire* (Nouveau Monde, 1960), *Le songe d'une nuit d'été* (Théâtre du Rideau Vert, Montréal, 15 Sept. 1965), Natalia in *Les trois soeurs* (Théâtre du Rideau Vert, 15 Apr. 1966).

FILMS

Played in several Canadian films, and *Ultima amor de Goya* (Mexico, 1950), *Una mujer* (Mexico, 1950).

TELEVISION

Played in several productions, e.g. Laura in *The glass menagerie* (CBC, 1954).

SALEMKA, Irene* 1931—

(Irene Salemka Roney)
Singer (soprano); b. 3 Oct. 1931 in Steinbach, Man.; daughter of A.P. and Mathilda (Smith) Salemka; m. Louis Roney 3 June 1964 (marriage dissolved).

EDUCATION

Attended Biggar primary school, Sask.; Weyburn High School, Sask.; studied voice with Marjorie Cathcart, Weyburn; Lloyd Slind and Mme. A. Birkett, Regina; Ernesto Barbini, Toronto, Ont.; Fred J. Smith, Montreal, PQ; Hans Löwlein, Germany.

RELIGION

Protestant.

HOME

c/o Rev. A.P. Salemka, 1364 Argyle St., Regina, Sask.

CAREER

Department of Social Welfare, Regina, stenographer; McGill University, stenographer 1949; Canadian Opera Company, Toronto, soloist 1953, guest artist 1960/61; New Orleans Opera Company, La., soloist 1955; Washington Opera Society, DC, soloist 1956; Sadler's Wells Opera Company, London, England, guest soloist 1956/57; Basel State Opera, Switzerland, soloist 1956; Frankfurt State Opera, Germany, leading lyric soprano 1957-64; Edinburgh Festival, Scotland, soloist 1961; Schwetzingen Festival, Germany, soloist 1963; Covent Garden Opera Company, London, soloist 1963; Bolshoi Theatre, Moscow, USSR, guest soloist 1963; Rome Opera Company, Italy, soloist 1963; Vienna State Opera, Austria, soloist 1963; Hamburg Opera Company, Germany, soloist 1963; toured extensively in North America and Europe.

AWARDS, HONOURS

First prize from Weyburn music festival, 1947; first prize from Saskatchewan music festival, Regina, 1947; scholarship from Kinsmen, Regina; "Singing stars of tomorrow" award, 1953, 1955; award from Canadian National Exhibition, Toronto, 1954; first place in New Orleans Opera Company competition, New York, NY, 1955.

THEATRE
Formal debut as Cio-Cio-San in *Madama Butterfly* (Canadian Opera Company, 1953; Frankfurt State Opera, 1963); sang in numerous productions, e.g. *Messiah* (Barcelona, Spain), *Symphony no. 4* by Mahler (Frankfurt Symphony Orchestra under Georg Solti), Anne in *The rake's progress* (Frankfurt State Opera), fifth Maid in *Electra* (Frankfurt State Opera), Cleopatra in *Julius Caesar* (Frankfurt State Opera), Monica in *The medium* (Canadian première, 1953), Adele in *Die Fledermaus* (Montreal Music Festival, 1954), Juliet in *Romeo and Juliet* (Montreal Music Festival, 1954), Mélisande in *Pelléas and Mélisande* (Frankfurt State Opera, 1957), Pamina in *The magic flute* (Sadler's Wells Opera Company, 1957; Frankfurt State Opera, 1964), Mimi in *La bohème* (Sadler's Wells Opera Company, 1957), Suzanna in *The marriage of Figaro* (Canadian Opera Company, 1960/61), Helena in *A midsummer night's dream* (Royal Opera House, Covent Garden, London, 1961), Olympia, Giulietta, Antonia, and Stella in *The tales of Hoffman* (Vancouver Opera Association, BC, 11 Oct. 1961), Lauretta in *Gianni Schicchi* (Frankfurt State Opera, 1961), Sophie in *Der Rosenkavalier* (Frankfurt State Opera, 1961), Violetta in *La traviata* (Vienna State Opera, 1963), *The merry widow* (Berlin and Bremen, Germany, c.1963), Concepcion in *L'heure espagnole* (Frankfurt State Opera, 1964), Blumenmädchen in *Parsifal* (Frankfurt State Opera, 1965), Micaela in *Carmen* (Frankfurt State Opera, 1966), Donna Elvira in *Don Giovanni* (Stratford, Ont. Festival, 8 July 1966), *Orlow* (Basel, 1967), *Madame Dubarry* (Basel, 1967), *Flower of Hawaii* (Basel, 1967), *Der Vogelhändler* (Basel, 1967), *Czardasfürstin* (Basel, 1967).

FILM
The merry widow (CCC film, Berlin, Spandau, West Germany).

RADIO
Sang in many European and North American productions, e.g. Suzanna in *The marriage of Figaro* (CBC, 19 Oct. 1960), *Frauenliebe und Leben* ("Distinguished artists," CBC, 29 June.1966), *Don Giovanni* excerpts ("Opera time," CBC, 2, 10 July 1966).

TELEVISION
Sang in many European and North American productions, e.g. *The medium* (CBC), *La bohème* (CBC), *Faust* (CBC), "Opportunity knocks" (series, CBC, 1951), *Kate Smith show* (New York, 1955), "L'heure du concert" (series, CBC, 1955), Marguerite in *Faust* (BBC, 1957), *Countess Maritza* (BBC, 1957), Suzanna in *The marriage of Figaro* ("Showcase for music," CBC, 11 Dec. 1960), Olympia, Giulietta, Antonia, and Stella in *The tales of Hoffman* ("Bazaar,"

CBC, 11 Oct. 1961), Hanna in *The merry widow* (Germany, 1965), *Madame Dubarry* (Germany, 1965).

RECORDINGS
Don Giovanni, Deutsche Grammophon, 1964. *Arias of Rameau*, Germany, 1964. *Musical soirée with John van Kesteren*, Philips, 1967.

SCHAEFER, Carl Fellman* 1903–
Artist; b. 30 Apr. 1903 in Hanover, Ont.; son of John D. and Mamie (Fellman) Schaefer; m. Lillian Marie Evers 17 Mar. 1927; children: Mark b. 6 July 1929, Paul b. 30 Oct. 1933.

EDUCATION
Attended primary school and secondary school in Hanover; studied under Arthur Lismer (*q.v.*), J.E.H. MacDonald (*q.v.*), C.M. Manly (*q.v.*), George A. Reid (*q.v.*), and J.W. Beatty, Ontario College of Art, Toronto, 1921-24; studied lithography under Ray Nash, Dartmouth College Workshop, Hanover, NH, 1940-41; studied at the Central School of Arts and Crafts, London, England, 1944-45.

RELIGION
Protestant.

HOME
157 St. Clements Ave., Toronto 12, Ont.

CAREER
Freelance artist and designer in Toronto 1921-30; stage and set designer for Hart House Theatre, Royal Alexandra Theatre, Princess Theatre, and Grand Opera House in Toronto 1921-26; carried out decorations for J.E.H. MacDonald in St. Anne's Church 1923-24, Claridge Apartments 1928, and Concourse Building 1928-29 in Toronto; Central Technical School, Toronto, part-time instructor in art 1930-40; Hart House, University of Toronto, director of art 1934-40 and 1947-56; Trinity College School, Port Hope, Ont., part-time instructor in art 1936-40; painted in Vermont 1940-41; RCAF, 1943-46, became flight lieutenant; appointed official war artist in Europe and Iceland 1943-46; Queen's University Summer School, instructor in painting 1946-50; Doon School of Fine Arts, Ont., instructor 1952-64; Upper Canada Academy, Goodwood, Ont., instructor 1965; Schneider School of Fine Arts, Actinolite, Ont., 1967–; Ontario College of Art, Toronto, instructor in art 1948-56, head of drawing and painting department 1956–.

COMMISSIONS
Series of paintings, Canada Packers Limited, Toronto, 1942.

MEMBER
International Institute of Arts and Letters (elected life fellow, 1958); Canadian Group of Painters (elected, 1936); Canadian Society of Graphic Art (charter member, 1932); Canadian Society of

Painters in Water Colour (elected, 1933; president, 1938-41); Royal Canadian Academy (Associate 1949; Academician 1964).

AWARDS, HONOURS
Fellowship in painting, John Simon Guggenheim Memorial Foundation, New York, NY., USA, 1940-41; Queen's Coronation medal, 1953; second prize, fifth annual exhibition of National Council of Jewish Women, Ottawa, 1962; Centennial medal, 1967.

EXHIBITIONS
ONE-MAN: Picture Loan Society, Toronto, 1937 and on twelve other occasions during 1937-58; Grace Horne Galleries, Boston, Mass., 1940; Feragil Galleries, New York, 1940; Canadian Club, New York, 1948; Virginia Museum of Fine Arts, Richmond, 1949; Hart House, University of Toronto, 1951; Roberts Gallery, Toronto, 1963; McIntosh Memorial Gallery, University of Western Ontario, 1964.

GROUP
Represented in group exhibitions held in Canada since 1925 including annual exhibitions of Canadian Group of Painters, Ontario Society of Artists, Canadian Society of Graphic Art, Royal Canadian Academy, Canadian Society of Painters in Water Colour, and Canadian National Exhibitions; represented in group exhibitions organized by National Gallery of Canada, Ottawa, Ont., including its Annual Exhibitions, International Exposition of Wood Engraving, Warsaw and Cracow, Poland, 1933 and 1936; Exhibition of Contemporary Canadian Painting Arranged ... for Circulation in the Southern Dominions of the British Empire, 1936; Exhibition of Paintings, Drawings and Sculpture by Artists of the British Empire Overseas, Royal Institute Galleries, London, England, 1937; Royal Scottish Society of Painters in Water Colour, Edinburgh, Scotland, 1938-39; A Century of Canadian Art, Tate Gallery, London, 1938; Great Lakes Exhibition Assembled by the Albright-Knox Art Gallery, Buffalo, NY, 1939; Exhibition of Water Colours by Canadian Artists, Gloucester, England, 1939; nineteenth and twentieth International Exhibitions of Water Colours, Art Institute of Chicago Ill., 1939 and 1941; Phildelphia Water Color Exhibition, Pennsylvania Academy of Fine Arts, 1940 and 1946; American Water Color Society, New York, 1941; eleventh International Water Colour Exhibition, Brooklyn Museum, NY, 1941; Aspects of Contemporary Painting in Canada, Addison Gallery, Andover, Mass., 1942-43; Exhibition of Print Makers, Seattle Art Museum, Wash., 1942; United Nations Print Exhibition, Philadelphia Art Alliance, 1943; Canadian Art 1760-1943, Yale University Art Gallery, 1944; War Art, National Gallery, London, 1944 and 1945; Development of Canadian Painting, American Federation of Arts, toured USA, 1944; Art of

the United Nations, San Francisco Palace of the Legion of Honour, Calif., 1945; Exhibition of Canadian Graphic Arts, São Paulo and Rio de Janeiro, Brazil, 1946; *UNESCO ... Exposition internationale d'art moderne, peinture, graphique et décoratif, architecture,* Musée d'Art Moderne, Paris, France, 1946; Canadian Water Colors, Arnot Art Gallery, Elmira, NY, 1946; Contemporary Canadian Painting, Canadian Club, New York; 1948; Canadian Water Colours in New Zealand, 1948-50; Painters of Canada ... 1668-1948, Virginia Museum of Fine Arts, Richmond, 1949; Forty Years of Canadian Painting, Museum of Fine Arts, Boston, 1949; Canadian Painting, National Gallery of Art, Washington, DC, 1950; São Paulo Biennial, Museo de Arte Moderna, São Paulo, 1951; German Industries Exhibition, Berlin, Germany 1953; Joint Canadian-American Water Colour exhibition, 1954; exhibition of Canadian painting shown in Pakistan, India, and Ceylon, 1954-55; An Exhibition of Canadian Paintings held at Fortnum and Mason Ltd., London, 1955; A Canadian Portfolio, Dallas Museum, Tex., 1958; fourth International Hallmark Exhibition, Wildenstein Gallery, New York, 1957; Canadian Paintings, Detroit Museum of Fine Arts, Mich., 1958; Inter-American Biennial of Painting and Graphic Art Museum of Fine Arts, Mexico City, Mexico, 1960; Commonwealth Arts Festival, Cardiff, Wales, 1965.

COLLECTIONS IN WHICH REPRESENTED
Agnes Etherington Art Centre, Queen's University; Art Gallery of Hamilton, Ont.; Art Gallery of Ontario, Toronto; Dalhousie University; Department of External Affairs, Ottawa; Canadian Embassy, Athens, Greece; Glyndhurst Art Gallery, Brantford, Ont.; Hart House Permanent Collection, University of Toronto; London Public Library and Art Museum, Ont.; Memorial University; McIntosh Memorial Gallery, University of Western Ontario; National Gallery of Canada; Pickering College, Newmarket, Ont.; Ridley College, St. Catharines, Ont.; Rodman Hall Art Gallery, St. Catharines; University College, University of Toronto; Upper Canada College, Toronto; Vancouver Art Gallery, BC; Virginia Museum of Fine Arts; Tom Thomson Memorial Gallery, Owen Sound, Ont.; Rothmans Company, Ltd.

SCHAFER, Murray* 1933—
(R. Murray Schafer)
Composer; b. 18 Feb. 1933 in Sarnia, Ont.; son of Harold J. and Belle (Rose) Schafer; m. Phyllis Mailing 2 Feb. 1960.

EDUCATION
Attended Humewood primary school, 1939-47 and Vaughan Road Collegiate School, 1948-53, in Toronto, Ont.; studied composition with John Weinzweig (q.v.), piano with Alberto Guerrero, Royal Conservatory of Music, Toronto, 1950-55;

studied composition with Peter Racine Fricker in England, 1958.

OFFICE

Communications Centre, Simon Fraser University, Burnaby, BC.

CAREER

Freelance journalist and broadcaster in Europe 1956-60; Ten Centuries Concerts, founder and organizer, 1961, president 1961-62; Memorial University, artist in residence 1962-64; Simon Fraser University, resident in music 1965–.

MEMBER

BMI Canada; Canadian League of Composers.

AWARDS, HONOURS

Canada Council arts scholarship, 1960, arts award, 1968.

COMPOSITIONS

Principal works: *Concerto for harpsichord and eight wind instruments*, 1954, first performed 1959 on CBC Montreal by wind ensemble under Kelsey Jones, recorded by CBC IS, no. 193; *Three contemporaries*, voice and piano, 1956; *Minnelieder*, mezzo-soprano and woodwind quintet, 1956, recorded by RCA Victor; *In memoriam Alberto Guerrero*, strings, 1959, first performed 1962 in Vancouver, BC, by CBC Orchestra under John Avison, recorded with the same performers; *Protest and incarceration*, mezzo-soprano and orchestra, 1960; *Brébeuf*, cantata, baritone and orchestra, 1961; *Dithyramb*, string orchestra, 1961; *The judgement of Jael*, cantata, soprano, mezzo-soprano, and orchestra, 1961; *Canzoni for prisoners*, timpani and strings, 1961-62; *Five studies on texts by Prudentius*, soprano and four flutes, 1962, BMI Canada, first performed 1963 at University of Toronto at a concert of electronic music by Mary Morrison and Robert Aitken; *Divisions for baroque trio*, 1963, first performed 1964 on CBC Montreal by Montreal Baroque Trio, commissioned by CBC; *The geography of Eros*, soprano, piano, harp, and percussion, 1963, first performed 1964 at Ten Centuries Concerts, Toronto by Mary Morrison and percussion under Howard Cable, recorded on air-check tapes with Phyllis Mailing; *Statement in blue*, youth orchestra, 1964, BMI Canada; *Air Ishtar*, soprano, piano, and percussion, first performed 1965 on CBC TV with Margot MacKinnon and ensemble under Serge Garant; *Modesty*, mezzo-soprano and strings (some pre-recorded), 1965, first performed 1965 on CBC TV Montreal with Evelyn Maxwell and ensemble under Serge Garant; *Vanity*, mezzo-soprano, strings, and percussion, 1965, first performed on CBC TV Montreal with Huguette Tourangeau and ensemble under Serge Garant; *Loving/Toi*, bilingual opera, 1966, first performed 1966 on CBC TV Montreal with orchestra under Serge Garant, commissioned by CBC; *Requiems for the party girl*, mezzo-soprano

and nine instruments, 1966, first performed 21 Nov. 1967 on CBC Vancouver with orchestra under Norman Nelson, commissioned by CBC for Canada's centennial; *Threnody*, youth choir and orchestra, electronic tape and narrators, 1967, first performed in Vancouver under Simon Streatfeild, commissioned by Vancouver Alumni of the Royal Conservatory of Music for Canada's centennial; *Gita*, chorus, brass, and prepared tape, 1967, first performed 1967 at Tanglewood, Mass., under Ira Dee Hiat, commissioned by Berkshire Music Center; *Sonorities for brass sextet*, baritone, tape recorder, and brass, 1967, first performed 4 Dec. 1967 at Memorial University, commissioned by St. John's Brass Consort for Canada's centennial; *Kaleidoscope*, music for exhibition pavilion, 1967, commissioned for Expo 67; *Man and life*, music for exhibition pavilion, 1967, commissioned for Expo 67.

WORK IN PROGRESS

Orchestral work commissioned by Montreal Symphony Orchestra; chamber work commissioned by Serge Koussevitzky Foundation; radiophonic work commissioned by CBC; "Patria," opera.

WRITINGS

British composers in interview, Faber & Faber, 1963; *The composer in the classroom*, BMI Canada, 1965; *Ear cleaning*, BMI Canada, 1967. CONTRIBUTED: Articles to *Canadian music journal, Tamarck review, Queen's quarterly, Canadian forum, West coast review, Musicanada, The music scene*.

WORK IN PROGRESS

"The cosmology of romantic music," book on the music of Ezra Pound.

SCHAFER, R. Murray
see SCHAFER, Murray

SCHULL, John Joseph
see SCHULL, Joseph

SCHULL, Joseph*   1910–
(John Joseph Schull)
Playwright and poet; b. 6 Feb. 1910 in Watertown, S. Dak.; son of Charles Henry and Alice Aveline (Travers) Schull; came to Canada in 1913; m. Helen Gougeon 8 Jan. 1955; children: Christiane b. 26 Apr. 1959, Joseph b. 2 Mar. 1961, Michael b. 4 Apr. 1964.

EDUCATION

Attended King George Public School and Ross Collegiate in Moose Jaw, Sask; Queen's University; University of Saskatchewan.

RELIGION

Roman Catholic.

HOME

544 Grande Côte, Rosemere, PQ.

OFFICE
42 Eleventh Ave., St.-Eustache-sur-le-lac, PQ.

CAREER
Mainly literary; moved to Montreal and worked in advertising 1935-41; RCNVR, 1941-45, became lieutenant commander (special branch), intelligence and information officer; freelance author, 1945—.

AWARDS, HONOURS
Award for *Shadow of the tree*; University of British Columbia medal for popular biography and Quebec government cultural award for *Laurier*, 1965.

WRITINGS
The legend of ghost lagoon (poem), Macmillan, 1937; *I, Jones, soldier* (poem), Macmillan, 1944; *The far distant ships; an official account of the Canadian naval operations in the Second World War*, King's Printer, 1950; *The salt water men, Canada's deep sea sailors*, Macmillan, 1957; *100 years of banking in Canada; a history of the Toronto-Dominion Bank*, Copp Clark, 1958; *Battle for the rock; the story of Wolfe and Montcalm*, Macmillan, 1960; *Ships of the great days*, Macmillan, 1962; *Laurier: The first Canadian*, Macmillan, 1965; *The nation makers*, Macmillan, 1967; *The jinker* (novel), Macmillan, 1968; *Shadow of the tree* (play; produced London Little Theatre, Ont., 1952); *Counterpoint* (play; produced Greystone Theatre, University of Saskatchewan, 1967); numerous radio and TV plays for CBC.

CONTRIBUTED: Poems and stories to *Heroic tales in verse*, edited by E.J. Pratt, Macmillan, 1941; *Anthology of Canadian poetry*, compiled by R. Gustafson, Penguin, 1942; *Twentieth century Canadian poetry*, edited by E. Birney, Ryerson, 1953; *Canadian poetry in English*, rev. and enl. ed., chosen by B. Carman, Ryerson, 1954; *Maclean's, Saturday night.*

SCOTT, David Robert* 1928—
Dancer; b. 2 Feb. 1928 in Colombo, Ceylon; son of Robert and Jessica (Thompson) Scott; m. Joanne Nisbet (*q.v.*) 15 Apr. 1957; came to Canada in 1959.

EDUCATION
Attended school in Newcastle upon Tyne, England; studied ballet with Nora Fearn, Newcastle upon Tyne; Espinosa School, Stanislas Idzikowski, Kathleen Crofton, Anna Northcote (Severskayal), Lubov Tchernicheva, and Serge Grigoriev in London, England.

RELIGION
Church of England.

HOME
7 Playter Blvd., Toronto 6, Ont.

OFFICE
National Ballet of Canada, 157 King St. E., Toronto 1, Ont.

CAREER
Original Ballet Russe, London, dancer 1949; London's Festival Ballet, corps de ballet 1950-54, soloist 1954-59; National Ballet of Canada, Toronto, soloist 1959-63, ballet master 1963—.

MEMBER
AEA.

THEATRE
First danced Poet in *Les sylphides* (Fokine, Théâtre Champs Élysées, Paris, France, 1955), Pas de deux in *Études* (Lander, 1955), Prince in *Cassenoisette*, act I (Ivanov, 1956), Prince Siegfried in *Le lac des cygnes* (Petipa-Ivanov, 1956), Romeo in *Romeo and Juliet* pas de deux (Briansky, 1957), *Variations for four* (Dolin, 1957), Captain Belaye in *Pineapple Poll* (Cranko, 1959), His Imperial Excellency in *Offenbach in the underworld* (Tudor, 1959), Florestan in *Princess Aurora* (Franca after Petipa, 1960), Groom in *Antic spring* (Strate, 1960).

TELEVISION
Danced in many BBC productions in the 1950s; Lord Montague in *Romeo and Juliet* (Cranko, "Festival," CBC, 15 Sept. 1965; 2 Mar. 1966).

SCOTT, Duncan Campbell 1862-1947
Author; b. 2 Aug. 1862 in Ottawa, Ont.; son of William and Janet (MacCallum) Scott; m. Belle Warner Botsford 1894 (d. 1929); m. Désirée Elise Aylen 1931; children: (first marriage) Elizabeth Duncan b. 1895 (d. 1907); d. 19 Dec. 1947 in Ottawa.

EDUCATION
Attended primary school in Smith's Falls, Ont.; Wesleyan College, Stanstead, PQ.

CAREER
Department of Indian Affairs, Ottawa, clerk 1879-93, chief accounting clerk 1893-1909, superintendent of Indian education 1909-13, deputy superintendent general, 1913-32; *Globe*, Toronto, Ont., columnist 1892-93; travelled extensively 1936-42.

MEMBER
Dominion Drama Festival (governor); Royal Society of Literature of Great Britain (fellow); Canadian Authors Association (president, 1931-33); Ottawa Drama League (president, 1925); Royal Society of Canada (elected fellow, 1899; president of section two, 1902-3; honorary secretary, 1911-21; president, 1921-22); Canadian Writers Foundation (board of governors).

AWARDS, HONOURS
Globe contest prize for "Lundy's Lane," 1908; D Litt from University of Toronto, 1922; Lorne Pierce medal, 1927; Companion of the Order of St. Michael and St. George, 1934; LL D from Queen's University, 1939.

WRITINGS
At Scarboro Beach (poem), p.p., n.d.; *Reality* (poem), n.p., n.d.; *The magic house and other*

poems, Durie, 1893; (with Archibald Lampman) *Two poems*, n.p., 1896; *In the village of Viger* (short stories) Copeland & Day, 1896; (with Archibald Lampman) *These poems*, n.p., 1897; *Labour and the angel* (poems), Copeland & Day, 1898; *New world lyrics and ballads*, Morang, 1905; *The life of John Graves Simcoe* (non-fiction), Morang, 1906; *Via Borealis* (poems), Tyrrell, 1906; *Spring on Mattagami* (poems), 1906; *Notes on the meeting place of the first parliament of Upper Canada and the early buildings at Niagara* (non-fiction), Royal Society, 1913; *Lines in memory of Edmund Morris* (poem), n.p., 1915; *Lundy's Lane and other poems*, Doran, 1916; *To the Canadian mothers, and three other poems*, p.p., 1917; *Beauty and life* (poems), McClelland & Stewart, 1921; *The witching of Elspie* (short stories), Doran, 1923; *Byron on Wordsworth* (poem), p.p., 1924; *The poems of Duncan Campbell Scott*, McClelland & Stewart, 1926; *The administration of Indian affairs in Canada ...* (non-fiction), Canadian Institute of International Affairs, 1931; *The green cloister; later poems*, McClelland & Stewart, 1935, *Walter J. Phillips, R.C.A.* (biography), Ryerson, 1947; *The circle of affection and other pieces in prose and verse*, McClelland & Stewart, 1947; *Joy! joy! joy!* (play; produced Hart House Theatre, Toronto, 1927).

EDITED: *The poems of Archibald Lampman*, Morang, 1900; A.A. Paget's *The people of the plains* (non-fiction), W. Briggs, 1909; *Lyrics of earth: sonnets and ballads by Archibald Lampman*, Musson, 1925; (with P. Edgar) *The makers of Canada* (non-fiction), Oxford, 1926; A. Lampman's *At the Long Sault and other new poems*, Ryerson, 1943; *Selected poems of Archibald Lampman*, Ryerson, 1947.

CONTRIBUTED: Poems, short stories, plays, and biographies to *Songs of the great Dominion*, edited by W.D. Lighthall, W. Scott, 1889; *A Victorian anthology*, *1837-1895*, edited by E.C. Stedman, Houghton Mifflin, 1895; *Werner's readings and recitations*, Edgar S. Werner, 1910; *A sailor's garland*, edited by J. Masefield, rev. ed., Macmillan, 1924; *The poetry cure*, compiled by R.H. Schauffler, Dodd, 1925; *The home book of verse*, edited by B.E. Stevenson, Holt, 1925; *Magic casements*, compiled by G.S. Carhart and P.A. McGhee, Macmillan, 1926; *Canadian poets*, edited by J.W. Garvin, rev. ed., McClelland & Stewart, 1926; *Canadian plays from Hart House Theatre*, Macmillan, 1926; *Armistice day*, edited by A.P. Sanford and R.H. Schauffler, Dodd, 1927; *Canadian short stories*, edited by R. Knister, Macmillan, 1928; *Modern lyric poetry*, edited by H. Bates, Row & Peterson, 1929; *Off to Arcady*, edited by M.J. Herzberg, American Book, 1933; *The modern muse*, Oxford, 1934; *What I like in poetry*, compiled by W.L. Phelps, Scribner, 1934;

Our Canadian literature, edited by B. Carman and L. Pierce, rev. ed., Ryerson, 1935; *Poems, chiefly narrative*, edited by W.L. Macdonald and F.C. Walker, rev. ed., Dent, 1938; *Poems worth knowing*, compiled by C.E. Lewis, Copp Clark, 1941; *Flying colours*, edited by C.G.D. Roberts, Ryerson, 1942; *Anthology of Canadian poetry*, compiled by R. Gustafson, Penguin, 1942; *The book of Canadian poetry*, edited by A.J.M. Smith, University of Chicago, 1943; *The new treasury of war poetry: poems of the second world war*, edited by G.H. Clarke, Houghton Mifflin, 1943; *Twentieth century verse*, edited by I. Dilworth, Clarke, Irwin, 1945; *The eternal sea; an anthology of sea poetry*, edited by W.H. Williamson, Coward-McCann, 1946; *The golden book of Catholic poetry*, edited by A. Noyes, Lippencott, 1946; *Leading Canadian poets*, compiled by W.P. Percival, Ryerson, 1948; *Queen's quarterly, Saturday night, Canadian poetry, Canadian magazine, Proceedings and transactions of the Royal Society of Canada, Scribner's magazine, Two tales, Truth, Youth's companion*.

SCOTT, Frederick George   1861-1944

Poet; b. 7 Apr. 1861 in Montreal, PQ; son of William Edward Scott and Elizabeth (Sproston) Scott; m. Amy Brooks 27 Apr. 1887; children: William B., Elton, Francis Reginald, Mrs. A.R. Kelly, Arthur; d. 19 Jan. 1944 in Quebec, PQ.

EDUCATION

Attended Montreal high school; Bishop's College, Lennoxville, PQ, BA, 1881, MA, 1884; King's College, University of London, DD.

RELIGION

Anglican.

CAREER

Ordained deacon 1884; St. John's School, master 1884; ordained in the Church of England 1886; Coggleshall, Essex, England, curate 1886-87; Drummondville, PQ, rector 1887-96; St. Matthew's Church, Quebec, curate and rector 1896-1934; Cathedral of Quebec, canon 1906-25; Canadian Army, 8th Royal Rifles, Quebec, 1906, chaplain, honorary rank of captain, First Canadian Division, 1914, became major and senior chaplain, repeatedly mentioned in dispatches, awarded DSO 1918, and VD; Canadian Legion and the Army and Navy Veterans, elected Dominion chaplain; Archdeacon of Quebec 1925.

MEMBER

Royal Society of Canada (elected fellow, 1900); Canadian Landmarks Association, councillor.

AWARDS, HONOURS

Sandford gold medal for life saving, Royal Canadian Humane Society, 1898; LLD from McGill University; DCL from King's College, Windsor, NS; DCL from Bishop's College, 1902; CMG, 1916.

WRITINGS

The soul's guest and other poems, Paul, 1888;

Elton Hazelwood; a memoir by his friend Harry Vane (novel), Whittaker, 1891; *My lattice and other poems*, Briggs, 1894; *The unnamed lake and other poems*, Briggs, 1897; *A hymn of Empire and other poems*, Briggs, 1906; *The key of life; a mystery play*, Dussault, 1907; *Poems*, Constable, 1910; *In the battle of silences; poems written at the front*, Constable, 1916; *The great war as I saw it* (non-fiction), Goodchild, 1922; *In sun and shade*, Dussault & Proulx, 1926; *New poems*, Lafrance, 1929; *Selected poems*, Robitaille, 1933; *Collected poems*, Clarke & Stuart, 1934; *Poems*, Society for Promoting Christian Knowledge, 1936.
CONTRIBUTED: Poems to many anthologies, e.g. *A Victorian anthology 1837-1895*, edited by E. C. Stedman, Houghton Mifflin, 1895; *Canadian poets*, edited by J.W. Garvin, rev. ed., McClelland & Stewart, 1926; *Quotable poems*, v.I, edited by T.C. Clark and E.A. Gillespie, Willett Clark, 1928; *Our Canadian literature*, edited B. Carman and L. Pierce, rev. ed., Ryerson, 1935; *1000 quotable poems*, edited by T.C. Clark, Willett Clark, 1937; *Poems worth knowing*, edited by C.E. Lewis, Copp Clark, 1941; *Flying colours*, edited by Sir C.G.D. Roberts, Ryerson, 1942; *Anthology of Canadian poetry*, edited by R. Gustafson, Penguin, 1942; *The book of Canadian poetry*, edited by A.J.M. Smith, University of Chicago, 1943; *Unseen wings, the living poetry of man's immortality*, edited by S.A. Coblentz, Beechhurst, 1949; *Transactions of the Royal Society of Canada, McGill fortnightly review, Saturday night, Maclean's, Royal Architectural Institute of Canada journal*.

SCOTT, Joanne Nisbet
see NISBET, Joanne

SECTER, David* 1943–
Film director and writer; b. 24 Mar. 1943 in Brandon, Man.; son of Joseph and Gwen (Feinstein) Secter.
EDUCATION
Attended St. Michael's Academy, Brandon, 1947-48; King George V primary school, Brandon, 1948-49; Grosvenor Primary School, Winnipeg, Man., 1949-50; Brock-Corydon Primary School, Winnipeg, 1950-56; River Heights Junior High School, Winnipeg, 1956-59; Kelvin High School, Winnipeg, 1959-61; University of Manitoba, 1961-63; University of Toronto, BA in English, 1963-65.
RELIGION
Jewish.
HOME
171 Spadina Rd., Toronto 7, Ont.
OFFICE
54 W. 71, Apt. 2F, New York City, NY, USA.

CAREER
The varsity, Toronto, film critic and entertainment writer 1962-64; freelance critic and entertainment writer; CBC, radio producer and interviewer; Cannes Film Festival, France, Canadian representative 1966; toured northwestern USA with features, speaking to universities and film societies on student film production 1967.
AWARDS, HONOURS
David Secter Festival, Ryerson Institute, Toronto, 1967.
FILMS
Wrote, produced, and directed *Love with the proper guppy* (1964), *Winter kept us warm* (c.1965; feature film, University of Toronto; world première, Commonwealth Arts Festival, Cardiff, Wales, 1965; special jury prize, Montreal International Film Festival, PQ, 1966; special award, Cinestudy '67, Amsterdam, The Netherlands; selected for festivals in Pesaro, Italy, Edinburgh, Scotland, London, England, Sidney and Melbourne, Australia, Chicago, Ill., and San Antonio, Tex.); produced and directed *The offering* (Toronto, 1966; selected as opening presentation, Hemis-film '68, San Antonio, Tex., and Vancouver, BC International Film Festival).
WORK IN PROGRESS: Producing, writing lyrics for and joint author of "Get thee to Canterbury!", opening Sept. 1968 off-Broadway, New York, NY; collaborating on "Zodiak"; writing feature film script for fall production.

SERRES, Marthe des, pseud.
see CHARBONNEAU, Hélène

SETON, Ernest Thompson 1860-1946
(Ernest Evan Seton Thompson; Ernest Seton-Thompson)
Novelist, artist, and naturalist; b. 14 Aug. 1860 in South Shields, Durham, England; son of Joseph Logan and Alice (Snowdon) Thompson; came to Canada in 1865; m. Grace Gallatin 1 June 1896 (marriage dissolved 1935); m. Julia Moss Buttree 22 Jan. 1935; children: (first marriage) Ann b. c. 1916; (second marriage) Beulah (adopted); became US citizen 6 Nov. 1931; d. 23 Oct. 1946 in Seton Village, Sante Fe, NM.
EDUCATION
Attended school in Toronto, Ont.; studied art at Ontario Art School, Toronto, 1879; Royal Academy of Painting and Sculpture, London, England, 1880; Académie Julian, Paris, France, 1890-96.
CAREER
Mainly literary; Manitoba government, official naturalist 1892–?; illustrated *Century dictionary*, Century, 1885 and *Bird life* by F.M. Chapman, Appleton, 1897; Woodcraft Indians (later League of American Woodcraft Indians, The Woodcraft

League of America), founder 1902; Boy Scouts of America, chairman of founding committee 1910, chief scout 1910-15; Seton Institute, Santa Fé, founder and president 1930-46.

MEMBER

American Ornithologists' Union; Royal Canadian Academy (Associate); National Institute of Arts and Letters.

AWARDS, HONOURS

Ontario Art School gold medal, 1879; Camp Fire gold medal for *Life-histories of northern animals*, 1909; Société d'Acclimatation de France silver medal, 1918; John Burroughs medal for *Lives of game animals*, v. 2 c.1928; Daniel Giraud Elliott gold medal for *Lives of game animals*, v. 3 1927; David Girou medal for contribution to natural sciences, 1930.

EXHIBITIONS

GROUP: Represented in group exhibitions held in Toronto area during his lifetime; Universal Exposition, Paris, 1889; Grand Salon, Paris, 1891; World's Columbian Exposition, Chicago, Ill., 1893.

WRITINGS

Prairie fires (non-fiction), Manitoba Historical and Scientific Society; *A list of mammals of Manitoba*, Oxford, 1886; *The birds of Manitoba*, US National Museum, 1891; *Studies in the art anatomy of animals*, Macmillan, 1896; *Wild animals I have known*, Scribner, 1898; *Lobo, Rag and Vixen*, Scribner, 1899; *The trail of the sandhill stag*, Scribner, 1899; *The biography of a grizzly*, Century, 1900; *The wild animal play for children*, Doubleday, Page, 1900; *Bird portraits*, Ginn, 1901; *Lives of the hunted*, Scribner, 1901; *The national zoo at Washington*, Smithsonian Institute, 1901; *Pictures of wild animals*, Scribner, 1901; *Krag and Johnny bear*, Scribner, 1902; *How to play Indian*, Curtis, 1903 (also published under title *The red book; or How to play Indian*); *Two little savages*, Doubleday, Page, 1903; *Monarch, the big bear of Tallac*, Scribner, 1904; *Animal heroes*, Scribner, 1905; *Woodmyth and fables*, Century, 1905; *The birch-bark rool of the Woodcraft Indians*, Doubleday, Page, 1906 (also published under titles *The birch-bark roll of the Woodcraft, The American Boy Scout; the official handbook of woodcraft for the Boy Scouts of America, Manual of Woodcraft Indians, The woodcraft manual for girls, The woodcraft manual for boys*); *The natural history of the Ten Commandments*, Scribner, 1907 (also published under title *The Ten Commandments in the animal world*); *The biography of a silver fox*, Century, 1909; *Life histories of northern animals, an account of the mammals of Manitoba*, Scribner, 1909; *Boy Scouts of America; a handbook of woodcraft, scouting and life-craft*, Doubleday, Page, 1910; *The war dance and the fire-fly dance*, Doubleday,

Page, 1910; *The Arctic prairies; a canoe journey of 2,000 miles in search of the caribou*, Scribner, 1911; *Rolf in the woods*, Doubleday, Page, 1911; *The book of woodcraft and Indian lore*, Doubleday, Page, 1912; *The forester's manual; or The forest trees of eastern North America*, Doubleday, Page 1912; *Wild animals at home*, Doubleday, Page, 1913; *Woodcraft boys, woodcraft girls*, Edgar, 1915; *Wild animal ways*, Doubleday, Page, 1916; *The preacher of Cedar mountain*, Doubleday, Page, 1917; *Sign talk; a universal signal code*, Doubleday, Page, 1918; *Woodland tales*, Doubleday, Page, 1921; *Bannertail*, Scribner, 1922; *Lives of game animals*, 4 v., Doubleday, Page, 1925-28; *Animals, selected from life histories of northern animals*, Doubleday, Page, 1926; *Billy the dog*, Hodder & Stoughton, 1930; *Cute coyote and other animal stories*, Hodder & Stoughton, 1930; *Lobo, Bingo and the racing mustang*, State Pub. House, 1930; *Famous animal stories*, Brentano, 1932; *Animals worth knowing, selected from Life histories of northern animals*, Doubleday, Doran, 1934; *Johnny bear, Lobo and other stories*, Scribner, 1935; *The gospel of the Red man; an Indian Bible*, Doubleday, Doran, 1936; *The biography of an Arctic fox*, Appleton-Century, 1937; *Great historic animals, mainly about wolves*, Scribner, 1937; *The buffalo wind*, Seton Village Press, 1938; *Ernest Thompson Seton's trail and camp-fire stories*, Appleton-Century, 1940; *The trail of an artist-naturalist* (autobiography), Scribner, 1940; *Santana, the hero dog of France*, Phoenix, 1945. Works have been extensively translated.

CONTRIBUTED: Short stories to numerous anthologies, e.g. *The Queen's gift book*, Hodder & Stoughton, 1916; *Modern short stories*, edited by F.H. Law, Century, 1918; *Real dogs; an anthology of short stories*, edited by C.W. Gray, Holt, 1926; *Hosses; an anthology of short stories*, edited by C.W. Gray, Holt, 1927; *Just cats; stories grave and gay of the hearthside tyrant*, edited by R. Miller, Doubleday, Doran, 1934; *Century of nature stories*, Hutchinson, 1937; *A treasury of cat stories*, compiled by E. Zistel, Greenberg, 1944; *Animal tales, an anthology of animal literature of all countries*, edited by I.T. Sanderson, Knopf, 1946; numerous periodicals, e.g. *Canadian journal, St. Nicholas, Forest and stream, Century magazine, Ladies home journal, Scribner's magazine, Outing, Dial, Nation, Athenaeum, Country life.*

SETON-THOMPSON, Ernest
see SETON, Ernest Thompson

SEYMOUR, Lynn 1939–
(Lynn Berta Springbett Jones; Lynn Berta Springbett Valtz)
Dancer; b. 8 Mar. 1939 in Wainwright, Alta.;

daughter of Edward Victor and Marjorie Isabelle (McIvor) Springbett; m. Colin Edward Jones 16 July 1963; m. Eike Valtz; children: (second marriage) twin sons b. 1968.

EDUCATION

Attended school in Vancouver, BC; studied ballet with Jean Jepson and Nicolai Svetlanoff, Vancouver; Sadler's Wells (now Royal) Ballet School, London, England, 1953-57; Valentina Perejaslavec, New York, NY.

OFFICE

German Opera Ballet, Berlin Opera House, West Berlin, Germany.

CAREER

Covent Garden Opera Ballet, London, dancer 1956-57; Royal Ballet, London, corps de ballet 1957-58; soloist 1958-?, principal 19?-66; Stuttgart National Ballet, Germany, guest artist 1964; National Ballet of Canada, Toronto, guest artist 1964; German Opera Ballet, West Berlin, principal 1966–.

THEATRE

First danced Tarantella in *Veneziana* (Howard, 1958), *A blue rose* (Wright, 1958), Dancer in *First impression* (Beale, Sunday Ballet Club, London, 1958); created Young lover in *The burrow* (MacMillan, 2 Jan. 1958); first danced Odette-Odile in *Le lac des cygnes* (Petipa-Ivanov, Australian tour 1958), title role in *Giselle* (Coralli-Perrot, 1960), title role in *The sleeping beauty* (Petipa, 1960); created Bride in *Le baiser de la fée* (MacMillan, 12 Apr. 1960), Girl in *The invitation* (MacMillan, New Theatre, Oxford, England, 10 Nov. 1960), Young girl in *Les deux pigeons* (Ashton, 1961); first danced title role in *Cinderella* (Ashton, 1961), Ophelia in *Hamlet* (Helpmann, 1961), Bride in *La fête étrange* (Howard, 1961), Girl in *Solitaire* (MacMillan, 1963), *Danses concertantes* (MacMillan, 1963); created role in *Symphony* (MacMillan, 1963, did not dance première), "Love is blind" and "Two loves I have" in *Images of love* (MacMillan, 2 Apr. 1964), Juliet in *Romeo and Juliet* (MacMillan, 1965, did not dance première).

TELEVISION

Danced in several CBC productions, e.g. ballet excerpts ("Parade," 26 July 1960), ballet excerpts ("Thursday special," 20 Oct. 1960), *Our dancing export* ("Telescope," 31 Jan. 1964; 31 July 1964), *Variety show* ("Show of the week," 28 Sept. 1964), *Première* ("Festival," 28 Oct. 1964), *Four faces of ballet* ("Compass," 22 Aug. 1965).

SHADBOLT, Jack Leonard* 1909–
Artist; b. 4 Feb. 1909 in Shoeburyness, England; son of Edmund and Alice Mary Maude (Healy) Shadbolt; came to Canada with his parents in 1912 and settled in Victoria, BC; m. Doris Meisel.

EDUCATION

Attended Victoria High School, 1924-27; Victoria College, 1925-27; Provincial Normal School, Vic-

toria, 1927-28; studied under Victor Pasmore, William Coldstream, and Claude Rogers, Euston Road School, London, England, 1937-38; André Lhate, School of Art, Paris, France, 1938; Vaclav Vytacil, Art Students League, New York, NY, 1948-49.

RELIGION

Protestant.

HOME AND STUDIO

461 North Glynde St., Vancouver, BC .

CAREER

Duncan Consolidated Elementary School, BC, art teacher 1929-31; Kitsilano High School, Vancouver, art teacher 1931 and 1934-37; Danforth Technical School, Toronto, Ont., art teacher in evening course 1933; John Oliver High School, Vancouver, art teacher for five months 1934; Vancouver School of Art, instructor 1938-42, head of drawing and painting section 1945-66; Canadian Army, 1942-45, became lieutenant; official war artist 1945 and acting administration officer for army war artists; Victoria College Summer School, instructor 1953; University of Saskatchewan Emma Lake Workshop, instructor 1955; University of Alberta summer painting workshop, instructor 1967; painter in Vancouver 1931–.

COMMISSIONS

Mural, Alcazar Hotel, Vancouver, 1947; mural, Dominion Hotel, Victoria, 1951; murals, Queen Elizabeth Theatre restaurant, Vancouver, 1961; mural, Edmonton International Airport, Alta., 1964; mural, Confederation Memorial Centre, Charlottetown, PEI, 1964; painting, Canadian pavilion, International Trade Fair, Tokyo, Japan, 1965; Artists for Billboards Project, Vancouver, 1965; posters for 1967-68 season, Playhouse Theatre, Vancouver, 1967.

MEMBER

BC Society of Artists; Federation of Canadian Artists (founding member); Canadian Group of Painters; International Society of Artists; Canadian Society of Painters in Water Colour.

AWARDS, HONOURS

Beatrice Stone gold medal, Vancouver Art Gallery, 1941; Jessie Dow Memorial award, Montreal Museum of Fine Arts, 1952; prize, Northwest Artists Annual Exhibition, Seattle Art Museum, Wash., 1957; Canada Council fellowship for study in France, 1957; Carnegie International award, 1958; Guggenheim International award, 1958; prize, Winnipeg Show, Winnipeg Art Gallery, Man., 1964.

EXHIBITIONS

ONE-MAN: Vancouver, 1936; Laing Fine Art Galleries, Toronto, 1948; Laurel Galleries, New York, 1949; University of British Columbia, 1949; School of Fine Arts Gallery, San Francisco, Calif., 1953; Art Gallery of Greater Victoria, 1954 and 1961; Seattle Art Museum, 1958; Vancouver Art Gallery, 1959; Winnipeg, Man., 1961; Galerie

Agnès Lefort, Montréal, PQ, 1964; Jerrold Morris Gallery, Toronto, 1965.

GROUP: Represented in group exhibitions held in Canada including annual exhibitions of Canadian Group of Painters, Canadian Society of Painters in Water Colour, and BC Society of Artists; represented in group exhibitions organized by National Gallery of Canada, Ottawa, Ont., including its first, second, third, fourth, and sixth Biennial Exhibitions of Canadian Painting, 1955, 1957, 1959, 1961, and 1965; Caracas Biennial Exhibition, Venezuela, 1953; São Paulo Biennial Exhibition, Brazil, 1953; Canadian Section, Biennale, Venice, Italy, 1954; International Exhibition, Carnegie Institute, Pittsburgh, Pa., 1955; International Exhibition of Paintings, Athenee of Valencia, Venezuela, 1955; Exhibition of Canadian Art, Canadian pavilion, Brussels International Exposition, Belgium, 1958; Canadian travelling exhibition, Mexico City, Mexico, 1958; Paintings and Sculptures of the Pacific Northwest, Portland Art Museum, Ore., 1959; International Water Color Exhibition, Brooklyn Museum, NY, 1959; Canadian Painting, Dallas, Tex., 1960; World's Fair, Seattle, 1962; Four Canadians, San Francisco Museum, 1962; Warsaw, Poland, 1963; Canadian Exhibition, Buffalo, NY, 1963; A Quarter Century of Canadian Art, Tate Gallery, London, 1964.

COLLECTIONS IN WHICH REPRESENTED
Art Gallery of Greater Victoria; Art Gallery of Hamilton, Ont.; Art Gallery of Ontario, Toronto; Brooklyn Museum; Beaverbrook Art Gallery, Fredericton, NB; Hart House Permanent Collection, University of Toronto; Mills College, Oakland, Calif.; Montreal Museum of Fine Arts; National Gallery of Canada; Portland Art Museum; Sarnia Public Library and Art Gallery, Ont.; Seattle Art Museum; Smith College Art Museum, Northampton, Mass.; University of Birtish Columbia; University of Saskatchewan; University of Victoria; Vancouver Art Gallery; Winnipeg Art Gallery; Musée d'Art Contemporain, Montréal; Agnes Etherington Art Centre, Queen's University.

SHUMSKY, Oscar
Violinist, conductor, and director; b. in Philadelphia, Pa.

EDUCATION
Studied violin with Leopold Auer; studied with Efrem Zimbalist, Curtis Institute, Philadelphia.

CAREER
Concert violinist in recitals; Peabody Conservatory of Music, Baltimore, Md., professor to 1953; Stratford, Ont. Festival of Music, teacher of master classes summer 1959, artist-in-residence 1960, co-director of music 1961-64, director of music 1965-67; Juilliard School of Music, New York, NY, faculty member 1953–; Westchester Symphony Orchestra, White Plains, NY, director of music.

AWARDS, HONOURS
Ford Foundation fellowship, 1962.

CONCERT STAGE
Soloist with Philadelphia Orchestra at the age of eight; (with Glenn Gould and Leonard Rose) played and conducted chamber music programs, Stratford, Ont. Festival, 1959, 1960, 1961; (with Claudio Arrau and Leonard Rose) played Beethoven program, Stratford, Ont. Festival, 1962; conducted Ford Foundation Award concert, New York, Dec. 1963.

TELEVISION
Appearances on CBC TV in music from Stratford, Ont. Festival.

SHUSTER, Frank   1916–
Comedian; b. 1916; m. Ruth 1942; children: Rosalind b. 1947, Stephen b. 1950.

EDUCATION
Attended Harbord Collegiate in Toronto; University of Toronto, BA in English.

HOME
33 Ridelle Ave., Toronto 19, Ont.

CAREER
CBC, Toronto, comedian 1939–; Canadian Army, 1942- ?, sergeant; Capitol Films, vice-president 1951; Charlottetown Festival, PEI, co-director 1965.

MEMBER
ACTRA; Canadian Theatre Centre.

AWARDS, HONOURS
Canadian Association for Adult Education award for *The lost comic book weekend*, 1960; *Motion picture daily and television today* award for best TV comedy team, 1962, 1963; Silver rose (2nd prize) at International Variety Show Festival, Montreux, Switzerland, 1965.

THEATRE
Wrote and played in *The Army show* (tour 1942- ?); played in *Royal variety concert* (Confederation Centre, Charlottetown, 6 Oct. 1964), *An evening with Wayne and Shuster* (Charlottetown Festival, 1965; trans-Canada tour 1965); produced *Mother Goose* (Eaton Auditorium, Toronto, 1950-51).

RADIO
Played in numerous CBC programs, e.g. "Wife preservers" (series, 1939), "The Johnny home show" (Beaver award), "The Wayne and Shuster show" (1948- ?).

TELEVISION
Played in many programs, e.g. *The Wayne and Shuster show* (CBC, 1954–), guest on *The Rosemary Clooney show* (1957), "Chelsea at nine" (series, Granada, London, England, 1957), *The Ed Sullivan show* (CBS, 4 May 1958–), *Holiday Lodge* (serial, CBS, 1961), *Wayne and Shuster take an affectionate look at ...* (CBC, 1964–).

SHUTTLEWORTH, Gisèle
see MacKENZIE, Gisèle

SIDGWICK, John Robert Lindsay 1923–
Organist and choirmaster; b. 29 Jan. 1923 in
Surrey, England; son of John Benson and Dolores
(Young) Sidgwick; m. Mary Sibly 12 Apr. 1947;
children: Helen, Rosemary, Peter.

EDUCATION
Attended St. George's Choir School, Windsor
Castle, England, 1931-37; Felstead School,
Essex, England 1937-41; Clare College, University
of Cambridge, 1941-42; BMus, 1948, BA, 1949,
MA, 1954; Royal College of Music, London, Eng-
land, associate, 1946; Royal College of Organists,
associate, 1946, fellow, 1953; studied with Sir
Walford Davies and Sir William Harris.

RELIGION
Anglican.

HOME
26 Chipping Rd., Don Mills, Ont.

OFFICE
Royal Conservatory of Music, Toronto, Ont.

CAREER
Royal Air Force, 1941-45, flight lieutenant;
Upper Canada College, Toronto, head of music
department 1949-51; English Madrigal Singers,
founder 1950; All Saints, Kingsway, Toronto,
organist 1951-52; Metropolitan United Church,
Toronto, organist 1952-60; Toronto Mendelssohn
Choir, conductor of a capella section 1953-55;
Bach-Elgar Choir, Hamilton, Ont., conductor
1955-60; Royal Conservatory of Music, Toronto,
lecturer 1955–; Toronto Orpheus Choir, director;
St. Clements Church, Toronto, organist and
choirmaster.

MEMBER
Toronto Musicians Association.

AWARDS, HONOURS
St. George's Choir School choral scholarship,
1931; Clare College organ scholarship, 1941.

SIDIMUS, Joysanne* 1938–
Dancer; b. 21 June 1938 in New York, NY;
daughter of Jerome Hillel and Bessie (Brodsky)
Sidimus; came to Canada in 1963 and returned to
USA in 1968.

EDUCATION
Attended Public School 139, Brooklyn, 1944-
46; Adelphi Academy, Brooklyn, 1946-55; Bar-
nard College, New York, 1955-57; studied piano
with Rosalie Cassell, New York, 1940-60; School
of American Ballet, New York, 1947-63; studied
ballet with Robert Joffrey, Beatrice Tompkins,
Vera Nemtchinova, and Antony Tudor in New
York.

RELIGION
Jewish.

HOME
c/o 1800 Albermarle Rd., Brooklyn, NY 11226, USA.

CAREER
New York City Ballet, 1958-62; London's Festi-
val Ballet, England, Jan.-Aug. 1963; National
Ballet of Canada, Toronto, 1963-68; Pennsylvania
Ballet, Pittsburgh, guest artist summer 1964.

MEMBER
ACTRA; AEA; AGMA.

AWARDS, HONOURS
School of American Ballet scholarship, 1955-58.

THEATRE
First danced *Pastorale* (Moncion, Mar. 1958),
Sister in *The prodigal son* (Balanchine, Apr. 1960),
Mother in *Casse-noisette* (Balanchine, Dec. 1961),
Tsarevna in *L'oiseau de feu* (Balanchine, July
1962), *Bourée fantasque* (Balanchine, Feb. 1963),
Napoli (Lander after Bournonville, Mar. 1963),
The snow maiden (Bourmeister, Mar. 1963),
Mazurka in *Les sylphides* (Fokine, Apr. 1963),
Debutante in *Offenbach in the underworld*
(Tudor, Sept. 1963), *Giselle* (Coralli-Perrot, Sept.
1963), *Concerto barocco* (Balanchine, Sept.
1963), *Sérénade* (Balanchine, Sept. 1963), Electra in *The house of Atreus* (Strate, Mar. 1964),
title role in *Electre* (Strate, Stratford, Ont. Festival, 1964), *Triptych* (Strate, Nov. 1964), Colum-
bine and Spanish dance in *Casse-noisette* (Franca
after Ivanov, Dec. 1964), Pimpinella in *Pulcinen-
ella* (Strate, Sept. 1965), Betrayed girl in *The
rake's progress* (de Valois, Mar. 1966), Woman in
his past in *Le jardin aux lilas* (Tudor, Mar. 1966),
Prince's friend in *Le lac des cygnes* (Bruhn, Apr.
1967), Lady Capulet in *Romeo and Juliet*
(Cranko, July 1967), Black Queen in *Le lac des
cygnes* (Bruhn, July 1967).

TELEVISION
Danced Mrs. Noah in *Noah and the flood* (Balanchine, CBS), *Casse-noisette* (Balanchine, CBS, 25
Dec. 1958; Dec. 1960), Fury in *Orpheus* (Balanchine, CBC), Pimpinella in *Pulcinella* (Strate, CTV),
Spanish dance in *Casse-noisette* (Franca after
Ivanov, CBC, Dec. 1965?), Prince's friend in *Le
lac des cygnes* (Bruhn, "Festival," CBC, 27 Dec.
1967).

SIMPSON, Charles Walter 1878-1942
Artist; b. 16 Apr. 1878 in Montreal, PQ; son of
Thomas and Rebecca (Spear) Simpson; m. Mabel
Mary Baile 1903; d. 16 Sept. 1942 in Montreal.

EDUCATION
Attended public school and high school in
Montreal; studied under William Brymner (*q.v.*),
Edmund Dyonnet (*q.v.*), and Maurice Cullen
(*q.v.*), School of the Art Association of Montreal;
studied under G.B. Bridgman and W.A. Clark, Art
Students League, New York, NY.

RELIGION
Anglican.

CAREER
Montreal star, illustrator 1899-1901; *Halifax
chronicle*, illustrator 1902-03; commercial artist,
illustrator, and landscape painter in Montreal,

1903-42; painted in England for the Canadian War Memorials, 1918-19; executed paintings for the railways in Canada including illustrations for *The spirit of Canada*, prepared by the CPR, 1939; illustrated books including *Maria Chapdelaine* by Louis Hémon and *Here and there in Montreal* by Charles W. Stokes; travelled in USA 1928-31; illustrated series of articles on American cities published in *Ladies home journal*, 1929-32.

MEMBER
Royal Canadian Academy (Associate 1913; Academician 1920; treasurer); Montreal Art Association Guild of Artists.

AWARDS, HONOURS
Jessie Dow award, Art Association of Montreal, 1921.

EXHIBITIONS
GROUP: Represented in group exhibitions, 1910-42, including exhibitions of Royal Canadian Academy and Spring Exhibitions of Art Association of Montreal; A Century of Canadian Art, Tate Gallery, London, England, 1938.

COLLECTIONS IN WHICH REPRESENTED
Art Gallery of Western Australia, Perth; Montreal Museum of Fine Arts; National Gallery of Canada, Ottawa, Ont.

SINGER, Emmy Heim
see HEIM, Emmy

SMALACOMBE, John, pseud.
see MacKAY, Louis Alexander

SMITH, Arthur James Marshall* 1902—
Poet, critic, and teacher; b. 1902 in Westmount, Montreal, PQ; m. Jeannie Dougall Robins; children: Peter b. 1941.

EDUCATION
Attended Westmount High School; McGill University, BSc., 1925, MA, 1926; University of Edinburgh, PhD, 1931.

OFFICE
Department of English, Michigan State University, East Lansing, Mich. 48823, USA.

CAREER
Ball State (now University) Teachers College, Muncie, Ind. and Doane College, Crete, Neb., teacher; Michigan State University, instructor in English 1936- ?, associate professor 1944-46, professor 1946—, poet in residence 1961—; Dalhousie University, Canada Council professor 1966/67.

AWARDS, HONOURS
Guggenheim fellowship, 1941-43; Harriet Monroe memorial prize for *Poetry: a magazine of verse*, 1943; Governor General's literary award for *News of the phoenix*, 1943; Rockefeller fellowship, 1944-46; D Litt from McGill University, 1958; Lorne Pierce medal, 1966; LL D from Queen's University, 1966; DCL from Bishop's University,

1967; Canada Council medal for outstanding cultural achievement, 1968.

WRITINGS
News of the phoenix and other poems, Ryerson, 1943; *A sort of ecstasy, poems: new and selected*, Ryerson, 1954; (with M.L. Rosenthal) *Exploring poetry*, Macmillan, 1955; *Collected poems*, Oxford, 1962; *Poems: new and collected*, Oxford, 1967.

EDITED: (with F.R. Scott) *New provinces*, Macmillan, 1936; *The book of Canadian poetry; a critical and historical anthology*, University of Chicago, 1943; *The wordly muse: an anthology of serious light verse*, Abelard, 1951; (with F.R. Scott) *The blasted pine*, Macmillan, 1957; *Seven centuries of verse, English and American*, Scribner, 1957; *The Oxford book of Canadian verse in English and French*, Oxford, 1960; *Masks of fiction*, McClelland & Stewart, 1961; *Masks of poetry*, McClelland & Stewart, 1962; *Essays for college writing*, St. Martin's, 1965; *100 poems: Chaucer to Dylan Thomas*, Scribner, 1965; *The book of Canadian prose: v.1 Early beginnings to Confederation*, Gage, 1965; *Modern Canadian verse in English and French*, Oxford, 1967; *The collected poems of Anne Wilkinson*, Macmillan, 1968.

CONTRIBUTED: Poetry and articles to *Best poems of 1934*, edited by T. Moult, Cape, 1935; *New verse; an anthology*, edited by G. Grigson, Faber, 1939; *Twentieth century verse*, edited by I. Dilworth, Oxford, 1945; *Canadian poems 1850-1952*, edited by L. Dudek and I. Layton, Contact, 1952; *Twentieth century Canadian poetry*, edited by E. Birney, Ryerson, 1953; *Our sense of identity*, edited by M. Ross, Ryerson, 1954; *Writing in Canada*, edited by G. Whalley, Macmillan, 1956; *The undergraduate essay*, edited by R.S. Harris and others, University of Toronto, 1956; *Silver treasury of light verse*, edited by O. Williams, New American Library, 1957; *The Penguin book of Canadian verse*, edited by R. Gustafson, Penguin, 1958; *Canadian anthology*, edited by C.F. Klinck and R.E. Watters, Gage, 1958; *The pocket book of modern verse*, edited by O. Williams, Washington Square, 1958; *Our living tradition*, edited by R.L. McDougall, 2nd and 3rd series, University of Toronto, 1959; *Anthology of Commonwealth verse*, edited by M.J. O'Donnell, Blackie, 1963; *Encyclopedia of poetry and poetics*, edited by A.S. Preminger, Princeton, 1965; *Master poems of the English language*, edited by O. Williams, Trident, 1966; *A choice of critics*, edited by G. Woodcock, Oxford, 1966; *Poets between the wars*, edited by M.T. Wilson, McClelland & Stewart, 1967; *The new modern poetry*, edited by M.L. Rosenthal, Macmillan, 1967; *University of Toronto quarterly*,

Queen's quarterly, Dalhousie review, Canadian forum, Canadian literature, McGill fortnightly review, The Times (London), *Tamarack review, Here and now, Contemporary verse, Northern review, Dial, Measure, Poetry, Commonwealth, Hound & horn, Nation, Rocking horse, Viceversa, Voices, New York times, Adelphi, Bermondsey book, London Aphrodite, New verse, Twentieth century verse, Contemporary poetry and prose, Meanjin papers, Sur.*

WORK IN PROGRESS

"The book of Canadian prose: v.2 One hundred years," to be published by Gage.

SMITH, Dorothy Dumbrille
see DUMBRILLE, Dorothy

SMITH, Gord* 1937—
(Gordon Hammond Smith)
Sculptor; b. 8 Oct. 1937 in Montreal, PQ; son of Cyril John and Mildred Viola (MacCullough) Smith; m. Wendy Jane Mathews 1 Oct. 1960; children: Christopher Gordon b. 21 Dec. 1962, Kimberley Anne b. 20 Aug. 1964.

EDUCATION
Attended Kings School, Westmount, PQ, 1942-49; attended Westmount Junior and Senior High School, 1949-55; studied architecture at Sir George Williams University, 1956-59; self-taught as an artist.

RELIGION
Protestant.

HOME
RR2, Arundel, PQ.

CAREER
Sculptor in Montreal 1959—.

COMMISSIONS
Sculpture, Fraser-Hickson Library, Montreal, 1959; two sculptures, Governor Metcalfe apartment building, Ottawa, Ont., 1959; sculpture, Les Habitations Jeanne Mance, Montréal, 1960; sculpture, Pall Corporation, New York, NY, 1960, 1968; sculpture, Imperial West Apartment building, Westmount, 1961; relief, Arts and Science Building, McMaster University, 1962; sculpture for Mrs. J.A. Huston, Toronto, Ont., 1962; sculpture, Planned Estates Ltd., Toronto, 1962; relief, Waterloo Trust Co., Kitchener, Ont., 1963; sculpture, Montreal Star building, 1964; sculpture, Sault Ste. Marie Airport, Ont., 1965; two sculptures, Westmount Life Building, 1965; sculpture, Carlingwood Public Library, Ottawa, 1966; screen, Canadian Pavilion, Expo 67, Montreal, 1967; relief, Argentia Ferry, 1967; sculpture and relief, International Nickel Co. of Canada, Toronto, 1967; sculpture for Mrs. G. Nicholls, Halifax, NS, 1967.

MEMBER
Quebec Sculptors' Society; Royal Canadian Academy (Associate* 1967).

AWARDS, HONOURS
Grand prize for painting, National Federation of Canadian Universities, 1957; purchase award, Quebec Hydro mural competition, 1961; first prize for sculpture, Salon de la Jeune Peinture et Sculpture, 1962; finalist for Mews Fountain Competition, Toronto, 1964; Canada Council grant, 1964; second prize, fountains and monuments competition, Expo 67, 1964.

EXHIBITIONS
ONE-MAN: Waddington Galleries, Montreal, 1959, 1961, 1963, 1964, and 1967; Isaacs Gallery, Toronto, 1963.

GROUP: Represented in group exhibitions held in Canada since 1959 including exhibitions organized by National Gallery of Canada, Ottawa.

COLLECTIONS IN WHICH REPRESENTED
Montreal Museum of Fine Arts; National Gallery of Canada; Musée d'Art Contemporain, Montréal; Sir George Williams University.

SMITH, John Ivor* 1927—
Sculptor; b. 28 Jan. 1927 in London, England; son of Albert Sidney and Frances (Warrior) Smith; m. Colleen Mary Kenney 3 Aug. 1957 (marriage dissolved); children: Fraser Matthew b. 2 Apr. 1959.

EDUCATION
Attended Tottenham Hall School, London, until 1938; Glendale County School, London, 1938-40; West Hill High School, Montreal, until 1944; McGill University, B Sc, 1948; studied under Jacques de Tonnancour (*q.v.*), Arthur Lismer (*q.v.*), and Eldon Grier (*q.v.*), School of Art and Design, Montreal Museum of Fine Arts; self-taught as a sculptor.

RELIGION
Church of England.

HOME
PO Box 49, Piedmont, PQ.

OFFICE
Fine Arts Department, Henry Hall Bldg., Sir George Williams University, Montreal, PQ.

CAREER
Worked in Italy 1957-58; Northern Electric Company, Montreal, technical writer and film maker 1958-66; sculptor in Montreal 1955—; Sir George Williams University, assistant professor of fine arts and head of the sculpture department 1966—.

COMMISSIONS
Sculpture, Canadian Pavilion, Expo 67, Montreal; sculpture, Expo Corporation, Expo 67, Montreal.

MEMBER
Sculptors' Society of Canada.

AWARDS, HONOURS
Scholarship in drawing, School of Art and Design, Montreal Museum of Fine Arts, 1954; scholarship in sculpture, School of Art and Design, Montreal Museum of Fine Arts, 1955; prizes, Quebec Provincial Competition, 1956 and

1959; Canada Council fellowship (forfeited) 1957, senior fellowship, 1967; first prize, Winnipeg Shows, Winnipeg Art Gallery, Man., 1959, 1960, and 1961; grand centennial award, Spring Exhibition, Montreal Museum of Fine Arts, 1960; silver medal, Vancouver Contemporary Exhibition, BC, 1961.

EXHIBITIONS

ONE-MAN: Isaacs Gallery, Toronto, Ont., 1962 and 1968.

GROUP: Represented in Spring Exhibitions of Montreal Museum of Fine Arts, Winnipeg Shows of the Winnipeg Art Gallery, and group exhibitions held elsewhere in Canada including exhibitions organized by National Gallery of Canada, Ottawa, Ont.

COLLECTIONS IN WHICH REPRESENTED

Agnes Etherington Art Centre, Queen's University; Art Gallery of Ontario, Toronto; Calgary Allied Arts Centre, Alta.; Edmonton Art Gallery, Alta.; London Public Library and Art Museum, Ont.; McMaster University; Musée du Québec, PQ; Rodman Hall Art Centre, St. Catharines, Ont.; Sir George Williams University; Winnipeg Art Gallery; Art Gallery of Hamilton, Ont.; Imperial Bank of Commerce, Montreal; Imperial Oil Collection, Montreal; Seagrams Collection, Montreal.

SMITH, John Meredith
see MEREDITH, John

SNOW, John Harold Thomas*   **1911—**
Artist; b. 12 Dec. 1911 in Vancouver, BC; son of Harold Thomas and Sophie Beatrice (Thompson) Snow; m. Bula Mae Forcade 2 Apr. 1949 (deceased); m. Kathleen Mary Allen 12 July 1963; children: (first marriage) John Vance Forcade b. 17 July 1952.

EDUCATION

Attended primary school in Olds, Alta. and Gordon School in Alberta; attended secondary school in Innisfail, Alta.; studied under Maxwell Bates (*q.v.*), Provincial Institute of Technology and Art evening classes, Calgary, 1947-49.

RELIGION

Church of England.

HOME

915 18th Ave. S.W., Calgary, Alta.

OFFICE

411 8th Ave. S.W., Calgary, Alta.

CAREER

RCAF, 1940-45, became flight lieutenant, mentioned in dispatches; Royal Bank of Canada, various positions 1928—, presently assistant manager, main branch, Calgary.

COMMISSIONS

Special lithograph, Canada Council, 1966; medal, Calgary Medical Society, 1967.

MEMBER

International Institute of Arts and Letters (elected fellow, 1960); Alberta Society of Artists; Canadian Society of Graphic Art (elected, 1956); Royal Canadian Academy (Associate 1965).

AWARDS, HONOURS

Adrian Seguin award, Canadian Society of Graphic Art, 1957 and 1959; C.W. Jefferys award, Canadian Society of Graphic Art, 1961; top award, Winnipeg Show, Winnipeg Art Gallery, Man., 1961; Jessie Dow prize, Spring Exhibition, Montreal Museum of Fine Arts, PQ, 1962; award, Calgary Graphics, 1962 and 1963; honourable mention, *Salon des Beaux-Arts*, Paris, France, 1965; purchase award, Vancouver Print International, 1967.

EXHIBITIONS

ONE-MAN: Dorothy Cameron Gallery, Toronto, Ont., 1962 and 1965; Fleet Gallery, Winnipeg, 1965; Medicine Hat Community Arts Club, Alta., 1966; University of Calgary, 1966 and 1967; exhibition toured four universities in the Atlantic Provinces, 1967-68; Manitoba Theatre Centre, Winnipeg, 1968; Gallery Pascal, Toronto, 1968; Pandora's Box Gallery, Victoria, BC, 1968.

GROUP: Represented in group exhibitions held in Canada including annual exhibitions of Canadian Group of Painters, Winnipeg Shows of the Winnipeg Art Gallery, and Spring Exhibitions of Montreal Museum of Fine Arts; represented in group exhibitions organized by National Gallery of Canada, Ottawa, Ont., including its second and third Biennial Exhibitions of Canadian Painting, 1957 and 1959; First International Biennial Exhibition of Prints, Tokyo, Japan, 1957; Fifth International Biennial of Colour Lithography, Cincinnati, Ohio, 1958; *Primera Bienal Interamericana de Pintura y Grabado*, Mexico City, Mexico, 1958; Northwest Printmakers, Seattle, Wash., 1959, 1960, and 1965; New Directions in Printmaking, Chicago, Ill., 1960; Royal Institute of British Artists, London, England, 1960, 1962, and 1967; New English Art Club, London, 1961; *Salon des Beaux-Arts*, Paris, 1961, 1963, 1965, and 1967; Canadian Exhibition of Prints, Pratt Institute, New York, NY, 1962; Royal Academy of Arts, London, 1963 and 1967; Canadian Drawings and Prints, Commonwealth Arts Festival, Cardiff, 1965; Canadian Prints Exhibition, organized by the Victoria and Albert Museum, London, toured England, 1965; Royal Scottish Academy, Glasgow, Scotland, 1966; Society of Graphic Arts, London, 1966; Second Biennial of Modern Engraving, Santiago, Chile, 1965; Centennial Exhibition of Canadian Prints and Drawings, Australia, 1967.

COLLECTIONS IN WHICH REPRESENTED

National Gallery of Canada; Victoria and Albert Museum, London; Department of External Affairs, Ottawa; University of Victoria; Norman Mackenzie Art Gallery, Regina, Sask.; Winnipeg Art Gallery; Art Gallery of Hamilton, Ont.; Imperial Oil Limited, Toronto; Art Gallery of Greater Victoria; University of Oregon; London Public Library and Art Museum, Ont.; Edmonton Art Gallery, Alta.; University of Saskatchewan, Regina Campus; Vancouver Art Gallery; Art Gallery of Ontario, Toronto; University of Calgary; Memorial University; Owens Museum, Mount Allison University; Canada Council, Ottawa.

SOBINOVA, Natasha, pseud.
see DEVESON, Rosemary

SOREL, Ruth
Dancer, choreographer, and teacher; b. in Poland; came to Canada c.1944 and settled in Montreal, PQ; m. Michel Choromanski; returned to Poland.

CAREER
Les Ballets de Ruth Sorel, Montréal, founder and director c.1946.

THEATRE
Choreographed *La Gaspésienne, Biographie dansée, Mea culpa, mea culpa, Ombres shakespeariennes.*

SOUCY, Jean-Baptiste* 1915–
Artist; b. 21 July 1915 in Isle-Verte, PQ.

EDUCATION
Attended Collège Ste. Anne de la Pocatière, PQ; studied under Lucien Martial and Jean-Paul Lemieux, École des Beaux-Arts de Québec, diplôme, 1939; École des Arts Décoratifs, Paris, France, diplôme architecte; studied under André Planson, Académie Julian, Paris, 1946-50; studied under Jean Cassou, École du Louvre, Paris, 1946-50; attended Grande-Chaumière, Paris, 1946-50.

HOME
31, rue des Remparts, Québec, PQ.

CAREER
École Normale Laval, teacher of design and art history 1939-65; Salon d'Hiver de Paris, full member, 1948; École des Beaux-Arts de Québec, professeur titulaire du cours de psycho-pédagogie 1950-67, director; Université Laval école de pédagogie, teacher of art history; Musée du Québec, PQ, director.

MEMBER
Fellow of Royal Architectural Institute of Canada; Société des Décorateurs Ensembliers du Québec (honorary member); Architecture Association of Quebec; Association des professeurs de l'École des Beaux-Arts de Québec.

AWARDS, HONOURS
Silver medal, 1939; grand prix de peinture de la province, 1945; boursier de la province, 1946; prix, Sociétaire du Salon d'Hiver de Paris, 1948; Officier de l'Ordre du Mérite Scolaire, 1962.

EXHIBITIONS
ONE-MAN: Québec, PQ; Mont Orford, PQ, 1966; Blue Barn Gallery, Ottawa, Ont., 1967.

GROUP: Represented in group exhibitions held in Canada; Galerie Jean de Ruaz, Paris, 1947; Sociétaire du Salon d'Hiver, Paris, 1948; Galerie Montjois, Paris, 1948; Maison du Canada, Paris, 1948.

COLLECTIONS IN WHICH REPRESENTED
Musée du Québec; National Gallery of Canada, Ottawa; Galerie de Ruaz.

SPARKS, Judith Rosemary
see CRAWLEY, Judith

SPATZ, Christa Mertins
see MERTINS, Christa

SPOHR, Arnold*
Dancer, choreographer, and director; b. in Rhein, Sask.

EDUCATION
Royal Conservatory of Music, Toronto, Ont., associates' diploma in piano; studied ballet in Moscow and Leningrad, USSR, Copenhagen, Denmark, London, England, New York, NY, and Hollywood, Calif.; Royal Academy of Dancing, London, advanced certificate and solo seal.

HOME
Apt. 1211, 411 Cumberland Ave., Winnipeg 2, Man.

OFFICE
Royal Winnipeg Ballet, 322 Smith St., Winnipeg 2, Man.

CAREER
(now Royal) Winnipeg Ballet, corps de ballet 1945-47, premier danseur 1947-54, director 1958–; taught piano in Winnipeg, 1948-53; CBC, choreographer and dancer 1955; Rainbow Stage, Winnipeg, choreographer 1955-58; School of Fine Arts, Nelson, BC, director 1965-67; Banff School of Fine Arts, Alta., co-director and artistic adviser of ballet division 1967–; travelled extensively.

MEMBER
AEA; Canadian Theatre Centre.

AWARDS, HONOURS
Canada Council arts scholarship, 1959, short-term grant in the arts, 1962/63, arts fellowship, 1965/66; Centennial medal, 1967.

THEATRE
Danced Poet in *Les sylphides* (Fokine), *The shooting of Dan McGrew* (Lloyd, Playhouse, Winnipeg, 2 May 1950), *Where the rainbow ends* (Coliseum, London, Dec. 1956); choreographed *Hansel and Gretel* (commissioned by Winnipeg Children's Theatre), *Ballet premier* (Playhouse, Winnipeg, 2 May 1950), *Intermède* (1951), *E minor* (Playhouse, Winnipeg, 15 Jan. 1959).

SPRINGBETT, Lynn Berta
see SEYMOUR, Lynn

STARK, Ethel*   1916–

Conductor and violinist; b. 25 Aug. 1916 in Montreal; daughter of Adolph and Laura (Haupt) Stark.

EDUCATION
Attended Mount Royal School, Montreal; studied violin with Carl Flesch, Léa Luboschutz, Louis Bailly, Artur Rodzinski and conducting with Fritz Reiner, Curtis Institute, Philadelphia, Pa., graduated with distinction, 1934; Saul Brant and Alfred de Sève, McGill Conservatory of Music; Académie de Musique de Québec, lauréat avec distinction; studied with Ernest Bloch, Geneva, Switzerland.

HOME
5501 Adalbert Ave., Apt. 1110, Côte St. Luc, Montréal 267, PQ.

CAREER
Debut at Windsor Hotel, Montreal, 1928; guest soloist with many orchestras, e.g. Montreal, Toronto, and CBC Symphonies, Curtis Symphony, Philadelphia; guest conductor with many orchestras, e.g. Toronto Symphony, Quebec Symphony, CBC Symphony, Miami Symphony, Fla., Tokyo Asahi Philharmonic, and Nippon Hoso Kyokai Symphony, Japan, Kol Israel Symphony, Jerusalem, and New York City Symphony; concert tours as soloist and conductor in Canada, USA, Europe, and Far East; New York Women's Chamber Orchestra, founding director and conductor 1938; Montreal Women's Symphony Orchestra, founding director and conductor 1940; The Canadian Choir, founding director and conductor 1952; Catholic University of Washington, DC, guest lecturer 1952; Conservatory of Music and Dramatic Art, Montreal, teacher of violin 1952; Montreal Women's Symphonietta, founding director and conductor 1955; Cardinal Léger Institute, Montreal, lecturer 1964; Ethel Stark Symphonietta, founding director and conductor 1968.

MEMBER
Ladies Morning Musical Club; Quebec Music Teachers Association; Musicians Guild of Montreal (honorary life member, 1942); International Society of Contemporary Music (honorary member); Sigma Alpha Iota, USA (honorary member).

AWARDS, HONOURS
McGill Conservatory of Music, Sir William MacDonald memorial scholarship; Curtis Institute scholarship; Canada Council short-term grant, 1962/63.

RADIO
Violin soloist and conductor in many programs, e.g. soloist with Curtis Symphony Orchestra (NBC), in series of sonata programs (WEVD, New York), recital series (CBC), shortwave recitals to South America, Central America, and Europe; conductor of Toronto Symphony Pop concerts (CBC), Summer symphonies (CBC), Kol Israel Symphony (Jerusalem, 1952, 1954), *Orchestral concert* (Wednesday night." CBC, 20 Mar. 1957), Tokyo Asahi Philharmonic (NHK, Japan, 1960).

TELEVISION
Conducted several concerts of Montreal Women's Orchestra ("Concert hour," Mar. 1957).

STEAD, Robert James Campbell   1880-1959

Author; b. 4 Sept. 1880 in Middleville, Ont.; son of Richard Thompson and Mary (Campbell) Stead; m. Nettie May Wallace 31 Dec. 1901; children: Richard L., Stanley W., Robert A.; d. 25 June 1959 in Ottawa, Ont.

EDUCATION
Attended public schools in Manitoba; Winnipeg Business College, Man.

RELIGION
United Church.

CAREER
Review, Cartwright, Man., founder and publisher c.1898; *Courier*, Crystal City, Man., publisher 1908; *Albertan*, Calgary, Alta., editorial staff 1912; CPR, assistant director of publicity, colonization department in Calgary 1913-16, publicity director 1916-19; Department of Immigration and Colonization, Ottawa, publicity director 1919-36; Department of Mines and Resources, Ottawa, superintendent of information and resources publicity 1936-46; British Empire Exhibition, London, England, organizer of Canadian literary production; *Canadian geographical journal*, editorial committee 1942- ?.

MEMBER
Canadian Authors Association (past president of Ottawa branch; national president, 1923; honorary life member, 1958); Canadian Club; Royal Canadian Geographical Society (elected fellow, 1929); Rotary Club (Ottawa president, 1932-33).

WRITINGS
The empire builders and other poems, W. Briggs, 1908; *Songs of the prairie* (poems), W. Briggs, 1911; *Prairie born and other poems*, W. Briggs, 1911; *The bail jumper* (novel), W. Briggs, 1914; *The homesteaders* (novel), Musson, 1916; *Kitchener and other poems*, Musson, 1917; *Why don't they cheer?* (poems), T.F. Unwin, 1918; *The cow puncher* (novel), Harper, 1918; *Dennison Grant* (novel), Musson, 1920; *Neighbours* (novel), Hodder, 1922; *The smoking flax* (novel), McClelland, 1924; *Grain* (novel), McClelland, 1926; *The copper disc* (novel), Doubleday, Doran, 1931; (with D. Dumbrille and N.A. Benson) *The maple's praise of Franklin Delano Roosevelt, 1882-1945, Canadian tributes*, Tower Books, 1945; *Words* (essays), Public Press, 1945.
CONTRIBUTED: Poetry, articles and short stories to *Saturday night* and *Canadian geographical journal*.

STEELE, Patricia Joudry
see JOUDRY, Patricia

STRATAKIS, Anastasia
see STRATAS, Teresa

STRATAS, Teresa 1938–
(Anastasia Stratakis)
Singer (soprano); b. 26 May 1938 in Toronto;
daughter of Emanuel and Argero Stratakis.

EDUCATION
Attended Malvern Collegiate, Toronto; Royal
Conservatory of Music, Toronto, 1954-58; studied
with Irene Jessner, Toronto; Kathrin Long
School, New York, NY.

RELIGION
Greek Orthodox.

HOME
19 Brookside Dr., Toronto, Ont.

CAREER
Canadian Opera Company chorus member, Texas
tour; Nova Scotia Festival of the Arts, Halifax,
guest soloist; Covent Garden Opera Company,
London, England, soloist; La Scala, Milan, Italy,
soloist; Metropolitan Opera Company, New York,
soloist 1958–; Toronto Symphony Orchestra,
guest soloist, 1959; Montreal Symphony Orchestra, PQ; USSR tour, Apr. 1962; Munich Festival,
Germany, 1965.

AWARDS, HONOURS
Winner of amateur contest, Oshawa, Ont., 1942;
Royal Conservatory of Music scholarship, 1955-
58; Eaton award, 1958; Metropolitan Opera
Audition winner, 1959; Canada Council arts
scholarship, 1959/60; University of Toronto
Faculty of Music scholarships, c.1959.

THEATRE
Sang in numerous productions, e.g. Zerlina in
Don Giovanni, Composer in *Ariadne auf Naxos*,
Boris Godunov, Mimi in *La bohème* (Toronto
Opera Festival, 1958; Metropolitan Opera, Feb.
1962, 1964/65; Cincinnati Summer Opera Festival,
Ohio, July 1962; Covent Garden Opera, 1963;
Canadian Opera Company, 13 Oct. 1964), Cio-
Cio-San in *Madama Butterfly* (Vancouver Inter-
national Festival, 22 July 1960; Metropolitan
Opera, late spring 1968), *Turandot* (Metropolitan
Opera, Mar. 1961), *Nausicaa* (world première,
Athens Festival, Greece, Aug. 1961), *Atlantida*
(world première, La Scala, 1962), *The merry widow*
selections (Canadian National Exhibition, Toron-
to, Aug. 1962), opening recital (Concert Hall,
Edward Johnson Building, Toronto, 1962),
Tatania in *Eugene Onegin* (Bolshoi Theatre,
Moscow, USSR, 1963), Sardulla in *The last savage*
(Metropolitan Opera, 1963/64), *Queen of spades*
(Metropolitan Opera, 1965), title role in *La
périchole* (Metropolitan Opera, 1965), *Promenade
concerts* (New York Philharmonic Orchestra,
1965), *Manon* (Metropolitan Opera, 1965),
Cherubino in *The marriage of Figaro* (Jan. 1967),
Otello (Montreal Opera Company, Expo 67,
summer 1967), *Centennial concert* (Montreal
Symphony Orchestra, July 1967).

FILM
The performer (National Film Board of Canada,
106B 0159050 1957), *The Canadians* (Twentieth
Century Fox, 1960).

RADIO
Sang in many productions, e.g. "Terry Toons"
(series), "Voice of America" (series), "Songs of
my people" (series, CBC), Cio-Cio-San in *Madama
Butterfly* (CBC, 27 July 1960), "Symphony Hall"
(series, CBC, 24 Feb. 1963), *Music in G* (CBC, 27
Feb. 1963), Lisa in *Pique dame* (CBC, 15 Jan.
1966), L'italiana in *Algeri* ("Opera time," CBC,
4 June 1966), *Otello* (CBC, 1967), *Centennial
concert* (CBC, 24 Aug. 1967), Gretel in *Hansel
and Gretel* (CBC, 23 Dec. 1967).

TELEVISION
Sang in many CBC productions, e.g. *An hour of
stars* (8 June 1960), *Swing gently* (29 Aug. 1960),
Opera highlights ("Parade," 24 Oct. 1962),
Teresa Stratas 1967 ("Festival," 25 Jan. 1967),
"Ed Sullivan show."

RECORDINGS
Nausicaa, Composers Recordings CRI 175, 1964.

STRATE, Grant Elroy* 1927–
Dancer, choreographer, and teacher; b. 7 Dec.
1927 in Cardston, Alta.; son of Alfred and Mabel
(Wilson) Strate.

EDUCATION
University of Alberta, BA, LL B, 1950; studied
modern dance with Laine Metz in Edmonton,
Alta.; ballet with Celia Franca and Betty
Oliphant in Toronto.

RELIGION
None.

HOME
105 Belsize Dr., Toronto 7, Ont.

OFFICE
National Ballet of Canada, 157 King St. E.,
Toronto 1, Ont.

CAREER
National Ballet of Canada, Toronto (charter
member), corps de ballet 1951-53, character and
dramatic soloist 1953–, assistant to artistic
director 1958-60, resident choreographer 1960–;
National Ballet School of Canada, Toronto,
teacher 1967–; Koninklijke Vlaamse Opera Ballet
School, Antwerp, Belgium, guest teacher and
choreographer 1967; Studio Ballet, Antwerp,
co-founder 1967.

MEMBER
AEA; Canadian Theatre Centre.

AWARDS, HONOURS
Canada Council senior arts fellowship for study
abroad, 1962/63; National Ballet Guild of Canada,

Toronto branch grant for three months study abroad, 1966.

THEATRE

Danced title role in *L'après-midi d'un faune*, Dr. Coppélius in *Coppélia* (Franca after Ivanov, Capitol, Ottawa, Ont., 30 Oct. 1958), Prince of Verona in *Romeo and Juliet* (Cranko, 1963/64), Father in *Cinderella* (Franca, 1968); choreographed *Jeune pas de deux* (1956), *The fisherman and his soul* (1956), *Ballad* (Capitol, Ottawa, 29 Oct. 1958), *The willow* (1959), *Antic spring* (Palace, Hamilton, Ont., 24 Oct. 1960), *Sequel* and *Time cycle* (Stratford, Ont. Festival, 13 July 1962), *Patterns* (National Ballet School of Canada, 1962), *The house of Atreus* (Dance Department of Juilliard School of Music, New York, NY, 1963; National Ballet of Canada, 13 Jan. 1964), *Electre* (Stratford, Ont. Festival, 1964), *Triptych* (1965), *Bird-life* (National Ballet School of Canada, 1966; Studio Ballet, 1967), *Pulcinella* (1966), *Cyclus* (Studio Ballet, 1967; National Ballet of Canada, 1968), *Pretendant* (Studio Ballet, 1967), *Sun, sea and wind* (Studio Ballet, 1967), *Studies in white* (Concert Ballet of National Ballet of Canada, 1967), *Arena* (Concert Ballet of National Ballet of Canada, 1968).

TELEVISION

Danced Friar Laurence and Prince of Verona in *Romeo and Juliet* (Cranko, "Festival," CBC, 15 Sept. 1965; 2 Mar. 1966); choreographed *Studies* (CBC, 1963).

STRIKE, Maurice 1945–

Designer; b. 1945 in Bournemouth, England.

EDUCATION

Wimbledon School of Art, England, for 5 years.

HOME

PO Box 774, Niagara-on-the-Lake, Ont.

OFFICE

Neptune Theatre, 1593 Argyle St., Halifax, NS.

CAREER

Citizens' Theatre, Glasgow, Scotland, designer; Great Malvern Festival, designer; Colchester Theatre, England, designer; Manitoba Theatre Centre, Winnipeg, designer; Shaw Festival, Niagara-on-the-Lake, designer 1967-68; Neptune Theatre, Halifax, resident designer 1969–.

MEMBER

Royal Society of Arts, England; Canadian Theatre Centre.

AWARDS, HONOURS

Wimbledon School of Art intermediate award in arts and crafts; National diploma in theatre design; Royal Society of Arts, England, bursary; British Arts Council designers' award.

THEATRE

Designed *Live like pigs* (Citizens' Theatre), *Misalliance* (Citizens' Theatre), *Little Malcolm and his struggle against the eunuchs* (Citizens' Theatre), *Playboy of the western world* (Citizens' Theatre), *Inadmissible evidence* (Citizens' Theatre), *Nightmare Abbey* (Citizens' Theatre), *False confessions* (Great Malvern Festival), *The laundry* (Great Malvern Festival), *The castaway* (Great Malvern Festival), *Androcles and the lion* (Great Malvern Festival), *Man of destiny* (Great Malvern Festival), *Who's afraid of Virginia Woolf?* (Colchester Theatre), *The merry fools* (Manitoba Theatre Centre), *Luv* (Manitoba Theatre Centre), *Major Barbara* (Manitoba Theatre Centre; Shaw Festival, 16 Aug. 1967; Expo 67, Montreal, PQ); sets for *Arms and the man* (Shaw Festival, 21 June 1967), *The circle* (Shaw Festival, 19 July 1967), *The knack* (Studio Arena Theatre, Buffalo, NY), *Charley's aunt* (Studio Arena Theatre, Buffalo, NY), *Heartbreak house* (Shaw Festival, 27 June 1968).

WORK IN PROGRESS: Design for *In good king Charles' golden days* (Theatre Toronto, 1969/70) and for 1969 Shaw Festival.

STRINGER, Arthur John Arbuthnott 1874-1950

Author; b. 26 Feb. 1874 in Chatham, Ont.; son of Hugh Arbuthnott and Sally (Delmege) Stringer; m. Jobyna Howland Oct. 1900 (marriage dissolved 1914); m. Margaret Arbuthnott Stringer 1914; children: (second marriage) Robert A., Hugh A., John A.; became American citizen in 1937; d. 14 Sept. 1950 in Mountain Lakes, NJ.

EDUCATION

Attended London Collegiate Institute, Ont.; Wycliffe College, University of Toronto; University of Oxford.

CAREER

Père Marquette Railway, Saginaw, Mich., car-record officer *c.*1896-97; *Herald*, Montreal, editorial staff 1897-98; American Press Association, New York, NY, editorial staff 1898-1901; *Success*, literary editor 1903-04; fruit farming at Cedar Springs, Ont.; ranching near Calgary, Alta., *c.*1915-21; resided at Mountain Lakes, NJ, 1921-50; travelled in Alaska, Labrador, Hudson Bay country, South America, Africa, and Europe.

MEMBER

Canadian Authors Association; New Jersey Library Commission; Mountain Lakes Dramatic Guild (founder and first president, director); Canadian Club, New York, NY; Macauley Club; University of Toronto Club (former vice-president); Cambridge Club; Rockaway River Country Club; Mountain Lakes Club.

AWARDS, HONOURS

D Litt from University of Western Ontario, 1946.

WRITINGS

Watchers of twilight and other poems, Warren, 1894; *Pauline and other poems*, Warren, 1895; *Epigrams* (poems), Warren, 1896; *A study in King Lear* (non-fiction), American Shakespeare Press, 1897; *The loom of destiny* (essays), Small,

Maynard, 1899; *Hephaestus; Persephone at Enna; and Sappho in Leucadia* (poems), Methodist Books, 1903; *The silver poppy* (novel), Appleton, 1903 (dramatized under title *The narrow door*); *Lonely O'Malley* (novel), Houghton, Mifflin, 1905; *The wire tappers* (novel), Little, Brown, 1906; *Phantom wires* (novel), Little, Brown, 1907; *The woman in the rain and other poems*, Little, Brown, 1907; *The under groove* (novel), McClure, 1908; *The gun runner* (novel), B.W. Dodge, 1909; *Irish poems*, M. Kennerley, 1911; *The shadow* (novel), Century, 1913; *Open water* (poems), J. Lane, 1914; *The prairie wife* (novel), Bobbs-Merrill, 1915; *The hand of peril* (novel), Macmillan, 1915; *Door of dread* (novel), Bobbs-Merrill, 1916; *House of intrigue* (novel), Bobbs-Merrill, 1918; *The man who couldn't sleep* (novel), Bobbs-Merrill, 1919; *The stranger* (prose), Dominion Publicity Committee, 1919; *Prairie mother* (novel), Bobbs-Merrill, 1920; *The wine of life* (novel), Knopf, 1921; *Twin tales: Are all men alike? and The lost Titian* (novel), Bobbs-Merrill, 1921; *Prairie child* (novel), Bobbs-Merrill, 1922; *City of peril* (novel), Knopf, 1923; *The diamond thieves* (novel), Bobbs-Merrill, 1923; *Empty hands* (novel), Bobbs-Merrill, 1924; *Never fail Blake* (novel), Burt, 1924; (with R. Holman) *The story without a name* (novel), Bobbs-Merrill, 1924; (with R. Holman) *Manhandled* (novel), Bobbs-Merrill, 1924; *Power* (novel), Bobbs-Merrill, 1925; *Night hawk* (novel), Burt, 1926; *In bad with Sinbad* (novel), Bobbs-Merrill, 1926; *White hands* (novel), Bobbs-Merrill, 1927; *Confessions of an author's wife* (prose), Bobbs-Merrill, 1927; *The wolf woman* (novel), Bobbs-Merrill, 1928; *A woman at dusk and other poems*, Bobbs-Merrill, 1928; *Cristina and I*, (prose), Bobbs-Merrill, 1929; *The woman who couldn't die* (novel), Bobbs-Merrill, 1929; *Out of Erin, songs in exile* (poems), Bobbs-Merrill, 1930; *A lady quite lost* (novel), Bobbs-Merrill, 1931; *The mud lark* (novel), Bobbs-Merrill, 1932; *Marriage by capture* (novel), Bobbs-Merrill, 1933; *Dark soil* (poems), Bobbs-Merrill, 1933; *Man lost* (novel), Bobbs-Merrill, 1934; *The wife traders* (novel), Bobbs-Merrill, 1936; *Tooloona* (novel), Methuen, 1936; *Heather of the high hand* (novel), Bobbs-Merrill, 1937; *Alexander was great* (play), French, 1937; *The old woman remembers and other Irish poems*, Bobbs-Merrill, 1937; *The lamp in the valley* (novel), Bobbs-Merrill, 1938; *The dark wing* (novel), Bobbs-Merrill, 1939; *The cleverest woman in the world and other one act plays*, Bobbs-Merrill, 1939; *The ghost plane* (novel), Bobbs-Merrill, 1940; *The king who loved old clothes and other Irish poems*, Bobbs-Merrill, 1941; *Intruders in Eden* (novel), Bobbs-Merrill, 1942; *Shadowed victory* (poems), Bobbs-Merrill, 1943; *Star in a mist* (novel), Bobbs-Merrill, 1943; *The devastator* (novel), Bobbs-Merrill, 1944; *Red wine of youth, life of Rupert Brooke* (non-fiction), Bobbs-Merrill, 1948; *New York nocturnes* (poems), Ryerson, 1948 (Ryerson chap-book); *Peace triumphant, a pageant*; *The blot* (play); *The changing world* (play); *The wishing well* (play); *Smuggled in* (play); *Bruised lady* (play); *The fireside* (play); *The house of Oedipus* (play); *The lady intervenes* (play).

CONTRIBUTED: Poetry, short stories, and articles to *The week, Sun, Post, Commercial advertiser, Everybody's magazine, Success magazine, Saturday night, Canadian magazine, Oxford magazine, Pall Mall gazette, New York times, Ainslee's magazine, Chronicle, Harper's magazine, Atlantic monthly, Maclean's, Saturday evening post*.

STUART, Eleanor

Actress and teacher; b. Montreal.

HOME
#4, 50 Academy Rd., Westmount, Montreal 6, PQ.

CAREER
Comédie-Française, Paris, France, actress; Montreal Repertory Theatre, actress; Stratford, Ont. Festival, actress 1953–; National Theatre School of Canada, Montreal, teacher.

MEMBER
ACTRA (life member).

THEATRE
Played in many productions, e.g. *The kingdom of God, Cymbeline, Le marcheur,* Duchess of York in *Richard III* (Stratford, Ont. Festival, 1953), Countess of Rossillion in *All's well that ends well* (Stratford, Ont. Festival, 1953), Jocasta in *Oedipus rex* (Stratford, Ont. Festival, 1954, 1955), Francisca in *Measure for measure* (Stratford, Ont. Festival, 1954), Calpurnia in *Julius Caesar* (Stratford, Ont. Festival 1955), Queen Isabel in *Henry V* (Stratford, Ont. Festival, 1956), Volumnia in *Coriolanus* (Stratford, Ont. Festival, 1961).

FILM
Played Jocasta in *King Oedipus* (Oedipus Rex Productions, Toronto, Ont., 1957).

RADIO
Played in several CBC productions, e.g. Judge in *The fate of a poet* ("Sunday night," 31 Jan. 1965), Grandmother in *Men of the mountain* ("Midweek theatre," 23 Mar. 1966).

SUKIS, Lilian* 1942–

Singer (soprano); b. 29 June 1942 in Kaunas, Lithuania; daughter of Vincentas and Zinaïda (Grabauskas) Sukis.

EDUCATION
Attended Holy Saviour Academy, Val d'Or, PQ; St. Patrick's School, Hamilton, Ont; Cathedral High School, Hamilton, 1953-58; McMaster University, 1958-62; Royal Conservatory of

Music, Toronto, Ont., ARCT 1960; University of Toronto Faculty of Music, 1962-65; studied with Irene Jessner.

OFFICE

Metropolitan Opera Company, 1865 Broadway, New York, NY 10023, USA.

CAREER

Guest soloist in USA, e.g. Jordan Hall, Boston, Mass., New York, Chicago, Ill., Cleveland, Ohio, Detroit, Mich., Rochester, NY, Philadelphia, Pa.; CBC Symphony Orchestra, soloist 1964; Toronto Symphony Orchestra, soloist 1965; New York Philharmonic Orchestra, soloist 1967; Westchester Symphony Orchestra, NY, soloist 1968.

AWARDS, HONOURS

Scholarship from the Royal Society of Canada, 1962; Rose bowl trophy from Kiwanis Festival, 1964; "CBC Talent festival" second place, 1964; Canada Council arts scholarship, 1964/65, travel grant, 1967/68.

THEATRE

Sang in many productions, e.g. Alice Ford in *Falstaff* (Banff School of Fine Arts, Alta., tour 1964), Lady Billows in *Albert Herring* (Canadian première, opening of Edward Johnson Building, Toronto, 1964), title role in *Deirdre of the sorrows* (world première, Royal Conservatory of Music Opera School, Toronto, Apr. 1965), Countess Rosina in *The marriage of Figaro* (Stratford, Ont. Festival, 1965), Mimi in *La bohème* (Canadian Opera Company, O'Keefe Centre, Toronto, 23 Sept. 1965), Violetta in *La traviata* (Chicago Opera Company, 1966), Lauretta in *Gianni Schicchi* (Baltimore Civic Opera, Md., 1967), Maria in *La guerra* (Baltimore Civic Opera, 1967), title role in *Grazina* (North American première, Chicago Lyric Theater, 1967); created Helen Niles in *Mourning becomes Electra* (world première, Metropolitan Opera, 1966/67, 1967/68); sang Micaela in *Carmen* (Metropolitan Opera, 1968 and on tour 1968, 1968/69).

RADIO

Sang in several CBC productions, e.g. aria from *Andrea Chénier* ("Talent festival," 9 Dec. 1964); *Hypolite et Aricie* and *Orfeo ed Euridice* excerpts ("Opera time," 11 June 1966), songs by Beckwith and Morawetz ("Tuesday night," 11 July 1967), *The great song* ("Encore" part I, 16 July 1967).

TELEVISION

Sang in several CBC productions, e.g. Mimi in *La bohème* (1965), *Sounds of Chicago* ("Bell telephone hour," 1968), *Grazina* excerpts (1968).

SURDIN, Morris*

Composer; b. in Toronto; son of Benjamin and Basha Surdin; m. Hazel Stephens 24 Apr. 1939; children: Paul b. 2 June 1957.

EDUCATION

Attended Ogden Public School and Harbord Collegiate Institute, Toronto; studied with Louis Gesensway, Philadelphia, Pa., 1938-39; with Henry Brant, New York, NY.

HOME

2 Totteridge, New Toronto, Ont.

CAREER

CBC, Toronto, music arranger, conductor, composer 1939-41, 1949–; Philadelphia Pop concerts, arranger; CBS, New York, composer, conductor 1949-54.

COMPOSITIONS

Softly as the flute blows, flute and strings. *Five shades of brass*, trumpet and symphony orchestra. *Concerto for accordion and strings*, first performed by Hart House String Orchestra under Boyd Neel, Toronto, 29 Jan. 1967, commissioned by Hart House Orchestra, 1967. *Concerto for mandolin and strings. Credo*, suite for small orchestra, performed at Canadian Jewish Congress. *Prairie boy*, Boosey & Hawkes. Many scores for musicals, e.g. *The rookie; Top level; The gallant greenhorn; The fever and the glory*, produced on "Wednesday night," CBC, 1949; "Once upon a time," series of 39 musicals, produced on CBC radio, 1949. *The remarkable rocket*, ballet for symphony orchestra, 1960, first performed by National Ballet of Canada, 1960/61, commissioned by National Ballet of Canada, 1960, recorded, *Wild rose*, musical comedy, first performed by The MAC 14 Theatre Society, Calgary, Alta., 2 May 1967, commissioned on a grant from the Centennial Commission. Numerous scores for CBC radio and TV productions, e.g. *Never look back; Foothill fables; Voice for Victor; Curtaintime; In search of ourselves;* "Once upon a tune," series, CBS; "Mr. Ace and Jane," series, CBS; *The dream of Peter Mann; Tempo 13*, 1952; "CBC playhouse," 1952; *A Spanish tragedy*, soprano and orchestra, 1955, performed by CBC Symphony Orchestra, recorded; *A beach of strangers*, 1959; *Epitaph for a one-roomer*, "Project '63," 7 Oct. 1962; *A symbol of the people*, "Stage," 2 Dec. 1962; *The endless echo*, 11 Mar. 1963; *The tempest*, 14 June 1964; Impressionistic trio in *Summer is icumen in*, 21 June 1964; *Juana la loca*, Jan. 1966; *Charged to your account*, "Stage," 6 Feb. 1966; *Can I speak to Shirley?*, 20 Feb. 1966; *Everyman*, "Stage," 3 Apr. 1966; *The widow of Mississagi*, "Stage," 4 Dec. 1966; *Huckleberry Finn*, "Adventure theatre," 11 Oct. 1967; "Hatch's mill," series, 1967; *The devil's instrument*, "Festival," 5 Nov. 1962; *The great hunger*, "Stage," 25 Feb. 1968; *The Revenge and the Nabara*, "Stage," 19 May 1968; *Turtle island*, "Stage," 19 Oct. 1968; *The incoherent*, "Stage," 3 Nov. 1968.

SURMEJAN, Hazaros* 1943–

Dancer; b. 21 Jan. 1943 in Skopje, Yugoslavia;

son of Artur and Radmila (Sake) Surmejan; came to Canada in 1966.

EDUCATION
Attended school in Skopje; studied ballet with Alexander Dobrohotov, Skopje, 1956-60.

HOME
81 Isabella St., Toronto, Ont.

OFFICE
National Ballet of Canada, 157 King St. E., Toronto 1, Ont.

CAREER
National Ballet of Skopje, 1960; Mannheim State Opera, Germany, 1961; partnered Rosella Hightower in Vichy and Cannes, France, 1962; Cologne Opera Ballet, Germany, principal 1963-66; guest artist in Munich, Germany, 1966; National Ballet of Canada, Toronto, principal 1966—.

MEMBER
AEA.

THEATRE
First danced Benvolio in *Romeo and Juliet* (Dimitrie Parlié, 1960), *Don Quixote* pas de deux (Petipa, 1960), Köstchei in *L'oiseau de feu* (Fokine, 1960), *Giselle* pas de deux (Coralli-Perrot, 1960), *Casse-noisette* pas de deux (Ivanov, 1961), Colas in *La fille mal gardée* (Dauberval, 1961), St. Francis in *Nobilissime visione* (Massine, 1961), *Argon* pas de deux (1961), Solo boy in *The bitter weird* (de Mille, 1963), *Études* (Lander, 1963), Romeo in *Romeo and Juliet* (Cranko, 1966/67), *Le corsaire* pas de deux (Klavin, 1966/67), *Adagio cantabile* (Poll, 1966/67), Prince in *Casse-noisette* (Franca after Ivanov, 1966/67), Prince Siegfried in *Le lac des cygnes* (Bruhn, 1967), Solor in *La bayadère* (Petipa, 1967), *Concerto barocco* (Balanchine, 1967), *Sérenade* (Balanchine, 1967), Prince in *Cinderella* (Franca, 1968).

TELEVISION
Danced in *Le corsaire* pas de deux (Klavin, "INCO centennial performance," CBC, 4 Oct. 1967), Master of ceremonies in *Le lac des cygnes* (Bruhn, "Festival," CBC, 27 Dec. 1967).

SURREY, Philip Henry* 1910—
(Philip Henry Howard Surrey)
Artist; b. 10 Oct. 1910 in Calgary, Alta.; son of Henry Philip and Katherine (de Guèrin) Surrey; m. Margaret Day 22 June 1939.

EDUCATION
Studied under Lemoine Fitzgerald, Winnipeg School of Art, Man., 1926-27; F.H. Varley, Vancouver School of Art, BC, evenings 1930-32; Alexander Abels, Art Students League, New York, NY, 1936-37.

HOME
478 Grosvenor Ave., Montreal 6, PQ.

OFFICE
231 St. James St. W., Montreal 1, PQ.

CAREER
Travelled in Java, Malaya, India, and England, 1911-1921; Brigden's of Winnipeg Ltd., commercial artist 1926-29; Cleland-Kent Engraving, Vancouver, commercial artist 1929-36; *Weekend magazine*, photograph editor, feature editor 1937-64, associate editor 1964—; International Plastic Arts Association, UNESCO, secretary, 1958-60.

MEMBER
Eastern Group; Canadian Society of Graphic Art (elected, *c.*1940) Contemporary Art Society (founding member); Federation of Canadian Artists (elected, *c.*1938).

AWARDS, HONOURS
First prize for painting, Montreal Museum of Fine Arts Spring Show, 1953; third prize, Winnipeg Show, 1959.

EXHIBITIONS
ONE-MAN: Galerie Antoine, Montréal, 1940; Contempo Studios, Ottawa, Ont., 1942; Gaierie l'Art Français, Montréal, 1945; Musée des Beaux-Arts (with Louise Gadbois), Montréal, 1949; Watson Galleries (with John Lyman), Montreal, 1951; Roberts Gallery, Toronto, 1953; Musée des Beaux-Arts (with York Wilson) 1955, (with G. Fiori) 1961, Montréal; Penthouse Gallery, Montreal, 1962; Jerrold Morris International Art Gallery, Toronto, 1964; Galerie Martin, Montreal, 1965 and 1967; Musée du Québec, PQ, 1966.
GROUP: Represented in group exhibitions held in Canada since 1941 including exhibitions held by Eastern Group, Contemporary Art Society, Montreal Museum of Fine Arts Spring Show, Hamilton Winter Exhibition, Ont., Canadian Society of Graphic Art, and Salon des Indépendants; represented in group exhibitions organized by National Gallery of Canada, Ottawa, including the second biennial, 1957; World's Fair, New York, NY, 1936; Aspects of Contemporary Painting in Canada, Addison Gallery, Andover, Mass., 1942-43; Yale University Art Gallery, 1944; Rio de Janeiro, Brazil, 1946.

COLLECTIONS IN WHICH REPRESENTED
National Gallery of Canada; Musée du Québec; Musée des Beaux-Arts, Montréal; Art Gallery of Ontario, Toronto; Art Gallery of Hamilton; London Public Library and Art Museum, Ont.; Winnipeg Art Gallery; Sir George Williams University; Séminaire de Joliette, PQ; Willistead Art Gallery, Windsor, Ont.; Rodman Hall, St. Catharines, Ont.; Musée Bezalel, Jerusalem, Isreal.

SUSSKIND, Walter* 1913—
Conductor and pianist; b. 1 May 1913 in Prague, Czecho-Slovakia; son of Bronislav and Gertrude (Seger) Susskind; m. Diane Hartman 2 Aug. 1961.

EDUCATION
Studied conducting with Georg Szell, composition

with Josef Suk and Alois Hába, piano at State Conservatory, Prague, until 1933.

OFFICE

c/o Mr. Bailey Bird, Leeds Music, 215 Victoria St., Toronto, Ont.; c/o Wilfrid Van Wyck Ltd., 80 Wigmore St., London, England.

CAREER

German Opera House, Prague, assistant conductor 1933-38; toured as pianist 1938; Strand Theatre, London, conductor 1941; Carl Rosa Opera Company, England, principal conductor c.1942-45; Sadler's Wells Opera Company, London, conductor during German tour 1945; Liverpool Philharmonic Orchestra, England, conductor 1945; London Symphony, London Philharmonic, BBC Symphony, Birmingham Symphony Orchestras, England, and Scottish National Orchestra, Glasgow, Scotland, conductor 1946-52; Victoria Symphony Orchestra, Melbourne, Australia, conductor 1953-56; Toronto Symphony Orchestra, conductor 1956-65; Toronto Mendelssohn Choir, conductor 1960-64; Concertgebouw Orchestra, Amsterdam, The Netherlands, guest conductor 1957; Israel Philharmonic Orchestra, guest conductor 1957; Canadian Opera Company, Toronto, conductor 1957-64; travelled extensively in Europe, Asia, and Africa c.1957 and 1966-67; Glyndebourne Festival, England and Edinburgh Festival, Scotland, guest conductor; Statford, Ont. Festival, guest conductor 1957; Houston Symphony Orchestra, Tex., conductor 1958; Stokowski Orchestra, conductor touring southwestern states and at Gulbenkian Music Festival, Lisbon, Portugal, 1959; National Youth Orchestra of Canada, founder, organizer, music director 1960; Aspen Music Festival, Colo., principal conductor and music director 1961–; St. Louis Symphony Orchestra, Mo., principal conductor and music director 1968–.

RADIO

Conductor and pianist in numerous CBC concerts, e.g. pianist in *Archduke trio* (12 June 1960); conducted *The marriage of Figaro* ("Wednesday night," 19 Oct. 1960), *Aïda* ("Wednesday night," 19 Apr. 1961), *Mass in C minor* by Mozart (21 Nov. 1962), "Sunday concert" (series, 17 Feb. 1963), "Symphony hall" (series, 10 Mar. 1963; 9, 23 Jan. 1964; 2 Apr. 1964); guest pianist in *Canadian String Quartet* (24 July 1963); conducted *National Youth Orchestra* (13 Aug. 1963; 8 Sept. 1966); guest on "Opera time" (series, 25 Apr. 1964); conducted "Radio international" (series, 11 July 1964), *The magic flute* ("Festival," fall 1964), "Thursday concert" (series, 29 Oct. 1964; 5, 26 Nov. 1964; 10 Dec. 1964; 14 Jan. 1965; 11 Mar. 1965; 22 Apr. 1965), "Concert from two worlds" (series, 1 Nov. 1964; 5 Apr. 1965; 5 Jan. 1967), *War requiem* ("Sunday night," 15 Nov. 1964), "Toronto Symphony Or-

chestra" (series, 18 Dec. 1964; 22 Jan. 1965), "Opera theatre" (series, 19 Sept. 1965; 1 Sept. 1968), *The art of Glenn Gould* (12 Mar. 1967), "Thursday music" (11 May 1967), *The concerto* (15 July 1968); pianist in *Musica viva* (19 July 1968); conducted *Canadian concerts* (29 Aug. 1968), "BBC concert" (series, 14 Sept. 1968; 16 Nov. 1968).

TELEVISION

Conducted several programs, e.g. Overture to *Theodora and Lulu*, final movement ("Music in the mirror," 15 Apr. 1962).

RECORDINGS

Numerous recordings, e.g. *Concerto*, harpsichord and strings, by Bach, Columbia ML 4782. *Rhapsody on a theme of Paganini*, RCA Victor ERB 1 (549-5031-549-5032). Tatiana's letter scene from *Eugene Onegin*, Columbia ML 2048, 1949. *Concerto no. 2*, A major, by Liszt, Angel Records, ANG 35031, 1953. *Orchestral suite from Prince Igor*, MGM Records, E 3008, 1953. *Concerto in C minor*, oboe and string orchestra by B. Marcello, Columbia ML 4782, 1954(?). *The wooden prince*, Bartok Records BR 308, 1954. *Bluebeard's castle*, Bartok Records BR 310-311, 1955. *Concerto in D*, violin, by Tchaikovsky, RCA Victor LM 1832, 1955. *Concerto in B minor* by Dvořák, Angel Records ANG 35417, 1957. *Élégie* by Fauré, Angel Records ANG 35417, 1957. *Spirituals*, Everest SDBR 3002, 1958. *Konzertstück*, violoncello and orchestra, by Dohnanyi, Angel Records ANG 35627, 1958. *Appalachian spring*, Everest SDBR 3002, 1958. Canzone del gondolier and Assisa a piè d'un salice, *Otello*, RCA Victor LM 6146, 1958. *Concerto no. 1*, D flat major, by Prokofiev, Angel Records ANG 35568, 1958. *Symphony no. 6*, by Schubert, Mercury MG 50196, 1959. *Concerto no. 3*, C minor, by Beethoven, Capitol P 8468, 1959. *Third piano concerto* in D major, Capitol P 8524, 1960. *Opera arias* by Wagner, Angel Records ANG 35715, 1960. *Concerto no. 2*, in F minor, by Chopin, Angel Records S 35729, 1960. *Concerto no. 24*, in C minor, piano and orchestra, by Mozart, Columbia ML 5739, 1962.

COMPOSITIONS

Wrote several film scores.

SUTTO, Jeanine (Janine?)

Actress.

HOME

393 Prince Albert St., Montreal 215, PQ.

CAREER

L'Équipe, Montréal, actress 1943-47; Théâtre du Nouveau Monde, Montréal, actress 1951–; Théâtre du Rideau Vert, Montréal, actress 1958–; La Comédie Canadienne, Montréal, actress 1966–.

MEMBER

Union des Artistes de Montréal.

THEATRE

Played in many productions, e.g. *Les mal aimés* (Compagnons de Saint-Laurent, Montréal, 1941), *Tessa ou la nymphe au coeur fidèle* (Équipe, 1943), title role in *Fanny* (Équipe, Dec. 1944), Hermia in *Le songe d'une nuit d'été* (Équipe, 1945), *Liliom* (Équipe, 1946), *Les parents terribles* (Équipe, Oct. 1947), *La cathédrale* (Monument National, Montréal, 1950), Vivette in *L'Arlésienne* (Société des Festivals de Montréal, 1950), *L'avare* (Nouveau Monde, 1951), *Célimare le bien-aimé* (Nouveau Monde, 1951), *La folle* (Montreal Repertory Theatre, 1953?), *Pygmalion* (Montreal Repertory Theatre, 1953?), *Le barrage* (Le Théâtre Club, Montréal, Oct. 1955), Ines de Castro in *La reine morte* (Rideau Vert, 1958), *Le dindon* (Nouveau Monde, Montreal Festival, 1960), Mme. Frola in *Chacun sa vérité* (Nouveau Monde, 1960), Stéphane in *Fleur de cactus* (Rideau Vert, 15 Oct. 1965), Ann Putnam in *Les sorcières de Salem* (Nouveau Monde, 20 Oct. 1965), Femme in *Les temples* (Comédie, 16 Jan. 1966), Coco in *Croque-Monsieur* (Rideau Vert, 15 Mar. 1966), *Retour des oies blanches* (Comédie, 19 Oct. 1966), *Je veux voir Mioussov* (Rideau Vert, 15 Mar. 1967), *Docile* (Comédie, 10 May 1968), *Bilan* (Nouveau Monde, 4 Oct. 1968).

SYMONDS, Norm 1920–

(Norman A. Symonds)

Composer; b. 23 Dec. 1920 near Nelson, BC.

EDUCATION

Studied theory, harmony, counterpoint, and clarinet at Royal Conservatory of Music, Toronto, 1946-48; with Gordon Delamont (*q.v.*), Toronto, 1948- ? .

HOME

529 Yonge St., Toronto 284, Ont.

CAREER

RCN, 1938-45; played with Ron Collier (*q.v.*) and Gordon Delamont *c.*1948-51; Norman Symonds Jazz Octet, Toronto, founder and director 1953-57; CBC, Toronto, director for "Ten centuries concerts" series 1962.

AWARDS, HONOURS

Canadian Department of Veterans' Affairs study grant, 1946-48, Canada Council arts fellowship 1965/66, award, 1968/69.

COMPOSITIONS

Dance suite. Boy meets girl, ms. at Canadian Music Centre. *Tension*, ballet score. *Concerto for Dixieland group*, performed by Metro Stompers, Toronto. *Fair wind*, 1952, recorded on *In Canada* with Duke Ellington on Decca 75069, 1968. *Fugue for reeds and brass*, 1952, performed on CBC series "Jazz unlimited." *Concerto no. 1 for jazz octet*, 1955. *Concerto no. 2 for jazz octet*, 1956. *The cocktail party*, a piece for mim-

ing, 1956. *Experiments for improvising*, 1957. *Bordello ballad*, 1957. *Fugue for Shearing*, 1957. *Fugue and fantasy*, performed at Stratford, Ont. Festival, 1957. *Concerto grosso for jazz quintet and symphony orchestra*, first performed by Ron Collier Jazz Quintet and CBC Symphony Orchestra under Victor Feldbrill (*q.v.*) on CBC, Jan. 1958, commissioned by CBC. *Pastel and Hambourg suite*, commissioned by Ron Collier Jazz Quintet, 1958. *The age of anxiety*, interludes, performed on CBC series "Wednesday night," 4 Feb. 1959, commissioned by John Reeves through CBC. *Shepherd's lament*, for jazz quartet, 1959. *She gently moves*, for jazz dancer and jazz quintet, 1959. *Autumn nocturne*, three interludes for tenor saxophone and string orchestra, first performed by CBC Orchestra, fall 1960 and recorded on air-check tape, 1961. *Opera for six voices*, jazz opera, 1960/61, first performed on CBC series "Wednesday night," 29 Nov. 1961. *Perspectives*, essay for jazz octet, 1962. *Pastel for string orchestra*, 1963, ms. at Canadian Music Centre. *Elegy for string orchestra*, ms. at Canadian Music Centre, first performed 1963. *Big lonely*, for orchestra, singer, and narrator, 1965/66. *The umbrella*, for jazz quartet and string quartet, third stream program score, performed on CBC TV, 12 Dec. 1966. *The nameless hour*, jazz for flugelhorn and strings, Leeds Music Company, first performed by Toronto Symphony Orchestra and soloist Fred Stone under Victor Feldbrill, broadcast on CBC series "Concerts from two worlds," 15 Dec. 1966, recorded on *In Canada* with Duke Ellington on Decca 75069, 1968, commissioned by CBC. *Duet for violin and all the percussion that can be carried across town by one man – blues*, first performed by Toronto Symphony Orchestra at Lincoln Center, New York, NY, Mar. 1967. *Citérama*, third stream music, commissioned for the Man in the Community pavilion, Expo 67, Montreal, 1967. *The democratic concerto*, for jazz quartet and symphony orchestra, 1967, first performed by Winnipeg Symphony Orchestra and Fred Stone Quartet under Victor Feldbrill, 14 Dec. 1967, broadcast on CBC series "Friday concert," 22 Dec. 1967, commissioned by Winnipeg Symphony Orchestra for Canadian centennial. *L'âge de Pierre*, drama score, performed in Le Centre, Montréal, Jan. 1968. *Inscribed with love*, film score, performed on CBC TV, 12 Apr. 1968. *Bongos for Bill*, performed by Toronto Symphony Orchestra on CBC series "Symphony hall," winter 1968, commissioned by R.W. Finlayson. *Impulse*, 1969, first performed by Toronto Symphony Orchestra under Seiji Ozawa on CBC series "Symphony hall," 23 Mar. 1968, commissioned by R.W. Finlayson for Toronto Symphony Orchestra.

SYSAK, Juliette Augustina

see JULIETTE

TAKASHIMA, Shizuye Violet*   1928–
Artist; b. 12 June 1928 in Vancouver, BC; daughter
of Senji and Teru (Fujiwara) Takashima.

EDUCATION
Attended Henry Hudson School and Kitsilano
Junior High School in Vancouver; Notre Dame
High School, New Denver, BC; Westdale Colleg-
iate, Hamilton, Ont., 1945-46; Central Technical
School, Toronto, Ont., 1946-48, studied under J.
W.G. Macdonald (q.v.), Will Ogilvie (q.v.), Ontario
College of Art, Toronto, 1951-53.

HOME
429 W. 46th St., Apt. 5D, New York, NY 10036,
USA.

CAREER
Bell Telephone of Canada, Toronto, draftsman
1953-56; travelled and painted in Europe 1956-
59; painted in Toronto 1959-64, travelled in Mexico 1964-65; painter in Toronto and later in New
York.

EXHIBITIONS
ONE-MAN: Upstairs Gallery, Toronto, 1959,
1960, and 1961; Waddington Galleries, Montreal,
PQ, 1963 and 1967; Jerrold Morris International
Art Gallery, Toronto, 1963 and 1964.
GROUP: Represented in group exhibitions held
in Canada since 1959; sixth Biennial Exhibition of
Canadian Painting, National Gallery of Canada,
Ottawa, Ont., 1965.

COLLECTIONS IN WHICH REPRESENTED
Department of External Affairs, Ottawa; National
Gallery of Canada; Montreal *Star*; Montreal Stan-
dard Publishing Co.; Canadian Titanium Pigments
Ltd., Montreal.

TANABE, Takao*   1926–
Artist; b. 16 Sept. 1926 in Prince Rupert, BC; son
of Naojiro Izumi and Tomie Tanabe; m. Patricia
Anne White 7 Mar. 1956.

EDUCATION
Studied under Joseph Plaskett (q.v.), Winnipeg
School of Art, Man., diploma, 1946-49; Reuben
Tam, Brooklyn Museum Art School, New York,
NY, 1951-52; attended University of Manitoba Art
School, 1950; studied under Hans Hofmann, New
York, 1951; attended New School of Social Re-
search, New York, 1952; studied under William
Scott, Banff School of Fine Arts, Alta., 1953;
attended Central School of Arts and Crafts, Lon-
don, England, 1954; studied under Iao Hirayama,
Tokyo University of Fine Arts, Japan, 1959.

RELIGION
Agnostic.

HOME
3939 Viewridge, West Vancouver, BC.

CAREER
Sometime printer, publisher, and typographic
designer 1956–; Vancouver School of Art,
teacher 1961-65, 1967–.

COMMISSIONS
Mural, Fine Arts Gallery, University of British
Columbia, 1953; mosaic mural, Sir John Carling
Building, Ottawa, Ont., 1966; six Thailand silk
banners, Winnipeg Centennial Concert Hall, 1967.

MEMBER
Royal Canadian Academy (Associate 1967).

AWARDS, HONOURS
Emily Carr Foundation scholarship to study in
Europe, 1953; Canada Council fellowship to
study in Japan, 1959.

EXHIBITIONS
ONE-MAN: Winnipeg Art Gallery, 1952; Banff
School of Fine Arts, 1952; Richardson's Gallery,
Winnipeg, 1953; Robertson Galleries, Ottawa,
1953 and 1955; University of Alberta, 1953;
Coste House, Calgary, Alta., 1953; McGill Univer-
sity School of Architecture Gallery, 1955; Univer-
sity of Manitoba Art School Gallery, 1956; Van-
couver Art Gallery, 1957; Gallery of Contemporary
Art, Toronto, 1957 and 1958; New Design Gallery,
Vancouver, 1959, 1961, 1962, and 1966; Art
Gallery of Greater Victoria, BC, 1959; Nihonbashi
Gallery, Tokyo, 1960; Galerie Agnès Lefort,
Montréal, PQ, 1962 and 1966; Blue Barn Gallery,
Ottawa, 1963; Western Art Circuit, eight-city tour
of four western provinces, 1965; Yellow Door
Gallery, Winnipeg, 1966; Lofthouse Galleries,
Ottawa, 1967; Atlantic Provinces Art Circuit,
1967.
GROUP: Represented in group exhibitions held
in Canada since 1951 including annual exhibi-
tions of Montreal Museum of Fine Arts Spring
Show, Canadian Group of Painters, Burnaby Art
Society, and Winnipeg Show; represented in group
exhibitions organized by National Gallery of Canada, Ottawa, since 1953 including the second, third,
fourth, fifth, and sixth biennials, 1957, 1959,
1961, 1963, and 1965; São Paulo Bienal, Brazil,
1953 and 1957; Caracas Exhibition, Venezuela,
1953; summer show, Aia Gallery, London, 1955;
Guggenheim International Exhibition, Paris,
France and New York, 1956; Canadian Abstract
Painters, Smithsonian Institute, Washington, DC,
1956; Milan Triennial, Italy, 1957; World's Fair,
Brussels, Belgium, 1958; Canadian Painters,
Geneva, Switzerland, Cologne, Germany, Utrecht
and Groningen, The Netherlands, 1958; First
Inter-American Biennial of Arts and Crafts,
Mexico City, Mexico, 1958; Twentieth Internat-
ional Biennial of Watercolors, Brooklyn Museum,
New York, 1959; Northwest Art Today, World's
Fair, Seattle, Wash., 1962; Commonwealth Art
Today, Commonwealth Centre, London, 1962;
Contemporary Canadian Painting and Sculpture,
Rochester Memorial Art Gallery, 1963; Pacific
Northwest Annual, Seattle Art Museum, 1964 and
1965; Canadian Prints and Drawings, Cardiff
Commonwealth Arts Festival, Wales, 1965;

Seventh Annual Northwest Painters, University of Oregon, 1967.

COLLECTIONS IN WHICH REPRESENTED
National Gallery of Canada; Art Gallery of Ontario, Toronto; Art Gallery of Greater Victoria; Sir George Williams University; Brock Hall Collection, University of British Columbia; Alumni Collection, University of Victoria; Art Gallery, Dalhousie University; Carlton University; Agnes Etherington Art Centre, Queen's University; Department of External Affairs, Ottawa; Musée d'Art Contemporain, Montréal; Geigg Ltd., Montreal; Canadian Imperial Bank of Commerce, Montreal; J.W. Thompson Ltd., New York.

TATLOW, Josephine Barrington
see BARRINGTON, Josephine

TAVERNER, Sonia*   1936–
Dancer; b. 18 May 1936 in Byfleet, Surrey, England; daughter of Herbert Frank and Evelyn Norah (Powell) Taverner; came to Canada in 1956 and became Canadian citizen.

EDUCATION
Attended school in England; Elmhurst Ballet School, Camberley, Surrey, three major Royal Academy of Dancing examinations, 1952-54; Sadler's Wells (now Royal) Ballet School, London, England, 1954-55; studied with Henry Danton and Vladimir Dokoudovsky at Ballet Arts, William Dollar at (now American) Ballet Theatre, and Felia Doubrovska and Muriel Stuart at School of American Ballet, New York, NY; Gweneth Lloyd and Betty Farrally (*q.v.*) at Banff School of Fine Arts, Alta.

RELIGION
Roman Catholic.

HOME
The Drake, 1512 Spruce St., Philadelphia, Pa. 19102, USA.

OFFICE
Les Grands Ballets Canadiens, 5415 Chemin de la Reine Marie, Montréal 248, PQ.

CAREER
Sadler's Wells (now Royal) Ballet, London, 1955-56; Royal Winnipeg Ballet, Man., corps de ballet 1956-57, soloist 1957-62, prima ballerina 1962-66; Jacob's Pillow Dance Festival, Lee, Mass., 1963, 1967; Les Grands Ballets Canadiens, Montréal, leading 1966–.

MEMBER
ACTRA: AEA: Union des Artistes de Montréal.

AWARDS, HONOURS
Scholarship to Elmhurst Ballet School, 1952; scholarship to Sadler's Wells (now Royal) Ballet School, 1954; Adeline Genée silver medal from Royal Academy of Dancing, London, 1954; Canada Council arts scholarship for study abroad, 1963/64.

THEATRE
First danced *Casse-noisette* pas de deux (Ivanov, 1957), *The sleeping beauty* pas de deux (Petipa, 1958), Black Swan pas de deux from *Le lac des cygnes* (Petipa-Ivanov, 1958), *Don Quixote* pas de deux (Petipa, 1958), Spanish girl in *The comedians* (Boris, 1958); created Young girl in *Grasslands* (Moulton, Playhouse, Winnipeg, 18 Oct. 1958); first danced *Ballet premier* (Spohr, 1959), *Concerto* (Lloyd, 1959), *Romance* (Lloyd, 1959); created title role in *The Chinese nightingale* (Heiden, 15 Jan. 1959), Maiden in *Brave song* (Moulton, Playhouse, Winnipeg, 28 Dec. 1959), Witch in *Variations for a lonely theme* (Conte, Playhouse, Winnipeg, 18 Mar. 1960), Trumpet in *A court occasion* (Macdonald, Playhouse, Winnipeg, 26 Dec. 1961), Young girl in *Recurrence* (Clouser, Winnipeg, 27 Dec. 1961); first danced *Pas de dix* (Balanchine, 10 Mar. 1962), Princess Naissa in *Pas d'action* (Macdonald, 1963), Polly Peachum in *The beggar's ballet* (Moulton, 1965), *Divertissement Glazounov* (Nault, Place des Arts, Montréal, 1966), *Carmina burana* (Nault, 1966), *The three sisters* (Paige, 1966), Girl in *Quintan* (Nault, 1966), title role in *Giselle* (Dolin after Coralli, 1967), *Suite canadienne* (Chiriaeff, 1967), Young girl in *Gehenne* (Nault, 1967), Sugar Plum Fairy in *Casse-noisette* (Nault, 1967), Odette in *Le lac des cygnes*, act II (Boston Ballet, Mass., 1967), *Theme and variations* (Balanchine, 1968).

TELEVISION
Danced in several CBC productions, e.g. "Toes in tempo" (series, 1957), "Dancing storybook" (series, 1958-59), Black Swan pas de deux from *Le lac des cygnes* (Petipa-Ivanov, "Patronage in music," 4 Mar. 1962), *Recurrence* (Clouser, *Royal Winnipeg Ballet*, 26 Aug. 1962).

TEKAHIONWAKE
see JOHNSON, Pauline

THOMAS, Lionel Arthur John   1915–
Artist; b. 3 Apr. 1915 in Toronto, Ont.; m. Patricia Simmons; children: three children.

EDUCATION
Canadian College of Music, diploma, 1930; John Russell School of Fine Arts, Toronto, 1933-35; Ontario College of Art, Toronto, 1936-37; Karl Godwin School of Illustration, Toronto, 1937; Hans Hofmann School of Fine Art, Provincetown, Mass., 1947; studied under Mark Rothko, California School of Fine Art, San Francisco, Calif., 1949.

OFFICE
Dept. of Fine Arts, University of British Columbia, Vancouver 8, BC.

CAREER
Canadian Army, Reserve Forces, 1943-45; Boeing

Aircraft Company, draftsman; Vancouver School of Art, instructor for five years; University of British Columbia, summer session instructor 1947, 1963, 1964, and 1965, school of architecture instructor 1950-59, assistant professor 1959-64, department of university extension instructor and lecturer 1951-55, department of fine arts associate professor 1964–; colour consultant for Vancouver Public Library 1957; Committee on Applied Art chairman, BC Archives and Museum Building, Victoria, BC, 1965.

COMMISSIONS
Mural, Mercantile Bank of Canada, Vancouver, 1954; two murals, St. John's Cathedral, Winnipeg, Man., 1956; mural, Vancouver Public Library, 1957; fountain, Edmonton City Hall, Alta., 1957; Stations of the Cross and doors, St. Thomas More College, University of Saskatchewan; mural, St. Paul's College, University of Manitoba, 1958; sculpture, St. Mark's College, University of British Columbia, 1958; Stations of the Cross, Lady of Perpetual Help Church, Calgary, Alta., 1958; bas-relief, St. Mary's Church, Saskatoon, Sask., 1959; bas-relief, Great West Life, Winnipeg, 1959; bas-relief, York University, 1961; bas-relief, Brock Hall, University of British Columbia, 1962; bas-relief, Vancouver Public Library, 1962; bas-relief, Phillips Barrett Engineering Building; bas-relief and doors, St. Thomas More College, University of Saskatchewan, 1963; bas-relief and mural, Block Bros. Building, Vancouver, 1965.

MEMBER
BC Society of Artists; Canadian Group of Painters; Pacific Artists Association (Pacific Coast Region); Royal Canadian Academy (Associate); Northwest Institute of Sculptors.

AWARDS, HONOURS
Scholarship, John Russell School of Fine Arts, Toronto, 1935; Emily Carr scholarship, 1949-50; top award and purchase, International Division of the Florida International Art Exhibition, Lakeland; award, Pacific Northwest Artists Exhibition, Seattle, Wash., 1952; Allied Arts medal, Royal Architectural Institute of Canada, 1956.

EXHIBITIONS
ONE-MAN: Vancouver Art Gallery, 1942 and 1948; University of British Columbia Fine Arts Gallery, 1947, 1948, and 1951; Art Gallery of Toronto, 1953.
GROUP: Represented in group exhibitions held in Canada since 1941; Florida International Art Exhibition, 1952; Grand Central Galleries, New York, NY, 1952; São Paulo Biennial, Brazil, 1954; Caracas, Venezuela, 1954; Seattle Art Museum, 1954; University of California, San Francisco, 1960.

COLLECTIONS IN WHICH REPRESENTED
National Gallery of Canada; Art Gallery of Ontario, Toronto; Vancouver Art Gallery; University of Victoria; Florida Southern College.

THOMAS, Powys*   1925–
Actor, director, and teacher; b. 31 Dec. 1925 in Cwmbach, Glamorganshire, Wales; son of William Bryn and Mary Olinda (Jones) Thomas; m. Ann Morrish 20 July 1951 (marriage dissolved 1968); children: Nicholas Owain and Sian Rebecca b. 20 Sept. 1953, Sara Mair b. 15 Nov. 1959; came to Canada in 1956.

EDUCATION
Attended Mountain School, Port Talbot, S. Wales, 1930-38; Rendcomb College, Cirencester, England, 1939-44; studied theatre with Michael Saint-Denis, George Devine, and Glen Byam Shaw at Old Vic Theatre School, London, England, 1947-48.

OFFICE
Festival Theatre, Stratford, Ont.

CAREER
Royal Navy, 1946, mental nurse; Young Vic Company, England, actor 1948-51; Perth Theatre Company, Scotland, actor 1951; Shakespeare Memorial (now Royal Shakespeare) Theatre Company, Stratford-upon-Avon, England, actor 1952-56; Crest Theatre, Toronto, Ont., actor 1956-60; American Shakespeare Festival, Stratford, Conn., actor 1957; Stratford, Ont. Festival, actor 1957–; National Theatre School of Canada, Montreal, PQ, co-founder and artistic director of English section 1960-65; Canadian Players, Toronto, actor 1965; Manitoba Theatre Centre, Winnipeg, actor 1966–.

MEMBER
AEA; ACTRA.

THEATRE
Played Shylock in *The merchant of Venice* (Young Vic, 1951), Oberon in *A midsummer night's dream* (Young Vic, 1950; Shakespeare Memorial Theatre, 1954), Sicinius in *Coriolanus* (Shakespeare Memorial Theatre, 1952), Duke Frederick in *As you like it* (Shakespeare Memorial Theatre, 1952), Prince of Arragon in *The merchant of Venice* (Shakespeare Memorial Theatre, 1953), Cornwall in *King Lear* (Shakespeare Memorial Theatre, 1953), Proculeius in *Antony and Cleopatra* (Shakespeare Memorial Theatre, 1953; Princes, London, 4 Nov. 1953), Roderigo in *Othello* (Shakespeare Memorial Theatre, 1954), Benvolio in *Romeo and Juliet* (Shakespeare Memorial Theatre, 1954), Arnolphe in *School for wives* (Arts Council Midland Theatre, Coventry, England, 1956; Manitoba Theatre Centre, 1968), *An Italian straw hat* (Crest, 1956), Kolyghin in *The three sisters* (Crest, 1956), Lepidus in *Antony and Cleopatra* (Crest, 1956), Player King in *Hamlet* (Stratford, Ont. Festival, 1957), Reverend Eli Jenkins in *Under Milkwood* (Henry Miller's, New York, NY, 15 Oct. 1957), Panthino in *Two gentlemen of Verona* (Phoenix, New York, 18 Mar. 1958), Achille De Moulinville in *The broken jug*

Phoenix, New York, 1 Apr. 1958), First voice
in *Under Milkwood* (Crest, 1959/60), title role in
Macbeth (Crest, 1959/60), Sorin in *The seagull*
(Crest, 1959/60), Captain Shotover in *Heartbreak
House* (Crest, 1959/60), Owen Glendower in
Henry IV, part I (Stratford, Ont. Festival, 14 June
1965), Cinna the poet and Ligarius in *Julius
Caesar* (Stratford, Ont. Festival, 16 June 1965),
Firs in *The cherry orchard* (Stratford, Ont. Fes-
tival, 26 July 1965), Thomas à Becket in *Murder
in the Cathedral* (Canadian Players, 21 Oct. 1965),
Eisenring in *The firebugs* (Canadian Players, 19
Nov. 1965), Pistol in *Henry V* (Stratford, Ont.
Festival, 6 June 1966), Henry Beaufort in *Henry
VI* (Stratford, Ont. Festival, 7 June 1966), Gri-
gori Rasputin in *The last of the Tsars* (Stratford,
Ont. Festival, 12 July 1966), Friar Laurence in
Romeo and Juliet (Manitoba Theatre Centre,
1967), Creon in *Antigone* (Manitoba Theatre
Centre, 1967), Colonel Vershinin in *The three
sisters* (Manitoba Theatre Centre, 1967), Solness
in *The master builder* (Ipswich Arts Theatre,
England, 1967), Athos in *The three musketeers*
(Stratford, Ont. Festival, 22 July 1968), Vlad-
imir in *Waiting for Godot* (Stratford, Ont. Festival, 13 Aug. 1968), Hieronymus in *Red magic*
(Manitoba Theatre Centre, 1968).

FILM
Played in *The last of the Mohicans* (Normandie
Productions, Toronto, 1956), Fox in *The luck of
Ginger Coffey* (Continental Distributing Inc.,
1964).

RADIO
Played in many CBC productions, e.g. *Tomorrow's
actors* ("Wednesday night," 19 June 1963),
Shakespeare in *The trumpets of summer* ("Sunday
night," 29 Nov. 1964), Public Prosecutor in *The
fate of a poet* ("Sunday night," 31 Jan. 1965),
Lucifer in *The black spider* ("Sunday night," 2
May 1965), Glendower in *Henry IV*, part I ("Open-
ing of Stratford, Ontario Festival," 14 June 1965),
Yeats in Dublin ("Tuesday night," 14 Mar. 1967),
Wilf in *The front room* ("Midweek theatre," 15
Mar. 1967), *Benny the bashful boxcar* ("Between
ourselves," 20 Dec. 1967).

TELEVISION
Played in many CBC productions, e.g. title role in
Lord Durham ("Explorations," 17 May 1961),
Leader in *Stop the world and let me off* ("Play-
date," 4 Oct. 1961), Painter in *Masterpiece*
("Playdate," 15 Nov. 1961), Duncan in *Macbeth*
("National school telecast," 30 Nov., 5, 7, 12, 14
Dec. 1961; "Festival," 23 Apr. 1962), Pistol in
Henry V (CTV, 1966), Butler in *Traveller without
luggage* ("Festival," 10 Apr. 1968); directed
Orpheus (Gluck, "Festival," 13 Mar. 1961).

THOMPSON, Ernest Evan Seton
see SETON, Ernest Thompson

THOMSON, Edward William 1849-1924
Author; b. 12 Feb. 1849 in York Township, Peel
County, Upper Canada (now Ont.); son of William
and Margaret Hamilton (Foley) Thomson; m.
Adelaide L.G. St. Denis 1873; children: son; d. 5
Mar. 1924 in Boston, Mass.

EDUCATION
Attended Brantford Grammar School and
Trinity College School in Weston, Ont.

CAREER
3rd and 5th Pennsylvania Cavalry, 1864-65;
Queen's Own Rifles, 1866; land surveyor and civil
engineer 1868-78; *Globe*, Toronto, editorial
writer 1878-91; *Youth's companion*, revising
editor 1891-1901; *Star*, Montreal, 1901-02; *Tran-
script*, Boston, Canadian correspondent in Ottawa,
Ont. 1902-22.

MEMBER
Royal Society of Literature of the United King-
dom (elected fellow, 1909); Royal Society of
Canada (elected fellow, 1910).

AWARDS, HONOURS
Youth's companion short story prize for "Pether-
ick's peril," 1885.

WRITINGS
Old man Savarin and other stories, W. Briggs, 1895;
Smoky days (juvenile fiction), Thomas & Crowell,
1896; *Walter Gibbs, The young boss and other
stories* (juvenile fiction), W. Briggs, 1896; *Between
earth and sky and other strange stories of deliver-
ance* (juvenile fiction), A.J. Roland, 1897; *Peter
Ottawa* (poem), p.p., 1908; *When Lincoln died
and other poems*, Houghton, Mifflin, 1909 (also
published under title *The many mansioned house
and other poems*, W. Briggs, 1909).
TRANSLATED: M.S. Henry's *Aucassin and Nico-
lette*, Copeland, 1895.
CONTRIBUTED: Poetry and short stories to *Canadian poems and lays*, edited by W.D. Lighthall,
W. Scott, 1893; *A treasury of Canadian verse*,
edited by T.H. Rand, W. Briggs, 1900; *Songs of
French Canada*, compiled by L.J. Burpee, Musson,
1909; *The Oxford book of Victorian verse*, edited
by A.T. Quiller-Couch, Oxford, 1913; *The Oxford
book of Canadian verse*, chosen by W. Campbell,
Oxford, 1913; *The book of sorrow*, edited by A.
Macphail, Oxford, 1916; *Canadian singers and
their songs*, edited by E.S. Caswell, McClelland &
Stewart, 1919; *A book of Canadian prose and
verse*, compiled by E.K. and E.H. Broadus, Macmillan, 1923; *Atlantic monthly*, *University
magazine* (Montreal), *Collier's weekly*, *Youth's
companion*.

THORNE, Joy Coghill
see COGHILL, Joy

TILL, Eric Stanley* 1929—
Film director; b. 24 Nov. 1929 in London, Eng-

land; son of William and Beatrice (Porter) Till; m. Betty Ann Pope 14 July 1957; children: Alison, Douglas, David, Justine.

FILMS
Produced *Great expectations* ("Festival," CBC, 27 Mar. 1961), *Pictures in the hallway* ("Festival," CBC, 24 Apr. 1961), *The offshore island* ("Festival," CBC, Mar. 1962; nomination for international award, National Academy of TV Arts and Sciences, 1963), *A book with chapters in it* ("Festival," CBC, 8 Oct. 1962), *The devil's instrument* ("Festival," CBC, 5 Nov. 1962), *Serjeant Musgrave's dance* ("Festival," CBC, 26 Nov. 1962), *The Royal Winnipeg Ballet* ("Festival," CBC, 5 Feb. 1964), *Pale horse, pale rider* ("Festival," CBC, 18 Mar. 1964; nomination for Emmy award, National Academy of TV Arts and Sciences), *The diary of a scoundrel* ("Festival," CBC, 1 Apr. 1964), *The master builder* ("Festival," CBC, 18 Nov. 1964); produced and directed *A game – like – only a game* ("Festival," CBC, 29 Sept. 1965); produced *Silent night, lonely night* ("Festival," CBC, 1 Dec. 1965), *Ashes to ashes* ("Festival," CBC, 1 Feb. 1966), special ("Festival," CBC, 18 May 1966), *Miss Julie* ("Festival," CBC, 14 Sept. 1966); produced and directed *Tea party* ("Festival," CBC, 11 Oct. 1967).

TOBIAS, Sally Brayley
see BRAYLEY, Sally

TONDINO, Gentile* 1923–
Artist; b. 3 Sept. 1923 in Montreal; son of Antonio and Lucia (Liberatore) Tondino; m. Livia Helen Martucci 15 Nov. 1947; children: Guido Paul b. 13 Mar. 1951, Tristan Christopher, Lisa Lucia.

EDUCATION
Attended Holy Family School in Montreal, 1929-36; studied full-time under Adam Sheriff Scott in Montreal, 1943-46; studied under Ghitta Caiserman and Alfred Pinsky, Montreal School of Art, 1947-48; Arthur Lismer (*q.v.*), Marian Scott, Eldon Grier (*q.v.*), Jacques de Tonnancour (*q.v.*), Goodridge Roberts (*q.v.*), Gordon Webber (*q.v.*), and Louis Archambault, Montreal Museum of Fine Arts School of Art and Design, diploma, 1949-51; studied child art teaching under Arthur Lismer (*q.v.*), 1951-52.

HOME
5905 Côté des Neiges, Apt. 4, Montréal, PQ.

CAREER
Montreal Museum of Fine Arts School of Art and Design, instructor 1952-67; Queen's University, summer school instructor 1955-59; School of Community Arts, Tatamagouche, NS, painting instructor summers 1956-61; YMCA, Montreal, instructor 1957-59; YMHA, Montreal, evening class instructor 1960-65; McGill University, fine

arts department part-time instructor 1961-68; Sir George Williams University, part-time instructor 1967-68; McGill University School of Architecture, lecturer 1958–.

COMMISSIONS
Mural, St. Marguerite Hotel, Montreal?, 1947; mural, Laurentian Hotel, Montreal, 1953.

MEMBER
Canadian Group of Painters (elected, 1952); Royal Canadian Academy (Associate 1963).

AWARDS, HONOURS
Second prize, Canadian Painting, Vancouver Art Gallery, BC, 1960; first prize, Hadassah exhibition, 1964.

EXHIBITIONS
ONE-MAN: Robertson Gallery, Ottawa, Ont., 1955; Festival of the Arts, Tatamagouche, 1957. GROUP: Represented in group exhibitions held in Canada including exhibitions of Canadian Group of Painters, Royal Canadian Academy, and Montreal Museum of Fine Arts; first and fourth Biennial Exhibitions of Canadian Painting, National Gallery of Canada, Ottawa, 1955 and 1961; World's Fair, Brussels, Belgium, 1958.

COLLECTIONS IN WHICH REPRESENTED
National Gallery of Canada; Montreal Museum of Fine Arts; Canadian Industries Ltd. Collection Montreal; Reader's Digest Collection.

TONNANCOUR, Jacques Godefroy de 1917–
Artist; b. 3 Jan. 1917 in Montreal, PQ; m. Margot Clerk in 1944.

EDUCATION
Studied under Father R. Fortin, Collège Jean-de-Brébeuf, Montréal, 1935; École des Beaux-Arts de Montréal, 1937; studied with Goodridge Roberts (*q.v.*), Montreal School of Art and Design.

HOME
211 ave. Walnut, St. Lambert, PQ.

CAREER
Montreal School of Art and Design, teacher 1942; painted in Rio de Janeiro, Brazil, 1945/46; Canadian delegate to 5th UNESCO Conference, Florence, Italy, 1950; École des Beaux-Arts de Montréal, teacher; University of British Columbia, teacher summer session 1960.

COMMISSIONS
Mural, Dow Planetarium, Montreal, 1965.

MEMBER
Contemporary Art Society.

AWARDS, HONOURS
Brazilian government scholarship, 1945; major prize, Second Winnipeg Show, Man., 1956; prize, Second Biennial Exhibition, National Gallery of Canada, Ottawa, Ont., 1957; prize, Third Winnipeg Show, 1958; Canadian government fellowship, 1958; Canada Council grant, 1958/59; second

prize, Concours Artistique de la Province de Québec, 1963.

EXHIBITIONS

ONE-MAN: Dominion Gallery, Montreal, 1942; Collège Jean-de-Brébeuf, 1943; Hart House, University of Toronto, 1944; Galerie Parizeau, Montréal, 1945; Rio de Janeiro, sponsored by the Ministry of Education, 1946; Montreal Museum of Fine Arts, 1949 and 1956; Laing Gallery, Toronto, 1958 and subsequent years; Galerie Denyse Delrue, Montréal, 1958 and subsequent years; Galerie Camille Hébert, Montréal, 1964; Vancouver Art Gallery, BC, 1966; Galerie Agnès Lefort, Montréal, 1966; Musée d'Art Contemporain, Montréal, 1966.

GROUP: Represented in group exhibitions held in Canada since 1942 including exhibitions of Montreal Museum of Fine Arts Spring Show and National Gallery of Canada; Rio de Janeiro, 1944; Canadian Graphic Arts Exhibition, Rio de Janeiro, 1946; Canadian Club, New York, NY, 1948; Painters of Canada ... 1668-1948; Virginia Museum of Fine Arts, Richmond, 1949; Canadian Painting, National Gallery of Art, Washington, DC; Florida State Fair, Tampa, 1952; *Biennale de Venise*, Italy, 1958; Canadian Exhibition, World's Fair, Brussels, Belgium, 1958; *Art Contemporain au Canada*, Germany and Switzerland, 1959; *Arte Canadiense*, Mexico, 1960; Galerie Arnaud, Paris, France, 1964.

COLLECTIONS IN WHICH REPRESENTED

National Gallery of Canada; Art Gallery of Ontario, Toronto; Montreal Museum of Fine Arts.

WRITINGS

Roberts, L'Arbre, 1943; *Refus global*, Mithra-Mythe, 1948; *Manifesto for prisme d'yeux*, p.p., 1948.

CONTRIBUTED: Articles to *La presse, La relève, Le quartier latin, Amérique-française, La nouvelle relève, JEC, Gants du ciel, Le devoir, World affairs, Canadian art, Queen's quarterly*.

TOUSIGNANT, Serge* 1942–
Artist; b. 28 May 1942 in Montreal; son of André-J. and Claire (Brisebois) Tousignant.

EDUCATION

Attended Montreal primary schools, 1948-54; attended Collège classique Sainte-Croix, 1955-58; École des Beaux-Arts, Montréal, diploma, 1958-62; worked and studied under Albert Dumouchel, Atelier Libres and École des Beaux-Arts, Montréal, 1962-65; attended Slade School of Fine Arts, London, England and University College, University of London, 1965-66.

HOME

827 Marie-Anne, Montréal, PQ.

CAREER

Travelled in Mexico, 1964-65; studied and travelled in England, 1965-66; travelled to Spain and Paris, France, 1966.

AWARDS, HONOURS

Painting award, École des Beaux-Arts, Montréal, 1962; purchase award, Fifth Calgary Graphics Exhibition, Alta., 1965; Leverhulme Canadian Painting scholarship, 1965; Brigestone Art Gallery prize, Fifth Tokyo International Prints Biennial, Japan, 1966; Canada Council grants, 1967, 1968, and 1969; sculpture prize, Perspective 67, Centennial Visual Arts Competition, 1967; grant, Ministère des Affaires Culturelles du Québec, 1968-69.

EXHIBITIONS

ONE-MAN: Galerie Camille Hébert, Montréal, 1964; Musée d'Art Contemporain, Montréal, 1965; Edifice Radio-Canada, Montréal, 1966.

GROUP: Represented in group exhibitions held in Canada since 1963 including annual exhibitions of Montreal Museum of Fine Arts Spring Show, Concours artistique de la Province de Québec, Calgary Graphics Exhibitions; represented in group exhibitions organized by National Gallery of Canada, Ottawa, Ont., including the Fifth Biennial of Canadian Painting, 1965; Canadian Prints and Drawings Exhibition, Cardiff Commonwealth Festival of Arts, Wales, 1965; Second and Third American Biennial of Prints, Santiago, Chile, 1966 and 1968; Contemporary Canadian Prints and Drawings Exhibition in Australia, 1966; Fifth International Biennial of Prints of Tokyo; Museum of Modern Art of Tokyo, 1967; Canada 67, Museum of Modern Art, New York, NY, 1967.

COLLECTIONS IN WHICH REPRESENTED

National Gallery of Canada; Victoria and Albert Museum, London; Musée d'Art Contemporain, Montréal; Canada Council of Arts; London Public Library and Art Museum, Ont.; Art Gallery of Greater Victoria, BC; Regina Public Library and Museum of Fine Arts, Sask.; Brigestone Art Gallery of Tokyo; Museum of Modern Art, New York.

TOWN, Harold Barling* 1924–
Artist; b. 13 June 1924 in Toronto; son of William Harry and Ellen Noelice (Watson) Town; m. Trudella Carol Tredwell 3 Sept. 1957; children: Heather b. 18 June 1958, Shelley b. 27 Apr. 1962.

EDUCATION

Attended Swansea Public School and Regal Road Public School, Toronto; Western Technical Commercial School, Toronto, graduated 1942; Ontario College of Art, Toronto, graduated 1944, post graduate work, 1945.

HOME

9 Castle Frank Cres., Toronto 5, Ont.

STUDIO

Studio 4, 25 Severn St., Toronto 5, Ont.

CAREER

McCall Frontenac oil tanker, *Cyclo Chief*, deck

hand and ship's painter 1943; Sinnot News, Toronto, comic strip artist (drew Minute Man of *Whiz comics*) 1943; Canada Steamship Lines, ticket salesman 1944; Eaton's, College St., Toronto, freelance artist (doing backdrops, large illustrations, rug design, directing construction and creation of model interiors, sculptures objects); *Mayfair*, Toronto, freelance illustrator 1947; editorial freelance illustrator till *c*.1957; entirely artistic 1957–; illustrated for *Maclean's, Chatelaine, Saturday night, Liberty, National home monthly, Weekend magazine, Canadian home journal, Globe and mail, Bride's book, Men's wear* and some advertising illustration for agencies; illustrated *Love where the nights are long: Canadian love poems,* comp. by I. Layton, McClelland & Stewart, 1962; designed décors and costumes for *House of Atreus* (National Ballet of Canada, 1964); illustrated jacket cover for *Beautiful losers* by L. Cohen, Viking Press, 1966; *Toronto life magazine,* columnist 1966-67.

COMMISSIONS
Mural, commissioned by Robert H. Saunders, Ontario Hydro for St. Lawrence Generating Station, Cornwall, Ont., 1958; mural, North York Public Library, Ont., 1959; two-part, double-sided painting and hand-etched brass screen, Malton International Airport, Toronto, 1963-64; mural and collage, lobby, Telegram Building, Toronto, 1963; banners, Founders College, York University, 1965; mural, Queens Park Project, Toronto, 1968.

MEMBER
Ontario Society of Artists (resigned); Canadian Society of Graphic Art (1953-54; member of executive; resigned, 1955); Toronto Art Directors Club (1954-56; executive member; resigned, 1959; honorary member, 1960); Painters Eleven (founding member); Royal Canadian Academy (Academician 1967).

AWARDS, HONOURS
Prize, first Winnipeg Show, Winnipeg Art Gallery, Man.; two awards, Second Canadian Biennial, National Gallery of Canada, Ottawa, Ont., 1957; honourable mention, Second International Exhibition of Drawings and Prints, Yugoslavia, 1957; Arno Prize, São Paulo Biennale, Brazil, 1957; prize, International Exhibition of Drawings and Prints, Lugano, Switzerland, 1958; Canada Council Purchase award, Montreal Museum of Fine Arts Spring Show, PQ, 1960; honourable mention, National Section, Canada, Guggenheim International award, New York, NY, 1960; Baxter award, 1961; fellowship, Instituto de Cultura Hispanica, Arte de America y Espana, Madrid, Spain, 1963; group honourable mention, Canadian section of the first Bienal Americana de Grabado, Museo de Arte Contemporaneo, Uni-

versidad de Chile, Santiago, Chile, 1963; merit award, Royal Canadian Academy, 1963; grand prix, Albert H. Robinson award, Montreal Museum of Fine Arts Spring Show, 1963; prize, Women's Committee, Art Gallery of Ontario, Toronto, 1963; medal award, Montreal Art Director's Club, 1963; DLitt from York University, 1966; Centennial medal, 1967.

EXHIBITIONS
ONE-MAN: Picture Loan Society, Toronto, 1954 and 1956; Gallery of Contemporary Art, Toronto, 1957; Galerie l'Actuelle, Montreal, 1957; Loranger Gallery, Ottawa; Jordan Gallery, Toronto, 1958; Laing Galleries, Toronto, 1959 and 1961; Norman Mackenzie Memorial Gallery, Regina, Sask., 1960; Vancouver Art Gallery, BC, 1960; Montreal Museum of Fine Arts, 1961; Dresdnere Gallery, Montreal, 1961 and 1964; Kitchener-Waterloo Gallery, Ont., 1962 and 1966; Jerrold Morris Gallery, Toronto, 1964 and 1966; Andrew Morris Gallery, New York, 1962; Fairleigh Dickenson University, Madison, NJ, 1963; St. Catharines Art Council, Ont., 1963; Galeria Bonino, New York, 1964; Bendale Branch, Scarborough Public Library, Ont., 1965; Studio Art Gallery, Vancouver, 1965; Blue Barn Gallery, Ottawa, 1966; Waddington Galleries, Montreal, 1966; Mazelow Gallery, Toronto, 1966; Memorial University, 1966; Community Festival of Arts, Waterloo, 1966; Sears Vincent Price Gallery, Chicago, Ill., 1967; Douglas Gallery, Vancouver, 1967; Yellow Door Gallery, Winnipeg, 1967; Scarborough College, Toronto, 1967; Hart House, University of Toronto, 1967; Winnipeg Art Gallery, 1967; Kensington Art Gallery, Calgary, Alta., 1967.

GROUP: Represented in group exhibitions held in Canada since 1960 including annual exhibitions of Canadian National Exhibition, Royal Canadian Academy, and Ontario Society of Artists; represented in group exhibitions organized by National Gallery of Canada, including the first, second, third, fourth, sixth, and seventh Biennials of Canadian Painting, 1955, 1957, 1959, 1961, 1965, and 1967; Venice Biennale, Italy, 1956; Painters 11, Riverside Museum, New York, 1956; São Paulo Biennale, 1957; 2nd Exposition de Gravure, Ljubljana, Yugoslavia, 1957; *Triennale de Milano,* Italy, 1957; Canadian Abstract Paintings Exhibition, Smithsonian Tour, USA, 1957; Canadian Contemporary Painting, Australia, 1957; International Exhibition of Drawings and Prints, Lugano, 1958; First International Triennial of Original Coloured Graphics, Grenchen, Switzerland, 1958; Brussels Universal and International Exhibition, Belgium, 1958; First Biennial of Inter-American Painting, Grabado, Mexico, 1958; Art in Canada, Dallas Museum of Contemporary

Art, Tex.; Walker Art Center, Minneapolis, Minn., 1958; Contemporary Art in Canada, Palais des Beaux-Arts, Brussels, 1958; Borduas and Town, Tooth Gallery, London, England, 1958; Musée d'Art Histoire, Geneva, Switzerland, 1959; Musée Rath, Geneva, and Walraf-Richartz Museum, Cologne, Germany, 1959; 20th Biennial International Watercolour Exhibition, Brooklyn Museum, NY, 1959; 3rd International Exposition de Gravure, Ljubljana, 1959; Canadian Graphics, Ljubljana, 1959; Canadian Watercolours and Prints, American Federation of Arts Tours, 1959-60; International Biennial of Prints, Cincinnati, Ohio, 1960; Guggenheim Awards Exhibition, New York, 1960; International Prints, American Federation of Arts, 1960; Canadian Art, Instituto National de Bellas Artes, Mexico City, Mexico, 1960-61; Dayton Art Institute, Ohio, 1960-61; *VI Biennale de São Paulo,* 1961; International Arts Festival, Pittsburgh, Pa., 1961; 4th International Exposition de Gravure, Ljubljana, 1961; Canadian Art, Warsaw Museum, Poland, 1962; International Exhibition, Tunisian Artists Association, Tunis, 1962; International Print Biennial, Tokyo, Japan, 1962; Pratt Institute, Brooklyn, Canadian Prints, 1962; J.B. Speed Art Museum, Louisville, Ky., 1962; Recent Acquisitions, Museum of Modern Art, New York, 1962; Canadian Prints, Pratt Graphic Art Center, New York, 1962; Brooklyn Museum, 1962; Recent Acquisitions, Guggenheim Museum, New York, 1963; Cézannne and Structure in Modern Painting, Guggenheim Museum, 1963; Canadian Biennial, London, 1963; *Arte de America y Espana,* Madrid, Barcelona, Spain, Naples, Italy, 1963; 5th International Exposition de Gravure, Ljubljana, 1963; Dunn International Exhibition, Fredericton, NB, and Tate Gallery, London, 1963; Graphik 1963, Albertina, Vienna, Austria, 1963; Fifteen Canadian Artists, Museum of Modern Art tour, 1963; Two Sculptors, Four Painters, Galerie Bonino, New York, 1963; *Primera Bienal Americana de Grabado,* Santiago, 1963; Mixed Media and Pop Art, Buffalo, NY, 1963; Contemporary Canadian Painting and Sculpture, Rochester Memorial Art Gallery, NY, 1963; *Primera Bienal Americana de Grabado,* Lima, Peru, 1964; Canadian Painting Tate Gallery, London, 1964; *Arte de America y Espana,* Rome and Milan, Italy, Berlin, Germany, Paris, France, 1964; Venice Biennale, 1964; *Dokumenta,* Kassel, Germany, 1964; Carnegie International, Pittsburgh, 1964; Print Biennale, Prague, Czecho-Slovakia, 1965; 1+1=3 Retinal, Austin, Tex., 1965; 6th International Exposition de Gravure, Ljubljana, 1965; Contemporary American Painting and Sculpture, University of Illinois, 1965; Cardiff Commonwealth Arts Festival, Wales, 1965; Canadian Graphic Art, Victoria and Albert Museum, London, tour of British Isles, 1965; 2nd Biennial of Contemporary Graphic Art, University of Chile, 1965; Selections from the Carnegie International, Pittsburgh, Detroit, Mich., 1965; *1ère Biennale Internationale de la Gravure,* Cracow, Poland, 1966; International Art Exhibition and Auction, UNESCO, and Brandeis University, 1966; Recent Acquisitions, Painting and Sculpture, Museum of Modern Art, New York, 1967; Painting in the 60s, Museum of Modern Art, New York, 1967; Eleven Canadian Printmakers, Hopkins Center Art Galleries, Dartmouth College, Hanover, NH, 1967; Town, McEwen Exhibition, National Gallery of Canada, Canadian and US Tour, 1967; Canada 67 Exhibition, New York and Detroit, 1967; Canadian Government pavilion, Expo 67, Montreal 1967.

COLLECTIONS IN WHICH REPRESENTED
Museum of Modern Art, New York; National Gallery of Canada; Museum of Modern Art, São Paulo; Stedelijk Museum, Amsterdam, The Netherlands; Cleveland Museum of Art, Ohio; Detroit Art Institute; Art Gallery of Ontario, Toronto; Montreal Museum of Fine Arts; Vancouver Art Gallery; Winnipeg Art Gallery; Beaverbrook Art Gallery, Fredericton, NB; Edmonton Art Gallery, Alta.; Art Gallery of Hamilton, Ont.; Art Gallery of London, Ont.; Galleria d'Arte di Villa Ciani, Lugano; Agnes Etherington Art Centre, Queen's University; Hart House, University of Toronto; University of British Columbia; Norman Mackenzie Art Gallery, Regina; York University; Toronto Dominion Bank Collection, Toronto; National Film Board of Canada, Ottawa; Kingston Art Society, Ont.; Canadian Industries Ltd. Collection, Montreal; Imperial Oil Collection, Toronto; Tate Gallery, London; Museo d'Arte Contemporaneo, Santiago; Guggenheim Museum, New York; Brooklyn Museum; Art Gallery of Greater Victoria, BC; Mount Allison University Collection; Sir George Williams University; Victoria College, University of Toronto; Adam Scott Collegiate, Peterborough, Ont.; Hirshorn Collection, Washington, DC; Mendel Art Collection, Saskatoon, Sask.; Willistead Art Gallery, Windsor, Ont.; Upper Canada College, Toronto; Albright-Knox Art Gallery, Buffalo; Canada Council Collection, Ottawa; Des Moines Art Center, Iowa; Department of External Affairs, Ottawa; Musée du Québec, PQ; Toronto Public Library; Metropolitan Museum, New York; Musée d'Art Contemporain, Montréal.

WRITINGS
Enigmas, McClelland & Stewart, 1964.
CONTRIBUTED: Articles to *The globe, Canadian art, Maclean's, Canadian forum, Toronto life, Gambit magazine, Chatelaine,* and *Canadian homes and gardens.*

TREMBLAY, Monique
see LEYRAC, Monique

TROTTIER, Pierre* 1925–

Poet; b. 21 Mar. 1925 in Montreal, PQ; son of
Louis and Marie-Rose (Lalumière) Trottier; m.
Barbara Theis 1952; children: Anne-Hélène b.
1955, Maxime b. 1960, Jean-Philippe b. 1963.

EDUCATION
Attended Collège Sainte-Marie and Collège Jean-
de-Brébeuf, Montréal; Université de Montréal,
faculté de droit.

RELIGION
Roman Catholic.

HOME
834 Echo Dr., Ottawa, Ont.

OFFICE
Canadian Embassy, 35 ave. Montaigne, Paris 8e,
France.

CAREER
Lawyer and diplomat; Department of External
Affairs, Ottawa 1949; Canadian Embassy, Moscow, USSR 1951, Djakarta, Indonesia 1956, London, England 1957, Paris, France, cultural coun-
sellor 1964–; Liberté, editorial consultant.

AWARDS, HONOURS
Prix David, 1960.

WRITINGS
Le combat contre Tristan, Malte, 1951; Poèmes
de Russie, Hexagone, 1957; Les belles au bois dor-
mant, Hexagone, 1960; Le retour d'Oedipe, Écrits
du Canada français, 1962; Mon Babel (non-fiction),
HMH, 1963.
CONTRIBUTED: Poetry to several anthologies, e.g.
The Oxford book of Canadian verse, edited by A.
J.M. Smith, Oxford, 1960; Anthologie de la
poésie canadienne française, edited by G. Sylvestre, Beauchemin, 1963; Liberté, Tamarack review.

TRUDEAU, Yves* 1930–

Artist; b. 3 Dec. 1930 in Montreal; son of Armand
and Berthe (Bonhommé) Trudeau; m. Huguette
Lefebvre 15 Jan. 1955; children: Marie b. 22 Dec.
1955, François b. 1 Feb. 1959, Gilles b. 19 Dec.
1963.

EDUCATION
Attended Jardin d'Enfance, Soeurs de la Providence, École St. Jean Baptiste, École Supérieure St. Viateur, Montréal; Séminaire Marie Méd-
iatrice, Montréal, 1952-54; studied ceramics with
Gaétan Beaudin, North Hatley, PQ; attended
École des Beaux-Arts, Montréal; studied anatomy
with Father Juan Lang, Collège Jean-de-Brébeuf,
Montréal, 1954-55; studied welding (gas and electric), Centre d'Apprentissage des Métiers de la
Construction, Montréal; studied forging, Institut
des Arts Appliqués, Montréal.

RELIGION
Roman Catholic.

HOME AND STUDIO
5429 ave. Durocher, Outremont, Montréal 8, PQ.

CAREER
Illustrated for a Scout magazine until 1954; Bell
Telephone Company, Montreal, 1957-59; travelled
through England, France, Belgium, The Netherlands, Switzerland, Italy and Yugoslavia, 1963-
64, stayed in Paris, France, for nine months (has
own studio in Auxerre); École des Beaux-Arts,
Montréal, part-time teacher of sculpture, Feb.
1967–.

COMMISSIONS
Bronze group, Auditorium Jeunesses Musicales du
Canada, Mount Orford, PQ, 1961; murals, piscine
"Claire Fontaine," Sherbrooke, PQ, 1961; claustre,
Chapelle des F.F. du Sacré-Coeur, Arthabaska,
PQ, 1961; "Corpus," fer soudé, Soeurs-Grises de
la Croix, Rockcliffe, Ottawa, Ont., 1962; ceramic
reliefs, Chapelle des Professeurs, Université de
Sherbrooke, 1962; murals, Hotel de Ville, Mégan-
tic, PQ, 1962; bronze group, Science de l'Édu-
cation, Université de Sherbrooke, 1963; Chemin
de la Croix, Chapelle de la Maison de Détention
Soeurs du Bon Pasteur, Montréal, 1963; Chemin
de la Croix et brise lumière, Chapelle des Soeurs
Servites de Marie, Sherbrooke, 1963; murals,
Centre d'Apprentissage, Sherbrooke, 1963; autels
et retable, Chapelle Notre Dame de l'Enfant,
Sherbrooke, 1965; facade, Notre-Dame de l'Enfant,
Sherbrooke, 1966; Maitre autel, autel du St.
Sacrement and Corpus, and exterior decoration of
Église St. Gaétan, Montréal, 1967; sculpture
mécanisée à effets sonores, Expo 67 Montreal,
Place de l'Univers, 1967; relief en béton,
Hôpital Universitaire et Centre de Recherche et
de Diagnostique de l'Université de Sherbrooke,
1968; Mérite Annuel des Diplômés de l'Université
de Montréal, 1968.

AWARDS, HONOURS
Senior fellowship for research, Province of Quebec, 1957; third prize, Concours Artistique de la
Province de Québec, 1959 and 1962; lauréat,
Concours Artistique de la Province de Québec,
1959 and 1962; purchase award, Association des
Artisans Professionels du Québec, 1961; Canada
Council senior fellowship, 1963/64, grant 1965/
66, 1966/67; Forma VIVA, Symposium International de la Sculpture, Yugoslavia, 1964; purchase award, Concours Artistique de la Province
de Québec, 1966.

MEMBER
Association des Sculpteurs du Québec (co-founder,
1961; president, 1961-65; vice-president, 1965-
68); Société des Sculpteurs du Canada, Société
des Artistes Professionnels du Québec (treasurer,
1967).

EXHIBITIONS
ONE-MAN: Institut des Arts Appliqués, Montréal,
1960; Canadian Handicraft Guild, Toronto, 1960;
Sherbrooke, 1962; Galerie Agnès Lefort, Montréal,
1962 and 1965; Exposition solo en plein air,

Mount Orford, 1963; Galerie Suzanne de Coninck, Paris, 1965.

GROUP: Represented in group exhibitions held
in Canada since 1958 including annual exhibitions of Association des Sculpteurs du Québec,
Montreal Museum of Fine Arts Spring Show, Concours Artistiques de la Province de Québec, and
Winnipeg Biennials, Man.; represented in group
exhibitions organized by National Gallery of Canada, Ottawa, Ont.; *16ème Salon de la Jeune
Sculpture*, Salle Balzac, Galerie Creuze, Paris,
1964; *Symposium International de Sculpture*,
Ravne, Yugoslavia, 1964; *17ème Salon de la Jeune
Sculpture*, Musée Rodin, Paris, 1965; *4ème Bien-
nale de Paris*, Musée d'Art Moderne de la Ville de
Paris, 1965; *Nouvelle École de Paris*, Bohmans-
Bohmans Konsthandel, Stockholm, Sweden, 1965;
10 Sculpteurs de Montréal, Bundy Art Gallery,
Waitsfield, Vt., 1965; *Biennale de Sculpture Con-
temporaine*, Musée Rodin, Paris, 1966; *2a Mostra
Internazionale di Sculpture* all'aperto Fondazione
Pagani-Legnano, Milan, Italy, 1966; Festival 1966,
Mulhouse, France, 1966; Maison Canadienne,
Paris, 1966; *Festival International des Arts Plas-
tiques*, Nice, France, 1966; Galerie Suzanne de
Coninck, Paris, 1967.

COLLECTIONS IN WHICH REPRESENTED
Musée du Québec; National Gallery of Canada;
Musée d'Art Contemporain, Montréal; La Maison
du Québec à Paris; Musée en plein air, Ravne,
Yugoslavia; Maison du Québec, New York, NY;
Collection du Ministère de l'Éducation, PQ; Art
Institute of Ontario; Dunkelman Gallery, Toronto;
Collection of Monumental Pieces for Expo 67;
Seagram's Collection, Montreal; Collection de
l'Institut des Arts Appliqués.

TURGEON, Bernard*

Singer (baritone); b. in Edmonton, Alta.; m.;
children: son b. *c.*1959, daughters b. *c.*1964 and
1967.

EDUCATION
Attended St. Jean's College, Edmonton; St. Boniface College, Winnipeg, Man.; Royal Conservatory
of Music, Toronto, Ont., 1951-55; studied voice
with George Lambert, Ernesto Barbini,
Ernesto Vinci, and Herman Geiger-Torel;
with Walter Jensch, London, England; with Guis-
ella Rathausher and F. Grossman, Vienna, Austria,
1959.

CAREER
Guest soloist with many organizations, e.g. Montreal Opera Company, PQ, Montreal Symphony
Orchestra, Edmonton Opera Association, Vancouver Opera Association, BC, Vancouver Symphony
Orchestra, Toronto Symphony Orchestra, Royal
Philharmonic Orchestra, London, England; Canadian Opera Company, Toronto, leading baritone
1952–; Stratford, Ont. Festival, guest soloist

1956, 1965; Vancouver International Festival,
guest soloist 1958, 1962, 1964; Sadler's Wells
Opera Company, London, England, leading baritone 1960–; Glyndebourne Festival, England,
guest soloist 1960; Edinburgh Festival, Scotland,
guest soloist 1961; Welsh National Opera, guest
soloist 1962; USSR tour, 1970-71; University of
Alberta, assistant professor, head of vocal and
opera department, 1 July 1969–.

AWARDS, HONOURS
Canada Council senior arts fellowship, 1959, grant
1963, travel grant, 1967/68.

THEATRE
Sang in many productions, e.g. Junius in *The rape
of Lucretia* (Stratford, Ont. Festival, 1956),
Masetto in *Don Giovanni* (Vancouver International
Festival, 1958), Papageno in *The magic flute* (Van-
couver International Festival, 1962), *Tosca* (Mon-
treal Opera Company, 1963), *La bohème* (Van-
couver Opera Association, 1964), *The consul*
(Vancouver Opera Association, 1964), Count
Almaviva in *The marriage of Figaro* (Stratford,
Ont. Festival, 1965), Alaska Wolf Joe in *Mahag-
onny* (Stratford, Ont. Festival, 1965), Ping in
Turandot (Canadian Opera Company, 17 Sept.
1965), Dr. Bartolo in *The barber of Seville*
(Canadian Opera Company, 18 Sept. 1965),
Prince Yamadori in *Madama Butterfly* (Vancouver
Opera Association, 28 Oct. 1965), Tonio in *I
Pagliacci* (Canadian Opera Company, 1966), *Mac-
beth* (Canadian Opera Company, 16 Sept. 1966),
Alfio in *Cavalleria rusticana* (Canadian Opera
Company, 17 Sept. 1966), *La traviata* (Canadian
Opera Company, 20 Sept. 1966), Conochar in
Deirdre (Canadian Opera Company, 24 Sept.
1966), *Don Pasquale* (Central City Opera, Color-
ado Opera Festival, 1967), title role in *Louis Riel*
(world première, Canadian Opera Company, 23
Sept. 1967; 16 Sept. 1968), Amonasro in *Aïda*
(Canadian Opera Company, 13 Sept. 1968).

RADIO
Sang in several CBC productions, e.g. *Just a gigolo*
(13 Sept. 1962), "Distinguished concert" (series,
10 Dec. 1962), *Broadway holiday* (29 July
1963), "Distinguished artists" (series, 19 Aug.
1963; 12 Feb. 1967), "Music in G" (series, 20 May
1964; 13 Apr. 1966), *Mr. Bach in London* ("Saturday evening," 11 July 1964), *Songs and dances
of death* ("Music in G," 3 Feb. 1965), *Mahagonny*
(8 Aug. 1965), title role in *Louis Riel* (19 Oct.
1967; Oct. 1969), and BBC productions.

TELEVISION
Sang in several CBC productions, e.g. "Summer
concert" (series, 1 July 1964; 7 July 1965; 6 July
1966), *Carols anyone?* (25 Dec. 1964), and BBC
opera productions.

RECORDINGS
Trial by jury, Angel 35966; s 35966.

TURP, André   1925–
Singer (tenor); b. 1925 in Montreal, PQ; m.; children: two sons.

HOME
83 Castleton Rd., Wembley, Middlesex, England.

OFFICE
c/o John Coast, 1 Park Close, Knightsbridge, London S.W.1, England.

CAREER
Metropolitan Opera Company, New York, NY, soloist; San Francisco Opera Company, Calif., soloist; Covent Garden Opera Company, London, England, soloist 1960–; Opéra Comique, Paris, France, soloist; Paris Opera, France, soloist; Grand Theatre, Geneva, Switzerland, guest soloist; Edinburgh Festival, Scotland, guest soloist; Canadian Opera Company, Toronto, soloist 1967–.

MEMBER
Union des Artistes de Montréal.

AWARDS, HONOURS
Quebec government scholarship for studies in Italy, 1949.

THEATRE
Sang in many productions, e.g. *Carmen*, title role in *Werther*, *La traviata* (Varese, Italy, *c.* 1950), Fenton in *Falstaff* (New Orleans, La., 1956), *Lakmé* (New Orleans, 1959), Edgardo in *Lucia di Lammermoor* (Covent Garden Opera, *c.* 1960), Turiddu in *Cavalleria rusticana* (Covent Garden Opera, *c.* 1960), Macduff in *Macbeth* (Covent Garden Opera, *c.* 1960), des Grieux in *Manon* (Covent Garden Opera, *c.* 1960), Rodolfo in *La bohème* (Covent Garden Opera, *c.* 1960), Cavaradossi in *Tosca* (Covent Garden Opera, *c.* 1960), Singer in *Der Rosenkavalier* (Covent Garden Opera, *c.* 1960), Lysander in *A midsummer night's dream* (Covent Garden Opera, *c.* 1960), Don Ottavio in *Don Giovanni* (Covent Garden Opera, *c.* 1960), Prince Andrei in *Khovanshina* (Covent Garden Opera, *c.* 1960), Pylade in *Iphigénie en Tauride* (Covent Garden Opera, *c.* 1960), Pinkerton in *Madama Butterfly* (Covent Garden Opera, *c.* 1960), *The damnation of Faust* (Grand Theatre, Geneva, *c.* 1966), *Iphigénie* (Lima, Peru, 1967), title role in *The tales of Hoffmann* (Canadian Opera Company, 18 Oct. 1967).

RADIO
Sang in several CBC productions, e.g. Toni in *Elegy for young lovers* ("Wednesday night," 23 Aug. 1961.)

TELEVISION
Sang in several CBC productions, e.g. *A gala performance* ("Music Canada," 7 Dec. 1966).

RECORDINGS
Macbeth, 1958. *Médée*, Columbia ML 5325, 1958; Columbia MS 6032, 1959. *Roméo et Juliette*, Westminster XWN 2233, 1963?.

UNDERWOOD, Miles, pseud.
see GLASSCO, John

VAILLANCOURT, Armand   1931–
(Armand Joseph Robert Vaillancourt)
Sculptor; b. 4 Sept. 1931 in Black Lake, PQ.

EDUCATION
Attended University of Ottawa, 1948-49; Montreal Museum of Fine Arts School, PQ, for four years; École des Beaux-Arts, Montréal, 1954.

CAREER
Employed by the Merchant Marine for two years; Place des Arts, Montréal, active member; Ste-Adèle Art Centre, PQ, teacher; First International Sculpture Symposium in North America, Mount Royal, Montreal, Canadian representative 1964; International Sculpture Symposium, Musée d'Art Contemporain, Montréal, participant 1965; International Sculpture Symposium, Toronto, participant 1967; member of the jury of several art and sculpture competitions in Canada.

COMMISSIONS
Sculpture, Dorval Airport, Montreal, 1958; sculpture, Chicoutimi, PQ, 1958; mural, Ile Ste Hélène, Montréal, 1958; marble fountain, Lac des Castors, Montréal; sculpture, Malton Airport, Toronto, Ont., 1963-64; sculpture, commissioned by the Provincial Government of Quebec, School of Arts and Crafts, Asbestos, PQ, 1963-64; commission from the Federal Government, School of Architecture, University of Manitoba, 1965; mural in concrete, Administrative Building, Expo 67, Montreal, 1966; outdoor casting of a sculpture, Saint-Jean-Baptiste Festivals, 1966; two sculptures, Ministry of Education, Quebec, PQ, 1966; bronze screen, Musée d'Art Contemporain, Montréal, 1966; project for the maquette for the Embarcadero Center, San Francisco Development Center, San Francisco, Calif.; sculpture for Place des Nations, Expo 67, Montreal, 1967.

MEMBER
Association des Arts Plastiques (founder member; vice-president, 1956); Quebec Sculptors' Association; Association des Étudiants de l'École de Beaux-Arts de Montréal (president, 1953-54).

AWARDS, HONOURS
First prize, Hadassah Exhibition, Montreal, 1959, 1962, 1963, and 1966; first prize, Montreal Museum of Fine Arts Spring Show, 1960, 1962, and 1963; scholarship, Federal Government, 1961; third prize, Concours Provincial, Musée du Québec, 1963; Quebec government scholarship, 1963-64; first prize, project for the maquette for the Embarcadero Center, San Francisco Development Center, 1967.

EXHIBITIONS

ONE-MAN: Galerie Libre, Montréal, 1959; Galerie Denyse Delrue, Montréal, 1960; Dorothy Cameron Gallery, Toronto, 1961; Here and Now Gallery, Toronto, 1962 and 1967; Collège Notre-Dame, Montréal, 1962; Collège de Rigaud, PQ, 1962; Galerie Camille Hébert, Montréal, 1963; University of Ottawa, 1963; Collège du Sacré-Coeur, Victoriaville, PQ, 1963; Galerie du Sacré-Coeur, Victoriaville, 1963; École d'Architecture, Montréal, 1966; Université de Sherbrooke, 1966.

GROUP: Represented in group exhibitions held in Canada including exhibions of Association des non-figuratifs and Montreal Museum of Fine Arts Spring Show; represented in group exhibitions organized by National Gallery of Canada, Ottawa, Ont., including the third Biennial of Canadian Painting, 1959; Art in Architecture, American Institute of Artists, 1961; *Salon de la Jeune Sculpture*, Musée Rodin, Paris, France, 1962; *Salon de Mai*, Museum of Modern Art, Paris, 1962; Tokyo International Trade Fair, Japan, 1965; *Salon de la Jeune Sculpture*, Paris, 1966; Maison du Québec, New York, NY, 1966; *3a Mostra Internazionale di Sculpture,* pour la Fondation Pagani, Musée d'Art Moderne, Milan, Italy, 1967.

COLLECTIONS IN WHICH REPRESENTED

Agnes Etherington Art Centre, Queen's University; Montreal Museum of Fine Arts; Musée d'Art Contemporain, Montréal; Museé du Québec, PQ; International Museum of Occidental Art, Tokyo.

VALCOURT, Jean

Actor, director, and composer.

EDUCATION

Attended Conservatoire de Paris, France, 19?-30; studied music composition with George Caussade, Charles Tournemire, and André Caplet.

CAREER

La Comédie Française, Paris, actor 1930-44; Conservatoire d'Art Dramatique de la Province de Québec, director in Montreal and founding director in Quebec, PQ, 1958−; Théâtre Populaire du Québec, Montréal, artistic director; toured Egypt, Lebanon, and South America.

AWARDS, HONOURS

First medal from Concours de Théâtre Lyrique, Paris, 1950; Quintette de Cuivres prize for *Pentaphonie,* Montréal, 1962.

THEATRE

Played in numerous productions, e.g. Alceste in *Le misanthrope* (Comédie Française); directed numerous productions, e.g. *L'âge de fer* (Comédie Française), *Père humilié* (Théâtre des Champs-Elysées, Paris), *Oedipe roi, Polyeucte, Les femmes savantes, La nuit des rois, Othello, La paix d'Aris-*

tophane, Faisons un rêve, Banco, Cinna (Le Théâtre Club, Montréal, 1961), *On ne badine pas avec l'amour* (Théâtre Populaire, 15 Apr. 1967), *L'avare* (Théâtre Populaire, 31 Oct. 1968), *Antigone* (Théâtre Populaire, 11 Feb. 1969).

COMPOSITIONS

Satni, opera. *Oedipe roi*, musique de scène, performed by Orchestre des Concerts Colonne Orange, 1952. *Pièce d'orgue pour une messe de mariage*, 1954. *Ariettes pour les anges* pour soli et choeur de femmes, 4 ondes martenot. 2 *Quatuors à cordes*, one with voice, 1958. *L'illusion comique*, pour ondes martenot, performed by Yvonne Loriot, 1956. *Pentaphonie*, performed by Quintette de Cuivres, Montréal, 1962. *Mise en scène de ...,* commissioned by CBC, 1962.

VALDOMBRE, pseud.

see GRIGNON, Claude-Henri

VALLERAND, Jean   1915−

Composer; b. 1915 in Montreal, PQ.

EDUCATION

Attended University of Montreal, graduated in journalism; studied violin with Lucien Sicotte and harmony with Claude Champagne (*q.v.*), Montreal.

OFFICE

Délégation Générale du Québec, 19 rue Barbet-de-Jony, Paris, France.

CAREER

Conservatory of Music and Dramatic Art, Montreal, secretary-general 1942−; University of Montreal faculty of music, council member and teacher of music history and orchestration; CBC, lecturer on music, general supervisor of music broadcasts 1965; Royal Conservatory of Music, Toronto, Ont., summer session lecturer *c.*1965; *Le Canada, Matin, Le devoir, Le nouveau journal,* Montreal, music critic; Quebec House, Paris, France, cultural attaché, 1966.

MEMBER

CAPAC.

COMPOSITIONS

Numerous scores for CBC radio and TV productions. *Le magicien,* 1961, first performed by Les Jeunesses Musicales du Canada Music Camp, Mount Orford, PQ, 1961, recorded on air-check tape, 1962, broadcast on "Wednesday night," CBC, 6 June 1962, with revised score on "Tuesday night," CBC, 26 Mar. 1968, commissioned by Les Jeunesses Musicales du Canada. *Quatuor, Le diable dans le beffroi,* orchestra. *Strings in motion,* 1961, first performed by McGill Chamber Orchestra under Alexander Brott, 1961, commissioned by Lapitzky Foundation.

WRITINGS

La musique et les tout petits, Éditions Chantecler, 1950.

VALTZ, Lynn Berta Springbett
see SEYMOUR, Lynn

VAN HAMEL, Martine* 1945—
Dancer; b. 16 Nov. 1945 in Brussels, Belgium;
daughter of Diederick A. and Manette (Cramer)
van Hamel; came to Canada in 1959 and settled
in Toronto.
EDUCATION
Attended schools in The Netherlands, Venez-
uela, and Canada; studied ballet with Edith Dam,
Copenhagen, Denmark, 1949; Javanese dancing in
Indonesia, 1951; ballet at The Hague Conser-
vatory, The Netherlands, 1952-53; with Henry
Danton at National Ballet of Venezuela, Caracas,
1956-58; Betty Oliphant, Toronto, 1959;
National Ballet School of Canada, Toronto,
1959-63.
OFFICE
National Ballet of Canada, 157 King St. E.,
Toronto 1, Ont.
CAREER
National Ballet of Venezuela, Caracas, 1956-58;
National Ballet of Canada, Toronto, soloist 1963-
67, principal 1967—.
MEMBER
AEA.
AWARDS, HONOURS
Scholarships (declined) from George Balanchine
and Lucia Chase Schools in New York, NY, 1958;
first prize in Junior Class and prize for best artis-
tic interpretation at Third International Ballet
Competition, Varna, Bulgaria, 26 July 1966;
International Nickel Company of Canada Cen-
tennial scholarship, 1967.
THEATRE
Made debut as Sugar Plum Fairy in *Casse-noisette*
(Franca after Ivanov, 1963); first danced Odette
in *Le lac des cygnes*, act II, IV (Petipa-Ivanov,
1963), Queen of the Wilis in *Giselle* (Coralli-Perrot,
1963), *Don Quixote* pas de deux (after Petipa,
1963), *Sérénade* (Balanchine, 1963), *Concerto
barocco* (Balanchine, 1963), Queen of the carriage
trade in *Offenbach in the underworld* (Tudor,
1964), title role in *La sylphide* (Bruhn, 1965),
Girl in *Solitaire* (MacMillan, 1965), *Le corsaire*
pas de deux (Klavin, 1966), title role in *La bayadère* (Petipa, 1967), Odette-Odile in *Le lac des
cygnes* (Bruhn, 1967), Autumn fairy in *Cinderella*
(Franca, 1968).
TELEVISION
Danced in several CBC productions, e.g. Gypsy in
Romeo and Juliet (Cranko, "Festival," 15 Sept.
1965; 2 Mar. 1966), *Le corsaire* pas de deux
(Klavin, "INCO centennial performance," 4 Oct.
1967), solo in *George Burns and Canada's loveliest stars* ("O'Keefe Centre presents," 16 Jan.
1968).

VERREAU, Richard 1926—
Singer (tenor); b. 1926 in Château Richer, PQ.
EDUCATION
Attended Laval University School of Music;
studied voice in Rome, Italy, 1952-54.
HOME
800 rue du Château, St-Hilaire, PQ.
CAREER
Choir boy in Château Richer; Canadian Opera
Company, Toronto, Ont., soloist; Philadelphia
Symphony Orchestra, Pa., guest soloist; New
Orleans Opera Company, La., guest soloist;
Théâtre Lyrique de Nouvelle France, Québec, PQ,
soloist; Lyon Opera Company, France, soloist
1951; Montreal Symphony Orchestra, PQ, soloist
1953-60; Covent Garden Opera Company, London,
England, soloist 1956; Vienna Opera Company,
Austria, guest soloist 1960; New York City Opera,
NY, leading tenor c.1960-63; San Francisco Opera
Company, Calif., guest soloist 19-? and 1963/64;
Bolshoï Theatre, Moscow, USSR, guest soloist
1964.
MEMBER
Union des Artistes de Montréal.
AWARDS, HONOURS
Quebec government scholarship, 1949.
THEATRE
Sang in many productions, e.g. *Mireille* (Lyon
Opera, 1951), *Mignon* (New York City Opera,
1956), *Requiem* by Verdi (Hollywood Bowl,
Calif., 1958), *The damnation of Faust* (Paris
Opera, France, 1959), Rodolfo in *La bohème*
(Vancouver International Festival, BC, 1960),
Madama Butterfly (Vancouver International
Festival, Queen Elizabeth Theatre, 22 July 1960),
Tosca (Montreal Symphony Orchestra, 1963),
title role in *Faust* (Metropolitan Opera, New York,
28 Nov. 1963; Montreal Symphony Orchestra,
Expo 67, Montreal, 1967), *Manon* (Metropolitan
Opera, 1965).
RADIO
Sang in several CBC productions, e.g. Pinkerton in
Madama Butterfly (1958; 27 July 1960), *Richard
Verreau* ("Music diary," 28 June 1964).
TELEVISION
Sang in several CBC productions, e.g. Pinkerton in
Madama Butterfly (1958), des Grieux in *Manon*
("Heure du concert," 11 Feb. 1960), *La bohème,
Faust, Show from two cities* (17 Nov. 1963).

VIGNEAULT, Gilles 1928—
Chansonnier and poet; b. 13 Oct. 1928 in Nata-
shquan, PQ; son of Willie and Marie (Landry)
Vigneault; m. Rachel Cloutier 13 July 1955;
children: Michel, Louis, François, Pascale.
EDUCATION
Attended Séminaire Rimouski, PQ, to 1950;
Laval University, BA, 1953.

HOME
941 ave. Bougainville, Québec, PQ.

OFFICE
Université Laval, Québec, PQ.

CAREER
Émourie, review, co-founder 1953; teacher of English and French, Valcartier, PQ, 1954-56; Institut de Technologie de Québec, teacher of algebra and French 1957-61; Éditions de l'Arc, founder and proprietor 1959–; Laval University, teacher of modern French literature summer 1961; toured France, Belgium, and Luxembourg 1968.

MEMBER
CAPAC; Union des Artistes de Montréal.

AWARDS, HONOURS
Congrès du Spectacle, first prize, 1962; Grand Prix du Disque canadien, first prize, 1963; International Song Festival, Sopot, Poland, second prize for *Jack Monnoloy*, 1964, first prize for *Mon pays*, 1965; Festival du Disque, Prix Félix Leclerc for *Mon pays*, 1965; Prix Calixa Lavallée, 1966; Governor General's literary award for *Quand les bateaux s'en vont*, 1966.

CONCERT STAGE
Chansonnier in numerous boîtes à chansons, e.g. La Boîte à Chansons, Québec, 1960, Chat Noir, Montréal, PQ, 1961, Cro-Magnon, Québec, 9-14 Jan. 1967; open-air concert, Ile d'Orléans, PQ, 18 July 1961; recital, Comédie Canadienne, Montréal, 1-3 Nov. 1963, 15-20 Sept. 1964, 7-26 Sept. 1965, Sept. 1966, July-Aug. 1967; Arena Maurice Richard, Montréal, 3 Sept. 1965, Apr. 1968; Bobino, Paris, France, fall, 1966; Expo 67, May 1967; open-air concert, Ottawa, Ont., 1967; Olympia, Paris, Sept. 1967; Mariposa Folk Festival Orillia, Ont., 9-11 Aug. 1968.

FILM
Engineer in *La neige a fondu sur la Manicouagan* (1965).

TELEVISION
Appearances on CBC French network, e.g. Télès in *Sans atout* (1958); guest artist, "Le sel de la semaine" (20 Nov. 1967), *Au bout de mon âge* (25 Feb. 1968).

RECORDINGS
Recorded by Columbia: *Gilles Vigneault enregistré à Paris*, FL 348; *Gilles Vigneault* v. 1, FS 538, FS 544; *Gilles Vigneault*, arrangé Gaston Rochon, FS 612; *Gilles Vigneault à la Comédie Canadienne*, FS 632; *La Manikoutai*, FS 652; *Le nord du nord*, FS 681; two records by CBS, France; more than 12 long-play records.

COMPOSITIONS
Numerous chansons, e.g. *Mon pays, L'air du voyageur, Le vent, C'est le temps, Tire mon coeur, Le nord du nord, Les gens de mon pays, Tam ti delam, Avec les vieux mots;* many published by Éditions du vent qui vire.

WRITINGS
Étraves, Éditions de l'Arc, 1959; *Contes sur la pointe des pieds*, Éditions de l'Arc, 1960; *Balises*, Éditions de l'Arc, 1964; *Quand les bateaux s'en vont*, Éditions de l'Arc, 1965; *Pour un soirée de chansons*, Éditions de l'Arc, 1965; *Contes du coin de l'oeil*, Éditions de l'Arc, 1966; (with F. Lafortune) *Où la lumière chante*, Université Laval, 1966; *Les gens de mon pays*, Éditions de l'Arc, 1967; *Tam ti delam*, Éditions de l'Arc, 1967.

VISCOUNT, Bill Martin
see MARTIN-VISCOUNT, Bill

VOGT, Augustus Stephen   1861-1926
Organist, choir director, and conductor; b. 14 Aug. 1861 in Washington, Upper Canada (now Ont.); son of John George and Mariana (Zingg) Vogt; m. Georgia Adelaide McGill 19 Aug. 1891; children: 1 son, 1 daughter; d. 17 Sept. 1926 in Toronto, Ont.

EDUCATION
Attended public schools in Elmira and Hamilton, Ont.; New England Conservatory of Music, Boston, Mass., 1878-81; studied piano with Adolf Ruthardt, organ with Dr. Papperitz, theory with Dr. Judassohn, theory and composition with Paul Quasdorf at Royal Conservatory of Leipzig, Germany, 1885-88.

RELIGION
Anglican.

CAREER
St. James Lutheran Church, Elmira, organist 1873-78; First Methodist Church, St. Thomas, Ont., organist c. 1881-85; Jarvis St. Baptist Church, Toronto, organist and choirmaster 1888-1906; Royal College of Organists, Toronto, secretary 1889-92; Moulton Ladies College, Ont. [?], teacher of piano and organ; Dufferin House, Winnipeg, Man. [?], teacher of piano and organ; *Saturday night*, musical editor; World's Fair, Chicago, Ill., organ recitals, only Canadian organist 1893; Toronto Mendelssohn Choir, founder and conductor 1894-1907, retired 1917; Earl Grey Amateur Musical Competition, judge 1909; Royal Conservatory of Music, Toronto, teacher of piano and organ, principal 1913-26; University of Toronto, dean of faculty of music 1919-26.

MEMBER
Arts & Letters Club; St. Andrew's Society; National Club; Royal Conservatory of Music Alumni Association (former vice-president); University of Toronto Alumni Association (councillor); Canadian Society of Musicians (president, 1893-95); Toronto Clef Club (president, 1897).

AWARDS, HONOURS
MusD from University of Toronto, 1906.

WRITINGS
Modern pianoforte technique, 1900.

EDITED: Standard anthem book, 1894.

VOLKOFF, Catherine Janet Baldwin
see BALDWIN, Janet

VON GENCSY, Eva* 1924—
(Eva von Gencsy Murray)
Dancer, teacher, and choreographer; b. 11 Mar.
1924 in Budapest, Hungary; daughter of Joseph
and Valerie (Kromer) von Gencsy; came to Can-
ada in 1948; m. John Murray 13 May 1957
(marriage dissolved 1967).
EDUCATION
Attended school in Hungary; studied ballet with
V.G. Troyanoff at Russian Ballet Academy, Bud-
apest, 1934-41; Dramatic School, Budapest, 1941-
44; Mozarteum Summer School, Salzburg, Aus-
tria, 1944.
RELIGION
Roman Catholic.
HOME
Apt. 605, 3650 Mountain St., Montreal 109, PQ.
OFFICE
Académie des Grands Ballets Canadiens, 5415
Chemin de la Reine Marie, Montréal 248, PQ;
Banff School of Fine Arts, Banff, Alta.
CAREER
Landes Theatre, Salzburg Opera House, soloist
1945-48; (now Royal) Winnipeg Ballet, Man.,
soloist 1948-53, guest artist 1959—; Banff School
of Fine Arts, ballet division instructor 1953-54,
jazz division assistant instructor 1962-65, head of
jazz division 1966—; Les Ballets Chiriaeff (now
Les Grands Ballets Canadiens) Montréal, soloist
1954-57, leading dancer 1957-59, guest artist and
instructor 1959—; CBC, Montreal, dancer 1959—;
Jacob's Pillow Dance Festival, Lee, Mass., 1959;
Montreal Professional Dance Centre, instructor in
jazz 1966—; Saidye Bronfman Centre, Montreal,
instructor in jazz 1967—; Classical Ballet Studio,
Ottawa, Ont., instructor 1968—; Canadian College
of Dance, Montreal, guest instructor 1968.
MEMBER
AEA; Union des Artistes de Montréal.
AWARDS, HONOURS
Scholarship to Mozarteum Summer School,
Salzburg, 1944; advanced and solo seal with
honours of Royal Academy of Dancing, London,
England, 1951; Congrès du Spectacle trophy for
best television dancer of the year, Montreal, 1963.
THEATRE
First danced Odette in *Le lac des cygnes*, act II
(Petipa-Ivanov, 1948-53), Black Swan pas de deux
from *Le lac des cygnes* (Petipa, 1948-53), Lady
known as Lou in *The shooting of Dan McGrew*
(Lloyd, 1952), *Suite canadienne* (Chiriaeff,
1957), Echo in *Hangup* (Jones, Banff School
Festival Ballet, 1968).

TELEVISION
Danced in numerous CBC productions, e.g.
Odette in *Le lac des cygnes*, act II (Hyrst after
Petipa-Ivanov, "Heure du concert"), Swanhilda in
Coppélia (Hyrst after St. Leon).

WADDINGTON, Geoffrey 1904-66
Conductor and violinist; b. 1904 in Leicester,
England; came to Canada in 1907; m. Mildred
Baker; children: two; d. Jan. 1966.
EDUCATION
Attended school in Lethbridge, Alta.; studied
violin from 1911.
CAREER
Canadian tour, violinist 1921; CKCL, Truro, NS,
1922; Toronto Symphony Orchestra, Ont., first
violinist c.1922; Toronto Chamber Music Society,
organizer and director; Royal Conservatory of
Music, Toronto, faculty member 1922; CKNC,
Toronto, music director 1926-33; CKNX, Wingham, Ont., music director 1926-36; Canadian
Radio Broadcasting Commission (now CBC)
music director 1933-35, music director in Manitoba 1936 (1938?), 1943, music adviser in Toronto 1947-52, CBC Opera Company co-founder
1949, CBC Symphony Orchestra organizer and
sometime conductor 1952, director of music
1952—; Royal York Hotel Orchestra, Toronto,
founder and conductor 1935-36; Winnipeg Sum-
mer Symphony, Man., conductor 1939-40; Army
Show, music director 1941-42; all-Canada Radio
Facilities, music director 1944; freelance con-
ductor, Toronto, 1945-47.
MEMBER
Arts & Letters Club.
AWARDS, HONOURS
LLD from Dalhousie University, 1956.
RADIO
Conducted numerous CBC productions, e.g. "The
Neilson hour" (series), *White empire & specials*
(1945-46), *Geoffrey Waddington show* (1946-47),
Just a song (1946-47), *Hockridge show* (1946-47),
Canadian party (1946-47), "National school broad-
cast" (series 1946-47), *Morgan and Weston* (1948);
Deirdre of the sorrows (c.1949), *Summer strings*
(1950), *Cosi fan tutte* ("Wednesday night," 18
Apr. 1951), *CBC Symphony Orchestra* (14 Aug.
1958; 12 May 1961), *16th anniversary of United
Nations concert* (23 Oct. 1961), "Conductor's
choice" (series, 1 Apr. 1962), *Antiphonie, Horo-
scope* (16 May 1962), *Divertimento no. 5* (28
Oct. 1962), *Concertos for string quartet and orchestra* (28 Nov. 1962), *Cantata for a joy* ("Distinguished artists," 4 Mar. 1963), *Winnipeg pops
concert* (28 Apr. 1963), "Encore," part II

(series, 30 Apr. 1967; 7 May 1967), *The concerto* (10 July 1967).

TELEVISION

Conducted "Portrait of an orchestra" (series, 6 Jan. 1962).

WRITINGS

CONTRIBUTED: "Music and radio" in *Music in Canada*, edited by E. MacMillan, University of Toronto, 1955.

WAINWRIGHT, Ruth* 1902–

(Ruth Salter Wainwright)

Artist; b. 5 May 1902 in North Sydney, NS; daughter of Joseph and Isabel (Nisbet) Salter; m. Inglis Lough Wainwright 21 Oct. 1929; children: Harold b. 31 Mar. 1932, Isabel b. 25 July 1935.

EDUCATION

Attended secondary school in North Sydney; Halifax Ladies College, NS, graduated in concert harp, teacher's certificate in art, 1917-21; studied under Gentile Tondino (*q.v.*), summer school of Tatamagouche, NS, 1956-57; studied under Hans Hofmann, Provincetown, Mass., summer 1958-59.

RELIGION

Anglican.

HOME

6570 Waegwoltic Ave., Halifax, NS.

CAREER

Halifax Ladies College, art teacher 1924; illustrated Margaret Nickerson's child verses for *Chatelaine*, 1929; CBC, harpist 1932-41; travelled to England, 1951; teaching privately since 1952; travelled through eastern USA and Canada many times, Italy 1963, Greece 1965, Portugal and Spain 1968; Nova Scotia Museum of Fine Arts, Dalhousie University, member 1966.

MEMBER

Nova Scotia Society of Artists (elected, 1930).

AWARDS, HONOURS

Second prize, Maritime Art Exhibition, Beaverbrook Gallery, Fredericton, NB, 1960; prize, Beaverbrook Gallery, 1964; prize Summer Festival, Tatamagouche, 1964.

EXHIBITIONS

ONE-MAN: Robert Harris Gallery, Charlottetown, PEI, 1960s; Mount Allison University, 1960s. Maritime Art Association, NS, 1960s; Acadia University, 1960s; Granville Gallery, Halifax, 1960s; Dalhousie University, 1965.

GROUP: Represented in group exhibitions held in Canada including annual exhibitions of Nova Scotia Society of Artists, Maritime Art Association, Montreal Museum of Fine Arts Spring Show, Canadian Society of Painters in Water Colour; represented in group exhibitions organized by National Gallery of Canada, Ottawa, Ont., including the second, third, and sixth Biennial Exhibition of Canadian Painting, 1957, 1959, and

1965; Canadian Woman's Club of New York, NY, 1961 and 1962; Halifax Board of Trade, London, England, 1965.

COLLECTIONS IN WHICH REPRESENTED

Dalhousie University; Acadia University; Mount Allison University.

WALKER, Horatio 1858-1938

Artist; b. 12 May 1858 in Listowel, Ont.; son of Thomas Walker; m. in 1883; d. 27 Sept. 1838 in Sainte Pétronille, Ile d'Orléans, PQ.

EDUCATION

Studied under J.A. Fraser *c.*1873-76; studied in New York, NY, *c.*1877; largely self-taught.

CAREER

Employed by Notman and Fraser, photographers, Toronto, Ont., 1873-76; set up a studio in New York, 1878; walking trip from Montreal to Quebec, PQ, 1880; made several trips to Europe *c.* 1881-83; settled on Ile d'Orléans, 1883.

COMMISSIONS

Banner, Orange Lodge of Listowel, Perth County, *c.*1888.

MEMBER

National Academy (1891); Royal Canadian Academy (Academician 1918; president, 1925); American Water Color Society; Royal Institute of Painters in Water Colour; Union Internationale des Beaux-Arts et des Lettres, Paris, France; National Academy of Design; National Institute of Arts and Letters, New York.

AWARDS, HONOURS

Bronze medal, Paris Exhibition, 1899; gold medal and diploma, Columbia Exhibition, Chicago, Ill., 1893; gold medal, Pan American Exhibition, Buffalo, NY, 1901; gold medal, Charleston Exhibition, SC, 1902; gold medal, Universal Exhibition, St. Louis, Mo., 1904; gold medal of honour, Pennsylvania Academy of Fine Arts, Philadelphia, 1906; gold medal, Panama Pacific International Exhibition, San Francisco, Calif., 1915; LLD from University of Toronto, 1915; Doctor of Arts from Laval University, 1938.

EXHIBITIONS

ONE-MAN: Montross Gallery, New York, 1919; National Gallery of Canada, Ottawa, Ont., 1941.

GROUP: Represented in group exhibitions held in Canada since 1910 including annual exhibitions of Royal Canadian Academy and Canadian Art Club; Paintings by Canadian Artists, City Art Museum, St. Louis, 1918; Canadian Section of Fine Arts, British Empire Exhibition, London, England, 1924; International Exposition, Ghent, Belgium, 1925; *Exposition d'art canadien*, Musée du Jeu de Paume, Paris, 1927; A Century of Canadian Art, Tate Gallery, London, 1938; Canadian Painting, National Gallery of Art, Washington, DC, 1950; An Exhibition of Canadian Paintings held at Fortnum and Mason, Ltd., London, 1955.

COLLECTIONS IN WHICH REPRESENTED
Metropolitan Museum, New York; Corcoran Gallery of Art, Washington; National Gallery of Art, Washington; Peabody Institute, Baltimore, Md.; Baltimore Fine Arts Academy; City Art Museum, St. Louis; Toledo Museum of Art, Ohio; Carnegie Institute, Pittsburgh, Pa.; National Gallery of Canada; Art Gallery of Ontario, Toronto.

WARREN, Vincent
Dancer; b. in Jacksonville, Fla.

EDUCATION
Studied ballet with Betty Hyatt Linton in Jacksonville; Ballet Theatre School and Metropolitan Opera Ballet School in New York, NY.

OFFICE
Les Grands Ballets Canadiens, 5415 Chemin de la Reine Marie, Montréal 248, PQ.

CAREER
Jacksonville Ballet Guild, soloist; Metropolitan Opera Ballet, New York; Santa Fe Opera Company, NM, premier danseur; Pennsylvania Ballet, Philadelphia, guest artist; Guatemala National Theatre, guest artist; Les Grands Ballets Canadiens, Montréal, soloist 1961-64, leading dancer 1964–.

MEMBER
AEA; Union des Artistes de Montréal.

AWARDS, HONOURS
Scholarship to Ballet Theatre School and Metropolitan Opera Ballet School, New York.

THEATRE
Danced in *La fille mal gardée* (Hyrst-Chiriaeff after Caton), *Graduation ball* (Lichine), *Gehenne* (Nault), Jason in *Medea* (Paige), Albrecht in *Giselle* (Dolin after Coralli), Prince Siegfried in *Le lac des cygnes* (Hyrst after Petipa-Ivanov), Ivan Tsarevich in *L'oiseau de feu* (Nault), Poet in *Les sylphides* (Nault after Fokine); created male role in *The swan of Tuonela* (Dolin, Jacobs Pillow Dance Festival, Lee, Mass.); danced in *Quintan* (Nault, Opus 66, Place Ville-Marie, Montréal), *Carmina burana* (Nault), *Catulli carmina* (Butler).

TELEVISION
Danced in several CBC productions, e.g. *Prelude to Expo* ("Music Canada," 19 Oct. 1966).

WATSON, Wilfred* 1911–
Poet, playwright, and teacher; b. 1 May 1911 in Rochester, England; son of Frederick Walter and Louisa (Claydon) Watson; came to Canada in 1926; m. Sheila Doherty.

EDUCATION
Attended Maldon Grammar School, Essex, England; Duncan High School, BC; University of British Columbia, BA, 1943; University of Toronto, MA, 1946, PhD, 1951.

HOME
8918 Windsor Rd., Edmonton, Alta.

OFFICE
Department of English, University of Alberta, Edmonton, Alta.

CAREER
Sawmill worker until 1941; University of British Columbia, special lecturer in English 1949/50; University of Alberta, Calgary, lecturer in English *c.* 1951-53; University of Alberta, Edmonton, assistant professor of English 1954-57, associate professor 1958-66, professor 1967–; Interface, co-founder 1962.

MEMBER
Canadian University Theatre Association; University of Edmonton Studio Players (honorary life member, 1968).

AWARDS, HONOURS
British Council award in poetry, 1953-55; Canadian government overseas fellowship, 1955-56; Governor General's literary award for *Friday's child*, 1955; University of Western Ontario President's medal for "The necklace," 1960.

WRITINGS
Friday's child (poems), Faber & Faber, 1955; *Cockcrow and the gulls* (play; produced Studio Theatre, Edmonton, 29 Mar. 1962); *Trial of Corporal Adam* (play; produced Coachhouse Theatre, Toronto, Ont., 1963); *Wail for two pedestals* (play; produced Yardbird Suite, Edmonton, 1964); *Thing in black* (play; produced Yardbird Suite, Edmonton, 1967); *The Canadian fact* (play; produced Walterdale Playhouse, Edmonton, 1967); *O, holy ghost, dip your finger in the blood of Canada, and write, I love you* (play; produced Studio Theatre, Edmonton, 1967); *Two teardrops frozen in the rearview mirror* (play; produced Walterdale Playhouse, Edmonton, 1968); *Soul is my button* (play; produced Acadia University Student's Union, 1969).
CONTRIBUTED: Poetry, short stories, and articles to *The Penguin book of Canadian verse*, edited by R. Gustafson, Penguin, 1958; *Oxford book of Canadian verse*, edited by A.J.M. Smith, Oxford, 1960; *Modern Canadian verse*, edited by A.J.M. Smith, Oxford, 1967; *Canadian literature, Canadian forum, Fiddlehead, Contemporary verse, Delta, Alphabet, Paris review, Prism, Humanities bulletin of Canada, Explorations.*
WORK IN PROGRESS: (with Marshall McLuhan) "From cliché to archetype," *c.* 1969.

WAYNE, Johnny 1918–
Comedian; b. 1918; m. Bea 1943; children: Michael, James, Brian b. 25 Dec. 1951.

EDUCATION
Attended Harbord Collegiate in Toronto; University of Toronto, BA in English.

HOME
15 Forest Ridge Dr., Toronto 19, Ont.

CAREER

CBC, Toronto, comedian 1939–; Canadian Army, 1942–?, sergeant; Capitol Films, vice-president 1951; Charlottetown Festival, PEI, co-director 1965.

MEMBER

ACTRA; Canadian Theatre Centre.

AWARDS, HONOURS

Canadian Association for Adult Education award for *The lost comic book weekend*, 1960; *Motion picture daily and television today* award for the best TV comedy team, 1962, 1963; Silver Rose (2nd prize) at International Variety Show Festival, Montreux, Switzerland, 1965.

THEATRE

Wrote and played in *The Army show* (tour 1942–?); played in *Royal variety concert* (Confederation Centre, Charlottetown, 6 Oct. 1964), *An evening with Wayne and Shuster* (Charlottetown Festival, 1965; trans-Canada tour 1965); produced *Mother Goose* (Eaton Auditorium, Toronto, 1950-51).

RADIO

Played in numerous CBC programs, e.g. "Wife preservers" (series, 1939), "The Johnny home show" (Beaver award), "The Wayne and Shuster show" (1948–?).

TELEVISION

Played in many programs, e.g. *The Wayne and Shuster show* (CBC, 1954–), guest on *The Rosemary Clooney show* (1957), "Chelsea at nine" (series, Granada, London, England, 1957), *The Ed Sullivan show* (CBS, 4 May 1958–), *Holiday Lodge* (serial, CBS, 1961), *Wayne and Shuster take an affectionate look at ...* (CBC, 1964–).

WEBBER, Gordon McKinley 1909-66

Artist; b. 12 Mar. 1909 in Sault Ste. Marie, Ont.; son of William George and Martha (McKinley) Webber; d. 1966.

EDUCATION

Attended Ontario College of Art and Art Students' League, Toronto, Ont.; studied under Kepes and Moholy-Nagy, Chicago School of Design, Ill., 1939-42.

CAREER

Pickering College, Newmarket, Ont., art teacher 1930-33; Art Gallery of Toronto children's art classes, teacher 1935-39; Montreal Museum of Fine Arts School of Art and Design, PQ, instructor 1942-[?] ; McGill University School of Architecture, lecturer 1942-[?]; Macdonald College, Ste. Anne de Bellevue, PQ, director of adult art programme 1943-46; National Film Board, special designer 1945-46; McGill University, department of Fine arts lecturer 1948-?; University of British Columbia, extension courses lecturer 1950; theatre designer in Toronto; ballet designer 1947-50.

COMMISSIONS

Murals, Hart House, University of Toronto, 1927; murals, Canadian Youth Congress, 1936; murals, Ottawa City Hall, Ont.; frescoe, Ottawa Civic Hospital.

MEMBER

Canadian Group of Painters (elected, 1937; president, 1959-60); Canadian Society of Graphic Art (elected, 1942); Canadian Federation of Artists; Canadian Association of Industrial Designers.

AWARDS, HONOURS

Scholarships, Ontario College of Art, 1924 and 1927; Carnegie fellowship for study at Chicago School of Design, 1939-42.

EXHIBITIONS

GROUP: Represented in group exhibitions held in Canada since 1931 including annual exhibitions of Ontario Society of Artists and Canadian Group of Painters; First Biennial of Canadian Painting, National Gallery of Canada, Ottawa, 1955; Exhibition of Contemporary Canadian Painting ... Southern Dominions, 1936; Great Lakes Exhibition, Buffalo, NY, 1938-39; World's Fair, New York, NY, 1939; Exhibition of Water Colours, Gloucester, England, 1939.

COLLECTIONS IN WHICH REPRESENTED

Art Gallery of Ontario, Toronto; Hart House Permanent Collection, University of Toronto; Montreal Museum of Fine Arts; Guggenheim Museum, New York; National Gallery, Auckland, New Zealand; Glasgow, Scotland.

WRITINGS

CONTRIBUTED: Articles to *School arts, Canadian art,* and *Theatre arts.*

WEINZWEIG, John Jacob* 1913–

Composer; b. 11 Mar. 1913 in Toronto; son of Joseph and Rose (Burshtyn) Weinzweig; m. Helen Tenenbaum 19 July 1940; children: Paul b. 6 Jan. 1943, Daniel b. 23 July 1947.

EDUCATION

Attended Grace Street Public School, Harbord Collegiate Institute, and Central High School of Commerce in Toronto; studied piano with Gertrude V. Anderson, harmony with Leo Smith, counterpoint with Healey Willan (*q.v.*), orchestration with Sir Ernest MacMillan, conducting with Reginald Stewart at University of Toronto, BMus, 1934-37; studied orchestration with Bernard Rogers, conducting with Paul White at Eastman School of Music, University of Rochester, NY, MMus, 1938.

RELIGION

Hebrew.

HOME

107 Manor Rd. E., Toronto, Ont.

OFFICE

Edward Johnson Building, University of Toronto, Toronto, Ont.

CAREER
Harbord Collegiate Institute, Toronto, orchestra
member; Central High School of Commerce,
Toronto, orchestra member; Toronto Philhar-
monic Orchestra, Vancouver Symphony Orchestra, BC, guest conductor of own compositions;
Inter-American Composer's Seminar, University
of Indiana, guest speaker; Canadian Conference
of the Arts, member of the national executive;
Canadian Jewish Congress, member of educational and cultural committee; travelled in
England, Wales, and Scotland as guest of
Composer's Guild of Great Britain and British
Council; John Adaskin Memorial Fund, trustee;
University of Toronto Symphony Orchestra,
founder and conductor 1934-37; Royal Conservatory of Music, Toronto, teacher of
composition and orchestration 1939-60; RCAF,
1943-45; University of Toronto, assistant
professor of music 1952, professor of composition and orchestration 1968–; International
Conference of Composers, Stratford, Ont. Festival, chairman 1960; World Assembly of Choirs,
Israel, guest 1964; Inter-American Festival of the
Arts, San Juan, Puerto Rico, guest of honour 1966.

MEMBER
Canadian Music Council; CAPAC (member of
board of directors); Canadian League of Composers (founder and president, 1951); Canadian
Music Centre (member of board of directors,
c.1959).

AWARDS, HONOURS
London Olympiad silver medal for *Divertimento
no. 1*, 1948; Canada Council grant, 1965/66,
award, 1967/68; Centennial citation for creative
achievements, 1967.

COMPOSITIONS
Quartet no. 1, strings, 1937, first performed by
Kilbourn Quartet, Rochester, 1938. *The whirling
dwarf*, orchestra, 1937, first performed under S.
Hersenhoren, CBC, Toronto, 1939. *Legend*, orchestra, 1937. *The enchanted hill*, orchestra, 1938,
first performed by Rochester Civic Orchestra
under Howard Hanson, 1938. *Suite*, orchestra,
1938, first performed by Rochester Civic Orchestra under Howard Hanson, NBC, 1938. *Spectre,*
string orchestra and solo timpani, 1938, first performed under A. Chuhaldin, CBC Toronto, 1939.
A tale of Tuamotu, orchestra and solo bassoon,
1939. *Suite no. 1*, paino, 1939. *Waltzling*, Frederick Harris Music Co., 1955. *Dirgeling, Themes with
variables,* first performed by Sophie Cait, Toronto,
1940. *Symphony*, orchestra, 1940. Score for
Mackenzie River, 1941, commissioned by National
Film Board of Canada. *Rhapsody*, orchestra,
1941, first performed by CBC Symphony Orchestra under Victor Feldbrill (*q.v.*) Toronto, 1957.
Sonata, violin and piano, 1941, first performed
by Harry Adaskin (*q.v.*) and Frances Marr, 1942,

Oxford University Press, 1953. Score for *West-
wind*, 1942, commissioned by National Film
Board of Canada. *Improvisation on an Indian
tune*, organ, 1942, first performed New York,
NY, 1942, commissioned by Temple Emanuel
for the Three Choir Festival. *Our Canada*, music
for radio no. 1, orchestra, 1943, first performed
under S. Hersenhoren, CBC, Toronto, 1943, commissioned by CBC, recorded by CBC IS. *Intermis-
sions*, flute and oboe, 1943, first performed by
Keetbaas and Freedman (*q.v.*), CBC, Toronto,
1949, Southern Music Pub. Co., 1964. *Fanfare*,
3 trumpets and three trombones, 1943, first performed by Toronto Symphony Orchestra under
Sir Ernest MacMillan, 1943. *Interlude in an artist's life*, string orchestra, 1943, first performed
under Ettore Mazzoleni (*q.v.*), CBC, Toronto,
1944, Leeds, 1961, recorded by CBC IS. *Band-hut
sketches*, band, 1944, first performed by RCAF
Rockcliffe Central Band under the composer,
CBC, 1944. *Prelude to a new day*, orchestra, 1944,
first performed under S. Hersenhoren, CBC, Toronto, 1945, commissioned by CBC. Scores for
The great Canadian Shield and *Turner Valley*,
1945, commissioned by National Film Board of
Canada. *To the lands over yonder*, mixed chorus
a capella, 1945, first performed under G. Waddington (*q.v.*) CBC, Toronto, 1946, Harris Music
Co., 1953. *Divertimento no. 1*, flute and string
orchestra, 1946, first performed by Albert Steinberg and N. Fiore, CBC, Vancouver, 1946, Boosey
& Hawkes, 1950, recorded by CBC IS. *Edge of
the world*, music for radio no. 2, orchestra, 1946,
first performed under G. Waddington, CBC, Toronto, 1946, Leeds, 1967. *Quartet no. 2*,
strings, 1946, first performed by Parlow Quartet,
Toronto, 1947, commissioned by Forest Hill
Community Centre. *Of time, rain and the world*,
soprano and piano, 1947, first performed by
Frances James and Earle Moss, Toronto, 1948.
Divertimento no. 2, oboe and string, 1948; first
performed by Harold Sumberg and Perry Baum,
CBC, 1948, Boosey & Hawkes, 1951, recorded
by CBC IS. *Red ear of corn*, ballet, orchestra,
1949, first performed by CBC under S. Hersenhoren, Royal Alexandra Theatre, Toronto, 1949,
commissioned by Volkoff Canadian Ballet. *Red
ear of corn suite*, orchestra, 1949, first performed
Toronto, 1951. *Sonata*, cello and piano, 1949,
first performed by Mamott and Barkin, CBC, Toronto, 1950. *Suite no. 2: Conversation piece*,
Oxford University Press, 1965, *Berceuse*, Oxford
University Press, 1956 and *Toccata dance*, 1950,
all three first performed by Neil Van Allen, CBC,
Toronto, 1950. *Round dance*, orchestra, 1950,
first performed by CBC Orchestra under John
Adaskin (*q.v.*) Toronto, 1950, commissioned by
CBC, recorded by RCA Victor, 1964. *Sonata*,
piano, 1950, first performed by Reginald

Godden, Canadian League of Composers concert, Toronto, 1951, Leeds, 1950. *Dance of the Massadah*, baritone and piano, 1951, first performed by Felton and Kushner, Toronto, 1952, commissioned by Canadian Jewish Congress. *Am Yisrael Chai*, mixed chorus and piano, 1952, first performed under Gordon Kushner, Toronto, 1953, commissioned by Canadian Jewish Congress, Leeds, 1964. *Violin concerto*, violin and orchestra, 1954, first performed by Albert Pratz and CBC Symphony Orchestra under Ettore Mazzoleni, Toronto, 30 May 1955, recorded by CBC IS. *Wine of peace*, dedicated to the United Nations, soprano and orchestra, 1957, first performed by Mary Simmons and CBC Symphony Orchestra under Walter Susskind (*q.v.*), Toronto, 1958, commissioned by CBC, recorded by CBC IS. *Symphonic ode*, orchestra, 1958, commissioned and first performed by Saskatoon Symphony Orcestra under the composer, 1959, Leeds, 1961. *Divertimento no. 3*, bassoon and string orchestra, 1959, first performed by Jane Taylor and Saskatoon Orchestra under Murray Adaskin, 1959, commissioned by Saskatoon Festival, Leeds, 1963. *Divertimento no. 5*, trumpet, trombone, wind orchestra, 1961, commissioned and first performed by American Wind Symphony Orchestra, Pittsburgh, Pa., under Robert Boudreau, 9 June 1961, Leeds 1968. *Concerto for harp and chamber orchestra*, 1967, first performed by Judy Loman and Toronto Repertory Ensemble under Milton Barnes, Edward Johnson Concert Hall, Toronto, 30 Apr. 1967, centennial commission, Leeds, 1968. *String quartet no. 3*, 1962, first performed by Canadian String Quartet, Edward Johnson Concert Hall, Toronto, 17 Jan. 1963, commissioned by Albert Pratz, Canada Council. *Woodwind quintet*, 1963-64, first performed by Toronto Woodwind Quintet, Ten centuries concerts, Edward Johnson Concert Hall, Toronto, 10 Jan. 1965. *Clarinet quartet*, 1964-65, commissioned by Canadian Music on a grant from Canada Council. *Piano concerto*, 1966, first performed by Paul Helmer and Toronto Symphony Orchestra under Victor Feldbrill, 15 Dec. 1966, commissioned by CBC.

RECORDINGS
String quartet no. 2, Columbia, 1962. *Barn dance*, Columbia, 1965. *Woodwind quartet*, RCA Victor, 1966.

WENTWORTH, John, pseud.
see CHILD, Philip Albert

WESTERFIELD, Rosemary Deveson
see DEVESON, Rosemary

WESTON, Bill
see WESTON, William Percy

WESTON, William Percy   1879-1967
(Bill Weston)
Artist; b. 30 Nov. 1879 in London, England; son of William and Jane (Smith) Weston; m. Jessie Clara Bennett 11 Apr. 1908; children: Betty b. 31 May 1909, Doris b. 9 Feb. 1912; came to Canada in 1909 and settled in Vancouver, BC; d. 20 Dec. 1967 in Vancouver.

EDUCATION
Attended Borough Road College, London; Putney School of Art, London; largely self-taught.

CAREER
King Edward High School, Vancouver, art teacher *c.* 1909-10; Vancouver Normal School, art adviser *c.*1914-46; Vancouver School of Art, night school teacher; University of British Columbia, extension teacher; Education Department, Victoria, BC, teacher; Council of Vancouver Art Gallery, member 1938-67.

MEMBER
British Columbia Society of Artists (president, 1931-38); Canadian Group of Painters (co-founder, 1933); Royal Canadian Academy (Associate 1936); Royal Society of Arts, London.

EXHIBITIONS
ONE-MAN: Vancouver Art Gallery, 1946 and 1959; Vancouver Arts Club, 1966.
GROUP: Represented in group exhibitions held in Canada since 1930 including British Columbia Society of Artists, Canadian National Exhibition, Canadian Group of Painters, and Royal Canadian Academy; represented in group exhibitions organized by National Gallery of Canada, Ottawa, Ont.; World's Fair, NY, 1939; A Century of Canadian Art, Tate Gallery, London, 1938.

COLLECTIONS IN WHICH REPRESENTED
National Gallery of Canada; Hart House, University of Toronto.

WRITINGS
Teachers manual of drawing, Nelson.

WILD, Eric*   1910–
(Eric Lees Wild)
Conductor and composer; b. 11 Feb. 1910 in Sault Ste. Marie, Ont.; son of Isaac Ashton and Sarah Ann (Brook) Wild; m. Anna Linnea Hartz 1 July 1932; children: Eric Ashton b. 5 Apr. 1933, James Lynn b. 23 Sept. 1936, John Lees b. 23 Sept. 1936, Elizabeth Angela b. 29 July 1938.

EDUCATION
Attended Sault Ste. Marie Collegiate; Royal College of Music, London, England, Associate, 1925; University of Michigan, BMus, 1928-32.

RELIGION
Anglican.

HOME
74 Roslyn Cres., Winnipeg 13, Man.

CAREER
CBC, 1934-35, 1940, CBC Winnipeg Concert Or-

chestra organizer and conductor 1947-68, CBC, Halifax Orchestra, NS, guest conductor 1967; Billy Bissett Orchestra, Monte Carlo tour, Monaco, 1935; BBC, London, England, assistant conductor 1936-39; toured England and France with entertainment group for troops, 1939; Alan Young Show, musical director 1940; Wrigley Air Band, musical director 1940; RCNVR, 1943-46, *Meet the Navy* conductor, became lieutenant; Rainbow Stage, Winnipeg, musical director; Royal Winnipeg Ballet, conductor 1949-56, musical director; Toronto Symphony Orchestra, Ont., guest conductor 1957-58; London Studio Players, England, guest conductor 1965; Toronto Philharmonic Orchestra, guest conductor 1966; Saskatchewan Symphony Orchestra, guest conductor 1966-67.

MEMBER
Phi Mu Alpha; Sinfonia.

FILM
Meet the Navy conductor, became lieutenant;

RADIO
Conducted numerous CBC programs, e.g. *Alan Young show* (1940), *Wayne & Shuster* (1940), *Time on my hands* (1940), "Curtain time" (series, 1943-46), *Vets show* (1943-46), "Winnipeg Sunday concerts" (series, 1950), *Music by Eric Wild* (1950), *Overture, please* (1951), *The lowland sea* ("Wednesday night," 16 June 1954), *Christian frontiers* (25 Mar. 1964), *Advance democracy* (22 Nov. 1966), "Pops concert" (series, c.1963-66), *The widow* (17 Jan. 1967).

TELEVISION
Conducted many CBC programs, e.g. "Interlude" (first TV musical series), *Royal Winnipeg Ballet* (26 Aug. 1962), *The seven last words* (27 Mar. 1964), *Hymn sing* (Sept. 1965–), *And then we wrote* ("Music Canada," 8 Feb. 1967).

COMPOSITIONS
The shooting of Dan McGrew, ballet score, first performed by (now Royal) Winnipeg Ballet, Playhouse, Winnipeg, 1 May 1950. Scores for several CBC programs and productions, e.g. "Opportunity knocks"; *Paola and Francesca,* 1951; *Saddle for a Stony,* 14 July 1963.

RECORDINGS
Hymn sing, RCA Victor, 1966. *The widow,* RCA Victor, LSC 2981, 1967. *Light Canadian orchestral classics,* Capitol, 1967.

WILKINSON, Anne Cochran Gibbons 1910-61
Author; b. 21 Sept. 1910 in Toronto, Ont.; daughter of George Sutton and Mary Elizabeth Lammond (Osler) Gibbons; m. Frederik Robert Wilkinson 23 July 1932 (marriage dissolved 1953); children: Robert Jeremy b. 11 July 1935, Heather Anne b. 7 Sept. 1938, Alan Gurd b. 8 Jan. 1941; d. 10 May 1961 in Toronto.

EDUCATION
Attended private schools in Canada and USA.

CAREER
Purely literary; travelled extensively; *Tamarack review,* co-founding editor, 1956.

WRITINGS
Counterpoint to sleep (poems), First Statement Press, 1951; *The hangman ties the holly* (poems), Macmillan, 1955; *Lions in the way: a discursive history of the Oslers,* Macmillan, 1956; *Swann and Daphne* (juvenile fiction), Oxford, 1960.

CONTRIBUTED
Poetry and articles to *Twentieth century Canadian poetry,* edited by E. Birney, Ryerson, 1953; *Canadian poetry in English,* chosen by B. Carman and others, rev. and enl. ed., Ryerson, 1954; *Penguin book of Canadian verse,* edited by R. Gustafson, Penguin, 1958; *The first five years: a selection from the Tamarack review,* edited by R. Weaver, Oxford, 1962; *Contemporary verse, Tamarack review, Canadian forum, Outposts, Canadian poetry magazine, Here and now, Fiddlehead, Northern review, Poetry Commonwealth, Reading.*

WILLAN, Healey 1880-1968
(James Healey Willan)
Composer and organist; b. 12 Oct. 1880 in London, England; son of James Henry Burton and Eleanor (Healey) Willan; m. Gladys Ellen 1905; children: Michael, Bernard, Patrick, Mary; came to Canada in 1913; d. 16 Feb. 1968 in Toronto, Ont.

EDUCATION
Attended St. Saviour's Choir School, Eastbourne, England; privately educated; advanced musical studies with William Stevenson Hoyte, London; Royal College of Organists, London, Associate, 1896, Fellow, 1898.

RELIGION
Anglican.

CAREER
St. Saviour's Church, St. Alban's, England, organist 1897-1900; Christ Church, Wanstead, England, organist 1900-03; St. John the Baptist Church, Kensington, London, organist 1903-13; St. Paul's Anglican Church, Toronto, organist 1913-21; St. Mary Magdalene Church, Toronto, organist and choir master, music director 1921-68; Royal Conservatory of Music, Toronto, head of theory department 1913-36, vice-principal 1920-36; University of Toronto, Hart House music director 1919-25, organist 1932-65, professor of music 1938-50; Tudor Singers, founder and director 19?-40; University of California, Los Angeles, special lecturer on choral music 1949; adjudicator at many of the principal competitive music festivals in Canada.

MEMBER
Fellow of the Royal Society of Church Music; Royal Canadian College of Organists (president, 1921-22, 1933-35); Arts & Letters Club, Toronto (president, 1922-23); Canadian League of

Composers (honorary member, 1955).

AWARDS, HONOURS

Mus D from University of Cambridge; D Litt from McMaster University; D Litt from University of Manitoba; Mus D from University of Toronto, 1921; LL D from Queen's University, 1952; Lambeth Doctorate of Music, England, 1956; Canada Council medal, 1961; Companion of the Order of Canada, 1967.

COMPOSITIONS

Composed numerous works, e.g. motets, anthems, carols, masses, settings for the Anglican liturgy, song cycles, choral works with orchestra, orchestral works, chamber and piano works, incidental music to Hart House plays, including *Prelude and fugue in* B minor, Western Music, 1909; *Prelude and fugue in C minor,* Novello, 1909; *Trio in B minor,* violin, cello, piano, 1917; *Introduction, passacaglia and fugue,* Oxford University Press, 1919; *Sonata in E minor,* violin, piano, c.1920, BMI Canada, 1950, Harris, 1928; *An apostrophe to the heavenly hosts,* 1921, Harris, 1936; *Theme and variations,* 2 pianos, c.1922; *The constitution of the Arts and Letters Club,* 1922; *School and community song book,* W.J. Gage, 1922; *Sonata no. 2 in E major,* violin and piano, c.1923, Bosworth, 1923; *Mystery of Bethlehem,* cantata, 1923; *Series of 11 liturgical motets,* 1928-37; *L'ordre de bon temps,* Harris, 1928; *Songs of the British Isles,* Harris, 1928; *Chansons canadiennes,* Harris, 1929; *Symphony no. 1* in D minor, 1936; *Suite for rhythm band,* Harris, 1938; *Te Deum Laudamus,* for the coronation of George VI, Harris, 1938; *The trumpet call,* Oxford University Press, 1941; *Transit through fire,* radio opera, 1942; *Brébeuf and his brethren,* pageant, voices, orchestra, narrator, 1943; *Deidre,* opera, 1943, BMI Canada, first performed by CBC 1946 and Canadian Opera Company, 24 Sept. 1966; *Symphony no. 2* in C minor, 1943-49; *Concerto in C minor,* piano and orchestra, 1944; *12 Chorale preludes,* Concordia, 1950-51; *5 Preludes on plainchant melodies,* Oxford University Press, 1951; *Royce Hall suite,* symphonic band, BMI Canada, 1951; *Gloria Deo per immensa saecula,* double choir, 1952; *Coronation suite,* BMI Canada, 1953; *Song of welcome,* for Stratford, Ont. Festival, 1955; *30 Hymn preludes,* Peters, 1956, 1957, 1958; *A fugal trilogy,* Oxford University Press, 1959, *Five pieces,* BMI Canada, 1959; *Passacaglia and fugue no. 2* in E minor, Peters, 1959; *36 Short preludes and postludes,* Peters, 1960; *The Canadian psalter,* 1963, Gregorian Association, Canada, edition with accompaniments, Anglican Book Centre; *Andante fugue and chorale,* Peters, 1965; *An anthem for the centennial of Canadian confederation,* BMI Canada, 1966; *A centennial march,* orchestra, 1967.

WILLAN, James Healey
see WILLAN, Healey

WILLIS, James Frank 1909-69
Producer; b, 15 May 1909 in Halifax, NS; son of Alexander Samuel and Emma Graham (Pushie) Willis; m. Gladys Winchcombe 22 Aug. 1934; d. 26 Oct. 1969 in Toronto, Ont.

EDUCATION

Attended King's College School, Windsor, NS; Royal Victoria School of Art, Halifax, 1916-19; studied at Art Students League, Cooper Union and Grand Central School of Art, New York, NY.

RELIGION

Anglican.

CAREER

Paramount, Long Island Studios, New York, outdoor advertising artist 1930-31; CHNS, Halifax, 1931-33; Canadian Radio Broadcasting Commission (now CBC), maritime regional director in Halifax 1933-38, feature broadcast supervisor in Toronto 1939-58, senior producer of features and documentaries 1958-69; Australian Broadcasting Commission, exchange senior radio producer 1938-39.

MEMBER

ACTRA; Celebrity Club.

AWARDS, HONOURS

Ohio State University first awards 1942, 1945, 1947, 1949, 1952, 1956, 1957 and honourable mentions 1946, 1952, 1955; Canadian radio first awards 1950, 1951 and honourable mentions 1949, 1950, 1951.

RADIO

Produced numerous CBC programs, e.g. "The white empire," "Comrades in arms," "Carry on Canada," "The quiet victory," "The Johnny home show," "In reply," *Murder by court martial* ("Sunday night," 27 Oct. 1963), *The winter nobody got younger* ("Sunday night," 31 May 1964), "Living words" (series, 5 July 1964-?), *The trial of Henry Fauntleroy* ("Sunday night," 12 July 1964); produced, directed, and narrated *Design for a nation* ("Sunday night," 18 Oct. 1964); produced an narrated "Flanders' Fields" (17-week series, 11 Nov. 1964-); produced *Hot days in Dayton* ("Sunday night," 19 Sept. 1965), *The bold ones* ("Tuesday night," 16 Nov. 1965); produced and host on "As time goes by" (series, 28 Nov. 1965-?); produced *Big Geordie* ("Tuesday night," 8 Mar. 1966), *The life of Joseph Howe* ("Tuesday night," 6, 13 June 1967), *Little George* ("Tuesday night," 14 Nov. 1967), *The fantastic emperor* ("Tuesday night," 20 Feb. 1968), *A man? No, an element* ("Tuesday night," 29 Oct. 1968); host on "Voice of the pioneer" (series, 1968).

TELEVISION

Produced and/or host on many CBC programs, e.g. "Tabloid," "Close-up," "Horizon," "Public eye,"

"Canada 98," "Canada 99," "Canada 100,"
"Question mark," *Wall of ice* (13 Sept. 1964),
The Dumbells ("Camera Canada," 16 June 1965),
A sense of truth ("Telescope," 23 Feb. 1967), *A
century of song* (3 Sept. 1967), *One per cent plus*
(25 Dec. 1968).
RECORDINGS
Vimy, CBC, 1965.

WILSON, Ethel Davis Bryant*   1888–

Novelist; b. 20 Jan. 1888 in Port Elizabeth, South
Africa; daughter of Robert William and Lila (Mal-
kin) Bryant; came to Canada in 1898 and settled
in Vancouver; m. Wallace Wilson 4 Jan. 1921 (d.
12 Mar. 1966).
EDUCATION
Attended Miss Gordon's School (now Crofton
House), Vancouver, 1898-?; Trinity Hall School,
Southport, England, London matriculation,
1902-06; Vancouver Normal School, teacher's
certificate, 1907.
RELIGION
Anglican.
HOME
2890 Point Grey Rd., Apt. 308, Vancouver, BC.
CAREER
Mainly literary; Kitsilano Elementary School,
Vancouver, teacher 1907-09; Model School, Van-
couver, teacher 1909-12; Lord Roberts School,
Vancouver, teacher 1914-18; Dawson Elementary
School, Vancouver, teacher 1918-20; edited maga-
zine for Red Cross, Vancouver, 1940-45; travelled
extensively.
AWARDS, HONOURS
D Litt from University of British Columbia, 1955;
Canada Council medal for contribution to Cana-
dian literature, 1961; Lorne Pierce medal, 1964.
WRITINGS
Hetty Dorval, Macmillan, 1947; *The innocent
traveller,* Macmillan, 1949; *The equations of love,*
Macmillan, 1952 (translated into French, German,
and Italian); *Swamp angel,* Macmillan, 1954; *Love
and salt water,* Macmillan, 1956; *Mrs. Golightly
and other stories,* Macmillan, 1961.
CONTRIBUTED
Short stories and articles to *Best British short
stories,* edited by E. O'Brien, Houghton, Mifflin,
1938; *A book of Canadian stories,* school ed.,
edited by D. Pacey, Ryerson, 1952; *Canadian
short stories,* edited by R. Weaver and Helen
James, Oxford, 1952; *Canadian anthology,* edited
by C.F. Klinck and R.E. Watters, Gage, 1955; *British Columbia: a centennial anthology,* edited by
R.E. Watters, McClelland & Stewart, 1958; *A
century of Canadian literature,* edited by H.G.
Green and G. Sylvestre, Ryerson, 1967; *Canadian
winter's tales,* edited by N. Levine, Macmillan,
1968; *Chatelaine, New Statesman and nation,
Royal Architectural Institute of Canada journal,*
*Canadian literature, Northern review, Canadian
forum, Tamarack review, Saturday night.*

WINTER, William   1909–

(William Arthur Winter)
Artist; b. 27 Aug. 1909 in Winnipeg, Man.
EDUCATION
Studied under Lemoine Fitzgerald and Franz
Johnson, Winnipeg School of Art; Ontario
College of Art, Toronto, 1925-28.
HOME
15 Pricefield Rd., Toronto 5, Ont.
CAREER
Worked in advertising and book design; Wookey,
Bush and Winter, advertising artist.
MEMBER
Ontario Society of Artists (elected, 1942); Royal
Canadian Academy (Associate 1949; Academician
1953); Canadian Group of Painters (elected,
1946); Canadian Society of Painters in Water-
colour (elected, 1936; president, 1946-47).
AWARDS, HONOURS
J.W.L. Forster award, 1943.
EXHIBITIONS
ONE-MAN: Roberts Gallery, Toronto, 1959.
GROUP: Represented in group exhibitions held
in Canada since 1927 including exhibitions of
Royal Canadian Academy, Canadian Group of
Painters, Manitoba Society of Artists, Canadian
Society of Painters in Watercolour; represented in
group exhibitions organized by National Gallery
of Canada, Ottawa, Ont., including the first Bien-
nial of Canadian Painting, 1955; World's Fair,
New York, NY, 1939; Exhibition of Water Colours
by Canadian Artists, Gloucester, England, 1939;
Rio de Janeiro, Brazil, 1939; Exhibition of Inter-
national Modern Art, Musée d'Art Moderne,
Paris, France, originated by UNESCO, 1946; An
Exhibition of Canadian Paintings held at Fortnum
and Mason Ltd., London, England, 1955.
COLLECTIONS IN WHICH REPRESENTED
National Gallery of Canada; Art Gallery of
Ontario, Toronto; Vancouver Art Gallery, BC; Na-
tional Gallery, Auckland, New Zealand; Mel-
bourne, Australia.
WRITINGS
CONTRIBUTED: Articles to *Maclean's.*

WISEMAN, Adele   1928–

Novelist; b. 1928 in Winnipeg, Man.; daughter of
Pesach and Chaika Wiseman.
EDUCATION
University of Manitoba, BA honours in English
and psychology.
RELIGION
Jewish.
OFFICE
Macdonald College, McGill University, Ste. Anne
de Bellevue, PQ.

CAREER

Royal Winnipeg Ballet, executive secretary; Overseas School of Rome, Italy, teacher; Stepney Jewish Girls' Club, London, England, welfare worker and magazine editor c.1956; Sir George Williams University, 1963-?; Macdonald College, McGill University, assistant professor of English 1963–.

AWARDS, HONOURS

University of Manitoba Chancellor's prize for short story; Governor General's literary award for *The sacrifice*, 1956; Canada Foundation fellowship, Brotherhood award, Beta Sigma Phi award, and Guggenheim fellowship for *The sacrifice*, 1957.

WRITINGS

The sacrifice, Viking, 1956; (with J. Rosenthal) *Old markets, new world* (non-fiction), Macmillan, 1964.

CONTRIBUTED

Short stories and articles to *Modern Canadian stories*, edited by G. Rimanelli and R. Ruberto, Ryerson, 1966; *Maclean's, Alphabet, Tamarack review, Jewish chronicle, Weekend magazine, Transactions of Royal Society of Canada*.

WOOD, William John   1877-1954

Artist; b. 26 May 1877 in Ottawa, Ont.; m. 1906; children: five; d. 4 Jan. 1954 in Midland, Ont.

EDUCATION

Studied under G.A. Reid (*q.v.*) and William Cruikshank, Central Ontario School of Art, Toronto, 1904-05; attended Eric Pape's School, Boston, Mass., for short night class course.

CAREER

Worked as a sailor, Great Lakes c.1900; construction work around Washago, Ont.; lived in northern Ontario and Orillia, Ont., 1910; carriage painter with Frank Carmichael (*q.v.*) in Orillia; moved to Midland 1913, worked as a carriage painter; Canadian Army 1914-18; worked in the shipyards c.1918; also worked in Boston, Mass., Galveston, Tex., Toledo, Ohio, Crowsnest Pass, Alta., and Portage la Prairie, Man.; did restoration work on the Martyrs Shrine, Midland.

MEMBER

Arts and Letters Club, Toronto (elected, c.1912); Canadian Group of Painters (co-founder, 1933; non-resident member), Canadian Society of Painter-Etchers and Engravers (elected, 1920); Canadian Society of Graphic Art (elected, 1913).

EXHIBITIONS

ONE-MAN: Represented in group exhibitions held in Canada since 1921 including annual exhibitions of Ontario Society of Artists, Canadian National Exhibition, Canadian Society of Graphic Art, Arts and Letters Club, Toronto, Art Association of Montreal Spring Show, Canadian Society of Painter-Etchers and Engravers, Canadian Group

of Painters, Group of Seven; represented in group exhibitions organized by National Gallery of Canada, Ottawa; Canadian Section of Fine Arts, British Empire Exhibition, London, England, 1924.

COLLECTIONS IN WHICH REPRESENTED

National Gallery of Canada; Hart House, University of Toronto; Art Gallery of Ontario, Toronto.

WYERS, Jan G.*   1888–

(Jan Gerrit Wyers)

Artist; b. 20 July 1888 in Steenderen, The Netherlands; son of Herman Otto and Johana (Kets) Wyers; went to USA in 1913; came to Canada June 1916 and settled in Windthorst.

EDUCATION

Attended public school in Hatteren, Gelderland, The Netherlands, 1893-1902; self-taught as an artist.

RELIGION

Dutch Reformed Church.

ADDRESS

c/o General Delivery, Windthorst, Sask.

CAREER

Lived in North Dakota 1913-16; came to Saskatchewan; spent three winters in Ontario lumber camps c.1942-44; night-watchman in a prisoner-of-war camp in Ontario, winter 1944/45; began painting c.1936; farmer and folk painter in Windthorst, 1916–.

AWARDS, HONOURS

Various prizes after 1950.

EXHIBITIONS

GROUP: Folk Painters of the Canadian West, toured Canada and USA, 1959-60; fifth Biennial Exhibition of Canadian Painting, National Gallery of Canada, Ottawa, Ont., 1963.

COLLECTIONS IN WHICH REPRESENTED

Norman Mackenzie Art Gallery, Regina, Sask.; National Gallery of Canada; Department of External Affairs, Ottawa.

WYLE, Florence   1881-1968

Sculptor; b. 24 Nov. 1881 in Trenton, Ill.; daughter of Solomon B. and Libbie Armstrong (Sandford) Wyle; came to Canada in 1913 and settled in Toronto, Ont.; d. 14 Jan. 1968 in Newmarket, Ont.

EDUCATION

Attended University of Illinois; studied under C.J. Mulligan and Lorado Tuft, Chicago Art Institute, Ill.

CAREER

Chicago Art Institute, teacher for six years; met Frances Loring (*q.v.*) at Chicago Art Institute in 1910, worked and shared studio with her in New York, NY; came to Canada in 1913; shared studio with Frances Loring in Toronto from 1913; Central Technical School, Toronto, teacher; worked on Canadian War Memorials 1918-19.

COMMISSIONS

Bust, Vincent Massey, 1934; Edith Cavell Memorial, Toronto; memorials for Mrs. Timothy Eaton, Eaton Memorial Church, Toronto; memorial, Royal Canadian Academy; sculpture, Bank of Montreal, Toronto; portrait relief of Barbara Robertson and fountains, Canadian Mothercraft Society, Toronto, 1947; garden fountain, H.R. Baine, Toronto, 1948; student with sheep, Ontario Veterinary College, Guelph, Ont., 1950; garden fountain, Clara Wood, Toronto, 1952; memorial tablet, McNabb, Guelph, 1953; fountain, Marjorie Gibbons Counsell Garden, London, Ont., 1957; bird panels, Harry Oaks Park Pavilion, Niagara Falls, Ont., 1958-59; coat-of-arms, Rainbow Bridge, Niagara Falls, 1959; three floral designs and three landscapes, Rainbow Bridge, Niagara Falls, 1959; tombstone, Dr. Frederick Banting, Toronto; tombstone, Sir Edward Walker, Toronto.

MEMBER

Ontario Society of Artists (elected, 1920; resigned, 1933); Sculptors' Society of Canada (founder member, 1928); Royal Canadian Academy (Associate 1920; Academician 1938); Potters' Guild, Toronto.

AWARDS, HONOURS

Medal from Queen Elizabeth II, 1953.

EXHIBITIONS

GROUP: Represented in group exhibitions held in Canada including annual exhibitions of Royal Canadian Academy, Sculptors' Society of Canada, Ontario Society of Artists, Canadian Art Club, Montreal Museum of Fine Arts Spring Show; Canadian Section of Fine Arts, British Empire Exhibition, Wembley, England, 1925; *Exposition d'art canadien*, Musée du Jeu de Paume, Paris, France, 1927; A Quarter Century of Canadian Art, Tate Gallery, London, England, 1938; Coronation, 1937; World's Fair, New York, 1939.

COLLECTIONS IN WHICH REPRESENTED

National Gallery of Canada, Ottawa, Ont.; Art Gallery of Winnipeg, Man.; Art Gallery of Ontario, Toronto; Art Gallery of Chicago.

YARWOOD, A. Walter Hawley
see YARWOOD, Walter

YARWOOD, Walter* 1917–
(A. Walter Hawley Yarwood)
Sculptor and artist; b. 19 Sept. 1917 in Toronto; m. Helen; children: five.

EDUCATION

Largely self-taught; studied under L.A.C. Panton and Herbert C. Clark, Western Technical School, Toronto.

HOME

39 McMurrich St., Toronto 5, Ont.

CAREER

Advertising artist and designer; illustrated for *Mayfair*; illustrated *Annual advertising and editorial art,* MacEachern, 1949; devoted time exclusively to sculpture since 1960.

COMMISSIONS

War memorial, Chicoutimi, PQ, 1959; sculpture, Cedarbrae Shopping Centre, Ont., 1962; sculpture, Winnipeg International Airport, Man., 1963; Sculptural mural, Sydney Smith Hall, University of Toronto, 1964; sculptural mural, Maynards (Canada) Ltd., Yorkdale, Ont., 1964; sculptures, Pharmacy Building, University of Toronto, 1965; sculpture, Coca Cola Head Office, Thornecliffe Park, Toronto, 1965; Structural Steel Award, National Design Council and Department of Industry, 1965; York University; Badminton and Racquets Club, Toronto, Ont.; Ontario Pavilion Restaurant, Expo 67, Montreal, PQ; Hon. Alexander Mackenzie Monument, Sarnia, Ont.; Queen's Park, Toronto.

MEMBER

Ontario Society of Artist (elected, 1950); Painters Eleven (co-founder); Canadian Group of Painters (elected, 1957); Art Directors' Club, Toronto; Sculpture Society (Associate); Royal Canadian Academy.

AWARDS, HONOURS

Taber Dulmage Feheley award for progressive painting, Ontario Society of Artists, 1948; medal award for distinctive merit, Art Directors' Club, Toronto, 1949; honorable mention, Winnipeg, 1958.

EXHIBITIONS

ONE-MAN: Jerrold Morris Gallery, Toronto, 1962; Hart House Gallery, University of Toronto, 1967.

GROUP: Represented in group exhibitions held in Canada since 1936 including exhibitions of Ontario Society of Artists, Canadian Group of Painters, Canadian National Exhibition, Painters Eleven; represented in exhibitions organized by National Gallery of Canada, Ottawa, Ont., including third Biennial Exhibition of Canadian Painting, 1957.

COLLECTIONS IN WHICH REPRESENTED

Agnes Etherington Art Centre, Queen's University; National Gallery of Canada; Art Gallery of Ontario, Toronto; Montreal Museum of Fine Arts, PQ; Sir George Williams University; Oshawa Art Gallery, Ont.

YOUNG, Marilyn 1936–
(Marilyn Young Marshall)
Dancer; b. 1936 in Winnipeg, Man.; m. Grant Marshall.

EDUCATION

Studied ballet at Canadian School of Ballet, Winnipeg; Robert Joffrey, School of American Ballet, and Ballet Theatre School in New York, NY; Banff School of Fine Arts, Alta., 1951, 1952, 1958.

CAREER

(now Royal) Winnipeg Ballet, corps de ballet, soloist 1952-?, guest artist 1964; Theatre Under the Stars, Vancouver, BC, dancer 1954, 1955, 1957; Rainbow Stage, Winnipeg, dancer 1956, 1958.

AWARDS, HONOURS

Royal Winnipeg Ballet scholarship to Banff School of Fine Arts, 1958.

THEATRE

Made debut in *Casse-noisette* pas de deux (Ivanov, 1952); danced *The sleeping beauty* pas de deux (Petipa), *Le jazz hot* (Boris), *Pasticcio* (Boris), *Ballet premier* (Spohr), *Intermède* (Spohr), *Roundelay* (Boris), *Romance* (Lloyd); created Girl in *The darkling* (Macdonald, 17 Oct. 1958), Floozie in *Grasslands* (Moulton, 18 Oct. 1958), *E minor* (Spohr, 15 Jan. 1959); first danced Yellow girl in *The comedians* (Boris, 24 June 1959); created *Variations for a lonely theme* (Conte, Playhouse, Winnipeg, 18 Mar. 1960); first danced Maiden in *The bitter weird* (de Mille, Playhouse, Winnipeg, 9 Mar. 1962).

TELEVISION

Danced in several CBC productions, e.g. Girl in *The darkling* (Macdonald, *Royal Winnipeg Ballet*, 14 Aug. 1961), *Les whoops-de-doo* (Macdonald, *Royal Winnipeg Ballet,* 26 Aug. 1962).

Index